# REPAIRS AND OVERHAUL

## Engine and Associated Systems

## Transmission

## Brakes, Suspension and Steering

## Body Equipment

# REFERENCE

## Index

All models have fully-independent front suspension, incorporating shock absorbers, coil springs and an anti-roll bar. The rear beam axle has a built-in anti-roll bar, with separate shock absorbers and coil springs.

A wide range of standard and optional equipment is available within the range to suit most tastes, including central locking, electric windows and front, side and curtain airbags. An air conditioning system is available on all models.

Provided that regular servicing is carried out in accordance with the manufacturer's recommendations, the vehicle should prove reliable and very economical. The engine compartment is well-designed, and most of the items requiring frequent attention are easily accessible.

## Your Citroën C3 Manual

The aim of this manual is to help you get the best value from your vehicle. It can do so in several ways. It can help you decide what work must be done (even should you choose to get it done by a garage), provide information on routine maintenance and servicing, and give a logical course of action and diagnosis when random faults occur. However, it is hoped that you will use the manual by tackling the work yourself. On simpler jobs it may even be quicker than booking the car into a garage and going there twice, to leave and collect it. Perhaps most important, a lot of money can be saved by avoiding the costs a garage must charge to cover its labour and overheads.

The Citroën C3 was introduced into the UK in five-door Hatchback form in early 2002. At its launch, the C3 was offered with a choice of 1.4 (1360cc) and 1.6 (1587cc) petrol engines or 1.4 litre (1398cc) HDi turbo-diesel engine. Later that year a 1.1 litre (1124cc) petrol engine and a 16-valve version of the 1.4 litre HDi diesel engine were added to the range. The engines are all versions of the well-proven units which have appeared in many Citroën/Peugeot vehicles over the years, with the exception of the 1.4 litre HDi engine, newly developed in a joint venture with the Ford Motor Co. In 2005 a 1.6 litre HDi diesel engine was added to the range.

The engine is mounted transversely at the front of vehicle, with the transmission mounted on its left-hand end. All engines are fitted with a manual transmission as standard, with an automatic transmission being optionally available on some models.

The manual has drawings and descriptions to show the function of the various components so that their layout can be understood. Tasks are described and photographed in a clear step-by-step sequence.

References to the 'left-hand' and 'right-hand' sides of the vehicle are always in the sense of when viewed by a person sat in the driver's seat, facing forwards.

## Acknowledgements

Thanks are due to Draper Tools Limited, who provided some of the workshop tools, and to all those people at Sparkford who helped in the production of this Manual.

**We take great pride in the accuracy of information given in this manual, but vehicle manufacturers make alterations and design changes during the production run of a particular vehicle of which they do not inform us. No liability can be accepted by the authors or publishers for loss, damage or injury caused by errors in, or omissions from, the information given.**

Working on your car can be dangerous. This page shows just some of the potential risks and hazards, with the aim of creating a safety-conscious attitude.

# General hazards

### Scalding

• Don't remove the radiator or expansion tank cap while the engine is hot.
• Engine oil, transmission fluid or power steering fluid may also be dangerously hot if the engine has recently been running.

### Burning

• Beware of burns from the exhaust system and from any part of the engine. Brake discs and drums can also be extremely hot immediately after use.

### Crushing

• When working under or near a raised vehicle, always supplement the jack with axle stands, or use drive-on ramps. *Never venture under a car which is only supported by a jack.*

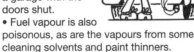

• Take care if loosening or tightening high-torque nuts when the vehicle is on stands. Initial loosening and final tightening should be done with the wheels on the ground.

### Fire

• Fuel is highly flammable; fuel vapour is explosive.
• Don't let fuel spill onto a hot engine.
• Do not smoke or allow naked lights (including pilot lights) anywhere near a vehicle being worked on. Also beware of creating sparks (electrically or by use of tools).
• Fuel vapour is heavier than air, so don't work on the fuel system with the vehicle over an inspection pit.
• Another cause of fire is an electrical overload or short-circuit. Take care when repairing or modifying the vehicle wiring.
• Keep a fire extinguisher handy, of a type suitable for use on fuel and electrical fires.

### Electric shock

• Ignition HT and Xenon headlight voltages can be dangerous, especially to people with heart problems or a pacemaker. Don't work on or near these systems with the engine running or the ignition switched on.

• Mains voltage is also dangerous. Make sure that any mains-operated equipment is correctly earthed. Mains power points should be protected by a residual current device (RCD) circuit breaker.

### Fume or gas intoxication

• Exhaust fumes are poisonous; they can contain carbon monoxide, which is rapidly fatal if inhaled. Never run the engine in a confined space such as a garage with the doors shut.

• Fuel vapour is also poisonous, as are the vapours from some cleaning solvents and paint thinners.

### Poisonous or irritant substances

• Avoid skin contact with battery acid and with any fuel, fluid or lubricant, especially antifreeze, brake hydraulic fluid and Diesel fuel. Don't syphon them by mouth. If such a substance is swallowed or gets into the eyes, seek medical advice.
• Prolonged contact with used engine oil can cause skin cancer. Wear gloves or use a barrier cream if necessary. Change out of oil-soaked clothes and do not keep oily rags in your pocket.
• Air conditioning refrigerant forms a poisonous gas if exposed to a naked flame (including a cigarette). It can also cause skin burns on contact.

### Asbestos

• Asbestos dust can cause cancer if inhaled or swallowed. Asbestos may be found in gaskets and in brake and clutch linings. When dealing with such components it is safest to assume that they contain asbestos.

# Special hazards

### Hydrofluoric acid

• This extremely corrosive acid is formed when certain types of synthetic rubber, found in some O-rings, oil seals, fuel hoses etc, are exposed to temperatures above 4000C. The rubber changes into a charred or sticky substance containing the acid. *Once formed, the acid remains dangerous for years. If it gets onto the skin, it may be necessary to amputate the limb concerned.*
• When dealing with a vehicle which has suffered a fire, or with components salvaged from such a vehicle, wear protective gloves and discard them after use.

### The battery

• Batteries contain sulphuric acid, which attacks clothing, eyes and skin. Take care when topping-up or carrying the battery.
• The hydrogen gas given off by the battery is highly explosive. Never cause a spark or allow a naked light nearby. Be careful when connecting and disconnecting battery chargers or jump leads.

### Air bags

• Air bags can cause injury if they go off accidentally. Take care when removing the steering wheel and trim panels. Special storage instructions may apply.

### Diesel injection equipment

• Diesel injection pumps supply fuel at very high pressure. Take care when working on the fuel injectors and fuel pipes.

⚠️ *Warning: Never expose the hands, face or any other part of the body to injector spray; the fuel can penetrate the skin with potentially fatal results.*

---

# Remember...

## DO

• Do use eye protection when using power tools, and when working under the vehicle.

• Do wear gloves or use barrier cream to protect your hands when necessary.

• Do get someone to check periodically that all is well when working alone on the vehicle.

• Do keep loose clothing and long hair well out of the way of moving mechanical parts.

• Do remove rings, wristwatch etc, before working on the vehicle – especially the electrical system.

• Do ensure that any lifting or jacking equipment has a safe working load rating adequate for the job.

## DON'T

• Don't attempt to lift a heavy component which may be beyond your capability – get assistance.

• Don't rush to finish a job, or take unverified short cuts.

• Don't use ill-fitting tools which may slip and cause injury.

• Don't leave tools or parts lying around where someone can trip over them. Mop up oil and fuel spills at once.

• Don't allow children or pets to play in or near a vehicle being worked on.

The following pages are intended to help in dealing with common roadside emergencies and breakdowns. You will find more detailed fault finding information at the back of the manual, and repair information in the main chapters.

# If your car won't start and the starter motor doesn't turn

- [ ] If it's a model with automatic transmission, make sure the selector is in P or N.
- [ ] Open the bonnet and make sure that the battery terminals are clean and tight.
- [ ] Switch on the headlights and try to start the engine. If the headlights go very dim when you're trying to start, the battery is probably flat. Get out of trouble by jump starting (see next page) using a friend's car.

# If your car won't start even though the starter motor turns as normal

- [ ] Is there fuel in the tank?
- [ ] Is there moisture on electrical components under the bonnet? Switch off the ignition, then wipe off any obvious dampness with a dry cloth. Spray a water-repellent aerosol product (WD-40 or equivalent) on ignition and fuel system electrical connectors like those shown in the photos. (Note that diesel engines don't usually suffer from damp).

**A** Remove the plastic covers and check the security and condition of the battery connections.

**B** Check the fuel/ignition system (as applicable) wiring connectors are securely connected (1.6 litre petrol model shown).

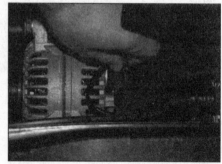

**C** Check that the alternator wiring connectors are securely connected.

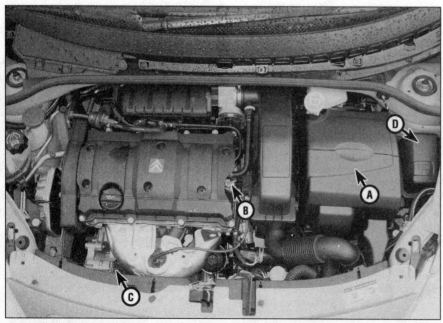

Check that electrical connections are secure (with the ignition switched off) and spray them with a water-dispersant spray like WD-40 if you suspect a problem due to damp

**D** Check that all fuses are still in good condition and none have blown.

# Jump starting

When jump-starting a car using a booster battery, observe the following precautions:

✔ Before connecting the booster battery, make sure that the ignition is switched off.

**Caution: Remove the key in case the central locking engages when the jump leads are connected**

✔ Ensure that all electrical equipment (lights, heater, wipers, etc) is switched off.

✔ Take note of any special precautions printed on the battery case.

✔ Make sure that the booster battery is the same voltage as the discharged one in the vehicle.

✔ If the battery is being jump-started from the battery in another vehicle, the two vehicles MUST NOT TOUCH each other.

✔ Make sure that the transmission is in neutral (or PARK, in the case of automatic transmission).

 **Jump starting will get you out of trouble, but you must correct whatever made the battery go flat in the first place. There are three possibilities:**

**1** The battery has been drained by repeated attempts to start, or by leaving the lights on.

**2** The charging system is not working properly (alternator drivebelt slack or broken, alternator wiring fault or alternator itself faulty).

**3** The battery itself is at fault (electrolyte low, or battery worn out).

**1** Connect one end of the red jump lead to the positive (+) terminal of the flat battery

**2** Connect the other end of the red lead to the positive (+) terminal of the booster battery.

**3** Connect one end of the black jump lead to the negative (-) terminal of the booster battery

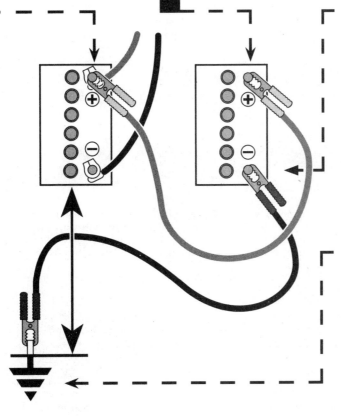

**4** Connect the other end of the black jump lead to a bolt or bracket on the engine block, well away from the battery, on the vehicle to be started.

**5** Make sure that the jump leads will not come into contact with the fan, drive-belts or other moving parts of the engine.

**6** Start the engine using the booster battery and run it at idle speed. Switch on the lights, rear window demister and heater blower motor, then disconnect the jump leads in the reverse order of connection. Turn off the lights etc.

# Wheel changing

⚠️ *Warning: Do not change a wheel in a situation where you risk being hit by other traffic. On busy roads, try to stop in a lay-by or a gateway. Be wary of passing traffic while changing the wheel – it is easy to become distracted by the job in hand.*

## Preparation

☐ When a puncture occurs, stop as soon as it is safe to do so.

☐ Park on firm level ground, if possible, and well out of the way of other traffic.

☐ Use hazard warning lights if necessary.

☐ If you have one, use a warning triangle to alert other drivers of your presence.

☐ Apply the handbrake and engage first or reverse gear (or Park on models with automatic transmission).

☐ Chock the wheel diagonally opposite the one being removed – a couple of large stones will do for this.

☐ If the ground is soft, use a flat piece of wood to spread the load under the jack.

## Changing the wheel

**1** The spare wheel and tools are stored in the luggage compartment. Lift up the carpet, release the retaining strap and remove the tool kit and jack from the centre of the spare wheel. Remove the spare wheel.

**2** Remove the wheel trim/hub cap (as applicable). On models where anti-theft wheel bolts are fitted, pull off the plastic cover using the plastic tool in the tool kit, then unscrew the anti-theft bolt using the special tool provided.

**3** Using the wheelbrace, slacken each wheel bolt by half a turn. On models with alloy wheels, use the special tool to undo the locking wheel nuts.

**4** Make sure the jack is located on firm ground, and engage the jack head correctly with the reinforced area on the sill (indicated by a triangle). Then raise the jack until the wheel is raised clear of the ground.

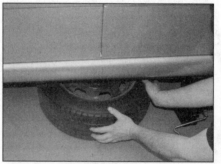

**5** Unscrew the wheel bolts and remove the wheel. Place the wheel under the vehicle sill in case the jack fails. Fit the spare wheel and screw in the bolts. Lightly tighten the bolts with the wheelbrace then lower the car to the ground.

**6** Securely tighten the wheel bolts in a diagonal sequence then refit the wheel trim/hub cap/wheel bolt covers (as applicable).

## Finally...

☐ Remove the wheel chocks.

☐ Stow the jack and tools in the correct locations in the car.

☐ Check the tyre pressure on the wheel just fitted. If it is low, or if you don't have a pressure gauge with you, drive slowly to the nearest garage and inflate the tyre to the right pressure.

☐ Have the damaged tyre or wheel repaired as soon as possible.

# Identifying leaks

Puddles on the garage floor or drive, or obvious wetness under the bonnet or underneath the car, suggest a leak that needs investigating. It can sometimes be difficult to decide where the leak is coming from, especially if an engine undershield is fitted. Leaking oil or fluid can also be blown rearwards by the passage of air under the car, giving a false impression of where the problem lies.

 *Warning: Most automotive oils and fluids are poisonous. Wash them off skin, and change out of contaminated clothing, without delay.*

 *The smell of a fluid leaking from the car may provide a clue to what's leaking. Some fluids are distinctively coloured. It may help to remove the engine undershield, clean the car carefully and to park it over some clean paper overnight as an aid to locating the source of the leak. Remember that some leaks may only occur while the engine is running.*

## Sump oil

Engine oil may leak from the drain plug...

## Oil from filter

...or from the base of the oil filter.

## Gearbox oil

Gearbox oil can leak from the seals at the inboard ends of the driveshafts.

## Antifreeze

Leaking antifreeze often leaves a crystalline deposit like this.

## Brake fluid

A leak occurring at a wheel is almost certainly brake fluid.

## Power steering fluid

Power steering fluid may leak from the pipe connectors on the steering rack.

# Towing

When all else fails, you may find yourself having to get a tow home – or of course you may be helping somebody else. Long-distance recovery should only be done by a garage or breakdown service. For shorter distances, DIY towing using another car is easy enough, but observe the following points:

☐ Use a proper tow-rope – they are not expensive. The vehicle being towed must display an ON TOW sign in its rear window.

☐ Always turn the ignition key to the 'On' position when the vehicle is being towed, so that the steering lock is released, and the direction indicator and brake lights work.

☐ Only attach the tow-rope to the towing eye provided. This can be found in the tool kit in the luggage compartment, and is screwed into the front or rear towing locations on the body, as required. Lift up the access cover from the towing eye location and use the wheel brace to screw the towing eye firmly into place.

☐ Before being towed, release the handbrake and select neutral on the transmission.

*On models with automatic transmission, if towing with the front wheels on the ground, the towing speed must be limited to 30 mph (48 kph) and the distance must not exceed 30 miles (48 km). If in doubt, do not tow, or transmission damage may result.*

☐ Note that greater-than-usual pedal pressure will be required to operate the brakes, since the vacuum servo unit is only operational with the engine running.

☐ Greater-than-usual steering effort will also be required.

☐ The driver of the car being towed must keep the tow-rope taut at all times to avoid snatching.

☐ Make sure that both drivers know the route before setting off.

☐ Only drive at moderate speeds and keep the distance towed to a minimum. Drive smoothly and allow plenty of time for slowing down at junctions.

# Introduction

There are some very simple checks which need only take a few minutes to carry out, but which could save you a lot of inconvenience and expense.

These *Weekly checks* require no great skill or special tools, and the small amount of time they take to perform could prove to be very well spent, for example:

☐ Keeping an eye on tyre condition and pressures, will not only help to stop them wearing out prematurely, but could also save your life.

☐ Many breakdowns are caused by electrical problems. Battery-related faults are particularly common, and a quick check on a regular basis will often prevent the majority of these.

☐ If your car develops a brake fluid leak, the first time you might know about it is when your brakes don't work properly. Checking the level regularly will give advance warning of this kind of problem.

☐ If the oil or coolant levels run low, the cost of repairing any engine damage will be far greater than fixing the leak, for example.

# Underbonnet check points

◀ **1.1 and 1.4 litre petrol (1.6 litre similar)**

**A** *Engine oil level dipstick*

**B** *Engine oil filler cap*

**C** *Coolant expansion tank*

**D** *Brake and clutch fluid reservoir*

**E** *Washer fluid reservoir*

**F** *Battery*

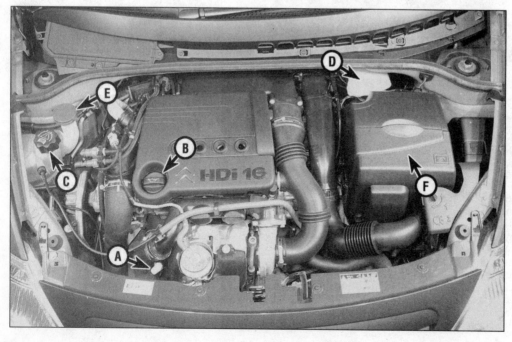

◀ **1.4 litre 16-valve diesel (1.4 litre 8-valve and 1.6 litre similar)**

**A** *Engine oil level dipstick*

**B** *Engine oil filler cap*

**C** *Coolant expansion tank*

**D** *Brake and clutch fluid reservoir*

**E** *Washer fluid reservoir*

**F** *Battery*

# Engine oil level

## Before you start

✔ Make sure that the car is on level ground.
✔ Check the oil level before the car is driven, or at least 5 minutes after the engine has been switched off.

 **If the oil is checked immediately after driving the vehicle, some of the oil will remain in the upper engine components, resulting in an inaccurate reading on the dipstick.**

## The correct oil

Modern engines place great demands on their oil. It is very important that the correct oil for your car is used (see *Lubricants and fluids*).

## Car care

● If you have to add oil frequently, you should check whether you have any oil leaks. Place some clean paper under the car overnight, and check for stains in the morning. If there are no leaks, then the engine may be burning oil.
● Always maintain the level between the upper and lower dipstick marks (see photo 3). If the level is too low, severe engine damage may occur. Oil seal failure may result if the engine is overfilled by adding too much oil.

**1** The dipstick is often brightly coloured for easy identification. Withdraw the dipstick.

**2** Using a clean rag or paper towel, wipe all the oil from the dipstick. Insert the clean dipstick into the tube as far as it will go, then withdraw it again.

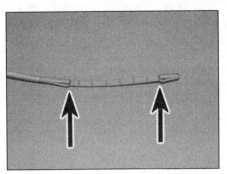

**3** Note the oil level on the end of the dipstick, which should be between the upper (MAX) mark and lower (MIN) mark. Approximately 1.5 litres of oil (petrol engines) or 1.8 litres of oil (diesel engines) will raise the level from the lower mark to the upper mark.

**4** Oil is added through the filler cap. Unscrew the cap and top up the level; a funnel may help to reduce spillage. Add the oil slowly, checking the level on the dipstick often. Don't overfill (see *Car Care*).

# Coolant level

 **Warning: Do not attempt to remove the expansion tank pressure cap when the engine is hot, as there is a very great risk of scalding. Do not leave open containers of coolant about, as it is poisonous.**

## Car Care

● With a sealed-type cooling system, adding coolant should not be necessary on a regular basis. If frequent topping-up is required, it is likely there is a leak. Check the radiator, all hoses and joint faces for signs of staining or wetness, and rectify as necessary.

● It is important that antifreeze is used in the cooling system all year round, not just during the winter months. Don't top up with water alone, as the antifreeze will become diluted.

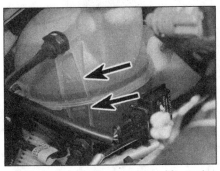

**1** The coolant level varies with engine temperature. The level is checked in the expansion tank, which is located on the right-hand side of the engine compartment. When the engine is cold, the coolant level should be between the MAXI and MINI marks.

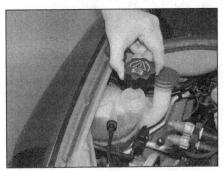

**2** If topping-up is necessary, wait until the engine is cold then turn the expansion tank cap slowly anti-clockwise, and pause until any pressure remaining in the system is released. Unscrew the cap and lift off.

**3** Add a mixture of water and antifreeze to the expansion tank, until the coolant level is up to the MAXI level mark. Refit the cap, turning it clockwise as far as it will go until it is secure.

# Washer fluid level

● Screenwash additives not only keep the windscreen clean during bad weather, they also prevent the washer system freezing in cold weather – which is when you are likely to need it most. Don't top-up using plain water, as the screenwash will become diluted, and will freeze in cold weather.

 *Warning: On no account use engine coolant antifreeze in the screen washer system – this may damage the paintwork.*

**1** The washer fluid reservoir is located at the front right-hand side of the engine compartment. If topping-up is necessary, open the cap.

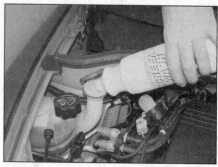

**2** When topping-up the reservoir a screenwash additive should be added in the quantities recommended on the bottle.

# Brake and clutch fluid level

 *Warning:*
● *Brake fluid can harm your eyes and damage painted surfaces, so use extreme caution when handling and pouring it.*
● *Do not use fluid that has been standing open for some time, as it absorbs moisture from the air, which can cause a dangerous loss of braking effectiveness.*

**HAYNES HiNT**
● *Make sure that your car is on level ground.*

● *The fluid level in the reservoir will drop slightly as the brake pads and shoes wear down, but the fluid level must never be allowed to drop below the MIN mark.*

## Safety first!

● If the reservoir requires repeated topping-up, this is an indication of a fluid leak somewhere in the system, which should be investigated immediately.

● If a leak is suspected, the car should not be driven until the braking system has been checked. Never take any risks where brakes are concerned.

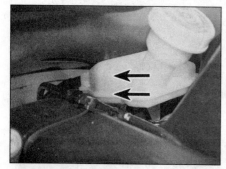

**1** The MAX and MIN marks are indicated on the side of the reservoir, which is located on the front of the vacuum servo unit in the engine compartment. The fluid level must be kept between these two marks.

**2** If topping-up is necessary, first wipe the area around the filler cap with a clean rag before removing the cap. When adding fluid, it's a good idea to inspect the reservoir. The system should be drained and refilled if dirt is seen in the fluid (see Chapter 9).

**3** Carefully add fluid, avoiding spilling it on surrounding paintwork. Use only the specified hydraulic fluid; mixing different types of fluid can cause damage to the system and/or a loss of braking effectiveness. After filling to the correct level, refit the cap securely and wipe off any spilt fluid.

# Tyre condition and pressure

It is very important that tyres are in good condition, and at the correct pressure - having a tyre failure at any speed is highly dangerous. Tyre wear is influenced by driving style - harsh braking and acceleration, or fast cornering, will all produce more rapid tyre wear. As a general rule, the front tyres wear out faster than the rears. Interchanging the tyres from front to rear ("rotating" the tyres) may result in more even wear. However, if this is completely effective, you may have the expense of replacing all four tyres at once!

Remove any nails or stones embedded in the tread before they penetrate the tyre to cause deflation. If removal of a nail does reveal that the tyre has been punctured, refit the nail so that its point of penetration is marked. Then immediately change the wheel, and have the tyre repaired by a tyre dealer.

Regularly check the tyres for damage in the form of cuts or bulges, especially in the sidewalls. Periodically remove the wheels, and clean any dirt or mud from the inside and outside surfaces. Examine the wheel rims for signs of rusting, corrosion or other damage. Light alloy wheels are easily damaged by "kerbing" whilst parking; steel wheels may also become dented or buckled. A new wheel is very often the only way to overcome severe damage.

New tyres should be balanced when they are fitted, but it may become necessary to re-balance them as they wear, or if the balance weights fitted to the wheel rim should fall off. Unbalanced tyres will wear more quickly, as will the steering and suspension components. Wheel imbalance is normally signified by vibration, particularly at a certain speed (typically around 50 mph). If this vibration is felt only through the steering, then it is likely that just the front wheels need balancing. If, however, the vibration is felt through the whole car, the rear wheels could be out of balance. Wheel balancing should be carried out by a tyre dealer or garage.

**1 Tread Depth - visual check**
The original tyres have tread wear safety bands (B), which will appear when the tread depth reaches approximately 1.6 mm. The band positions are indicated by a triangular mark on the tyre sidewall (A).

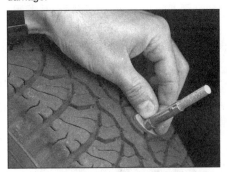

**2 Tread Depth - manual check**
Alternatively, tread wear can be monitored with a simple, inexpensive device known as a tread depth indicator gauge.

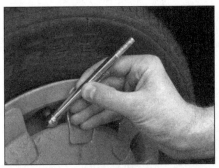

**3 Tyre Pressure Check**
Check the tyre pressures regularly with the tyres cold. Do not adjust the tyre pressures immediately after the vehicle has been used, or an inaccurate setting will result.

# Tyre tread wear patterns

### Shoulder Wear

**Underinflation (wear on both sides)**
Under-inflation will cause overheating of the tyre, because the tyre will flex too much, and the tread will not sit correctly on the road surface. This will cause a loss of grip and excessive wear, not to mention the danger of sudden tyre failure due to heat build-up.
*Check and adjust pressures*
**Incorrect wheel camber (wear on one side)**
*Repair or renew suspension parts*
**Hard cornering**
*Reduce speed!*

### Centre Wear

**Overinflation**
Over-inflation will cause rapid wear of the centre part of the tyre tread, coupled with reduced grip, harsher ride, and the danger of shock damage occurring in the tyre casing.
*Check and adjust pressures*

*If you sometimes have to inflate your car's tyres to the higher pressures specified for maximum load or sustained high speed, don't forget to reduce the pressures to normal afterwards.*

### Uneven Wear

Front tyres may wear unevenly as a result of wheel misalignment. Most tyre dealers and garages can check and adjust the wheel alignment (or "tracking") for a modest charge.
**Incorrect camber or castor**
*Repair or renew suspension parts*
**Malfunctioning suspension**
*Repair or renew suspension parts*
**Unbalanced wheel**
*Balance tyres*
**Incorrect toe setting**
*Adjust front wheel alignment*
**Note:** *The feathered edge of the tread which typifies toe wear is best checked by feel.*

# Battery

**Caution: Before carrying out any work on the vehicle battery, read the precautions given in 'Safety first!' at the start of this manual.**

✔ Make sure that the battery tray is in good condition, and that the clamp is tight. Corrosion on the tray, retaining clamp and the battery itself can be removed with a solution of water and baking soda. Thoroughly rinse all cleaned areas with water. Any metal parts damaged by corrosion should be covered with a zinc-based primer, then painted.

✔ Periodically (approximately every three months), check the charge condition of the battery as described in Chapter 5A.

✔ If the battery is flat, and you need to jump start your vehicle, see *Roadside Repairs*.

**1** The battery is located on the left-hand side of the engine compartment, in a plastic box. Lift off the front part of the cover followed by the rear part, to gain access to the battery. The exterior of the battery should be inspected periodically for damage such as a cracked case or cover.

**2** Check the tightness of the battery cable clamps to ensure good electrical connections. You should not be able to move them. Also check each cable for cracks and frayed conductors.

HAYNES HiNT

*Battery corrosion can be kept to a minimum by applying a layer of petroleum jelly to the clamps and terminals after they are reconnected.*

**3** If corrosion (white, fluffy deposits) is evident, remove the cables from the battery terminals, clean them with a small wire brush, then refit them. Automotive stores sell a useful tool for cleaning the battery post . . .

**4** . . . as well as the battery cable clamps.

---

# Electrical systems

✔ Check all external lights and the horn. Refer to the appropriate Sections of Chapter 12 for details if any of the circuits are found to be inoperative.

✔ Visually check all accessible wiring connectors, harnesses and retaining clips for security, and for signs of chafing or damage.

HAYNES HiNT

*If you need to check your brake lights and indicators unaided, back up to a wall or garage door and operate the lights. The reflected light should show if they are working properly.*

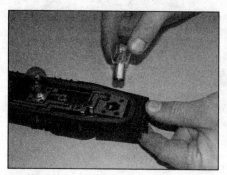

**1** If a single indicator light, brake light or headlight has failed, it is likely that a bulb has blown and will need to be renewed. Refer to Chapter 12 for details. If both brake lights have failed, it is possible that the brake light switch operated by the brake pedal has failed. Refer to Chapter 9 for details.

**2** If more than one indicator light or tail light has failed it is likely that either a fuse has blown or that there is a fault in the circuit (see Chapter 12). The main fuses are located in the fuse/relay boxes situated behind the cover in the facia on the driver's side, and in the engine compartment (refer to Chapter 12).

**3** To renew a blown fuse, remove it, where applicable, using the plastic tool provided. Fit a new fuse of the same rating, available from car accessory shops. It is important that you find the reason that the fuse blew (see *Electrical fault finding* in Chapter 12).

# Wiper blades

**Note:** *On 2005-on models, set the wiper blades to their vertical (maintenance) position by first switching the ignition on and off, then within one minute move the wiper control stalk. To return the blades to their normal position, switch the ignition on and move the wiper control stalk.*

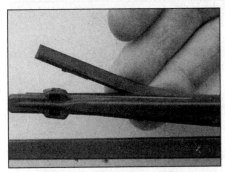

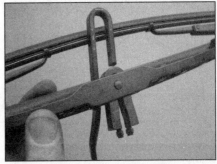

**1** Check the condition of the wiper blades; if they are cracked or show any signs of deterioration, or if the glass swept area is smeared, renew them. Wiper blades should be renewed annually.

**2** To remove a windscreen wiper blade, pull the arm fully away from the screen until it locks. Swivel the blade through 90°, then depress the locking clip at the base of the mounting block.

**3** Move the blade down the arm to disengage the mounting block, then slide the blade from the arm. Don't forget to check the tailgate wiper blade as well (where applicable).

## Lubricants and fluids

**Engine**

| | |
|---|---|
| Petrol . . . . . . . . . . . . . . . . . . . . . . . . . . . . . . . . . . . . . . | Synthetic or semi-synthetic multigrade engine oil, viscosity SAE 5W-40 or 10W-40 to specification API SH/SJ and/or ACEA A3: ESSO ULTRA/ULTRON or TOTAL QUARTZ |
| Diesel . . . . . . . . . . . . . . . . . . . . . . . . . . . . . . . . . . . . . . | Synthetic or semi-synthetic multigrade engine oil, viscosity SAE 10W-40 to specification API CF/CD and/or ACEA B3: ESSO ULTRA DIESEL or TOTAL QUARTZ DIESEL 7000 |
| **Cooling system** . . . . . . . . . . . . . . . . . . . . . . . . . . . . . | Mixture of monoethylene glycol based antifreeze (PROCOR TM 108, GLYSANTIN G33 or REVKOGEL 2000) and clean de-ionised water |
| **Manual gearbox**. . . . . . . . . . . . . . . . . . . . . . . . . . . . . . | ESSO BV 75W-80W or TOTAL TRANSMISSION BV 75W-80 only |
| **Automatic transmission** . . . . . . . . . . . . . . . . . . . . . . | ESSO ATF 4HP20-AL4 only |
| **Brake and clutch fluid reservoir** . . . . . . . . . . . . . . . . | Hydraulic fluid to SAE J1703, DOT 4 |
| **Particulate filter additives**. . . . . . . . . . . . . . . . . . . . . | Eolys DPX42 or Eolys 176 |

## Tyre pressures

**Note:** *The latest tyre pressure recommendations are marked on a label attached to the front door pillar on the left-hand side. The following pressures are included as a guide, and apply to original-equipment tyres. The pressures may vary if any other make or type of tyre is fitted; check with the tyre manufacturer or supplier for correct pressures if necessary.*

| | **Front** | **Rear** |
|---|---|---|
| **All models** . . . . . . . . . . . . . . . . . . . . . . . . . . . . . . . . . | 2.1 bar (30 psi) | 2.1 bar (30 psi) |

# Chapter 1 Part A:
# Routine maintenance and servicing – petrol models

## Contents

## Degrees of difficulty

| | | | | |
|---|---|---|---|---|
| **Easy,** suitable for novice with little experience  | **Fairly easy,** suitable for beginner with some experience | **Fairly difficult,** suitable for competent DIY mechanic | **Difficult,** suitable for experienced DIY mechanic | **Very difficult,** suitable for expert DIY or professional 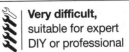 |

**Lubricants and fluids**........................................ Refer to end of *Weekly checks* on page 0•16

## Capacities

### Engine oil
Including filter:
1.1 litre (TU1) and 1.4 litre (TU3) engines ..................... 3.0 litres
1.4 litre (ET3) engine............................................... 3.75 litres
1.6 litre (TU5) engine.............................................. 3.25 litres
Difference between MAX and MIN dipstick marks:
All engines except 1.4 litre (ET3) ......................... 1.5 litres
1.4 litre (ET3) engine............................................. 1.2 litres

### Cooling system
All engines except 1.4 litre (ET3) ......................... 7.0 litres
1.4 litre (ET3) engine............................................. 6.0 litres

### Transmission
Manual ................................................................ 2.0 litres
Automatic:
Refilling after draining........................................ 4.5 litres
From dry ............................................................. 6.0 litres

### Fuel tank
Early models....................................................... 45 litres
Later models....................................................... 50 litres

## Engine
Auxiliary drivebelt tensions (for use with belt tensioning tool – see text):
Without air conditioning:
New belt:
1.1 and 1.4 litre engines ................................. 55 SEEM units
1.6 litre engine................................................ 120 SEEM units
Used belt:                                                            SEEM units
1.1 and 1.4 litre engines ................................. N/A
1.6 litre engine................................................ 60 to 80 SEEM units
With air conditioning:
New belt:
1.1 and 1.4 litre engines ................................. 120 SEEM units
1.6 litre engine................................................ 100 SEEM units
Used belt:
1.1 and 1.4 litre engines ................................. 60 to 80 SEEM units
1.6 litre engine................................................ 75 SEEM units

## Cooling system
Antifreeze mixture:
50% antifreeze .................................................... Protection down to –35°C
**Note:** *Refer to antifreeze manufacturer for latest recommendations.*

## Ignition system
Spark plugs:
1.1 (TU1) and 1.4 litre (TU3) engines .................... Bosch FR7DE, Eyquem RFN58LZ or Champion RC8YLC
1.4 litre (ET3) engines......................................... Bosch VR8SE
1.6 litre (TU5) engines......................................... Bosch FR7ME or Eyquem RFN58HZ
Electrode gap........................................................ 0.9 mm

## Brakes
Brake pad and shoe friction material minimum thickness ........... 2.0 mm

## Tyre pressures ............................................... See end of *Weekly checks* on page 0•16

## Torque wrench settings

| | Nm | lbf ft |
| --- | --- | --- |
| Alternator mounting bolts | 37 | 27 |
| Automatic transmission: | | |
| Filler plug | 24 | 18 |
| Level plug | 24 | 18 |
| Manual transmission filler/level plug | 25 | 18 |
| Oil filter cover | 25 | 18 |
| Roadwheel bolts | 90 | 66 |
| Spark plugs | 25 | 18 |
| Sump drain plug | 30 | 22 |

**Note:** *This maintenance schedule is a guide recommended by Haynes, for servicing your own vehicle. For the manufacturer's maintenance schedule, check with your local dealer.*

The maintenance intervals in this manual are provided with the assumption that you, not the dealer, will be carrying out the work. These are the minimum maintenance intervals recommended by us for vehicles driven daily. If you wish to keep your vehicle in peak condition at all times, you may wish to perform some of these procedures more often. We encourage frequent maintenance, because it enhances the efficiency, performance and resale value of your vehicle.

If the vehicle is driven in dusty areas, used to tow a trailer, or driven frequently at slow speeds (idling in traffic) or on short journeys, more frequent maintenance intervals are recommended.

When the vehicle is new, it should be serviced by a dealer service department (or other workshop recognised by the vehicle manufacturer as providing the same standard of service) in order to preserve the warranty. The vehicle manufacturer may reject warranty claims if you are unable to prove that servicing has been carried out as and when specified, using only original equipment parts or parts certified to be of equivalent quality.

## Every 250 miles (400 km) or weekly
☐ Refer to *Weekly checks*

## Every 10 000 miles (15 000 km) or 12 months – whichever comes sooner
☐ Renew the engine oil and filter* (Section 3).
☐ Check all underbonnet components and hoses for fluid leaks (Section 4).
☐ Check the condition of the driveshaft rubber gaiters and CV joints (Section 5).
☐ Lubricate all hinges and locks (Section 6).
☐ Carry out a road test (Section 7).

***Note:** Citroën recommend the engine oil and filter are changed every 20 000 miles or two years. However, oil and filter changes are good for the engine and we recommend that the oil and filter are renewed more frequently, especially if the vehicle is used on a lot of short journeys.*

## Every 20 000 miles (30 000 km) or two years – whichever comes sooner
☐ Reset the service interval indicator (Section 8).
☐ Renew the pollen filter (Section 9).
☐ Check the condition of the auxiliary drivebelt (Section 10).
☐ Check the condition of the brake pads (Section 11).
☐ Check the condition of the rear brake shoes – models with rear drum brakes (Section 12).
☐ Check the operation of the handbrake (Section 13).
☐ Check the condition of the exhaust system (Section 14).
☐ Check the steering and suspension components (Section 15).

## Every 40 000 miles (60 000 km)
☐ Renew the timing belt (Section 16).

**Note:** *Although the normal interval for timing belt renewal is 80 000 miles (120 000 km) or 10 years, it is strongly recommended that the interval is reduced to 40 000 miles (60 000 km), especially on vehicles which are subjected to intensive use, ie, mainly short journeys or a lot of stop-start driving. The actual belt renewal interval is therefore very much up to the individual owner, but bear in mind that severe engine damage will result if the belt breaks.*

## Every 40 000 miles (60 000 km) or two years – whichever comes sooner
☐ Renew the brake fluid (Section 17).

**Note:** *A hydraulic clutch shares its fluid reservoir with the braking system, and may also need to be bled.*

## Every 40 000 miles (60 000 km) or four years – whichever comes sooner
☐ Renew the spark plugs (Section 18).
☐ Renew the air cleaner filter element (Section 19).
☐ Check the manual transmission oil level (Section 20).
☐ Check the automatic transmission fluid level (Section 21).
☐ Check the exhaust emissions (Section 22).
☐ Renew the coolant* (Section 23).

***Note:** The cooling system is initially 'filled-for-life' and does not require regular renewal.*

## Every ten years
☐ Renew the airbags and seat belt pretensioners (Section 24).

## Underbonnet view of a 1.4 litre (TU3) model (1.1 litre and 1.4 litre (ET3) similar)

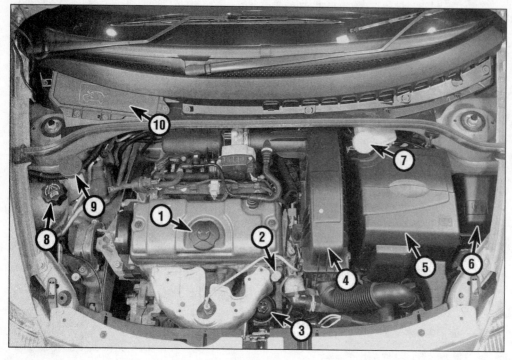

1  Engine oil filler cap
2  Engine oil level dipstick
3  Engine oil filter
4  Air cleaner assembly
5  Battery
6  Fuse/relay box
7  Brake/clutch fluid
   reservoir
8  Coolant expansion tank
9  Washer fluid reservoir
10 Pollen filter housing

## Underbonnet view of a 1.6 litre model

1  Engine oil filler cap
2  Engine oil level dipstick
3  Engine oil filter
4  Air cleaner assembly
5  Battery
6  Fuse/relay box
7  Brake/clutch fluid
   reservoir
8  Coolant expansion tank
9  Washer fluid reservoir
10 Pollen filter housing

## Front underbody view

1 Engine oil drain plug
2 Air conditioning compressor
3 Catalytic converter
4 Radiator electric cooling fan
5 Manual transmission oil filler/level plug
6 Brake caliper
7 Suspension lower arm
8 Front suspension subframe
9 Driveshaft inner constant velocity joint
10 Subframe bracing strut
11 Track rod balljoint
12 Anti-roll bar connecting link

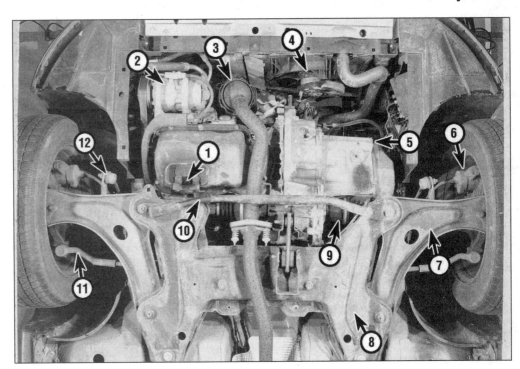

## Rear underbody view

1 Fuel tank
2 Anti-roll bar
3 Rear axle beam
4 Shock absorber lower mounting
5 Coil spring
6 Exhaust rear silencer
7 Handbrake cable

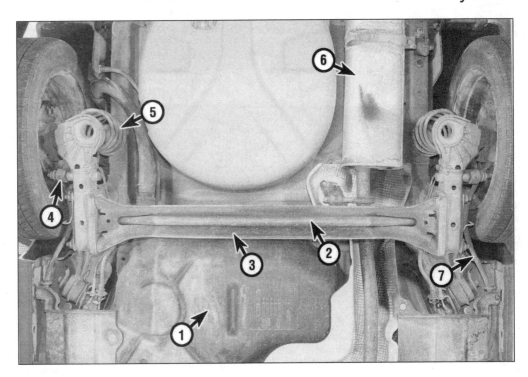

## 1  General information

**1** This Chapter is designed to help the home mechanic maintain his/her vehicle for safety, economy, long life and peak performance.

**2** The Chapter contains a master maintenance schedule, followed by Sections dealing specifically with each task in the schedule. Visual checks, adjustments, component renewal and other helpful items are included. Refer to the accompanying illustrations of the engine compartment and the underside of the vehicle for the locations of the various components.

**3** Servicing your vehicle in accordance with the mileage/time maintenance schedule and the following Sections will provide a planned maintenance programme, which should result in a long and reliable service life. This is a comprehensive plan, so maintaining some items but not others at the specified service intervals will not produce the same results.

**4** As you service your vehicle, you will discover that many of the procedures can – and should – be grouped together, because of the particular procedure being performed, or because of the close proximity of two otherwise-unrelated components to one another. For example, if the vehicle is raised for any reason, the exhaust can be inspected at the same time as the suspension and steering components.

**5** The first step in this maintenance programme is to prepare yourself before the actual work begins. Read through all the Sections relevant to the work to be carried out, then make a list and gather together all the parts and tools required. If a problem is encountered, seek advice from a parts specialist, or a dealer service department.

## 2  Regular maintenance

**1** If, from the time the vehicle is new, the routine maintenance schedule is followed closely, and frequent checks are made of fluid levels and high-wear items, as suggested throughout this manual, the engine will be kept in relatively good running condition, and the need for additional work will be minimised.

**2** It is possible that there will be times when the engine is running poorly due to the lack of regular maintenance. This is even more likely if a used vehicle, which has not received regular and frequent maintenance checks, is purchased. In such cases, additional work may need to be carried out, outside of the regular maintenance intervals.

**3** If engine wear is suspected, a compression test (refer to Chapter 2A) will provide valuable information regarding the overall performance of the main internal components. Such a test can be used as a basis to decide on the extent of the work to be carried out. If, for example, a compression test indicates serious internal engine wear, conventional maintenance as described in this Chapter will not greatly improve the performance of the engine, and may prove a waste of time and money, unless extensive overhaul work (Chapter 2C) is carried out first.

**4** The following series of operations are those often required to improve the performance of a generally poor-running engine:

### Primary operations

a) *Clean, inspect and test the battery (See 'Weekly checks').*
b) *Check all the engine-related fluids (See 'Weekly checks').*
c) *Check the condition of all hoses, and check for fluid leaks (Section 4).*
d) *Check the condition and tension of the auxiliary drivebelt (Section 10).*
e) *Renew the spark plugs (Section 18).*
f) *Check the condition of the air cleaner filter element, and renew if necessary (Section 19).*

**5** If the above operations do not prove fully effective, carry out the following operations:

### Secondary operations

All items listed under Primary operations, plus the following:

a) *Check the charging system (Chapter 5A).*
b) *Check the ignition system (Chapter 5B).*
c) *Check the fuel system (Chapter 4A).*

# Every 10 000 miles (15 000 km) or 12 months

## 3  Engine oil and filter renewal

**Note:** *A suitable square-section wrench may be required to undo the sump drain plug. These wrenches can be obtained from most motor factors or your Citroën dealer.*

**1** Frequent oil and filter changes are the most important preventative maintenance procedures which can be undertaken by the DIY owner. As engine oil ages, it becomes diluted and contaminated, which leads to premature engine wear.

**2** Before starting this procedure, gather together all the necessary tools and materials. Also make sure that you have plenty of clean rags and newspapers handy, to mop-up any spills. Ideally, the engine oil should be warm, as it will drain better, and any impurities suspended in the oil will be removed with it. Take care, however, not to touch the exhaust or any other hot parts of the engine when working under the vehicle. To avoid any possibility of scalding, and to protect yourself from possible skin irritants and other harmful contaminants in used engine oils, it is advisable to wear gloves when carrying out this work. Access to the underside of the vehicle will be greatly improved if it can be raised on a lift, driven onto ramps, or jacked up and supported on axle stands (see *Jacking and vehicle support*). Whichever method is chosen, make sure that the vehicle remains level, or if it is at an angle, that the drain plug is at the lowest point.

**3** Undo the screws and remove the engine undershield, where fitted.

**4** Some engines have a metal guard plate bolted to the sump directly over the drain plug **(see illustration)**. If a long square-section wrench is available, it is just possible to remove the drain plug through the aperture in the guard plate. Alternatively, undo the retaining bolts and remove the guard plate. To further improve access to the drain plug, undo the two bolts and remove the subframe bracing strut.

**5** Slacken the drain plug about half a turn **(see illustration)**. Position the draining container under the drain plug, then remove the plug completely. If possible, try to keep the plug pressed into the sump while unscrewing it by hand the last couple of turns **(see Haynes Hint)**. Recover the sealing ring from the drain plug.

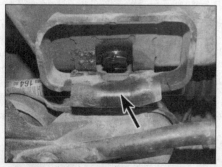

**3.4  Metal guard plate (arrowed) located over the sump drain plug on certain models**

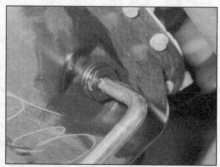

**3.5  Slackening the sump drain plug with a square-section wrench**

*As the drain plug releases from the threads, move it away sharply so the stream of oil issuing from the sump runs into the container, not up your sleeve.*

**6** Allow some time for the old oil to drain, noting that it may be necessary to reposition the container as the oil flow slows to a trickle.
**7** After all the oil has drained, wipe off the drain plug with a clean rag, and fit a new sealing washer. Clean the area around the drain plug opening, and refit the plug, tightening it to the specified torque. Where applicable, refit the guard plate and subframe bracing strut and tighten the retaining bolts securely.
**8** Move the container into position under the oil filter, which is located on the front of the cylinder block.
**9** On these engines, the filter element is contained within a filter cover. Using a socket or spanner, slacken and remove the filter cover from above. Be prepared for fluid spillage, and recover the O-ring seal from the cover **(see illustrations)**.
**10** Pull the filter element from the filter cover.
**11** Use a clean rag to remove all oil, dirt and sludge from the inside and outside of the filter cover.
**12** Insert the new filter element in to the cover, then apply a little clean engine oil to the new O-ring seal, and fit it to the filter cover **(see illustrations)**.
**13** Refit the filter/cover to the housing and tighten the cover to the specified torque.
**14** Remove the old oil and all tools from under the car, then lower the car to the ground (if applicable).
**15** Remove the dipstick, then unscrew the oil filler cap from the cylinder head cover. Fill the engine, using the correct grade and type of oil (see *Lubricants and fluids*). An oil can spout or funnel may help to reduce spillage. Pour in half the specified quantity of oil first, then wait a few minutes for the oil to run to the sump. Continue adding oil a small quantity at a time until the level is up to the lower mark on the dipstick. Refit the filler cap.
**16** Start the engine and run it for a few minutes; check for leaks around the oil filter and the sump drain plug. Note that there may be a delay of a few seconds before the oil pressure warning light goes out when the engine is first started, as the oil circulates through the engine oil galleries and the new oil filter before the pressure builds-up.

**3.9a  Slacken and remove the filter cover . . .**

**3.12a  Fit the new element into the cover . . .**

**17** Refit the engine undershield (where applicable), and secure it in place with the screw fasteners.
**18** Switch off the engine, and wait a few minutes for the oil to settle in the sump once more. With the new oil circulated and the filter completely full, recheck the level on the dipstick, and add more oil as necessary.
**19** Dispose of the used engine oil and filter safely, with reference to *General repair procedures* at the rear of this manual. Do not discard the old filter with domestic household waste. The facility for waste oil disposal provided by many local council refuse tips generally has a filter receptacle alongside.

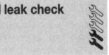

**4   Hose and fluid leak check**

### Cooling system

⚠️ *Warning: Refer to the safety information given in 'Safety first!' and Chapter 3 before disturbing any of the cooling system components.*

**1** Carefully check the radiator and heater coolant hoses along their entire length. Renew any hose which is cracked, swollen or which shows signs of deterioration. Cracks will show up better if the hose is squeezed. Pay close attention to the clips that secure the hoses to the cooling system components. Hose clips that have been over-tightened can pinch and puncture hoses, resulting in cooling system leaks.

**3.9b  . . . and recover the O-ring seal**

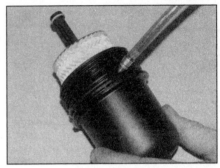

**3.12b  . . . and apply a little clean engine oil to the O-ring seal**

**2** Inspect all the cooling system components (hoses, joint faces, etc) for leaks. Where any problems of this nature are found on system components, renew the component or gasket with reference to Chapter 3.
**3** A leak from the cooling system will usually show up as white or rust-coloured deposits, on the area surrounding the leak **(see Haynes Hint)**.

### Fuel

⚠️ *Warning: Refer to the safety information given in 'Safety first!' and Chapter 4A before disturbing any of the fuel system components.*

**4** From within the engine compartment, check the security of all fuel pipe attachments and unions, and inspect the fuel pipes for kinks, chafing and deterioration.

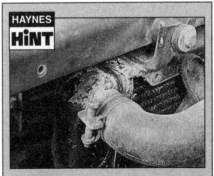

*A leak in the cooling system will usually show up as white- or rust-coloured deposits on the area adjoining the leak.*

**5** To identify fuel leaks between the fuel tank and the engine bay, the vehicle should be raised and securely supported on axle stands (see *Jacking and vehicle support*). Inspect the fuel tank and filler neck for punctures, cracks and other damage. The connection between the filler neck and tank is especially critical. Sometimes a rubber filler neck or connecting hose will leak due to loose retaining clamps or deteriorated rubber.

**6** Carefully check all rubber hoses and metal fuel lines leading away from the fuel tank. Check for loose connections, deteriorated hoses, kinked lines, and other damage. Pay particular attention to the vent pipes and hoses, which often loop up around the filler neck and can become blocked or kinked, making tank filling difficult. Follow the fuel supply and return lines to the front of the vehicle, carefully inspecting them all the way for signs of damage or corrosion. Renew damaged sections as necessary.

### Engine oil

**7** Inspect the area around the cylinder head cover, cylinder head, oil filter and sump joint faces. Bear in mind that, over a period of time, some very slight seepage from these areas is to be expected – what you are really looking for is any indication of a serious leak caused by gasket failure. Engine oil seeping from the base of the timing belt cover or the transmission bellhousing may be an indication of crankshaft or input shaft oil seal failure. Should a leak be found, renew the failed gasket or oil seal by referring to the appropriate Chapters in this manual.

### Air conditioning refrigerant

⚠️ **Warning: Refer to the safety information given in 'Safety first!' and Chapter 3, regarding the dangers of disturbing any of the air conditioning system components.**

**8** The air conditioning system is filled with a liquid refrigerant, which is retained under high pressure. If the air conditioning system is opened and depressurised without the aid of specialised equipment, the refrigerant will immediately turn into gas and escape into the atmosphere. If the liquid comes into contact with your skin, it can cause severe frostbite. In

**5.1 Check the driveshaft gaiters for damage or deterioration**

addition, the refrigerant contains substances which are environmentally damaging; for this reason, it should not be allowed to escape into the atmosphere.

**9** Any suspected air conditioning system leaks should be immediately referred to a Citroën dealer or air conditioning specialist. Leakage will be shown up as a steady drop in the level of refrigerant in the system.

**10** Note that water may drip from the condenser drain pipe, underneath the car, immediately after the air conditioning system has been in use. This is normal, and should not be cause for concern.

### Brake (and clutch) fluid

⚠️ **Warning: Refer to the safety information given in 'Safety first!' and Chapter 9, regarding the dangers of handling brake fluid.**

**11** With reference to Chapter 9, examine the area surrounding the brake pipe unions at the master cylinder for signs of leakage. Check the area around the base of fluid reservoir, for signs of leakage caused by seal failure. Also examine the brake pipe unions at the ABS hydraulic unit.

**12** If fluid loss is evident, but the leak cannot be pinpointed in the engine bay, the brake calipers and underbody brake lines and should be carefully checked with the vehicle raised and supported on axle stands. Leakage of fluid from the braking system is serious fault that must be rectified immediately.

**13** Refer to Chapter 6 and check for leakage around the hydraulic fluid line connections to the clutch master cylinder at the bulkhead, and to the clutch slave cylinder, bolted to the side of the transmission bellhousing.

**14** Brake/clutch hydraulic fluid is a toxic substance with a watery consistency. New fluid is almost colourless, but it becomes darker with age and use.

### Unidentified fluid leaks

**15** If there are signs that a fluid of some description is leaking from the vehicle, but you cannot identify the type of fluid or its exact origin, park the vehicle overnight and slide a large piece of card underneath it. Providing that the card is positioned in roughly in the right location, even the smallest leak will show up on the card. Not only will this help you to pinpoint the exact location of the leak, it should be easier to identify the fluid from its colour. Bear in mind, though, that the leak may only be occurring when the engine is running!

### Vacuum hoses

**16** Although the braking system is hydraulically-operated, the brake servo unit amplifies the effort you apply at the brake pedal, by making use of the vacuum created in the inlet manifold. Vacuum is ported to the servo by means of a large-bore hose. Any leaks that develop in this hose will reduce the effectiveness of the braking system.

**17** In addition, many of the underbonnet

components, particularly the emission control components, are driven by vacuum supplied from the inlet manifold via narrow-bore hoses. A leak in a vacuum hose means that air is being drawn into the hose (rather than escaping from it) and this makes leakage very difficult to detect. One method is to use an old length of vacuum hose as a kind of stethoscope – hold one end close to (but not in) your ear and use the other end to probe the area around the suspected leak. When the end of the hose is directly over a vacuum leak, a hissing sound will be heard clearly through the hose. Care must be taken to avoid contacting hot or moving components, as the engine must be running, when testing in this manner. Renew any vacuum hoses that are found to be defective.

### 5 Driveshaft gaiter and CV joints check

**1** With the vehicle raised and securely supported on stands (see *Jacking and vehicle support*), turn the steering onto full lock, then slowly rotate the roadwheel. Inspect the condition of the outer constant velocity (CV) joint gaiters, squeezing the gaiters to open out the folds (see illustration). Check for signs of cracking, splits or deterioration of the gaiter, which may allow the grease to escape, and lead to water and grit entry into the joint. Also check the security and condition of the retaining clips. Repeat these checks on the inner CV joints. If any damage or deterioration is found, the gaiters should be renewed (see Chapter 8).

**2** At the same time, check the general condition of the CV joints themselves by first holding the driveshaft and attempting to rotate the wheel. Repeat this check by holding the inner joint and attempting to rotate the driveshaft. Any appreciable movement indicates wear in the joints, wear in the driveshaft splines, or a loose driveshaft retaining nut.

### 6 Hinge and lock lubrication

**1** Work around the vehicle and lubricate the hinges of the bonnet, doors and tailgate with a small amount of general-purpose oil.

**2** Lightly lubricate the bonnet release mechanism and exposed section of inner cable with a smear of grease.

**3** Check carefully the security and operation of all hinges, latches and locks, adjusting them where required. Check the operation of the central locking system.

**4** Check the condition and operation of the tailgate struts, renewing them if either is leaking or no longer able to support the tailgate securely when raised.

## 7 Road test

### Instruments and electrical equipment

**1** Check the operation of all instruments and electrical equipment.

**2** Make sure that all instruments read correctly, and switch on all electrical equipment in turn to check it functions properly.

### Steering and suspension

**3** Drive the vehicle, and check that there are no unusual vibrations or noises.

**4** Check for any abnormalities in the steering, suspension, handling or road 'feel'.

**5** Check that the steering feels positive, with no excessive 'sloppiness', or roughness, and check for any suspension noises when cornering, or when driving over bumps.

### Drivetrain

**6** Check the performance of the engine, clutch, transmission and driveshafts.

**7** Listen for any unusual noises from the engine, clutch and transmission.

**8** Make sure the engine idles smoothly, and that there is no hesitation when accelerating.

**9** Check that the clutch action is smooth and progressive, that the drive is taken up smoothly, and that the pedal travel is not excessive. Also listen for any noises when the clutch pedal is depressed.

**10** Check that all gears can be engaged smoothly, without noise, and that the gear lever action is smooth and not vague or 'notchy'.

**11** On automatic transmission models, make sure that all gearchanges occur smoothly, without snatching, and without an increase in engine speed between changes. Check that all the gear positions can be selected with the vehicle at rest. If any problems are found, they should be referred to a Citroën dealer.

**12** Listen for a metallic clicking sound from the front of the vehicle, as the vehicle is driven slowly in a circle with the steering on full lock. Carry out this check in both directions. If a clicking noise is heard, this generally indicates lack of lubrication or wear in a driveshaft outer constant velocity joint (see Chapter 8).

### Braking system

**13** Make sure that the vehicle does not pull to one side when braking, and that the wheels do not lock when braking hard.

**14** Check that there is no vibration through the steering when braking.

**15** Check that the handbrake operates correctly, without excessive movement of the lever, and that it holds the vehicle on a slope.

**16** Test the operation of the brake servo unit as follows. With the engine off, depress the footbrake four or five times to exhaust the vacuum. Start the engine, holding the brake pedal depressed. As the engine starts, there should be a noticeable 'give' in the brake pedal as vacuum builds-up. Allow the engine to run for at least two minutes, and then switch it off. If the brake pedal is depressed now, it should be possible to detect a hiss from the servo as the pedal is depressed. After about four or five applications, no further hissing should be heard, and the pedal should feel considerably firmer.

# Every 20 000 miles (30 000 km) or two years

## 8 Resetting the service indicator

**1** On completion of the service, reset the service interval indicator as follows.

**2** With the ignition switched off, press and hold the trip meter button.

**3** Turn on the ignition switch, and the display begins a countdown. When the countdown reaches 0, release the trip meter button, and the spanner service symbol in the display will disappear.

**4** Turn off the ignition switch.

**5** Turn on the ignition switch and check the correct mileage to the next service interval is displayed on the indicator.

**Note:** *If you need to disconnect the battery after carrying out this procedure, lock the vehicle and wait at least 5 minutes. Otherwise the display reset may not register.*

## 9 Pollen filter renewal

**1** The pollen filter is located behind a plastic cover at the rear right-hand corner of the engine compartment.

**2** Undo the three retaining screws and remove the plastic cover **(see illustration)**.

**3** Release the filter retaining plate and pull the plate from its location **(see illustrations)**.

**4** Withdraw the filter from the housing **(see illustration)**.

**5** Wipe clean the inside of the housing and fit the new pollen filter element, making sure that it is correctly seated.

**6** Refit the filter retaining plate and the plastic cover.

**9.2 Undo the three retaining screws and remove the pollen filter plastic cover**

**9.3a Release the filter retaining plate . . .**

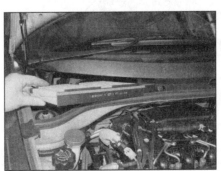

**9.3b . . . and pull the plate from its location**

**9.4 Withdraw the filter from the housing**

## 10 Auxiliary drivebelt check and renewal

**Note:** *On models with a manually adjusted drivebelt, Citroën specify the use of a special electronic tool (SEEM C.TRONIC type 105.5 belt tension measuring tool) to correctly*

set the auxiliary drivebelt tension. If access to this equipment cannot be obtained, an approximate setting can be achieved using the method described below. If this method is used, the tension should be checked using the special electronic tool at the earliest opportunity.

1  A single multi-ribbed drivebelt is used to drive the alternator and, where fitted, the air conditioning compressor, from the crankshaft pulley. The belt is adjusted either manually, or by means of an automatic, spring-loaded tensioner mechanism.

### Check

2  Apply the handbrake, slacken the front right-hand roadwheel bolts, then jack up the front of the car and support it on axle stands (see Jacking and vehicle support). Remove the right-hand front roadwheel.

3  Remove the plastic expanding rivets (pull out the centre pin then remove the complete rivet) securing the wheel arch liner to the body then manoeuvre the liner out from underneath the wing.

4  Using a suitable socket and extension bar fitted to the crankshaft sprocket bolt, rotate the crankshaft so that the entire length of the drivebelt can be examined. Examine the drivebelt for cracks, splitting, fraying or damage. Check also for signs of glazing (shiny patches) and for separation of the belt plies. Renew the belt if worn or damaged.

5  If the condition of the belt is satisfactory, on models with a manually adjusted drivebelt, check the drivebelt tension as described in the appropriate sub-Section below.

6  Refit the wheel arch liner, securing it in position with the plastic expanding rivets.

7  Refit the roadwheel then lower the vehicle

to the ground and tighten the wheel bolts to the specified torque.

### Manual adjuster on the alternator mounting

#### Renewal

8  If not already done, proceed as described in paragraphs 2 and 3.

9  Slacken both the alternator upper and lower mounting bolts.

10  Back off the adjuster bolt, located on the alternator lower mounting, to relieve the tension in the drivebelt. Slip the drivebelt from the pulleys. Note: If the belt is going to be re-used, mark the direction of rotation on the belt prior to removal. This will ensure it is refitted the correct way around.

11  If the belt is being renewed, ensure that the correct type is used. If the original belt is being refitted, use the mark made on removal to ensure it is fitted the correct way around.

12  Fit the belt around the pulleys, and take up the slack in the belt by tightening the adjuster bolt. Tension the drivebelt as described in the following paragraphs.

#### Tensioning

13  If not already done, proceed as described in paragraphs 2 and 3.

14  If the special measuring tool is available, fit the measuring equipment to the 'lower run' of the belt, approximately midway between the crankshaft and alternator pulleys. The belt tension should be set to the figure given in the Specifications at the start of this Chapter.

15  If the measuring tool is not available, the belt should be tensioned so that, under firm thumb pressure, there is about 5.0 mm of free movement at the mid-point between the pulleys on the lower belt run.

**Caution: Correct tensioning of the drivebelt will ensure it has a long life. A belt which is too slack will slip and squeal. Beware of overtightening, as this can cause wear in the alternator bearings.**

16  To adjust the belt tension, with the mounting bolt(s) just slackened, turn the adjuster bolt until the correct tension is achieved.

17  Rotate the crankshaft a couple of times, recheck the tension, then tighten the alternator mounting bolt(s) to the specified torque.

18  Refit the wheel arch liner, securing it in position with the plastic expanding rivets.

19  Refit the roadwheel then lower the vehicle to the ground and tighten the wheel bolts to the specified torque.

### Manually-adjusted tensioner pulley

#### Renewal

20  If not already done, proceed as described in paragraphs 2 and 3.

21  Slacken the tensioner pulley bracket bolts and rotate the adjuster bolt at the base of the pulley bracket to release the tension in the drivebelt. Remove the belt from the pulleys (see illustration). Note: If the belt is to be re-used, mark the direction of rotation on the belt prior to removal. This will ensure it is refitted the correct way around.

22  If the belt is being renewed, ensure that the correct type is used. If the original belt is being refitted, use the mark made on removal to ensure it is fitted the correct way around. Fit the drivebelt around the pulleys in the following order:

  a) Air conditioning compressor.
  b) Crankshaft.
  c) Alternator.
  d) Idler pulley.
  e) Tensioner pulley.

23  Ensure that the ribs on the belt are correctly engaged with the grooves in the pulleys, and that the drivebelt is correctly routed. Tension the belt as follows.

#### Tensioning

24  If not already done, proceed as described in paragraphs 2 and 3.

25  If the special measuring tool is available, fit the measuring equipment to the belt, approximately midway between the crankshaft and air conditioning compressor pulleys. Check the belt tension is as given in the Specifications at the start of this Chapter.

26  If the measuring tool is not available, the belt should be tensioned so that, under firm thumb pressure, there is about 5.0 mm of free movement at the mid-point between the crankshaft and air conditioning compressor pulleys.

**Caution: Correct tensioning of the drivebelt will ensure it has a long life. A belt which is too slack will slip and squeal. Beware of overtightening, as this can cause wear in the alternator bearings.**

27  To adjust the tension, rotate the adjuster bolt until the correct tension is achieved. Once the belt is correctly tensioned, tighten the tensioner pulley

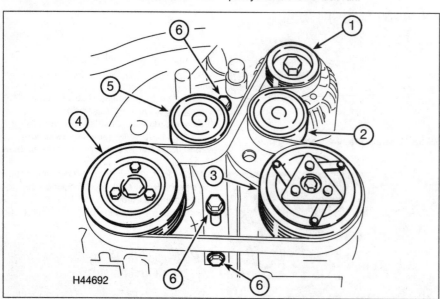

**10.21 Auxiliary drivebelt details (models with a manually-adjusted tensioner pulley)**

| 1 | Alternator pulley | 4 | Crankshaft | 6 | Tensioner pulley |
|---|---|---|---|---|---|
| 2 | Idler pulley | | pulley | | bracket bolts and |
| 3 | Compressor pulley | 5 | Tensioner pulley | | adjuster bolt |

H44692

bracket bolts securely. Rotate the crankshaft a couple of times and recheck the tension.

**28** When the belt is correctly tensioned, refit the wheel arch liner, securing it in position with the plastic expanding rivets.

**29** Refit the roadwheel then lower the vehicle to the ground and tighten the wheel bolts to the specified torque.

### Automatic spring-loaded tensioner pulley

#### Renewal

**30** If not already done, proceed as described in paragraphs 2 and 3.

**31** Rotate the tensioner pulley clockwise, away from the drivebelt, using a spanner on the tensioner pulley retaining bolt.

**32** Once the tension is released, disengage the belt from all the pulleys, noting its correct routing. Remove the drivebelt from the engine. **Note:** *If the belt is going to be re-used, mark the direction of rotation on the belt prior to removal. This will ensure it is refitted the correct way around.*

**33** If the belt is being renewed, ensure that the correct type is used. If the original belt is being refitted, use the mark made on removal to ensure it is fitted the correct way around. Fit the drivebelt around the pulleys in the following order:

a) *Air conditioning compressor.*
b) *Crankshaft.*
c) *Alternator.*
d) *Idler pulley.*
e) *Automatic tensioner pulley.*

**34** Ensure that the ribs on the belt are correctly engaged with the grooves in the pulleys.

**Caution: Do not allow the tensioner pulley to spring forcefully onto the belt as this could result in damage.**

**35** Refit the wheel arch liner, securing it in position with the retaining plastic expanding rivets.

**36** Refit the roadwheel then lower the vehicle to the ground and tighten the wheel bolts to the specified torque.

### 11 Brake pad condition check
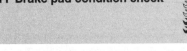

**1** Firmly apply the handbrake, then jack up the front of the car and support it securely on axle stands (see *Jacking and vehicle support*). Remove the front roadwheels.

**2** A quick check of the pad thickness can be carried out via the aperture in the caliper body **(see Haynes Hint)**. Using a steel rule, measure the thickness of the pad friction material. This must not be less than the specified minimum thickness given in the Specifications.

**3** If any pad's friction material is worn to the specified minimum thickness or less, all four pads must be renewed as a set.

**4** For a comprehensive check, the brake pads should be removed and cleaned. The operation of the caliper can then be checked, and the brake disc itself can be fully examined on both sides. Refer to Chapter 9 for details.

**5** On completion, refit the roadwheels, then lower the car to the ground and tighten the wheel bolts to the specified torque.

**6** On models with rear disc brakes, chock the front wheels then jack up the rear of the car and securely support it on axle stands (see *Jacking and vehicle support*). Remove the rear roadwheels. Repeat the procedure described in paragraphs 2 to 5 to check the condition of the rear brake pads.

### 12 Rear brake shoe condition check

**1** Chock the front wheels then jack up the rear of the car and support it on axle stands (see *Jacking and vehicle support*).

**2** For a quick check, the thickness of friction material remaining on one of the brake shoes can be measured through the slot in the brake backplate that is exposed by prising out its sealing grommet. If a rod of the same diameter as the specified minimum thickness is placed against the shoe friction material, the amount of wear can quickly be assessed – a small mirror may help observation. If any shoe's friction material is worn to the specified thickness or less, all four shoes must be renewed as a set.

**3** For a comprehensive check, the brake drums should be removed and cleaned. This will permit the wheel cylinders to be checked and the condition of the brake drum itself to be fully examined. Refer to Chapter 9 for further information.

### 13 Handbrake check and adjustment

**1** The handbrake should be fully applied before 8 clicks can be heard from the lever ratchet mechanism. Check and, if necessary, adjust the handbrake as described in Chapter 9.

### 14 Exhaust system check

**1** With the engine cold (at least an hour after the vehicle has been driven), check the complete exhaust system from the engine to the end of the tailpipe. The exhaust system is most easily checked with the vehicle raised on a hoist, or suitably supported on axle stands, so that the exhaust components are readily visible and accessible (see *Jacking and vehicle support*).

**2** Check the exhaust pipes and connections for evidence of leaks, severe corrosion and damage. Make sure that all brackets and mountings are in good condition, and that all relevant nuts and bolts are tight. Leakage at any of the joints or in other parts of the system will usually show up as a black sooty stain in the vicinity of the leak.

**3** Rattles and other noises can often be traced to the exhaust system, especially the brackets and mountings. Try to move the pipes and silencers. If the components are able to come into contact with the body or suspension parts, secure the system with new mountings. Otherwise separate the joints (if possible) and twist the pipes as necessary to provide additional clearance.

### 15 Steering and suspension check

### Front suspension and steering

**1** Raise the front of the vehicle, and securely support it on axle stands (see *Jacking and vehicle support*).

**2** Visually inspect the balljoint dust covers and the steering gear gaiters for splits, chafing or deterioration.

**3** Any wear of these components will cause loss of lubricant, together with dirt and water entry, resulting in rapid deterioration of the balljoints or steering gear.

**4** Grasp the roadwheel at the 12 o'clock and 6 o'clock positions, and try to rock it **(see illustration)**. Very slight free play may be felt,

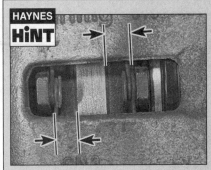

*For a quick check, the thickness of friction material on each brake pad can be measured through the aperture in the caliper body.*

**15.4 Check for wear in the hub bearings by grasping the wheel and trying to rock it**

but if the movement is appreciable, further investigation is necessary to determine the source. Continue rocking the wheel while an assistant depresses the footbrake. If the movement is now eliminated or significantly reduced, it is likely that the hub bearings are at fault. If the free play is still evident with the footbrake depressed, then there is wear in the suspension joints or mountings.

5 Now grasp the wheel at the 9 o'clock and 3 o'clock positions, and try to rock it as before. Any movement felt now may again be caused by wear in the hub bearings or the steering track rod balljoints. If the inner or outer balljoint is worn, the visual movement will be obvious.

6 Using a large screwdriver or flat bar, check for wear in the suspension mounting bushes by levering between the relevant suspension component and its attachment point. Some movement is to be expected as the mountings are made of rubber, but excessive wear should be obvious. Also check the condition of any visible rubber bushes, looking for splits, cracks or contamination of the rubber.

7 With the car standing on its wheels, have an assistant turn the steering wheel back-and-forth about an eighth of a turn each way. There should be very little, if any, lost movement between the steering wheel and roadwheels. If this is not the case, closely observe the joints and mountings previously described, but in addition, check the steering column universal joints for wear, and the steering gear itself.

### Strut/shock absorber

8 Check for any signs of fluid leakage around the suspension strut/shock absorber body, or from the rubber gaiter around the piston rod. Should any fluid be noticed, the suspension strut/shock absorber is defective internally, and should be renewed. **Note:** *Suspension struts/ shock absorbers should always be renewed in pairs on the same axle, or the handling of the vehicle will be adversely affected.*

9 The efficiency of the suspension strut/ shock absorber may be checked by bouncing the vehicle at each corner. Generally speaking, the body will return to its normal position and stop after being depressed. If it rises and returns on a rebound, the suspension strut/shock absorber is probably suspect. Examine also the suspension strut/ shock absorber upper and lower mountings for any signs of wear.

# Every 40 000 miles (60 000 km)

## 16 Timing belt renewal

1 Refer to Chapter 2A.

# Every 40 000 miles (60 000 km) or two years

## 17 Brake fluid renewal

⚠ *Warning: Brake hydraulic fluid can harm your eyes and damage painted surfaces, so use extreme caution when handling and pouring it. Do not use fluid that has been standing open for some time, as it absorbs moisture from the air. Excess moisture can cause a dangerous loss of braking effectiveness.*
**Note:** *The hydraulic clutch shares its fluid reservoir with the braking system, and may also need to be bled (see Chapter 6).*

1 The procedure is similar to that for the bleeding of the hydraulic system as described in Chapter 9, except that the brake fluid reservoir should be emptied by syphoning, using a clean ladle or similar before starting, and allowance should be made for the old fluid to be expelled when bleeding a section of the circuit.

2 Working as described in Chapter 9, open the first bleed screw in the sequence, and pump the brake pedal gently until nearly all the old fluid has been emptied from the master cylinder reservoir.

 **HAYNES HiNT** *Old hydraulic fluid is invariably much darker in colour than the new, making it easy to distinguish the two.*

3 Top-up to the MAX level with new fluid, and continue pumping until only the new fluid remains in the reservoir, and new fluid can be seen emerging from the bleed screw. Tighten the screw, and top the reservoir level up to the MAX level line.

4 Work through all the remaining bleed screws in the sequence until new fluid can be seen at all of them. Be careful to keep the master cylinder reservoir topped-up to above the MIN level at all times, or air may enter the system and increase the length of the task.

5 When the operation is complete, check that all bleed screws are securely tightened, and that their dust caps are refitted. Wash off all traces of spilt fluid, and recheck the master cylinder reservoir fluid level.

6 Check the operation of the brakes before taking the car on the road.

# Every 40 000 miles (60 000 km) or four years

## 18 Spark plug renewal

1 The correct functioning of the spark plugs is vital for the correct running and efficiency of the engine. It is essential that the plugs fitted are appropriate for the engine (see Specifications). If this type is used and the engine is in good condition, the spark plugs should not need attention between scheduled renewal intervals. Spark plug cleaning is rarely necessary, and should not be attempted unless specialised equipment is available, as damage can easily be caused to the firing ends.

2 To gain access to the spark plugs, remove the ignition HT coil as described in Chapter 5B.

3 Unscrew the plugs using a spark plug spanner, suitable box spanner or a deep socket and extension bar **(see illustration)**. Keep the socket aligned with the spark plug – if it is forcibly moved to one side, the ceramic insulator may be broken off. As each plug is removed, examine it as follows.

4 Examination of the spark plugs will give a good indication of the condition of the engine **(see illustration)**. If the insulator nose of the spark plug is clean and white, with no

**18.3 Unscrew the spark plugs**

**18.4 Examine the spark plugs to check the condition of the engine – see text**

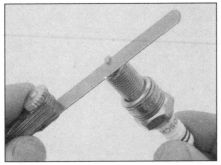

**18.8 Measure the spark plug electrode gap with a feeler gauge**

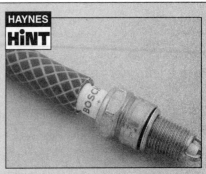

*It is very often difficult to insert spark plugs into their holes without cross-threading them. To avoid this possibility, fit a short length of 8 mm internal diameter rubber hose over the end of the spark plug. The flexible hose acts as a universal joint to help align the plug with the plug hole. Should the plug begin to cross-thread, the hose will slip on the spark plug, preventing thread damage to the cylinder head.*

deposits, this is indicative of a weak mixture or too hot a plug (a hot plug transfers heat away from the electrode slowly, a cold plug transfers heat away quickly).

**5** If the tip and insulator nose are covered with hard black-looking deposits, then this is indicative that the mixture is too rich. Should the plug be black and oily, then it is likely that the engine is fairly worn, as well as the mixture being too rich.

**6** If the insulator nose is covered with light tan to greyish-brown deposits, then the mixture is correct and it is likely that the engine is in good condition.

**7** The spark plug electrode gap is of considerable importance as, if it is too large or too small, the size of the spark and its efficiency will be seriously impaired. The gap should be set to the value given in the Specifications at the beginning of this Chapter. **Note:** *The electrode gap on multi-electrode spark plugs cannot be adjusted.*

**8** To set the gap on single-electrode plugs, measure the gap with a feeler blade, and then bend open, or closed, the outer plug electrode until the correct gap is achieved **(see illustration)**. The centre electrode should never be bent, as this may crack the insulator and cause plug failure, if nothing worse. If using feeler blades, the gap is correct when the appropriate-size blade is a firm sliding fit.

**9** Special spark plug electrode gap adjusting tools are available from most motor accessory shops, or from spark plug manufacturers.

**10** Before fitting the spark plugs, check that the threaded connector sleeves are tight, and

that the plug exterior and threads are clean **(see Haynes Hint)**.

**11** Remove the rubber hose (if used), and tighten the plug to the specified torque using the spark plug socket and a torque wrench. Refit the remaining spark plugs in the same manner.

**12** Refit the ignition HT coil as described in Chapter 5B.

## 19 Air cleaner filter element renewal

**1** Remove the air cleaner assembly from the car as described in Chapter 4A.

**2** With the air cleaner assembly on the bench, undo the screws securing the air cleaner lid to the base. Lift off the lid and remove the air filter element, noting which way up it is fitted **(see illustrations)**.

**3** Wipe clean the inside of the air cleaner lid and base then fit the new element, ensuring it is correctly located.

**4** Locate the lid correctly on the base and securely tighten the retaining screws.

**5** Refit the air cleaner assembly to the car as described in Chapter 4A.

## 20 Manual transmission oil level check

**Note:** *On later transmissions, the oil level cannot be checked, as there is no filler/level*

plug fitted. These transmissions do not require regular maintenance and are filled-for-life. If the transmission develops a leak or is removed for other work, the oil needs to be completely drained and the transmission refilled with the correct amount of oil. The transmission is then refilled through the vent/breather on the top of the transmission.

**Note:** *A suitable square-section wrench may be required to undo the transmission filler/level plug on some models. These wrenches can be obtained from most motor factors or your Citroën dealer.*

**1** Park the car on a level surface. The oil level must be checked before the car is driven, or at least 5 minutes after the engine has been switched off. If the oil is checked immediately after driving the car, some of the oil will remain distributed around the transmission, resulting in an inaccurate level reading.

**2** Push in the centre pins a little, then prise out the complete expanding plastic rivets, and remove the left-hand wheel arch liner.

**3** Wipe clean the area around the filler/level plug, which is on the left-hand end of the

**19.2a Undo the screws (arrowed) securing the air cleaner lid to the base . . .**

**19.2b . . . lift off the air cleaner lid . . .**

**19.2c . . . and remove the air filter element**

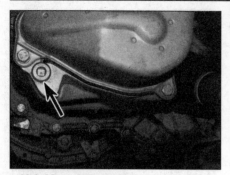

**20.3 Manual transmission oil level/filler plug (arrowed)**

**21.2 Automatic transmission fluid filler plug location (arrowed)**

transmission. Unscrew the plug and clean it; discard the sealing washer **(see illustration)**.

**4** The oil level should reach the lower edge of the filler/level hole. A certain amount of oil will have gathered behind the filler/level plug, and will trickle out when it is removed; this does **not** necessarily indicate that the level is correct. To ensure that a true level is established, wait until the initial trickle has stopped, then add oil as necessary until a trickle of new oil can be seen emerging. The level will be correct when the flow ceases; use only good-quality oil of the specified type (see *Lubricants and fluids*).

**5** Filling the transmission with oil is an extremely awkward operation; above all, allow plenty of time for the oil level to settle properly before checking it. If a large amount is added to the transmission, and a large amount flows out on checking the level, refit the filler/level plug and take the vehicle on a short journey so that the new oil is distributed fully around

the transmission components, then recheck the level when it has settled again.

**6** If the transmission has been overfilled so that oil flows out as soon as the filler/level plug is removed, check that the car is completely level (front-to-rear and side-to-side), and allow the surplus to drain off into a container.

**7** When the level is correct, fit a new sealing washer to the filler/level plug. Refit the plug, tightening it to the specified torque setting. Wash off any spilt oil then refit the wheel arch liner, securing it in position with the screws and fasteners.

**21 Automatic transmission fluid level check**

**Note 1:** *Refer to Chapter 7B for information regarding fluid renewal and modifications to later transmissions.*
**Note 2:** *A suitable square section wrench may*

be required to undo the transmission filler plug. These wrenches can be obtained from most motor factors or your Citroën dealer.

**1** Take the vehicle on a short journey, to warm the transmission up to normal operating temperature, then park the vehicle on level ground. Firmly apply the handbrake and place the selector lever in the P position.

**2** Wipe clean the area around the filler plug, which is situated on the top of the transmission, directly beneath the air cleaner assembly. Remove the air cleaner assembly as described in Chapter 4A, then unscrew the filler plug from the transmission and recover the sealing washer **(see illustration)**.

**3** Carefully add 0.5 litre of the specified type of fluid to the transmission via the filler plug aperture. Fit a new sealing washer to the filler plug then refit the plug, tightening it to the specified torque.

**4** Undo the screws and remove the engine undershield – where fitted.

**5** Position a suitable container under the drain/filler plug arrangement, situated on the base of the transmission. On early transmissions, the level plug is the smaller plug fitted to the centre of the larger drain plug. On later transmissions, only a level plug is fitted **(see illustrations)**.

**Caution: On early transmissions, do not remove the drain plug by mistake.**

**6** Start the engine and allow it to idle. With the engine running, retain the drain plug (where fitted) then slacken and remove the level plug and sealing washer.

⚠️ **Warning: The fluid will be hot, take precautions against scalding.**

**7** If there is sufficient fluid in the transmission unit, fluid should trickle out of the level plug orifice before slowing to a drip. **Note:** *If no fluid trickles out, or just a few drips appear when the plug is removed, the fluid level is too low. Refit the level plug then switch off the engine. Add a further 0.5 litre of fluid to the transmission then refit the filler plug and repeat the check (see paragraph 3).*

**8** Once the flow of fluid stops, the level is correct. Fit a new sealing washer to the level plug then refit the plug and tighten it to the specified torque. Switch off the engine, refit the air cleaner assembly and, where applicable, the engine undershield.

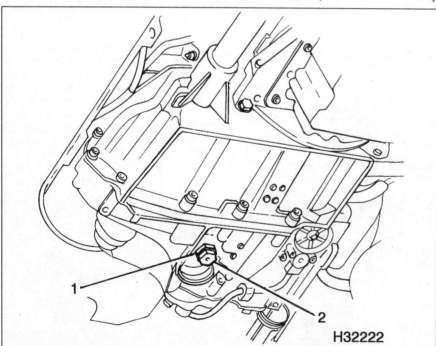

**21.5a Automatic transmission fluid level plug (2) is located inside the drain plug (1) – early models**

**21.5b Automatic transmission fluid level plug (arrowed) – later models**

**23.4 Release the retaining clamp and disconnect the lower hose from the radiator**

**23.5a Undo the bleed screw from the heater matrix outlet hose union (arrowed) . . .**

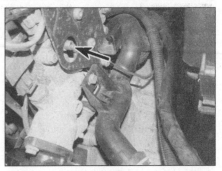

**23.5b . . . and the bleed screw and sealing washer (arrowed) from the coolant housing**

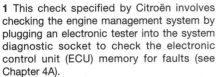

## 22 Emissions control systems check

**1** This check specified by Citroën involves checking the engine management system by plugging an electronic tester into the system diagnostic socket to check the electronic control unit (ECU) memory for faults (see Chapter 4A).

**2** In reality, if the vehicle is running correctly and the engine management warning light on the instrument panel is functioning normally, then this check need not be carried out.

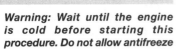

## 23 Coolant renewal

⚠️ *Warning: Wait until the engine is cold before starting this procedure. Do not allow antifreeze to come in contact with your skin, or with the painted surfaces of the vehicle. Rinse off spills immediately with plenty of water. Never leave antifreeze lying around in an open container, or in a puddle in the driveway or on the garage floor. Children and pets are attracted by its sweet smell, but antifreeze can be fatal if ingested.*

**Note:** *The cooling system is initially 'filled-for-life' and does not require regular renewal.*

### Cooling system draining

**1** With the engine completely cold, unscrew the expansion tank filler cap.

**2** Undo the screws and remove the engine undershield – where fitted.

**3** Position a suitable container beneath the coolant drain outlet at the lower left-hand side of the radiator.

**4** Release the retaining clamp and disconnect the lower hose from the radiator, then allow the coolant to drain into the container **(see illustration)**.

**5** To assist draining, remove the cooling system bleed screw from the heater matrix outlet hose union on the engine compartment bulkhead and the bleed screw and sealing washer from the coolant housing on the left-hand end of the cylinder head **(see**

**illustrations)**. To gain access to the bleed cap and screw, remove the air cleaner assembly as described in Chapter 4A.

**6** If the coolant is one of those specified by Citroen it can be saved for re-use.

**7** Refit the radiator hose and secure it with the hose clamp.

### Cooling system flushing

**8** If the antifreeze mixture has become diluted, then in time, the cooling system may gradually lose efficiency, as the coolant passages become restricted due to rust, scale deposits, and other sediment. The cooling system efficiency can be restored by flushing the system clean.

**9** The radiator should be flushed separately from the engine, to avoid excess contamination.

### Radiator flushing

**10** Disconnect the top and bottom hoses and any other relevant hoses from the radiator (see Chapter 3).

**11** Insert a garden hose into the radiator top inlet. Direct a flow of clean water through the radiator, and continue flushing until clean water emerges from the radiator bottom outlet.

**12** If after a reasonable period, the water still does not run clear, the radiator can be flushed with a good proprietary cleaning agent. It is important that their manufacturer's instructions are followed carefully. If the contamination is particularly bad, insert the hose in the radiator bottom outlet, and reverse-flush the radiator.

### Engine flushing

**13** To flush the engine, remove the thermostat (see Chapter 3).

**14** With the bottom hose disconnected from the radiator, insert a garden hose into the coolant housing. Direct a clean flow of water through the engine, and continue flushing until clean water emerges from the radiator bottom hose.

**15** When flushing is complete, refit the thermostat and reconnect the hoses (see Chapter 3).

### Cooling system filling

**16** Before attempting to fill the cooling system, make sure that all hoses and clips are in good condition, and that the clips are

tight. Note that an antifreeze mixture must be used all year round, to prevent corrosion of the engine components (see following sub-Section).

**17** Remove the expansion tank filler cap.

**18** Remove the cooling system bleed screws (see paragraph 5).

**19** Citroën recommend the use of a 'header tank' when refilling the cooling system, to reduce the possibility of air being trapped in the system. Although Citroën dealers use a special header tank which screws onto the expansion tank, the same effect can be achieved by using a suitable 1.0 litre bottle, with a seal between the bottle and the expansion tank **(see illustration)**.

**20** Fit the header tank to the expansion tank and slowly fill the system whilst observing the bleed holes. Coolant will emerge from each of the bleed holes in turn, starting with the heater matrix hose. As soon as coolant free from air bubbles emerges from the heater matrix hose outlet, securely refit the cap/screw (as applicable) then watch the bleed hole on the coolant housing. Once coolant free from air bubbles emerges from the housing hole, refit the bleed screw and sealing washer and tighten securely.

**21** Continue to fill the cooling system until bubbles stop appearing in the expansion tank. Help to bleed the air from the system by repeatedly squeezing the radiator bottom hose.

**22** When no more bubbles appear, ensure the header tank is full (at least 1.0 litre of coolant) then start the engine. Run the engine at a fast idle speed (do not exceed 2000 rpm) until the cooling fan cuts in and out TWICE, then when

**23.19 Use a 1.0 litre plastic bottle as a header tank**

the fan has stopped for the second time, switch the engine off.

*Caution: The coolant will be hot. Take great care not to scald yourself.*

**23** Allow the engine to cool, then remove the header tank. Wash off any spilt coolant with cold water.

**24** When the engine has cooled, check the coolant level with reference to *Weekly checks*. Top-up the level if necessary, and refit the expansion tank cap. Where removed, refit the engine undershield.

### Antifreeze mixture

**25** The cooling system is initially 'filled-for-life', but any other brand of antifreeze should always be renewed at the specified intervals. This is necessary not only to maintain the antifreeze properties, but also to prevent corrosion which would otherwise occur as the corrosion inhibitors become progressively less effective.

**26** Always use an ethylene-glycol based antifreeze of the specified type (see *Lubricants and fluids*). The quantity of antifreeze and level of protection are indicated in the Specifications.

**27** Before adding antifreeze, the cooling system should be completely drained, preferably flushed, and all hoses checked for condition and security.

**28** After filling with antifreeze, a label should be attached to the expansion tank, stating the type and concentration of antifreeze used, and the date installed. Any subsequent topping-up should be made with the same type and concentration of antifreeze.

**29** Do not use engine antifreeze in the windscreen/tailgate washer system, as it will damage the vehicle paintwork. A screenwash additive should be added to the washer system in the quantities stated on the bottle.

# Every ten years

**24 Airbags and seat belt pretensioners renewal**

**1** Citroën recommend that the airbags and seat belt pretensioners are renewed regardless of their condition every ten years. Refer to Chapter 12 for airbag renewal, and Chapter 11 for seat belt pretensioner renewal.

# Chapter 1 Part B:
# Routine maintenance and servicing – diesel models

## Contents

## Degrees of difficulty

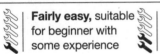

| Easy, suitable for novice with little experience | Fairly easy, suitable for beginner with some experience | Fairly difficult, suitable for competent DIY mechanic | Difficult, suitable for experienced DIY mechanic | Very difficult, suitable for expert DIY or professional |
|---|---|---|---|---|

## Servicing specifications – diesel models

**Lubricants and fluids** . . . . . . . . . . . . . . . . . . . . . . . . . . . . . . . Refer to end of *Weekly checks* on page 0•16

### Capacities

**Engine oil**
| | |
|---|---|
| Including filter | 3.8 litres |
| Difference between MAX and MIN dipstick marks | 1.8 litres |

**Cooling system**
| | |
|---|---|
| 1.4 litre models | 5.7 litres |
| 1.6 litre non-FAP models | 5.9 litres |
| 1.6 litre FAP models | 6.2 litres |

**Manual transmission (after draining)**
| | |
|---|---|
| MA5 | 2.0 litres |
| BE4/5 | 1.8 litres |

**Fuel tank**
| | |
|---|---|
| Early models | 45 litres |
| Later models | 50 litres |

### Cooling system
Antifreeze mixture:
50% antifreeze . . . . . . . . . . . . . . . . . . . . . . . . . . . . . . . . . . . . Protection down to –35°C
**Note:** *Refer to antifreeze manufacturer for latest recommendations.*

### Brakes
Brake pad and shoe friction material minimum thickness . . . . . . . . . . 2.0 mm

### Tyre pressures  . . . . . . . . . . . . . . . . . . . . . See end of *Weekly checks* on page 0•16

### Torque wrench settings
| | Nm | lbf ft |
|---|---|---|
| Engine oil filter cover | 25 | 18 |
| Engine sump drain plug | 16 | 12 |
| Manual transmission filler/level plug | 20 | 15 |
| Roadwheel bolts | 90 | 66 |

**Note:** *These maintenance schedules are a guide recommended by Haynes, for servicing your own vehicle. For the manufacturer's maintenance schedule, check with your local dealer.*

The maintenance intervals in this manual are provided with the assumption that you, not the dealer, will be carrying out the work. These are the minimum maintenance intervals recommended by us for vehicles driven daily. If you wish to keep your vehicle in peak condition at all times, you may wish to perform some of these procedures more often. We encourage frequent maintenance, because it enhances the efficiency, performance and resale value of your vehicle.

If the vehicle is driven in dusty areas, used to tow a trailer, or driven frequently at slow speeds (idling in traffic) or on short journeys, more frequent maintenance intervals are recommended.

When the vehicle is new, it should be serviced by a dealer service department (or other workshop recognised by the vehicle manufacturer as providing the same standard of service) in order to preserve the warranty. The vehicle manufacturer may reject warranty claims if you are unable to prove that servicing has been carried out as and when specified, using only original equipment parts or parts certified to be of equivalent quality.

# 1.4 litre SOHC models to RPO 10247, and all 1.4 and 1.6 litre DOHC models

## Every 250 miles (400 km) or weekly

☐ Refer to *Weekly checks*

## Every 6250 miles (10 000 km) or 12 months

☐ Engine oil and filter – renewal (Section 3)

**Note:** *Citroën recommend that the engine oil and filter are changed every 12 500 miles (20 000 km). However, oil and filter changes are good for the engine and we recommend that the oil and filter are renewed more frequently, especially if the vehicle is used on a lot of short journeys.*

## Every 12 500 miles (20 000 km) or two years, whichever comes sooner

☐ Drain any water from the fuel filter (Section 4).
☐ Check all underbonnet components and hoses for fluid leaks (Section 5).
☐ Check the condition of the driveshaft rubber gaiters and CV joints (Section 6).
☐ Lubricate all hinges and locks (Section 7).
☐ Carry out a road test (Section 8).
☐ Reset the service interval indicator (Section 9).
☐ Renew the pollen filter (Section 10).
☐ Check the condition of the auxiliary drivebelt (Section 11).
☐ Check the condition of the brake pads (Section 12).
☐ Check the condition of the rear brake shoes – models with rear drum brakes (Section 13).
☐ Check the operation of the handbrake (Section 14).
☐ Check the condition of the exhaust system (Section 15).
☐ Check the steering and suspension components (Section 16).
☐ Renew the brake fluid* (Section 17).

**\* Note:** *A hydraulic clutch shares its fluid reservoir with the braking system, and may also need to be bled.*

## Every 37 500 miles (60 000 km) or six years, whichever comes sooner

☐ Renew the air cleaner filter element (Section 18).
☐ Renew the fuel filter (Section 19).
☐ Check the manual transmission oil level (Section 20).
☐ Renew the coolant* (Section 21).

**\* Note:** *The cooling system is initially 'filled-for-life' and does not require regular renewal.*

## Every 75 000 miles (120 000 km)

☐ Renew the timing belt* (Section 22).
☐ Renew the particulate filter on 1.6 litre models with 9HZ engine (Section 23).

**\* Note:** *Although the normal interval for timing belt renewal is 150 000 miles (240 000 km) or 10 years, it is strongly recommended that the interval is reduced to 75 000 miles (120 000 km), especially on vehicles which are subjected to intensive use, ie. mainly short journeys or a lot of stop-start driving. The actual belt renewal interval is therefore very much up to the individual owner, but bear in mind that severe engine damage will result if the belt breaks.*

## Every 10 years

☐ Renew the airbags and seat belt pretensioners (Section 24).

## 1.4 litre SOHC models from RPO 10248

### Every 250 miles (400 km) or weekly
☐ Refer to Weekly checks

### Every 10 000 miles (15 000 km) or 12 months – whichever comes sooner
☐ Renew the engine oil and filter* (Section 3).
☐ Drain any water from the fuel filter (Section 4).
☐ Check all underbonnet components and hoses for fluid leaks (Section 5).
☐ Check the condition of the driveshaft rubber gaiters and CV joints (Section 6).
☐ Lubricate all hinges and locks (Section 7).
☐ Carry out a road test (Section 8).
**\* Note:** *Frequent oil and filter changes are good for the engine. We recommend changing the oil at least once a year.*

### Every 20 000 miles (30 000 km) or two years, whichever comes sooner
☐ Reset the service interval indicator (Section 9).
☐ Renew the pollen filter (Section 10).
☐ Check the condition of the auxiliary drivebelt (Section 11).
☐ Check the condition of the brake pads (Section 12).
☐ Check the condition of the rear brake shoes – models with rear drum brakes (Section 13).
☐ Check the operation of the handbrake (Section 14).
☐ Check the condition of the exhaust system (Section 15).
☐ Check the steering and suspension components (Section 16).

### Every 40 000 miles (60 000 km) or two years, whichever comes sooner
☐ Renew the brake fluid* (Section 17).
**\* Note:** *A hydraulic clutch shares its fluid reservoir with the braking system, and may also need to be bled.*

### Every 40 000 miles (60 000 km) or four years, whichever comes sooner
☐ Renew the air cleaner filter element (Section 18).
☐ Renew the fuel filter (Section 19).
☐ Check the manual transmission oil level (Section 20).
☐ Renew the coolant* (Section 21).
**\* Note:** *The cooling system is initially 'filled-for-life' and does not require regular renewal.*

### Every 80 000 miles (120 000 km)
☐ Renew the timing belt* (Section 20).
**\* Note:** *Although the normal interval for timing belt renewal is 150 000 miles (240 000 km) or 10 years, it is strongly recommended that the interval is reduced to 80 000 miles (120 000 km), especially on vehicles which are subjected to intensive use, ie, mainly short journeys or a lot of stop-start driving. The actual belt renewal interval is therefore very much up to the individual owner, but bear in mind that severe engine damage will result if the belt breaks.*

### Every 10 years
☐ Renew the airbags and seat belt pretensioners (Section 24).

## Underbonnet view of an 8-valve engine model

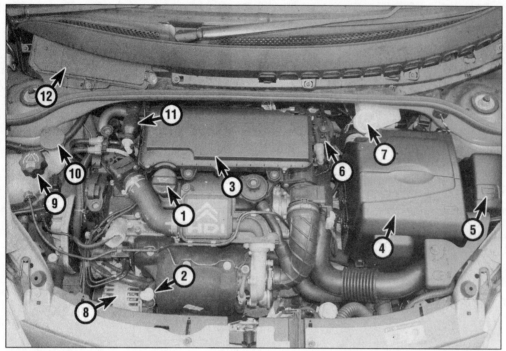

1   Engine oil filler cap
2   Engine oil level dipstick
3   Air cleaner assembly
4   Battery
5   Fuse/relay box
6   Fuel filter
7   Brake/clutch fluid reservoir
8   Alternator
9   Coolant expansion tank
10  Washer fluid reservoir
11  Hand priming pump
12  Pollen filter housing

## Underbonnet view of a 1.4 litre 16-valve engine model

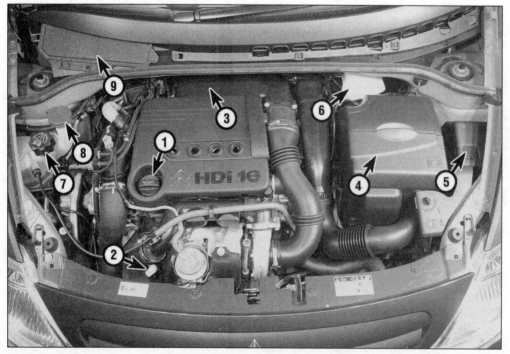

1   Engine oil filler cap
2   Engine oil level dipstick
3   Air cleaner assembly
4   Battery
5   Fuse/relay box
6   Brake/clutch fluid reservoir
7   Coolant expansion tank
8   Washer fluid reservoir
9   Pollen filter housing

## Underbonnet view of a 1.6 litre engine model

1  Engine oil filler cap
2  Engine oil level dipstick
3  Air cleaner assembly
4  Battery
5  Fuse/relay box
6  Brake/clutch fluid
   reservoir
7  Coolant expansion tank
8  Washer fluid reservoir
9  Pollen filter housing

## Front underbody view

1  Engine oil drain plug
2  Air conditioning
   compressor
3  Catalytic converter
4  Radiator electric cooling
   fan
5  Manual transmission oil
   filler/level plug
6  Brake caliper
7  Suspension lower arm
8  Front suspension
   subframe
9  Driveshaft inner constant
   velocity joint
10 Subframe bracing strut
11 Track rod balljoint
12 Anti-roll bar connecting
   link

## Rear underbody view

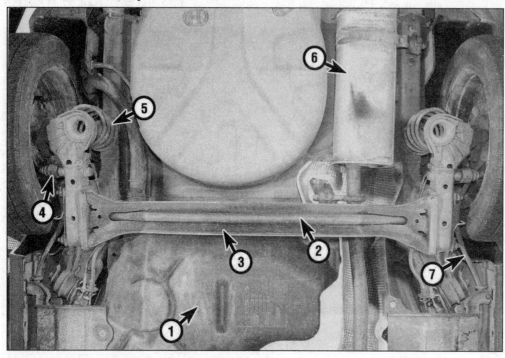

| | |
|---|---|
| **1** | *Fuel tank* |
| **2** | *Anti-roll bar* |
| **3** | *Rear axle beam* |
| **4** | *Shock absorber lower mounting* |
| **5** | *Coil spring* |
| **6** | *Exhaust rear silencer* |
| **7** | *Handbrake cable* |

# Maintenance procedures

### 1 General information

This Chapter is designed to help the home mechanic maintain his/her vehicle for safety, economy, long life and peak performance.

The Chapter contains a master maintenance schedule, followed by Sections dealing specifically with each task in the schedule. Visual checks, adjustments, component renewal and other helpful items are included. Refer to the accompanying illustrations of the engine compartment and the underside of the vehicle for the locations of the various components.

Servicing your vehicle in accordance with the mileage/time maintenance schedule and the following Sections will provide a planned maintenance programme, which should result in a long and reliable service life. This is a comprehensive plan, so maintaining some items but not others at the specified service intervals, will not produce the same results.

As you service your vehicle, you will discover that many of the procedures can – and should – be grouped together, because of the particular procedure being performed, or because of the proximity of two otherwise-unrelated components to one another. For example, if the vehicle is raised for any reason, the exhaust can be inspected at the same time as the suspension and steering components.

The first step in this maintenance programme is to prepare yourself before the actual work begins. Read through all the Sections relevant to the work to be carried out, then make a list and gather all the parts and tools required. If a problem is encountered, seek advice from a parts specialist, or a dealer service department.

### 2 Regular maintenance

**1** If, from the time the vehicle is new, the routine maintenance schedule is followed closely, and frequent checks are made of fluid levels and high-wear items, as suggested throughout this manual, the engine will be kept in relatively good running condition, and the need for additional work will be minimised.

**2** It is possible that there will be times when the engine is running poorly due to the lack of regular maintenance. This is even more likely if a used vehicle, which has not received regular and frequent maintenance checks, is purchased. In such cases, additional work may need to be carried out, outside of the regular maintenance intervals.

**3** If engine wear is suspected, a compression or leakdown test (refer to Chapter 2B or 2C) will provide valuable information regarding the overall performance of the main internal components. Such a test can be used as a basis to decide on the extent of the work to be carried out. If, for example, a compression test indicates serious internal engine wear, conventional maintenance as described in this Chapter will not greatly improve the performance of the engine, and may prove a waste of time and money, unless extensive overhaul work is carried out first.

**4** The following series of operations are those most often required to improve the performance of a generally poor-running engine:

#### Primary operations

a) *Clean, inspect and test the battery (refer to 'Weekly checks').*
b) *Check all the engine-related fluids (refer to 'Weekly checks').*
c) *Check the condition of all hoses, and check for fluid leaks (Section 5).*
d) *Check the condition of the auxiliary drivebelt (Section 11).*
e) *Check the condition of the air cleaner filter element, and renew if necessary (Section 17).*
f) *Renew the fuel filter (Section 18).*

**5** If the above operations do not prove fully effective, carry out the following secondary operations:

#### Secondary operations

All items listed under *Primary operations*, plus the following:

a) *Check the charging system (refer to Chapter 5A).*
b) *Check the preheating system (refer to Chapter 5C).*
c) *Check the fuel system (refer to Chapter 4B).*

## 3 Engine oil and filter renewal

**1.4 litre SOHC models from RPO 10248: Every 10 000 miles (15 000 km)**

**All other models: Every 6250 miles (10 000 km)**

**1** Frequent oil and filter changes are the most important preventative maintenance procedures which can be undertaken by the DIY owner. As engine oil ages, it becomes diluted and contaminated, which leads to premature engine wear.

**2** Before starting this procedure, gather together all the necessary tools and materials. Also make sure that you have plenty of clean rags and newspapers handy, to mop up any spills. Ideally, the engine oil should be warm, as it will drain better, and any impurities suspended in the oil will be removed with it. Take care, however, not to touch the exhaust or any other hot parts of the engine when working under the vehicle. To avoid any possibility of scalding, and to protect yourself from possible skin irritants and other harmful contaminants in used engine oils, it is advisable to wear gloves when carrying out this work. Access to the underside of the vehicle will be greatly improved if it can be raised on a lift, driven onto ramps, or jacked up and supported on axle stands. Whichever method is chosen, make sure that the vehicle remains level, or if it is at an angle, that the drain plug is at the lowest point. Where fitted, release the screws and remove the engine undershield.

**3** Slacken the drain plug about half a turn, position the draining container under the drain plug, then remove the plug completely **(see illustration)**. If possible, try to keep the plug pressed into the sump while unscrewing it by hand the last couple of turns **(see Haynes Hint)**. Recover the sealing ring from the drain plug.

**4** Allow some time for the old oil to drain, noting that it may be necessary to reposition the container as the oil flow slows to a trickle.

**5** After all the oil has drained, wipe off the drain plug with a clean rag, and fit a new sealing washer. Clean the area around the drain plug opening, and refit the plug. Tighten the plug securely.

**6** Move the container into position under the oil filter, which is located in a housing on the front of the cylinder block.

**7** Refer to Chapter 4B and remove the air cleaner air intake ducts as necessary for access to the filter.

**8** Using a socket or spanner, unscrew the filter housing cover and withdraw the cover complete with the filter element **(see illustrations)**.

**9** Pull the filter element out of the cover, then remove the cover O-ring seal **(see illustration)**.

**10** Use a clean rag to remove all oil, dirt and sludge from the inside and outside of the filter housing and cover.

**11** Locate the new filter element into the filter housing, ensuring that the non-return valve on the base of the filter engages with the corresponding orifice in the housing **(see illustrations)**.

**12** Apply a little clean engine oil to the new O-ring seal, and fit it to the filter housing cover.

**13** Refit the cover to the housing and tighten the cover to the specified torque.

**14** Remove the old oil and all tools from under the car, then lower the car to the ground (if applicable).

**15** Remove the dipstick, then unscrew the oil filler cap from the top of the engine. Fill the engine, using the correct grade and type of oil (see Lubricants and fluids). An oil can spout or funnel may help to reduce spillage. Pour in half the specified quantity of oil first, then wait a few minutes for the oil to run to the sump. Continue adding oil a small quantity at a time until the level is up to the lower mark on the dipstick. Adding approximately 1.8 litres will bring the level up to the upper mark on the dipstick. Refit the filler cap.

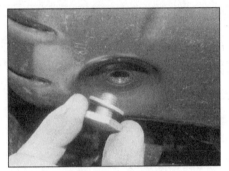

**3.3 Unscrew the sump drain plug**

*As the drain plug releases from the threads, move it away sharply so the stream of oil issuing from the sump runs into the container, not up your sleeve.*

**3.8a Unscrew the oil filter housing cover . . .**

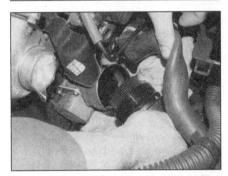

**3.8b . . . and withdraw the cover complete with the filter element**

**3.9 Remove the cover O-ring seal**

**3.11a Ensure that the non-return valve (arrowed) on the base of the filter . . .**

**3.11b . . . engages with the corresponding orifice (arrowed) in the housing**

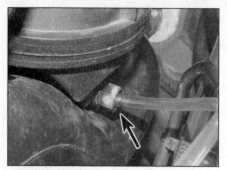

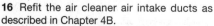

**4.2a Fuel filter water drain tap (arrowed) on 8-valve engines . . .**

**4.2b . . . and on 16-valve engines (arrowed)**

**16** Refit the air cleaner air intake ducts as described in Chapter 4B.

**17** Start the engine and run it for a few minutes; check for leaks around the oil filter and the sump drain plug. Note that there may be a delay of a few seconds before the oil pressure warning light goes out when the engine is first started, as the oil circulates through the engine oil galleries and the new oil filter (where fitted) before the pressure builds-up.

**18** Switch off the engine, and wait a few minutes for the oil to settle in the sump once more. With the new oil circulated and the filter completely full, recheck the level on the dipstick, and add more oil as necessary.

**19** Dispose of the used engine oil and filter safely, with reference to *General repair procedures* at the rear of this manual. Do not discard the old filter with domestic household waste. The facility for waste oil disposal provided by many local council refuse tips generally has a filter receptacle alongside.

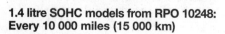

**4 Fuel filter water draining**

**1.4 litre SOHC models from RPO 10248: Every 10 000 miles (15 000 km)**

**All other models: Every 12 500 miles (20 000 km)**

**1** The fuel filter is mounted on a support bracket on the left-hand side of the engine. On 16-valve engines, refer to Chapter 4B and remove the air cleaner air intake ducts as necessary, for access to the filter.

**2** Place a suitable container under the engine, beneath the filter housing water drain tube. If a drain tube is not fitted, take care not to allow fuel to enter the transmission bellhousing which is just below. If possible, fit a suitable length of clear plastic hose over the drain tap outlet, and direct the hose under the engine.

**3** Open the drain tap on the filter housing and allow fuel and water to drain. On 8-valve engines the drain tap is located on the base of the filter housing and on 16-valve engines the tap is on the top of the housing **(see illustrations)**. When fuel which is free from

water emerges from the end of the tube, close the drain tap.

**4** Remove the container from under the engine and dispose of the drained fuel safely.

**5** On 16-valve engines, refit the air intake ducts removed for access, as described in Chapter 4B.

**6** Start the engine. If difficulty is experienced, bleed the fuel system (Chapter 4B).

**5 Hose and fluid leak check**

**1.4 litre SOHC models from RPO 10248: Every 10 000 miles (15 000 km)**

**All other models: Every 12 500 miles (20 000 km)**

### Cooling system

> ⚠ **Warning: Refer to the safety information given in 'Safety first!' and Chapter 3 before disturbing any of the cooling system components.**

**1** Carefully check the radiator and heater coolant hoses along their entire length. Renew any hose which is cracked, swollen or which shows signs of deterioration. Cracks will show up better if the hose is squeezed. Pay close attention to the clips that secure the hoses to the cooling system components. Hose clips that have been over-tightened can pinch and

*A leak in the cooling system will usually show up as white- or rust-coloured deposits on the area adjoining the leak.*

puncture hoses, resulting in cooling system leaks.

**2** Inspect all the cooling system components (hoses, joint faces, etc) for leaks. Where any problems of this nature are found on system components, renew the component or gasket with reference to Chapter 3.

**3** A leak from the cooling system will usually show up as white or rust-coloured deposits, on the area surrounding the leak **(see Haynes Hint)**.

### Fuel

> ⚠ **Warning: Refer to the safety information given in 'Safety first!' and Chapter 4B before disturbing any of the fuel system components.**

**4** Check all fuel lines at their connections to the injection pump, injectors and fuel filter housing.

**5** Examine each fuel hose/pipe along its length for splits or cracks. Check for leakage from the union nuts and examine the unions between the metal fuel lines and the fuel filter housing. Also check the area around the fuel injectors for signs of leakage.

**6** To identify fuel leaks between the fuel tank and the engine bay, the vehicle should raised and securely supported on axle stands (see *Jacking and vehicle support*). Inspect the fuel tank and filler neck for punctures, cracks and other damage. The connection between the filler neck and tank is especially critical. Sometimes a rubber filler neck or connecting hose will leak due to loose retaining clamps or deteriorated rubber.

**7** Carefully check all rubber hoses and metal fuel lines leading away from the fuel tank. Check for loose connections, deteriorated hoses, kinked lines, and other damage. Pay particular attention to the vent pipes and hoses, which often loop up around the filler neck and can become blocked or kinked, making tank filling difficult. Follow the fuel supply and return lines to the front of the vehicle, carefully inspecting them all the way for signs of damage or corrosion. Renew damaged sections as necessary.

### Engine oil

**8** Inspect the area around the cylinder head cover, cylinder head, oil filter and sump joint faces. Bear in mind that, over a period of time, some very slight seepage from these areas is to be expected – what you are really looking for is any indication of a serious leak caused by gasket failure. Engine oil seeping from the base of the timing belt cover or the transmission bellhousing may be an indication of crankshaft or input shaft oil seal failure. Should a leak be found, renew the failed gasket or oil seal by referring to the appropriate Chapters in this manual.

### Air conditioning refrigerant

> ⚠ **Warning: Refer to the safety information given in 'Safety first!' and Chapter 3, regarding**

*the dangers of disturbing any of the air conditioning system components.*

**9** The air conditioning system is filled with a liquid refrigerant, which is retained under high pressure. If the air conditioning system is opened and depressurised without the aid of specialised equipment, the refrigerant will immediately turn into gas and escape into the atmosphere. If the liquid comes into contact with your skin, it can cause severe frostbite. In addition, the refrigerant contains substances which are environmentally damaging; for this reason, it should not be allowed to escape into the atmosphere.

**10** Any suspected air conditioning system leaks should be immediately referred to a Citroën dealer or air conditioning specialist. Leakage will be shown up as a steady drop in the level of refrigerant in the system.

**11** Note that water may drip from the condenser drain pipe, underneath the car, immediately after the air conditioning system has been in use. This is normal, and should not be cause for concern.

### Brake (and clutch) fluid

*Warning: Refer to the safety information given in 'Safety first!' and Chapter 9, regarding the dangers of handling brake fluid.*

**12** With reference to Chapter 9, examine the area surrounding the brake pipe unions at the master cylinder for signs of leakage. Check the area around the base of fluid reservoir, for signs of leakage caused by seal failure. Also examine the brake pipe unions at the ABS hydraulic unit.

**13** If fluid loss is evident, but the leak cannot be pinpointed in the engine bay, the brake calipers and underbody brake lines and should be carefully checked with the vehicle raised and supported on axle stands. Leakage of fluid from the braking system is serious fault that must be rectified immediately.

**14** Refer to Chapter 6 and check for leakage around the hydraulic fluid line connections to the clutch master cylinder at the bulkhead, and to the clutch slave cylinder, bolted to the side of the transmission bellhousing.

**15** Brake/clutch hydraulic fluid is a toxic substance with a watery consistency. New fluid is almost colourless, but it becomes darker with age and use.

### Unidentified fluid leaks

**16** If there are signs that a fluid of some description is leaking from the vehicle, but you cannot identify the type of fluid or its exact origin, park the vehicle overnight and slide a large piece of card underneath it. Providing that the card is positioned in roughly in the right location, even the smallest leak will show up on the card. Not only will this help you to pinpoint the exact location of the leak, it should be easier to identify the fluid from its colour. Bear in mind, though, that the leak may only be occurring when the engine is running!

### Vacuum hoses

**17** Although the braking system is hydraulically-operated, the brake servo unit amplifies the effort you apply at the brake pedal, by making use of the vacuum created by the pump (see Chapter 9). Vacuum is ported to the servo by means of a large-bore hose. Any leaks that develop in this hose will reduce the effectiveness of the braking system.

**18** In addition, many of the underbonnet components, particularly the emission control components, are driven by vacuum supplied from the vacuum pump via narrow-bore hoses. A leak in a vacuum hose means that air is being drawn into the hose (rather than escaping from it) and this makes leakage very difficult to detect. One method is to use an old length of vacuum hose as a kind of stethoscope – hold one end close to (but not in) your ear and use the other end to probe the area around the suspected leak. When the end of the hose is directly over a vacuum leak, a hissing sound will be heard clearly through the hose. Care must be taken to avoid contacting hot or moving components, as the engine must be running when testing in this manner. Renew any vacuum hoses that are found to be defective.

## 6 Driveshaft gaiter and CV joints check

**1.4 litre SOHC models from RPO 10248: Every 10 000 miles (15 000 km)**

**All other models: Every 12 500 miles (20 000 km)**

**1** With the vehicle raised and securely supported on stands (see *Jacking and vehicle support*), turn the steering onto full lock, then slowly rotate the roadwheel. Inspect the condition of the outer constant velocity (CV) joint gaiters, squeezing the gaiters to open out the folds **(see illustration)**. Check for signs of cracking, splits or deterioration of the gaiter, which may allow the grease to escape, and lead to water and grit entry into the joint. Also check the security and condition of the retaining clips. Repeat these checks on the

**6.1 Check the driveshaft gaiter for damage**

inner CV joints. If any damage or deterioration is found, the gaiters should be renewed (see Chapter 8).

**2** At the same time, check the general condition of the CV joints themselves by first holding the driveshaft and attempting to rotate the wheel. Repeat this check by holding the inner joint and attempting to rotate the driveshaft. Any appreciable movement indicates wear in the joints, wear in the driveshaft splines, or a loose driveshaft retaining nut.

## 7 Hinge and lock lubrication

**1.4 litre SOHC models from RPO 10248: Every 10 000 miles (15 000 km)**

**All other models: Every 12 500 miles (20 000 km)**

**1** Lubricate the hinges of the bonnet, doors and tailgate with a light general-purpose oil. Similarly, lubricate all latches, locks and lock strikers – don't overdo it, or it will get on your clothes as you get in! At the same time, check the security and operation of all the locks, adjusting them if necessary (see Chapter 11).

**2** Lightly lubricate the bonnet release mechanism and cable with a suitable grease.

## 8 Road test

**1.4 litre SOHC models from RPO 10248: Every 10 000 miles (15 000 km)**

**All other models: Every 12 500 miles (20 000 km)**

### Instruments and electrical equipment

**1** Check the operation of all instruments and electrical equipment.

**2** Make sure that all instruments read correctly, and switch on all electrical equipment in turn, to check that it functions properly.

### Steering and suspension

**3** Check for any abnormalities in the steering, suspension, handling or road 'feel'.

**4** Drive the vehicle, and check that there are no unusual vibrations or noises.

**5** Check that the steering feels positive, with no excessive 'sloppiness', or roughness, and check for any suspension noises when cornering and driving over bumps.

### Drivetrain

**6** Check the performance of the engine, clutch, transmission and driveshafts.

**7** Listen for any unusual noises from the engine, clutch and transmission.

**10.2 Undo the three retaining screws and remove the pollen filter plastic cover**

**8** Make sure that the engine runs smoothly when idling, and that there is no hesitation when accelerating.

**9** Check that the clutch action is smooth and progressive, that the drive is taken up smoothly, and that the pedal travel is not excessive. Also listen for any noises when the clutch pedal is depressed.

**10** Check that all gears can be engaged smoothly without noise, and that the gear lever action is smooth and not abnormally vague or 'notchy'.

### Braking system

**11** Make sure that the vehicle does not pull to one side when braking, and that the wheels do not lock when braking hard.

**12** Check that there is no vibration through the steering when braking.

**13** Check that the handbrake operates correctly without excessive movement of the lever, and that it holds the vehicle stationary on a slope.

**14** Test the operation of the brake servo unit as follows. With the engine off, depress the footbrake four or five times to exhaust the vacuum. Hold the brake pedal depressed, then start the engine. As the engine starts, there should be a noticeable 'give' in the brake pedal as vacuum builds-up. Allow the engine to run for at least two minutes, and then switch it off. If the brake pedal is depressed now, it should be possible to detect a hiss from the servo as the pedal is depressed. After about four or five applications, no further hissing should be heard, and the pedal should feel considerably harder.

## 9 Resetting the service indicator

**1.4 litre SOHC models from RPO 10248: Every 20 000 miles (30 000 km)**

**All other models: Every 12 500 miles (20 000 km)**

**1** On completion of the service, reset the service interval indicator as follows.

**2** With the ignition switched off, press and hold the trip meter button.

**3** Turn on the ignition switch, and the display begins a countdown. When the countdown reaches 0, release the trip meter button, and the spanner service symbol in the display will disappear.

**4** Turn off the ignition switch.

**5** Turn on the ignition switch and check the correct mileage to the next service interval is displayed on the indicator.

**Note:** *If you need to disconnect the battery after carrying out this procedure, lock the vehicle and wait at least 5 minutes. Otherwise the display reset may not register.*

## 10 Pollen filter renewal

**1.4 litre SOHC models from RPO 10248: Every 20 000 miles (30 000 km)**

**All other models: Every 12 500 miles (20 000 km)**

**1** The pollen filter is located behind a plastic cover at the rear right-hand corner of the engine compartment.

**2** Undo the three retaining screws and remove the plastic cover **(see illustration)**.

**3** Release the filter retaining plate and pull the plate from its location **(see illustrations)**.

**4** Withdraw the filter from the housing **(see illustration)**.

**5** Wipe clean the inside of the housing and fit the new pollen filter element, making sure that it is correctly seated.

**6** Refit the filter retaining plate and the plastic cover.

## 11 Auxiliary drivebelt check and renewal

**1.4 litre SOHC models from RPO 10248: Every 20 000 miles (30 000 km)**

**All other models: Every 12 500 miles (20 000 km)**

**Note:** *Some later models may be fitted with an elastic auxiliary drivebelt which can only be fitted using special tools. Do not attempt to remove and refit this type of drivebelt using any other tools as the belt ribs may not be correctly located on the pulley grooves and the belt may be irreversibly damaged in the process. Note that the pulleys and idler for this type of drivebelt are different from the earlier type, and it is prohibited to combine the two versions. Also note that removal for subsequent re-use is only allowed with the engine cold.*

**1** A single multi-ribbed drivebelt is used to drive the alternator and, where fitted, the air conditioning compressor, from the crankshaft pulley. The belt tension is adjusted automatically by means of a spring-loaded tensioner mechanism.

### Check

**2** Slacken the right-hand front roadwheel bolts. Apply the handbrake, then jack up the front of the car and support it securely on axle stands (see *Jacking and vehicle support*). Remove the right-hand front roadwheel.

**3** Remove the plastic expanding rivets (push in the centre pin a little, then prise out the rivet) and remove the wheel arch liner from under the right-hand front wing for access to the crankshaft pulley bolt.

**4** Using a suitable socket and bar fitted to the crankshaft pulley bolt, rotate the crankshaft so that the entire length of the drivebelt can be examined. Examine the drivebelt for cracks, splitting, fraying or damage. Check also for signs of glazing (shiny patches) and for separation of the belt plies. Renew the belt if worn or damaged.

**5** On 1.6 litre models, the automatic tensioner has markings which align with each other when the belt is in need of renewal. The small

**10.3a Release the filter retaining plate . . .**

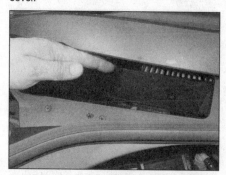

**10.3b . . . and pull the plate from its location**

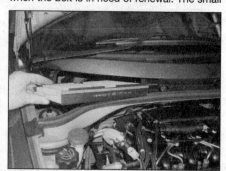

**10.4 Withdraw the filter from the housing**

**11.8 Use an open-ended spanner to rotate the tensioner arm clockwise, then lock it in place by inserting a drill into the hole in the tensioner body (arrowed)**

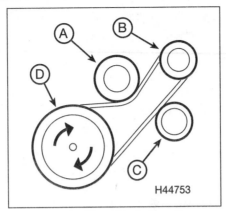

**11.11a Auxiliary drivebelt routing – models without air conditioning**

A  Tensioner      C  Idler pulley
B  Alternator     D  Crankshaft

**11.11b Auxiliary drivebelt routing – models with air conditioning**

A  Tensioner      C  Compressor
B  Alternator     D  Crankshaft

square lug aligns with the large square on the front of the tensioner body.

**6** If the condition of the belt is satisfactory, refit the wheel arch liner, securing it in position with the plastic expanding rivets. Refit the roadwheel then lower the vehicle to the ground and tighten the wheel bolts to the specified torque.

### Renewal

**7** If not already done, proceed as described in paragraphs 2 and 3.

**8** Using an open-ended spanner, reach down and rotate the tensioner arm clockwise to release the belt tension. Insert a 3.0 mm drill bit or rod into the hole in the tensioner body, so that the tensioner arm rests against it, and locks it in this position **(see illustration)**. It is useful to have a small mirror available to enable the alignment of the locking holes to be more easily seen in the limited space available.

**9** Remove the belt from the pulleys. Note that if the belt is to be re-used, mark the direction of rotation. The belt must be refitted the same way around.

**10** If the belt is being renewed, ensure that the correct type is used. If the original belt is being refitted, use the mark made on removal to ensure it is fitted the correct way around.

**11** Fit the belt around the pulleys, ensuring that the ribs on the belt are correctly engaged with the grooves in the pulleys, and the drivebelt is correctly routed **(see illustrations)**.

**12** Using an open-ended spanner, hold the tensioner arm so that the locking drill bit/rod can be removed, then release the pressure on the spanner so that the automatic tensioner takes up the slack in the drivebelt.

**13** Refit the wheel arch liner, securing it in position with the retaining plastic expanding rivets.

**14** Refit the roadwheel then lower the vehicle to the ground and tighten the wheel bolts to the specified torque.

---

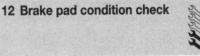

## 12 Brake pad condition check

### 1.4 litre SOHC models from RPO 10248: Every 20 000 miles (30 000 km)

### All other models: Every 12 500 miles (20 000 km)

**1** Firmly apply the handbrake, then jack up the front of the car and support it securely on axle stands (see *Jacking and vehicle support*). Remove the front roadwheels.

**2** A quick check of the pad thickness can be carried out via the aperture in the caliper body **(see Haynes Hint)**. Using a steel rule, measure the thickness of the pad friction material. This must not be less than the specified minimum thickness given in the Specifications.

**3** If any pad's friction material is worn to the specified minimum thickness or less, all four pads must be renewed as a set.

**4** For a comprehensive check, the brake pads should be removed and cleaned. The

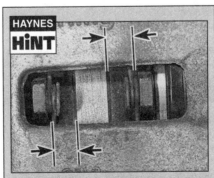

*For a quick check, the thickness of the friction material remaining on each brake pad can be measured through the aperture in the caliper body.*

operation of the caliper can then be checked, and the brake disc itself can be fully examined on both sides. Refer to Chapter 9 for details.

**5** On completion, refit the roadwheels, then lower the car to the ground and tighten the wheel bolts to the specified torque.

**6** On models with rear disc brakes, chock the front wheels then jack up the rear of the car and securely support it on axle stands (see *Jacking and vehicle support*). Remove the rear roadwheels. Repeat the procedure described in paragraphs 2 to 5 to check the condition of the rear brake pads.

## 13 Rear brake shoe condition check

### 1.4 litre SOHC models from RPO 10248: Every 20 000 miles (30 000 km)

### All other models: Every 12 500 miles (20 000 km)

**1** Chock the front wheels then jack up the rear of the car and support it on axle stands (see *Jacking and vehicle support*).

**2** For a quick check, the thickness of friction material remaining on one of the brake shoes can be measured through the slot in the brake backplate that is exposed by prising out its sealing grommet. If a rod of the same diameter as the specified minimum thickness is placed against the shoe friction material, the amount of wear can quickly be assessed – a small mirror may help observation. If any shoe's friction material is worn to the specified thickness or less, all four shoes must be renewed as a set.

**3** For a comprehensive check, the brake drums should be removed and cleaned. This will permit the wheel cylinders to be checked and the condition of the brake drum itself to be fully examined. Refer to Chapter 9 for further information.

**16.4 Check for wear in the hub bearings by grasping the wheel and trying to rock it**

## 14 Handbrake check and adjustment

**1.4 litre SOHC models from RPO 10248: Every 20 000 miles (30 000 km)**

**All other models: Every 12 500 miles (20 000 km)**

1 The handbrake should be fully applied before 8 clicks can be heard from the lever ratchet mechanism. Check and, if necessary, adjust the handbrake as described in Chapter 9.

## 15 Exhaust system check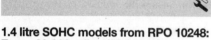

**1.4 litre SOHC models from RPO 10248: Every 20 000 miles (30 000 km)**

**All other models: Every 12 500 miles (20 000 km)**

1 With the engine cold (at least an hour after the vehicle has been driven), check the complete exhaust system from the engine to the end of the tailpipe. The exhaust system is most easily checked with the vehicle raised on a hoist, or suitably supported on axle stands, so that the exhaust components are readily visible and accessible (see *Jacking and vehicle support*).

2 Check the exhaust pipes and connections for evidence of leaks, severe corrosion and damage. Make sure that all brackets and mountings are in good condition, and that all relevant nuts and bolts are tight. Leakage at any of the joints or in other parts of the system will usually show up as a black sooty stain in the vicinity of the leak.

3 Rattles and other noises can often be traced to the exhaust system, especially the brackets and mountings. Try to move the pipes and silencers. If the components are able to come into contact with the body or suspension parts, secure the system with new mountings. Otherwise separate the joints (if possible) and twist the pipes as necessary to provide additional clearance.

## 16 Steering and suspension check

**1.4 litre SOHC models from RPO 10248: Every 20 000 miles (30 000 km)**

**All other models: Every 12 500 miles (20 000 km)**

### Front suspension and steering

1 Raise the front of the vehicle, and securely support it on axle stands (see *Jacking and vehicle support*).

2 Visually inspect the balljoint dust covers and the steering gear gaiters for splits, chafing or deterioration.

3 Any wear of these components will cause loss of lubricant, together with dirt and water entry, resulting in rapid deterioration of the balljoints or steering gear.

4 Grasp the roadwheel at the 12 o'clock and 6 o'clock positions, and try to rock it **(see illustration)**. Very slight free play may be felt, but if the movement is appreciable, further investigation is necessary to determine the source. Continue rocking the wheel while an assistant depresses the footbrake. If the movement is now eliminated or significantly reduced, it is likely that the hub bearings are at fault. If the free play is still evident with the footbrake depressed, then there is wear in the suspension joints or mountings.

5 Now grasp the wheel at the 9 o'clock and 3 o'clock positions, and try to rock it as before. Any movement felt now may again be caused by wear in the hub bearings or the steering track rod balljoints. If the inner or outer balljoint is worn, the visual movement will be obvious.

6 Using a large screwdriver or flat bar, check for wear in the suspension mounting bushes by levering between the relevant suspension component and its attachment point. Some movement is to be expected as the mountings are made of rubber, but excessive wear should be obvious. Also check the condition of any visible rubber bushes, looking for splits, cracks or contamination of the rubber.

7 With the car standing on its wheels, have an assistant turn the steering wheel back-and-forth about an eighth of a turn each way. There should be very little, if any, lost movement between the steering wheel and roadwheels. If this is not the case, closely observe the joints and mountings previously described, but in addition, check the steering column universal joints for wear, and the steering gear itself.

### Strut/shock absorber

8 Check for any signs of fluid leakage around the suspension strut/shock absorber body, or from the rubber gaiter around the piston rod. Should any fluid be noticed, the suspension strut/shock absorber is defective internally, and should be renewed. **Note:** *Suspension struts/shock absorbers should always be renewed in pairs on the same axle, or the handling of the vehicle will be adversely affected.*

9 The efficiency of the suspension strut/shock absorber may be checked by bouncing the vehicle at each corner. Generally speaking, the body will return to its normal position and stop after being depressed. If it rises and returns on a rebound, the suspension strut/shock absorber is probably suspect. Examine also the suspension strut/shock absorber upper and lower mountings for any signs of wear.

## 17 Brake fluid renewal

**1.4 litre SOHC models from RPO 10248: Every 40 000 miles (60 000 km)**

**All other models: Every 12 500 miles (20 000 km)**

⚠️ *Warning: Brake hydraulic fluid can harm your eyes and damage painted surfaces, so use extreme caution when handling and pouring it. Do not use fluid that has been standing open for some time, as it absorbs moisture from the air. Excess moisture can cause a dangerous loss of braking effectiveness.* **Note:** *The hydraulic clutch shares its fluid reservoir with the braking system, and may also need to be bled (see Chapter 6).*

1 The procedure is similar to that for the bleeding of the hydraulic system as described in Chapter 9, except that the brake fluid reservoir should be emptied by syphoning, using a clean ladle or similar before starting, and allowance should be made for the old fluid to be expelled when bleeding a section of the circuit.

2 Working as described in Chapter 9, open the first bleed screw in the sequence, and pump the brake pedal gently until nearly all the old fluid has been emptied from the master cylinder reservoir.

> **HAYNES HiNT** *Old hydraulic fluid is invariably much darker in colour than the new, making it easy to distinguish the two.*

3 Top-up to the MAX level with new fluid, and continue pumping until only the new fluid remains in the reservoir, and new fluid can be seen emerging from the bleed screw. Tighten the screw, and top the reservoir level up to the MAX level line.

4 Work through all the remaining bleed screws in the sequence until new fluid can be seen at all of them. Be careful to keep the master cylinder reservoir topped-up to above the MIN level at all times, or air may enter the system and increase the length of the task.

5 When the operation is complete, check that all bleed screws are securely tightened, and that their dust caps are refitted. Wash off all traces of spilt fluid, and recheck the master cylinder reservoir fluid level.

6 Check the operation of the brakes before taking the car on the road.

**18.2a Undo the three air cleaner lid screws (arrowed), lift off the lid . . .**

**18.2b . . . and remove the filter element – 8-valve engines**

**18.4 Lift off the engine cover by pulling it upwards – 16-valve engines**

**18.5 Release the tabs securing the hand priming pump support brackets to the air cleaner lid – 16-valve engines**

**18.6a Slacken the retaining clips . . .**

**18.6b . . . and disconnect the air intake duct from the turbocharger and air mass meter – 16-valve engines**

## 18 Air cleaner filter element renewal

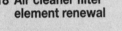

**1.4 litre SOHC models from RPO 10248: Every 40 000 miles (60 000 km)**

**All other models: Every 37 500 miles (60 000 km)**

### 8-valve engines

1 Undo the three screws at the front securing the air cleaner lid to the base, then lift off the lid and withdraw the filter element. Note which way up the element was fitted **(see illustrations)**.

2 Position the new element in the air cleaner base and refit the lid. Note the three lugs at the rear of the lid which engage with the base. Tighten the retaining screws securely.

### 16-valve engines

3 Disconnect the battery (see Chapter 5A).

4 Remove the plastic cover from the top of the engine. The cover is retained by rubber grommets, and pulls upwards to release **(see illustration)**.

5 Using a small screwdriver, release the tabs securing the diesel hand priming pump support brackets to the front of the air cleaner lid **(see illustration)**. Move the priming pump forwards slightly clear of the air cleaner assembly.

6 Slacken the retaining clips and disconnect the air intake duct from the turbocharger and air mass meter **(see illustrations)**.

7 Disconnect the air mass meter wiring connector **(see illustration)**.

8 Undo the three screws at the front securing the air cleaner lid to the base. Lift the air cleaner lid, complete with air mass meter upwards, disengage the locating

**18.7 Disconnect the air mass meter wiring connector – 16-valve engines**

lugs at the rear, and remove the lid **(see illustrations)**.

9 Lift out the filter element, noting which way up it was fitted **(see illustration)**.

10 Position the new element in the air cleaner base and refit the lid. Ensure that the rear

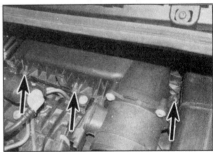

**18.8a Undo the three screws (arrowed) securing the air cleaner lid to the base – 16-valve engines**

**18.8b Lift the lid, complete with air mass meter and disengage the locating lugs at the rear – 16-valve engines**

**18.9 Lift out the filter element – 16-valve engines**

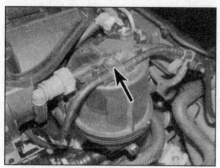

**19.3 Undo the vacuum pipe bracket screw (arrowed) – 8-valve engines**

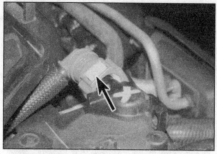

**19.6 Depress the tab (arrowed) and disconnect the fuel inlet and outlet hoses – 8-valve engines**

**19.7a Undo the filter retaining screw (arrowed) . . .**

**19.7b . . . then disengage the filter lug from the bracket – 8-valve engines**

**19.15 Remove the turbocharger-to-air mass meter air duct (A), and the cold air intake duct (B) – 16-valve engines**

locating lugs engage correctly and secure the lid with the three retaining screws.

**11** Reconnect the air mass meter wiring connector, then refit the air intake duct.

**12** Locate the hand priming pump back into position then refit the plastic engine cover.

**13** Reconnect the battery on completion.

---

## 19 Fuel filter renewal

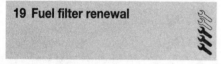

**1.4 litre SOHC models from RPO 10248: Every 40 000 miles (60 000 km)**

**All other models: Every 37 500 miles (60 000 km)**

 *Warning: Refer to the special information given in Chapter 4B, Section 2, before proceeding.*

*Note: The fuel filter element and housing are only supplied as a complete assembly. The filter element is not available separately.*

### 8-valve engines

**1** Disconnect the battery (see Chapter 5A). Undo the three screws at the front securing the air cleaner lid to the base and remove the lid for access to the filter housing.

**2** Thoroughly clean the fuel inlet and outlet hose unions on the filter, and the surrounding area with a suitable degreasing fluid.

**3** Undo the screw, release the retaining bracket, and position the brake servo vacuum pipe to one side **(see illustration)**.

**4** Place a suitable container under the engine, beneath the filter housing water drain tube. If a drain tube is not fitted, take care not to allow fuel to enter the transmission bellhousing which is just below. If possible, fit a suitable length of clear plastic hose over the drain tap

outlet, and direct the hose under the engine **(see illustration 4.2a)**.

**5** Open the drain tap by turning it anti-clockwise. Allow fuel and water to drain, then close the drain tap.

**6** Depress the tabs on the side of the quick-release fittings and disconnect the fuel inlet and outlet hoses from the filter **(see illustration)**. Plug the hoses and unions to prevent dirt ingress and fuel loss. Note that suitable protective caps to plug the hoses and unions are normally supplied with the new filter.

**7** Undo the single filter retaining screw, and manoeuvre the filter from the bracket. Disconnect the fuel heater and water detector wiring connectors (where fitted) as the filter is withdrawn **(see illustrations)**.

**8** Unscrew the fuel heater and water detector (where fitted) from the filter. Discard the O-ring seals, new ones must be fitted.

**9** Renew the water detector and fuel heater O-ring seals, and refit them to the new filter, tightening them securely.

**10** Manoeuvre the filter into position and secure it in place with the fixing screw.

**11** Reconnect the fuel inlet and outlet hoses and the wiring plugs.

**12** Resecure the brake servo vacuum pipe and refit the air cleaner lid.

**13** Reconnect the battery, then prime the fuel system as described in Chapter 4B.

### 16-valve engines

**14** Disconnect the battery (see Chapter 5A).

**15** Remove the air duct connecting the turbocharger to the air mass meter, and the cold air intake duct to the air cleaner base as described in Chapter 4B **(see illustration)**.

**16** Thoroughly clean the fuel inlet and outlet hose unions on the filter, and the surrounding area with a suitable degreasing fluid.

**17** Place a container under the engine, beneath the filter housing water drain tube. If a drain tube is not fitted, take care not to allow fuel to enter the transmission bellhousing which is just below. If possible, fit a length of clear plastic hose over the drain tap outlet, and direct the hose under the engine **(see illustration 4.2b)**.

**18** Open the drain tap by turning it anti-clockwise. Allow fuel and water to drain, then close the drain tap.

**19.19 Depress the tabs and disconnect the fuel inlet and outlet hoses – 16-valve engines**

**19.20 Disconnect the fuel heater unit wiring connector – 16-valve engines**

**19.22a  Lift the filter from its location . . .**

**19.22b  . . . then disconnect the water detector wiring connector . . .**

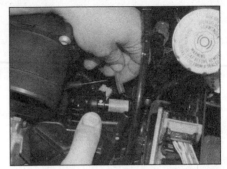

**19.22c  . . . and water drain tube – 16-valve engines**

**19.24a  Depress the locking tab . . .**

**19.24b  . . . and slide the fuel heater off the filter housing – 16-valve engines**

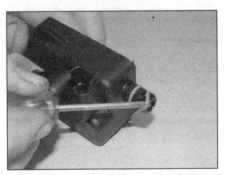

**19.25  Renew the two fuel heater O-rings – 16-valve engines**

**19** Depress the tabs on the side of the quick-release fittings and disconnect the fuel inlet and outlet hoses from the filter **(see illustration)**. Plug the hoses and unions to prevent dirt ingress and fuel loss. Note that suitable protective caps to plug the hoses and unions are normally supplied with the new filter.

**20** Disconnect the wiring connector from the fuel heater unit on the side of the filter housing **(see illustration)**.

**21** Release the retaining clips on the front, and left-hand side of the air cleaner assembly. Lift the assembly upwards slightly until there is sufficient clearance to remove the fuel filter.

**22** Depress the plastic locking tab to release the filter from its mounting bracket. Lift the filter up and out of its location, then disconnect the water detector wiring connector and water drain tube as the filter is withdrawn **(see illustrations)**.

**23** Open the drain tap and drain any remaining fuel from the filter.

**24** Using a screwdriver, depress the locking tab and slide the fuel heater off the filter housing **(see illustrations)**.

**25** Remove and discard the two O-rings on the fuel heater and fit the new O-rings supplied with the new filter **(see illustration)**.

**26** Remove the protective caps from the new filter and slide the fuel heater into position until it can be heard to click into place.

**27** Fit the new filter to the engine using a reversal of the removal procedure.

**28** Close the fuel drain tap and prime the fuel system as described in Chapter 4B.

## 20  Manual transmission oil level check

**1.4 litre SOHC models from RPO 10248: Every 40 000 miles (60 000 km)**

**All other models: Every 37 500 miles (60 000 km)**

**Note:** *On later MA transmissions, the oil level cannot be checked, as there is no filler/level plug fitted. These transmissions do not require regular maintenance and are filled for life. If the transmission develops a leak or is removed for other work, the oil needs to be completely drained and the transmission refilled with the correct amount of oil. The transmission is then refilled through the vent/breather on the top of the transmission.*

**Note:** *A suitable square-section wrench may*

*be required to undo the transmission filler/level plug on some models. These wrenches can be obtained from most motor factors or your Citroën dealer. A new sealing washer will be required for the transmission filler/level plug, when refitting.*

**1** Slacken the left-hand front road wheels bolts. Jack up the front and rear of the car and securely support it on axle stands so that it remains level (see *Jacking and vehicle support*). If the car has been recently driven, wait at least 5 minutes after the engine has been switched off. If the oil level is checked immediately after driving the car, some of the oil will remain distributed around the transmission components, resulting in an inaccurate level reading.

**2** Remove the left-hand front roadwheel then push in the centre pins a little, prise out the complete plastic expanding rivet, and remove the wheel arch liner from under the wing for access to the filler/level plug.

**3** Wipe clean the area around the filler/level

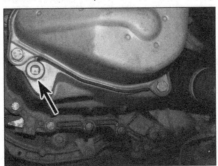

**20.3a  Transmission oil level filler plug (arrowed) – 8-valve engines**

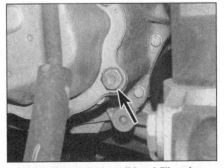

**20.3b  Transmission oil level filler plug (arrowed) – 16-valve engines**

**21.21 Use a 1.0 litre plastic bottle as a header tank**

plug which is on the left-hand end of the transmission. Unscrew the plug and clean it; discard the sealing washer **(see illustrations)**.
**4** The oil level should reach the lower edge of the filler/level hole. A certain amount of oil will have gathered behind the filler/level plug, and will trickle out when it is removed; this does *not* necessarily indicate that the level is correct. To ensure that a true level is established, wait until the initial trickle has stopped, then add oil as necessary until a trickle of new oil can be seen emerging. The level will be correct when the flow ceases; use only good-quality oil of the specified type (see *Lubricants and fluids*).
**5** Filling the transmission with oil is an extremely awkward operation; above all, allow plenty of time for the oil level to settle properly before checking it. If a large amount had is added to the transmission, and a large amount flows out on checking the level, refit the filler/level

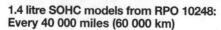

**21.4 Squeeze together the tabs to release the hose retaining clip**

**21.6a Prise out the retaining clip . . .**

plug and take the vehicle on a short journey. With the new oil distributed fully around the transmission components, recheck the level after allowing time for it to settle again.
**6** If the transmission has been overfilled so that oil flows out as soon as the filler/level plug is removed, first check that the car is completely level (front-to-rear and side-to-side). Allow any surplus oil to drain off into a suitable container.
**7** When the level is correct, fit a new sealing washer to the filler/level plug. Tighten the plug to the specified torque wrench setting. Wash off any spilt oil. Refit the wheel arch liner, and secure it in position with its plastic rivets. Refit the roadwheel then lower the car to the ground.
**8** Frequent need for topping-up indicates a leak, which should be found and corrected before it becomes serious.

---

### 21 Coolant renewal

**1.4 litre SOHC models from RPO 10248: Every 40 000 miles (60 000 km)**

**All other models: Every 37 500 miles (60 000 km)**

⚠️ *Warning: Wait until the engine is cold before starting this procedure. Do not allow antifreeze to come in contact with your skin, or with the painted surfaces of the vehicle. Rinse off spills immediately with plenty of water.*

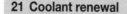

**21.5 Undo the heater outlet hose union bleed screw cap (arrowed)**

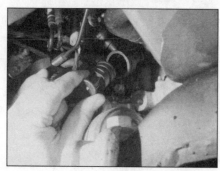

**21.6b . . . and pull out the drain plug**

*Never leave antifreeze lying around in an open container, or in a puddle in the driveway or on the garage floor. Children and pets are attracted by its sweet smell, but antifreeze can be fatal if ingested.*

#### Cooling system draining

**1** With the engine completely cold, unscrew the expansion tank filler cap.
**2** Undo the screws and remove the engine undershield – where fitted.
**3** Position a suitable container beneath the radiator lower hose outlet at the lower left-hand side of the radiator.
**4** Release the retaining clip and disconnect the lower hose from the radiator, then allow the coolant to drain into the container **(see illustration)**.
**5** To assist draining, unscrew the cooling system bleed screw from the heater matrix outlet hose union on the engine compartment bulkhead **(see illustration)**.
**6** To drain the engine, pull out the clip and remove the plug located in the coolant manifold at the rear of the cylinder block **(see illustrations)**. The plug must be refitted with a new clip and O-ring.
**7** If the coolant has been drained for a reason other than renewal, then provided it is clean and less than four years old, it can be re-used, though this is not recommended.
**8** Refit the radiator hose and secure it with the hose clamp.

#### Cooling system flushing

**9** If coolant renewal has been neglected, or if the antifreeze mixture has become diluted, then in time, the cooling system may gradually lose efficiency, as the coolant passages become restricted due to rust, scale deposits, and other sediment. The cooling system efficiency can be restored by flushing the system clean.
**10** The radiator should be flushed independently of the engine, to avoid unnecessary contamination.

#### Radiator flushing

**11** To flush the radiator, disconnect the top hose and any other relevant hoses from the radiator, with reference to Chapter 3.
**12** Insert a garden hose into the radiator top inlet. Direct a flow of clean water through the radiator, and continue flushing until clean water emerges from the radiator bottom outlet.
**13** If after a reasonable period, the water still does not run clear, the radiator can be flushed with a good proprietary cleaning agent. It is important that their manufacturer's instructions are followed carefully. If the contamination is particularly bad, insert the hose in the radiator bottom outlet, and reverse-flush the radiator.

#### Engine flushing

**14** To flush the engine, first refit the plug located in the coolant manifold at the rear of the cylinder block, and tighten the cooling system bleed screw.
**15** Remove the thermostat as described in Chapter 3.

**16** With the bottom hose disconnected from the radiator, insert a garden hose into the thermostat housing aperture. Direct a clean flow of water through the engine, and continue flushing until clean water emerges from the radiator bottom hose.

**17** On completion of flushing, refit the thermostat and reconnect the hoses with reference to Chapter 3.

### Cooling system filling

**18** Before attempting to fill the cooling system, make sure that all hoses and clips are in good condition, and that the clips are tight. Note that an antifreeze mixture must be used all year round, to prevent corrosion of the engine components (see following sub-Section).

**19** Remove the expansion tank filler cap.

**20** Open the cooling system bleed screw (see paragraph 5).

**21** Citroën recommend the use of a 'header tank' when refilling the cooling system, to reduce the possibility of air being trapped in the system. Although Citroën dealers use a special header tank which screws onto the expansion tank, the same effect can be achieved by using a suitable 1.0 litre bottle, with a seal between the bottle and the expansion tank **(see illustration)**.

**22** Fit the 'header tank' to the expansion tank and slowly fill the system. Coolant will emerge from the bleed screw. As soon as coolant free from air bubbles emerges from the screw, tighten the screw.

**23** Ensure that the 'header tank' is full (at least 1.0 litre of coolant). Start the engine, and run it at a fast idle speed (do not exceed 2000 rpm) until the cooling fan cuts in, and then cuts out. Stop the engine.

*Caution: The coolant will be hot. Take great care not to scald yourself.*

**24** Allow the engine to cool, then remove the 'header tank'.

**25** When the engine has cooled, check the coolant level as described in *Weekly checks*. Top-up the level if necessary, and refit the expansion tank cap. Where removed, refit the engine undershield.

### Antifreeze mixture

**26** The antifreeze should always be renewed at the specified intervals. This is necessary not only to maintain the antifreeze properties, but also to prevent corrosion which would otherwise occur as the corrosion inhibitors become progressively less effective.

**27** Always use an ethylene-glycol based antifreeze of the specified type (see *Lubricants and fluids*). The quantity of antifreeze and level of protection are indicated in the Specifications.

**28** Before adding antifreeze, the cooling system should be completely drained, preferably flushed, and all hoses checked for condition and security.

**29** After filling with antifreeze, a label should be attached to the expansion tank, stating the type and concentration of antifreeze used, and the date installed. Any subsequent topping-up should be made with the same type and concentration of antifreeze.

**30** Do not use engine antifreeze in the washer system, as it will cause damage to the vehicle paintwork. A screenwash additive should be added to the washer system in the quantities stated on the bottle.

## 22 Timing belt renewal

**1.4 litre SOHC models from RPO 10248: Every 80 000 miles (120 000 km)**

**All other models: Every 75 000 miles (120 000 km)**

**1** Refer to Chapter 2B or 2C (as applicable).

## 23 Particulate filter renewal

### Every 75 000 miles (120 000 km)

**1** A particulate filter is fitted to 1.6 litre models with the DV6TED4 engine (code 9HZ). This filter is combined with the catalytic converter in the exhaust front pipe.

**2** Renewal of the particulate filter is described in Chapter 4B.

**3** An additive is used to help clean the filter element. This additive is stored in a separate reservoir adjacent to the fuel tank. However, checking the filter and refilling the reservoir should be entrusted to a Citroën dealer or specialist, as parameters of the engine management ECU must be re-initialised, and special equipment/tools must be used due to the hazardous nature of the additive.

**4** Citroën recommends that the additive is topped-up at the same interval the particulate filter is renewed (see *Lubricants and fluids*).

## 24 Airbags and seat belt pretensioners renewal

### Every 10 years

**1** Citroën recommend that the airbags and seat belt pretensioners are renewed regardless of their condition every ten years. Refer to Chapter 12 for airbag renewal, and Chapter 11 for seat belt pretensioner renewal.

# Chapter 2 Part A:
# Petrol engine in-car repair procedures

## Contents

## Degrees of difficulty

| Easy, suitable for novice with little experience 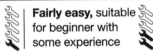 | Fairly easy, suitable for beginner with some experience | Fairly difficult, suitable for competent DIY mechanic | Difficult, suitable for experienced DIY mechanic | Very difficult, suitable for expert DIY or professional  |
|---|---|---|---|---|

## Specifications

| Engine (general) | Designation | Code* |
|---|---|---|
| 1.1 litre engine . . . . . . . . . . . . . . . . . . . . . . . . . . . . . . . . . . . . . . . . . | TU1JP | HFX |
| 1.4 litre engines: | | |
|   SOHC. . . . . . . . . . . . . . . . . . . . . . . . . . . . . . . . . . . . . . . . . . . . . . . . | TU3JP | KFV |
|   DOHC. . . . . . . . . . . . . . . . . . . . . . . . . . . . . . . . . . . . . . . . . . . . . . . . | ET3J4 and ET3JA | KFU |
| 1.6 litre engine . . . . . . . . . . . . . . . . . . . . . . . . . . . . . . . . . . . . . . . . . | TU5JP4 | NFU |

Capacity:
  1.1 litre engine . . . . . . . . . . . . . . . . . . . . . . . . . . . . . . . . . . . . . . . . . 1124 cc
  1.4 litre engine . . . . . . . . . . . . . . . . . . . . . . . . . . . . . . . . . . . . . . . . . 1360 cc
  1.6 litre engine . . . . . . . . . . . . . . . . . . . . . . . . . . . . . . . . . . . . . . . . . 1587 cc

Bore:
  1.1 litre engine . . . . . . . . . . . . . . . . . . . . . . . . . . . . . . . . . . . . . . . . . 72.00 mm
  1.4 litre engine . . . . . . . . . . . . . . . . . . . . . . . . . . . . . . . . . . . . . . . . . 75.00 mm
  1.6 litre engine . . . . . . . . . . . . . . . . . . . . . . . . . . . . . . . . . . . . . . . . . 78.50 mm

Stroke:
  1.1 litre engine . . . . . . . . . . . . . . . . . . . . . . . . . . . . . . . . . . . . . . . . . 69.00 mm
  1.4 litre engine . . . . . . . . . . . . . . . . . . . . . . . . . . . . . . . . . . . . . . . . . 77.00 mm
  1.6 litre engine . . . . . . . . . . . . . . . . . . . . . . . . . . . . . . . . . . . . . . . . . 82.00 mm

Direction of crankshaft rotation . . . . . . . . . . . . . . . . . . . . . . . . . . . . Clockwise (viewed from right-hand side of vehicle)
No 1 cylinder location. . . . . . . . . . . . . . . . . . . . . . . . . . . . . . . . . . . . At transmission end of the block

Compression ratio:
  1.1 and 1.4 litre SOHC engines . . . . . . . . . . . . . . . . . . . . . . . . . . . 10.5 : 1
  1.4 litre DOHC and 1.6 litre engine. . . . . . . . . . . . . . . . . . . . . . . . . 11.0 : 1

Maximum power output:
  1.1 litre engine . . . . . . . . . . . . . . . . . . . . . . . . . . . . . . . . . . . . . . . . . 44 kW @ 5500 rpm
  1.4 litre engines:
    SOHC. . . . . . . . . . . . . . . . . . . . . . . . . . . . . . . . . . . . . . . . . . . . . . . . 54 kW @ 5400 rpm
    DOHC. . . . . . . . . . . . . . . . . . . . . . . . . . . . . . . . . . . . . . . . . . . . . . . . 65 kW @ 5250 rpm
  1.6 litre engine . . . . . . . . . . . . . . . . . . . . . . . . . . . . . . . . . . . . . . . . . 80 kW @ 5800 rpm

Maximum torque output:
  1.1 litre engine . . . . . . . . . . . . . . . . . . . . . . . . . . . . . . . . . . . . . . . . . 94 Nm @ 3400 rpm
  1.4 litre engines:
    SOHC. . . . . . . . . . . . . . . . . . . . . . . . . . . . . . . . . . . . . . . . . . . . . . . . 120 Nm @ 3400 rpm
    DOHC. . . . . . . . . . . . . . . . . . . . . . . . . . . . . . . . . . . . . . . . . . . . . . . . 133 Nm @ 3250 rpm
  1.6 litre engine . . . . . . . . . . . . . . . . . . . . . . . . . . . . . . . . . . . . . . . . . 147 Nm @ 4000 rpm

*The engine code is situated on the front, left-hand end of the cylinder block.*

## Camshaft(s)

Drive . . . . . . . . . . . . . . . . . . . . . . . . . . . . . . . . . . . . . . . . . . . . .   Toothed belt

## Valve clearances (engine cold)

1.1 and 1.4 litre SOHC engines:
   Inlet. . . . . . . . . . . . . . . . . . . . . . . . . . . . . . . . . . . . . . . . . . . .   0.20 mm
   Exhaust. . . . . . . . . . . . . . . . . . . . . . . . . . . . . . . . . . . . . . . . . .   0.40 mm
1.4 and 1.6 litre DOHC engines . . . . . . . . . . . . . . . . . . . . . . . . . .   Hydraulic adjusters

## Lubrication system

Oil pump type. . . . . . . . . . . . . . . . . . . . . . . . . . . . . . . . . . . . . . . .   Gear type, chain-driven off the crankshaft
Minimum oil pressure at 80°C . . . . . . . . . . . . . . . . . . . . . . . . . .   4 bars @ 4000 rpm
Oil pressure warning switch operating pressure . . . . . . . . . . . . . . .   0.8 bars

## Torque wrench settings

| | Nm | lbf ft |
|---|---|---|
| Big-end bearing cap nuts*: | | |
|   1.1 & 1.4 litre SOHC and 1.6 litre engines . . . . . . . . . . . . . . . . . . . | 40 | 30 |
|   1.4 litre DOHC engine: | | |
|     Stage 1 . . . . . . . . . . . . . . . . . . . . . . . . . . . . . . . . | 30 | 22 |
|     Stage 2 . . . . . . . . . . . . . . . . . . . . . . . . . . . . . . . . | Angle-tighten a further 45° | |
| Camshaft bearing housing to cylinder head (DOHC engines) . . . . . . . . | 10 | 7 |
| Camshaft sprocket retaining bolt(s): | | |
|   1.1 & 1.4 litre SOHC and 1.6 litre engines . . . . . . . . . . . . . . . . . . . | 45 | 33 |
|   1.4 litre DOHC engine: | | |
|     Exhaust sprocket retaining bolt . . . . . . . . . . . . . . . . . . . . . . . | 45 | 33 |
|     Inlet sprocket retaining bolt: | | |
|       Stage 1 . . . . . . . . . . . . . . . . . . . . . . . . . . . . . . . . | 20 | 15 |
|       Stage 1 . . . . . . . . . . . . . . . . . . . . . . . . . . . . . . . . | 60 | 44 |
|     Inlet sprocket retaining bolt cover . . . . . . . . . . . . . . . . . . . . . . | 40 | 30 |
| Camshaft thrust fork retaining bolt (SOHC engine) . . . . . . . . . . . . . | 16 | 12 |
| Crankshaft oil seal housing bolts. . . . . . . . . . . . . . . . . . . . . . . . . . . | 8 | 6 |
| Crankshaft pulley retaining bolts . . . . . . . . . . . . . . . . . . . . . . . . . . . | 25 | 18 |
| Crankshaft sprocket retaining bolt*: | | |
|   Stage 1 . . . . . . . . . . . . . . . . . . . . . . . . . . . . . . . . . . . . . . . | 40 | 30 |
|   Stage 2 . . . . . . . . . . . . . . . . . . . . . . . . . . . . . . . . . . . . . . . | Angle-tighten a further 45° | |
| Cylinder head bolts: | | |
|   1.1 & 1.4 litre SOHC engines: | | |
|     Stage 1 . . . . . . . . . . . . . . . . . . . . . . . . . . . . . . . . . | 20 | 15 |
|     Stage 2 . . . . . . . . . . . . . . . . . . . . . . . . . . . . . . . . . | Angle-tighten a further 240° | |
|   1.4 litre DOHC engine: | | |
|     Stage 1 . . . . . . . . . . . . . . . . . . . . . . . . . . . . . . . . . | 15 | 11 |
|     Stage 2 . . . . . . . . . . . . . . . . . . . . . . . . . . . . . . . . . | 25 | 18 |
|     Stage 3 . . . . . . . . . . . . . . . . . . . . . . . . . . . . . . . . . | Angle-tighten a further 200° | |
|   1.6 litre engine: | | |
|     Stage 1 . . . . . . . . . . . . . . . . . . . . . . . . . . . . . . . . . | 20 | 15 |
|     Stage 2 . . . . . . . . . . . . . . . . . . . . . . . . . . . . . . . . . | Angle-tighten a further 260° | |
| Cylinder head cover bolts (DOHC engines) . . . . . . . . . . . . . . . . . . . | 10 | 7 |
| Cylinder head cover screws/nuts (SOHC engine) . . . . . . . . . . . . . . . | 8 | 6 |
| Driveplate bolts . . . . . . . . . . . . . . . . . . . . . . . . . . . . . . . . . . . . . . | 67 | 49 |
| Engine-to-transmission bolts: | | |
|   Manual transmission models . . . . . . . . . . . . . . . . . . . . . . . . . . . | 40 | 30 |
|   Automatic transmission models. . . . . . . . . . . . . . . . . . . . . . . . . . | 35 | 26 |
| Engine/transmission left-hand mounting: | | |
|   Mounting arm-to-transmission bracket bolts. . . . . . . . . . . . . . . . . | 60 | 44 |
|   Mounting assembly-to-body bolts. . . . . . . . . . . . . . . . . . . . . . . . | 55 | 41 |
|   Transmission bracket-to-transmission bolts . . . . . . . . . . . . . . . . | 55 | 41 |
| Engine/transmission rear mounting: | | |
|   Connecting link-to-transmission bracket bolt . . . . . . . . . . . . . . . | 60 | 44 |
|   Connecting link-to-subframe bolt . . . . . . . . . . . . . . . . . . . . . . . | 60 | 44 |
| Engine/transmission right-hand mounting: | | |
|   Mounting-to-body bolts . . . . . . . . . . . . . . . . . . . . . . . . . . . . . | 50 | 37 |
|   Mounting bracket-to-cylinder head bolts. . . . . . . . . . . . . . . . . . . | 45 | 33 |
|   Cylinder head bracket-to-cylinder head bolts . . . . . . . . . . . . . . . | 45 | 33 |
| Flywheel bolts* . . . . . . . . . . . . . . . . . . . . . . . . . . . . . . . . . . . . . . | 70 | 52 |
| Main bearing cap bolts (1.6 litre engine): | | |
|   Stage 1 . . . . . . . . . . . . . . . . . . . . . . . . . . . . . . . . . . . . . . . | 20 | 15 |
|   Stage 2 . . . . . . . . . . . . . . . . . . . . . . . . . . . . . . . . . . . . . . . | Angle-tighten a further 49° | |

## Torque wrench settings (continued)

| | Nm | lbf ft |
|---|---|---|
| Main bearing ladder casting (1.1 & 1.4 litre engines): | | |
| M11 bolts: | | |
| Stage 1 .................................................... | 20 | 15 |
| Stage 2 .................................................... | Angle-tighten a further 44° | |
| M6 bolts ...................................................... | 8 | 6 |
| Oil filter ......................................................... | 25 | 18 |
| Oil filter housing to engine block (1.6 litre engine) ................. | 10 | 7 |
| Oil pressure switch: | | |
| SOHC engines ............................................... | 30 | 22 |
| DOHC engines ............................................... | 20 | 15 |
| Oil pump retaining bolts..................................... | 9 | 7 |
| Piston oil jet spray tube bolts ............................. | 10 | 7 |
| Roadwheel bolts............................................... | 90 | 66 |
| Sump drain plug............................................... | 30 | 22 |
| Sump retaining nuts and bolts .............................. | 8 | 6 |
| Timing belt cover bolts....................................... | 8 | 6 |
| Timing belt tensioner pulley nut: | | |
| 1.1 and 1.4 litre engines.................................... | 20 | 15 |
| 1.6 litre engine ............................................. | 22 | 16 |

*New nuts/bolts must be used*

## 1  General information

### How to use this Chapter

This Part of Chapter 2 describes those repair procedures that can reasonably be carried out on the engine while it remains in the car. If the engine has been removed from the car and is being dismantled, as described in Part D, any preliminary dismantling procedures can be ignored.

Note that, while it may be possible physically to overhaul items such as the piston/connecting rod assemblies while the engine is in the car, such tasks are not normally carried out as separate operations. Usually, several additional procedures (not to mention the cleaning of components and of oilways) have to be carried out. For this reason, all such tasks are classed as major overhaul procedures, and are described in Part D of this Chapter.

Part D describes the removal of the engine/ transmission from the vehicle, and the full overhaul procedures that can then be carried out.

### Engine description

The petrol engines in this Part of Chapter 2 are from the TU and ET series, and are well-proven engines which have been fitted to many previous Citroën and Peugeot vehicles. 1.1 and 1.4 litre single overhead camshaft (SOHC) 8-valve, or 1.4 and 1.6 litre double overhead camshaft (DOHC) 16-valve, in-line four cylinder engines are fitted, being mounted transversely at the front of the car with the transmission attached to the left-hand end. All 1.1 and 1.4 litre engines share the same block incorporating wet liners. Both 1.4 and 1.6 litre DOHC engines have similar cylinder heads and repair procedures are identical, except

in the area of the hydraulic followers. On the 1.6 litre, the camshaft operates directly on the hydraulic followers which are located in the cylinder head beneath the camshaft. On the 1.4 litre, the valves are operated by roller rocker arms between the camshaft and the tops of the valves – one end of the rocker arm is clipped to the hydraulic follower and the other end rests on top of the valve stem.

The crankshaft runs in five main bearings. Thrustwashers are fitted to No 2 main bearing (upper half) to control crankshaft endfloat.

The connecting rods rotate on horizontally-split bearing shells at their big-ends. The pistons are attached to the connecting rods by gudgeon pins, which are an interference fit in the connecting rod small-end eyes. The aluminium-alloy pistons are fitted with three piston rings – two compression rings and an oil control ring.

On 1.1 and 1.4 litre engines, the cylinder block is made of aluminium, and wet liners are fitted to the cylinder bores. Sealing O-rings are fitted at the base of each liner, to prevent the escape of coolant into the sump.

On 1.6 litre engines, the cylinder block is made from cast-iron, and the cylinder bores are an integral part of the cylinder block. On this type of engine, the cylinder bores are sometimes referred to as having dry liners.

The inlet and exhaust valves are each closed by coil springs, and operate in guides pressed into the cylinder head; the valve seat inserts are also pressed into the cylinder head, and can be renewed separately if worn.

On SOHC engines, the camshaft is driven by a toothed timing belt, and operates the eight valves via rocker arms. Valve clearances are adjusted by a screw-and-locknut arrangement. The camshaft rotates directly in the cylinder head. The timing belt also drives the coolant pump.

On DOHC engines, the camshafts are driven by a timing belt, and operate the 16 valves. The camshafts rotate directly in the cylinder

head and are retained by a one-piece bearing housing. The belt also drives the coolant pump.

Lubrication is by means of an oil pump, which is driven (via a chain and sprocket) off the right-hand end of the crankshaft. It draws oil through a strainer located in the sump, and then forces it through an externally-mounted filter into galleries in the cylinder block/ crankcase. From there, the oil is distributed to the crankshaft (main bearings) and camshaft. The big-end bearings are supplied with oil via internal drillings in the crankshaft, while the camshaft bearings also receive a pressurised supply. On 1.6 litre engines, piston cooling oil spray jets are fitted to spray oil on the underside of each piston. The camshaft lobes and valves are lubricated by splash, as are all other engine components.

### Operations with engine in car

The following work can be carried out with the engine in the car:

a) Compression pressure – testing.
b) Cylinder head cover – removal and refitting.
c) Timing belt covers – removal and refitting.
d) Timing belt – removal, refitting and adjustment.
e) Timing belt tensioner and sprockets – removal and refitting.
f) Camshaft oil seal(s) – renewal.
g) Camshaft(s) and rocker arms/followers – removal, inspection and refitting.
h) Cylinder head – removal and refitting.
i) Cylinder head and pistons – decarbonising.
j) Sump – removal and refitting.
k) Oil pump – removal, overhaul and refitting.
l) Crankshaft oil seals – renewal.
m) Engine/transmission mountings – inspection and renewal.
n) Flywheel/driveplate – removal, inspection and refitting.

## 2 Compression test – description and interpretation

**1** When engine performance is down, or if misfiring occurs which cannot be attributed to the ignition or fuel systems, a compression test can provide diagnostic clues as to the engine's condition. If the test is performed regularly, it can give warning of trouble before any other symptoms become apparent.
**2** The engine must be fully warmed-up to normal operating temperature, the battery must be fully charged. The aid of an assistant will also be required.
**3** Remove the ignition HT coil assembly (see Chapter 5B) then remove the spark plugs (see Chapter 1A).
**4** Fit a compression tester to the No 1 cylinder spark plug hole – the type of tester which screws into the plug thread is to be preferred.
**5** Have the assistant hold the throttle wide open, and crank the engine on the starter motor; after one or two revolutions, the compression pressure should build-up to a maximum figure, and then stabilise. Record the highest reading obtained.
**6** Repeat the test on the remaining cylinders, recording the pressure in each.
**7** All cylinders should produce very similar pressures; a difference of more than 2 bars between any two cylinders indicates a fault. Note that the compression should build-up quickly in a healthy engine; low compression on the first stroke, followed by gradually-increasing pressure on successive strokes, indicates worn piston rings. A low compression reading on the first stroke, which does not build-up during successive strokes, indicates leaking valves or a blown head gasket (a cracked head could also be the cause). Deposits on the undersides of the valve heads can also cause low compression.
**8** Although Citroën do not specify exact compression pressures, as a guide, any cylinder

pressure of below 10 bars can be considered as less than healthy. Refer to a Citroën dealer or other specialist if in doubt as to whether a particular pressure reading is acceptable.
**9** If the pressure in any cylinder is low, carry out the following test to isolate the cause. Introduce a teaspoonful of clean oil into that cylinder through its spark plug hole, and repeat the test.
**10** If the addition of oil temporarily improves the compression pressure, this indicates that bore or piston wear is responsible for the pressure loss. No improvement suggests that leaking or burnt valves, or a blown head gasket, may be to blame.
**11** A low reading from two adjacent cylinders is almost certainly due to the head gasket having blown between them; the presence of coolant in the engine oil will confirm this.
**12** If one cylinder is about 20 percent lower than the others and the engine has a slightly rough idle, a worn camshaft lobe could be the cause.
**13** If the compression reading is unusually high, the combustion chambers are probably coated with carbon deposits. If this is the case, the cylinder head should be removed and decarbonised.
**14** On completion of the test, refit the spark plugs and ignition HT coil (see Chapters 1A and 5B).

## 3 Engine assembly/ valve timing holes – general information and usage

**Note:** *Do not attempt to rotate the engine whilst the crankshaft/camshaft are locked in position. If the engine is to be left in this state for a long period of time, it is a good idea to place warning notices inside the vehicle, and in the engine compartment. This will reduce the possibility of the engine being accidentally cranked on the starter motor, which is likely to cause damage with the locking pins in place.*

**1** On all models, timing holes are drilled in the camshaft sprocket(s) and in the rear of the flywheel/driveplate. The holes are used to ensure that the crankshaft and camshaft(s) are correctly positioned when assembling the engine (to prevent the possibility of the valves contacting the pistons when refitting the cylinder head), or refitting the timing belt. When the timing holes are aligned with access holes in the cylinder head and the front of the cylinder block, suitable diameter bolts/pins can be inserted to lock both the camshaft and crankshaft in position, preventing them from rotating. Proceed as follows.
**2** Remove the timing belt upper cover as described in Section 5.

### SOHC engines

**3** The crankshaft must now be turned until the timing hole in the camshaft sprocket is aligned with the corresponding hole in the cylinder head. The holes are aligned when the camshaft sprocket hole is in the 2 o'clock position, when viewed from the right-hand end of the engine. The crankshaft can be turned by using a spanner on the crankshaft sprocket bolt, noting that it should always be rotated in a clockwise direction (viewed from the right-hand end of the engine).
**4** With the camshaft sprocket hole correctly positioned, insert a 6 mm diameter stud or pin, 90 mm long, welded to a length of weld rod bent to the appropriate shape, through the hole in the front left-hand flange of the cylinder block, and locate it in the timing hole in the rear of the flywheel **(see illustration)**. A purpose-made Citroën tool No 0132-QY is available from dealers. Note that it may be necessary to rotate the crankshaft slightly to get the holes to align.
**5** With the flywheel correctly positioned, insert a 10 mm diameter bolt or pin through the timing hole in the camshaft sprocket, and locate it in the hole in the cylinder head **(see illustration)**.

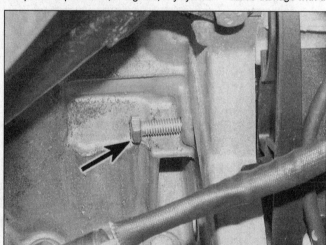

**3.4 Insert a 6 mm diameter bolt/pin (arrowed) into the hole in the cylinder block flange and into the flywheel hole**

**3.5 Lock the camshaft sprocket in position with a 10 mm diameter bolt/pin (arrowed) – SOHC engines**

## DOHC engines

**6** Turn the crankshaft until the holes in the camshaft sprockets align with the corresponding holes in the cylinder head. The crankshaft can be turned by using a spanner on the crankshaft sprocket bolt, noting that it should always be rotated in a clockwise direction (viewed from the right-hand end of the engine).

**7** With the camshaft sprocket holes correctly positioned, insert a 6 mm diameter stud or pin, 90 mm long, welded to a length of weld rod bent to the appropriate shape, through the hole in the front left-hand flange of the cylinder block, and locate it in the timing hole in the rear of the flywheel/driveplate **(see illustrations)**. A purpose-made Citroën tool No 0132-QY is available from dealers. Note that it may be necessary to rotate the crankshaft slightly to get the holes to align.

**8** With the crankshaft correctly positioned, insert suitable bolts or pins through the timing holes in the camshaft sprockets, and locate them in the holes in the cylinder head **(see illustrations)**. **Note:** *The holes on all engines are 8 mm diameter except for the inlet camshaft sprocket hole on 1.4 litre DOHC engines which is 5 mm.*

## All models

**9** The crankshaft and camshaft are now locked in position, preventing unnecessary rotation.

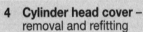 

### 4  Cylinder head cover – removal and refitting

## SOHC engines

### Removal

**1** Disconnect the battery (see Chapter 5A).

**2** Depress the clip and disconnect the breather hose from the cylinder head cover **(see illustration)**.

**3** Remove the ignition HT coil as described in Chapter 5B.

**4** Undo the two retaining nuts and sealing washers (where fitted) then lift off the cylinder head cover, complete with its rubber seal. Examine the seal for signs of damage and deterioration, and if necessary, renew it.

**5** Remove the spacer from each cover stud then lift off the oil baffle plate **(see illustrations)**.

### Refitting

**6** Carefully clean the cylinder head and cover mating surfaces, and remove all traces of oil.

**7** Fit the rubber seal over the edge of the cylinder head cover, ensuring that it is correctly located along its entire length **(see illustration)**.

**8** Refit the oil baffle plate then fit the spacers to the cover studs.

**9** Carefully refit the cylinder head cover to the engine, taking great care not to displace the rubber seal.

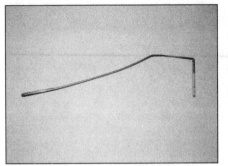

**3.7a  Weld a 90 mm length of 6 mm rod/ stud to a length of weld rod . . .**

**3.8a  Use 10 mm diameter bolts/pins (arrowed) to lock the camshaft sprockets in position – 1.6 litre DOHC engines**

**10** Fit the sealing washers (where fitted) and cover retaining nuts, tightening them to the specified torque.

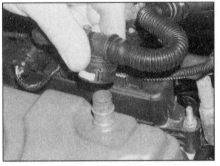

**4.2  Disconnect the breather hose from the cylinder head cover**

**4.5b  . . . then lift off the baffle plate**

**3.7b  . . . and insert it into the hole in the cylinder block flange (arrowed)**

**3.8b  Lock the camshaft sprockets in position using 5 mm and 8 mm diameter drill bits/bolts – 1.4 litre DOHC engines**

**11** Refit the ignition HT coil then reconnect the breather hose securely to the cylinder head cover. On completion reconnect the battery.

**4.5a  Remove the spacers (arrowed) from the studs . . .**

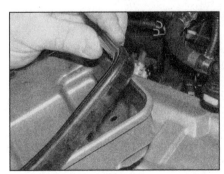

**4.7  Ensure the rubber seal is correctly located on the cylinder head cover**

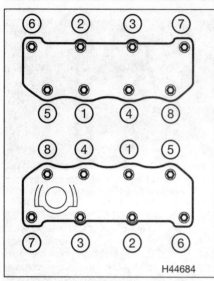

**4.16 Cylinder head cover bolts tightening sequence**

### DOHC engines

#### Removal

**12** Disconnect the battery (see Chapter 5A), and remove the ignition coil as described in Chapter 5B.

**13** Working in a spiral pattern, progressively and evenly slacken the cylinder head cover bolts, and remove the covers. Recover the gaskets.

#### Refitting

**14** Carefully clean the cylinder head and cover mating surfaces, and remove all traces of oil.

**5.1 Timing belt upper cover retaining bolts (arrowed) – SOHC engines**

**15** Check the condition of the cover's composite gasket, and re-use it if undamaged. If it is damaged, a repair may be effected using silicone sealing compound.

**16** Refit the cover(s) and tighten the bolts in sequence **(see illustration)**.

**17** Refit the ignition coils (Chapter 5B).

**18** Reconnect the battery.

---

**5 Timing belt covers –** removal and refitting

## Upper cover removal

### SOHC engines

**1** Slacken and remove the two retaining bolts (one at the front and one at the rear), and remove the upper timing cover from the cylinder head **(see illustration)**.

### DOHC engines

**2** Position a trolley jack under the engine, with a block of wood between the jack head and the sump to prevent damage. Raise the jack to take the weight of the engine.

**3** Undo the three bolts securing the right-hand engine mounting assembly to the bracket on the engine, and the two bolts securing the mounting to the body **(see illustration)**. Remove the mounting assembly from the car and recover the reinforcing plate. Undo the three bolts and remove the engine mounting bracket from the engine.

**4** Slacken the two lower bolts, the undo the five upper bolts and remove the upper timing belt cover **(see illustration)**.

### Lower cover removal

**5** Remove the upper cover as described previously.

**6** Remove the auxiliary drivebelt as described in Chapter 1A.

**7** Undo the three crankshaft pulley retaining bolts and remove the pulley, noting which way round it is fitted **(see illustrations)**.

**8** Slacken and remove the retaining bolts then remove the lower cover from the engine **(see illustration)**.

### Inner cover removal

#### DOHC engines

**9** Remove the camshaft sprockets and tensioner pulley as described in Section 7.

**10** Undo the bolts and remove the inner cover **(see illustration)**.

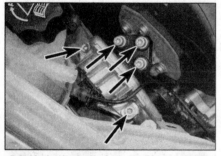

**5.3 Undo the bolts (arrowed) and remove the right-hand engine mounting assembly – DOHC engines**

**5.4 Timing belt upper cover retaining bolts (arrowed) – DOHC engines**

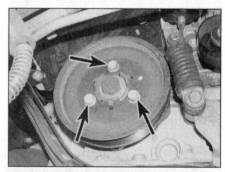

**5.7a Undo the retaining bolts (arrowed) . . .**

**5.7b . . . and remove the crankshaft pulley**

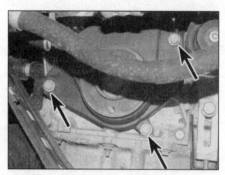

**5.8 Undo the bolts (arrowed) and remove the timing belt lower cover**

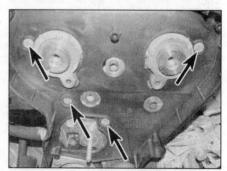

**5.10 Undo the bolts (arrowed) and remove the inner cover – DOHC engines**

## Refitting

### Upper cover

**11** Refitting is the reverse of removal.

### Lower cover

**12** Locate the lower cover over the timing belt sprocket, and tighten its retaining bolts.
**13** Fit the pulley to the end of the crankshaft, ensuring it is fitted the correct way round, and tighten its bolts to the specified torque.
**14** Refit the upper cover as described above.
**15** Refit and tension the auxiliary drivebelt as described in Chapter 1A.

### Inner cover

**16** Refitting is a reversal of removal. Ensure that the cupped lower edge of the cover engages correctly with the lip at the top of the crankshaft oil seal housing as the cover is refitted.

### 6 Timing belt – general information, removal and refitting

## General information

**1** The timing belt drives the camshaft(s) and coolant pump from a toothed sprocket on the front of the crankshaft. If the belt breaks or slips in service, the pistons are likely to hit the valve heads, resulting in extensive (and expensive) damage.
**2** The timing belt should be renewed at the specified intervals (see Chapter 1A), or earlier if it is contaminated with oil or if it is at all noisy in operation (a 'scraping' noise due to uneven wear).
**3** If the timing belt is being removed, it is a wise precaution to check the condition of the coolant pump at the same time (check for signs of coolant leakage). This may avoid the need to remove the timing belt again at a later stage, should the coolant pump fail.

## Removal

**4** Disconnect the battery (see Chapter 5A).
**5** Align the engine assembly/valve timing holes as described in Section 3, and lock both the camshaft sprocket(s) and the flywheel/driveplate in position.
**Caution: Do not attempt to rotate the engine whilst the locking tools are in position.**
**6** Remove the timing belt lower cover as described in Section 5.

### SOHC engines

**7** Position a trolley jack under the engine, with a block of wood between the jack head and the sump to prevent damage. Raise the jack to take the weight of the engine.
**8** Undo the three bolts securing the right-hand engine mounting assembly to the bracket on the engine, and the two bolts securing the mounting to the body **(see illustration)**. Remove the mounting assembly from the

**6.8 Undo the retaining bolts (arrowed) and remove the right-hand engine mounting assembly – SOHC engines**

car and recover the reinforcing plate. Undo the engine mounting bracket retaining bolts and remove the mounting bracket from the engine.
**9** Loosen the timing belt tensioner pulley retaining nut **(see illustration)**. Pivot the pulley approximately 60° in a clockwise direction, using a hexagonal key fitted to the hole in the pulley hub, then retighten the retaining nut.

### DOHC engines

**10** Slacken the timing belt tensioner pulley retaining nut and, using a hexagonal key, rotate the pulley clockwise until the index arm is in the minimum tension position **(see illustration)**. Temporarily tighten the tensioner pulley nut in this position.

### All models

**11** If the timing belt is to be re-used, use white paint or similar to mark the direction of rotation on the belt (if markings do not already exist). Slip the belt off the sprockets.
**12** Check the timing belt carefully for any signs of uneven wear, splitting, or oil contamination. Pay particular attention to the roots of the teeth. Renew the belt if there is the slightest doubt about its condition. If the engine is undergoing an overhaul, and has covered more than 40 000 miles (60 000 km) with the existing belt fitted, renew the belt as a matter of course, regardless of its apparent condition. The cost of a new belt is nothing when compared to the cost of repairs, should the belt break in service. If signs of oil contamination are found, trace the source of the oil leak, and rectify it. Wash down the engine timing belt area and all related components, to remove all traces of oil.
**13** Prior to refitting, thoroughly clean the timing belt sprockets. Check that the tensioner and pulleys rotate freely, without any sign of roughness. If necessary, renew the pulleys as described in Section 7. Make sure that the locking tools are still in place, as described in Section 3.

### Refitting – early SOHC engines with manual tensioner

**14** Manoeuvre the timing belt into position, ensuring that the arrows on the belt are pointing in the direction of rotation (clockwise, when viewed from the right-hand end of the engine).

**6.9 Slacken the nut then pivot the tensioner pulley clockwise to relieve the timing belt tension – early SOHC engines**

**15** Do not twist the timing belt sharply while refitting it. Fit the belt over the crankshaft and camshaft sprockets. Make sure that the 'front run' of the belt is taut – ie, ensure that any slack is on the tensioner pulley side of the belt. Fit the belt over the coolant pump sprocket and tensioner pulley. Ensure that the belt teeth are seated centrally in the sprockets.
**16** Loosen the tensioner pulley retaining nut. Pivot the pulley anti-clockwise to remove all freeplay from the timing belt, and then retighten the nut **(see illustration 6.9)**. Tension the timing belt as described under the following relevant sub-heading.

### Tensioning without the electronic tool

**Note:** *If this method is used, ensure that the belt tension is checked by a Citroën dealer at the earliest possible opportunity.*

**17** If the special tool is not available, an approximate setting may be achieved by pivoting the tensioner pulley anti-clockwise until it is just possible to twist the timing belt through 90° by finger and thumb (without using excessive force), midway between the crankshaft and

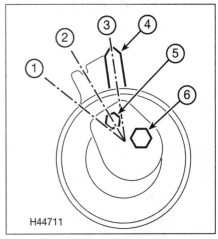

H44711

**6.10 Timing belt tensioner – DOHC engines**

1 Minimum tension position
2 Normal tension position
3 Maximum tension position
4 Index arm
5 Hole for hexagonal key
6 Tensioner pulley bolt

**TOOL TiP**

*To hold their arms clear of the camshaft, fix a stout metal bar to the cylinder head cover studs with the nuts, and lift the arms using shorter lengths of metal bar pivoted on large sockets.*

camshaft sprockets. The deflection of the belt at the mid-point between the sprockets should be approximately 6.0 mm.

**18** Remove the locking tools from the camshaft sprocket and flywheel.

**19** Using a suitable socket and extension bar on the crankshaft sprocket bolt, rotate the crankshaft through four complete rotations in a clockwise direction (viewed from the right-hand end of the engine). Refit the flywheel locking tool and check that the camshaft timing hole is correctly aligned with the cylinder head hole.

*Caution: Do not at any time rotate the crankshaft anti-clockwise.*

**20** Slacken the tensioner pulley nut, retension the belt as described in paragraph 17, then tighten the tensioner pulley nut to the specified torque.

**21** Remove the flywheel locking tool then rotate the crankshaft through a further two turns clockwise.

**22** Check that both the camshaft sprocket and flywheel timing holes are still correctly aligned.

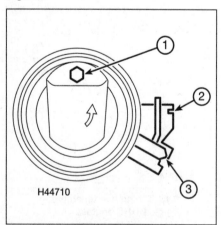

H44710

**6.37 Timing belt tensioner – SOHC engines**

1  *Hole for hexagonal key*
2  *Normal tension position*
3  *Maximum tension position*

**23** If all is well, refit the timing belt covers as described in Section 5.

**24** Clip the wiring harness back into position then reconnect the battery.

### Tensioning with the electronic tool

**25** Fit the special belt tensioning measuring equipment to the 'front run' of the timing belt, approximately midway between the camshaft and crankshaft sprockets. Position the tensioner pulley so that the belt is tensioned to a setting of 44 SEEM units, then retighten its retaining nut.

**26** Remove the locking tools from the camshaft sprocket and flywheel, and remove the measuring tool from the belt.

**27** Using a suitable socket and extension bar on the crankshaft sprocket bolt, rotate the crankshaft through four complete rotations in a clockwise direction (viewed from the right-hand end of the engine). Refit the flywheel locking tool and check that the camshaft timing hole is correctly aligned with the cylinder head hole.

*Caution: Do not at any time rotate the crankshaft anti-clockwise.*

**28** To ensure an accurate reading, it is necessary to remove the valve spring load from the camshaft by fitting the rocker arm plate tool (0132-AE). Remove the cylinder head cover (see Section 4) then back off all the rocker arm contact bolts on the plate (0132-AE). Fit the plate to the cylinder head cover studs, ensuring it is fitted the correct way around then secure it in position with the cylinder head cover nuts. Tighten each rocker arm contact bolt until all rockers are lifted clear of the camshaft lobes. If the rocker arm plate is not available, obtain clearance between the rocker arms and camshaft by slackening the locknut and backing off the adjusting screws on all the necessary rocker arms. It will be found that two of the rocker arms remain in contact with the camshaft, even with the adjusting screws backed fully off. To hold these arms clear of the camshaft, use an arrangement similar to that shown **(see Tool Tip).**

*Caution: Do not overtighten the contact bolts any more than is necessary to obtain a small amount of clearance between the rocker arm roller and cam lobe. If the bolts are overtightened, there is a risk of the valves being forced into contact with the pistons, resulting in serious engine damage.*

**29** Refit the tensioning measuring equipment to the front run of the belt.

**30** Slacken the tensioner pulley retaining nut whilst holding the pulley stationary. Gradually release the tensioner pulley until a tension setting of between 29 and 33 SEEM units is indicated on the measuring equipment. With the belt correctly tensioned, hold the pulley stationary and tighten its retaining nut to the specified torque.

**31** Remove the measuring tool from the belt then unscrew the nuts and remove the rocker

arm contact plate (or home-made alternative) from the cylinder head.

**32** Remove the flywheel locking tool, then rotate the crankshaft through another four complete rotations in a clockwise direction. Refit the flywheel locking tool and check that the camshaft timing hole is correctly aligned with the cylinder head hole.

**33** If all is well, refit the timing belt covers and cylinder head cover as described in Sections 4 and 5. **Note:** *If the rocker arm adjusting screws were moved, adjust the valve clearances before refitting the cylinder head cover.*

### Refitting – later SOHC engines with automatic tensioner

**34** These engines are equipped with a spring-loaded tensioner, so access to the belt tensioning gauge is unnecessary.

**35** Manoeuvre the timing belt into position, ensuring that the arrows on the belt are pointing in the direction of rotation (clockwise, when viewed from the right-hand end of the engine).

**36** Do not twist the timing belt sharply while refitting it. Fit the belt over the crankshaft and camshaft sprockets. Make sure that the 'front run' of the belt is taut – ie, ensure that any slack is on the tensioner pulley side of the belt. Fit the belt over the coolant pump sprocket and tensioner pulley. Ensure that the belt teeth are seated centrally in the sprockets.

**37** Remove the crankshaft and camshaft locking tools, then slacken the tensioner pulley nut and, using a hexagonal key, rotate the pulley anti-clockwise until the index arm is in the maximum tension position **(see illustration)**. Tighten the pulley retaining nut.

**38** Using a socket on the crankshaft pulley bolt, rotate the crankshaft clockwise 10 complete revolutions, and refit the crankshaft locking tool as described in Section 3.

**39** Check the timing is correct by inserting the camshaft sprocket locking tool (Section 3). If the tool cannot be inserted, slacken the tensioner, remove the belt, refit the locking tools, and start again from Paragraph 35.

**40** Remove the crankshaft and camshaft locking tools.

**41** Hold the hexagonal key in the tensioner pulley to maintain the tension, then slacken the pulley nut, and rotate the tensioner to bring the index arm to the normal tension position **(see illustration 6.37)**. Tighten the pulley nut to the specified torque.

**42** Rotate the crankshaft two complete revolutions, and check that the crankshaft and camshaft locking tools can still be inserted.

**43** The remainder of refitting is a reversal of removal.

### Refitting – DOHC engines

**44** Manoeuvre the timing belt into position, ensuring that the arrows on the belt are pointing in the direction of rotation (clockwise, when viewed from the right-hand end of the engine). Note that there are three marks on a new belt, which correspond to marks on the crankshaft and camshaft sprockets (see illustration).

45 Do not twist the timing belt sharply while refitting it. Fit the belt over the crankshaft and camshaft sprockets aligning the marks on the belt with those on the crankshaft and camshaft sprockets. Make sure that the 'front run' of the belt is taut – ie, ensure that any slack is on the tensioner pulley side of the belt. Fit the belt over the coolant pump sprocket and tensioner pulley. Ensure that the belt teeth are seated centrally in the sprockets.

46 Insert the hexagonal key on the tensioner pulley, slacken the pulley nut and rotate the key to bring the index arm to the maximum tension position (see illustration 6.10). Tighten the tensioner roller nut securely.

47 Remove the camshaft and crankshaft locking tools, and rotate the crankshaft 4 complete revolutions clockwise, and refit the crankshaft locking tool.

48 Insert the hexagon key in the tensioner, slacken the nut and rotate the tensioner using the key, until the index arm is in the normal tension position (see illustration 6.10). Tighten the tensioner nut to the specified torque.

49 Remove the crankshaft locking tool, and rotate the crankshaft two complete revolutions clockwise. Check the position of the tensioner index arm – it should be no more than 2.0 mm away from the normal tension position. If it is not, repeat the belt fitting procedure from Paragraph 44.

50 The remainder of refitting is a reversal of removal.

## 7 Timing belt tensioner and sprockets – removal, inspection and refitting

### Removal

#### Camshaft sprocket – SOHC engines

1 Remove the timing belt as described in Section 6.

2 Withdraw the crankshaft and camshaft locking tools, and using a spanner or socket on the crankshaft pulley bolt, rotate the crankshaft backwards (anti-clockwise) 90°.

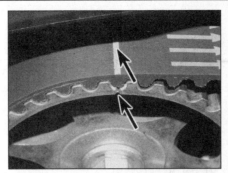

**6.44 Note the timing belt marks which correspond to the camshaft sprockets and crankshaft sprocket – DOHC engines**

This is to prevent any accidental contact between the pistons and valves.

3 Slacken the camshaft sprocket retaining bolt and remove it, along with its washer. To prevent the camshaft rotating as the bolt is slackened, a sprocket-holding tool will be required. In the absence of the special Citroën tool, an acceptable substitute can be fabricated as follows. Use two lengths of steel strip (one long, the other short), and three nuts and bolts; one nut and bolt forms the pivot of a forked tool, with the remaining two nuts and bolts at the tips of the 'forks' to engage with the sprocket spokes (see Tool Tip).

*Caution: Do not attempt to use the sprocket locking pin to prevent the sprocket from rotating whilst the bolt is slackened.*

4 With the retaining bolt removed, slide the sprocket off the end of the camshaft. If the sprocket locating pin is a loose fit, remove it for safe-keeping. Examine the camshaft oil seal for signs of oil leakage and, if necessary, renew it as described in Section 8.

#### Camshaft sprockets – DOHC engines

5 Remove the cylinder head covers as described in Section 4.

6 Remove the timing belt as described in Section 6.

7 Withdraw the crankshaft and camshaft locking tools, and using a spanner or socket on the crankshaft pulley bolt, rotate the crankshaft backwards (anti-clockwise) 90°. This is to prevent any accidental contact between the pistons and valves.

**TOOL TiP**

*Using a home-made tool to hold the camshaft sprocket stationary whilst the bolt is tightened (shown with the cylinder head removed).*

8 Using an open-ended spanner on the square section to counterhold the camshaft, undo the sprocket retaining bolt (see illustration).

*Caution: Do not attempt to use the sprocket locking pin to prevent the sprocket from rotating whilst the bolt is slackened.*

9 With the retaining bolt removed, slide the sprocket off the end of the camshaft. Note that the key is integral with the sprocket. Examine the camshaft oil seals for signs of oil leakage and, if necessary, renew it as described in Section 8.

#### Crankshaft sprocket

10 Remove the timing belt as described in Section 6.

11 Slacken the crankshaft sprocket bolt. To prevent crankshaft rotation on manual transmission models, select top gear, and have an assistant apply the brakes firmly. If the engine has been removed from the vehicle or the vehicle is equipped with an automatic transmission unit, it will be necessary to lock the flywheel/driveplate (see Section 15).

*Caution: Do not be tempted to use the flywheel/driveplate locking pin to prevent the crankshaft from rotating; temporarily remove the locking pin prior to slackening the pulley bolt, then refit it once the bolt has been slackened.*

12 Unscrew the retaining bolt and washer, then slide the sprocket off the end of the crankshaft (see illustrations).

**7.8 Use an open-ended spanner to counterhold the camshaft whilst slackening the sprocket bolt – DOHC engines**

**7.12a Remove the retaining bolt and washer . . .**

**7.12b . . . then slide off the crankshaft sprocket**

**7.13 Remove the Woodruff key and flanged spacer (where fitted) from the crankshaft**

**13** If the Woodruff key is a loose fit in the crankshaft, remove it and store it with the sprocket for safe-keeping. If necessary, also slide the flanged spacer (where fitted) off the end of the crankshaft (see illustration). Examine the crankshaft oil seal for signs oil leakage and, if necessary, renew as described in Section 14.

### Tensioner pulley

**14** Remove the lower timing belt cover (see Section 5).

**15** Lock the camshaft and crankshaft at TDC on No 1 cylinder as described in Section 3.

**16** Slacken and remove the timing belt tensioner pulley retaining nut, and slide the pulley off its mounting stud. Examine the mounting stud for signs of damage and, if necessary, renew it.

### Idler pulley – ET3 DOHC engine only

**17** Remove the lower timing belt cover (see Section 5).

**18** Lock the camshaft and crankshaft at TDC on No 1 cylinder as described in Section 3.

**19** Slacken the timing belt tensioner pulley retaining nut, to release the tension from the timing belt.

**20** Slacken and remove the timing belt idler pulley retaining nut, and slide the pulley off its mounting stud. Examine the mounting stud for signs of damage and, if necessary, renew it.

### Inspection

**21** Clean the sprockets thoroughly, and renew any that show signs of wear, damage or cracks.

**22** Clean the tensioner/idler pulleys, but do not use any strong solvent which may enter the pulley bearings. Check that the pulleys rotate freely about their hubs, with no sign of stiffness or of free play. Renew them if there is any doubt about their condition, or if there are any obvious signs of wear or damage.

**23** Inspect the timing belt (see Section 6). Renew the belt is there is any doubt about its condition.

### Refitting

#### Camshaft sprocket

**24** Refit the locating pin (where removed) then locate the sprocket on the end of the camshaft. Ensure that the locating pin is correctly engaged with the sprocket and the cut-out in the camshaft end. Note that on DOHC engines, the exhaust sprocket is marked E and the inlet sprocket marked A (see illustrations).

**25** Refit the sprocket retaining bolt and washer. Tighten the bolt to the specified torque, whilst retaining the sprocket/camshaft with the method used on removal.

**26** Realign the timing hole in the camshaft sprocket (see Section 3) with the corresponding hole in the cylinder head, and refit the locking pin.

**27** Rotate the crankshaft 90° in the normal direction of rotation (clockwise), until the crankshaft locking pin can be inserted.

**28** Refit the timing belt as described in Section 6. On DOHC engines, refit the cylinder head covers as described in Section 4.

#### Crankshaft sprocket

**29** Locate the Woodruff key in the crankshaft end, then slide on the flanged spacer (where fitted) aligning its slot with the Woodruff key.

**30** Align the crankshaft sprocket slot with the Woodruff key, and slide it onto the end of the crankshaft.

**31** Temporarily remove the locking pin from the rear of the flywheel/driveplate, then refit the crankshaft sprocket retaining bolt and washer. Tighten the bolt to the specified torque, whilst preventing crankshaft rotation using the method employed on removal. Refit the locking pin to the rear of the flywheel/driveplate.

**32** Refit the timing belt as described in Section 6.

### Idler pulley – ET3 DOHC engine only

**33** Refit the idler pulley to its mounting stud, refit the retaining nut and tighten it to the specified torque.

**34** Ensure that the 'front run' of the timing belt is taut – ie, ensure that any slack is on the pulley side of the belt. Check that the belt is centrally located on all its sprockets. Rotate the tensioner pulley anti-clockwise to remove all free play from the timing belt, then tighten the pulley retaining nut securely.

**35** Tension the timing belt as described in Section 6.

**36** Once the belt is correctly tensioned, refit the timing belt covers as described in Section 5.

### Tensioner pulley

**37** Refit the tensioner pulley to its mounting stud, ensuring the cut-out aligns with the pin (see illustration), and fit the retaining nut.

**38** Ensure that the 'front run' of the belt is taut – ie, ensure that any slack is on the pulley side of the belt. Check that the belt is centrally located on all its sprockets. Rotate the pulley anti-clockwise to remove all free play from the timing belt, then tighten the pulley retaining nut securely.

**39** Tension the timing belt as described in Section 6.

**40** Once the belt is correctly tensioned, refit the timing belt covers as described in Section 5.

## 8 Camshaft oil seal(s) – renewal

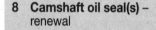

**Note:** *If the camshaft oil seal has been leaking, check the timing belt for signs of oil contamination; the belt must be renewed if signs of oil contamination are found. Ensure that all traces of oil are removed from the sprockets and surrounding area before the new belt is fitted.*

**1** Remove the camshaft sprocket as described in Section 7.

**2** Punch or drill two small holes opposite each other in the oil seal. Screw a self-tapping screw into each, and pull on the screws with pliers to extract the seal. Alternatively, carefully prise the seal out using a flat-bladed screwdriver (see illustration).

**7.24a The locating pin must engage with the slot (arrowed)**

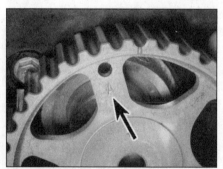

**7.24b On DOHC engines, the inlet sprocket is marked A (arrowed) and the exhaust E**

**7.37 The cut-out aligns the locating pin (arrowed)**

**3** Clean the seal housing, and polish off any burrs or raised edges, which may have caused the seal to fail in the first place.

**4** Lubricate the lips of the new seal with clean engine oil, and drive it into position until it seats on its locating shoulder. Use a suitable tubular drift, such as a socket, which bears only on the hard outer edge of the seal. Take care not to damage the seal lips during fitting. Note that the seal lips should face inwards.

**5** Refit the camshaft sprocket as described in Section 7.

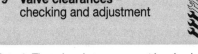

## 9 Valve clearances – checking and adjustment

**Note 1:** *The valve clearances must be checked and adjusted only when the engine is cold.*
**Note 2:** *This procedure applies only to the SOHC engines – the valve clearances on the DOHC engine are maintained by hydraulic compensator units built into the cam followers.*

**1** The importance of having the valve clearances correctly adjusted cannot be overstressed, as they vitally affect the performance of the engine. If the clearances are too big, the engine will be noisy (characteristic rattling or tapping noises) and engine efficiency will be reduced, as the valves open too late and close too early. A more serious problem arises if the clearances are too small, however. If this is the case, the valves may not close fully when the engine is hot, resulting in serious damage to the engine (eg, burnt valve seats and/or cylinder head warping/cracking). The clearances are checked and adjusted as follows.

**2** Remove the cylinder head cover as described in Section 4.

**3** The engine can now be turned using a suitable socket and extension bar fitted to the crankshaft sprocket bolt.

**4** It is important that the clearance of each valve is checked and adjusted only when the valve is fully closed, with the rocker arm resting on the heel of the cam (directly opposite the peak). This can be ensured by carrying out the adjustments in the following sequence, noting that No 1 cylinder is at the transmission end of the engine. The correct valve clearances are given in the Specifications at the start of this Chapter. The valve locations can be determined from the position of the manifolds.

| Valve fully open | Adjust valves |
|---|---|
| *No 1 exhaust* | *No 3 inlet and No 4 exhaust* |
| *No 3 exhaust* | *No 4 inlet and No 2 exhaust* |
| *No 4 exhaust* | *No 2 inlet and No 1 exhaust* |
| *No 2 exhaust* | *No 1 inlet and No 3 exhaust* |

**5** With the relevant valve fully open, check the clearances of the two valves specified. The clearances are checked by inserting a feeler blade of the correct thickness between the valve stem and the rocker arm adjusting screw. The feeler blade should be a light,

**8.2 Carefully prise the camshaft oil seal out with a flat-bladed screwdriver**

sliding fit. If adjustment is necessary, slacken the adjusting screw locknut, and turn the screw as necessary **(see illustration)**. Once the correct clearance is obtained, hold the adjusting screw and tighten the locknut securely. Once the locknut has been tightened, recheck the valve clearance, and adjust again if necessary.

**6** Rotate the crankshaft until the next valve in the sequence is fully open, and check the clearances of the next two specified valves.

**7** Repeat the procedure until all eight valve clearances have been checked (and if necessary, adjusted), then refit the cylinder head cover as described in Section 4.

## 10 Camshaft(s) and rocker arms/followers – removal, inspection and refitting

### General information

**1** On DOHC engines, the valves are operated by followers incorporating hydraulic compensator units between the camshafts and the top of the valves. On SOHC engines, the valves are operated by rockers arms between the camshaft and the top of the valves. The rocker arm assembly is secured to the top of the cylinder head by the cylinder head bolts. Although in theory it is possible to undo the head bolts and remove the rocker arm assembly without removing the head, in practice, this is not recommended. Once the bolts have been

**10.4 Remove the circlip and slide the components from the rocker shaft – SOHC engines**

**9.5 Check the valve clearances using feeler gauges**

removed, the head gasket will be disturbed, and the gasket will almost certainly leak or blow after refitting. For this reason, removal of the rocker arm assembly cannot be done without removing the cylinder head and renewing the head gasket.

**2** On DOHC engines, the camshafts can be removed upwards from the cylinder head. On SOHC engines, the camshaft is slid out of the right-hand end of the cylinder head, and it therefore cannot be removed without first removing the cylinder head, due to a lack of clearance.

### Removal

#### Rocker arms – SOHC engines

**3** Remove the cylinder head as described in Section 11.

**4** To dismantle the rocker arm assembly, carefully prise off the circlip from the right-hand end of the rocker shaft; retain the rocker pedestal, to prevent it being sprung off the end of the shaft. Slide the various components off the end of the shaft, keeping all components in their correct fitted order **(see illustration)**. Make a note of each component's correct fitted position and orientation as it is removed, to ensure it is fitted correctly on reassembly.
**Note:** *Avoid touching the rocker arm roller bearing surfaces with your fingers.*

**5** To separate the left-hand pedestal and shaft, first unscrew the cylinder head cover retaining stud from the top of the pedestal; this can be achieved using a stud extractor, or two nuts locked together **(see illustration)**. With the stud removed, unscrew the grub screw

**10.5 Lock two nuts together to enable the stud to be unscrewed from the left-hand end pedestal – SOHC engines**

**10.9 Undo the bolt and slide out the camshaft thrust fork (arrowed) – SOHC engines**

**10.10b . . . then slide out the camshaft from the cylinder head – SOHC engines**

from the top of the pedestal, and withdraw the rocker shaft.

### Camshaft – SOHC engines

**6** Remove the cylinder head as described in Section 11.

**7** With the head on a bench, remove the locking tool, then remove the camshaft sprocket as described in Section 7.

**8** Unbolt the coolant housing from the left-hand end of the cylinder head.

**9** Undo the retaining bolt and slide out the camshaft thrust fork **(see illustration)**.

**10** Using a large flat-bladed screwdriver, carefully prise the oil seal out of the right-hand end of the cylinder head, then slide out the camshaft **(see illustrations)**.

### Camshafts/followers – DOHC engines

**11** Remove the camshaft sprockets as described in Section 7, then remove the timing belt inner cover as described in Section 5.

**10.15a Remove the rocker arms complete with hydraulic lifter . . .**

**10.10a Prise out the oil seal . . .**

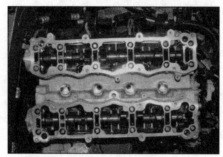

**10.12 Evenly and progressively slacken the camshaft housing retaining bolts – DOHC engines**

**12** Starting from the outside, working in a spiral pattern, progressively and evenly slacken the camshaft bearing housing retaining bolts, and lift the housing from cylinder head **(see illustration)**.

**13** Identify each camshaft for position – the inlet camshaft is at the rear and the exhaust camshaft is at the front of the cylinder head. Also note the TDC position of each camshaft for correct refitting.

**14** Remove the camshafts by pressing on the transmission ends to release the opposite ends from their bearings. Withdrawn the camshafts from the cylinder head and slide the oil seals from the ends.

**15** Obtain 16 small, clean plastic containers, and number them inlet 1 to 8 and exhaust 1 to 8; alternatively, divide a larger container into 16 compartments and number each compartment accordingly. On 1.6 litre DOHC engines, use a rubber sucker to withdraw

**10.15b . . . and keep them in a clean container**

each follower in turn, and place it in its respective container. On 1.4 litre DOHC engines, withdraw each rocker arm complete with hydraulic follower, and place it in its respective container **(see illustrations)**. Don't interchange the followers; the wear rate will be much increased.

### Inspection

#### Rocker arm assembly

**16** Examine the rocker arm roller surfaces which contact the camshaft lobes for wear ridges and scoring. Renew any rocker arms on which the rollers show signs of damage. If a rocker arm roller surface is badly scored, also examine the corresponding lobe on the camshaft for wear, as both will likely be worn. Renew worn components as necessary. The rocker arm assembly can be dismantled as described in paragraphs 4 and 5.

**17** Inspect the ends of the (valve clearance) adjusting screws for signs of wear or damage, and renew as required.

**18** If the rocker arm assembly has been dismantled, examine the rocker arm and shaft bearing surfaces for wear ridges and scoring. If there are obvious signs of wear, the relevant rocker arm(s) and/or the shaft must be renewed.

#### Camshaft(s)

**19** Examine the camshaft bearing surfaces and cam lobes for signs of wear ridges and scoring. Renew the camshaft if any of these conditions are apparent. Examine the condition of the bearing surfaces, both on the camshaft journals and in the cylinder head/bearing housing. If the head bearing surfaces are worn excessively, the cylinder head will need to be renewed. If the necessary measuring equipment is available, camshaft bearing journal wear can be checked by direct measurement, noting that No 1 journal is at the transmission end of the head.

**20** On SOHC engines, examine the thrust fork for signs of wear or scoring, and renew as necessary.

**21** On DOHC engines, examine the hydraulic follower surfaces which contact the camshaft lobes for wear ridges and scoring. Renew any follower where these conditions are apparent. If a follower bearing surface is badly scored,

**10.21 Check the roller surface (arrowed) on the rocker arm**

10.31a  Refit the rocker arm and hydraulic lifter . . .

10.31b  . . . making sure the hydraulic lifter is clipped into the rocker arm securely

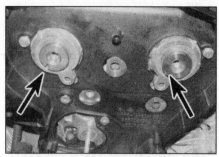

10.32  Position the inlet camshaft locking notch at the 7 o'clock position and the exhaust camshaft at 8 o'clock (arrowed)

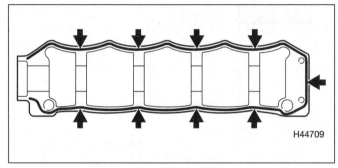

H44709

10.33  Apply a bead of silicone sealant to the cylinder head mating surface (arrowed) – DOHC engines

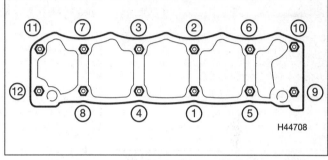

H44708

10.34  Camshaft bearing housing bolts tightening sequence – DOHC engines

also examine the corresponding lobe on the camshaft for wear, as it is likely that both will be worn **(see illustration)**. Renew any components as necessary.

### Refitting

#### Rocker arms – SOHC engines

**22** If the rocker arm assembly was dismantled, refit the rocker shaft to the left-hand pedestal, aligning its locating hole with the pedestal threaded hole. Refit the grub screw, and tighten it securely. With the grub screw in position, refit the cylinder head cover mounting stud to the pedestal, and tighten it securely. Apply a smear of clean engine oil to the shaft, then slide on all removed components, ensuring each is correctly fitted in its original position. **Note:** *Avoid touching the rocker arm roller bearing surfaces with your fingers*. Once all components are in position on the shaft, compress the right-hand pedestal and refit the circlip. Ensure that the circlip is correctly located in its groove on the shaft.

**23** Refit the cylinder head and rocker arm assembly as described in Section 11.

#### Camshaft – SOHC engines

**24** Ensure that the cylinder head and camshaft bearing surfaces are clean, then liberally oil the camshaft bearings and lobes. Slide the camshaft back into position in the cylinder head.

**25** Locate the thrust fork with the left-hand end of the camshaft. Refit the fork retaining bolt, tightening it to the specified torque setting.

**26** Ensure that the coolant housing and cylinder head mating surfaces are clean and dry, then apply a smear of sealant to the housing mating surface. Refit the housing to the left-hand end of the head, and securely tighten its retaining bolts.

**27** Lubricate the lips of the new seal with clean engine oil, then drive it into position until it seats on its locating shoulder. Use a suitable tubular drift, such as a socket, which bears only on the hard outer edge of the seal. Take care not to damage the seal lips during fitting. Note that the seal lips should face inwards.

**28** Refit the camshaft sprocket as described in Section 7.

**29** Refit the cylinder head as described in Section 11.

#### Camshafts/followers – DOHC engines

**30** Before commencing refitting, remove all traces of oil from the bearing housing retaining bolts holes in the cylinder head, using a clean rag. Also ensure that both the cylinder head and bearing housing mating faces are clean and free from oil.

**31** Liberally oil the cylinder head hydraulic follower bores and the followers. Carefully refit the followers to the cylinder head, ensuring that each follower is refitted to its original bore. Some care will be required to enter the followers squarely into their bores. Check that each follower rotates freely. On the 1.4 litre engine, make sure the rocker arms are clipped to the hydraulic follower securely **(see illustrations)**.

**32** Liberally oil the camshaft bearings in the cylinder head and the camshaft lobes, then

refit the camshafts to the cylinder head in the previously noted positions. The locating notch in the right-hand end of the camshafts should be positioned at the 7 o'clock position on the inlet camshaft, and the 8 o'clock position on the exhaust camshaft **(see illustration)**.

**33** Apply a bead of silicone-based jointing compound around the perimeter of the mating faces and around the retaining bolt hole locations **(see illustration)**.

**34** Refit the bearing housing, and tighten the bolts progressively, in sequence, to the specified torque **(see illustration)**.

**35** Fit new oil seals with reference to Section 8.

**36** Ensure that the lower edge of the inner timing belt cover engages correctly with the upper edge of the crankshaft oil seal housing **(see illustration)**.

**37** Refit the camshaft sprockets as described in Section 7.

10.36  Ensure the lower edge of the inner timing belt cover engages correctly (arrowed)

**11.11  Slacken and remove the cylinder head bolts – SOHC engines**

**11.13  Lift off the rocker arm assembly – SOHC engines**

## 11  Cylinder head – removal and refitting

**Note:** *Ensure the engine is cold before removing the cylinder head.*

### Removal

**1** Disconnect the battery (see Chapter 5A).

**2** Drain the cooling system as described in Chapter 1A.

**3** Remove the ignition HT coil assembly (see Chapter 5B) then remove the spark plugs (see Chapter 1A).

**4** Remove the cylinder head cover(s) as described in Section 4.

**5** Align the engine assembly/valve timing holes as described in Section 3, and lock both the camshaft sprocket(s) and flywheel/driveplate in position.

**Caution: Do not attempt to rotate the engine whilst the tools are in position.**

**6** Note that the following text assumes that the cylinder head will be removed with both inlet and exhaust manifolds attached; this is easier, but makes it a bulky and heavy assembly to handle. If it is wished to remove the manifolds first, proceed as described in Chapter 4A.

**7** Carry out the following operations as described in Chapter 4A:

a) *Disconnect the exhaust system front pipe from the manifold. Disconnect or release the oxygen sensor wiring.*

b) *Remove the air cleaner housing and inlet duct assembly.*

c) *Disconnect the fuel feed and return hoses from the fuel rail (plug all openings, to prevent loss of fuel and entry of dirt into the fuel system).*

d) *Note their fitted positions, then disconnect the relevant electrical connectors and vacuum/breather hoses from the inlet manifold.*

e) *Where necessary unbolt the support bracket from the inlet manifold.*

f) *Disconnect the accelerator cable (where fitted).*

**8** Remove the timing belt and timing belt inner cover as described in Sections 5 and 6.

**9** Undo the mounting bolt and remove the upper section of the oil dipstick guide tube. Note their fitted positions, then slacken the retaining clips, and disconnect the coolant hoses from the cylinder head. Likewise, note the routing, and then disconnect all electrical connectors from the cylinder head.

**10** On DOHC engines, remove the camshafts as described in Section 10.

**11** Working in the *reverse* of the tightening sequence **(see illustration 11.30a or 11.30b)**, progressively slacken the cylinder head bolts by half a turn at a time, until all bolts can be unscrewed by hand **(see illustration)**.

**12** On DOHC engines, lift the cylinder head away; seek assistance if possible, as it is a heavy assembly, especially if it is being removed complete with the manifolds.

**13** On SOHC engines, with all the cylinder head bolts removed, lift the rocker arm assembly off the cylinder head **(see illustration)**. **Note:** *Avoid touching the rocker arm roller bearing surfaces with your fingers.*

Note the locating pins, which are fitted to the base of each rocker arm pedestal. If any pin is a loose fit in the head or pedestal, remove it for safekeeping.

**14** On all 1.1 and 1.4 litre engines, the joint between the cylinder head and gasket, and the cylinder block/crankcase, must now be broken without disturbing the wet liners. To break the joint, obtain two stout screwdrivers, which fit into the cylinder head bolt holes. Gently 'rock' the cylinder head free towards the front of the car **(see illustration)**. Do not try to swivel the head on the cylinder block/crankcase; it is located by dowels, as well as by the tops of the liners. **Note:** *If care is not taken and the liners are moved, there is also a possibility of the bottom seals being disturbed, causing leakage after refitting the head.* When the joint is broken, lift the cylinder head away; seek assistance if possible, as it is a heavy assembly, especially if it is being removed complete with the manifolds.

**15** On all models, remove the gasket from the top of the block, noting the two locating dowels. If the locating dowels are a loose fit, remove them and store them with the head for safekeeping. Do not discard the gasket – on some models it will be needed for identification purposes (see paragraphs 20 and 21). Operations that require the rotation of the crankshaft (eg, cleaning the piston crowns) should only be carried out on 1.1 and 1.4 litre engines once the cylinder liners are firmly clamped in position **(see illustration)**. In the absence of the special Citroën liner clamps, the liners can be clamped in position using large flat washers positioned underneath suitable-length bolts. Alternatively, the original head bolts could be temporarily refitted, with suitable spacers fitted to their shanks.

**Caution: On 1.1 and 1.4 litre engines, do not attempt to rotate the crankshaft with the cylinder head removed, otherwise the wet liners may be displaced.**

**16** If the cylinder head is to be dismantled for overhaul, refer to Part D of this Chapter.

### Preparation for refitting

**17** The mating faces of the cylinder head and cylinder block/crankcase must be perfectly clean before refitting the head. Use a hard plastic or wood scraper to remove all traces of gasket and carbon; also clean the piston crowns. **Note:** *On all 1.1 and 1.4 litre engines, clamp the liners in position before turning the crankshaft (see paragraph 15).* Take particular care during the cleaning operations, as aluminium alloy is easily damaged. Also, make sure that the carbon is not allowed to enter the oil and water passages – this is particularly important for the lubrication system, as carbon could block the oil supply to the engine's components. Using adhesive tape and paper, seal the water, oil and bolt holes in the cylinder block/crankcase. To prevent carbon entering the gap between the pistons and bores, smear a little grease in the gap. After cleaning each piston, use a small brush to remove all traces

**11.14  Use two stout screwdrivers to rock the cylinder head free from the block – SOHC engines**

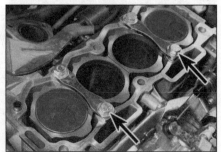

**11.15  Clamp the cylinder liners in position before rotating the crankshaft (clamps arrowed) – all 1.1 and 1.4 litre engines**

of grease and carbon from the gap, then wipe away the remainder with a clean rag. Clean all the pistons in the same way.

**18** Check the mating surfaces of the cylinder block/crankcase and the cylinder head for nicks, deep scratches and other damage. If slight, they may be removed carefully with a file, but if excessive, machining may be the only alternative to renewal.

**19** If warpage of the cylinder head gasket surface is suspected, use a straight-edge to check it for distortion. Refer to Part D of this Chapter if necessary.

**20** When purchasing a new cylinder head gasket, it is essential that a gasket of the correct thickness is obtained. On some models only one thickness of gasket is available, so this is not a problem. On other models, there are two different thicknesses available – the standard gasket, and a slightly thicker 'repair' gasket (+ 0.2 mm). The gaskets can be identified as described in the following paragraph, using the cut-outs on the left-hand end of the gasket.

**21** With the gasket fitted the correct way up on the cylinder block, there will be a single or double cut-out at the rear of the left-hand side of the gasket identifying the engine type (eg, TU3JP engine). In the centre of the gasket there will likely be another series of between 0 and 4 cut-outs, identifying the manufacturer of the gasket and whether or not it contains asbestos (these cut-outs are of little importance). The important cut-out location is at the front of the gasket; on the standard gasket there will be no cut-out in this position, whereas on the thicker 'repair' gasket there will be a single cut-out **(see illustration)**. Identify the gasket type, and ensure that the new gasket obtained is of the correct thickness. If there is any doubt as to which gasket is fitted, take the old gasket along to your Citroën dealer, and have him confirm the gasket type.

**22** Check the condition of the cylinder head bolts, and particularly their threads, whenever they are removed. Wash the bolts in suitable solvent, and wipe them dry. Check each for any sign of visible wear or damage, renewing any bolt if necessary. Measure the length of each bolt, from the underside of its head to the bolt end, to check for stretching **(see illustration)**.

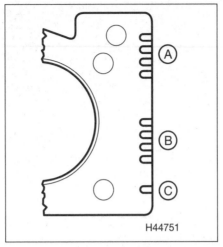

**11.21 Cylinder head gasket identification markings**

*A Engine type identification cut-out locations*
*B Gasket manufacturer identification cut-out locations*
*C Gasket thickness identification cut-out locations*

The bolts for the SOHC engines are 175.5 mm in length when new; if any bolt has stretched to more than 176.5 mm, renew all the cylinder head bolts as a set. On the 1.4 litre DOHC engine, the maximum length for the bolts is 118.6 mm and they can only be re-used 2 times. On 1.6 litre DOHC engines, the maximum length for the bolts is 122.6 mm. Although Citroën do not actually specify that the bolts must be renewed, it is strongly recommended that the bolts should be renewed as a complete set, regardless of their apparent condition, whenever they are disturbed.

**23** On all 1.1 and 1.4 litre engines, prior to refitting the cylinder head, check the cylinder liner protrusion as described in Chapter 2D.

## Refitting

**24** Wipe clean the mating surfaces of the cylinder head and cylinder block/crankcase. Check that the two locating dowels are in position at each end of the cylinder block/crankcase surface and, if necessary, remove the cylinder liner clamps **(see illustration)**.

**25** Position a new gasket on the cylinder block/crankcase surface, ensuring that its

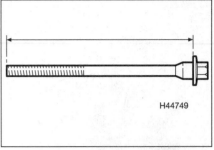

**11.22 Measure the bolt length from the underside of the bolt head to the end of the bolt**

identification cut-outs are at the left-hand end of the gasket, and the side marked TOP is uppermost.

**26** Check that the flywheel/driveplate and camshaft sprocket(s) are still correctly locked in position with their respective tools then, with the aid of an assistant, carefully refit the cylinder head assembly to the block, aligning it with the locating dowels. On DOHC engines, ensure that the inner timing cover lower edge engages correctly with the upper edge of the crankshaft oil seal housing.

**27** On SOHC engines, ensure that the locating pins are in position in the base of each rocker pedestal, and then refit the rocker arm assembly to the cylinder head.

**28** On all engines, lubricate the threads and underside of the heads of the cylinder head bolts lightly with clean engine oil.

**29** Carefully enter each bolt into its relevant hole (*do not drop them in*) and screw in, by hand only, until finger-tight.

**30** Working progressively and in the sequence shown, tighten the cylinder head bolts to their Stage 1 torque setting, using a torque wrench and suitable socket **(see illustrations)**.

**31** Once all the bolts have been tightened to their Stage 1 setting, working again in the given sequence, angle-tighten the bolts through the specified Stage 2 angle, using a socket and extension bar. It is recommended that an angle-measuring gauge be used during this stage of the tightening, to ensure accuracy. If a gauge is not available, use white paint to make alignment marks between the bolt head and cylinder head prior to tightening; the marks can then be used to check that the

**11.24 Ensure the locating dowels (arrowed) are in position then fit the new head gasket**

**11.30a Cylinder head bolt tightening sequence – SOHC engines**

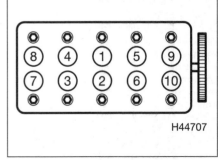

**11.30b Cylinder head bolt tightening sequence – DOHC engines**

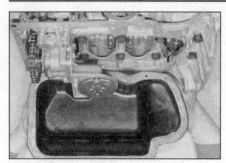

**12.4a Undo the nuts and bolts, then remove the sump from the engine – 1.1 and 1.4 litre engines**

bolt has been rotated through the correct angle during tightening.

**32** Refit the timing belt inner cover and timing belt as described in Sections 5 and 6. Reconnect the all wiring plugs and coolant hoses to the cylinder head and manifold.

**33** On DOHC engines, refit the camshafts with reference to Section 10.

**34** Working as described in the Chapter 4A, carry out the following tasks:

a) Refit all disturbed wiring, fuel hoses and control cable(s) to the inlet manifold and fuel system components.

b) Reconnect and adjust the accelerator cable (where fitted).

c) Reconnect the exhaust system front pipe to the manifold and reconnect the oxygen sensor wiring connector.

d) Refit the air cleaner assembly and intake ducts.

**35** On SOHC engines, check and, if necessary, adjust the valve clearances as described in Section 9.

**36** Refit the cylinder head cover(s) as described in Section 4.

**37** Refit the spark plugs and install the ignition HT coil (see Chapters 1A and 5B).

**38** On completion, reconnect the battery (Chapter 5A), and refill the cooling system as described in Chapter 1A.

## 12 Sump –
removal and refitting

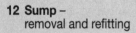

### *Removal*

**1** Firmly apply the handbrake, then jack up the front of the vehicle and support it on axle stands (see *Jacking and vehicle support*). Where fitted, undo the screws and remove the engine undershield.

**2** Drain the engine oil, then clean and refit the engine oil drain plug, tightening it to the specified torque. If the engine is nearing its service interval when the oil and filter are due for renewal, it is recommended that the filter is also removed, and a new one fitted. After reassembly, the engine can then be refilled with fresh oil. Refer to Chapter 1A for further information.

**3** Remove the exhaust system front pipe as described in Chapter 4A.

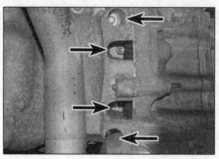

**12.4b Access to the sump end bolts/nuts is through holes in the casing (arrowed) – 1.6 litre engines**

**4** Progressively slacken and remove all the sump nuts and bolts/nuts and position the wiring harness guide clear of the sump **(see illustrations)**.

**5** Break the joint by striking the sump with the palm of your hand, then lower and withdraw the sump from under the car. On 1.1 and 1.4 litre engines, it may be necessary to use a putty knife or similar carefully inserted between the sump and block. Ease the knife along the joint until the sump is released. On 1.6 litre engines, recover the gasket

**6** While the sump is removed, take the opportunity to check the oil pump pick-up/ strainer for signs of clogging or splitting. If necessary, remove the pump as described in Section 13, and clean or renew the strainer.

### *Refitting*

**7** Clean all traces of sealant from the mating surfaces of the cylinder block/crankcase and sump, then use a clean rag to wipe out the sump and the engine's interior.

**8** Ensure that the sump and cylinder block/ crankcase mating surfaces are clean and dry then, on 1.1 and 1.4 litre engines, apply a coating of suitable sealant to the sump mating surface. On 1.6 litre engines, if the gasket is undamaged, refit it to the sump, otherwise fit a new gasket.

**9** Offer up the sump and locate it on its studs. Locate the wiring harness guide back in position then refit the sump retaining nuts and bolts. Tighten the nuts and bolts evenly and progressively to the specified torque.

**10** Refit the exhaust front pipe as described in Chapter 4A, and refit the engine undershield (where applicable).

**11** Replenish the engine oil (see Chapter 1A).

**13.2 Unscrew the three bolts securing the oil pump in position**

## 13 Oil pump –
removal, inspection and refitting

### *Removal*

**1** Remove the sump (see Section 12).

**2** Slacken and remove the three bolts securing the oil pump in position **(see illustration)**. Disengage the pump sprocket from the chain, and remove the oil pump. If the pump locating dowel is a loose fit, remove and store it with the bolts for safe-keeping.

### *Inspection*

**3** Examine the oil pump sprocket for signs of damage and wear, such as chipped or missing teeth. If the sprocket is worn, the pump assembly must be renewed, as the sprocket is not available separately. It is also recommended that the chain and drive sprocket, fitted to the crankshaft, are renewed at the same time. On 1.1 and 1.4 litre engines, renewal of the chain and drive sprocket is an involved operation requiring the removal of the main bearing ladder, and therefore cannot be carried out with the engine still fitted to the vehicle. On 1.6 litre engines, the oil pump drive sprocket and chain can be removed with the engine *in situ*, once the crankshaft sprocket has been removed and the crankshaft oil seal housing has been unbolted.

**4** Slacken and remove the bolts securing the strainer cover to the pump body, then lift off the strainer cover. Remove the relief valve piston and spring (and guide pin – 1.6 litre engines only), noting which way round they are fitted.

**5** Examine the pump rotors and body for signs of wear ridges and scoring. If worn, the complete pump assembly must be renewed.

**6** Examine the relief valve piston for signs of wear or damage, and renew if necessary. The condition of the relief valve spring can only be measured by comparing it with a new one; if there is any doubt about its condition, it should also be renewed. Both the piston and spring are available individually.

**7** Thoroughly clean the oil pump strainer with a suitable solvent, and check it for signs of clogging or splitting. If the strainer is damaged, the strainer and cover assembly must be renewed.

**8** Locate the relief valve spring, piston and (where fitted) the guide pin in the strainer cover, then refit the cover to the pump body. Align the relief valve piston with its bore in the pump. Refit the cover retaining bolts, tightening them securely.

### *Refitting*

**9** Ensure that the locating dowel is in position, then engage the pump sprocket with its drive chain. Locate the pump on its dowel, and refit the pump retaining bolts, tightening them to the specified torque setting.

**10** Refit the sump as described in Section 12.

## 14 Crankshaft oil seals – renewal

### Right-hand oil seal

1 Remove the crankshaft sprocket and flanged spacer (where fitted) as described in Section 7.

2 Make a note of the correct fitted depth of the seal in its housing then carefully punch or drill two small holes opposite each other in the seal. Screw a self-tapping screw into each, and pull on the screws with pliers to extract the seal. Alternatively, the seal can be levered out of position using a suitable flat-bladed screwdriver, taking great care not to damage the crankshaft/oil pump drive gear shoulder or seal housing (see illustration).

3 Clean the seal housing, and polish off any burrs or raised edges, which may have caused the seal to fail in the first place.

4 Lubricate the lips of the new seal with clean engine oil, and carefully locate the seal on the end of crankshaft. Note that its sealing lip must face inwards. Take care not to damage the seal lips during fitting.

5 Using a suitable tubular drift (such as a socket) which bears only on the hard outer edge of the seal, tap the seal into position, to the same depth in the housing as the original was prior to removal. The inner face of the seal must be flush with the inner wall of the crankcase.

6 Wash off any traces of oil, then refit the crankshaft sprocket as described in Section 7.

### Left-hand oil seal

7 Remove the flywheel/driveplate (see Section 15).

8 Make a note of the correct fitted depth of the seal in its housing. Punch or drill two small holes opposite each other in the seal. Screw a self-tapping screw into each, and pull on the screws with pliers to extract the seal.

9 Clean the seal housing, and polish off any burrs or raised edges, which may have caused the seal to fail in the first place.

10 Lubricate the lips of the new seal with clean engine oil, and carefully locate the seal on the end of the crankshaft.

11 Using a suitable tubular drift, which bears only on the hard outer edge of the seal, drive the seal into position, to the same depth in the housing as the original was prior to removal.

12 Wash off any traces of oil, then refit the flywheel/driveplate as described in Section 15.

## 15 Flywheel/driveplate – removal, inspection and refitting

### Flywheel

#### Removal

1 Remove the transmission as described in Chapter 7A, then remove the clutch assembly as described in Chapter 6.

2 Prevent the flywheel from turning by locking the ring gear teeth (see illustration). Alternatively, bolt a strap between the flywheel and the cylinder block/crankcase.
Caution: *Do not attempt to lock the flywheel in position using the locking pin described in Section 3.*

3 Slacken and remove the flywheel retaining bolts.

4 Remove the flywheel. Do not drop it, as it is very heavy. If the locating dowel is a loose fit in the crankshaft end, remove and store it with the flywheel for safe-keeping.

#### Inspection

5 If the flywheel's clutch mating surface is deeply scored, cracked or otherwise damaged, the flywheel must be renewed. However, it may be possible to have it surface-ground; seek the advice of a Citroën dealer or engine reconditioning specialist.

6 If the ring gear is badly worn or has missing teeth, it must be renewed. This job is best left to a Citroën dealer or engine reconditioning specialist. The temperature to which the new ring gear must be heated for installation is critical and, if not done accurately, the hardness of the teeth will be destroyed.

#### Refitting

7 Clean the mating surfaces of the flywheel and crankshaft.

8 If the new flywheel retaining bolts are not supplied with their threads already precoated, apply a suitable thread-locking compound to the threads of each bolt.

9 Ensure that the locating dowel is in position. Offer up the flywheel, locating it on the dowel, and fit the retaining bolts.

10 Lock the flywheel using the method employed on dismantling, and tighten the retaining bolts evenly and progressively to the specified torque.

11 Refit the clutch as described in Chapter 6. Remove the locking tool, and refit the transmission as described in Chapter 7A.

### Driveplate

#### Removal

12 Remove the transmission as described in Chapter 7B.

13 Prevent the driveplate from turning by locking the ring gear teeth with a similar arrangement to that for the flywheel (see illustration 15.2). Alternatively, bolt a strap between the driveplate and the cylinder block/crankcase.
Caution: *Do not attempt to lock the driveplate in position using the locking pin described in Section 3.*

14 Slacken and remove the driveplate retaining bolts and remove the outer spacer plate and torque converter mounting plate.

15 Remove the driveplate and inner spacer plate from the end of the crankshaft. If the locating dowel is a loose fit in the crankshaft end, remove and store it with the driveplate for safe-keeping. Note: *The inner and outer spacer plates are different and are not interchangeable.*

**14.2 Use a screwdriver to lever out the crankshaft right-hand oil seal**

#### Inspection

16 Inspect the driveplate and torque converter mounting plate for signs of wear or damage. If damage is found, the worn component must be renewed (it is not possible to renew the driveplate ring gear separately).

#### Refitting

17 Ensure all mating surfaces are clean and dry.

18 Remove any traces of locking compound from the threads of the driveplate bolts and apply a small amount of fresh locking compound to the bolt threads.

19 Ensure that the locating dowel is in position then refit the inner spacer plate, driveplate, torque converter mounting plate and outer spacer plate. Ensure all components are correctly located on the dowel then fit the retaining bolts.

20 Lock the driveplate using the method employed on dismantling, and tighten the retaining bolts evenly and progressively to the specified torque.

21 Refit the transmission as described in Chapter 7B.

## 16 Engine/transmission mountings – inspection and renewal

### Inspection

1 If improved access is required, raise the front of the car and support it on axle stands (see *Jacking and vehicle support*).

**15.2 Use a tool to lock the flywheel ring gear and prevent rotation**

**16.6a  Right-hand engine mounting retaining bolts (arrowed) – 1.1 and 1.4 litre engines**

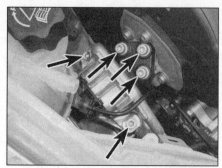

**16.6b  Right-hand engine mounting retaining bolts (arrowed) – 1.6 litre engines**

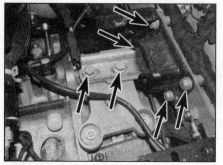

**16.14  Left-hand engine mounting retaining bolts (arrowed)**

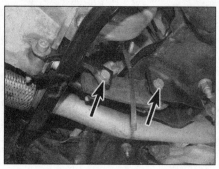

**16.21  Rear engine mounting connecting link through-bolts (arrowed)**

**2** Check the mounting rubber to see if it is cracked, hardened or separated from the metal at any point; renew the mounting if any such damage or deterioration is evident.

**3** Check that all the mounting's fasteners are securely tightened; use a torque wrench to check if possible.

**4** Using a large screwdriver or a crowbar, check for wear in the mounting by carefully levering against it to check for free play. Where this is not possible, enlist the aid of an assistant to move the engine/transmission back-and-forth, or from side-to-side, while you watch the mounting. While some free play is to be expected even from new components, excessive wear should be obvious. If excessive free play is found, check first that the fasteners are secure, then renew any worn components as described below.

### Renewal

**Right-hand mounting**

**5** Place a jack beneath the engine, with a block of wood on the jack head. Raise the jack until it is supporting the weight of the engine.

**6** Slacken and remove the bolts securing the mounting to the body, and the mounting bracket to the bracket bolted to the cylinder head **(see illustrations)**. Remove the mounting assembly from the car and recover the reinforcing plate.

**7** If required, undo the three bolts and remove the bracket from the cylinder head. Release the wiring loom and fuel lines from the retaining clips as it is removed.

**8** Check for signs of wear or damage on all components, and renew as necessary.

**9** On reassembly, refit the bracket to the cylinder head, tightening the bolts to the specified torque.

**10** Install the mounting and mounting bracket and tighten its retaining bolts to the specified torque setting.

**11** Remove the jack from under the engine.

### Left-hand mounting

**12** Remove the battery, and battery tray/box as described in Chapter 5A.

**13** Place a jack beneath the transmission, with a block of wood on the jack head. Raise the jack until it is supporting the weight of the transmission.

**14** Slacken and remove the two bolts securing the mounting arm to the bracket on the transmission **(see illustration)**. Undo the four bolts securing the mounting to the body and remove the complete mounting assembly from the engine compartment.

**15** If necessary, undo the retaining bolts and remove the mounting bracket from the transmission.

**16** Check carefully for signs of wear or damage on all components, and renew them where necessary.

**17** Refit the mounting assembly to the vehicle body and tighten its bolts to the specified torque.

**18** Locate the mounting arm over the transmission bracket and tighten its retaining bolts to the specified torque.

**19** Remove the jack from underneath the transmission, then refit the battery tray/box and battery as described in Chapter 5A.

### Rear mounting

**20** If not already done, firmly apply the handbrake, then jack up the front of the vehicle and support it securely on axle stands (see *Jacking and vehicle support*).

**21** Unscrew and remove the two through-bolts securing the rear mounting connecting link to the subframe and transmission bracket **(see illustration)**.

**22** Manoeuvre the connecting link from its location and remove it from under the car.

**23** Check carefully for signs of wear or damage on all components, and renew them where necessary.

**24** Refit the rear mounting connecting link, and tighten both its bolts to their specified torque settings.

**25** Lower the vehicle to the ground.

# Chapter 2 Part B:
## 1.4 litre diesel engine (DV4 series) in-car repair procedures

## Contents

## Degrees of difficulty

| | | | | |
|---|---|---|---|---|
| **Easy,** suitable for novice with little experience 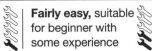 | **Fairly easy,** suitable for beginner with some experience | **Fairly difficult,** suitable for competent DIY mechanic | **Difficult,** suitable for experienced DIY mechanic | **Very difficult,** suitable for expert DIY or professional  |

## Specifications

### Engine (general)

| | Designation | Code* |
|---|---|---|
| 8-valve engines | DV4TD | 8HX and 8HZ |
| 16-valve engines | DV4TED4 | 8HY |
| Capacity | 1398 cc (1.4 litres) | |
| Bore | 73.70 mm | |
| Stroke | 82.00 mm | |
| Direction of crankshaft rotation | Clockwise (viewed from the right-hand side of vehicle) | |
| No 1 cylinder location | At transmission end of the block | |
| Maximum power output: | | |
|   8-valve engines | 50 kW @ 4000 rpm | |
|   16-valve engines | 66 kW @ 4000 rpm | |
| Maximum torque output: | | |
|   8-valve engines | 150 Nm @ 2000 rpm | |
|   16-valve engines | 200 Nm @ 2000 rpm | |
| Compression ratio: | | |
|   8-valve engines | 17.9 : 1 | |
|   16-valve engines | 18.2 : 1 | |

*\* The engine code is stamped on a plate attached to the front of the cylinder block, next to the oil filter.*

### Compression pressures (engine hot, at cranking speed)

| | |
|---|---|
| Normal | 15 to 25 bars (218 to 363 psi) |
| Maximum difference between any two cylinders | 5 bars (73 psi) |

### Camshaft(s)

| | |
|---|---|
| Drive: | |
|   8-valve engines | Toothed belt |
|   16-valve engines | Toothed belt/chain |

### Lubrication system

| | |
|---|---|
| Oil pump type | Gear type, driven directly by the right-hand end of the crankshaft |
| Minimum oil pressure | 3.5 bars @ 4000 rpm, 2.3 bars @ 2000 rpm (110°C) |
| Oil pressure warning switch operating pressure | 0.8 bars |

## Torque wrench settings

| | Nm | lbf ft |
|---|---|---|
| **8-valve engines** | | |
| Big-end bolts*: | | |
|     Stage 1 | 10 | 7 |
|     Stage 2 | Slacken 180° | |
|     Stage 3 | 10 | 7 |
|     Stage 4 | Angle-tighten a further 100° | |
| Camshaft bearing housing | 10 | 7 |
| Camshaft position sensor bolt | 5 | 4 |
| Camshaft sprocket: | | |
|     Stage 1 | 20 | 15 |
|     Stage 2 | Angle-tighten a further 50° | |
| Coolant outlet housing bolts | 10 | 7 |
| Crankshaft position/speed sensor bolt | 5 | 4 |
| Crankshaft pulley/sprocket bolt: | | |
|     Stage 1 | 35 | 26 |
|     Stage 2 | Angle-tighten a further 190° | |
| Cylinder head bolts: | | |
|     Stage 1 | 20 | 15 |
|     Stage 2 | 40 | 30 |
|     Stage 3 | Angle-tighten a further 260° | |
| Cylinder head cover bolts | 10 | 7 |
| Engine-to-transmission fixing bolts | 45 | 33 |
| Engine/transmission left-hand mounting: | | |
|     Mounting arm-to-transmission bracket bolts | 60 | 44 |
|     Mounting assembly-to-body bolts | 55 | 41 |
|     Transmission bracket-to-transmission bolts | 55 | 41 |
| Engine/transmission rear mounting: | | |
|     Connecting link-to-transmission bracket bolt | 60 | 44 |
|     Connecting link-to-subframe bolt | 60 | 44 |
| Engine/transmission right-hand mounting: | | |
|     Mounting-to body bolts | 45 | 33 |
|     Mounting bracket-to-cylinder head bracket bolts | 30 | 22 |
|     Cylinder head bracket-to-cylinder head bolts | 55 | 41 |
| Flywheel/driveplate bolts*: | | |
|     Stage 1 | 15 | 11 |
|     Stage 2 | Angle-tighten a further 75° | |
| Fuel pump sprocket nut | 50 | 37 |
| Main bearing ladder seam bolts: | | |
|     Stage 1 | 5 | 4 |
|     Stage 2 | 10 | 7 |
| Main bearing ladder to cylinder block*: | | |
|     Stage 1 | 10 | 7 |
|     Stage 2 | Slacken 180° | |
|     Stage 3 | 30 | 22 |
|     Stage 4 | Angle-tighten a further 140° | |
| Piston oil jet spray tube bolt | 20 | 15 |
| Oil pump to cylinder block | 10 | 7 |
| Roadwheel bolts | 90 | 66 |
| Sump bolts/nuts | 10 | 7 |
| Sump drain plug | 16 | 12 |
| Timing belt idler pulley | 45 | 33 |
| Timing belt tensioner pulley | 30 | 22 |
| **16-valve engines** | | |
| Big-end bolts*: | | |
|     Stage 1 | 5 | 4 |
|     Stage 2 | 10 | 7 |
|     Stage 3 | Angle-tighten a further 130° | |
| Camshaft bearing cap bolts | 10 | 7 |
| Camshaft bearing housing to cylinder head | 10 | 7 |
| Camshaft position sensor bolt | 5 | 4 |
| Camshaft sprocket | | |
|     Stage 1 | 20 | 15 |
|     Stage 2 | Angle-tighten a further 50° | |
| Coolant outlet housing bolts | 10 | 7 |
| Crankshaft position/speed sensor bolt | 5 | 4 |

## Torque wrench settings (continued)

| | Nm | lbf ft |
|---|---|---|
| **16-valve engines (continued)** | | |
| Crankshaft pulley/sprocket bolt: | | |
| Stage 1 ............................................ | 35 | 26 |
| Stage 2 ............................................ | Angle-tighten a further 190° | |
| Cylinder head bolts: | | |
| Stage 1 ............................................ | 20 | 15 |
| Stage 2 ............................................ | 40 | 30 |
| Stage 3 ............................................ | Angle-tighten a further 260° | |
| Cylinder head cover bolts ............................ | 10 | 7 |
| Engine-to-transmission fixing bolts .................... | 45 | 33 |
| Engine/transmission left-hand mounting: | | |
| Mounting arm-to-transmission bracket bolts............ | 60 | 44 |
| Mounting assembly-to-body bolts..................... | 55 | 41 |
| Transmission bracket-to-transmission bolts ............ | 55 | 41 |
| Engine/transmission rear mounting: | | |
| Connecting link-to-transmission bracket bolt ......... | 60 | 44 |
| Connecting link-to-subframe bolt .................... | 60 | 44 |
| Engine/transmission right-hand mounting: | | |
| Mounting-to body bolts ............................. | 60 | 44 |
| Mounting bracket-to-cylinder head bracket bolts ....... | 60 | 60 |
| Cylinder head bracket-to-cylinder head bolts .......... | 57 | 42 |
| Flywheel bolt*: | | |
| Dual mass flywheel: | | |
| Stage 1 ............................................ | 25 | 18 |
| Stage 2 ............................................ | Fully slacken | |
| Stage 3 ............................................ | 8 | 6 |
| Stage 4 ............................................ | 30 | 22 |
| Stage 5 ............................................ | Angle-tighten a further 90° | |
| Normal flywheel: | | |
| Stage 1 ............................................ | 25 | 18 |
| Stage 2 ............................................ | Fully slacken | |
| Stage 3 ............................................ | 8 | 6 |
| Stage 4 ............................................ | 17 | 13 |
| Stage 5 ............................................ | Angle-tighten a further 75° | |
| Fuel pump sprocket nut.............................. | 50 | 37 |
| Main bearing ladder seam bolts: | | |
| Stage 1 ............................................ | 5 | 4 |
| Stage 2 ............................................ | 10 | 7 |
| Main bearing ladder to cylinder block*: | | |
| Stage 1 ............................................ | 10 | 7 |
| Stage 2 ............................................ | Slacken 180° | |
| Stage 3 ............................................ | 30 | 22 |
| Stage 4 ............................................ | Angle-tighten a further 140° | |
| Piston oil jet spray tube bolt.......................... | 20 | 15 |
| Oil pump to cylinder block ............................ | 10 | 7 |
| Roadwheel bolts..................................... | 90 | 66 |
| Sump bolts/nuts..................................... | 10 | 7 |
| Sump drain plug..................................... | 16 | 12 |
| Timing belt idler pulley ............................... | 37 | 27 |
| Timing belt tensioner pulley .......................... | 23 | 17 |

*New nuts/bolts must be used.*

## 1  General information

### How to use this Chapter

This Part of Chapter 2 describes the repair procedures that can reasonably be carried out on the engine while it remains in the car. If the engine has been removed from the car and is being dismantled as described in Part D, any preliminary dismantling procedures can be ignored.

Note that, while it may be possible physically to overhaul items such as the piston/connecting rod assemblies while the engine is in the car, such tasks are not usually carried out as separate operations. Usually, several additional procedures are required (not to mention the cleaning of components and oilways); for this reason, all such tasks are classed as major overhaul procedures, and are described in Part D of this Chapter.

Part D describes the removal of the engine/transmission from the car, and the full overhaul procedures that can then be carried out.

### Engine description

The 1.4 litre DV series engine is the result of development collaboration between Peugeot/Citroën and Ford. The engine is of the turbo-charged, four-cylinder, single overhead cam-shaft (SOHC) 8-valve type, or double overhead camshaft (DOHC) 16-valve type, mounted transversely at the front of the car with the transmission attached to its left-hand end.

On 8-valve engines, a toothed timing belt drives the camshaft, high-pressure fuel pump and coolant pump. The camshaft operates the inlet and exhaust valves via rocker arms which are supported at their pivot ends by hydraulic self-adjusting tappets. The camshaft is supported by bearings machined directly in the upper and lower halves of the camshaft bearing housing.

On 16-valve engines, a toothed timing belt drives the inlet camshaft, high-pressure fuel pump and coolant pump. The exhaust camshaft is driven by the inlet camshaft via a short, hydraulically tensioned chain. One camshaft operates the inlet valves, with the other camshaft operating the exhaust valves. The valves are actuated via rocker arms which are supported at their pivot ends by hydraulic self-adjusting tappets. The camshafts are supported by bearings machined directly in the cylinder head and camshaft bearing housing.

The high-pressure fuel pump supplies fuel to the fuel rail, and subsequently to the electronically-controlled injectors which inject the fuel directly into the combustion chambers. This design differs from the previous type where an injection pump supplies the fuel at high-pressure to each injector. The earlier, conventional type injection pump required fine calibration and timing, and these functions are now completed by the high-pressure pump, electronic injectors and engine management ECU.

The crankshaft runs in five main bearings of the usual shell type. Endfloat is controlled by thrustwashers either side of No 2 main bearing.

The pistons are selected to be of matching weight, and incorporate fully-floating gudgeon pins retained by circlips.

The gear type oil pump is fitted over the end of the crankshaft, and is driven by interlocking machined flats on the crankshaft and pump gear.

Throughout the manual, it is often necessary to identify the engines not only by their cubic capacity, but also by their engine code. The engine code, consists of three letters (eg, 8HY). The code is stamped on a plate attached to the front of the cylinder block.

### Precautions

The engine is a complex unit with numerous accessories and ancillary components. The design of the engine compartment is such that every conceivable space has been utilised, and access to virtually all of the engine components is extremely limited. In many cases, ancillary components will have to be removed, or moved to one side, and wiring, pipes and hoses will have to be disconnected or removed from various cable clips and support brackets.

When working on this engine, read through the entire procedure first, look at the car and engine at the same time, and establish whether you have the necessary tools, equipment, skill and patience to proceed. Allow considerable time for any operation, and be prepared for the unexpected. Any major work on these engines is not for the faint-hearted!

Because of the limited access, many of the engine photographs appearing in this Chapter

were, by necessity, taken with the engine removed from the vehicle.

**⚠ Warning: It is essential to observe strict precautions when working on the fuel system components of the engine, particularly the high-pressure side of the system. Before carrying out any engine operations that entail working on, or near, any part of the fuel system, refer to the special information given in Chapter 4B, Section 2.**

### Operations with engine in car

a) Compression pressure – testing.
b) Cylinder head cover – removal and refitting.
c) Crankshaft pulley – removal and refitting.
d) Timing belt covers – removal and refitting.
e) Timing belt – removal, refitting and adjustment.
f) Timing belt tensioner and sprockets – removal and refitting.
g) Camshaft oil seal – renewal.
h) Camshaft(s), rocker arms and hydraulic tappets – removal, inspection and refitting.
i) Sump – removal and refitting.
j) Oil pump – removal and refitting.
k) Crankshaft oil seals – renewal.
l) Engine/transmission mountings – inspection and renewal.
m) Flywheel – removal, inspection and refitting.

### 2 Compression and leakdown tests – description and interpretation

### Compression test

**Note:** *A compression tester specifically designed for diesel engines must be used for this test.*

**1** When engine performance is down, or if misfiring occurs which cannot be attributed to the fuel system, a compression test can provide diagnostic clues as to the engine's condition. If the test is performed regularly, it can give warning of trouble before any other symptoms become apparent.

**2** A compression tester specifically intended for diesel engines must be used, because of the higher pressures involved. The tester is connected to an adapter which screws into the glow plug or injector hole. On these engines, an adapter suitable for use in the glow plug holes will be required, so as not to disturb the fuel system components. It is unlikely to be worthwhile buying such a tester for occasional use, but it may be possible to borrow or hire one – if not, have the test performed by a garage.

**3** Unless specific instructions to the contrary are supplied with the tester, observe the following points:

a) The battery must be in a good state of charge, the air filter must be clean, and the engine should be at normal operating temperature.

b) All the glow plugs should be removed as described in Chapter 5C before starting the test.
c) The wiring connector on the engine management system ECU (located in the plastic battery box) must be disconnected as described in Chapter 4B.

**4** The compression pressures measured are not so important as the balance between cylinders. Values are given in the Specifications.

**5** The cause of poor compression is less easy to establish on a diesel engine than on a petrol one. The effect of introducing oil into the cylinders ('wet' testing) is not conclusive, because there is a risk that the oil will sit in the swirl chamber or in the recess on the piston crown instead of passing to the rings. However, the following can be used as a rough guide to diagnosis.

**6** All cylinders should produce very similar pressures; any difference greater than that specified indicates the existence of a fault. Note that the compression should build-up quickly in a healthy engine; low compression on the first stroke, followed by gradually-increasing pressure on successive strokes, indicates worn piston rings. A low compression reading on the first stroke, which does not build-up during successive strokes, indicates leaking valves or a blown head gasket (a cracked head could also be the cause). Deposits on the undersides of the valve heads can also cause low compression.

**7** A low reading from two adjacent cylinders is almost certainly due to the head gasket having blown between them; the presence of coolant in the engine oil will confirm this.

**8** If the compression reading is unusually high, the cylinder head surfaces, valves and pistons are probably coated with carbon deposits. If this is the case, the cylinder head should be removed and decarbonised (see Part C).

### Leakdown test

**9** A leakdown test measures the rate at which compressed air fed into the cylinder is lost. It is an alternative to a compression test, and in many ways it is better, since the escaping air provides easy identification of where pressure loss is occurring (piston rings, valves or head gasket).

**10** The equipment needed for leakdown testing is unlikely to be available to the home mechanic. If poor compression is suspected, have the test performed by a suitably-equipped garage.

### 3 Engine assembly/ valve timing holes – general information and usage

**Note:** *Do not attempt to rotate the engine whilst the crankshaft and camshaft are locked in position. If the engine is to be left in this state for a long period of time, it is a good idea to place suitable warning notices inside the vehicle, and in the engine compartment. This will reduce the possibility of the engine*

*being accidentally cranked on the starter motor, which is likely to cause damage with the locking pins in place.*

**1** Timing holes are located in the crankshaft sprocket flange, and camshaft sprocket hub. The holes are used to align the crankshaft and camshaft in the assembly position with the pistons halfway up the cylinder bores. This will ensure that the valve timing is maintained during operations that require removal and refitting of the timing belt. When the holes are aligned with their corresponding holes in the cylinder block and cylinder head, suitable diameter bolts/pins can be inserted to lock the crankshaft and camshaft in position, preventing rotation.

**2** Note that the HDi type fuel system used on these engines does not have a conventional diesel injection pump, but instead uses a high-pressure fuel pump that does not have to be timed. The alignment of the fuel pump sprocket (and hence the fuel pump itself) with respect to crankshaft and camshaft position, is therefore irrelevant.

**3** To align the engine assembly/valve timing holes, proceed as follows.

**4** Apply the handbrake, then jack up the front of the vehicle and support it on axle stands (see *Jacking and vehicle support*). Remove the right-hand front roadwheel.

**5** To gain access to the crankshaft pulley area, to enable the engine to be turned, the wheel arch plastic liner must be removed. The liner is secured by several plastic expanding rivets. To remove the rivets, push in the centre pins a little, then prise the clips from place. Remove the liner from under the front wing. Where necessary, unclip the coolant hoses from under the wing to improve access further.

**6** Remove the upper and lower timing belt covers as described in Section 6.

**7** Refit the crankshaft pulley retaining bolt (without the pulley) to enable the crankshaft to be turned using a suitable socket and extension bar.

**8** Turn the crankshaft until the timing hole in the camshaft sprocket hub is aligned with the corresponding hole in the cylinder head. Note that the crankshaft must always be turned in a clockwise direction (viewed from the right-hand side of vehicle). Use a small mirror so that the position of the sprocket hub timing slot can be observed. When the slot is aligned with the corresponding hole in the cylinder head, the camshaft is positioned correctly.

**9** Insert a 5 mm diameter bolt, rod or drill through the hole in crankshaft sprocket flange and into the corresponding hole in the oil pump **(see illustration)**. If necessary, carefully turn the crankshaft either way until the rod enters the timing hole in the block.

**10** Insert an 8 mm bolt, rod or drill through the hole in the camshaft sprocket hub and into engagement with the cylinder head **(see illustration)**.

**11** The crankshaft and camshaft are now locked in position, preventing unnecessary rotation.

**3.9 Insert a 5 mm drill through the hole in the crankshaft sprocket flange (arrowed), and into the corresponding hole in the oil pump**

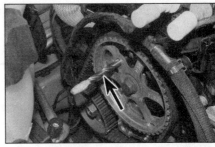

**3.10 Insert an 8 mm drill (arrowed) through the hole in the camshaft sprocket, and into the corresponding hole in the cylinder head**

## 4 Cylinder head cover – removal and refitting

> **Warning: Refer to the precautionary information contained in Section 1 before proceeding.**

### Removal

#### 8-valve engines

**Note:** *The cylinder head cover is integral with the inlet manifold and oil separator.*

**1** Disconnect the battery (see Chapter 5A).

**2** Remove the air cleaner assembly as described in Chapter 4B.

**3** Slacken the retaining clip, and disconnect the turbocharger outlet hose from the outlet flange adjacent to the oil filler cap **(see illustration)**.

**4** Release the small-bore coolant hose from

**4.3 Slacken the retaining clamps and disconnect the turbo outlet hose – 8-valve engines**

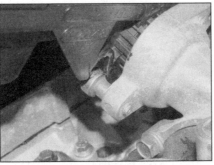

**4.4b . . . to disengage the resonator box from the turbocharger – 8-valve engines**

the clips at the front of the resonator. Undo the two retaining bolts, lift up the right-hand end and remove the resonator **(see illustrations)**. Recover the O-ring seal.

**5** Remove the diesel fuel filter as described in Chapter 1B, then undo the 3 bolts securing the diesel filter support bracket.

**6** Disconnect the wiring plugs from the top of each injector, then make sure all wiring harnesses are freed from any retaining brackets on the cylinder head cover/inlet manifold. Disconnect any vacuum pipes as necessary, having first noted their fitted positions.

**7** Prise out the retaining clips and disconnect the fuel return pipes from the injectors. Plug the openings to prevent dirt ingress.

**8** Thoroughly clean the fuel feed and return pipe connections located at the right-hand end of the cylinder head cover. Depress the tabs on the side of the quick-release fittings and disconnect the two pipes **(see illustration)**.

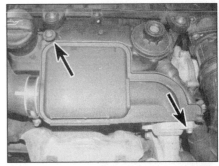

**4.4a Undo the bolts (arrowed) and lift up the right-hand end . . .**

**4.8 Depress the locking buttons (arrowed) and disconnect the fuel feed and return pipes – 8-valve engines**

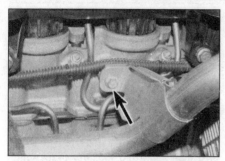

**4.10 Undo the bolt securing the EGR pipe to the rear of the block (arrowed) – 8-valve engines**

**4.12a Undo the 8 bolts (arrowed) at the front . . .**

**4.12b . . . and the two bolts (arrowed) at the rear – 8-valve engines**

**4.13 Remove the plastic cover from the top of the engine – 16-valve engines**

Plug the pipes and unions to prevent dirt ingress and fuel loss. Undo the Torx screw securing the fuel pipes to the support bracket.
**9** Unclip the fuel temperature sensor from the retaining bracket and move the pipe/hand priming pump assembly to the rear.

**4.14 Disconnect the air intake duct from the turbocharger and air mass meter – 16-valve engines**

**10** Undo the two screws securing the EGR pipe to the inlet manifold, and the bolt securing the pipe to the rear of the cylinder head **(see illustration)**.
**11** Undo the two bolts securing the EGR valve to the left-hand end of the cylinder head,

disconnect the vacuum hose, then remove the valve along with the EGR pipe. Recover the O-ring seal from the pipe.
**12** Undo the eight bolts securing the cylinder head cover and inlet manifold at the front, and the two retaining bolts along the rear edge of the cover. Lift the assembly away **(see illustrations)**. Recover the manifold rubber seals.

### 16-valve engines

**13** Remove the plastic cover from the top of the engine. The cover is retained by rubber grommets, and pulls upwards to release **(see illustration)**.
**14** Slacken the retaining clips and disconnect the air intake duct from the turbocharger and air mass meter **(see illustration)**.
**15** Undo the seven bolts and withdraw the cylinder head cover from the camshaft bearing housing. Cover the top of the camshaft bearing housing with a clean cloth to prevent dirt entry while the cylinder head cover is removed.

### *Refitting*

**16** Refitting is a reversal of removal, bearing in mind the following points:
a) *Examine the cover seal(s) for signs of damage and deterioration, and renew if necessary. On 8-valve engines, smear a little clean engine oil on the manifold seals.*
b) *Tighten the cylinder head cover bolts to the specified torque, in the order shown* **(see illustrations)**.

**4.16a Cylinder head cover tightening sequence – 8-valve engines**

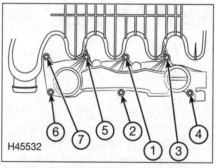

**4.16b Cylinder head cover tightening sequence – 16-valve engines**

## 5 Crankshaft pulley – removal and refitting

### *Removal*

**1** Remove the auxiliary drivebelt as described in Chapter 1B. Turn the tensioner anti-clockwise and insert a 3.0 mm diameter rod or drill to hold it away from the drivebelt **(see illustration)**.
**2** Slacken the retaining clamp and separate the exhaust system intermediate pipe from the catalytic converter.
**3** To lock the crankshaft, working underneath the engine, insert Citroën tool No 0194-C into the hole in the right-hand face of the engine block casting over the lower section of the flywheel. Rotate the crankshaft until the tool

**5.1 Insert a drill or pin to lock the auxiliary drivebelt tensioner in position**

**5.3a Insert a 12 mm bolt or rod into the hole in the right-hand face of the engine block casting . . .**

engages in the corresponding hole in the flywheel. In the absence of the Citroën tool, insert a 12 mm bolt or rod into the hole **(see illustrations)**. **Note:** *The hole in the casting and the hole in the flywheel are provided purely to lock the crankshaft whilst the pulley bolt is undone, it does **not** position the crankshaft at TDC or in a timing position.*

**4** Using a suitable socket and extension bar, unscrew the retaining bolt, then withdraw the pulley from the crankshaft sprocket **(see illustrations)**.

*Caution: Do not touch the outer magnetic sensor ring of the crankshaft sprocket with your fingers, or allow metallic particles to come into contact with it.*

### Refitting

**5** Refit the pulley to the crankshaft sprocket, ensuring that the notch on the pulley, engages with the key on the sprocket **(see illustration)**.

**6** Thoroughly clean the threads of the pulley retaining bolt, then apply a coat of locking compound to the bolt threads. Citroën recommend the use of Loctite (available from your dealer); in the absence of this, any good-quality locking compound may be used.

**7** Refit the crankshaft pulley retaining bolt and washer. Tighten the bolt to the specified torque, then through the specified angle, preventing the crankshaft from turning using the method employed on removal. Remove the crankshaft locking tool after tightening the bolt.

**8** Reconnect the exhaust system intermediate pipe to the catalytic converter.

**9** Refit the auxiliary drivebelt as described in Chapter 1B.

---

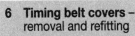

**6  Timing belt covers –**
   removal and refitting

⚠️ *Warning: Refer to the pre-cautionary information contained in Section 1 before proceeding.*

### Removal

#### Upper cover

**1** Disconnect the battery (see Chapter 5A).

**2** On 16-valve engines, remove the plastic cover from the top of the engine. The cover is retained by rubber grommets, and pulls upwards to release.

**3** Thoroughly clean the fuel feed and return pipe connections located above the timing belt upper cover. Depress the tabs on the side of the quick-release fittings and disconnect the two pipes **(see illustration)**. Plug the pipes and unions to prevent dirt ingress and fuel loss.

**4** On 16-valve engines, disconnect the wiring connector at the pressure sensor on the inlet manifold **(see illustration)**.

**5** Place a jack beneath the engine, with a block of wood on the jack head. Raise the jack until it is supporting the weight of the engine.

**6** Undo the three bolts securing the right-hand

**5.3b . . . and engage the bolt/rod (arrowed) into the hole in the flywheel (arrowed) to prevent rotation**

**5.4b . . . then withdraw the pulley from the crankshaft sprocket**

engine mounting assembly to the bracket on the engine, and the two bolts securing the mounting to the body.

**7** Remove the mounting assembly from the car and recover the reinforcing plate **(see illustration)**.

**6.3 Depress the tabs on the side of the quick-release fittings and disconnect the two fuel pipes**

**6.7 Undo the retaining bolts and remove the right-hand engine mounting**

**5.4a Unscrew the crankshaft pulley retaining bolt . . .**

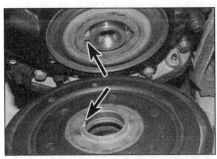

**5.5 The notch in the crankshaft pulley (arrowed) must align with the key in the sprocket (arrowed)**

**8** Release the wiring harness retaining clips, and the fuel pipes from the upper cover **(see illustrations)**.

**9** Slacken the four bolts securing the engine mounting bracket to the cylinder head. Move the bracket away from the cylinder head

**6.4 On 16-valve engines, disconnect the wiring connector at the manifold pressure sensor**

**6.8a Release the wiring harness retaining clips . . .**

**6.8b ... and the fuel pipes from the upper cover**

slightly to provide sufficient clearance for removal of the upper cover.

**10** Undo the five retaining bolts and manipulate the timing belt upper cover from its location **(see illustrations)**.

**Lower cover**

**11** Remove the crankshaft pulley as described in Section 5.

**12** Remove the upper cover as described previously.

**13** Using an open-ended spanner, hold the auxiliary drivebelt tensioner arm so that the locking drill bit/rod can be removed, then allow the tensioner to rotate to the fully released position.

**14** Undo the five cover retaining bolts, noting that the bolts are captive in the cover and cannot be removed completely. Manipulate the lower cover out from under the wheel arch **(see illustrations)**.

**Upper inner cover (16-valve engines)**

**15** Remove the camshaft sprocket as described in Section 8.

**16** Undo the nut and remove the wires from the terminal stud at the rear of the upper inner cover

**17** Undo the retaining bolts and remove the upper inner cover from the cylinder head.

**Refitting**

**18** Refitting of the covers is a reversal of the relevant removal procedure, bearing in mind the following points:

a) Ensure that each cover section is correctly located, and that the cover retaining bolts are securely tightened.

b) Ensure that all disturbed hoses are recon-nected and retained by their relevant clips.

c) Tighten the engine mounting bracket retaining bolts to the specified torque.

d) Before refitting the auxiliary drivebelt, return the tensioner to the retracted position and refit the locking drill bit/rod.

e) On completion, reconnect the battery, then prime the fuel system as described in Chapter 4B.

---

**7   Timing belt –**
removal, inspection, refitting and tensioning

**General**

**1** The timing belt drives the camshafts, high-pressure fuel pump, and coolant pump from a toothed sprocket on the end of the crankshaft. If the belt breaks or slips in service, the pistons are likely to hit the valve heads, resulting in expensive damage.

**2** The timing belt should be renewed at the specified intervals see Chapter 1B), or earlier if it is contaminated with oil or at all noisy in operation (a 'scraping' noise due to uneven wear).

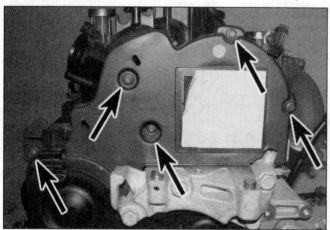

**6.10a  Upper timing belt cover retaining bolt locations (arrowed) – 8-valve engines**

**6.10b  Upper timing belt cover retaining bolt locations (arrowed) – 16-valve engines**

**6.14a  Undo the lower timing belt cover retaining bolts (arrowed) ...**

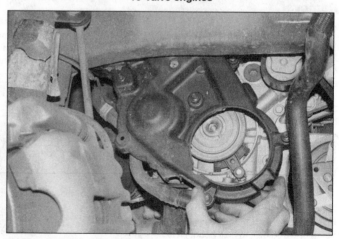

**6.14b  ... and manipulate the cover out from under the wheel arch**

**7.7  Undo the bolt securing the crankshaft position sensor (arrowed)**

**7.8  Timing belt protection bracket retaining bolt (arrowed)**

**7.10  Insert an Allen key into the hole (arrowed), slacken the pulley bolt and allow the tensioner to rotate**

**3**  If the timing belt is being removed, it is a wise precaution to check the condition of the coolant pump at the same time (check for signs of coolant leakage). This may avoid the need to remove the timing belt again at a later stage, should the coolant pump fail.

### Removal

**4**  Remove the auxiliary drivebelt as described in Chapter 1B.

**5**  Remove the crankshaft pulley as described in Section 5.

**6**  Remove the timing belt upper and lower covers as described in Section 6.

**7**  Undo the screw and remove the crankshaft position sensor adjacent to the crankshaft sprocket flange, and move it to one side **(see illustration)**.

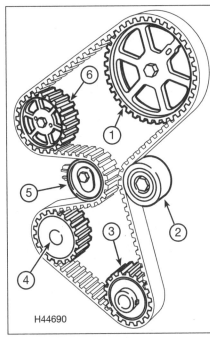

**7.16a  Timing belt routing**

1  *Camshaft sprocket*
2  *Idler pulley*
3  *Crankshaft sprocket*
4  *Coolant pump sprocket*
5  *Tensioner pulley*
6  *High-pressure fuel pump sprocket*

**8**  Undo the retaining screw and remove the timing belt protection bracket, again adjacent to the crankshaft sprocket flange **(see illustration)**.

**9**  Lock the crankshaft and camshaft in the assembly position as described in Section 3. If necessary, temporarily refit the crankshaft pulley bolt to enable the crankshaft to be rotated.

**10**  Insert an Allen key into the hexagonal hole on the timing belt tensioner pulley. Slacken the tensioner pulley retaining bolt and allow the tensioner to rotate, relieving the belt tension **(see illustration)**. With belt slack, temporarily tighten the pulley bolt.

**11**  Note its routing, then remove the timing belt from the sprockets and pulleys.

### Inspection

**12**  Renew the belt as a matter of course, regardless of its apparent condition. The cost of a new belt is nothing compared with the cost of repairs, should the belt break in service. If signs of oil contamination are found, trace the source of the oil leak and rectify it. Wash down the engine timing belt area and all related components, to remove all traces of oil. Check that the tensioner and idler pulleys rotate freely without any sign of roughness, and also check that the coolant pump pulley rotates freely. If necessary, renew these items. **Note:** *Citroën recommend that the tensioner and idler pulleys should not be re-used, regardless of apparent condition.*

### Refitting

**13**  Commence refitting by ensuring that the

**7.16b  Keep the belt taut and feed it around the sprockets and pulleys**

crankshaft and camshaft timing pins are still in position (see Section 3).

**14**  Align the hole in the high-pressure fuel pump sprocket with the corresponding hole in the mounting bracket. Lock the sprocket by inserting a 5 mm bolt, rod or drill through the sprocket hole and into the corresponding hole in the bracket.

**15**  Locate the timing belt on the crankshaft sprocket, then refit the timing belt protection bracket and tighten the retaining bolt securely.

**16**  Keep the belt taut and locate it around the idler pulley, camshaft sprocket, high-pressure fuel pump sprocket, coolant pump sprocket, and the tensioner pulley **(see illustrations)**.

**17**  Remove the locking tool from the high-pressure fuel pump sprocket.

**18**  Slacken the tensioner pulley bolt. Using an Allen key, rotate the tensioner anti-clockwise, which moves the index arm clockwise, until the index arm is aligned with the locating stud **(see illustration)**.

**19**  Remove the camshaft and crankshaft timing pins and, using a socket on the crankshaft pulley bolt, rotate the engine clockwise 10 complete revolutions. Refit the crankshaft and camshaft timing pins.

**20**  Check that the tensioner index arm is still aligned between the edges of the area **(see illustration 7.18)**. If it is not, remove the belt and begin the refitting process again, starting at Paragraph 13.

**21**  With the belt correctly fitted and tensioned, refit the crankshaft position sensor and tighten its retaining bolt securely.

**22**  Refit the timing belt lower and upper

**7.18  Align the index arm (A) with the locating stud (B)**

Tool Tip 1: A sprocket holding tool can be made from two lengths of steel strip (one long, the other short), and three nuts and bolts; one nut and bolt forms the pivot of a forked tool, with the remaining two nuts and bolts at the tips of the 'forks' to engage with the sprocket spokes.

covers as described in Section 6, then refit the crankshaft pulley as described in Section 5.
**23** Refit the auxiliary drivebelt as described in Chapter 1B.

## 8 Timing belt sprockets and tensioner – removal and refitting

### Camshaft sprocket

#### Removal

**1** Remove the timing belt as described in Section 7.
**2** Remove the engine assembly/valve timing locking pin from the camshaft sprocket and slacken the sprocket retaining bolt. To prevent the camshaft rotating as the bolt is slackened, a sprocket holding tool will be required. In the absence of the special Citroën tool, an acceptable substitute can be fabricated from steel strip **(see Tool Tip 1)**. *Do not* attempt to use the engine assembly/valve timing locking pin to prevent the sprocket from rotating whilst the bolt is slackened.

Tool Tip 2: Make a sprocket releasing tool from a short strip of steel. Drill two holes in the strip to correspond with the two holes in the sprocket. Drill a third hole just large enough to accept the flats of the sprocket retaining nut.

**8.3 Undo the retaining bolt and remove the camshaft sprocket**

**8.11a Slide the sprocket off the end of the crankshaft . . .**

**3** Remove the sprocket retaining bolt, and slide the sprocket off the end of the camshaft **(see illustration)**. Examine the camshaft oil seal for signs of oil leakage and, if necessary, renew it as described in Section 14.
**4** Clean the camshaft sprocket thoroughly, and renew it if there are any signs of wear, damage or cracks.

#### Refitting

**5** Locate the sprocket on the end of the camshaft, ensuring that the locating lug is correctly engaged with the cut-out in the camshaft end **(see illustration)**.
**6** Refit the sprocket retaining bolt and washer. Tighten the bolt to the specified torque, preventing the camshaft from turning as during removal.
**7** Align the engine assembly/valve timing slot in the camshaft sprocket hub with the hole in the cylinder head and refit the timing pin to lock the camshaft in position.
**8** Refit the timing belt as described in Section 7.

### Crankshaft sprocket

#### Removal

**9** Remove the timing belt as described in Section 7.
**10** Remove the crankshaft pulley retaining bolt (if temporarily refitted to allow the engine to be turned).
**11** Slide the sprocket off the end of the crankshaft and collect the Woodruff key **(see illustrations)**.
**12** Examine the crankshaft oil seal for signs of oil leakage and, if necessary, renew it as described in Section 14.

**8.5 Align the sprocket lug with the notch in the end of the camshaft (arrowed)**

**8.11b . . . and collect the Woodruff key**

**13** Clean the crankshaft sprocket thoroughly, and renew it if there are any signs of wear, damage or cracks.

#### Refitting

**14** Refit the Woodruff key to the end of the crankshaft, then refit the crankshaft sprocket with the flange facing the crankshaft pulley.
**15** Refit the timing belt as described in Section 7.

### Fuel pump sprocket

#### Removal

**16** Remove the timing belt as described in Section 7.
**17** Using a suitable socket, undo the pump sprocket retaining nut. The sprocket can be held stationary by using a suitable forked tool engaged with the holes in the sprocket **(see Tool Tip 1)**.
**18** The pump sprocket is a taper fit on the pump shaft and it will be necessary to make up another tool to release it from the taper **(see Tool Tip 2)**.
**19** Partially unscrew the sprocket retaining nut, fit the home-made tool, and secure it to the sprocket with two suitable bolts. Prevent the sprocket from rotating as before, and unscrew the sprocket retaining nut **(see illustrations)**. The nut will bear against the tool as it is undone, forcing the sprocket off the shaft taper. Once the taper is released, remove the tool, unscrew the nut fully, and remove the sprocket from the pump shaft.
**20** Clean the sprocket thoroughly, and renew it if there are any signs of wear, damage or cracks.

## Refitting

**21** Refit the pump sprocket and retaining nut, and tighten the nut to the specified torque. Prevent the sprocket rotating as the nut is tightened using the sprocket holding tool.
**22** Refit the timing belt as described in Section 7.

### Coolant pump sprocket

**23** The coolant pump sprocket is integral with the pump, and cannot be removed. Coolant pump removal is described in Chapter 3.

### Tensioner pulley

#### Removal

**24** Remove the timing belt as described in Section 7.
**25** Undo the tensioner pulley retaining bolt, and lift off the pulley.
**26** Clean the tensioner pulley, but do not use any strong solvent which may enter the pulley bearings. Check that the pulley rotates freely, with no sign of stiffness or free play. Renew the pulley if there is any doubt about its condition, or if there are any obvious signs of wear or damage.

#### Refitting

**27** Refit the tensioner pulley ensuring that the pulley arm engages over the locating peg (see illustration).
**28** Refit the timing belt as described in Section 7.

### Idler pulley

#### Removal

**29** Remove the timing belt as described in Section 7.
**30** Undo the retaining nut and withdraw the idler pulley from its mounting stud (see illustration).
**31** Clean the idler pulley, but do not use any strong solvent which may enter the bearings. Check that the pulley rotates freely, with no sign of stiffness or free play. Renew the idler pulley if there is any doubt about its condition, or if there are any obvious signs of wear or damage.

#### Refitting

**32** Locate the idler pulley on the engine, and fit the retaining bolt. Tighten the bolt/nut to the specified torque.

**8.19a Fit the home-made tool to the fuel pump sprocket . . .**

**8.27 Ensure that the tensioner pulley arm engages over the locating peg (arrowed) when refitting**

**33** Refit the timing belt as described in Section 7.

### 9 Camshaft(s), rocker arms and hydraulic tappets – removal, inspection and refitting

#### Removal

##### 8-valve engines

**1** Remove the cylinder head cover as described in Section 4.
**2** Remove the camshaft sprocket as described in Section 8.
**3** Refit the right-hand engine mounting, but only tighten the bolts moderately; this will keep the engine supported during the camshaft removal procedure.
**4** Undo the retaining bolts and remove the vacuum pump from the left-hand end of the

**8.19b . . . then unscrew the retaining nut to draw off the sprocket**

**8.30 Undo the retaining nut and withdraw the idler pulley from the mounting stud**

cylinder head. Recover the pump O-ring seals (see illustration).
**5** Disconnect the wiring plug, unscrew the retaining bolt, and remove the camshaft position sensor from the cylinder head.
**6** Working in a spiral pattern, progressively and evenly unscrew the camshaft upper bearing housing bolts (see illustration). Carefully lift the housing away.
**7** Note the orientation of the camshaft, then lift it upwards from the housing and slide off and discard the oil seal.
**8** To remove the rocker arms and hydraulic tappets, undo the 13 bolts and remove the lower half of the camshaft bearing housing.
**9** Obtain eight small, clean plastic containers, and number them 1 to 8; alternatively, divide a larger container into eight compartments.
**10** Lift out each rocker arm. Place the rocker arms in their respective positions in the box or containers (see illustration).

**9.4 Undo the vacuum pump bolts (arrowed) – 8-valve engines**

**9.6 Upper camshaft bearing housing bolts (arrowed) – 8-valve engines**

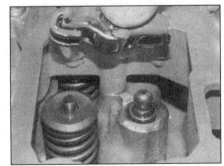

**9.10 Remove the rocker arms – 8-valve engines**

9.18 Undo the nut and remove the wires from the terminal stud on the timing belt upper inner cover – 16-valve engines

9.20 Undo the bolts (arrowed) and remove the fuel filter mounting bracket – 16-valve engines

9.21 Undo the retaining bolts and remove the timing belt upper inner cover – 16-valve engines

**11** A compartmentalised container filled with engine oil is now required to retain the hydraulic tappets while they are removed from the cylinder head. Withdraw each hydraulic follower and place it in the container, keeping them each identified for correct refitting. The tappets must be totally submerged in the oil to prevent air entering them.

**12** Recover the 5 O-ring seals between the housing and the cylinder head.

### 16-valve engines

**13** Remove the cylinder head cover as described in Section 4.

**14** Remove the inlet manifold as described in Chapter 4B.

**15** Remove the fuel injectors as described in Chapter 4B.

**16** Remove the camshaft sprocket as described in Section 8.

**17** Refit the right-hand engine mounting, but only tighten the bolts moderately; this will keep the engine supported during the camshaft removal procedure.

**18** Undo the nut and remove the wires from the terminal stud at the rear of the timing belt upper inner cover (see illustration).

**19** Disconnect the vacuum hose at the brake servo vacuum pump. Undo the retaining bolts and remove the vacuum pump from the left-hand end of the cylinder head. Recover the pump O-ring seals.

**20** Remove the fuel filter as described in Chapter 1B, then undo the three bolts and remove the filter mounting bracket (see illustration).

**21** Undo the retaining bolts and remove the timing belt upper inner cover (see illustration).

**22** Slacken the retaining screw and withdraw

the camshaft position sensor from its location (see illustration).

**23** Undo the six bolts and remove the lower heat shield from the front of the catalytic converter.

**24** Undo the three retaining bolts and manipulate the upper heat shield out from its location (see illustration).

**25** Working in the **reverse** of the tightening sequence (see illustration 9.72) progressively and evenly unscrew the camshaft bearing housing outer retaining bolts, followed by the inner retaining studs. Carefully lift the housing, complete with camshafts, off the cylinder head (see illustration). Place the housing on the bench with the camshafts uppermost.

**26** Obtain sixteen small, clean plastic containers, and number them inlet 1 to 8 and exhaust 1 to 8; alternatively, divide a larger container into sixteen compartments and number each compartment accordingly.

**27** Lift out each rocker arm. Place the rocker arms in their respective positions in the box or containers (see illustration).

**28** A compartmentalised container filled with engine oil is now required to retain the hydraulic tappets while they are removed from the cylinder head. Withdraw each hydraulic tappet and place it in the container, keeping them each identified for correct refitting (see illustration). The tappets must be totally submerged in the oil to prevent air entering them.

**29** Check for the presence of identification markings on the camshaft bearing caps. They should be marked A1 to A4 for the

9.22 Slacken the retaining screw (arrowed) and remove the camshaft position sensor – 16-valve engines

9.24 Remove the upper heat shield from the exhaust manifold and turbocharger – 16-valve engines

9.25 Lift the bearing housing, complete with camshafts, off the cylinder head – 16-valve engines

9.27 Lift out the rocker arms . . .

9.28 . . . followed by the hydraulic tappets – 16-valve engines

**9.29 Camshaft bearing cap identification markings (arrowed) – 16-valve engines**

**9.30 Lift both camshafts from the bearing housing together with the chain and tensioner – 16-valve engines**

**9.31 Extract the injector tube sealing rings using a hooked tool – 16-valve engines**

inlet camshaft, and E1 to E4 for the exhaust camshaft (see illustration). Also check the bearing cap orientation; the circular raised projection in the centre of each cap should be towards the exhaust manifold side of the engine. If no identification marks are present, or if the orientation can not be determined, suitably mark each cap for position and location.

**30** Progressively unscrew all the camshaft bearing cap retaining bolts, then unscrew the two bolts securing the drive chain tensioner assembly. Remove the bolts, then lift out both camshafts together with the chain and tensioner (see illustration). Withdraw the oil seal from the exhaust camshaft, slide out the tensioner assembly, then remove the chain from the camshaft sprockets.

**31** Using a hooked tool, carefully remove the four injector tube sealing rings from the camshaft bearing housing (see illustration). Note that four new sealing rings, together with four protector sleeves will be required for refitting. The protector sleeves (Citroën part number 198260) are used during reassembly only and ensure that the sealing rings locate correctly over the injector tubes when refitting the camshaft bearing housing.

### Inspection

**32** Thoroughly clean the sealant from the mating surfaces of the cylinder head and camshaft bearing housing. Use a suitable liquid gasket dissolving agent (available from Citroën dealers) together with a soft putty knife; do not use a metal scraper or the faces

will be damaged. As there is no conventional gasket used, the cleanliness of the mating faces is of the utmost importance.

**33** Clean off any oil, dirt or grease from both components and dry with a clean lint-free cloth. Ensure that all the oilways are completely clean.

**34** Inspect the cam lobes and the camshaft bearing journals for scoring or other visible evidence of wear. Once the surface hardening of the cam lobes has been eroded, wear will occur at an accelerated rate. Note: *If these symptoms are visible on the tips of the camshaft lobes, check the corresponding rocker arm, as it will probably be worn as well.*

**35** Examine the condition of the bearing surfaces in the cylinder head and/or camshaft bearing housing(s). If wear is evident, the mating components will both have to be renewed, as they are a matched assembly.

**36** Inspect the rocker arms and tappets for scuffing, cracking or other damage and renew any components as necessary. Also check the condition of the tappet bores in the cylinder head. As with the camshafts, any wear in this area will necessitate cylinder head renewal.

**37** On 16-valve engines, check the condition of the drive chain, camshaft sprockets and the tensioner assembly. Renew any components that show evidence of wear or deterioration.

**38** Renew all oil seals, O-rings and gaskets that were disturbed during removal and dismantling. A suitable sealing compound will be required for mating surfaces which are not sealed with a gasket. Citroën recommend Loctite Autojoint Noir for this purpose.

### Refitting

#### 8-valve engines

**39** Ensure that the crankshaft is still locked in the assembly position as described in Section 3, to prevent any possibility of the valves contacting the pistons during refitting.

**40** Liberally lubricate the hydraulic tappet bores in the cylinder head with clean engine oil.

**41** Insert the hydraulic tappets into their original bores in the cylinder head unless they have been renewed.

**42** Lubricate the rocker arms and place them over their respective tappets and valve stems.

**43** Sparingly apply a bead of sealant to the mating face of the cylinder head-to-camshaft lower bearing housing, and position the 5 new O-ring seals (see illustration).

**44** Insert two 12 mm rods or drill bits into the locating holes in the cylinder head to guide the bearing housing into position. Suitable guide rods, No 0194-N, are available from Citroën dealers. Refit the lower bearing housing over the tools, insert the bolts and finger-tighten them in order (see illustration).

**45** Remove the guide pins/rods and tighten the housing bolts in the sequence shown previously to the specified torque.

**46** Lubricate the camshaft bearing journals with clean engine oil, and lay the camshaft in position.

**47** Sparingly apply a bead of sealant to the mating face of the camshaft lower bearing housing (see illustration).

**48** Insert two 12 mm rods or drill bits into the

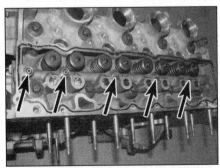

**9.43 Apply a bead of sealant, and fit the new O-rings (arrowed) – 8-valve engines**

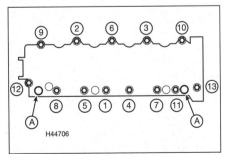

**9.44 Insert guide pins/rods into the guide holes (A), fit the housing and tighten the bolts in sequence – 8-valve engines**

**9.47 Lay the camshaft in position, and apply a bead of sealant to the housing mating face – 8-valve engines**

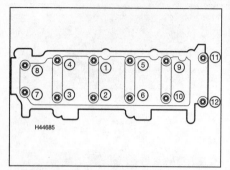

9.49  Upper camshaft housing bolts tightening sequence – 8-valve engines

9.53  When fitting a used sensor, the gap between the sensor end and the sensor ring web should be 1.2 mm – 8-valve engines

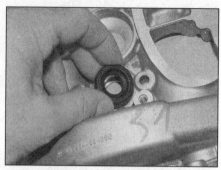

9.60a  Locate the new injector tube sealing rings in the camshaft bearing housing . . .

9.60b  . . . and push them into place using a suitable socket – 16-valve engines

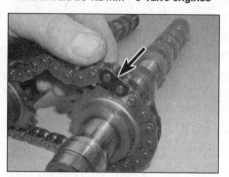

9.61a  Fit the drive chain over the camshaft sprockets, so that the dark link in the chain (arrowed) . . .

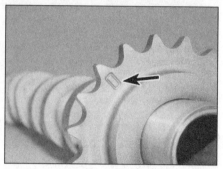

9.61b  . . . locates over the timing mark (arrowed) on each sprocket – 16-valve engines

locating holes in the lower camshaft bearing housing to guide the upper housing into position. Suitable guide rods, No 0194-N, are available from Citroën dealers.

**49** Locate the upper housing over the guide pins/rods, and finger-tighten the bolts gradually and evenly, in sequence until the upper housing makes firm contact with the lower housing **(see illustration)**.

**50** Remove the guides pins/rods and tighten the housing to the specified torque in the same sequence.

**51** Fit a new camshaft oil seal as described in Section 14.

**52** Refit the camshaft sprocket to the camshaft, ensuring that the sprocket lug engages with the camshaft slot, and tighten the bolt to the specified torque.

**53** Refit the camshaft position sensor to the camshaft housing, and position the sensor so that the gap between the sprocket and the sensor end is 1.2 mm for a used sensor. If fitting a new sensor, the small tip of the sensor must be just touching one of the three webs of the signal ring **(see illustration)**. Tighten the bolt to the specified torque.

**54** Turn the camshaft sprocket to the position where the timing tool can be inserted, then refit the timing belt as described in Section 7.

**55** The remainder of refitting is a reversal of removal.

### 16-valve engines

**56** Ensure that the crankshaft is still locked in the assembly position as described in Section 3, to prevent any possibility of the valves contacting the pistons during refitting.

**57** Liberally lubricate the hydraulic tappet

bores in the cylinder head with clean engine oil.

**58** Insert the hydraulic tappets into their original bores in the cylinder head unless they have been renewed.

**59** Lubricate the rocker arms and place them over their respective tappets and valve stems.

**60** Locate the new injector tube sealing rings in their locations in the camshaft bearing housing, with the flat face of each seal uppermost. Push the seals fully into place using a suitably sized socket **(see illustrations)**.

**61** Fit the drive chain over the camshaft sprockets, so that the two dark links in the chain locate over the timing mark on each sprocket **(see illustrations)**.

**62** Compress the tensioner assembly and insert a small drill bit through the slipper legs to hold the tensioner in the compressed position. Slide the tensioner into position between the two camshafts **(see illustrations)**.

**63** Lubricate the camshaft bearing journals in the bearing housing with clean engine oil and lay the camshafts, chain and tensioner assembly in position. Check that the dark links on the chain are still correctly engaged over the timing marks on each sprocket **(see illustrations)**.

**64** Lubricate the bearing journals in the camshaft bearing caps, then fit the caps to both camshafts. Ensure correct location and orientation as noted during removal.

**65** Refit the bearing cap retaining bolts and tighten them all finger tight. Working in

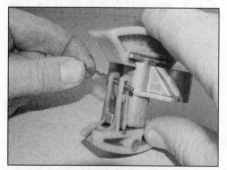

9.62a  Insert a small drill bit through the slipper legs to hold the tensioner in the compressed position . . .

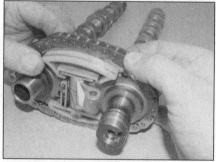

9.62b  . . . then slide the tensioner into position between the two camshafts – 16-valve engines

9.63a  Lubricate the camshaft bearing journals and lay the camshafts, chain and tensioner assembly in position – 16-valve engines

9.63b  Check that the dark links on the chain are still correctly engaged over the sprocket timing marks (arrowed) – 16-valve engines

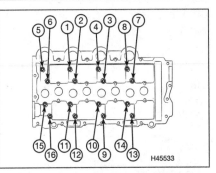

9.65  Camshaft bearing cap retaining bolt tightening sequence – 16-valve engines

9.66  Refit the chain tensioner retaining bolts, then pull out the drill bit to release the tensioner – 16-valve engines

9.68a  Lubricate the inner sealing lip of the injector tube sealing rings . . .

9.68b  . . . then insert a protector sleeve into the centre of each ring – 16-valve engines

sequence, progressively tighten the bearing cap retaining bolts to the specified torque **(see illustration)**.

**66**  Secure the chain tensioner assembly with the two retaining bolts tightened securely. Check that the chain dark links and sprocket timing marks are still correctly aligned, then pull out the drill bit to release the tensioner **(see illustration)**.

**67**  Temporarily refit the timing belt sprocket to the inlet camshaft together with its retaining bolt moderately tightened. Rotate the camshafts 40 times and check that the chain links and sprocket marks are once again aligned. If not repeat the complete refitting procedure from paragraph 61 onward. If all is satisfactory, remove the timing belt sprocket.

**68**  Apply a little multi-purpose grease to the inner sealing lip of the injector tube sealing

rings, then insert a protector sleeve into the centre of each ring **(see illustrations)**. Push the protector sleeve through the ring until only approximately 1 mm is left protruding.

**69**  Sparingly apply a bead of sealant to the mating face of the camshaft bearing housing, in the areas shown **(see illustration)**. Take great care not to allow the sealant to contaminate the lubrication hole for the chain tensioner.

**70**  Place the camshaft bearing housing assembly on the cylinder head and refit the retaining studs and bolts finger tight only.

**71**  As there are no locating dowels provided to align the bearing housing when refitting, temporarily refit the brake servo vacuum pump to its location and engage it with the camshaft. At the same time check that the edges of the bearing housing and cylinder head align in the area of the camshaft oil seal aperture.

**72**  Working in sequence, progressively tighten the bearing housing retaining studs and bolts to the specified torque **(see illustration)**. With the bearing housing secure, remove the temporarily refitted vacuum pump.

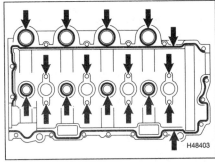

9.69  Apply a bead of sealant to the mating face of the camshaft bearing housing, in the areas shown (arrows) – 16-valve engines

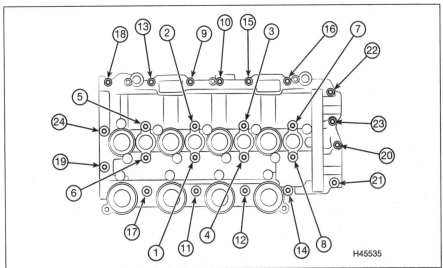

9.72  Camshaft bearing housing retaining bolt/stud tightening sequence – 16-valve engines

**9.73 Withdraw the protector sleeves from the injector tube sealing rings – 16-valve engines**

**73** Withdraw the protector sleeves from the injector tube sealing rings and check that the rings are correctly located around each tube **(see illustration)**.

**74** Fit a new camshaft oil seal as described in Section 14.

**75** Locate the timing belt upper inner cover in position and secure with the retaining bolts, tightened securely.

**76** Refit the wires to the terminal stud at the rear of the upper inner cover then refit and tighten the retaining nut.

**77** Locate the sprocket on the end of the camshaft, ensuring that the locating lug is correctly engaged with the cut-out in the camshaft end.

**78** Refit the sprocket retaining bolt and washer. Tighten the bolt to the specified torque, preventing the camshaft from turning as during removal.

**10.8 Auxiliary drivebelt tensioner bolts (arrowed) – 8-valve engines**

**10.13b . . . and front support bracket upper bolt – 8-valve engines**

**79** Refit the camshaft position sensor to the camshaft housing, and position the sensor so that the gap between the sprocket and the sensor end is 1.2 mm for a used sensor. If fitting a new sensor, the small tip of the sensor must be just touching one of the three webs of the signal ring. Tighten the bolt to the specified torque.

**80** Align the engine assembly/valve timing slot in the camshaft sprocket hub with the hole in the cylinder head and refit the timing pin to lock the camshaft in position.

**81** Refit the upper and lower heat shields to the turbocharger and catalytic converter.

**82** Refit the brake servo vacuum pump as described in Chapter 9.

**83** Refit the fuel filter mounting bracket and secure with the three bolts securely tightened. Refit the fuel filter with reference to Chapter 1B.

**84** Refit the timing belt as described in Section 7.

**85** Refit the fuel injectors and inlet manifold as described in Chapter 4B.

## 10 Cylinder head – removal and refitting

**Note:** *This is an involved procedure, and it is suggested that the Section is read thoroughly before starting work. To aid refitting, make notes on the locations of all relevant brackets and the routing of hoses and cables before removal.*

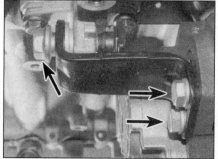

**10.13a Fuel pump rear support bracket bolts (arrowed) . . .**

**10.15 Coolant housing bolts (arrowed) – 8-valve engines**

### Removal

**1** Apply the handbrake, then jack up the front of the vehicle and support it on axle stands (see *Jacking and vehicle support*). Remove the front right-hand roadwheel, the engine undershield, and the front wheel arch liner. The undershield is secured by several screws, and the wheel arch liner is secured by several plastic expanding rivets. Push the centre pins in a little, then prise the rivet from place.

**2** Remove the battery (see Chapter 5A).

**3** Drain the cooling system as described in Chapter 1B. For improved general access, remove the bonnet as described in Chapter 11.

### 8-valve engines

**4** Remove the cylinder head cover as described in Section 4.

**5** Remove the timing belt as described in Section 7.

**6** Disconnect the exhaust intermediate pipe from the catalytic converter, as described in Chapter 4B. **Note:** *Do not allow any strain to be placed on the flexible section of the exhaust pipe, as damage will result.*

**7** Remove the glow plugs as described in Chapter 5C.

**8** Undo the three bolts and remove the auxiliary drivebelt tensioner from the front of the engine **(see illustration)**.

**9** Remove the catalytic converter as described in Chapter 4B.

**10** Remove the alternator (see Chapter 5A) and mounting bracket.

**11** Undo the union bolts and remove the oil feed pipe from the engine block and the turbocharger. Recover the unions sealing washers.

**12** Slacken the retaining clamp and disconnect the turbocharger oil return hose from the engine block.

**13** Slacken and remove the high-pressure fuel pump rear support bracket bolts and front support bracket upper bolt **(see illustrations)**.

**14** Remove the fuel injectors as described in Chapter 4B.

**15** Undo the coolant outlet housing (left-hand end of the cylinder head) retaining bolts, slacken the two bolts securing the housing support bracket to the top of the transmission bellhousing, and move the outlet housing away from the cylinder head a little **(see illustration)**. There is no need to disconnect the hoses.

**16** Disconnect the wiring plug, then undo the bolt and remove the camshaft position sensor from the cylinder head.

**17** Undo the 13 bolts and remove the camshaft bearing housing from the cylinder head, complete with camshaft. Recover the 5 small O-ring seals between the housing and the cylinder head.

**18** Obtain eight small, clean plastic containers, and number them 1 to 8; alternatively, divide a larger container into eight compartments.

**19** Lift out each rocker arm. Place the rocker arms in their respective positions in the box or containers **(see illustration 9.10)**.

**10.28a Undo the high-pressure fuel pump upper rear mounting bolt (arrowed) . . .**

**10.28b . . . and the upper mounting bolt at the front (arrowed) – 16-valve engines**

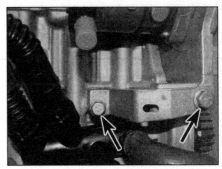

**10.29 Slacken the two lower pump mounting bracket bolts (arrowed) – 16-valve engines**

**20** A compartmentalised container filled with engine oil is now required to retain the hydraulic tappets while they are removed from the cylinder head. Withdraw each hydraulic follower and place it in the container, keeping them each identified for correct refitting. The tappets must be totally submerged in the oil to prevent air entering them.

**21** Working in the **reverse** of the tightening sequence **(see illustration 10.53)** undo the cylinder head bolts.

### 16-valve engines

**22** Remove the camshafts, rocker arms and hydraulic tappets as described in Section 9.

**23** Undo the three bolts and remove the auxiliary drivebelt tensioner.

**24** Remove the catalytic converter and inner heat shield as described in Chapter 4B.

**25** Remove the alternator as described in Chapter 5A.

**26** Undo the bolt securing the engine oil dipstick tube to the alternator mounting bracket. Undo the four bolts and remove the mounting bracket.

**27** Remove the high-pressure fuel pump sprocket as described in Section 8.

**28** Undo the high-pressure fuel pump upper rear mounting bolt, and the upper bolt at the front, securing the fuel pump mounting bracket to the cylinder head **(see illustrations)**.

**29** Slacken the two lower pump mounting bracket bolts and move the pump slightly away from the cylinder head **(see illustration)**.

**30** Remove the turbocharger as described in Chapter 4B.

**31** Undo the coolant outlet housing (left-hand end of the cylinder head) retaining bolts, slacken the two bolts securing the housing support bracket to the top of the transmission bellhousing, and move the outlet housing away from the cylinder head a little **(see illustration 10.15)**. There is no need to disconnect the hoses.

**32** Check that everything has been disconnected from the cylinder head to allow removal. Working in the **reverse** of the tightening sequence **(see illustration 10.53)** undo the cylinder head bolts.

### All engines

**33** Release the cylinder head from the cylinder

block and location dowels by rocking it. The Citroën tool for doing this consists simply of two metal rods with 90-degree angled ends **(see illustration)**. Do not prise between the mating faces of the cylinder head and block, as this may damage the gasket faces.

**34** Lift the cylinder head from the block, and recover the gasket.

**35** If necessary, remove the manifolds (if not already done so) with reference to Chapter 4B.

### Preparation for refitting

**36** The mating faces of the cylinder head and cylinder block must be perfectly clean before refitting the head. Citroën recommend the use of a scouring agent for this purpose, but acceptable results can be achieved by using a hard plastic or wood scraper to remove all traces of gasket and carbon. The same method can be used to clean the piston crowns. Take particular care to avoid scoring or gouging the cylinder head/cylinder block mating surfaces during the cleaning operations, as aluminium alloy is easily damaged. Make sure that the carbon is not allowed to enter the oil and water passages – this is particularly important for the lubrication system, as carbon could block the oil supply to the engine's components. Using adhesive tape and paper, seal the water, oil and bolt holes in the cylinder block. To prevent carbon entering the gap between the pistons

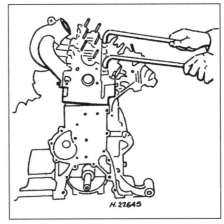

**10.33 Free the cylinder head using angled rods**

and bores, smear a little grease in the gap. After cleaning each piston, use a small brush to remove all traces of grease and carbon from the gap, then wipe away the remainder with a clean rag.

**37** Check the mating surfaces of the cylinder block and the cylinder head for nicks, deep scratches and other damage. If slight, they may be removed carefully with a file, but if excessive, machining may be the only alternative to renewal. If warpage of the cylinder head gasket surface is suspected, use a straight-edge to check it for distortion. Refer to Part C of this Chapter if necessary.

**38** Thoroughly clean the threads of the cylinder head bolt holes in the cylinder block. Ensure that the bolts run freely in their threads, and that all traces of oil and water are removed from each bolt hole.

### Gasket selection

**39** Remove the crankshaft timing pin, then turn the crankshaft until pistons 1 and 4 are at TDC (Top Dead Centre). Position a dial test indicator (dial gauge) on the cylinder block adjacent to the rear of No 1 piston, and zero it on the block face. Transfer the probe to the crown of No 1 piston (10.0 mm in from the rear edge), then slowly turn the crankshaft back-and-forth past TDC, noting the highest reading on the indicator. Record this reading as protrusion A.

**40** Repeat the check described in paragraph 39, this time 10.0 mm in from the front edge of the No 1 piston crown. Record this reading as protrusion B.

**41** Add protrusion A to protrusion B, then divide the result by 2 to obtain an average reading for piston No 1.

**42** Repeat the procedure described in paragraphs 39 to 41 on piston 4, then turn the crankshaft through 180° and carry out the procedure on the piston Nos 2 and 3 **(see illustration)**. Check that there is a maximum difference of 0.07 mm protrusion between any two pistons.

**43** If a dial test indicator is not available, piston protrusion may be measured using a straight-edge and feeler blades or Vernier calipers. However, this is much less accurate, and cannot therefore be recommended.

**10.42 Measure the piston protrusion using a DTI gauge**

**10.44 Cylinder head gasket thickness identification notches (arrowed)**

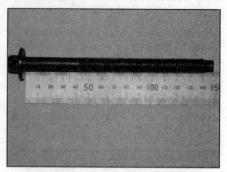

**10.45 Measure the length of each bolt from under the bolt head to its end**

**44** Note the greatest piston protrusion measurement, and use this to determine the correct cylinder head gasket from the following table. The series of notches/holes on the side of the gasket are used for thickness identification **(see illustration).**

| Piston protrusion | Gasket identification |
| --- | --- |
| 0.611 to 0.720 mm | 2 notches |
| 0.721 to 0.770 mm | 3 notches |
| 0.771 to 0.820 mm | 1 notch |
| 0.821 to 0.870 mm | 4 notches |
| 0.871 to 0.977 mm | 5 notches |

### Head bolt examination

**45** Carefully examine the cylinder head bolts for signs of damage to the threads or head, and for any sign of corrosion. If the bolts are in a satisfactory condition, measure the length of each bolt from the underside of the head, to the end of the shank. The bolts may be re-used providing that the measured length does not exceed 149.0 mm **(see illustration)**. **Note:** *Considering the stress to which the cylinder head bolts are subjected, it is highly recommended that they are all renewed, regardless of their apparent condition.*

### Refitting

**46** Turn the crankshaft and position Nos 1 and 4 pistons at TDC, then turn the crankshaft a quarter turn (90°) anti-clockwise.
**47** Thoroughly clean the surfaces of the cylinder head and block.
**48** Make sure that the locating dowels are in place, then fit the correct gasket the right way round on the cylinder block **(see illustration)**.
**49** If necessary refit the exhaust manifold to

the cylinder head as described in Chapter 4B.
**50** Carefully lower the cylinder head onto the gasket and block, making sure that it locates correctly onto the dowels.
**51** Apply a smear of grease to the threads, and to the underside of the heads, of the cylinder head bolts. Citroën recommend the use of Molykote G Rapid Plus (available from your Citroën dealer); in the absence of the specified grease, any good-quality high melting-point grease may be used.
**52** Carefully insert the cylinder head bolts into their holes (*do not drop them in*) and initially finger-tighten them.
**53** Working progressively and in sequence, tighten the cylinder head bolts to their Stage 1 torque setting, using a torque wrench and suitable socket **(see illustration)**.
**54** Once all the bolts have been tightened to their Stage 1 torque setting, working again in sequence, tighten each bolt to the specified Stage 2 setting. Finally, angle-tighten the bolts through the specified Stage 3 angle. It is recommended that an angle-measuring gauge is used during this stage of tightening, to ensure accuracy. **Note:** *Retightening of the cylinder head bolts after running the engine is not required.*
**55** The remainder of refitting is a reversal of removal, noting the following points.
a) *Refit the hydraulic tappets, rocker arms, and camshaft bearing housing (complete with camshaft(s) as described in Section 9.*
b) *Refit the timing belt as described in Section 7.*

c) *Use a new seal when refitting the coolant outlet housing.*
d) *When refitting a cylinder head, it is good practice to renew the thermostat.*
e) *Refit the camshaft position sensor and set the air gap with reference to Chapter 4B.*
f) *Tighten all fasteners to the specified torque where given.*
g) *Refill the cooling system as described in Chapter 1B.*
h) *The engine may run erratically for the first few miles, until the engine management ECU relearns its stored values.*

## 11 Sump –
removal and refitting

### Removal

**1** Drain the engine oil, then clean and refit the engine oil drain plug, tightening it securely. If the engine is nearing its service interval when the oil and filter are due for renewal, it is recommended that the filter is also removed, and a new one fitted. After reassembly, the engine can then be refilled with fresh oil. Refer to Chapter 1B for further information.
**2** Apply the handbrake, then jack up the front of the vehicle and support it on axle stands (see *Jacking and vehicle support*). Undo the screws and remove the engine undershield.
**3** With reference to Chapter 4B, disconnect the exhaust system intermediate pipe from the catalytic converter. Undo the mounting bolts and lower the system at the front for access to the sump.
**4** Progressively slacken and remove all the sump retaining bolts/nuts. Since the sump bolts vary in length, remove each bolt in turn, and store it in its correct fitted order by pushing it through a clearly-marked cardboard template. This will avoid the possibility of installing the bolts in the wrong locations on refitting.
**5** Try to break the joint by striking the sump with the palm of your hand, then lower and withdraw the sump from under the car. If the sump is stuck (which is quite likely) use a putty knife, or similar, carefully inserted between the sump and block. Ease the knife along the joint

**10.48 Ensure the gasket fits correctly over the locating dowels**

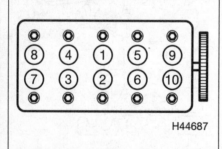

**10.53 Cylinder head bolt tightening sequence**

H44687

**12.4 Undo the three Allen bolts (arrowed) and remove the oil pick-up tube**

**12.5 Undo the 8 bolts (arrowed) and remove the oil pump**

**12.6 Undo the Torx screws and remove the pump cover**

until the sump is released. While the sump is removed, take the opportunity to check the oil pump pick-up/strainer for signs of clogging or splitting. If necessary, remove the pump as described in Section 12, and clean or renew the strainer.

### Refitting

**6** Clean all traces of sealant from the mating surfaces of the cylinder block/crankcase and sump, then use a clean rag to wipe out the sump and the engine's interior.
**7** Ensure that the sump mating surfaces are clean and dry, then apply a thin coating of suitable sealant to the sump mating surface.
**8** Offer up the sump to the cylinder block/crankcase. Refit the retaining bolts/nuts, then tighten the bolts evenly and progressively to the specified torque setting.
**9** Refit the exhaust system with reference to Chapter 4B.
**10** Lower the vehicle to the ground, then refill the engine with oil as described in Chapter 1B.

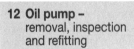

**12 Oil pump –**
removal, inspection and refitting

### Removal

**1** Remove the sump as described in Section 11.
**2** Remove the crankshaft sprocket as described in Section 8. Recover the locating key from the crankshaft.
**3** Disconnect the wiring plug, undo the bolts and remove the crankshaft position sensor,

located on the right-hand end of the cylinder block.
**4** Undo the three Allen bolts and remove the oil pump pick-up tube from the pump/block, complete with the dipstick guide tube **(see illustration)**. Discard the oil seal, a new one must be fitted.
**5** Undo the 8 bolts, and remove the oil pump **(see illustration)**.

### Inspection

**6** Undo and remove the Torx screws securing the cover to the oil pump **(see illustration)**. Examine the pump rotors and body for signs of wear and damage. If worn, the complete pump must be renewed.
**7** Remove the circlip, and extract the cap, valve piston and spring, noting which way around they are fitted **(see illustrations)**. The condition of the relief valve spring can only be measured by comparing it with a new one;

if there is any doubt about its condition, it should also be renewed.
**8** Refit the relief valve piston and spring, then secure them in place with the circlip.
**9** Refit the cover to the oil pump, and tighten the Torx screws securely.
**10** Prime the pump by filling it with clean engine oil before refitting.

### Refitting

**11** Remove all traces of sealant, and thoroughly clean the mating surfaces of the oil pump and cylinder block.
**12** Apply a 4 mm wide bead of silicone sealant to the mating face of the cylinder block **(see illustration)**. Ensure that no sealant enters any of the holes in the block.
**13** With a new oil seal fitted, refit the oil pump over the end of the crankshaft, aligning the flats in the pump drive gear with the flats machined in the crankshaft **(see illustrations)**. Note that

**12.7a Remove the circlip . . .**

**12.7b . . . cap . . .**

**12.7c . . . spring . . .**

**12.7d . . . and piston**

**12.12 Apply a bead of sealant to the cylinder block mating surface**

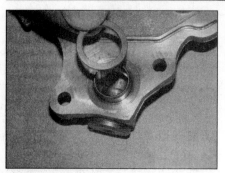

**12.13a Fit a new oil seal . . .**

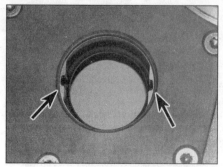

**12.13b . . . align the pump gear flats (arrowed) . . .**

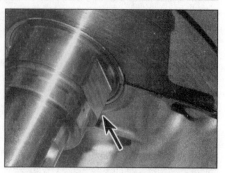

**12.13c . . . with those of the crankshaft (arrowed)**

new oil pumps are supplied with the oil seal already fitted, and a seal protector sleeve. The sleeve fits over the end of the crankshaft to protect the seal as the pump is fitted.

**14** Install the oil pump bolts and tighten them to the specified torque.

**15** Refit the oil pick-up tube to the pump/cylinder block using a new O-ring seal. Ensure the oil dipstick guide tube is correctly refitted.

**16** Refit the Woodruff key to the crankshaft, and slide the crankshaft sprocket into place.

**17** The remainder of refitting is a reversal of removal.

---

### 13 Oil cooler –
removal and refitting

#### *Removal*

**1** Apply the handbrake, then jack up the front

of the vehicle and support it on axle stands (see *Jacking and vehicle support*). Undo the screws and remove the engine undershield.

**2** The oil cooler is fitted to the front of the oil filter housing. Drain the coolant as described in Chapter 1B.

**3** Drain the engine oil as described in Chapter 1B, or be prepared for fluid spillage.

**4** Undo the bolts and remove the oil cooler. Recover the O-ring seals **(see illustrations)**.

#### *Refitting*

**5** Fit new O-ring seals into the recesses in the oil filter housing, and refit the cooler. Tighten the bolts securely.

**6** Refill or top-up the cooling system and engine oil level as described in Chapter 1B or *Weekly checks* (as applicable). Start the engine, and check the oil cooler for signs of leakage.

**13.4a Undo the bolts (arrowed), remove the oil cooler . . .**

**13.4b . . . and recover the O-ring seals**

**14.3 Drill a hole then use a self-tapping screw and pliers to extract the oil seal**

**14.12 The new oil seal comes with a protective sleeve (arrowed) which fits over the end of the crankshaft**

### 14 Oil seals --
renewal

#### *Crankshaft right-hand oil seal*

**1** Remove the crankshaft sprocket as described in Section 8.

**2** Measure and note the fitted depth of the oil seal.

**3** Pull the oil seal from the housing using a hooked instrument. Alternatively, drill a small hole in the oil seal, and use a self-tapping screw and a pair of pliers to remove it **(see illustration)**.

**4** Clean the oil seal housing and the crankshaft sealing surface.

**5** The seal has a Teflon lip and must not be oiled or marked. The new seal should be supplied with a protector sleeve, which fits over the end of the crankshaft to prevent any damage to the seal lip. With the sleeve in place, press the seal (open end first) into the pump to the previously noted depth, using a suitable tube or socket.

**6** Remove the protector sleeve from the end of the crankshaft.

**7** Refit the crankshaft sprocket as described in Section 8.

#### *Crankshaft left-hand oil seal*

**8** Remove the flywheel as described in Section 16.

**9** Measure and note the fitted depth of the oil seal.

**10** Pull the oil seal from the housing using a hooked instrument. Alternatively, drill a small hole in the oil seal, and use a self-tapping screw and a pair of pliers to remove it **(see illustration 14.3)**.

**11** Clean the oil seal housing and the crankshaft sealing surface.

**12** The seal has a Teflon lip and must not be oiled or marked. The new seal should be supplied with a protector sleeve, which fits over the end of the crankshaft to prevent any damage to the seal lip **(see illustration)**. With the sleeve in place, press the seal (open end first) into the housing to the previously noted depth, using a suitable tube or socket.

**13** Remove the protector sleeve from the end of the crankshaft.

**14.19 The new oil seal comes with a protective sleeve (arrowed) which fits over the end of the camshaft**

**15.3 The oil pressure switch is on the front face of the cylinder block**

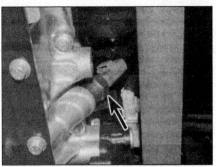

**15.5 Oil level sensor (arrowed)**

**14** Refit the flywheel as described in Section 16.

### Camshaft oil seal

**15** Remove the camshaft sprocket as described in Section 8. In principle there is no need to remove the timing belt completely, but remember that if the belt has been contaminated with oil, it must be renewed.

**16** On 16-valve engines, remove the timing belt upper inner cover as described in Section 6.

**17** Pull the oil seal from the housing using a hooked instrument. Alternatively, drill a small hole in the oil seal and use a self-tapping screw and a pair of pliers to remove it **(see illustration 14.3)**.

**18** Clean the oil seal housing and the camshaft sealing surface.

**19** The seal has a Teflon lip and must not be oiled or marked. The new seal should be supplied with a protector sleeve. which fits over the end of the camshaft to prevent any damage to the seal lip **(see illustration)**. With the sleeve in place, press the seal (open end first) into the housing to the previously noted depth, using a suitable tube or socket which bears only of the outer edge of the seal.

**20** On 16-valve engines, refit the timing belt upper inner cover as described in Section 6.

**21** Refit the camshaft sprocket as described in Section 8.

**22** Where necessary, fit a new timing belt with reference to Section 7.

### 15 Oil pressure switch and level sensor – removal and refitting

## Removal

### Oil pressure switch

**1** The oil pressure switch is located at the front of the cylinder block, adjacent to the oil dipstick guide tube. Note that on some models, access to the switch may be improved if the vehicle is jacked up and supported on axle stands (see *Jacking and vehicle support*), then undo the screws and remove the engine undershield so that the switch can be reached from underneath.

**2** Remove the protective sleeve from the

wiring plug (where applicable), then disconnect the wiring from the switch.

**3** Unscrew the switch from the cylinder block, and recover the sealing washer **(see illustration)**. Be prepared for oil spillage, and if the switch is to be left removed from the engine for any length of time, plug the hole in the cylinder block.

### Oil level sensor

**4** The oil level sensor is located at the rear of the cylinder block. Jack up the front of the vehicle and support it securely on axle stands (see *Jacking and vehicle support*). Undo the screws and remove the engine undershield.

**5** Reach up between the driveshaft and the cylinder block and disconnect the sensor wiring plug **(see illustration)**.

**6** Using an open-ended spanner, unscrew the sensor and withdraw it from position.

## Refitting

### Oil pressure switch

**7** Examine the sealing washer for any signs of damage or deterioration, and if necessary renew.

**8** Refit the switch, complete with washer, and tighten it securely.

**9** Refit the engine undershield, and lower the vehicle to the ground.

### Oil level sensor

**10** Smear a little silicone sealant on the threads and refit the sensor to the cylinder block, tightening it securely.

**11** Reconnect the sensor wiring plug.

**12** Refit the engine undershield, and lower the vehicle to the ground.

**16.6 If the new bolts are not supplied with their threads precoated, apply thread-locking compound to them . . .**

### 16 Flywheel – removal, inspection and refitting

## Removal

**1** Remove the transmission as described in Chapter 7A, then remove the clutch assembly as described in Chapter 6.

**2** Prevent the flywheel from turning by inserting a 12 mm diameter rod or drill bit through the hole in the flywheel cover casting, and into a slot in the flywheel **(see illustrations 5.3a and 5.3b)**.

**3** Make alignment marks between the flywheel and crankshaft to aid refitment. Slacken and remove the flywheel retaining bolts, and remove the flywheel from the end of the crankshaft. Be careful not to drop it; it is heavy. Discard the flywheel bolts; new ones must be used on refitting.

## Inspection

**4** Examine the flywheel for scoring of the clutch face, and for wear or chipping of the ring gear teeth. If the clutch face is scored, the flywheel may be surface-ground, but renewal is preferable. Seek the advice of a Citroën dealer or engine reconditioning specialist to see if machining is possible. If the ring gear is worn or damaged, it can be renewed separately, but this work must be entrusted to an engine reconditioning specialist.

## Refitting

**5** Clean the mating surfaces of the flywheel and crankshaft. Remove any remaining locking compound from the threads of the crankshaft holes, using the correct size of tap, if available.

> **HAYNES HINT** *If a suitable tap is not available, cut two slots along the threads of one of the old flywheel bolts, and use the bolt to remove the locking compound from the threads.*

**6** If the new flywheel retaining bolts are not supplied with their threads already precoated, apply a suitable thread-locking compound to the threads of each bolt **(see illustration)**.

**7** Offer up the flywheel, aligning the previously made marks if the original flywheel is being refitted, and fit the new retaining bolts.

**8** Lock the flywheel using the method employed on dismantling, and tighten the retaining bolts to the specified torque.

**9** Refit the clutch as described in Chapter 6. Remove the flywheel locking tool, and refit the transmission as described in Chapter 7A.

### 17 Engine/transmission mountings – inspection and renewal

### *Inspection*

**1** If improved access is required, raise the front of the car and support it on axle stands (see *Jacking and vehicle support*). Undo the screws and remove the engine undershield.

**2** Check the mounting rubber to see if it is cracked, hardened or separated from the metal at any point; renew the mounting if any such damage or deterioration is evident.

**3** Check that all the mounting's fasteners are securely tightened; use a torque wrench to check if possible.

**4** Using a large screwdriver or a crowbar, check for wear in the mounting by carefully levering against it to check for free play. Where this is not possible, enlist the aid of an assistant to move the engine/transmission back-and-forth, or from side-to-side, while you watch the mounting. While some free play is to be expected even from new components, excessive wear should be obvious. If

excessive free play is found, check first that the fasteners are secure, then renew any worn components as described below.

### *Renewal*

#### Right-hand mounting

**5** Place a jack beneath the engine, with a block of wood on the jack head. Raise the jack until it is supporting the weight of the engine.

**6** Slacken and remove the three bolts securing the mounting bracket to the bracket bolted to the cylinder head, and the two bolts securing the mounting to the body. Remove the mounting assembly from the car and recover the reinforcing plate **(see illustrations)**.

**7** If required, undo the three bolts and remove the bracket from the cylinder head.

**8** Check for signs of wear or damage on all components, and renew as necessary.

**9** On reassembly, refit the bracket to the cylinder head, tightening the bolts to the specified torque.

**10** Install the mounting and mounting bracket and tighten its retaining bolts to the specified torque setting.

**11** Remove the jack from under the engine.

#### Left-hand mounting

**12** Remove the battery, and battery tray/box as described in Chapter 5A.

**13** Place a jack beneath the transmission, with a block of wood on the jack head. Raise the jack until it is supporting the weight of the transmission.

**14** Slacken and remove the two bolts securing the mounting arm to the bracket on

the transmission **(see illustration)**. Undo the four bolts securing the mounting to the body and remove the complete mounting assembly from the engine compartment.

**15** If necessary, undo the retaining bolts and remove the mounting bracket from the transmission.

**16** Check carefully for signs of wear or damage on all components, and renew them where necessary.

**17** Refit the mounting assembly to the vehicle body and tighten its bolts to the specified torque.

**18** Locate the mounting arm over the transmission bracket and tighten its retaining bolts to the specified torque.

**19** Remove the jack from underneath the transmission, then refit the battery tray/box and battery as described in Chapter 5A.

#### Rear mounting

**20** If not already done, firmly apply the handbrake, then jack up the front of the vehicle and support it securely on axle stands (see *Jacking and vehicle support*).

**21** Unscrew and remove the two through-bolts securing the rear mounting connecting link to the subframe and transmission bracket **(see illustration)**.

**22** Manoeuvre the connecting link from its location and remove it from under the car.

**23** Check carefully for signs of wear or damage on all components, and renew them where necessary.

**24** Refit the rear mounting connecting link, and tighten both its bolts to their specified torque settings.

**25** Lower the vehicle to the ground.

**17.6a Undo the bolts (arrowed) securing the right-hand mounting bracket to the cylinder head bracket**

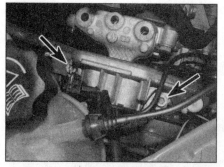

**17.6b . . . and the bolts (arrowed) securing the mounting to the body**

**17.6c Remove the mounting assembly . . .**

**17.6d . . . and recover the reinforcing plate**

**17.14 Left-hand engine mounting retaining bolts (arrowed)**

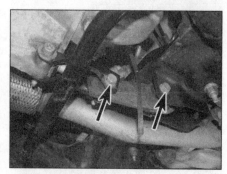

**17.21 Rear engine mounting connecting link through-bolts (arrowed)**

# Chapter 2 Part C:
# 1.6 litre diesel engine (DV6 series) in-car repair procedures

## Contents

## Degrees of difficulty

| **Easy,** suitable for novice with little experience | **Fairly easy,** suitable for beginner with some experience | **Fairly difficult,** suitable for competent DIY mechanic | **Difficult,** suitable for experienced DIY mechanic | **Very difficult,** suitable for expert DIY or professional |
|---|---|---|---|---|

## Specifications

### General

| | |
|---|---|
| Designation: | |
| Engine without intercooler | DV6TED4 |
| Engine with intercooler | DV6ATED4 |
| Engine codes*: | |
| DV6TED4: | |
| Without intercooler or particulate filter | 9HY |
| Without intercooler, but with particulate filter | 9HZ |
| DV6ATED4 (with intercooler) | 9HX |
| Capacity | 1560 cc |
| Bore | 75.0 mm |
| Stroke | 88.3 mm |
| Direction of crankshaft rotation | Clockwise (viewed from the right-hand side of vehicle) |
| No 1 cylinder location | At the transmission end of block |
| Maximum power output: | |
| DV6TED4: | |
| 9HY | 80 kW @ 4000 rpm |
| 9HZ | 80 kW @ 4000 rpm |
| DV6ATED4 (9HX) | 66 kW @ 4000 rpm |
| Maximum torque output: | |
| DV6TED4: | |
| 9HY | 240 Nm @ 1750 rpm |
| 9HZ | 240 Nm @ 1750 rpm |
| DV6ATED4 (9HX) | 215 Nm @ 1750 rpm |
| Compression ratio | 18.0 :1 |

*The engine code is stamped on a plate attached to the front of the cylinder block, next to the oil filter*

### Compression pressures (engine hot, at cranking speed)

| | |
|---|---|
| Normal | 20 ± 5 bar |
| Minimum | 15 bar |
| Maximum difference between any two cylinders | 5 bar |

## Camshaft

Drive:
  Inlet camshaft . . . . . . . . . . . . . . . . . . . . . . . . . . . . . . . . . . . . . . . . . . . . .   Toothed belt from crankshaft
  Exhaust camshaft . . . . . . . . . . . . . . . . . . . . . . . . . . . . . . . . . . . . . . . . . .   Chain-driven from inlet camshaft
Number of teeth . . . . . . . . . . . . . . . . . . . . . . . . . . . . . . . . . . . . . . . . . . . . .   19
Length:
  Inlet camshaft . . . . . . . . . . . . . . . . . . . . . . . . . . . . . . . . . . . . . . . . . . . . .   401.0 ± 0.15 mm
  Exhaust camshaft . . . . . . . . . . . . . . . . . . . . . . . . . . . . . . . . . . . . . . . . . .   389.0 ± 0.5 mm
Endfloat . . . . . . . . . . . . . . . . . . . . . . . . . . . . . . . . . . . . . . . . . . . . . . . . . . .   0.195 to 0.300 mm

## Lubrication system

Oil pump type . . . . . . . . . . . . . . . . . . . . . . . . . . . . . . . . . . . . . . . . . . . . . . .   Gear-type, driven directly by the right-hand end of the crankshaft, by two flats machined along the crankshaft journal

Minimum oil pressure at 80°C:
  1000 rpm . . . . . . . . . . . . . . . . . . . . . . . . . . . . . . . . . . . . . . . . . . . . . . . .   1.3 bar
  4000 rpm . . . . . . . . . . . . . . . . . . . . . . . . . . . . . . . . . . . . . . . . . . . . . . . .   3.5 bar

## Torque wrench settings

| | Nm | lbf ft |
|---|---|---|
| Ancillary drivebelt tensioner roller | 20 | 15 |
| Big-end bolts*: | | |
|   Stage 1 | 5 | 4 |
|   Stage 2 | 10 | 7 |
|   Stage 3 | Angle-tighten a further 130° | |
| Camshaft bearing caps | 10 | 7 |
| Camshaft cover/bearing ladder: | | |
|   Studs | 10 | 7 |
|   Bolts | 10 | 7 |
| Camshaft position sensor bolt | 5 | 4 |
| Camshaft sprocket: | | |
|   Stage 1 | 20 | 15 |
|   Stage 2 | Angle-tighten a further 50° | |
| Coolant outlet housing bolts | 7 | 5 |
| Crankshaft position/speed sensor bolt | 5 | 4 |
| Crankshaft pulley/sprocket bolt*: | | |
|   Stage 1 | 35 | 26 |
|   Stage 2 | Angle-tighten a further 190 ° | |
| Cylinder head bolts: | | |
|   Stage 1 | 20 | 15 |
|   Stage 2 | 40 | 30 |
|   Stage 3 | Angle-tighten a further 260° | |
| Cylinder head cover/manifold | 13 | 10 |
| EGR valve | 10 | 7 |
| Engine-to-transmission fixing bolts | 40 | 30 |
| Engine/transmission rear mounting: | | |
|   Connecting link-to-subframe nut/bolt | 60 | 44 |
|   Mounting/driveshaft intermediate bearing housing to cylinder block | 54 | 40 |
|   Mounting centre bolt | 60 | 44 |
| Flywheel bolt*: | | |
|   Dual mass flywheel: | | |
|     Stage 1 | 25 | 18 |
|     Stage 2 | Fully slacken | |
|     Stage 3 | 8 | 6 |
|     Stage 4 | 30 | 22 |
|     Stage 5 | Angle-tighten a further 90° | |
|   Normal flywheel: | | |
|     Stage 1 | 25 | 18 |
|     Stage 2 | Fully slacken | |
|     Stage 3 | 8 | 6 |
|     Stage 4 | 17 | 13 |
|     Stage 5 | Angle-tighten a further 75° | |
| Fuel pump sprocket | 50 | 37 |
| Left-hand engine/transmission mounting: | | |
|   Mounting bracket to transmission | 54 | 40 |
|   Mounting to body | 55 | 41 |
|   Mounting to transmission bracket | 60 | 44 |
| Main bearing ladder outer seam bolts: | | |
|   Stage 1 | 6 | 4 |
|   Stage 2 | 8 | 6 |

## Torque wrench settings (continued)

| | Nm | lbf ft |
| --- | --- | --- |
| Main bearing ladder to cylinder block: | | |
| Stage 1 . . . . . . . . . . . . . . . . . . . . . . . . . . . . . . . . . . . . . . . . . . . . . | 10 | 7 |
| Stage 2 . . . . . . . . . . . . . . . . . . . . . . . . . . . . . . . . . . . . . . . . . . . . . | Slacken 180° | |
| Stage 3 . . . . . . . . . . . . . . . . . . . . . . . . . . . . . . . . . . . . . . . . . . . . . | 30 | 22 |
| Stage 4 . . . . . . . . . . . . . . . . . . . . . . . . . . . . . . . . . . . . . . . . . . . . . | Angle-tighten a further 140° | |
| Piston oil jet spray tube bolt . . . . . . . . . . . . . . . . . . . . . . . . . . . . . | 20 | 15 |
| Oil filter cover . . . . . . . . . . . . . . . . . . . . . . . . . . . . . . . . . . . . . . . . | 25 | 18 |
| Oil pick-up pipe . . . . . . . . . . . . . . . . . . . . . . . . . . . . . . . . . . . . . . . | 10 | 7 |
| Oil pressure switch . . . . . . . . . . . . . . . . . . . . . . . . . . . . . . . . . . . . . | 32 | 24 |
| Oil pump to cylinder block: | | |
| Stage 1 . . . . . . . . . . . . . . . . . . . . . . . . . . . . . . . . . . . . . . . . . . . . . | 5 | 4 |
| Stage 2 . . . . . . . . . . . . . . . . . . . . . . . . . . . . . . . . . . . . . . . . . . . . . | 9 | 7 |
| Right-hand engine mounting: | | |
| Mounting-to-body bolts . . . . . . . . . . . . . . . . . . . . . . . . . . . . . . . . | 60 | 44 |
| Mounting to bracket on engine . . . . . . . . . . . . . . . . . . . . . . . . . . | 60 | 44 |
| Bracket to engine . . . . . . . . . . . . . . . . . . . . . . . . . . . . . . . . . . . . | 55 | 41 |
| Sump drain plug . . . . . . . . . . . . . . . . . . . . . . . . . . . . . . . . . . . . . . | 25 | 18 |
| Sump bolts/nuts . . . . . . . . . . . . . . . . . . . . . . . . . . . . . . . . . . . . . . | 12 | 9 |
| Timing belt idler pulley . . . . . . . . . . . . . . . . . . . . . . . . . . . . . . . . . | 37 | 27 |
| Timing belt tensioner pulley . . . . . . . . . . . . . . . . . . . . . . . . . . . . . | 23 | 17 |
| Timing chain tensioner . . . . . . . . . . . . . . . . . . . . . . . . . . . . . . . . . | 10 | 7 |
| Vacuum pump: | | |
| Stage 1 . . . . . . . . . . . . . . . . . . . . . . . . . . . . . . . . . . . . . . . . . . . . . | 3 | 2 |
| Stage 2 . . . . . . . . . . . . . . . . . . . . . . . . . . . . . . . . . . . . . . . . . . . . . | 5 | 4 |
| Stage 3 . . . . . . . . . . . . . . . . . . . . . . . . . . . . . . . . . . . . . . . . . . . . . | 20 | 15 |

*Do not re-use*

## 1  General information

### How to use this Chapter

This Part of Chapter 2 describes the repair procedures that can reasonably be carried out on the engine whilst it remains in the vehicle. If the engine has been removed from the vehicle and is being dismantled as described in Part D, any preliminary dismantling procedures can be ignored.

Note that, while it may be possible physically to overhaul items such as the piston/connecting rod assemblies while the engine is in the car, such tasks are not usually carried out as separate operations. Usually, several additional procedures are required (not to mention the cleaning of components and oilways); for this reason, all such tasks are classed as major overhaul procedures, and are described in Part D of this Chapter.

Part D describes the removal of the engine/transmission from the car, and the full overhaul procedures that can then be carried out.

### Engine description

The 1.6 litre DV6 series engine is the result of development collaboration between Citroën, Peugeot and Ford. The engine is of double overhead camshaft (DOHC) 16-valve design. The direct injection, turbocharged, four-cylinder engine is mounted transversely, with the transmission mounted on the left-hand side.

A toothed timing belt drives the inlet camshaft, high-pressure fuel pump and coolant pump. The inlet camshaft drives the exhaust camshaft via a chain. The camshafts operate the inlet and exhaust valves via rocker arms which are supported at their pivot ends by hydraulic self-adjusting tappets. The camshafts are supported by bearings machined directly in the cylinder head and camshaft bearing housing.

The high-pressure fuel pump supplies fuel to the fuel rail, and subsequently to the electronically-controlled injectors which inject the fuel direct into the combustion chambers. This design differs from the previous type where an injection pump supplies the fuel at high-pressure to each injector. The earlier conventional type injection pump required fine calibration and timing, and these functions are now completed by the high-pressure pump, electronic injectors and engine management ECU.

The crankshaft runs in five main bearings of the usual shell type. Endfloat is controlled by thrustwashers either side of No 2 main bearing.

The pistons are selected to be of matching weight, and incorporate fully-floating gudgeon pins retained by circlips.

### Repair operations precaution

The engine is a complex unit with numerous accessories and ancillary components. The design of the engine compartment is such that every conceivable space has been utilised, and access to virtually all of the engine components is extremely limited. In many cases, ancillary components will have to be removed, or moved to one side, and wiring, pipes and hoses will have to be disconnected or removed from various cable clips and support brackets.

When working on this engine, read through the entire procedure first, look at the car and engine at the same time, and establish whether you have the necessary tools, equipment, skill and patience to proceed. Allow considerable time for any operation, and be prepared for the unexpected.

Because of the limited access, many of the engine photographs appearing in this Chapter were, by necessity, taken with the engine removed from the vehicle.

⚠ **Warning: It is essential to observe strict precautions when working on the fuel system components of the engine, particularly the high-pressure side of the system. Before carrying out any engine operations that entail working on, or near, any part of the fuel system, refer to the special information given in Chapter 4B.**

### Operations with engine in vehicle

a) Compression pressure – testing.
b) Cylinder head cover – removal and refitting.
c) Crankshaft pulley – removal and refitting.
d) Timing belt covers – removal and refitting.
e) Timing belt – removal, refitting and adjustment.
f) Timing belt tensioner and sprockets – removal and refitting.
g) Camshaft oil seal – renewal.
h) Camshaft, rocker arms and hydraulic tappets – removal, inspection and refitting.
i) Sump – removal and refitting.
j) Oil pump – removal and refitting.
k) Crankshaft oil seals – renewal.
l) Engine/transmission mountings – inspection and renewal.
m) Flywheel – removal, inspection and refitting.

## 2  Compression and leakdown tests – description and interpretation

### Compression test

**1** When engine performance is down, or if misfiring occurs which cannot be attributed to the fuel system, a compression test can provide diagnostic clues as to the engine's condition. If the test is performed regularly, it can give warning of trouble before any other symptoms become apparent.

**2** A compression tester specifically intended for diesel engines must be used, because of the higher pressures involved. The tester is connected to an adapter which screws into the glow plug hole. On this engine, an adapter suitable for use in the glow plug holes will be required, so as not to disturb the fuel system components. It is unlikely to be worthwhile buying such a tester for occasional use, but it may be possible to borrow or hire one – if not, have the test performed by a garage.

**3** Unless specific instructions to the contrary are supplied with the tester, observe the following points:

a) *The battery must be in a good state of charge, the air filter must be clean, and the engine should be at normal operating temperature.*

b) *All the glow plugs should be removed as described in Chapter 5C before starting the test.*

c) *The wiring connectors on the engine management system ECU (located on the engine side of the battery) must be disconnected.*

**4** The compression pressures measured are not so important as the balance between cylinders. Values are given in the Specifications.

**5** The cause of poor compression is less easy to establish on a diesel engine than on a petrol one. The effect of introducing oil into the cylinders ('wet' testing) is not conclusive, because there is a risk that the oil will sit in the swirl chamber or in the recess on the piston crown instead of passing to the rings. However, the following can be used as a rough guide to diagnosis.

**6** All cylinders should produce very similar pressures; any difference greater than that specified indicates the existence of a fault. Note that the compression should build-up quickly in a healthy engine; low compression on the first stroke, followed by gradually-increasing pressure on successive strokes, indicates worn piston rings. A low compression reading on the first stroke, which does not build-up during successive strokes, indicates leaking valves or a blown head gasket (a cracked head could also be the cause). Deposits on the undersides of the valve heads can also cause low compression.

**7** A low reading from two adjacent cylinders is almost certainly due to the head gasket having blown between them; the presence of coolant in the engine oil will confirm this.

**8** If the compression reading is unusually high, the cylinder head surfaces, valves and pistons are probably coated with carbon deposits. If this is the case, the cylinder head should be removed and decarbonised (see Part D).

### Leakdown test

**9** A leakdown test measures the rate at which compressed air fed into the cylinder is lost. It is an alternative to a compression test, and in many ways it is better, since the escaping air provides easy identification of where pressure loss is occurring (piston rings, valves or head gasket).

**10** The equipment needed for leakdown testing is unlikely to be available to the home mechanic. If poor compression is suspected, have the test performed by a suitably-equipped garage.

## 3  Engine assembly/ valve timing holes – general information and usage

**Note:** *Do not attempt to rotate the engine whilst the crankshaft and camshaft are locked in position. If the engine is to be left in this state for a long period of time, it is a good idea to place suitable warning notices inside the vehicle, and in the engine compartment. This will reduce the possibility of the engine being accidentally cranked on the starter motor, which is likely to cause damage with the locking pins in place.*

**1** Timing holes or slots are located only in the crankshaft pulley flange and camshaft sprocket hub. The holes/slots are used to position the pistons halfway up the cylinder bores. This will ensure that the valve timing is maintained during operations that require removal and refitting of the timing belt. When the holes/slots are aligned with their corresponding holes in the cylinder block and cylinder head, suitable diameter boltseuins can be inserted to lock the crankshaft and camshaft in position, preventing rotation.

**2** Note that the HDi type fuel system used on these engines does not have a conventional

**3.9  Insert a 5.0 mm drill bit/bolt through the round hole in the sprocket flange, into the hole in the oil pump housing (lower timing belt cover removed for clarity)**

diesel injection pump, but instead uses a high-pressure fuel pump. Although it may be argued that timing of the fuel pump is irrelevant because it merely pressurises the fuel in the fuel rail, Citroën include this procedure for engines fitted with a Bosch high-pressure fuel pump, using the same timing rod/pin used for crankshaft sprocket timing. **Note:** *On the Bosch pump, the drive sprocket is keyed to the shaft. In addition, note that the hole in the fuel pump sprocket only aligns correctly with the hole in the mounting bracket every 12 revolutions of the crankshaft (or every 6 revolutions of the camshaft sprocket).*

**3** To align the engine assembly/valve timing holes, proceed as follows.

**4** Apply the handbrake then jack up the front of the vehicle and support it on axle stands (see *Jacking and vehicle support*). Remove the right-hand front roadwheel.

**5** To gain access to the crankshaft pulley, to enable the engine to be turned, the front right-hand wheel arch plastic liner must be removed. The liner is secured by several plastic expanding rivets/nut/screws. To remove the rivets, push in the centre pins a little, then prise the clips from place. Remove the liner from under the front wing. The crankshaft can then be turned using a suitable socket and extension bar fitted to the pulley bolt.

**6** Remove the upper and lower timing belt covers as described in Section 6.

**7** Temporarily refit the crankshaft pulley bolt, remove the crankshaft locking tool, then turn the crankshaft until the timing hole in the camshaft sprocket hub is aligned with the corresponding hole in the cylinder head. Note that the crankshaft must always be turned in a clockwise direction (viewed from the right-hand side of vehicle). Use a small mirror so that the position of the sprocket hub timing slot can be observed. When the slot is aligned with the corresponding hole in the cylinder head, the camshaft is positioned correctly.

**8** Remove the crankshaft drivebelt pulley as described in Section 5.

**9** Insert a 5 mm diameter bolt, rod or drill through the hole in crankshaft sprocket flange and into the corresponding hole in the oil pump **(see illustration)**, if necessary, carefully turn the crankshaft either way until the rod enters the timing hole in the block.

**10** Insert an 8 mm bolt, rod or drill through the hole in the camshaft sprocket hub and into engagement with the cylinder head. Note that a modified 3-segment camshaft sprocket is fitted to later models **(see illustrations)**.

**11** If using this procedure during refitting of the timing belt, insert a 5 mm diameter bolt, rod or drill through the hole in the fuel pump sprocket and into the corresponding hole in the cylinder head **(see illustration)**. **Note:** *On some engines, a hole is provided at the 5 o'clock position for locking purposes only, however, the timing hole is at the 12 o'clock position. Note the comment in paragraph 2 – if*

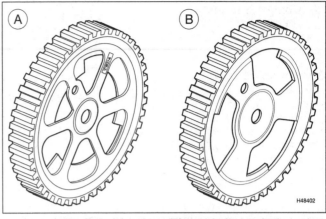

3.10a  Insert an 8.0 mm drill bit/bolt through the hole in the camshaft sprocket into the corresponding hole in the cylinder head

3.10b  Early (A) and late (B) camshaft sprocket

the fuel pump sprocket holes are not aligned during removal of the timing belt, it is of no consequence, however, it is important to align the holes during the refitting procedure. If timing alignment alone is being *checked* there is no need to check alignment of the pump sprocket.

**12** The crankshaft and camshaft are now locked in position, preventing unnecessary rotation.

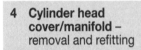

## 4  Cylinder head cover/manifold – removal and refitting

### Removal

**1** Pull the plastic cover upwards from the top of the engine.

**2** Disconnect the mass airflow meter wiring plug **(see illustration)**.

**3** Remove the inlet and outlet air ducting from the air filter housing **(see illustrations)**.

**4** Unscrew the air filter housing cover bolts, then remove the cover and filter element – refer to Chapter 4B **(see illustrations)**. Pull the air filter housing from its mountings.

**5** Disconnect the wiring plugs from the top of each injector, undo the guide bolts, then make sure all wiring harnesses are freed from any retaining brackets on the cylinder head cover/

3.11  Insert a 5.0 mm drill bit/bolt through the round hole in the fuel pump sprocket into the cylinder head

4.3a  Undo the screw (arrowed) and remove the inlet ducting

4.4a  ... then undo the cover screws (arrowed) ...

4.2  Release the clip (arrowed) and disconnect the mass airflow meter wiring plug

4.3b  Disconnect the hose to the turbocharger ...

4.4b  ... and remove the ducting/cover assembly

4.3c  ... release the clips (arrowed) and disconnect the breather hose ...

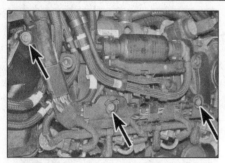

4.5 Undo the Allen screws (arrowed) and position the wiring harness/guide to one side

4.7a Depress the release buttons (arrowed) and disconnect the fuel feed and return hoses

4.7b Disconnect the fuel temperature sensor wiring plug (arrowed) . . .

4.7c . . . then unclip the fuel priming bulb/pipes (arrowed)

4.8a Slacken the left-hand turbocharger outlet hose bolt, undo the right-hand bolt (arrowed) . . .

4.8b . . . then slacken the hose clamps (arrowed), disconnect the wiring plugs . . .

inlet manifold (see illustration). Disconnect any vacuum pipes as necessary, having first noted their fitted positions.

6 Remove the EGR cooler as described in Chapter 4C.

7 Release and disconnect the fuel feed and return hoses at the right-hand end of the cylinder head, then disconnect the fuel temperature sensor wiring plug, and move the pipe/priming bulb assembly to the rear (see illustrations).

8 Release the clamps, undo the bolts and remove the inlet ducting between the turbocharger and the inlet manifold. Make a note of their fitted positions, then disconnect the various wiring plugs as the assembly is withdrawn (see illustrations).

9 Undo the retaining bolts and remove the oil separator from the top of the cylinder head (see illustration). Recover the rubber seal.

10 Prise out the retaining clips and disconnect the fuel return pipes from the injectors, then undo the unions and remove the high-pressure fuel pipes from the injectors and the common fuel rail at the rear of the cylinder head – counterhold the unions with a second spanner (see illustrations). Plug the openings to prevent dirt ingress.

11 Undo the 2 bolts securing the cylinder head cover/inlet manifold. Lift the assembly away (see illustration). Recover the manifold rubber seals.

4.8c . . . undo the bolt on the end (arrowed) . . .

4.8d . . . and the 2 at the front (arrowed), then remove the assembly

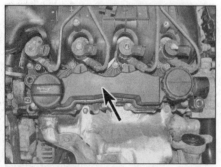

4.9 Undo the bolts and remove the oil separator (arrowed)

4.10a Prise out the clip and pull the return hose from the top of each injector

4.10b Use a second spanner to hold the injector port whilst slackening the fuel pipe unions

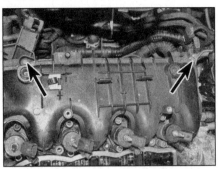

**4.11 Undo the 2 remaining bolts (arrowed) and pull the cover/manifold upwards**

## Refitting

**12** Refitting is a reversal of removal, bearing in mind the following points:

a) *Examine the seals for signs of damage and deterioration, and renew if necessary. Smear a little clean engine oil on the manifold seals.*

b) *Renew the fuel injector high-pressure pipes – see Chapter 4B.*

---

### 5  Crankshaft pulley – removal and refitting

## Removal

**1** Remove the auxiliary drivebelt as described in Chapter 1B.

**2** To lock the crankshaft, working underneath the engine, insert Citroën tool No 0194-C into the hole in the right-hand face of the engine block casting over the lower section of the flywheel. Rotate the crankshaft until the tool engages in the corresponding hole in the flywheel. In the absence of the Citroën tool, insert a 12 mm rod or drill into the hole (**see illustration**). Note: *The hole in the casting and the hole in the flywheel are provided purely to lock the crankshaft whilst the pulley bolt is undone, it does not position the crankshaft at TDC.*

**3** Using a suitable socket and extension bar, unscrew the retaining bolt, remove the washer, then slide the pulley off the end of the crankshaft (**see illustration**). If the pulley is tight fit, it can be drawn off the crankshaft using a suitable puller. If a puller is being used, refit the pulley retaining bolt without the washer to avoid damaging the crankshaft as the puller is tightened.

*Caution: Do not touch the outer magnetic sensor ring of the sprocket with your fingers, or allow metallic particles to come into contact with it.*

## Refitting

**4** Refit the pulley to the end of the crankshaft.

**5** Thoroughly clean the threads of the pulley retaining bolt, then apply a coat of locking compound to the bolt threads. Citroën recommend the use of Loctite (available from

**5.2 The locking pin/bolt (arrowed) must locate in the hole in the flywheel (arrowed) to prevent rotation**

your Citroën dealer); in the absence of this, any good-quality locking compound may be used.

**6** Refit the crankshaft pulley retaining bolt and washer. Tighten the bolt to the specified torque, then through the specified angle, preventing the crankshaft from turning using the method employed on removal.

**7** Refit and tension the auxiliary drivebelt as described in Chapter 1B.

---

### 6  Timing belt covers – removal and refitting

## Removal

### Upper cover

**1** Remove the plastic cover from the top of the engine.

**6.2a Unclip the fuel pipes (arrowed) . . .**

**6.3 Upper timing belt cover screws (arrowed)**

**5.3 Undo the crankshaft pulley retaining bolt (arrowed)**

**2** Release the wiring harness and fuel pipes from the upper cover (**see illustrations**).

**3** Undo the five screws and remove the timing belt upper cover (**see illustration**).

### Lower cover

**4** Remove the upper cover as described previously.

**5** Remove the crankshaft pulley as described in Section 5.

**6** Remove the auxiliary drivebelt tensioner locking tool (where applicable), then undo the five bolts and remove the lower cover (**see illustration**).

## Refitting

**7** Refitting of all the covers is a reversal of the relevant removal procedure, ensuring that each cover section is correctly located, and that the cover retaining bolts are securely tightened. Ensure that all disturbed hoses are reconnected and retained by their relevant clips.

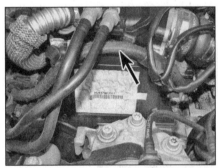

**6.2b . . . and the wiring harness (arrowed) from the timing belt upper cover**

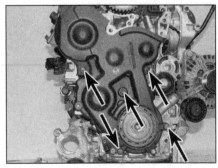

**6.6 Lower timing belt cover screws (arrowed)**

**7.10 Undo the bolt (arrowed) and remove the crankshaft position sensor**

**7.11 Remove the timing belt protection bracket**

**7.13 Slacken the bolt and allow the tensioner to rotate, relieving the tension on the belt**

**7   Timing belt –**
removal, inspection, refitting and tensioning

### General

**1** The timing belt drives the inlet camshaft, high-pressure fuel pump, and coolant pump from a toothed sprocket on the end of the crankshaft. If the belt breaks or slips in service, the pistons are likely to hit the valve heads, resulting in expensive damage.

**2** The timing belt should be renewed at the specified intervals, or earlier if it is contaminated with oil or at all noisy in operation (a 'scraping' noise due to uneven wear).

**3** If the timing belt is being removed, it is a wise precaution to check the condition of the coolant pump at the same time (check for signs of coolant leakage). This may avoid the need to remove the timing belt again at a later stage should the coolant pump fail.

### Removal

**4** Apply the handbrake then jack up the front of the vehicle and support it on axle stands (see *Jacking and vehicle support*). Remove the front right-hand roadwheel, wheel arch liner (to expose the crankshaft pulley), and the engine undershield. The wheel arch liner is secured by several plastic expanding rivets/nuts/plastic clips. Push the centre pins in a little then prise the rivets from place. The engine undershield is retained by several screws.

**5** Remove the auxiliary drivebelt as described in Chapter 1B.

**6** Remove the upper and lower timing belt covers, as described in Section 6.

**7** Refer to Chapter 4B and disconnect the front exhaust pipe at the flexible section.

**8** Position a trolley jack under the engine, and using a block of wood on the jack head, take the weight of the engine.

**9** Undo the bolts/nut and remove the right-hand engine mounting and support bracket – see Section 17.

**10** Undo the screw and remove the crankshaft position sensor adjacent to the crankshaft sprocket flange, and move it to one side **(see illustration)**.

**11** Undo the retaining screw and remove the timing belt protection bracket, again adjacent to the crankshaft sprocket flange **(see illustration)**.

**12** Lock the crankshaft and camshaft in the correct position as described in Section 3. If necessary, temporarily refit the crankshaft pulley bolt to enable the crankshaft to be rotated. At this stage, it is of no consequence that the fuel pump sprocket aligns correctly with the hole in the pump mounting bracket.

**13** Insert a hexagon key into the belt tensioner pulley centre, slacken the pulley bolt, and allow the tensioner to rotate, relieving the belt tension **(see illustration)**. With the belt slack, temporarily tighten the pulley bolt.

**14** Note its routing, then remove the timing belt from the sprockets.

### Inspection

**15** Renew the belt as a matter of course,

regardless of its apparent condition. The cost of a new belt is nothing compared with the cost of repairs should the belt break in service. If signs of oil contamination are found, trace the source of the oil leak and rectify it. Wash down the engine timing belt area and all related components, to remove all traces of oil. Check that the tensioner and idler pulleys rotate freely without any sign of roughness, and also check that the coolant pump pulley rotates freely. If necessary, renew these items.

### Refitting and tensioning

**16** Commence refitting by ensuring that the crankshaft and camshaft timing pins are still in position correctly. Also, where a Bosch high-pressure fuel pump is fitted, locate and lock the fuel pump sprocket in its correct position as described in Section 3.

**17** Locate the timing belt on the crankshaft sprocket, then keeping it taut, locate it around the idler pulley, camshaft sprocket, high-pressure pump sprocket, coolant pump sprocket, and the tensioner pulley **(see illustration)**. If the timing belt has directional arrows on it, make sure that they point in the direction of normal engine rotation.

**18** Refit the timing belt protection bracket and tighten the retaining bolt securely.

**19** Slacken the tensioner pulley bolt, and using a hexagonal key, rotate the tensioner anti-clockwise, which moves the index arm clockwise, until the index arm is aligned as shown **(see illustration)**.

**20** Remove the camshaft and crankshaft and fuel pump timing pins and, using a socket on the crankshaft pulley bolt, crankshaft clockwise 10 complete revolutions. Align the camshaft and crankshaft timing holes and check that the timing pins can be inserted, then remove them. There is no requirement to check the fuel pump sprocket alignment, as it will only be aligned after 12 complete revolutions.

**21** Check that the tensioner index arm is still aligned between the edges of the area shown **(see illustration 7.19)**. If it is not, remove and belt and begin the refitting process again, starting at Paragraph 19.

**22** The remainder of refitting is a reversal of removal. Tighten all fasteners to the specified torque where given.

**7.17 Timing belt routing**

**7.19 The index arm must align with the lug (arrowed)**

*Tool Tip 1: A sprocket holding tool can be made from two lengths of steel strip bolted together to form a forked end. Drill holes and insert bolts in the ends of the fork to engage with the sprocket spokes.*

## 8 Timing belt sprockets and tensioner – removal and refitting

### Camshaft sprocket

#### Removal

**1** Remove the timing belt as described in Section 7.

**2** Remove the locking tool from the camshaft sprocket/hub. Slacken the sprocket hub retaining bolt. To prevent the camshaft rotating as the bolt is slackened, a sprocket holding tool will be required. In the absence of the special Citroën tool, an acceptable substitute can be fabricated at home **(see Tool Tip 1)**. *Do not* attempt to use the engine assembly/valve timing locking tool to prevent the sprocket from rotating whilst the bolt is slackened.

**3** Remove the sprocket hub retaining bolt, and slide the sprocket and hub off the end of the camshaft.

**4** Clean the camshaft sprocket thoroughly, and renew it if there are any signs of wear, damage or cracks.

#### Refitting

**5** Refit the camshaft sprocket to the camshaft **(see illustration)**.

**6** Refit the sprocket hub retaining bolt. Tighten the bolt to the specified torque, preventing the camshaft from turning as during removal.

**7** Align the engine assembly/valve timing slot in the camshaft sprocket hub with the hole in the cylinder head and refit the timing pin to lock the camshaft in position.

**8** Fit the timing belt around the pump sprocket and camshaft sprocket, and tension the timing belt as described in Section 7.

### Crankshaft sprocket

#### Removal

**9** Remove the timing belt as described in Section 7.

**10** Check that the engine assembly/valve

**8.5 Ensure the lug on the sprocket hub engages with the slot on the end of the camshaft (arrowed)**

**8.11a Slide the sprocket from the crankshaft . . .**

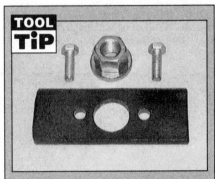

**8.11b . . . and recover the Woodruff key**

timing holes are still aligned as described in Section 3, and the camshaft sprocket and flywheel are locked in position.

**11** Slide the sprocket off the end of the crankshaft and collect the Woodruff key **(see illustrations)**.

**12** Examine the crankshaft oil seal for signs of oil leakage and, if necessary, renew it as described in Section 14.

**13** Clean the crankshaft sprocket thoroughly, and renew it if there are any signs of wear, damage or cracks. Recover the crankshaft locating key.

*Caution: Do not touch the outer magnetic sensor ring of the sprocket with your fingers, or allow metallic particles to come into contact with it.*

#### Refitting

**14** Refit the key to the end of the crankshaft, then refit the crankshaft sprocket (with the flange facing the crankshaft pulley).

**15** Fit the timing belt around the crankshaft sprocket, and tension the timing belt as described in Section 7.

### Fuel pump sprocket

#### Removal

**16** Remove the timing belt as described in Section 7.

**17** Using a suitable socket, undo the pump sprocket retaining nut. The sprocket can be held stationary by inserting a suitably-sized locking pin, drill or rod through the hole in the sprocket, and into the corresponding hole in the backplate **(see illustration)**, or by using a suitable forked tool engaged with the holes in

**8.17 Insert a suitable drill bit through the sprocket into the hole in the backplate**

the sprocket **(see Tool Tip 1)**. *Note: On some engines, a hole is provided at the 5 o'clock position for locking purposes only, however, the timing position hole is at the 12 o'clock position.*

**18** The pump sprocket is a taper fit on the pump shaft and it will be necessary to make up another tool to release it from the taper **(see Tool Tip 2)**.

**19** On late models where the sprocket is keyed to the shaft, unscrew the retaining nut and remove the sprocket, then recover the Woodruff key. On early models where the sprocket is **not** keyed to the shaft, partially unscrew the sprocket retaining nut, then fit the home-made tool, and secure it to the

*Tool Tip 2: Make a sprocket releasing tool from a short strip of steel. Drill two holes in the strip to correspond with the two holes in the sprocket. Drill a third hole just large enough to accept the flats of the sprocket retaining nut.*

**8.31  Timing belt idler pulley retaining nut (arrowed)**

sprocket with two suitable bolts. Prevent the sprocket from rotating as before, and unscrew the sprocket retaining nut. The nut will bear against the tool as it is undone, forcing the sprocket off the shaft taper. Once the taper is released, remove the tool, unscrew the nut fully, and remove the sprocket from the pump shaft.

**20** Clean the sprocket thoroughly, and renew it if there are any signs of wear, damage or cracks.

### Refitting

**21** Refit the Woodruff key (late models only) then refit the pump sprocket and retaining nut, and tighten the nut to the specified torque. Prevent the sprocket rotating as the nut is tightened using the sprocket holding tool.

**22** Fit the timing belt around the pump sprocket, and tension the timing belt as described in Section 7.

### Coolant pump sprocket

**23** The coolant pump sprocket is integral with the pump, and cannot be removed. Coolant pump removal is described in Chapter 3.

### Tensioner pulley

#### Removal

**24** Remove the timing belt as described in Section 7.

**25** Remove the tensioner pulley retaining bolt, and slide the pulley off its mounting stud.

**26** Clean the tensioner pulley, but do not use any strong solvent which may enter the pulley bearings. Check that the pulley rotates freely, with no sign of stiffness or free play. Renew the pulley if there is any doubt about its condition, or if there are any obvious signs of wear or damage.

**27** Examine the pulley mounting stud for signs of damage and if necessary, renew it.

#### Refitting

**28** Refit the tensioner pulley to its mounting stud, and fit the retaining bolt.

**29** Refit the timing belt as described in Section 7.

### Idler pulley

#### Removal

**30** Remove the timing belt as described in Section 7.

**31** Undo the retaining bolt/nut and withdraw the idler pulley from the engine (see illustration).

**32** Clean the idler pulley, but do not use any strong solvent which may enter the bearings.

Check that the pulley rotates freely, with no sign of stiffness or free play. Renew the idler pulley if there is any doubt about its condition, or if there are any obvious signs of wear or damage.

#### Refitting

**33** Locate the idler pulley on the engine, and fit the retaining bolt/nut. Tighten the bolt/nut to the specified torque.

**34** Refit the timing belt (see Section 7).

---

**9  Camshafts, rocker arms and hydraulic tappets** – removal, inspection and refitting

### Removal

**1** Remove the cylinder head cover/manifold as described in Section 4.

**2** Remove the injectors as described in Chapter 4B.

**3** Remove the camshaft sprocket as described in Section 8.

**4** Refit the right-hand engine mounting, but only tighten the bolts moderately; this will keep the engine supported during the camshaft removal.

**5** Undo the bolts and remove the vacuum pump. Recover the pump O-ring seals (see illustration).

**6** Remove the fuel filter (see Chapter 1B), then undo the bolts and remove the fuel filter mounting bracket.

**7** Release the wiring harness clips, then undo the 3 bolts and remove the timing belt inner, upper cover (see illustration).

**8** Disconnect the wiring plug, unscrew the retaining bolt, and remove the camshaft position sensor from the camshaft cover/bearing ladder.

**9** Undo the 5 bolts and remove the upper rear section of the turbocharger heat shield, then working progressively and in the **reverse** order to the tightening sequence in paragraph 26, slacken and remove the bolts securing the camshaft cover/bearing ladder to the cylinder head (see illustration). Lift the cover/ladder from position complete with the camshafts.

**10** Undo the retaining bolts and remove the bearing caps. Note their fitted positions, as they must be refitted into their original positions (see illustration). Note that the bearing caps are marked A for inlet, and E for exhaust, and 1 to 4 from the flywheel end of the cylinder head.

**11** Undo the bolts securing the chain tensioner assembly to the camshaft cover/bearing ladder, then lift the camshafts, chain and tensioner from place (see illustrations). Discard the camshaft oil seal.

**12** Obtain 16 small, clean plastic containers, and number them 1 to 8 inlet and 1 to 8 exhaust; alternatively, divide a larger container into 16 compartments.

**13** Lift out each rocker arm. Place the rocker arms in their respective positions in the box or containers.

**9.5  Vacuum pump bolts (arrowed)**

**9.7  Timing belt inner, upper cover bolts (arrowed)**

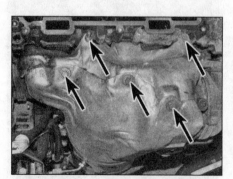

**9.9  Undo the bolts (arrowed) and remove the rear section of the heat shield**

**9.10  The camshaft bearing caps are numbered 1 to 4 from the flywheel end – A for inlet, and E for exhaust (arrowed)**

**14** A compartmentalised container filled with engine oil is now required to retain the hydraulic tappets while they are removed from the cylinder head. Withdraw each hydraulic follower and place it in the container, keeping them each identified for correct refitting. The tappets must be totally submerged in the oil to prevent air entering them.

## Inspection

**15** Inspect the cam lobes and the camshaft bearing journals for scoring or other visible evidence of wear. Once the surface hardening of the cam lobes has been eroded, wear will occur at an accelerated rate. **Note:** *If these symptoms are visible on the tips of the camshaft lobes, check the corresponding rocker arm, as it will probably be worn as well.*

**16** Examine the condition of the bearing surfaces in the cylinder head and camshaft bearing housing. If wear is evident, the cylinder head and bearing housing will both have to be renewed, as they are a matched assembly.

**17** Inspect the rocker arms and tappets for scuffing, cracking or other damage and renew any components as necessary. Also check the condition of the tappet bores in the cylinder head. As with the camshafts, any wear in this area will necessitate cylinder head renewal.

## Refitting

**18** Thoroughly clean the sealant from the mating surfaces of the cylinder head and camshaft bearing housing. Use a suitable liquid gasket dissolving agent (available from Citroën dealers) together with a soft putty knife; do not use a metal scraper or the faces will be damaged. As there is no conventional gasket used, the cleanliness of the mating faces is of the utmost importance. Prise out the oil injector oil seals from the camshaft bearing housing.

**19** Clean off any oil, dirt or grease from both components and dry with a clean

**9.11a Undo the tensioner bolts (arrowed) . . .**

**9.11b . . . then lift the camshafts, chain and tensioner from place**

**9.21 Refit the hydraulic tappets . . .**

**9.22 . . . and rocker arms to their original locations**

lint-free cloth. Ensure that all the oilways are completely clean.

**20** Liberally lubricate the hydraulic tappet bores in the cylinder head with clean engine oil.

**21** Insert the hydraulic tappets into their original bores in the cylinder head unless they have been renewed **(see illustration)**.

**22** Lubricate the rocker arms and place them over their respective tappets and valve stems **(see illustration)**.

**23** Engage the timing chain around the camshaft sprockets, aligning the black-coloured links with the marked teeth on the

camshaft sprockets **(see illustration)**. If the black colouring has been lost, there must be 12 chain link pins between the marks on the sprockets.

**24** Fit the chain tensioner between the upper and lower runs of the chain, then lubricate the bearing surfaces with clean engine oil, and fit the camshafts into position on the underside of the camshaft cover/bearing ladder. Refit the bearing caps to their original positions and tighten the retaining bolts progressively to the specified torque **(see illustrations)**. Tighten the tensioner retaining bolts to the specified torque.

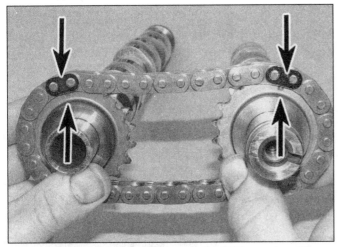

**9.23 Align the marks on the sprockets with the centre of the black-coloured chain links (arrowed). There must be 12 link pins between the sprocket marks**

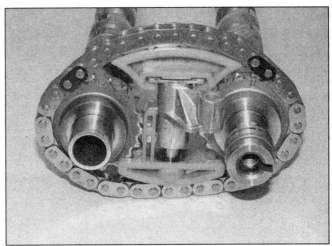

**9.24a Assemble the chain tensioner between the upper and lower runs of the chain . . .**

9.24b . . . and lower the camshafts, chain and tensioner into position

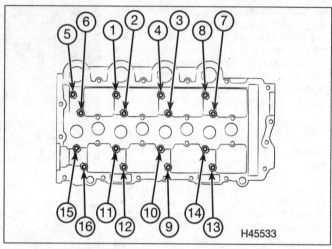

9.24c Camshaft bearing cap bolt tightening sequence

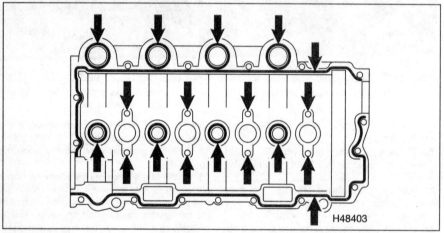

9.25 Apply a bead of sealant to the mating face of the camshaft bearing housing in the areas shown (arrows). Ensure sealant does not enter the hydraulic tensioner oil holes

**25** Apply a thin bead of sealant to the mating surface of the camshaft cover/bearing ladder as shown. Citroën recommend the use of Autojoint Noir **(see illustration)**. Do not allow the sealant to obstruct the oil channels for the hydraulic chain tensioner.

**26** Check that the black-coloured links on the chain are still aligned with the marks on the camshaft sprockets, then refit the camshaft cover/bearing ladder, and progressively tighten the retaining bolts until the cover/ladder is in contact with the cylinder head, then tighten the bolts to the specified torque in the sequence shown **(see illustration)**. Note: *Ensure the cover/ladder is correctly located by checking the bores of the vacuum pump and camshaft oil seal at each end of the cover/ladder.*

**27** Fit a new camshaft oil seal as described in Section 14.

**28** Refit the camshaft sprocket, and tighten the retaining bolt finger-tight.

**29** Using a spanner on the camshaft sprocket bolt, rotate the camshafts approximately 40 complete revolutions clockwise. Check the black-coloured links on the chain still align with the marks on the camshaft sprockets.

**30** If the marks still align, refit the camshaft sprocket as described in Section 8.

**31** Refit and adjust the camshaft position sensor as described in Chapter 4B.

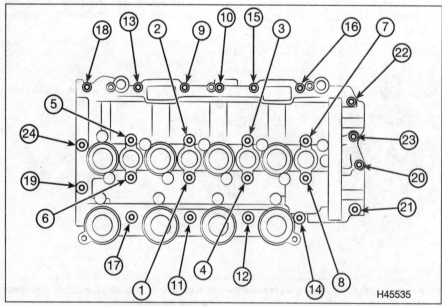

9.26 Camshaft cover/bearing ladder bolt tightening sequence

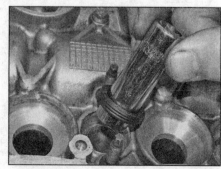

9.32a Fit the new seal around a 20 mm outside diameter socket . . .

**32** Press the new oil seals into the bearing housing, using a tube/socket of approximately 20 mm outside diameter, ensuring the inner lip of the seal fits around the injector guide tube (**see illustrations**). Refit the injectors as described in Chapter 4B.

**33** Refit the cylinder head cover/manifold as described in Section 4.

## 10 Cylinder head –
### removal and refitting

### Removal

**1** Apply the handbrake then jack up the front of the vehicle and support it on axle stands (see *Jacking and vehicle support*). Remove the front right-hand roadwheel, the engine undershield, and the front wheel arch liner. The undershield is secured by several screws, and the wheel arch liner is secured by several plastic expanding rivets/nuts/plastic clips. Push the centre pins in a little, then prise the rivet from place.

**2** Disconnect the battery negative lead as described in Chapter 5A.

**3** Drain the cooling system as described in Chapter 1B.

**4** Remove the camshafts, rocker arms and hydraulic tappets as described in Section 9.

**5** Remove the turbocharger as described in Chapter 4B.

**6** Remove the glow plugs as described in Chapter 5C.

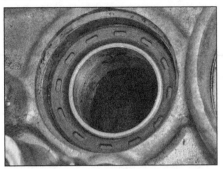

9.32b . . . and push it into place

**7** Where applicable, undo the 3 mounting bolts and move the power steering pump to one side (there's no need to disconnect the hoses).

**8** Undo the upper mounting bolts, and pivot the alternator away from the engine, undo the oil dipstick guide tube bolt, then undo the bolts securing the alternator/power steering pump mounting bracket to the cylinder head/block (**see illustration**).

**9** Undo the coolant outlet housing (left-hand end of the cylinder head) retaining bolts, slacken the two bolts securing the housing support bracket to the top of the transmission bellhousing, and move the outlet housing away from the cylinder head a little (**see illustration**). There is no need to disconnect the hoses.

**10** Disconnect the high-pressure fuel pipe from the common rail to the pump, and

disconnect the fuel supply and return hoses. Remove the bracket at the rear of the pump, then undo the bolt/nut and remove the pump and mounting bracket as an assembly (**see illustrations**). Note that a new high-pressure pipe must be fitted – see Chapter 4B.

**11** Working in the **reverse** of the sequence shown (**see illustration 10.32**) undo the cylinder head bolts.

**12** Release the cylinder head from the cylinder block and location dowels by rocking it. The Citroën tool for doing this consists simply of two metal rods with 90-degree angled ends (**see illustration**). Do not prise between the mating faces of the cylinder head and block, as this may damage the gasket faces.

**13** Lift the cylinder head from the block, and recover the gasket.

**14** If necessary, remove the exhaust manifold with reference to Chapter 4B.

### Preparation for refitting

**15** The mating faces of the cylinder head and cylinder block must be perfectly clean before refitting the head. Citroën recommend the use of a scouring agent for this purpose, but acceptable results can be achieved by using a hard plastic or wood scraper to remove all traces of gasket and carbon. The same method can be used to clean the piston crowns. Take particular care to avoid scoring or gouging the cylinder head/cylinder block mating surfaces during the cleaning operations, as aluminium alloy is easily damaged. Make sure that the carbon is not allowed to enter the oil and water passages – this is particularly important for the

10.8 The engine oil level dipstick is secured to the alternator bracket by a Torx bolt (arrowed)

10.9 Undo the bolts (arrowed) and pull the coolant outlet housing from the left-hand end of the cylinder head

10.10a Remove the high-pressure pipe (arrowed) . . .

10.10b . . . and the bracket (arrowed)

10.10c Pump mounting bracket upper nut and lower mounting bolt (arrowed)

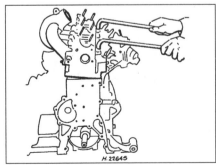

10.12 Free the cylinder head using angled rods

**10.17a  Pull the non-return valve from the cylinder head . . .**

**10.17b  . . . and push a new one into place**

lubrication system, as carbon could block the oil supply to the engine's components. Using adhesive tape and paper, seal the water, oil and bolt holes in the cylinder block. To prevent carbon entering the gap between the pistons and bores, smear a little grease in the gap. After cleaning each piston, use a small brush to remove all traces of grease and carbon from the gap, then wipe away the remainder with a clean rag.

16  Check the mating surfaces of the cylinder block and the cylinder head for nicks, deep scratches and other damage. If slight, they may be removed carefully with a file, but if excessive, machining may be the only alternative to renewal. If warpage of the cylinder head gasket surface is suspected, use a straight-edge to check it for distortion. Refer to Part D of this Chapter if necessary.

17  Thoroughly clean the threads of the cylinder head bolt holes in the cylinder

block. Ensure that the bolts run freely in their threads, and that all traces of oil and water are removed from each bolt hole. If required, pull the oil feed non-return valve from the cylinder head, and check the ball moves freely. Push a new valve into place if necessary **(see illustrations)**.

## Gasket selection

18  Remove the crankshaft timing pin, then turn the crankshaft until pistons 1 and 4 are at TDC (Top Dead Centre). Position a dial test indicator (dial gauge) on the cylinder block adjacent to the rear of No 1 piston, and zero it on the block face. Transfer the probe to the crown of No 1 piston (10.0 mm in from the rear edge), then slowly turn the crankshaft back-and-forth past TDC, noting the highest reading on the indicator. Record this reading as protrusion A.

19  Repeat the check described in paragraph 18, this time 10.0 mm in from the front edge of the

**10.21  Measure the piston protrusion using a DTI gauge**

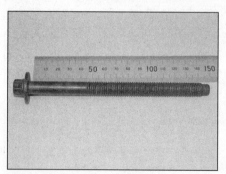

**10.24  Measure the length from under the bolt head to its end**

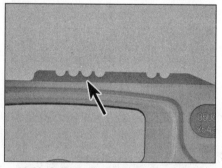

**10.23  Cylinder head gasket thickness identification notches (arrowed)**

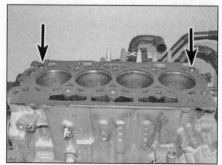

**10.27  Ensure the gasket locates over the dowels (arrowed)**

No 1 piston crown. Record this reading as protrusion B.

20  Add protrusion A to protrusion B, then divide the result by 2 to obtain an average reading for piston No 1.

21  Repeat the procedure described in paragraphs 18 to 20 on piston 4, then turn the crankshaft through 180° and carry out the procedure on the piston Nos 2 and 3 **(see illustration)**. Check that there is a maximum difference of 0.07 mm protrusion between any two pistons.

22  If a dial test indicator is not available, piston protrusion may be measured using a straight-edge and feeler blades or Vernier calipers. However, this is much less accurate, and cannot therefore be recommended.

23  Note the greatest piston protrusion measurement, and use this to determine the correct cylinder head gasket from the following table. The series of notches/holes on the side of the gasket are used for thickness identification **(see illustration)**.

| Piston protrusion | Gasket identification |
| --- | --- |
| 0.6115 to 0.720 mm | 2 notches |
| 0.721 to 0.770 mm | 3 notches |
| 0.771 to 0.820 mm | 1 notches |
| 0.821 to 0.870 mm | 4 notches |
| 0.871 to 0.977 mm | 5 notches |

## Head bolt examination

24  Carefully examine the cylinder head bolts for signs of damage to the threads or head, and for any sign of corrosion. If the bolts are in a satisfactory condition, measure the length of each bolt from the underside of the head to the end of the shank. The bolts may be re-used providing that the measured length does not exceed 149.0 mm **(see illustration)**. **Note:** *Considering the stress to which the cylinder head bolts are subjected, it is highly recommended that they are all renewed, regardless of their apparent condition.*

## Refitting

25  Turn the crankshaft and position Nos 1 and 4 pistons at TDC, then turn the crankshaft a quarter turn (90°) anti-clockwise.

26  Thoroughly clean the surfaces of the cylinder head and block.

27  Make sure that the locating dowels are in place, then fit the correct gasket the right way round on the cylinder block **(see illustration)**.

28  If necessary, refit the exhaust manifold to the cylinder head as described in Chapter 4B.

29  Carefully lower the cylinder head onto the gasket and block, making sure that it locates correctly onto the dowels.

30  Apply a smear of grease to the threads, and to the underside of the heads, of the cylinder head bolts. Citroën recommend the use of Molykote G Rapid Plus (available from your Citroën dealer); in the absence of the specified grease, any good-quality high melting-point grease may be used.

31  Carefully insert the cylinder head bolts into their holes (*do not drop them in*) and initially finger-tighten them.

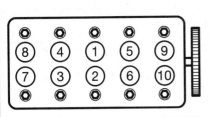

H44687

**10.32 Cylinder head bolt tightening sequence**

**32** Working progressively and in the sequence shown, tighten the cylinder head bolts to their Stage 1 torque setting, using a torque wrench and suitable socket **(see illustration)**.

**33** Once all the bolts have been tightened to their Stage 1 torque setting, working again in the specified sequence, tighten each bolt to the specified Stage 2 setting. Finally, angle-tighten the bolts through the specified Stage 3 angle. It is recommended that an angle-measuring gauge is used during this stage of tightening, to ensure accuracy. **Note:** *Retightening of the cylinder head bolts after running the engine is not required.*

**34** Refit the hydraulic tappets, rocker arms, and camshaft housing (complete with camshafts) as described in Section 9.

**35** Refit the timing belt as described in Section 7.

**36** The remainder of refitting is a reversal of removal, noting the following points.

a) *Use a new seal when refitting the coolant outlet housing.*

b) *When refitting a cylinder head, it is good practice to renew the thermostat.*

c) *Refit the camshaft position sensor and set the air gap with reference to Chapter 4B.*

d) *Tighten all fasteners to the specified torque where given.*

e) *Refill the cooling system as described in Chapter 1B.*

f) *The engine may run erratically for the first few miles, until the engine management ECU relearns its stored values.*

## 11 Sump – removal and refitting

### Removal

**1** Drain the engine oil, then clean and refit the engine oil drain plug, tightening it securely. If the engine is nearing the service interval when the oil and filter are due for renewal, it is recommended that the filter is also removed, and a new one fitted. After reassembly, the engine can then be refilled with fresh oil. Refer to Chapter 1B for further information.

**2** Apply the handbrake then jack up the front of the vehicle and support it on axle stands (see *Jacking and vehicle support*). Undo the screws and remove the engine undershield.

**3** Remove the exhaust front pipe as described in Chapter 4B.

**4** Where necessary, disconnect the wiring connector from the oil temperature sender unit, which is screwed into the sump. Also where necessary, unscrew the bolts securing the air conditioning compressor to the sump.

**5** Progressively slacken and remove all the sump retaining bolts/nuts. Since the sump bolts vary in length, remove each bolt in turn, and store it in its correct fitted order by pushing it through a clearly-marked cardboard template. This will avoid the possibility of installing the bolts in the wrong locations on refitting.

**6** Try to break the joint by striking the sump with the palm of your hand, then lower and withdraw the sump from under the car. If the sump is stuck (which is quite likely) use a putty knife or similar carefully inserted between the sump and block. Ease the knife along the joint until the sump is released. While the sump is removed, take the opportunity to check the oil

pump pick-up/strainer for signs of clogging or splitting. If necessary, remove the pump as described in Section 12, and clean or renew the strainer.

### Refitting

**7** Clean all traces of sealant from the mating surfaces of the cylinder block/crankcase and sump, then use a clean rag to wipe out the sump and the engine's interior.

**8** On engines where the sump was fitted without a gasket, ensure that the sump mating surfaces are clean and dry, then apply a thin coating of suitable sealant to the sump or crankcase mating surface **(see illustration)**.

**9** Offer up the sump to the cylinder block/crankcase. Refit its retaining bolts/nuts, ensuring that each bolt is screwed into its original location. Tighten the bolts evenly and progressively to the specified torque setting **(see illustration)**.

**10** Where necessary, align the air conditioning compressor with its mountings on the sump, and insert the retaining bolts. Securely tighten the compressor retaining bolts, then refit the drivebelt as described in Chapter 1B.

**11** Refit the exhaust front pipe as described in Chapter 4B.

**12** Reconnect the wiring connector to the oil temperature sensor (where fitted).

**13** Refit the undershield and lower the vehicle to the ground, then refill the engine with oil as described in Chapter 1B.

## 12 Oil pump – removal, inspection and refitting

### Removal

**1** Remove the crankshaft sprocket as described in Section 8. Recover the locating key from the crankshaft.

**2** Temporarily refit the right-hand engine mounting and support bracket, and remove

**11.8 Apply a bead of sealant to the sump or crankcase mating surface. Ensure the sealant is applied on the inside of the retaining bolt holes**

**11.9 Refit the sump and tighten the bolts**

12.4  Oil pick-up tube Allen screws
(arrowed)

12.5  Oil pump retaining bolts (arrowed)

12.6  Undo the Torx bolts and remove the
pump cover

12.7a  Remove the circlip . . .

12.7b  . . . cap . . .

### Inspection

**6** Undo and remove the Torx bolts securing the cover to the oil pump **(see illustration)**. Examine the pump rotors and body for signs of wear and damage. If worn, the complete pump must be renewed.

**7** Remove the circlip, and extract the cap, valve piston and spring, noting which way around they are fitted **(see illustrations)**. The condition of the relief valve spring can only be measured by comparing it with a new one; if there is any doubt about its condition, it should also be renewed.

**8** Refit the relief valve piston and spring, then secure them in place with the circlip.

**9** Refit the cover to the oil pump, and tighten the Torx bolts securely.

### Refitting

**10** Remove all traces of sealant, and thoroughly clean the mating surfaces of the oil pump and cylinder block.

**11** Apply a 4 mm wide bead of silicone sealant to the mating face of the cylinder block **(see illustration)**. Ensure that no sealant enters any of the holes in the block.

**12** With a new oil seal fitted, refit the oil pump over the end of the crankshaft, aligning the flats in the pump drivegear with the flats machined in the crankshaft **(see illustrations)**. Note that new oil pumps are supplied with the oil seal already fitted, and a seal protector sleeve. The sleeve fits over the end of the crankshaft to protect the seal as the pump is fitted.

**13** Install the oil pump bolts and tighten them to the specified torque.

the trolley jack, then remove the sump as described in Section 11.

**3** Disconnect the wiring plug, undo the bolts and remove the crankshaft position sensor, located on the right-hand end of the cylinder block.

**4** Undo the three Allen screws and remove the oil pump pick-up tube from the pump/block **(see illustration)**. Discard the oil seal, a new one must be fitted.

**5** Undo the 8 bolts, and remove the oil pump **(see illustration)**.

12.7c  . . . spring . . .

12.7d  . . . and piston

12.11  Apply a bead of sealant to the
cylinder block mating surface

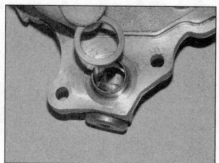

12.12a  Fit a new seal . . .

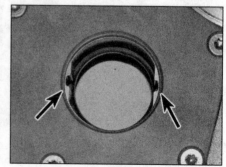

12.12b  . . . align the pump gear flats
(arrowed) . . .

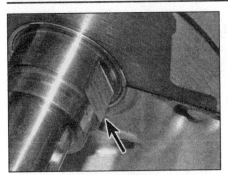

**12.12c ... with those of the crankshaft (arrowed)**

**13.4a Undo the oil cooler bolts/stud (arrowed)**

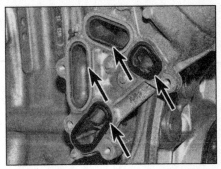

**13.4b Renew the O-ring seals (arrowed)**

**14** Refit the oil pick-up tube to the pump/cylinder block using a new O-ring seal. Ensure the oil dipstick guide tube is correctly refitted.
**15** Refit the Woodruff key to the crankshaft, and slide the crankshaft sprocket into place.
**16** The remainder of refitting is a reversal of removal.

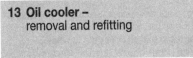

## 13 Oil cooler – removal and refitting

### Removal

**1** Apply the handbrake then jack up the front of the vehicle and support it on axle stands (see *Jacking and vehicle support*). Undo the screws and remove the engine undershield.
**2** The oil cooler is fitted to the front of the oil filter housing. Drain the coolant as described in Chapter 1B.
**3** Drain the engine oil as described in Chapter 1B, or be prepared for fluid spillage.
**4** Undo the 5 bolts/stud and remove the oil cooler. Recover the O-ring seals **(see illustrations)**.

### Refitting

**5** Fit new O-ring seals into the recesses in the oil filter housing, and refit the cooler. Tighten the bolts securely.
**6** Refill or top-up the cooling system and engine oil level as described in Chapter 1B or *Weekly Checks* (as applicable). Start the engine, and check the oil cooler for signs of leakage.

## 14 Oil seals – renewal

### Crankshaft

#### Right-hand oil seal

**1** Remove the crankshaft sprocket and Woodruff key as described in Section 8.
**2** Measure and note the fitted depth of the oil seal.
**3** Prise the oil seal from the housing using a screwdriver. Alternatively, drill a small hole in

the oil seal, and use a self-tapping screw and a pair of pliers to remove it **(see illustration)**.
**4** Clean the oil seal housing and the crankshaft sealing surface.
**5** The seal has a Teflon lip and must not be oiled or marked. The new seal should be supplied with a protector sleeve, which fits over the end of the crankshaft to prevent any damage to the seal lip. With the sleeve in place, press the seal (open end first) into the pump to the previously-noted depth, using a suitable tube or socket **(see illustrations)**.
**6** Where applicable, remove the plastic sleeve from the end of the crankshaft.
**7** Refit the timing belt crankshaft sprocket as described in Section 8.

#### Left-hand oil seal

**8** Remove the flywheel, as described in Section 16.

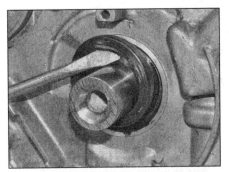

**14.3 Take great care not to mark the crankshaft whilst levering out the oil seal**

**14.5b ... and press the seal into place**

**9** Measure and note the fitted depth of the oil seal.
**10** Pull the oil seal from the housing using a screwdriver. Alternatively, drill a small hole in the oil seal, and use a self-tapping screw and a pair of pliers to remove it **(see illustration 14.3)**.
**11** Clean the oil seal housing and the crankshaft sealing surface.
**12** The seal has a Teflon lip and must not be oiled or marked. The new seal should be supplied with a protector sleeve, which fits over the end of the crankshaft to prevent any damage to the seal lip **(see illustration)**. With the sleeve in place, press the seal (open end first) into the housing to the previously-noted depth, using a suitable tube or socket.
**13** Where applicable, remove the plastic sleeve from the end of the crankshaft.
**14** Refit the flywheel, as described in Section 16.

**14.5a Slide the seal and protective sleeve over the end of the crankshaft ...**

**14.12 Slide the seal and protective sleeve over the left-hand end of the crankshaft**

**14.16  Drill a hole, insert a self-tapping screw, and pull the seal from place using pliers**

### Camshaft

**15** Remove the camshaft sprocket as described in Section 8. In principle there is no need to remove the timing belt completely, but remember that if the belt has been contaminated with oil, it must be renewed.

**16** Pull the oil seal from the housing using a hooked instrument. Alternatively, drill a small hole in the oil seal and use a self-tapping screw and a pair of pliers to remove it **(see illustration)**.

**17** Clean the oil seal housing and the camshaft sealing surface.

**18** The seal has a Teflon lip and must not be oiled or marked. The new seal should be supplied with a protector sleeve. which fits over the end of the camshaft to prevent any damage to the seal lip **(see illustration)**. With the sleeve in place, press the seal (open end first) into the housing, using a suitable tube or socket which bears only of the outer edge of the seal.

**19** Refit the camshaft sprocket as described in Section 8.

**20** Where necessary, fit a new timing belt with reference to Section 7.

---

### 15 Oil pressure switch and level sensor – removal and refitting

#### Removal

##### Oil pressure switch

**1** The oil pressure switch is located at the front of the cylinder block, adjacent to the oil dipstick guide tube. Note that on some

**15.3  The oil pressure switch is located on the front face of the cylinder block (arrowed)**

---

**14.18  Fit the protective sleeve and seal over the end of the camshaft**

models, access to the switch may be improved if the vehicle is jacked up and supported on axle stands, then undo the screws and remove the engine undershield so that the switch can be reached from underneath (see *Jacking and vehicle support*).

**2** Remove the protective sleeve from the wiring plug (where applicable), then disconnect the wiring from the switch.

**3** Unscrew the switch from the cylinder block, and recover the sealing washer **(see illustration)**. Be prepared for oil spillage, and if the switch is to be left removed from the engine for any length of time, plug the hole in the cylinder block.

##### Oil level sensor

**4** The oil level sensor is located at the rear of the cylinder block. Jack up the front of the vehicle and support it securely on axle stands (see *Jacking and vehicle support*). Undo the screws and remove the engine undershield.

**5** Reach up between the driveshaft and the cylinder block and disconnect the sensor wiring plug **(see illustration)**.

**6** Using an open-ended spanner, unscrew the sensor and withdraw it from position.

#### Refitting

##### Oil pressure switch

**7** Examine the sealing washer for any signs of damage or deterioration, and if necessary renew.

**8** Refit the switch, complete with washer, and tighten it to the specified torque.

**9** Refit the engine undershield, and lower the vehicle to the ground.

**15.5  The oil level sensor is located on the rear face of the cylinder block (arrowed)**

---

##### Oil level sensor

**10** Smear a little silicone sealant on the threads and refit the sensor to the cylinder block, tightening it securely.

**11** Reconnect the sensor wiring plug.

**12** Refit the engine undershield, and lower the vehicle to the ground.

---

### 16 Flywheel – removal, inspection and refitting

#### Removal

**1** Remove the transmission as described in Chapter 7A, then remove the clutch assembly as described in Chapter 6.

**2** Prevent the flywheel from turning by locking the ring gear teeth **(see illustration 5.2)**. Alternatively, bolt a strap between the flywheel and the cylinder block/crankcase. *Do not* attempt to lock the flywheel in position using the crankshaft pulley locking tool described in Section 3. Insert a 12 mm diameter rod or drill bit through the hole in the flywheel cover casting, and into a slot in the flywheel.

**3** Make alignment marks between the flywheel and crankshaft to aid refitting. Slacken and remove the flywheel retaining bolts, and remove the flywheel from the end of the crankshaft. Be careful not to drop it; it is heavy. If the flywheel locating dowel (where fitted) is a loose fit in the crankshaft end, remove it and store it with the flywheel for safe-keeping. Discard the flywheel bolts; new ones must be used on refitting.

#### Inspection

**4** Examine the flywheel for scoring of the clutch face, and for wear or chipping of the ring gear teeth. If the clutch face is scored, the flywheel may be surface-ground, but renewal is preferable. Seek the advice of a Citroën dealer or engine reconditioning specialist to see if machining is possible. If the ring gear is worn or damaged, the flywheel must be renewed, as it is not possible to renew the ring gear separately.

#### Refitting

**5** Clean the mating surfaces of the flywheel and crankshaft. Remove any remaining locking compound from the threads of the crankshaft holes, using the correct size of tap, if available.

**6** If the new flywheel retaining bolts are not supplied with their threads already pre-coated, apply a suitable thread-locking compound to the threads of each bolt.

**HAYNES HINT** *If a suitable tap is not available, cut two slots along the threads of one of the old flywheel bolts, and use the bolt to remove the locking compound from the threads.*

### All models except engines with dual mass flywheel

**7** Ensure that the locating dowel is in position. Offer up the flywheel, locating it on the dowel (where fitted), and fit the new retaining bolts. Where no locating dowel is fitted, align the previously-made marks to ensure the flywheel is refitted in its original position.

**8** Lock the flywheel using the method employed on dismantling, and tighten the retaining bolts to the specified torque **(see illustration)**.

### Engines with dual mass flywheel

**9** The dual mass flywheel is designed to reduce harshness and vibration in the action of the engine, clutch and transmission. With this type of flywheel, two flywheel centralising tools are needed (available from Citroën dealers). These are screwed into two opposite flywheel bolt holes in the crankshaft. As the tools are screwed down, their conical shape centralises the flywheel with regard to the crankshaft.

**10** With the flywheel centralised, fit the new bolts into the remaining flywheel holes, then lock the flywheel using the same method employed on dismantling, and tighten the bolts to the specified torque.

**11** Remove the two centralising tools, fit the new bolts and tighten them to the specified torque.

### All models

**12** Refit the clutch as described in Chapter 6. Remove the flywheel locking tool, and refit the transmission as described in Chapter 7A.

### 17 Engine/transmission mountings –
inspection and renewal

### Inspection

**1** Apply the handbrake then jack up the front of the car and support it on axle stands (see *Jacking and vehicle support*). Undo the screws and remove the engine undershield.

**2** Check the mounting rubbers to see if they are cracked, hardened or separated from the metal at any point; renew the mounting if any such damage or deterioration is evident.

**3** Check that all the mountings' fasteners are securely tightened; use a torque wrench to check if possible.

**4** Using a large screwdriver or a crowbar, check for wear in each mounting by carefully levering against it to check for free play. Where this is not possible, enlist the aid of an assistant to move the engine/transmission back-and-forth, or from side-to-side, while you watch the mounting. While some free play is to be expected even from new components, excessive wear should be obvious. If excessive free play is found, check first that the fasteners are correctly secured, then renew any worn components as described below.

**16.8 Flywheel retaining Torx bolts**

### Renewal

#### Right-hand mounting

**5** Place a jack beneath the engine, with a block of wood on the jack head. Raise the jack until it is supporting the weight of the engine.

**6** Slacken and remove the three bolts securing the mounting bracket to the bracket bolted to the cylinder head, and the two bolts securing the mounting to the body. Remove the mounting assembly from the car and recover the reinforcing plate **(see illustration)**.

**7** If required, undo the three bolts and remove the bracket from the cylinder head.

**8** Check for signs of wear or damage on all components, and renew as necessary.

**9** On reassembly, refit the bracket to the cylinder head, tightening the bolts to the specified torque.

**10** Install the mounting bracket and tighten its retaining bolts to the specified torque setting.

**11** Remove the jack from under the engine.

#### Left-hand mounting

**12** Remove the battery and battery tray/box as described in Chapter 5A.

**13** Place a jack beneath the transmission, with a block of wood on the jack head. Raise the jack until it is supporting the weight of the transmission/engine.

**14** Slacken and remove the two bolts securing the mounting arm to the bracket on the transmission **(see illustration)**. Undo the four bolts securing the mounting to the body

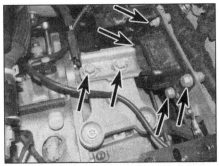

**17.14 Left-hand engine mounting retaining bolts (arrowed)**

**17.6 Right-hand engine mounting**

and remove the complete mounting assembly from the engine compartment.

**15** If necessary, undo the retaining bolts and remove the mounting bracket from the transmission.

**16** Check for signs of wear or damage on all components, and renew as necessary.

**17** Refit the mounting assembly to the vehicle body and tighten its bolts to the specified torque.

**18** Locate the mounting arm over the transmission bracket and tighten its retaining bolts to the specified torque.

**19** Remove the jack from underneath the transmission, then refit the battery tray/box and battery as described in Chapter 5A.

#### Rear engine mounting torque link

**20** If not already done, firmly apply the handbrake, then jack up the front of the vehicle and support it securely on axle stands (see *Jacking and vehicle support*).

**21** Unscrew and remove the two through-bolts securing the rear mounting connecting link to the subframe and transmission bracket **(see illustration)**.

**22** Manoeuvre the connecting link from its location and remove it from under the vehicle.

**23** Check carefully for signs of wear or damage on all components, and renew them where necessary.

**24** Refit the rear mounting connecting link, and tighten both its bolts to their specified torque settings.

**25** Lower the vehicle to the ground.

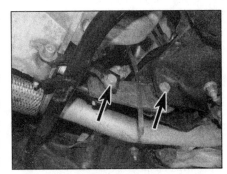

**17.21 Rear engine mounting connecting link through-bolts (arrowed)**

# Chapter 2  Part D:
# Engine removal and overhaul procedures

## Degrees of difficulty

| Easy, suitable for novice with little experience | Fairly easy, suitable for beginner with some experience | Fairly difficult, suitable for competent DIY mechanic | Difficult, suitable for experienced DIY mechanic | Very difficult, suitable for expert DIY or professional |
|---|---|---|---|---|

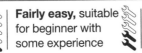

## Specifications

### Engine identification

| Petrol engines | Designation | Engine code |
|---|---|---|
| 1.1 litre SOHC (8-valve) ................................... | TU1JP and TU1A | HFX |
| 1.4 litre: | | |
| SOHC (8-valve)..................................... | TU3JP and TU3A | KFV |
| DOHC (16-valve)..................................... | ET3J4 and ET3JA | KFU |
| 1.6 litre DOHC (16-valve) ................................ | TU5JP4 | NFU |

| Diesel engines | | |
|---|---|---|
| 1.4 litre: | | |
| SOHC (8-valve)..................................... | DV4TD | 8HX and 8HZ |
| DOHC (16-valve)..................................... | DV4TED4 | 8HY |
| 1.6 litre: | | |
| DOHC (16-valve) with intercooler........................... | DV6ATED4 | 9HX |
| DOHC (16-valve) without intercooler ....................... | DV6TED4 | 9HY |
| DOHC (16-valve) without intercooler but with particulate filter ..... | DV6TED4 | 9HZ |

## Cylinder head

Maximum gasket face distortion:
    All engines . . . . . . . . . . . . . . . . . . . . . . . . . . . . . . . . . . . . . . . . . . . 0.05 mm
New cylinder head height:
    Petrol engines:
        1.1 and 1.4 litre. . . . . . . . . . . . . . . . . . . . . . . . . . . . . . . . . . . . . . 111.20 mm
        1.6 litre . . . . . . . . . . . . . . . . . . . . . . . . . . . . . . . . . . . . . . . . . . . . N/A
    Diesel engines:
        8-valve engines. . . . . . . . . . . . . . . . . . . . . . . . . . . . . . . . . . . . . . . 88.00 mm
        16-valve engines. . . . . . . . . . . . . . . . . . . . . . . . . . . . . . . . . . . . . . 124.0 mm
Minimum cylinder head height after machining:
    Petrol engines:
        1.1 and 1.4 litre. . . . . . . . . . . . . . . . . . . . . . . . . . . . . . . . . . . . . . 111.00 mm
        1.6 litre . . . . . . . . . . . . . . . . . . . . . . . . . . . . . . . . . . . . . . . . . . . . N/A
    Diesel engines:
        8-valve engines. . . . . . . . . . . . . . . . . . . . . . . . . . . . . . . . . . . . . . . 87.60 mm
        16-valve engines. . . . . . . . . . . . . . . . . . . . . . . . . . . . . . . . . . . . . . N/A
Valve head-to-cylinder head measurement – diesel engines:
    1.4 litre . . . . . . . . . . . . . . . . . . . . . . . . . . . . . . . . . . . . . . . . . . . . . . 1.25 mm maximum
    1.6 litre . . . . . . . . . . . . . . . . . . . . . . . . . . . . . . . . . . . . . . . . . . . . . . N/A

## Valves

| | Inlet | Exhaust |
|---|---|---|
| Valve head diameter: | | |
|   Petrol engines: | | |
|     1.1 and 1.4 litre. . . . . | 36.7 mm | 29.4 mm |
|     1.6 litre . . . . . | N/A | N/A |
|   Diesel engines . . . . . | 32.8 mm | 30.3 mm |
| Valve stem diameter: | | |
|   Petrol engines: | | |
|     1.1 and 14 litre . . . . . | 6.965 to 6.980 mm | 6.945 to 6.960 mm |
|     1.6 litre . . . . . | N/A | N/A |
|   Diesel engines: | | |
|     1.4 litre . . . . . | N/A | N/A |
|     1.6 litre . . . . . | 5.485 +0.0, -0.015 mm | 5.475 +0.0, -0.015 mm |

## Cylinder block

Cylinder bore diameter:
    Petrol engines:
        1.1.litre . . . . . . . . . . . . . . . . . . . . . . . . . . . . . . . . . . . . . . . . . . . 72.00 mm (nominal)
        1.4 litre . . . . . . . . . . . . . . . . . . . . . . . . . . . . . . . . . . . . . . . . . . . 75.00 mm (nominal)
        1.6 litre . . . . . . . . . . . . . . . . . . . . . . . . . . . . . . . . . . . . . . . . . . . 78.50 mm (nominal)
    Diesel engines:
        1.4 litre . . . . . . . . . . . . . . . . . . . . . . . . . . . . . . . . . . . . . . . . . . . 73.70 mm (nominal)
        1.6 litre (reboring not possible) . . . . . . . . . . . . . . . . . . . . . . . . . 75.00 mm (nominal)
Liner protrusion – 1.1 and 1.4 litre petrol engines:
    Standard. . . . . . . . . . . . . . . . . . . . . . . . . . . . . . . . . . . . . . . . . . . . . 0.03 to 0.10 mm
    Maximum difference between any two liners. . . . . . . . . . . . . . . . . . 0.05 mm

## Crankshaft

Endfloat:
    Petrol engines. . . . . . . . . . . . . . . . . . . . . . . . . . . . . . . . . . . . . . . . . 0.07 to 0.27 mm
    Diesel engines . . . . . . . . . . . . . . . . . . . . . . . . . . . . . . . . . . . . . . . . 0.10 to 0.30 mm (thrustwasher thickness 2.40 ± 0.05 mm)
Main bearing journal diameter:
    Petrol engines:
        TU1 and TU3 series . . . . . . . . . . . . . . . . . . . . . . . . . . . . . . . . . . . 49.981 +0.0 -0.016 mm
        TU5 and ET3 series . . . . . . . . . . . . . . . . . . . . . . . . . . . . . . . . . . . 49.981 +0.0 -0.019 mm
    Diesel engines . . . . . . . . . . . . . . . . . . . . . . . . . . . . . . . . . . . . . . . . 49.981 +0.0 -0.019 mm
Big-end bearing journal diameter:
    Petrol engines:
        TU1 and TU3 series . . . . . . . . . . . . . . . . . . . . . . . . . . . . . . . . . . . 45.000 ±0.008 mm
        TU5 and ET3 series . . . . . . . . . . . . . . . . . . . . . . . . . . . . . . . . . . . 45.000 -0.025, -0.009 mm
    Diesel engines . . . . . . . . . . . . . . . . . . . . . . . . . . . . . . . . . . . . . . . . 45.000 -0.025, -0.009 mm

## Pistons

Piston diameter:
Petrol engines:
1.1 litre . . . . . . . . . . . . . . . . . . . . . . . . . . . . . . . . . . . . . . . . . .   71.950 mm (nominal)
1.4 litre . . . . . . . . . . . . . . . . . . . . . . . . . . . . . . . . . . . . . . . . . .   74.950 mm (nominal)
1.6 litre . . . . . . . . . . . . . . . . . . . . . . . . . . . . . . . . . . . . . . . . . .   78.455 mm (nominal)
Diesel engines:
1.4 litre . . . . . . . . . . . . . . . . . . . . . . . . . . . . . . . . . . . . . . . . . .   73.528 mm (nominal)
1.6 litre . . . . . . . . . . . . . . . . . . . . . . . . . . . . . . . . . . . . . . . . . .   74.945 mm (nominal)
**Note:** *Check with your Citroën dealer or engine specialist regarding piston oversizes.*

## Piston rings

End gaps:
Petrol engines:
TU series:
Top compression ring . . . . . . . . . . . . . . . . . . . . . . . . . . . . . .   0.20 to 0.45 mm
Second compression ring . . . . . . . . . . . . . . . . . . . . . . . . . .   0.25 to 0.45 mm
Oil control ring . . . . . . . . . . . . . . . . . . . . . . . . . . . . . . . . .   0.25 to 0.45 mm
ET3 series:
Top compression ring . . . . . . . . . . . . . . . . . . . . . . . . . . . . . .   0.20 mm
Second compression ring . . . . . . . . . . . . . . . . . . . . . . . . . .   0.40 mm
Oil control ring . . . . . . . . . . . . . . . . . . . . . . . . . . . . . . . . .   0.25 mm
Diesel engines:
DV4 series:
Top compression ring . . . . . . . . . . . . . . . . . . . . . . . . . . . . . .   0.20 to 0.35 mm
Second compression ring . . . . . . . . . . . . . . . . . . . . . . . . . .   0.80 to 1.00 mm
Oil control ring . . . . . . . . . . . . . . . . . . . . . . . . . . . . . . . . .   0.20 to 0.40 mm
DV6 series:
Top compression ring . . . . . . . . . . . . . . . . . . . . . . . . . . . . . .   0.15 to 0.25 mm
Second compression ring . . . . . . . . . . . . . . . . . . . . . . . . . .   0.30 to 0.50 mm
Oil control ring . . . . . . . . . . . . . . . . . . . . . . . . . . . . . . . . .   0.35 to 0.55 mm

## Torque wrench settings

**Petrol engines**
Refer to Chapter 2A Specifications

**Diesel engines**
Refer to Chapter 2B or 2C Specifications

## 1  General information

Included in this Part of Chapter 2 are details of removing the engine/transmission from the car and general overhaul procedures for the cylinder head, cylinder block/crankcase and all other engine internal components.

The information given ranges from advice concerning preparation for an overhaul and the purchase of parts, to detailed step-by-step procedures covering removal, inspection, renovation and refitting of engine internal components.

After Section 5, all instructions are based on the assumption that the engine has been removed from the car. For information concerning in-car engine repair, as well as the removal and refitting of those external components necessary for full overhaul, refer to Part A, B or C of this Chapter, as applicable, and to Section 5. Ignore any preliminary dismantling operations described in Parts A, B or C that are no longer relevant once the engine has been removed from the car.

Apart from torque wrench settings, which are given at the beginning of Parts A, B or C, all specifications relating to engine overhaul are at the beginning of this Part of Chapter 2.

## 2  Engine overhaul –
general information

It is not always easy to determine when, or if, an engine should be completely overhauled, as a number of factors must be considered.

High mileage is not necessarily an indication that an overhaul is needed, while low mileage does not preclude the need for an overhaul. Frequency of servicing is probably the most important consideration. An engine which has had regular and frequent oil and filter changes, as well as other required maintenance, should give many thousands of miles of reliable service. Conversely, a neglected engine may require an overhaul very early in its life.

Excessive oil consumption is an indication that piston rings, valve seals and/or valve guides are in need of attention. Make sure that oil leaks are not responsible before deciding that the rings and/or guides are worn. Perform a compression test, as described in Part A or B of this Chapter (as applicable), to determine the likely cause of the problem.

Check the oil pressure with a gauge fitted in place of the oil pressure switch, and compare it with that specified. If it is extremely low, the main and big-end bearings, and/or the oil pump, are probably worn out.

Loss of power, rough running, knocking or metallic engine noises, excessive valve gear noise, and high fuel consumption may also point to the need for an overhaul, especially if they are all present at the same time. If a complete service does not remedy the situation, major mechanical work is the only solution.

A full engine overhaul involves restoring all internal parts to the specification of a new engine. During a complete overhaul, the pistons and the piston rings are renewed, and the cylinder bores are reconditioned. New main and big-end bearings are generally fitted; if necessary, the crankshaft may be reground, to compensate for wear in the journals. The valves are also serviced as well, since they are usually in less-than-perfect condition at this point. Always pay careful attention to the condition of the oil pump when overhauling the engine, and renew it if there is any doubt as to its serviceability. The end result should be an as-new engine that will give many trouble-free miles.

Critical cooling system components such as the hoses, thermostat and water pump should be renewed when an engine is overhauled. The radiator should be checked carefully, to ensure that it is not clogged or leaking. Also, it is a good idea to renew the oil pump whenever the engine is overhauled.

Before beginning the engine overhaul, read through the entire procedure, to familiarise yourself with the scope and requirements of the job. Check on the availability of parts and make sure that any necessary special tools and equipment are obtained in advance. Most work can be done with typical hand tools, although a number of precision measuring tools are required for inspecting parts to determine if they must be renewed.

The services provided by an engineering machine shop or engine reconditioning specialist will almost certainly be required, particularly if major repairs such as crankshaft regrinding or cylinder reboring are necessary. Apart from carrying out machining operations, these establishments will normally handle the inspection of parts, offer advice concerning reconditioning or renewal and supply new components such as pistons, piston rings and bearing shells. It is recommended that the establishment used is a member of the Federation of Engine Remanufacturers, or a similar society.

Always wait until the engine has been completely dismantled, and until all components (especially the cylinder block/crankcase and the crankshaft) have been inspected, before deciding what service and repair operations must be performed by an engineering works. The condition of these components will be the major factor to consider when determining whether to overhaul the original engine, or to buy a reconditioned unit. Do not, therefore, purchase parts or have overhaul work done on other components until they have been thoroughly inspected. As a general rule, time is the primary cost of an overhaul, so it does not pay to fit worn or sub-standard parts.

As a final note, to ensure maximum life and minimum trouble from a reconditioned engine, everything must be assembled with care, in a spotlessly-clean environment.

## 3 Engine/transmission removal – methods and precautions

If you have decided that the engine must be removed for overhaul or major repair work, several preliminary steps should be taken.

Locating a suitable place to work is extremely important. Adequate work space, along with storage space for the car, will be needed. If a workshop or garage is not available, at the very least, a flat, level, clean work surface is required.

Cleaning the engine compartment and engine/transmission before beginning the removal procedure will help keep tools clean and organised.

An engine hoist will also be necessary. Make sure the equipment is rated in excess of the combined weight of the engine and transmission. Safety is of primary importance, considering the potential hazards involved in removing the engine/transmission from the car.

The help of an assistant is essential. Apart from the safety aspects involved, there are many instances when one person cannot simultaneously perform all of the operations required during engine/transmission removal.

Plan the operation ahead of time. Before starting work, arrange for the hire of or obtain all of the tools and equipment you will need. Some of the equipment necessary to perform engine/transmission removal and installation safely (in addition to an engine hoist) is as follows: a heavy duty trolley jack, complete sets of spanners and sockets as described in the rear of this manual, wooden blocks, and plenty of rags and cleaning solvent for mopping-up spilled oil, coolant and fuel. If the hoist must be hired, make sure that you arrange for it in advance, and perform all of the operations possible without it beforehand. This will save you money and time.

Plan for the car to be out of use for quite a while. An engineering machine shop or engine reconditioning specialist will be required to perform some of the work which cannot be accomplished without special equipment. These places often have a busy schedule, so it would be a good idea to consult them before removing the engine, in order to accurately estimate the amount of time required to rebuild or repair components that may need work.

During the engine/transmission removal procedure, it is advisable to make notes of the locations of all brackets, cable ties, earthing points, etc, as well as how the wiring harnesses, hoses and electrical connections are attached and routed around the engine and engine compartment. An effective way of doing this is to take a series of photographs of the various components before they are disconnected or removed; the resulting photographs will prove invaluable when the engine/transmission is refitted.

Always be extremely careful when removing and refitting the engine/transmission. Serious injury can result from careless actions. Plan ahead and take your time, and a job of this nature, although major, can be accomplished successfully.

The engine and transmission assembly is removed downwards from the engine compartment on all models described in this manual.

## 4 Engine/transmission – removal and refitting

**Note:** *Such is the complexity of the power unit arrangement on these vehicles, and the*

variations that may be encountered according to model and optional equipment fitted, that the following should be regarded as a guide to the work involved, rather than a step-by-step procedure. Where differences are encountered, or additional component disconnection or removal is necessary, make notes of the work involved as an aid to refitting.

⚠️ **Warning: It is essential to observe strict precautions when working on the fuel system components of the diesel engines, particularly the high-pressure side of the system. Before carrying out any engine operations that entail working on, or near, any part of the fuel system, refer to the special information given in Chapter 4B, Section 2.**

### Removal

**1** Remove the battery and battery tray/box (see Chapter 5A). Wait five minutes, and then disconnect the engine wiring harness plugs at the fusebox or ECU depending on model. Remove the ECU as described in Chapter 4A or 4B.

**2** Apply the handbrake, then jack up the front of the vehicle and support it on axle stands (see *Jacking and vehicle support*). Remove both front roadwheels. Undo the screws and remove the engine undershield.

**3** Where fitted, remove the plastic cover from the top of the engine.

**4** To improve access, remove the bonnet as described in Chapter 11.

**5** Drain the cooling system with reference to Chapter 1A or 1B.

**6** Drain the transmission oil/fluid as described in Chapter 7A or 7B. Refit the drain and filler plugs, and tighten them to their specified torque settings.

**7** If the engine is to be dismantled, drain the engine oil and remove the oil filter as described in Chapter 1A or 1B. Clean and refit the drain plug, tightening it securely.

**8** Push the centre pins in a little, then prise out the complete plastic expanding rivets and remove the front wheel arch liners from both sides.

**9** Refer to Chapter 1A or 1B and remove the auxiliary drivebelt.

**10** Refer to Chapter 3 and remove the radiator electric cooling fan.

**11** Refer to Chapter 8 and remove both front driveshafts.

**12** On diesel engines with an intercooler, remove the air ducts leading from the turbocharger and inlet manifold to the intercooler.

**13** Remove the air cleaner housing and ducting as described in Chapter 4A or 4B.

**14** Disconnect the radiator top and bottom hoses, the heater hoses at the engine compartment bulkhead, the expansion tank hose and, where applicable, the automatic transmission fluid cooler hoses.

**15** On models with air conditioning, refer to Chapter 3 and unbolt the compressor from the engine. **Do not** disconnect the refrigerant lines. Support or tie the compressor to one side.

**16** Remove the exhaust system with reference to Chapter 4A or 4B.

**17** Note their fitted positions and harness routing, then disconnect all relevant wiring plugs from the transmission. If necessary label the connectors as they are unplugged.

**18** Disconnect the engine wiring harness connectors at the fusebox, and on diesel engines the three connectors at the pre/post-heating control unit (located under the left-hand wheel arch). Release the wiring harness from the retaining clips on the timing cover at the right-hand end of the engine (where applicable).

**19** Disconnect the engine earth leads at the fusebox, under the left hand wheel arch and on the left-hand chassis member.

**20** Disconnect the hose from the vacuum pump on the left-hand end of the cylinder head (diesel engines) or the brake servo unit vacuum pipe (petrol engines) – see Chapter 9.

**21** Disconnect the accelerator cable (where fitted) with reference to Chapter 4A.

**22** Disconnect the fuel feed and return hoses and plug the hoses and unions to prevent dirt ingress. Release the fuel hoses from the retaining clips on the engine and move them aside.

**23** Disconnect the selector cable(s) from the transmission as described in Chapter 7A or 7B.

**24** On manual transmission models, unbolt the clutch slave cylinder and release the fluid pipe from its retaining clips. Tie the cylinder to one side, without disconnecting the fluid pipe (see Chapter 6). Use an elastic band around the cylinder to prevent the piston from being discharged.

**25** Remove the front subframe as described in Chapter 10.

**26** Using a hoist attached to the lifting eyes on the cylinder head, take the weight of the engine and transmission.

**27** Remove the right-hand and left-hand engine mountings and support brackets as described in Chapter 2A, 2B or 2C.

**28** Make a final check to ensure all wiring, hoses and brackets that would prevent the removal of the assembly have been disconnected.

**29** Carefully lower the engine/transmission from the engine compartment taking care not to damage the surrounding components. Ideally lower the unit onto a low trolley so that it may be withdrawn from under the car. Disconnect the hoist from the engine/transmission assembly.

### Separation

**30** With the engine/transmission assembly removed, support the assembly on suitable blocks of wood on a workbench (or failing that, on a clean area of the workshop floor).

**31** Undo the retaining bolts, and remove the flywheel lower cover plate (where fitted) from the transmission.

**32** Slacken and remove the retaining bolts, and remove the starter motor from the transmission.

**33** Disconnect any remaining wiring connectors at the transmission, then move the main engine wiring harness to one side.

**34** On automatic transmission models, locate the access hole at the lower rear of the cylinder block, then turn the crankshaft by means of a socket on the crankshaft pulley bolt, until one of the three torque converter retaining nuts is accessible through the access hole. Undo the accessible torque converter bolt, then turn the crankshaft as necessary and undo the remaining two bolts.

**35** Ensure that both engine and transmission are adequately supported, then slacken and remove the remaining bolts securing the transmission housing to the engine. Note the correct fitted positions of each bolt (and the relevant brackets) as they are removed, to use as a reference on refitting. On diesel models, the left-hand catalytic converter mounting stud must be removed to access the front transmission-to-engine bolt.

**36** Carefully withdraw the transmission from the engine, ensuring that the weight of the transmission is not allowed to hang on the input shaft while it is engaged with the clutch friction disc (manual transmission models) or that the torque converter does not slip from the input shaft (automatic transmission models).

**37** If they are loose, remove the locating dowels from the engine or transmission, and keep them in a safe place.

### Refitting

**38** If the engine and transmission have not been separated, perform the operations described below from paragraph 45 onwards.

**39** Apply a smear of high melting-point grease (Citroën recommend the use of Molykote BR2 plus – available from your Citroën dealer) to the splines of the transmission input shaft. Do not apply too much, otherwise there is a possibility of the grease contaminating the clutch friction disc.

**40** Ensure that the locating dowels are correctly positioned in the engine or transmission.

**41** Carefully offer the transmission to the engine, until the locating dowels are engaged. On manual transmission models, ensure that the weight of the transmission is not allowed to hang on the input shaft as it is engaged with the clutch friction disc. On automatic transmission models, ensure the torque converter studs engage correctly with the corresponding holes in the driveplate.

**42** Refit the transmission housing-to-engine bolts, ensuring that all the necessary brackets are correctly positioned, and tighten them securely.

**43** Refit the starter motor, and securely tighten its retaining bolts.

**44** Refit the lower flywheel cover plate (where fitted) to the transmission, and securely tighten the bolts.

**45** Reconnect the hoist and lifting tackle to the engine lifting brackets. With the aid of an assistant, lift the assembly into the engine compartment, taking care not to damage surrounding components.

**46** Refit the right-hand and left-hand engine mountings and support brackets as described in Chapter 2A, 2B or 2C.

**47** Remove the hoist from the engine.

**48** Refit the front subframe as described in Chapter 10.

**49** The remainder of the refitting procedure is a direct reversal of the removal sequence, with reference to the relevant chapters and noting the following points:

a) Ensure that the wiring loom is correctly routed and retained by all the relevant retaining clips; all connectors should be correctly and securely reconnected.

b) Ensure that all coolant hoses are correctly reconnected, and securely retained by their retaining clips.

c) Refill the engine and transmission with the correct quantity and type of lubricant, as described in Chapters 1A or 1B, and 7A or 7B. On automatic transmission models check, and if necessary top-up the transmission fluid as described in Chapter 1B.

d) Refill the cooling system as described in Chapter 1A or 1B.

e) Pressurise/prime the fuel system as described in Chapter 4A (petrol engines), or Chapter 4B (diesel engines).

f) Initialise the engine management ECU as follows. Start the engine and run to normal temperature. Carry out a road test during which the following procedure should be made. Engage third gear and stabilise the engine at 1000 rpm. Now accelerate fully to 3500 rpm.

## 5  Engine overhaul – dismantling sequence

**1** It is much easier to dismantle and work on the engine if it is mounted on a portable engine stand. These stands can often be hired from a tool hire shop. Before the engine is mounted on a stand, the flywheel/driveplate should be removed, so that the stand bolts can be tightened into the end of the cylinder block/crankcase.

**2** If a stand is not available, it is possible to dismantle the engine with it blocked up on a sturdy workbench, or on the floor. Be extra careful not to tip or drop the engine when working without a stand.

**3** If you are going to obtain a reconditioned engine, all the external components must be removed first, to be transferred to the new engine (just as they will if you are doing a complete engine overhaul yourself). These components include the following:

a) Ancillary unit mounting brackets (oil filter, starter, alternator, power steering pump, etc).

**6.6a Compress the valve spring using a spring compressor . . .**

**6.6b . . . then extract the collets and release the spring compressor**

**6.6c Remove the spring retainer . . .**

**6.6d . . . followed by the valve spring**

b) Thermostat and housing (Chapter 3).
c) Dipstick tube/sensor.
d) All electrical switches and sensors.
e) Inlet and exhaust manifolds – where applicable (Chapter 4A or 4B).
f) Ignition coils and spark plugs – as applicable (Chapter 5B and 1A).
g) Flywheel/driveplate (Part A, B or C of this Chapter).

**Note:** When removing the external components from the engine, pay close attention to details that may be helpful or important during refitting. Note the fitted position of gaskets, seals, spacers, pins, washers, bolts, and other small items.

**4** If you are obtaining a 'short' engine (which consists of the engine cylinder block/crankcase, crankshaft, pistons and connecting rods all assembled), then the cylinder head, sump, oil pump, and timing belt will have to be removed also.

**5** If you are planning a complete overhaul,

**6.8a Withdraw the valve . . .**

the engine can be dismantled, and the internal components removed, in the order given below, referring to Part A, B or C of this Chapter unless otherwise stated.

a) Inlet and exhaust manifolds – where applicable (Chapter 4A or 4B).
b) Timing belts, sprockets and tensioner(s).
c) Cylinder head.
d) Flywheel/driveplate.
e) Sump.
f) Oil pump.
g) Piston/connecting rod assemblies (Section 9). **Note:** On diesel engines, remove the crankshaft main bearing ladder before the pistons.
h) Crankshaft (Section 10).

**6** Before beginning the dismantling and overhaul procedures, make sure that you have all of the correct tools necessary. Refer to Tools and working facilities for further information.

**6.8b . . . then use a pair of pliers to remove the valve stem oil seal. On diesel engines the spring seat is integral with the seal**

## 6 Cylinder head – dismantling

**Note:** New and reconditioned cylinder heads are available from the manufacturer, and from engine overhaul specialists. Be aware that some specialist tools are required for the dismantling and inspection procedures, and new components may not be readily available. It may therefore be more practical and economical for the home mechanic to purchase a reconditioned head, rather than dismantle, inspect and recondition the original head.

**1** Remove the cylinder head as described in Part A, B or C of this Chapter (as applicable).
**2** If not already done, remove the inlet and exhaust manifolds with reference to Chapter 4A or 4B. Remove any remaining brackets or housings as required.
**3** Remove the camshaft(s), hydraulic tappets and rockers (as applicable) as described in Part A, B or C of this Chapter.
**4** If not already done on petrol models, remove the spark plugs as described in Chapter 1A.
**5** If not already done on diesel models, remove the glow plugs as described in Chapter 5C.
**6** On all models, using a valve spring compressor, compress each valve spring in turn until the split collets can be removed. Release the compressor, and lift off the spring retainer, spring and, where fitted, the spring seat. Using a pair of pliers, carefully extract the valve stem oil seal from the top of the guide. On 16-valve engines, the valve stem oil seal also forms the spring seat and is deeply recessed in the cylinder head. It is also a tight fit on the valve guide making it difficult to remove with pliers or a conventional valve stem oil seal removal tool. It can be easily removed, however, using a self-locking nut of suitable diameter screwed onto the end of a bolt and locked with a second nut. Push the nut down onto the top of the seal; the locking portion of the nut will grip the seal allowing it to be withdrawn from the top of the valve guide. Access to the valves is limited, and it may be necessary to make up an adapter out of metal tube – cut out a 'window' so that the valve collets can be removed **(see illustrations)**.
**7** If, when the valve spring compressor is screwed down, the spring retainer refuses to free and expose the split collets, gently tap the top of the tool, directly over the retainer, with a light hammer. This will free the retainer.
**8** Withdraw the valve from the combustion chamber then, using a pair of pliers, carefully extract the valve stem oil seal from the top of the guide. Lift out the spring seat, where fitted, noting that on diesel engines, the valve stem oil seal also forms the spring seat **(see illustrations)**.
**9** It is essential that each valve is stored together with its collets, retainer, spring, and spring seat. The valves should also be kept in their correct sequence, unless they are so badly worn that they are to be renewed.

If they are going to be kept and used again, place each valve assembly in a labelled polythene bag or similar small container (see illustration). Note that No 1 valve is nearest to the transmission (flywheel/driveplate) end of the engine.

### 7  Cylinder head and valves – cleaning and inspection

1 Thorough cleaning of the cylinder head and valve components, followed by a detailed inspection, will enable you to decide how much valve service work must be carried out during the engine overhaul. **Note:** *If the engine has been severely overheated, it is best to assume that the cylinder head is warped – check carefully for signs of this.*

### Cleaning

2 Scrape away all traces of old gasket material from the cylinder head.
3 Scrape away the carbon from the combustion chambers and ports, then wash the cylinder head thoroughly with paraffin or a suitable solvent.
4 Scrape off any heavy carbon deposits that may have formed on the valves, then use a power-operated wire brush to remove deposits from the valve heads and stems.

### Inspection

**Note:** *Be sure to perform all the following inspection procedures before concluding that the services of a machine shop or engine overhaul specialist are required. Make a list of all items that require attention.*

#### Cylinder head

5 Inspect the head very carefully for cracks, evidence of coolant leakage, and other damage. If cracks are found, a new cylinder head should be obtained. Use a straight-edge and feeler blade to check that the cylinder head gasket surface is not distorted (see illustration). If it is, it may be possible to have it machined, provided that the cylinder head height is not significantly reduced.
6 Examine the valve seats in each of the combustion chambers. If they are severely pitted, cracked, or burned, they will need to be renewed or recut by an engine overhaul specialist. If they are only slightly pitted, this can be removed by grinding-in the valve heads and seats with fine valve-grinding compound, as described below. If in any doubt, have the cylinder head inspected by an engine overhaul specialist.
7 Check the valve guides for wear by inserting the relevant valve, and checking for side-to-side motion of the valve. A very small amount of movement is acceptable. If the movement seems excessive, remove the valve. Measure the valve stem diameter (see below), and renew the valve if it is worn. If the valve stem is not worn, the wear must be in the valve guide, and the guide must be renewed.

**6.9  Place each valve and its associated components in a labelled bag**

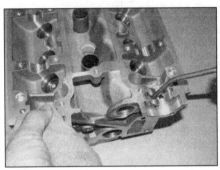
**7.9a  Apply compressed air to the oil feed bore of the inlet camshaft, seal the bore in the exhaust camshaft bore with a rag . . .**

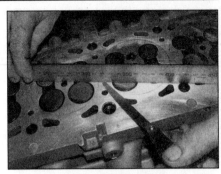
**7.5  Check the cylinder head gasket surface for distortion**

**7.9b  . . . and the camshaft oil supply non-return valve will be ejected from the underside of the cylinder head**

The renewal of valve guides is best carried out by an engine overhaul specialist, who will have the necessary tools available. Where no valve stem diameter is specified, seek the advice of a Citroën dealer or engine overhaul specialist on the best course of action.
8 If renewing the valve guides, the valve seats should be recut or reground only *after* the guides have been fitted.
9 Where applicable, examine the camshaft oil supply non-return valve in the oil feed bore at the timing belt end of the cylinder head. Check that the valve is not loose in the cylinder head and that the ball is free to move within the valve body. If the valve is a loose fit in its bore, or if there is any doubt about its condition, it should be renewed. The non-return valve can be removed (assuming it is not loose), using compressed air, such as that generated by a tyre foot pump. Place the pump nozzle over the oil feed bore of the camshaft bearing journal and seal the corresponding oil feed bore with a rag. Apply the compressed air and the valve will be forced out of its location in the underside of the cylinder head (see illustrations). Fit the new non-return valve to its bore on the underside of the head ensuring it is fitted the correct way. Oil should be able to pass upwards through the valve to the camshafts, but the ball in the valve should prevent the oil from returning back to the cylinder block. Use a thin socket or similar to push the valve fully into position.

#### Valves

10 Examine the head of each valve for pitting, burning, cracks, and general wear. Check the valve stem for scoring and wear ridges. Rotate the valve, and check for any obvious indication that it is bent. Look for pits or excessive wear on the tip of each valve stem. Renew any valve that shows any such signs of wear or damage.
11 If the valve appears satisfactory at this stage, measure the valve stem diameter at several points using a micrometer (see illustration). Any significant difference in the readings obtained indicates wear of the valve stem. Should any of these conditions be apparent, the valve must be renewed.
12 If the valves are in satisfactory condition, they should be ground (lapped) into their respective seats, to ensure a smooth, gas-tight seal. If the seat is only lightly pitted, or if it has been recut, fine grinding compound only should be used to produce the required finish.

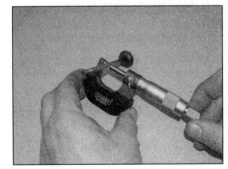
**7.11  Measure the valve stem diameter with a micrometer**

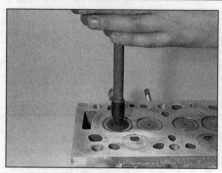

**7.14 Grinding-in a valve**

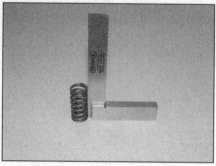

**7.18 Check each valve spring for squareness**

Coarse valve-grinding compound should not be used, unless a seat is badly burned or deeply pitted. If this is the case, the cylinder head and valves should be inspected by an expert, to decide whether seat recutting, or even the renewal of the valve or seat insert (where possible) is required.

**13** Valve grinding is carried out as follows. Place the cylinder head upside-down on a bench.

**14** Smear a trace of (the appropriate grade of) valve-grinding compound on the seat face, and press a suction grinding tool onto the valve head **(see illustration)**. With a semi-rotary action, grind the valve head to its seat, lifting the valve occasionally to redistribute the grinding compound. A light spring placed under the valve head will greatly ease this operation.

**15** If coarse grinding compound is being used, work only until a dull, matt even surface is produced on both the valve seat and the valve, then wipe off the used compound, and repeat the process with fine compound. When a smooth unbroken ring of light grey matt finish is produced on both the valve and seat, the grinding operation is complete. *Do not* grind-in the valves any further than absolutely necessary, or the seat will be prematurely sunk into the cylinder head.

**16** When all the valves have been ground-in, carefully wash off *all* traces of grinding compound using paraffin or a suitable solvent, before reassembling the cylinder head.

**Valve components**

**17** Examine the valve springs for signs of damage and discoloration. No minimum free length is specified by Citroën, so the only way of judging valve spring wear is by comparison with a new component.

**18** Stand each spring on a flat surface, and check it for squareness **(see illustration)**. If any of the springs are damaged, distorted

or have lost their tension, obtain a complete new set of springs. It is normal to renew the valve springs as a matter of course if a major overhaul is being carried out.

**19** Renew the valve stem oil seals regardless of their apparent condition.

**8 Cylinder head –**
**reassembly**

**1** Working on the first valve assembly, refit the spring seat then dip the new valve stem oil seal in fresh engine oil. Locate the seal on the valve guide and press the seal firmly onto the guide using a suitable socket **(see illustrations)**. Note that on diesel engines, the seal is integral with the lower spring seat.

**2** Lubricate the stem of the first valve, and insert it in the guide **(see illustration)**.

**3** Locate the valve spring on top of its seat, then refit the spring retainer.

**4** Compress the valve spring, and locate the split collets in the recess in the valve stem. Release the compressor, then repeat the procedure on the remaining valves. Ensure that each valve is inserted into its original location. If new valves are being fitted, insert them into the locations to which they have been ground.

> **HAYNES**
> **HiNT**
> *Use a little dab of grease to hold the collets in position on the valve stem while the spring compressor is released.*

**5** With all the valves installed, support the cylinder head and, using a hammer and interposed block of wood, tap the end of each valve stem to settle the components.

**6** Refit the camshafts, hydraulic tappets and rocker arms (as applicable) as described in Part A, B or C of this Chapter.

**7** Refit any remaining components using the reverse of the removal sequence and with new seals or gaskets as necessary.

**8** The cylinder head can then be refitted as described in Part A, B or C of this Chapter.

**9 Piston/connecting rod**
**assembly –**
**removal**

**1** Remove the cylinder head, sump and oil pump as described in Part A, B or C of this Chapter. **Note:** *On diesel engines, the main bearing ladder must be removed before the piston/connecting rods.*

**2** If there is a pronounced wear ridge at the top of any bore, it may be necessary to remove it with a scraper or ridge reamer to avoid piston damage during removal. Such a ridge indicates excessive wear of the cylinder bore.

**3** Using quick-drying paint, mark each connecting rod and big-end bearing cap with its respective cylinder number on the flat machined surface provided; if the engine has been dismantled before, note carefully

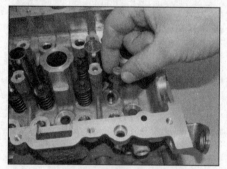

**8.1a Locate the valve stem oil seal on the valve guide . . .**

**8.1b . . . and press the seal firmly onto the guide using a suitable socket**

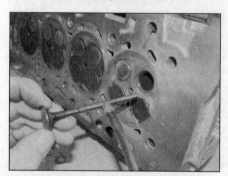

**8.2 Lubricate the valve stem and insert it in the guide**

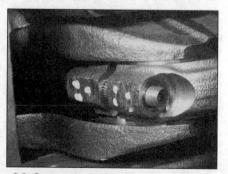

**9.3 Connecting rod and big-end bearing cap identification marks (No 3 shown)**

any identifying marks made previously **(see illustration)**. Note that No 1 cylinder is at the transmission (flywheel) end of the engine.

**4** Turn the crankshaft to bring pistons 1 and 4 to BDC (bottom dead centre). On diesel engines, remove the main bearing ladder as described in Section 10 of this Chapter.

**5** Unscrew the nuts or bolts, as applicable, from No 1 piston big-end bearing cap. Take off the cap, and recover the bottom half bearing shell **(see illustration)**. If the bearing shells are to be re-used, tape the cap and the shell together.

**6** Where applicable, to prevent the possibility of damage to the crankshaft bearing journals, tape over the connecting rod stud threads where fitted **(see illustration)**.

**7** Using a hammer handle, push the piston up through the bore, and remove it from the top of the cylinder block. Recover the bearing shell, and tape it to the connecting rod for safe-keeping.

**8** Loosely refit the big-end cap to the connecting rod, and secure with the nuts/bolts – this will help to keep the components in their correct order.

**9** Remove No 4 piston assembly in the same way.

**10** Turn the crankshaft through 180° to bring pistons 2 and 3 to BDC (bottom dead centre), and remove them in the same way.

## 10 Crankshaft – removal

**1** Remove the crankshaft sprocket and the oil pump as described in Part A, B or C of this Chapter (as applicable).

**2** Remove the pistons and connecting rods, as described in Section 9. If no work is to be done on the pistons and connecting rods, there is no need to remove the cylinder head, or to push the pistons out of the cylinder bores. The pistons should just be pushed far enough up the bores so that they are positioned clear of the crankshaft journals. **Note:** *On diesel engines, the main bearing ladder must be removed before the piston/connecting rods.*

**3** Check the crankshaft endfloat as described in Section 13, then proceed as follows.

### 1.1 and 1.4 litre petrol engines

**4** Work around the outside of the cylinder block, and unscrew all the small (M6) bolts securing the main bearing ladder to the base of the cylinder block. Note the correct fitted depth of both the left- and right-hand crankshaft oil seals in the cylinder block/main bearing ladder.

**5** Working in a diagonal sequence, evenly and progressively slacken the ten large (M11) main bearing ladder retaining bolts by a turn at a time. Once all the bolts are loose, remove them from the ladder.

**6** With all the retaining bolts removed, carefully lift the main bearing ladder casting away from the base of the cylinder block.

**9.5 Remove the big-end bearing shell and cap**

Recover the lower main bearing shells, and tape them to their respective locations in the casting. If the two locating dowels are a loose fit, remove them and store them with the casting for safe-keeping.

**7** Lift out the crankshaft, and discard both the oil seals. Remove the oil pump drive chain from the end of the crankshaft. Where necessary, slide off the drive sprocket, and recover the Woodruff key.

**8** Recover the upper main bearing shells, and store them along with the relevant lower bearing shell. Also recover the two thrustwashers (one fitted either side of No 2 main bearing) from the cylinder block.

### 1.6 litre petrol engines

**9** Unbolt and remove the crankshaft left- and right-hand oil seal housings from each end of the cylinder block, noting the correct fitted locations of the locating dowels. If the locating dowels are a loose fit, remove them and store them with the housings for safe-keeping.

**10** Remove the oil pump drive chain, and slide the drive sprocket off the end of the crankshaft. Remove the Woodruff key, and store it with the sprocket for safe-keeping.

**11** The main bearing caps should be numbered 1 to 5 from the transmission (flywheel/driveplate) end of the engine. If not, mark them accordingly using a centre-punch or paint.

**12** Unscrew and remove the main bearing cap retaining bolts, and withdraw the caps. Recover the lower main bearing shells, and tape them to their respective caps for safe-keeping.

**13** Carefully lift out the crankshaft, taking care not to displace the upper main bearing shell.

**14** Recover the upper bearing shells from the cylinder block, and tape them to their respective caps for safe-keeping. Remove the thrustwasher halves from the side of No 2 main bearing, and store them with the bearing cap.

### Diesel engines

**15** Work around the outside of the cylinder block, and unscrew all the small bolts securing the main bearing ladder to the base of the cylinder block. Note the correct fitted depth of the left-hand crankshaft oil seal in the cylinder block/main bearing ladder.

**9.6 To protect the crankshaft journals, tape over the connecting rod stud threads**

**16** Working in a diagonal sequence, evenly and progressively slacken the large main bearing ladder retaining bolts by a turn at a time. Once all the bolts are loose, remove them from the ladder. **Note:** *Prise up the two caps at the flywheel end of the ladder to expose the two end main bearing bolts **(see illustration)**.*

**17** With all the retaining bolts removed, carefully lift the main bearing ladder casting away from the base of the cylinder block. Recover the lower main bearing shells, and tape them to their respective locations in the casting. If the two locating dowels are a loose fit, remove them and store them with the casting for safe-keeping. Undo the big-end bolts and remove the pistons/connecting rods as described in Section 9.

**18** Lift out the crankshaft, and discard both the oil seals.

**19** Recover the upper main bearing shells, and store them along with the relevant lower bearing shell. Also recover the two thrustwashers (one fitted either side of No 2 main bearing) from the cylinder block.

## 11 Cylinder block/crankcase – cleaning and inspection

### Cleaning

**1** Remove all external components and electrical switches/sensors from the block. For complete cleaning, the core plugs

**10.16 On diesel engines, prise up the two caps to expose the main bearing bolts at the flywheel end**

**11.1 Cylinder block core plugs (arrowed)**

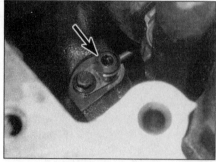

**11.3 Piston oil jet spray tube (arrowed) in the cylinder block**

should ideally be removed **(see illustration)**. Drill a small hole in the plugs, then insert a self-tapping screw into the hole. Pull out the plugs by pulling on the screw with a pair of grips, or by using a slide hammer.

**2** On aluminium block petrol engines with wet liners (1.1 and 1.4 litre), remove the liners – see paragraph 18.

**3** Where applicable, undo the retaining bolts and remove the piston oil jet spray tubes (there is one for each piston) from inside the cylinder block **(see illustration)**.

**4** Scrape all traces of gasket from the cylinder block/crankcase, and from the main bearing ladder/caps (as applicable), taking care not to damage the gasket/sealing surfaces.

**5** Remove all oil gallery plugs (where fitted). The plugs are usually very tight – they may have to be drilled out, and the holes retapped. Use new plugs when the engine is reassembled.

**6** If any of the castings are extremely dirty, all should be steam-cleaned.

**7** After the castings are returned, clean all oil holes and oil galleries one more time. Flush all internal passages with warm water until the water runs clear. Dry thoroughly, and apply a light film of oil to all mating surfaces, to prevent rusting. On cast-iron block engines, also oil the cylinder bores. If you have access to compressed air, use it to speed up the drying process, and to blow out all the oil holes and galleries.

 *Warning: Wear eye protection when using compressed air.*

**8** If the castings are not very dirty, you can do an adequate cleaning job with hot, soapy

water and a stiff brush. Take plenty of time, and do a thorough job. Regardless of the cleaning method used, be sure to clean all oil holes and galleries very thoroughly, and to dry all components well. On cast-iron block engines, protect the cylinder bores as described above, to prevent rusting.

**9** All threaded holes must be clean, to ensure accurate torque readings during reassembly. To clean the threads, run the correct-size tap into each of the holes to remove rust, corrosion, thread sealant or sludge, and to restore damaged threads **(see illustration)**. If possible, use compressed air to clear the holes of debris produced by this operation.

**10** Apply suitable sealant to the new oil gallery plugs, and insert them into the holes in the block. Tighten them securely. Also apply suitable sealant to new core plugs, and drive them into the block using a tube or socket.

**11** Where applicable, clean the threads of the piston oil jet retaining bolts, and apply a drop of thread-locking compound (Citroën recommend Loctite Frenetanch) to each bolt threads. Refit the piston oil jet spray tubes to the cylinder block, and tighten the retaining bolts to the specified torque setting.

**12** If the engine is not going to be reassembled right away, cover it with a large plastic bag to keep it clean; protect all mating surfaces and the cylinder bores as described above, to prevent rusting.

### Inspection

#### Cast-iron cylinder block

**13** Visually check the castings for cracks and

corrosion. Look for stripped threads in the threaded holes. If there has been any history of internal water leakage, it may be worthwhile having an engine overhaul specialist check the cylinder block/crankcase with special equipment. If defects are found, have them repaired if possible, or renew the assembly.

**14** Check each cylinder bore for scuffing and scoring. Check for signs of a wear ridge at the top of the cylinder, indicating that the bore is excessively worn.

**15** Accurate measuring of the cylinder bores requires specialised equipment and experience. We recommend having the bores measured by an engine reconditioning specialist who will also be able to supply appropriate pistons (where possible) should a rebore be necessary.

**16** If the cylinder bores and pistons are in reasonably good condition, and not worn beyond the specified limits, and if the piston-to-bore clearances can be maintained, then it will only be necessary to renew the piston rings. If this is the case, the cylinder bores must be honed to allow the new piston rings to bed in correctly and provide the best possible seal. An engine reconditioning specialist will carry out this work at moderate cost.

**17** At the time of writing, it was not clear whether oversize pistons were available for all models. Consult your Citroën dealer or engine specialist for the latest information on piston availability. If oversize pistons are available (either from Citroen, or from another source), then it may be possible to have the cylinder bores rebored and fit the oversize pistons. If oversize pistons are not available, and the bores are worn, renewal of the block seems to be the only option.

#### Aluminium cylinder block

**18** Remove the liner clamps (where used), then use a hardwood drift to tap out each liner from the inside of the cylinder block. When all the liners are released, tip the cylinder block/crankcase on its side and remove each liner from the top of the block. As each liner is removed, stick masking tape on its left-hand (transmission side) face, and write the cylinder number on the tape. No 1 cylinder is at the transmission (flywheel) end of the engine. Remove the sealing ring from the base of each liner, and discard **(see illustrations)**.

**11.9 Use a suitable tap to clean the cylinder block threaded holes**

**11.18a On aluminium block engines, remove each liner . . .**

**11.18b . . . and recover the bottom O-ring seal (arrowed)**

**19** Check each cylinder liner for scuffing and scoring. Check for signs of a wear ridge at the top of the liner, indicating that the bore is excessively worn.

**20** Take the liners to an engine reconditioning specialist and have their bores measured to determine if renewal is necessary. If it is, the specialist will be able to advise you regarding piston/liner availability.

**21** Prior to installing the liners, check the liner protrusion as follows. Thoroughly clean the mating surfaces of the liner and cylinder block. Insert the liners into the block ensuring each one is correctly seated; if the original liners are being refitted, ensure the liners are fitted in their original locations. With all four liners correctly installed, use a dial gauge (or a straight-edge and feeler blade) to check that the protrusion of each liner above the upper surface of the cylinder block is within the limits given in the Specifications. The maximum difference between any two liners must not be exceeded. **Note:** *If new liners are being fitted, it is permissible to interchange them to bring the difference in protrusion within limits. Remember to keep each piston with its respective liner.* If liner protrusion is not within the specified limits, seek the advice of an engine reconditioning specialist before proceeding with the engine rebuild.

**22** Once the protrusions have been checked, remove the liners from the block and fit a new sealing ring carefully to the base of each liner. Lubricate the base of each liner with a smear of oil to aid installation.

**23** Insert each liner into the cylinder block, taking care not to damage the O-ring, and press it home as far as possible by hand. Using a hammer and a block of wood, tap each liner lightly but fully onto its locating shoulder. If the original liners are being refitted, use the marks made on removal to ensure that each is refitted the correct way round, and is inserted into its original bore.

**24** Wipe clean, then lightly oil all exposed liner surfaces, to prevent rusting. Where necessary, clamp the liners back in position.

## 12 Piston/connecting rod assembly – inspection

**1** Before the inspection process can begin, the piston/connecting rod assemblies must be cleaned, and the original piston rings removed from the pistons.

**2** Carefully expand the old rings over the top of the pistons. The use of two or three old feeler blades will be helpful in preventing the rings dropping into empty grooves **(see illustration)**. Be careful not to scratch the piston with the ends of the ring. The rings are brittle, and will snap if they are spread too far. They are also very sharp – protect your hands and fingers. Note that the third ring incorporates an expander. Always remove the rings from the top of the piston. Keep each set of rings with its piston if the old rings are to be re-used.

**12.2  Remove the piston rings with the aid of a feeler gauge**

**3** Scrape away all traces of carbon from the top of the piston. A hand-held wire brush (or a piece of fine emery cloth) can be used, once the majority of the deposits have been scraped away.

**4** Remove the carbon from the ring grooves in the piston, using an old ring. Break the ring in half to do this (be careful not to cut your fingers – piston rings are sharp). Be careful to remove only the carbon deposits – do not remove any metal, and do not nick or scratch the sides of the ring grooves.

**5** Once the deposits have been removed, clean the piston/connecting rod assembly with paraffin or a suitable solvent, and dry thoroughly. Make sure that the oil return holes in the ring grooves are clear.

**6** If the pistons and cylinder bores are not damaged or worn excessively, and if the cylinder block does not need to be rebored (where possible), the original pistons can be refitted. Normal piston wear shows up as even vertical wear on the piston thrust surfaces, and slight looseness of the top ring in its groove. New piston rings should always be used when the engine is reassembled.

**7** Carefully inspect each piston for cracks around the skirt, around the gudgeon pin holes, and at the piston ring 'lands' (between the ring grooves).

**8** Look for scoring and scuffing on the piston skirt, holes in the piston crown, and burned areas at the edge of the crown. If the skirt is scored or scuffed, the engine may have been suffering from overheating, and/or abnormal combustion which caused excessively high operating temperatures. The cooling and lubrication

systems should be checked thoroughly. Scorch marks on the sides of the pistons show that blow-by has occurred. A hole in the piston crown, or burned areas at the edge of the piston crown, indicates that abnormal combustion (pre-ignition, knocking, or detonation) has been occurring. If any of the above problems exist, the causes must be investigated and corrected, or the damage will occur again. The causes are likely to be attributable to a faulty injector or engine management system fault.

**9** Corrosion of the piston, in the form of pitting, indicates that coolant has been leaking into the combustion chamber and/or the crankcase. Again, the cause must be corrected, or the problem may persist in the rebuilt engine.

**10** On aluminium block engines with wet liners, it is not possible to renew the pistons separately; pistons are only supplied with piston rings and a liner, as a part of a matched assembly (see Section 11). On iron-block engines, pistons can be purchased from a Citroën dealer or engine reconditioning specialist.

**11** Examine each connecting rod carefully for signs of damage, such as cracks around the big-end and small-end bearings. Check that the rod is not bent or distorted. Damage is highly unlikely, unless the engine has been seized or badly overheated. Detailed checking of the connecting rod assembly can only be carried out by an engine specialist with the necessary equipment.

**12** The connecting rod big-end cap nuts must be renewed whenever they are disturbed. Although Citroën do not specify that the bolts must also be renewed, it is recommended that the nuts and bolts are renewed as a complete set.

**13** On petrol engines, the gudgeon pins are an interference fit in the connecting rod small-end bearing. Therefore, piston and/or connecting rod renewal should be entrusted to an engine reconditioning specialist, who will have the necessary tooling to remove and install the gudgeon pins.

**14** On diesel engines, the gudgeon pins are of the floating type, secured in position by two circlips. On these engines, the pistons and connecting rods can be separated as follows.

**15** Using a small flat-bladed screwdriver, prise out the circlips, and push out the gudgeon pin **(see illustrations)**. Hand pressure should

**12.15a  Prise out the circlip . . .**

**12.15b  . . . and withdraw the gudgeon pin**

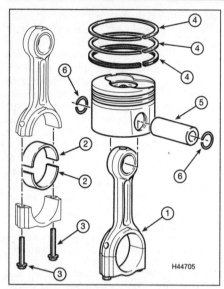

**12.19 Diesel engine piston and connecting rod assembly**

| | | | |
|---|---|---|---|
| *1* | *Connecting rod* | *4* | *Piston rings* |
| *2* | *Big-end shells* | *5* | *Gudgeon pin* |
| *3* | *Big-end bolt* | *6* | *Circlips* |

be sufficient to remove the pin. Identify the piston and rod to ensure correct reassembly. Discard the circlips – new ones *must* be used on refitting.

**16** Examine the gudgeon pin and connecting rod small-end bearing for signs of wear or damage. Wear can be cured by renewing both the pin and bush (where possible) or connecting rod. Bush renewal, however, is a specialist job – press facilities are required, and the new bush must be reamed accurately.

**17** The connecting rods themselves should not be in need of renewal, unless seizure or some other major mechanical failure has occurred. Check the alignment of the connecting rods visually, and if the rods are not straight, take them to an engine overhaul specialist for a more detailed check.

**18** Examine all components, and obtain any new parts accordingly. If new pistons are purchased, they will be supplied complete with gudgeon pins and circlips. Circlips can also be purchased individually.

**19** Ensure the piston and connecting rod are correctly positioned then apply a smear

of clean engine oil to the gudgeon pin **(see illustration)**. Slide it into the piston and through the connecting rod small-end. Check that the piston pivots freely on the rod, then secure the gudgeon pin in position with two new circlips. Ensure that each circlip is correctly located in its groove in the piston.

## 13 Crankshaft – inspection

### Checking endfloat

**1** If the crankshaft endfloat is to be checked, this must be done when the crankshaft is still installed in the cylinder block/crankcase, but is free to move (see Section 10).

**2** Check the endfloat using a dial gauge in contact with the end of the crankshaft. Push the crankshaft fully one way, and then zero the gauge. Push the crankshaft fully the other way, and check the endfloat. The result can be compared with the specified amount, and will give an indication as to whether new thrustwashers are required **(see illustration)**.

**3** If a dial gauge is not available, feeler blades can be used. First push the crankshaft fully towards the flywheel end of the engine, then use feeler blades to measure the gap between the web of No 2 crankpin and the thrustwasher **(see illustration)**.

### Inspection

**4** Clean the crankshaft using paraffin or a suitable solvent, and dry it, preferably with compressed air if available. Be sure to clean the oil holes with a pipe cleaner or similar probe, to ensure that they are not obstructed.

> ⚠ **Warning: Wear eye protection when using compressed air.**

**5** Check the main and big-end bearing journals for uneven wear, scoring, pitting and cracking.

**6** Big-end bearing wear is accompanied by distinct metallic knocking when the engine is running (particularly noticeable when the engine is pulling from low speed) and some loss of oil pressure.

**7** Main bearing wear is accompanied by severe engine vibration and rumble – getting

progressively worse as engine speed increases – and again by loss of oil pressure.

**8** Check the bearing journal for roughness by running a finger lightly over the bearing surface. Any roughness (which will be accompanied by obvious bearing wear) indicates that the crankshaft requires regrinding (where possible) or renewal.

**9** Check the oil seal contact surfaces at each end of the crankshaft for wear and damage. If the seal has worn a deep groove in the surface of the crankshaft, consult an engine overhaul specialist; repair may be possible, but otherwise a new crankshaft will be required.

**10** Take the crankshaft to an engine reconditioning specialist to have it measured for journal wear. If excessive wear is evident, they will be able to advise you with regard to regrinding the crankshaft and supplying new bearing shells.

**11** If the crankshaft has been reground, check for burrs around the crankshaft oil holes (the holes are usually chamfered, so burrs should not be a problem unless regrinding has been carried out carelessly). Remove any burrs with a fine file or scraper, and thoroughly clean the oil holes as described previously.

**12** At the time of writing, it was not clear whether Citroën produce oversize bearing shells for all of these engines. On some engines, if the crankshaft journals have not already been reground, it may be possible to have the crankshaft reconditioned, and to fit oversize shells. If no oversize shells are available and the crankshaft has worn beyond the specified limits, it will have to be renewed. Consult your Citroën dealer or engine specialist for further information on parts availability.

## 14 Main and big-end bearings – inspection

**1** Even though the main and big-end bearings should be renewed during the engine overhaul, the old bearings should be retained for close examination, as they may reveal valuable information about the condition of the engine. The bearing shells are graded by thickness, the grade of each shell being indicated by the colour code marked on it.

**2** Bearing failure can occur due to lack of lubrication, the presence of dirt or other foreign particles, overloading the engine, or corrosion **(see illustration)**. Regardless of the cause of bearing failure, the cause must be corrected (where applicable) before the engine is reassembled, to prevent it from happening again.

**3** When examining the bearing shells, remove them from the cylinder block/crankcase, the connecting rods and the connecting rod big-end bearing caps. Lay them out on a clean surface in the same general position as their location in the engine. This will enable you to match any bearing problems with the corresponding crankshaft journal. *Do not*

**13.2 The crankshaft endfloat can be checked with a dial gauge . . .**

**13.3 . . . or with feeler gauges**

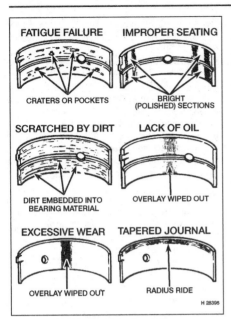

**14.2 Typical bearing failures**

touch any shell's bearing surface with your fingers while checking it, or the delicate surface may be scratched.

4 Dirt and other foreign matter gets into the engine in a variety of ways. It may be left in the engine during assembly, or it may pass through filters or the crankcase ventilation system. It may get into the oil, and from there into the bearings. Metal chips from machining operations and normal engine wear are often present. Abrasives are sometimes left in engine components after reconditioning, especially when parts are not thoroughly cleaned using the proper cleaning methods. Whatever the source, these foreign objects often end up embedded in the soft bearing material, and are easily recognised. Large particles will not embed in the bearing, and will score or gouge the bearing and journal. The best prevention for this cause of bearing failure is to clean all parts thoroughly, and keep everything spotlessly-clean during engine assembly. Frequent and regular engine oil and filter changes are also recommended.

5 Lack of lubrication (or lubrication breakdown) has a number of interrelated causes. Excessive heat (which thins the oil), overloading (which squeezes the oil from the bearing face) and oil leakage (from excessive bearing clearances, worn oil pump or high engine speeds) all contribute to lubrication breakdown. Blocked oil passages, which usually are the result of misaligned oil holes in a bearing shell, will also oil-starve a bearing, and destroy it. When lack of lubrication is the cause of bearing failure, the bearing material is wiped or extruded from the steel backing of the bearing. Temperatures may increase to the point where the steel backing turns blue from overheating.

6 Driving habits can have a definite effect on bearing life. Full-throttle, low-speed operation (labouring the engine) puts very high loads on bearings, tending to squeeze out the oil film. These loads cause the bearings to flex, which produces fine cracks in the bearing face (fatigue failure). Eventually, the bearing material will loosen in pieces, and tear away from the steel backing.

7 Short-distance driving leads to corrosion of bearings, because insufficient engine heat is produced to drive off the condensed water and corrosive gases. These products collect in the engine oil, forming acid and sludge. As the oil is carried to the engine bearings, the acid attacks and corrodes the bearing material.

8 Incorrect bearing installation during engine assembly will lead to bearing failure as well. Tight-fitting bearings leave insufficient bearing running clearance, and will result in oil starvation. Dirt or foreign particles trapped behind a bearing shell result in high spots on the bearing, which lead to failure.

9 *Do not* touch any shell's bearing surface with your fingers during reassembly; there is a risk of scratching the delicate surface, or of depositing particles of dirt on it.

10 As mentioned at the beginning of this Section, the bearing shells should be renewed as a matter of course during engine overhaul; to do otherwise is false economy.

## 15 Engine overhaul – reassembly sequence

1 Before reassembly begins, ensure that all new parts have been obtained, and that all necessary tools are available. Read through the entire procedure to familiarise yourself with the work involved, and to ensure that all items necessary for reassembly of the engine are at hand. In addition to all normal tools and materials, thread-locking compound will be needed. A tube of suitable liquid sealant will also be required for the joint faces that are fitted without gaskets. It is recommended that Citroën's own product(s) are used, which are specially formulated for this purpose; the relevant product names are quoted in the text of each Section where they are required.

2 In order to save time and avoid problems, engine reassembly can be carried out in the following order, referring to Part A, B or C of this Chapter unless otherwise stated:

a) *Crankshaft (See Section 17).* **Note:** *On diesel engines, the piston/connecting rods must be fitted before the crankshaft main bearing ladder.*
b) *Piston/connecting rod assemblies (See Section 18).*
c) *Oil pump.*
d) *Sump.*
e) *Flywheel/driveplate.*
f) *Cylinder head.*
g) *Injection pump and mounting bracket – diesel engines (Chapter 4B).*
h) *Timing belt tensioner pulley(s) and sprockets, and timing belt.*
i) *Engine external components.*

3 At this stage, all engine components should be absolutely clean and dry, with all faults repaired. The components should be laid out (or in individual containers) on a completely clean work surface.

## 16 Piston rings – refitting

1 Before fitting new piston rings, the ring end gaps must be checked as follows.

2 Lay out the piston/connecting rod assemblies and the new piston ring sets, so that the ring sets will be matched with the same piston and cylinder during the end gap measurement and subsequent engine reassembly.

3 Insert the top ring into the first cylinder, and push it down the bore using the top of the piston. This will ensure that the ring remains square with the cylinder walls. Position the ring near the bottom of the cylinder bore, at the lower limit of ring travel. Note that the top and second compression rings are different. The second ring can be identified by its taper; on petrol engines it also has a step on its lower surface. On diesel engines, the top ring has a chamfer on its upper/outer edge.

4 Measure the end gap using feeler blades.

5 Repeat the procedure with the ring at the top of the cylinder bore, at the upper limit of its travel **(see illustration)**, and compare the measurements with the figures given in the Specifications. If the end gaps are incorrect, check that you have the correct rings for your engine and for the cylinder bore size.

6 Repeat the checking procedure for each ring in the first cylinder, and then for the rings in the remaining cylinders. Remember to keep rings, pistons and cylinders matched up.

7 Once the ring end gaps have been checked, and if necessary corrected, the rings can be fitted to the pistons.

8 Fit the oil control ring expander (where fitted) then install the ring. The ring gap should be positioned 180° from the expander gap.

9 The second and top rings are different and can be identified from their cross-sections; the top ring is symmetrical whilst the second ring is tapered. Fit the second ring, ensuring its identification (TOP) marking is facing

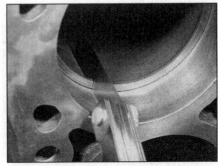

**16.5 Measure the piston rings end gaps with a feeler gauge**

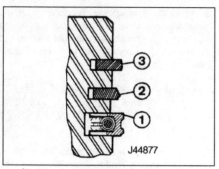

**16.9a  Typical piston ring fitting diagram –
petrol engines**

1  *Oil control ring*
2  *Second compression ring*
3  *Top compression ring*

upwards, then install the top ring **(see
illustrations)**. Arrange the oil control, second
and top ring end gaps so they are equally
spaced 120° apart. **Note:** *Always follow any
instructions supplied with the new piston ring
sets – different manufacturers may specify
different procedures. Do not mix up the top
and second compression rings, as they have
different cross-sections.*

## 17  Crankshaft – refitting

### Selection of bearing shells

**1**  Have the crankshaft inspected and measured
by an engine reconditioning specialist. They

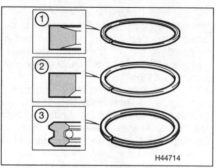

**16.9b  Piston ring fitting diagram –
diesel engines**

1  *Top compression ring*
2  *Second compression ring*
3  *Oil control ring*

will be able to carry out any regrinding/repairs,
and supply suitable main and big-end bearing
shells.

### Crankshaft refitting

**Note:** *New main bearing cap/lower crankcase
bolts must be used when refitting the
crankshaft.*

**2**  Where applicable, ensure that the oil spray
jets are fitted to the bearing locations in the
cylinder block.

#### 1.1 and 1.4 litre petrol engines

**3**  Using a little grease, stick the upper
thrustwashers to each side of the No 2 main
bearing upper location; ensure that the oilway
grooves on each thrustwasher face outwards
(away from the block).

**4**  Clean the backs of the bearing shells, and

the bearing locations in both the cylinder
block/crankcase and the main bearing ladder/
bearing caps.

**5**  Press the bearing shells into their locations,
ensuring that the tab on each shell engages in
the notch in the cylinder block/crankcase or
main bearing ladder/bearing cap. Take care not
to touch any shell's bearing surface with your
fingers. Note that the grooved bearing shells,
both upper and lower, are fitted to Nos 2 and 4
main bearings **(see illustration)**.

**6**  Liberally lubricate each bearing shell in the
cylinder block/crankcase with clean engine
oil.

**7**  Refit the Woodruff key, then slide on the
oil pump drive sprocket, and locate the drive
chain on the sprocket **(see illustration)**. Lower
the crankshaft into position so that Nos 2 and
3 cylinder crankpins are at TDC; Nos 1 and
4 cylinder crankpins will be at BDC, ready
for fitting No 1 piston. Check the crankshaft
endfloat as described in Section 13.

**8**  Thoroughly degrease the mating surfaces
of the cylinder block/crankcase and the main
bearing ladder. Apply a thin bead of suitable
sealant to the cylinder block mating surface of
the main bearing ladder casting, then spread
to an even film **(see illustration)**.

**9**  Ensure the locating dowels are in position
then lubricate the lower bearing shells with
clean engine oil. Refit the main bearing ladder
to the cylinder block, ensuring that the lower
bearings remain correctly fitted.

**10**  Install the main bearing ladder retaining
bolts, and tighten them all by hand only.
Working in a spiral pattern from the centre
bolts outwards, evenly and progressively
tighten the bolts to the specified Stage 1
torque wrench setting. Once all the bolts have
been tightened to the Stage 1 setting, working
in the same sequence, angle-tighten the bolts
through the specified Stage 2 angle using a
socket and extension bar. It is recommended
that an angle-measuring gauge is used
during this stage of the tightening, to ensure
accuracy **(see illustration)**. If a gauge is not
available, use a dab of white paint to make
alignment marks between the bolt head and
casting prior to tightening; the marks can
then be used to check that the bolt has been
rotated sufficiently during tightening.

**11**  Refit all the smaller bolts securing the
main bearing ladder to the base of the cylinder
block, and tighten them to the specified torque.
Check that the crankshaft rotates freely.

**12**  Refit the piston/connecting rod assemblies
to the crankshaft as described in Section 18.

**13**  Ensuring that the drive chain is correctly
located on the sprocket, refit the oil pump and
sump as described in Part A of this Chapter.

**14**  Fit two new crankshaft oil seals as
described in Part A of this Chapter.

**15**  Refit the flywheel as described in Part A of
this Chapter.

**16**  Refit the cylinder head (where removed)
as described in Part A of this Chapter. Also
refit the crankshaft sprocket and timing belt
(see Part A).

**17.5  Fit the grooved bearing shells to
No 2 and 4 main bearings –
1.1 and 1.4 litre petrol engines**

**17.7  Fit the oil pump drive chain and
sprocket – 1.1 and 1.4 litre petrol engines**

**17.8  Apply a thin film of sealant to the
cylinder block mating surface –
1.1 and 1.4 litre petrol engines**

**17.10  Tighten the ten main bearing bolts
to the specified torque –
1.1 and 1.4 litre petrol engines**

## 1.6 litre petrol engines

17  Using a little grease, stick the upper thrust-washers to each side of the No 2 main bearing upper location. Ensure that the oilway grooves on each thrustwasher face outwards (away from the cylinder block) **(see illustration)**.

18  Place the bearing shells in their locations as described in paragraphs 4 and 5 **(see illustration)**. If new shells are being fitted, ensure that all traces of protective grease are cleaned off using paraffin. Wipe dry the shells and connecting rods with a lint-free cloth. Liberally lubricate each bearing shell in the cylinder block/crankcase and cap with clean engine oil.

19  Lower the crankshaft into position so that Nos 2 and 3 cylinder crankpins are at TDC; Nos 1 and 4 cylinder crankpins will be at BDC, ready for fitting No 1 piston. Check the crank-shaft endfloat as described in Section 13.

20  Lubricate the lower bearing shells in the main bearing caps with clean engine oil. Make sure that the locating lugs on the shells engage with the corresponding recesses in the caps.

21  Fit the main bearing caps to their correct locations, ensuring that they are fitted the correct way round (the bearing shell lug recesses in the block and caps must be on the same side).

22  Lightly lubricate the threads and the underside of the heads of the main bearing cap bolts with engine oil then refit the bolts. Working in a spiral sequence from the centre bolts outwards, tighten the main bearing cap bolts evenly and progressively to the specified Stage 1 torque wrench setting. Once all the bolts have been tightened to the Stage 1 setting, working in the same sequence, angle-tighten the bolts through the specified Stage 2 angle, using a socket and extension bar. It is recommended that an angle-measuring gauge is used during this stage of the tightening, to ensure accuracy. If a gauge is not available, use a dab of white paint to make alignment marks between the bolt head and casting prior to tightening; the marks can then be used to check that the bolt has been rotated sufficiently during tightening.

23  Check that the crankshaft rotates freely.

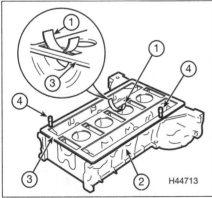

**17.34  Main bearing shell refitment – diesel engines**

*1  Bearing shell*
*2  Main bearing ladder*
*3  Citroën tool No 0194-Q*
*4  Aligning pins*

**17.17  Fit the thrustwashers to either side of the No 2 main bearing, with the oilway grooves facing outwards – 1.6 litre petrol engines**

24  Refit the piston/connecting rod assemblies to the crankshaft as described in Section 18.

25  Refit the Woodruff key to the crankshaft groove, and slide on the oil pump drive sprocket. Locate the drive chain on the sprocket.

26  Ensure that the mating surfaces of right-hand (timing belt end) oil seal housing and cylinder block are clean and dry. Note the correct fitted depth of the oil seal then, using a large flat-bladed screwdriver, lever the seal out of the housing.

27  Apply a smear of suitable sealant to the oil seal housing mating surface, and make sure that the locating dowels are in position. Slide the housing over the end of the crankshaft, and into position on the cylinder block. Tighten the housing retaining bolts securely.

28  Repeat the operations in paragraphs 26 and 27, and fit the left-hand (flywheel/driveplate end) oil seal housing.

29  Fit new crankshaft oil seals as described in Part A of this Chapter.

30  Ensuring that the chain is correctly located on the drive sprocket, refit the oil pump and sump as described in Part A of this Chapter.

31  Refit the flywheel/driveplate as described in Part A of this Chapter.

32  Refit the cylinder head (where removed) and install the crankshaft sprocket and timing belt as described in the relevant Sections of Part A of this Chapter.

## 1.4 litre diesel engine

**Note:** *On diesel engines, the piston/connecting rod assemblies must be fitted before refitting the crankshaft.*

33  Clean the backs of the bearing shells in both the cylinder block/crankcase and the main bearing ladder. If new shells are being fitted, ensure that all traces of protective grease are cleaned off using paraffin. Wipe dry the shells with a lint-free cloth.

34  Press the bearing shells into their locations, ensuring that the tab on each shell engages in the notch in the cylinder block/crankcase and bearing ladder. Take care not to touch any shell's bearing surface with your fingers. Note that the upper bearing shells all have a grooved surface, whereas the lower shells have a plain bearing surface. It is essential that the lower bearing shell halves are centrally located in the ladder. To ensure this use a Citroën tool No 0194-Q positioned

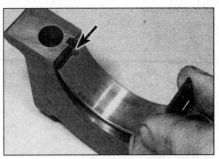

**17.18  Ensure the tab (arrowed) is located in the cut-out when fitting the bearing shells – 1.6 litre petrol engines**

over the ladder, and insert the bearing shells through the slots in the tool **(see illustration)**.

35  Liberally lubricate each bearing shell in the cylinder block with clean engine oil then lower the crankshaft into position.

36  Insert the thrustwashers to either side of No 2 main bearing upper location and push them around the bearing journal until their edges are horizontal. Ensure that the oilway grooves on each thrustwasher face outwards (away from the cylinder block). Now refit the piston and connecting rod assemblies as described in Section 18.

37  Thoroughly degrease the mating surfaces of the cylinder block and the crankshaft bearing cap housing/main bearing ladder. Apply a thin bead of RTV sealant to the bearing cap housing mating surface. Citroën recommend the use of Loctite Autojoint Noir for this purpose. Use two aligning pins (available from Citroën) inserted into the main bearing ladder, to ensure the correct positioning of the assembly.

38  Lubricate the lower bearing shells with clean engine oil, then refit the bearing cap housing, ensuring that the shells are not displaced, and that the locating dowels engage correctly. Remove the aligning pins from the bearing ladder.

39  Install the large and small crankshaft bearing cap housing/ladder retaining bolts, and screw them in until they are just making contact with the housing. Note that new large (M11) bolts must be used.

40  Tighten all the main bearing ladder bolts to their Stage 1 setting in sequence **(see illustration)**.

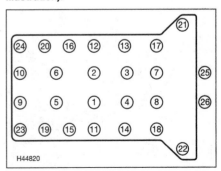

**17.40  Main bearing ladder bolts tightening sequence – diesel engines**

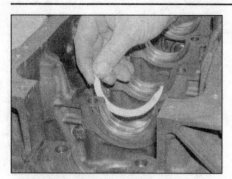

**17.49 Place the thrustwashers each side of the No 2 bearing upper location**

**41** Slacken (Stage 2) the large diameter bearing ladder bolts half a turn (180°), then tighten them in sequence to the Stage 3 torque setting, followed by the Stage 4 angle-tightening setting. Apply sealant to the two new bearing ladder bolt caps, and tap them into place over the two flywheel end bolts.

**42** Finally, tighten the small diameter bearing ladder bolts to their Stage 2 setting.

**43** With the bearing cap housing in place, check that the crankshaft rotates freely.

**44** Refit the oil pump and sump as described in Part B of this Chapter.

**45** Fit a new crankshaft left-hand oil seal, then refit the flywheel as described in Part B of this Chapter.

**46** Where removed, refit the cylinder head, crankshaft sprocket and timing belt also as described in Part B of this Chapter.

**1.6 litre diesel engine**

**Note:** *On diesel engines, the piston/connecting rod assemblies must be fitted before refitting the crankshaft.*

**47** Place the bearing shells in their locations. If new shells are being fitted, ensure that all traces of protective grease are cleaned off using paraffin. Wipe dry the shells with a lint-free cloth. The upper bearing shells all have a grooved surface, whereas the lower shells have a plain surface. On these engines, it's essential that the lower bearing shells are centrally located in the bearing cap housing/ladder. To ensure this, use Citroën tool No 0194-QZ positioned over the housing/ladder, and insert the

bearing shells through the slots in the tool **(see illustration 17.34)**.

**48** Liberally lubricate each bearing shell in the cylinder block with clean engine oil then lower the crankshaft into position.

**49** Insert the thrustwashers to either side of No 2 main bearing upper location and push them around the bearing journal until their edges are horizontal **(see illustration)**. Ensure that the oilway grooves on each thrustwasher face outwards (away from the bearing journal).

**50** Thoroughly degrease the mating surfaces of the cylinder block and the crankshaft bearing cap housing. Apply a thin bead of RTV sealant to the bearing cap housing mating surface. Citroën recommend the use of Loctite Autojoint Noir for this purpose.

**51** Lubricate the lower bearing shells with clean engine oil, then refit the bearing cap housing, ensuring that the shells are not displaced, and that the locating dowels engage correctly.

**52** Install the ten large diameter and sixteen smaller diameter crankshaft bearing cap housing retaining bolts, and screw them in until they are just making contact with the housing.

**53** Working in sequence, tighten the bolts to the torque settings given in the Specifications **(see illustration 17.40)**.

**54** With the bearing cap housing in place, check that the crankshaft rotates freely.

**55** Refit the piston/connecting rod assemblies to the crankshaft as described in Section 18.

**56** Refit the oil pump and sump.

**57** Fit a new crankshaft left-hand oil seal, then refit the flywheel.

**58** Where removed, refit the cylinder head, crankshaft sprocket and timing belt.

---

**18 Piston/connecting rod assembly – refitting**

**Note:** *New big-end cap nuts/bolts must be used on refitting.*

**1** Note that the following procedure assumes that the cylinder liners (aluminium block petrol engines) are in position in the cylinder block/crankcase as described in Section 11, and

that the crankshaft and main bearing ladder/caps are in place – except on diesel engines where the crankshaft is fitted after the pistons (see Section 17).

**2** Clean the backs of the bearing shells, and the bearing locations in both the connecting rod and bearing cap.

**Petrol engines**

**3** Press the bearing shells into their locations, ensuring that the tab on each shell engages in the notch in the connecting rod and cap. Take care not to touch any shell's bearing surface with your fingers **(see illustration)**.

**All engines**

**4** Lubricate the cylinder bores, the pistons, and piston rings, then lay out each piston/connecting rod assembly in its respective position.

**5** Start with assembly No 1. Make sure that the piston rings are still spaced as described in Section 16, then clamp them in position with a piston ring compressor.

**6** Insert the piston/connecting rod assembly into the top of cylinder/liner No 1, ensuring the piston is correctly positioned as follows.

a) On petrol engines, ensure that the arrow on the piston crown is pointing towards the timing belt end of the engine.

b) On diesel engines, ensure that the DIST mark or arrow on the piston crown is towards the timing belt end of the engine.

**7** Once the piston is correctly positioned, using a block of wood or hammer handle against the piston crown, tap the assembly into the cylinder/liner until the piston crown is flush with the top of the cylinder/liner **(see illustration)**.

**Petrol engines**

**8** Ensure that the bearing shell is still correctly installed. Liberally lubricate the crankpin and both bearing shells. Taking care not to mark the cylinder/liner bores, pull the piston/connecting rod assembly down the bore and onto the crankpin. Refit the big-end bearing cap and fit the new nuts, tightening them finger-tight at first **(see illustration)**. Note that the faces with the identification marks must match (which means that the bearing shell locating tabs abut each other).

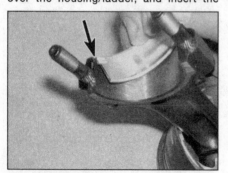

**18.3 Ensure the bearing shell tab (arrowed) locates correctly in the cut-out**

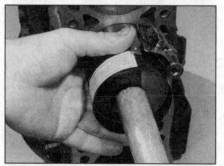

**18.7 Tap the piston into the bore using a hammer handle**

**18.8 Fit the big-end bearing cap, ensuring it is fitted the right way around, and screw on the new nuts**

**9** Tighten the bearing cap retaining nuts evenly and progressively to the specified torque setting.

### Diesel engines

**10** On diesel engines, the connecting rod is made in one piece, and the big-end bearing cap is 'cracked' off. This ensures that the cap fits onto the connecting rod only in one position, and with maximum rigidity. Consequently, there are no locating notches for the bearing shells to fit into.

**11** To ensure that the big-end bearing shells are centrally located in the connecting rod and cap, two special tools are available from Citroën. These half-moon shaped tools are pressed in from either side of the rod/cap and locate the shell exactly in the centre **(see illustration)**. Fit the shells into the connecting rods and big-end caps and lubricate them with plenty of clean engine oil.

**12** Pull the connecting rods and pistons down the bores and onto the crankshaft journals. Fit the big-end caps – they will only fit properly one way round (see paragraph 11), and insert the new bolts.

**13** Tighten the bolts to the Stage 1 torque setting, then slacken them 180° (Stage 2). Tighten the bolts to the Stage 3 setting, followed by the Stage 4 angle-tightening setting.

**14** Continue refitting the main bearing shells and ladder as described in Section 17.

### All engines

**15** Once the bearing cap retaining nuts have been correctly tightened, rotate the crankshaft. Check that it turns freely; some stiffness is to be expected if new components have been fitted, but there should be no signs of binding or tight spots.

**16** Refit the cylinder head and oil pump as described in Part A, B or C of this Chapter (as applicable).

---

**19 Engine –**
initial start-up after overhaul

**1** With the engine refitted in the vehicle, double-check the engine oil and coolant levels. Make a final check that everything has been reconnected, and that there are no tools or rags left in the engine compartment.

### Petrol engine models

**2** Remove the spark plugs and disable the fuel system by disconnecting the wiring connectors from the fuel injectors, referring to Chapter 4A for further information.

**3** Turn the engine on the starter until the oil pressure warning light goes out. Refit the spark plugs, and reconnect the wiring.

### Diesel engine models

**4** On the models covered in this Manual, the oil pressure warning light is linked to the STOP warning light, and is not illuminated when the ignition is initially switched on. Therefore it is not possible to check the oil pressure warning light when turning the engine on the starter motor.

**5** Prime the fuel system (refer to Chapter 4B). Although the system is self-priming, it will help if the ignition is switched on and off several times before attempting to start the engine in order to purge air from the system.

**6** Fully depress the accelerator pedal, turn the ignition key to position M, and wait for the preheating warning light to go out.

### All models

**7** Start the engine, noting that this may take a little longer than usual, due to the fuel system components having been disturbed.

**8** While the engine is idling, check for fuel, water and oil leaks. Don't be alarmed if there

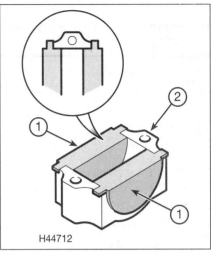

H44712

**18.11 Big-end bearing shell positioning – diesel engines**

*1 Citroën tool No 0194-P*
*2 Bearing shell*

are some odd smells and smoke from parts getting hot and burning off oil deposits.

**9** Assuming all is well, keep the engine idling until hot water is felt circulating through the top hose, then switch off the engine.

**10** After a few minutes, recheck the oil and coolant levels as described in *Weekly checks*, and top-up as necessary.

**11** Note that there is no need to retighten the cylinder head bolts once the engine has first run after reassembly.

**12** If new pistons, rings or crankshaft bearings have been fitted, the engine must be treated as new, and run-in for the first 500 miles (800 km). Do not operate the engine at full-throttle, or allow it to labour at low engine speeds in any gear. It is recommended that the oil and filter be changed at the end of this period.

# Chapter 3
# Cooling, heating and air conditioning systems

## Contents

## Degrees of difficulty

| Easy, suitable for novice with little experience | Fairly easy, suitable for beginner with some experience | Fairly difficult, suitable for competent DIY mechanic | Difficult, suitable for experienced DIY mechanic | Very difficult, suitable for expert DIY or professional |
|---|---|---|---|---|

## Specifications

### General
Maximum system pressure ................................ 1.4 bars

### Thermostat
Start of opening temperature:
    Petrol models .......................................... 89°C
    Diesel models .......................................... 83°C

### Air conditioning

**Compressor**
Make:
    Petrol engines......................................... Delphi 6CVC125
    Diesel engines ........................................ Sanden SD6V12
Compressor oil:
    Quantity:
        Petrol engines..................................... 150 cc
        Diesel engines.................................... 135 cc
    Type .............................................. SP10

**Refrigerant**
Quantity:
    Manual transmission models ............................ 450
    Automatic models...................................... 400
Type .................................................. R134a

| Torque wrench setting | Nm | lbf ft |
|---|---|---|
| Air conditioning compressor mounting bolts.................... | 25 | 17 |
| Coolant outlet housing................................... | 10 | 7 |
| Coolant pump: | | |
|     Petrol engines......................................... | 16 | 12 |
|     Diesel engines ........................................ | 10 | 7 |

## 1 General information and precautions

### General information

The cooling system is of pressurised type, comprising a coolant pump driven by the timing belt, an aluminium/plastic radiator, an expansion tank, an electric cooling fan, a thermostat, a heater matrix, and all associated hoses and switches.

The system functions as follows. Cold coolant in the bottom of the radiator passes through the bottom hose to the coolant pump, where it is pumped around the cylinder block and head passages. After cooling the cylinder bores, combustion surfaces and valve seats, the coolant reaches the underside of the thermostat, which is initially closed. The coolant passes through the heater, and is returned via the cylinder block to the coolant pump.

When the engine is cold, the coolant circulates

only through the cylinder block, cylinder head, and heater. When the coolant reaches a predetermined temperature, the thermostat opens, and the coolant passes through the top hose to the radiator. As the coolant passes down through the radiator, it is cooled by the inrush of air when the car is in forward motion. The airflow is supplemented by the action of the electric cooling fan when necessary. Upon reaching the bottom of the radiator, the coolant has now cooled, and the cycle is repeated.

On models with automatic transmission, a proportion of the coolant is recirculated through the transmission fluid cooler mounted on the transmission. On models fitted with an engine oil cooler, the coolant is also passed through the oil cooler.

The operation of the electric cooling fan is controlled by the engine management control unit.

## Precautions

⚠️ **Warning: Do not attempt to remove the expansion tank filler cap, or to disturb any part of the cooling system, while the engine is hot, as there is a high risk of scalding. If the expansion tank filler cap must be removed before the engine and radiator have fully cooled (even though this is not recommended), the pressure in the cooling system must first be relieved. Cover the cap with a thick layer of cloth to avoid scalding, and slowly unscrew the filler cap until a hissing sound is heard. When the hissing has stopped, indicating that the pressure has reduced, slowly unscrew the filler cap until it can be removed; if more hissing sounds are heard, wait until they have stopped before unscrewing the cap. At all times keep well away from the filler cap opening, and protect your hands.**

⚠️ **Warning: Do not allow antifreeze to come into contact with your skin, or with the painted surfaces of the vehicle. Rinse off spills immediately, with plenty of water. Never leave antifreeze lying around in an open container, or in a puddle in the driveway or on the garage floor. Children and pets are attracted by its sweet smell, but antifreeze can be fatal if ingested.**

⚠️ **Warning: If the engine is hot, the electric cooling fan(s) may start rotating even if the engine is not**

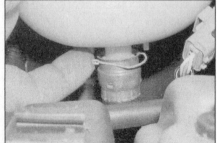

**2.5 Release the retaining clip and move it along the hose**

*running. Be careful to keep your hands, hair, and any loose clothing well clear when working in the engine compartment.*

⚠️ **Warning: Refer to Section 11 for precautions to be observed when working on models equipped with air conditioning.**

## 2 Cooling system hoses – disconnection and renewal

**Note:** *Refer to the warnings given in Section 1 of this Chapter before proceeding. Hoses should only be disconnected once the engine has cooled sufficiently to avoid scalding.*

1 If the checks described in the *Hose and fluid leak check* Section in Chapter 1A or 1B reveal a faulty hose, it must be renewed as follows.

2 First drain the cooling system (see Chapter 1A or 1B). If the coolant is not due for renewal, it may be re-used, providing it is collected in a clean container.

3 To disconnect a hose, proceed as follows, according to the type of hose connection.

### Conventional connections

4 On conventional connections, the clips used to secure the hoses in position may be either standard worm-drive clips, spring clips or disposable crimped types. The crimped type of clip is not designed to be re-used and should be renewed with a worm-drive type on reassembly.

5 To disconnect a hose, release the retaining clips and move them along the hose, clear

of the relevant inlet/outlet. Carefully work the hose free. The hoses can be removed with relative ease when new – on an older car, they may have stuck **(see illustration)**.

6 If a hose proves to be difficult to remove, try to release it by rotating its ends before attempting to free it. Gently prise the end of the hose with a blunt instrument (such as a flat-bladed screwdriver), but do not apply too much force, and take care not to damage the pipe stubs or hoses. Note in particular that the radiator inlet stub is fragile; do not use excessive force when attempting to remove the hose. If all else fails, cut the hose with a sharp knife, then slit it so that it can be peeled off in two pieces. Although this may prove expensive if the hose is otherwise undamaged, it is preferable to buying a new radiator. Check first, however, that a new hose is readily available.

7 When fitting a hose, first slide the clips onto the hose, then work the hose into position. If crimped-type clips were originally fitted, use standard worm-drive clips when refitting the hose.

8 Work the hose into position, checking that it is correctly routed, then slide each clip back along the hose until it passes over the flared end of the relevant inlet/outlet, before tightening the clip securely.

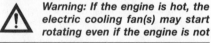 **HAYNES HiNT** *If the hose is stiff, use a little soapy water as a lubricant or soften the hose by soaking it in hot water. Do not use oil or grease as these may attack the rubber.*

9 Refill the cooling system (see Chapter 1A or 1B).

10 Check thoroughly for leaks as soon as possible after disturbing any part of the cooling system.

### Click-fit connections

**Note:** *New sealing ring should be used when reconnecting the hose.*

11 On certain models, some cooling system hoses are secured in position with click-fit connectors where the hose is retained by a large circlip.

12 To disconnect this type of hose fitting, carefully prise the wire clip out of position then disconnect the hose connection **(see illustration)**. Once the hose has been disconnected, refit the wire clip to the hose union. Inspect the hose unit sealing ring for signs of damage or deterioration and renew if necessary.

13 On refitting, ensure that the sealing ring is in position and wire clip is correctly located in the groove in the union **(see illustration)**. Lubricate the sealing ring with a smear of soapy water, to ease installation, then push the hose into its union until it is heard to click into position.

14 Ensure the hose is securely retained by the wire clip then refill the cooling system as described in Chapter 1A or 1B.

**2.12 Where click-fit connectors are used, prise out the circlip then disconnect the hose**

**2.13 Ensure the sealing ring and circlip (arrowed) are correctly fitted to the hose union before reconnecting a connector**

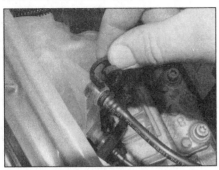

**3.2a  Slide up the retaining clip . . .**

15  Check thoroughly for leaks as soon as possible after disturbing any part of the cooling system.

### 3  Coolant expansion tank – removal and refitting

#### Removal

1  Referring to Chapter 1A or 1B, drain the cooling system sufficiently to empty the contents of the expansion tank. Do not drain any more coolant than is necessary.
2  Slide out the retaining clips, then pull the plastic hoses from the expansion tank **(see illustrations)**.
3  Where fitted, disconnect the wiring plug from the coolant level sensor on the side of the expansion tank.
4  Free the tank from the mounting lugs and withdraw it from its location.

5  Disconnect the remaining hose(s) as the expansion tank is removed.

#### Refitting

6  Refitting is the reverse of removal, ensuring the hoses are securely reconnected. On completion, top-up the coolant level as described in *Weekly checks*.

### 4  Radiator – removal, inspection and refitting

**Note:** *If leakage is the reason for removing the radiator, bear in mind that minor leaks can often be cured using a radiator sealant with the radiator in situ.*

#### Removal

1  Drain the cooling system (see Chapter 1A or 1B).
2  Remove the radiator electric cooling fan as described in Section 6.
3  Disconnect the lower coolant hose(s) from the radiator.
4  Undo the two bolts securing the bonnet lock to the radiator support frame. Withdraw the lock and disconnect the release cable **(see illustrations)**.
5  Undo the remaining bolt and remove the bonnet lock mounting bracket **(see illustration)**.
6  Slide out the retaining clip, then pull the expansion tank plastic hose from the connection on the right-hand end of the radiator **(see illustration)**.
7  Using two screwdrivers, depress the tabs

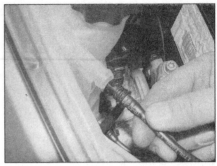

**3.2b  . . . and pull out the hose**

on each side of the two radiator upper plastic mounting brackets. Move the top of the radiator towards the engine to free the brackets from their locations **(see illustration)**.
8  Lift the radiator upwards to disengage the lower mounting lugs, then carefully remove the radiator from the engine compartment taking care not to damage the cooling fins **(see illustration)**. Recover the radiator lower mounting rubbers.

#### Inspection

9  If the radiator has been removed due to suspected blockage, reverse-flush it as described in Chapter 1A or 1B. Clean dirt and debris from the radiator fins, using an air line (in which case, wear eye protection) or a soft brush. Be careful, as the fins are sharp, and easily damaged.
10  If necessary, a radiator specialist can perform a 'flow test' on the radiator, to establish whether an internal blockage exists.

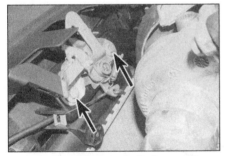

**4.4a  Undo the two bolts (arrowed) securing the bonnet lock to the radiator support frame**

**4.4b  Withdraw the lock and disconnect the release cable**

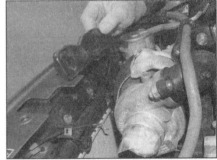

**4.5  Undo the remaining bolt and remove the bonnet lock mounting bracket**

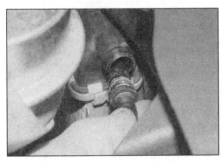

**4.6  Slide out the retaining clip, then pull the expansion tank hose from the radiator connection**

**4.7  Depress the tabs on radiator mounting brackets, then move the top of the radiator towards the engine**

**4.8  Lift the radiator upwards, then carefully remove it from the engine compartment**

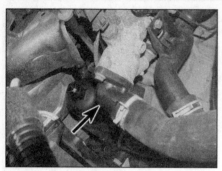

**5.2 Thermostat housing cover location (arrowed) on petrol engines**

**5.7a Press down the release button and disconnect the hose**

**5.7b Undo the coolant outlet housing retaining bolts (arrowed)**

**11** A leaking radiator must be referred to a specialist for permanent repair. Do not attempt to weld or solder a leaking radiator, as damage to the plastic components may result.

**12** Inspect the condition of the radiator mounting rubbers, and renew them if necessary.

### Refitting

**13** Refitting is a reversal of removal, bearing in mind the following points:
  a) *Ensure that the lower lugs on the radiator are correctly engaged with the mounting rubbers in the body panel.*
  b) *Reconnect the hoses with reference to Section 2, using new sealing rings where applicable.*
  c) *Refit the electric cooling fan as described in Section 6.*
  d) *On completion, refill the cooling system as described in Chapter 1A or 1B.*

## 5  Thermostat – removal, testing and refitting

### Removal

**1** Drain the cooling system (see Chapter 1A or 1B).

#### Petrol engines

**2** The thermostat is fitted to the coolant housing on the left-hand end of the cylinder head **(see illustration)**. For improved access on DOHC engines, remove the air cleaner intake duct as described in Chapter 4A.

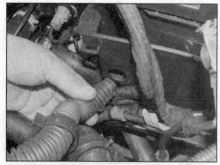

**6.3 Disconnect the air intake hose at the battery box**

**3** The thermostat is an integral part of the coolant housing cover. Where applicable, release the surrounding wiring harness from its retaining clips, then disconnect the radiator hose from the housing cover. Undo the two bolts and remove the cover and thermostat assembly. Recover the sealing ring.

#### Diesel engines

**4** The thermostat is integral with the coolant outlet housing on the left-hand end of the cylinder head.

**5** On 16-valve engines, remove the plastic cover from the top of the engine. The cover is retained by rubber grommets, and pulls upwards to release.

**6** Remove the air duct connecting the turbocharger to the air mass meter, and the cold air intake duct to the air cleaner base as described in Chapter 4B.

**7** Disconnect the coolant hoses from the outlet housing, and the wiring plug from the coolant temperature sensor. Note that some of the hoses are disconnected after pressing down on the white-coloured release button, or by extracting the small plastic retaining clip. Undo the four screws and remove the housing **(see illustrations)**.

### Testing

**8** A rough test of the thermostat may be made by submerging it in a container full of water. Heat the water to bring it to the boil – the thermostat must open by the time the water boils. If not, renew it.

**9** If a thermometer is available, the precise opening temperature of the thermostat may

**6.5 Disconnect the two wiring connectors at the top of the fan shroud**

be determined; compare with the figures given in the Specifications.

**10** A thermostat which fails to close as the water cools must also be renewed.

### Refitting

**11** Refitting is a reversal of removal, bearing in mind the following points.
  a) *Examine the sealing ring for damage or deterioration, and if necessary, renew.*
  b) *Where removed, refit the air intake ducting as described in Chapter 4A or 4B.*
  c) *On completion, refill the cooling system as described in Chapter 1A or 1B.*

## 6  Electric cooling fan – removal and refitting

### Removal

**1** Drain the cooling system (see Chapter 1A or 1B).

**2** On petrol engine models, remove the air cleaner assembly and air intake duct as described in Chapter 4A. On diesel engine models, remove the air duct connecting the turbocharger to the air mass meter, and the cold air intake duct to the air cleaner base as described in Chapter 4B.

**3** Disconnect the air intake hose at the battery box and move the hose to one side **(see illustration)**.

**4** Release the retaining clips and remove the radiator top hose.

**5** Disconnect the two wiring connectors at the top of the fan shroud **(see illustration)**. Where fitted, also release the cooling fan relay from the shroud and move it to one side.

**6** Undo the two upper mounting bolts, lift the fan shroud upward to disengage the lower lugs and remove the assembly from the engine compartment **(see illustrations)**.

### Refitting

**7** Refitting is a reversal of removal, bearing in mind the following points:
  a) *Refit the air cleaner and/or air intake ducting as described in Chapter 4A or 4B.*
  b) *On completion, refill the cooling system as described in Chapter 1A or 1B.*

## 7 Cooling system electrical sensors – general information, removal and refitting

### General information

**1** On petrol engine models, two coolant temperature sensors are fitted. One is fitted to the left-hand end of the cylinder head and provides the signal for temperature gauge operation. The second sensor is screwed into the coolant outlet housing on the left-hand end of the cylinder head and provides the engine coolant temperature signal for the engine management ECU. On diesel engine models, there is only one coolant temperature sensor, fitted to the coolant outlet housing. The coolant temperature gauge and the cooling fan are all operated by the engine management ECU using the signal supplied by this sensor **(see illustrations)**.

### Removal

**Note:** *Ensure the engine is cold before removing a temperature sensor.*

**2** On petrol engine models, remove the air cleaner assembly and air intake duct as described in Chapter 4A. On diesel engine models, remove the air duct connecting the turbocharger to the air mass meter, and the cold air intake duct to the air cleaner base as described in Chapter 4B.

**3** Partially drain the cooling system to just below the level of the sensor (as described in Chapter 1A or 1B). Alternatively, have ready a suitable bung to plug the sensor aperture whilst the sensor is removed. If this method is used, take great care not to damage the switch aperture or use anything which will allow foreign matter to enter the cooling system.

**4** Disconnect the wiring connector from the sensor.

**5** On petrol engines, unscrew the sensor and recover the sealing washer (where applicable). If the system has not been drained, plug the sensor aperture to prevent further coolant loss.

**6** On diesel engines, the sensor is clipped in place. Prise out the sensor retaining circlip then remove the sensor and sealing ring from the housing **(see illustration)**. If the system

**6.6a  Undo the two upper mounting bolts (arrowed) . . .**

has not been drained, plug the sensor aperture to prevent further coolant loss.

### Refitting

**7** On petrol engines, if the sensor was originally fitted using sealing compound, clean the sensor threads thoroughly, and coat them with fresh sealing compound. If the sensor was originally fitted using a sealing washer, use a new sealing washer. Fit the sensor and tighten securely.

**8** On diesel engines, fit a new sealing ring to the sensor. Push the sensor firmly into the housing and secure it in position with the circlip, ensuring it is correctly located in the housing groove.

**9** Reconnect the wiring connector then refit the air cleaner and/or air intake ducting as described in Chapter 4A or 4B.

**10** Top-up the cooling system as described in *Weekly checks*.

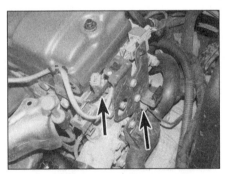

**7.1a  Coolant temperature sensors (arrowed) on petrol engine models . . .**

**6.6b  . . . then lift the fan shroud up and out of the engine compartment**

## 8 Coolant pump – removal and refitting

### Removal

**1** Drain the cooling system (see Chapter 1A or 1B).

**2** Remove the timing belt as described in Chapter 2A, 2B or 2C as applicable.

**3** Slacken and remove the retaining bolts and withdraw the pump assembly from the engine. Recover the pump sealing ring/gasket (as applicable) and discard it; a new one must be used on refitting **(see illustrations)**. Note that on some engines, the sealing ring is not available separately from the pump – check with your Citroën dealer.

**7.1b  . . . and diesel engine models**

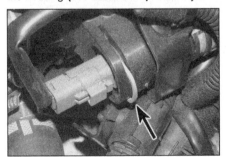

**7.6  Prise out the clip (arrowed) and pull out the diesel engine coolant temperature sensor**

**8.3a  Remove the coolant pump . . .**

**8.3b  . . . and recover the sealing ring (petrol engine models)**

**8.3c Undo the coolant pump bolts (arrowed) (diesel engine models)**

## Refitting

4 Ensure that the pump and cylinder block/housing mating surfaces are clean and dry.

5 Fit the new sealing ring/gasket (as applicable) to the pump then refit the pump assembly, tightening its retaining bolts to the specified torque.

6 Refit the timing belt as described in Chapter 2A, 2B or 2C (as applicable).

7 Refill the cooling system as described in Chapter 1A or 1B (as applicable).

## 9 Heating and ventilation system – general information

**Note:** *Refer to Section 11 for information on the air conditioning side of the system.*

### Manually-controlled system

The heating/ventilation system consists of a four-speed blower motor (housed behind the facia), face level vents in the centre and at each end of the facia, and air ducts to the front footwells.

The control unit is located in the facia, and the controls operate flap valves to deflect and mix the air flowing through the various parts of the heating/ventilation system. The flap valves are contained in the air distribution housing, which acts as a central distribution unit, passing air to the various ducts and vents.

Cold air enters the system through the grille in the scuttle. If required, the airflow is boosted by the blower, and then flows through the various ducts, according to the settings of the controls. Stale air is expelled through ducts at the rear of the vehicle. If warm air is required, the cold air is passed over the heater matrix, which is heated by the engine coolant.

A recirculation lever enables the outside air supply to be closed off, while the air inside the vehicle is recirculated. This can be useful to prevent unpleasant odours entering from outside the vehicle, but should only be used briefly, as the recirculated air inside the vehicle will soon become stale.

On some diesel engine models an electric heater is fitted into the heater housing. When the coolant temperature is cold, the heater warms the air before it enters the heater matrix. This quickly increases the temperature of the heater matrix on cold starts, resulting in warm air being available to heat the vehicle interior soon after start-up.

### Automatic climate control

A fully automatic electronic climate control system is optionally available on some models. The main components of the system are exactly the same as those described for the manual system, the only major difference being that the temperature and distribution flaps in the heating/ventilation housing are operated by electric motors rather than cables.

The operation of the system is controlled by the electronic control module (which is located in the control panel) along with the following sensors.

a) *The passenger compartment sensor – informs the control module of the temperature of the air inside the passenger compartment.*

b) *Evaporator temperature sensor – informs the control module of the evaporator temperature.*

c) *Heater matrix temperature sensor – informs the control module of the heater matrix temperature.*

Using the information from the above sensors, the control module determines the appropriate settings for the heating/ventilation system housing flaps to maintain the passenger compartment at the desired setting on the control panel.

If the system develops a fault, the vehicle should be taken to a Citroën dealer. A complete test of the system can then be carried out, using a special electronic diagnostic test unit which is simply plugged into the system's diagnostic connector (located next to the fusebox).

## 10 Heater/ventilation components – removal and refitting

### Control panel

**Removal**

1 Remove the audio unit (see Chapter 12).

2 Reach in through the audio unit aperture and push out the storage compartment, to release the retaining lugs each side **(see illustrations)**.

3 Push the control panel in at the top to release the upper locating lugs, then move the unit upwards to free the lower lugs **(see illustrations)**.

4 On models with a manual control panel, disconnect the wiring connectors from the rear of the control panel. Note the correct fitted location of each control cable (the end fittings are colour-coded) then unhook the cable retaining clips. Detach the cables and remove the control panel through the audio unit aperture.

5 On models with an automatic climate control system, disconnect the wiring connectors and remove the control panel through the audio unit aperture.

**Refitting**

6 Refitting is the reverse of removal. On

**10.2a Reach in through the audio unit aperture and push out the storage compartment . . .**

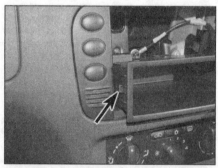

**10.2b . . . to release the retaining lugs (arrowed) each side**

**10.3a Release the control unit upper locating lugs . . .**

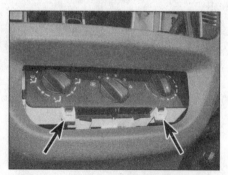

**10.3b . . . then move the unit upwards to free the lower lugs (arrowed)**

models with a manual control panel, ensure the control cables are correctly reconnected and securely held by the retaining clips; check the operation of the control knobs before securing the control panel to the facia.

### Control cables

#### Removal

**7** Remove the facia (see Chapter 11).
**8** Release the retaining clip and detach the relevant cable from the rear of the control panel and the heating/ventilation housing. Remove the cable, noting its correct routing.

#### Refitting

**9** Refitting is the reverse of removal, ensuring the cable is securely retained by its clips. Check the operation of the control panel and cables before refitting the facia (see Chapter 11).

### Heater matrix

#### Removal

**10** To improve access to the matrix unions on the bulkhead, remove the air cleaner assembly and/or air intake duct(s) as described in Chapter 4A or 4B.
**11** Drain the cooling system (see Chapter 1A or 1B). Alternatively, clamp the heater matrix coolant hoses to minimise coolant loss.
**12** Release the retaining clips and disconnect the coolant hoses from the heater matrix pipe unions on the engine compartment bulkhead **(see illustration)**.
**13** Slacken and remove the screw securing the heater matrix pipes to the bulkhead and remove the retaining plate and seal **(see illustration)**.
**14** Refer to Chapter 11 and remove the glovebox (right-hand drive models), or driver's side lower facia panel (left-hand drive models).
**15** Position a container beneath the heater matrix pipe union on the left-hand side of the heating/ventilation housing to catch any spilt coolant.
**16** Release the wiring harness from the clips on the side of the matrix pipes, then undo the screws securing the matrix and matrix pipes to the housing **(see illustration)**.
**17** Withdraw the matrix from the housing, then separate the pipes from the matrix, catching the coolant in the container. Recover the sealing rings fitted to the pipe unions and discard them; new ones should be used on refitting. Take care not to lose the bulkhead seal or retaining plate from the pipes.

#### Refitting

**18** Ensure the bulkhead seal and retaining plate are correctly fitted to the matrix pipes and fit a new sealing ring to each of the pipe unions.
**19** Manoeuvre the pipe assembly and matrix into position, engaging the pipes with the bulkhead and matrix. Refit the retaining screws and clip the wiring harness back into place.
**20** Working in the engine compartment, refit the seal and retaining plate to the heater

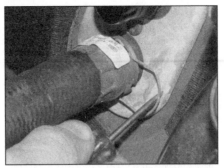

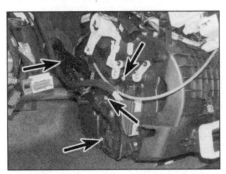

**10.16 Undo the screws (arrowed) securing the matrix and matrix pipes to the housing**

matrix pipes and securely tighten the retaining screw. Remove the clamps (where fitted) then reconnect the coolant hoses, securing them in position with the retaining clips.
**21** Refit the components removed for access, then refill the cooling system (see Chapter 1A or 1B).

### Heater blower motor

#### Removal

**22** The blower motor is fitted to the top of the heating/ventilation housing, on the left-hand side.
**23** On right-hand drive models, remove the glovebox as described in Chapter 11. Access to the motor can then be gained through the glovebox aperture.
**24** On left-hand drive models, remove driver's side lower facia panel as described in Chapter 11 to gain access to the motor.
**25** Where necessary, slacken and remove

**10.33 Heater/ventilation housing retaining bolt (arrowed)**

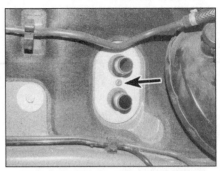

**10.12 Prise out the wire retaining clip and disconnect the heater hose**

**10.13 Undo the heater pipes retaining plate screw (arrowed)**

**10.27 Rotate the blower motor clockwise and withdraw it from the housing**

the retaining screw securing the motor to the housing (this screw may not be fitted).
**26** Disconnect the wiring connector(s) from the blower motor.
**27** Rotate the motor clockwise to free it from the housing then manoeuvre it out of position **(see illustration)**.

#### Refitting

**28** Refitting is the reverse of removal. If the motor is not a secure fit in the housing, fix it in position by fitting a self-tapping screw to the hole provided.

### Housing assembly

#### Removal without air conditioning

**29** To improve access to the matrix unions on the bulkhead, remove the air cleaner assembly and/or air intake duct(s) as described in Chapter 4A or 4B.
**30** Drain the cooling system (see Chapter 1A or 1B). Alternatively, working in the engine compartment, clamp the heater matrix coolant hoses to minimise coolant loss.
**31** Release the retaining clips and disconnect the coolant hoses from the heater matrix pipe unions on the engine compartment bulkhead **(see illustration 10.12)**.
**32** Slacken and remove the screw securing the heater matrix pipes to the bulkhead and remove the retaining plate and seal **(see illustration 10.13)**.
**33** Slacken and remove the bolt securing the heating/ventilation housing to the bulkhead **(see illustration)**.
**34** Remove the facia assembly as described in Chapter 11.

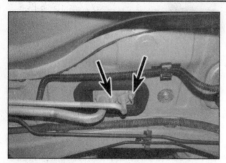

**10.40 Undo the two nuts (arrowed) securing the air conditioning pipes to the engine compartment bulkhead**

**35** Disconnect the wiring connectors from the heating/ventilation housing components then remove the housing and control panel assembly from the vehicle. Keep the heater matrix pipe unions uppermost as the assembly is removed to prevent coolant spillage.

**36** Recover the seal and retaining plate from the heater matrix pipes, and the seal from the housing mounting. Renew the seals if they show signs of damage or deterioration.

### Refitting without air conditioning

**37** Refitting is the reverse of removal ensuring the seals are in position on the pipes and housing mounting. On completion, refill the cooling system (see Chapter 1A or 1B).

### Removal with air conditioning

⚠ **Warning: Refer to Section 11 for precautions to be observed when working on models equipped with air conditioning. Do not attempt the following procedure unless the system has been professionally discharged.**

**38** Have the air conditioning system discharged by an air conditioning specialist and obtain suitable plugs to seal the air conditioning pipe unions whilst the system is disconnected.

**39** Carry out the operations described in paragraphs 29 to 32.

**40** Unscrew the two nuts securing the air conditioning pipe union to the bulkhead **(see illustration)**. Separate the pipes from the evaporator and quickly seal the pipe and evaporator unions to prevent the entry of moisture into the refrigerant circuit. Discard the sealing rings, new ones must be used on refitting.

⚠ **Warning: Failure to seal the refrigerant pipe unions will result in the dehydrator reservoir becoming saturated, necessitating its renewal.**

**41** Remove the heating/ventilation housing assembly as described in paragraphs 33 to 36 and recover the seal from the evaporator.

### Refitting with air conditioning

**42** Ensure the bulkhead seals are correctly fitted to the evaporator, matrix pipes and housing mounting. Manoeuvre the housing assembly into position, locating the housing drain hose correctly in its hole in the floor.

**43** Loosely refit the housing mounting bolt then refit the retaining plate to the heater matrix pipe and loosely install the retaining screw.

**44** Lubricate the new evaporator union sealing rings with compressor oil. Remove the plugs and install the sealing rings then quickly fit the refrigerant pipe union to the evaporator. Ensure the refrigerant pipes and evaporator are correctly joined then refit the retaining nuts, tighten them securely.

**45** Tighten the matrix pipe retaining screw securely and securely tighten the housing mounting bolt.

**46** The remainder of refitting is the reverse of removal. On completion, refill the cooling system (see Chapter 1A or 1B).

### Interior air temperature sensor

**47** The sensor is located at the base of the switch panel, situated to the right of the audio unit.

**48** Remove the audio unit as described in Chapter 12.

**49** Reach in through the audio unit aperture and push out the storage compartment, to release the retaining lugs each side **(see illustrations 10.2a and 10.2b)**. Similarly, reach through the aperture and push out the switch panel.

**50** Free the sensor from its location, and disconnect the wiring plug.

**51** Refitting is a reversal of removal.

### Diesel models additional heater

#### Removal

**52** Refer to Chapter 11 and remove the glovebox (right-hand drive models), or driver's side lower facia panel (left-hand drive models).

**53** Disconnect the heater wiring plug, then undo the screw, release the retaining clip at the base of the unit, and slide the heater from the housing.

#### Refitting

**54** Refitting is the reverse of removal.

---

**11 Air conditioning system –**
general information
and precautions

---

### General information

An air conditioning system is available on certain models. It enables the temperature of incoming air to be lowered, and also dehumidifies the air, which makes for rapid demisting and increased comfort.

The cooling side of the system works in the same way as a domestic refrigerator. Refrigerant gas is drawn into a belt-driven compressor, and passes into a condenser mounted on the front of the radiator, where it loses heat and becomes liquid. The liquid passes through an expansion valve to an evaporator, where it changes from liquid under high pressure to gas under low pressure. This change is accompanied by a drop in

temperature, which cools the evaporator. The refrigerant returns to the compressor, and the cycle begins again.

Air blown through the evaporator passes to the heating/ventilation housing, where it is mixed with hot air blown through the heater matrix to achieve the desired temperature in the passenger compartment.

The heating side of the system works in the same way as on models without air conditioning (see Section 9).

The operation of the system is controlled electronically by the ECU integral with the control panel. Any problems with the system should be referred to a Citroën dealer, or suitably-equipped specialist.

### Precautions

When an air conditioning system is fitted, it is necessary to observe special precautions whenever dealing with any part of the system, or its associated components. The refrigerant is potentially dangerous, and should only be handled by qualified persons. Uncontrolled discharging of the refrigerant is dangerous and damaging to the environment for the following reasons.

a) *If it is splashed onto the skin, it can cause frostbite.*

b) *The refrigerant is heavier then air and so displaces oxygen. In a confined space which is not adequately ventilated this could lead to a risk of suffocation. The gas is odourless and colourless so there is no warning of its presence in the atmosphere.*

c) *Although not poisonous, in the presence of a naked flame (including a cigarette) it forms a noxious gas which causes headaches, nausea, etc.*

⚠ **Warning: Never attempt to open any air conditioning system refrigerant pipe/hose union without first having the system fully discharged by an air conditioning specialist. On completion of work, have the system recharged by an air conditioning specialist.**

⚠ **Warning: Always seal disconnected refrigerant pipe/hose unions as soon as they are disconnected. Failure to form an air-tight seal on any union will result in the dehydrator reservoir becoming saturated, necessitating its renewal. Also renew all sealing rings disturbed.**

**Caution: Do not operated the air conditioning system if it is known to be short of refrigerant as this could damage the compressor.**

---

**12 Air conditioning system components –**
removal and refitting

---

⚠ **Warning: Refer to the precautions given in Section 11 and have the system discharged by an air**

*conditioning specialist before carrying out any work on the air conditioning system.*

## Compressor

### Removal

**1** Have the air conditioning system fully discharged by an air conditioning specialist.
**2** Remove the auxiliary drivebelt as described in Chapter 1A or 1B (as applicable).
**3** Disconnect the compressor wiring connector.
**4** Unscrew the nuts securing the refrigerant pipes retaining plates to the compressor (**see illustration**). Separate the pipes from the compressor and quickly seal the pipe and compressor unions to prevent the entry of moisture into the refrigerant circuit. Discard the sealing rings, new ones must be used on refitting.

⚠️ *Warning: Failure to seal the refrigerant pipe unions will result in the dehydrator reservoir becoming saturated, necessitating its renewal.*

**5** Unscrew the compressor mounting bolts then free the compressor from its mounting bracket and remove it from the engine (**see illustration**).
**6** If the compressor is to be renewed, drain the refrigerant oil from the old compressor. The specialist who recharges the refrigerant system will need to add this amount of oil to the system.

### Refitting

**7** If a new compressor is being fitted, drain the refrigerant oil.
**8** Manoeuvre the compressor into position and fit the mounting bolts. Tighten the mounting bolts securely working in a progressive diagonal sequence.
**9** Lubricate the new refrigerant pipe sealing rings with compressor oil. Remove the plugs and install the sealing rings then quickly fit the refrigerant pipes to the compressor. Ensure the refrigerant pipes are correctly joined then refit the retaining bolt, tighten it securely.
**10** Reconnect the wiring connector then refit the auxiliary drivebelt (see Chapter 1A or 1B).
**11** Have the air conditioning system recharged by a specialist before using the system.

**12.4  Unscrew the refrigerant pipes retaining plates nuts**

## Condenser

### Removal

**12** Have the air conditioning system fully discharged by an air conditioning specialist.
**13** Remove the front bumper and bumper bracket as described in Chapter 11.
**14** Remove the left-hand headlight unit as described in Chapter 12.
**15** Undo the retaining nuts and disconnect the refrigerant pipes from the right-hand side of the condenser. Recover the O-ring seals (**see illustrations**).

⚠️ *Warning: Failure to seal the refrigerant pipe unions will result in the dehydrator reservoir becoming saturated, necessitating its renewal.*

**16** Using two screwdrivers, depress the tabs on each side of the condenser upper plastic mounting bracket. Move the top of the condenser forwards to free the bracket from its location. Note that on some installations, there are two upper mountings (**see illustrations**).
**17** Lift the condenser upwards to disengage the lower mounting lugs, then carefully remove it from the car. Recover the condenser lower mounting rubbers.

### Refitting

**18** Refitting is a reversal of removal. Noting the following points:
a) Ensure the upper mounting bracket(s) and lower mounting rubbers are correctly fitted then seat the condenser in position in the front panel.
b) Lubricate the sealing rings with

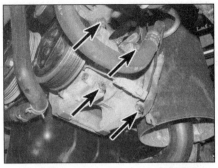

**12.5  Remove the compressor mounting bolts (arrowed) – TU3 petrol engine**

compressor oil. Remove the plugs and install the sealing rings then quickly fit the refrigerant pipes to the condenser. Securely tighten the dehydrator pipe union nut and ensure the compressor pipe is correctly joined.
c) Refit the headlight unit and front bumper as described in Chapter 12 and 11 respectively.
d) Have the air conditioning system recharged by a specialist before using the system.

## Receiver/drier

### Removal

**19** Have the air conditioning system fully discharged by an air conditioning specialist.
**20** The receiver/drier is located on the left-hand side of the condenser. Remove the radiator as described in Section 4.
**21** Undo the screw and remove the clip at the top then pull the top of the condenser rearwards slightly, and unscrew the receiver/drier cartridge using a Torx T70 bit. Take great care not to pull the condenser too far and damage the refrigerant pipes (**see illustrations**).

⚠️ *Warning: Prior to removal, clean the top of the condenser and wipe it dry, to avoid moisture/debris entering the air conditioning circuit.*

### Refitting

**22** Refitting is a reversal of removal noting the following points:
a) Lubricate the cartridge seals with compressor oil.

**12.15a  Undo the nuts (arrowed) securing the refrigerant pipes . . .**

**12.15b  . . . and plug the ends of the pipes**

**12.16  Release the condenser upper mountings**

12.21a Undo the screw and remove the clip (arrowed) . . .

12.21b . . . then unscrew the receiver/drier cartridge

12.21c Ensure the nut plate is in place when refitting the evaporator

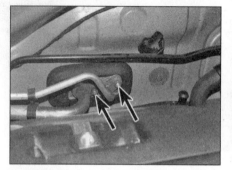

12.37 Undo the two nuts (arrowed) securing the air conditioning pipes

b) Have the air conditioning system recharged with the correct type and amount of refrigerant by a specialist prior to using the system.

### Evaporator

**Note:** *At the time of writing the evaporator was not available as a separate item and had to be supplied complete with the heater housing unit. See your local dealer for availability of parts.*

#### Removal

**23** Have the air conditioning system fully discharged by an air conditioning specialist.
**24** Remove the heating/ventilation housing as described in Section 10.
**25** Note their fitted positions, then disconnect the wiring plugs and harness from the housing.
**26** Remove any heater/ventilation components from the heater housing as described in Section 10.
**27** Undo the retaining screws and remove the plastic cover to access the evaporator.

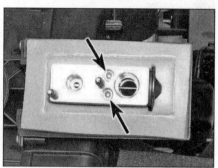

12.39 Expansion valve retaining bolts (arrowed)

#### Refitting

**28** Refitting is a reversal of removal but have the air conditioning system recharged with the correct type and amount of refrigerant by a specialist prior to using the system.

### Evaporator sensor

#### Removal

**29** The evaporator sensor is fitted to the lower part of the heating/ventilation housing, at the right-hand side.
**30** Remove the lower facia trim panel.
**31** Trace the wiring back from the sensor and disconnect the wiring connector. **Note:** *If a wiring connector is not available, it may be part of the wiring loom. In this case, the wiring will need to be cut approximately 50 mm from the sensor.*
**32** Rotate the sensor anti-clockwise and withdraw it from the heater housing.

#### Refitting

**33** Refit the sensor in the housing and connect the wiring connector. **Note:** *If required, join the wiring where it has been cut.*

**34** Refit any components removed for access.

### Expansion valve

#### Removal

**35** Have the air conditioning system fully discharged and evacuated by an air conditioning specialist.
**36** Remove the sound insulation material/ heat shield from the engine compartment bulkhead (where fitted).
**37** Undo the nuts securing the refrigerant pipes to the connection at the engine compartment bulkhead **(see illustration)**. Plug/cover the openings to prevent contamination/saturation. Recover and discard the O-ring seals – new ones must be fitted.

⚠️ *Warning: Failure to seal the refrigerant pipe unions will result in the receiver/drier becoming saturated, necessitating its renewal.*

**38** Pull the seal from around the pipes connection at the bulkhead.
**39** Undo the upper bolt and insert a piece of threaded rod (or stud), then undo the lower bolt and insert another piece of threaded rod (or stud). The expansion/relief valve can then be withdrawn out from the bulkhead along the length of the threaded rods. **Note:** *If the threaded rods (studs) are not used the spacer at the rear of the expansion/relief valve may drop down behind the heater unit housing (see illustration).* Recover and discard the O-ring seals – new ones must be fitted.

#### Refitting

**40** Refitting is a reversal of removal but have the air conditioning system recharged with the correct type and amount of refrigerant by a specialist prior to using the system.

# Chapter 4 Part A:
# Fuel and exhaust systems – petrol models

## Contents

## Degrees of difficulty

| Easy, suitable for novice with little experience | Fairly easy, suitable for beginner with some experience | Fairly difficult, suitable for competent DIY mechanic | Difficult, suitable for experienced DIY mechanic | Very difficult, suitable for expert DIY or professional |
|---|---|---|---|---|

## Specifications

### Engine identification

| | Designation | Engine code |
|---|---|---|
| 1.1 litre: | | |
| SOHC (8-valve) | TU1JP | HFX |
| SOHC (8-valve) | TU1A | HFV |
| 1.4 litre: | | |
| SOHC (8-valve) | TU3JP | KFV |
| SOHC (8-valve) | TU3A | KFT |
| DOHC (16-valve) | ET3J4 and ET3JA | KFU |
| 1.6 litre DOHC (16-valve) | TU5JP4 | NFU |

### System type

| | |
|---|---|
| 1.1 litre models (TU1) | Magnetti-Marelli MM48.P2 |
| 1.4 litre models: | |
| TU3 | Sagem S2000 PM1 |
| ET3 | Marelli 6LP2 |
| 1.6 litre models (TU5) | BOSCH ME 7.4.4 |

### Fuel system data

| | |
|---|---|
| Fuel pump type | Electric, immersed in tank |
| Fuel pump regulated constant pressure | 3.5 ± 0.2 bars |
| Specified idle speed | 850 ± 100 rpm (not adjustable – controlled by ECU) |
| Idle mixture CO content | Less than 1.0% (not adjustable – controlled by ECU) |

### Recommended fuel

| | |
|---|---|
| Minimum octane rating | 95 RON unleaded (UK unleaded premium). Leaded/lead replacement fuel (LRP) must **not** be used |

### Torque wrench settings

| | Nm | lbf ft |
|---|---|---|
| Exhaust manifold to catalytic converter: | | |
| Stage 1 | 20 | 15 |
| Stage 2 | 40 | 30 |
| Exhaust manifold-to-cylinder head nuts | 20 | 15 |
| Inlet manifold nuts: | | |
| M6 | 10 | 7 |
| M8 | 20 | 15 |
| Oxygen sensor | 45 | 33 |
| Roadwheel bolts | 90 | 66 |

**2.1  Slacken the clip securing the air cleaner lid to the throttle housing**

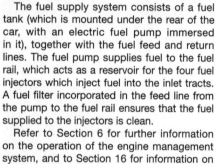

**2.3  Disconnect the plastic air inlet hose from the inlet duct or resonator**

## 1  General information and precautions

The fuel supply system consists of a fuel tank (which is mounted under the rear of the car, with an electric fuel pump immersed in it), together with the fuel feed and return lines. The fuel pump supplies fuel to the fuel rail, which acts as a reservoir for the four fuel injectors which inject fuel into the inlet tracts. A fuel filter incorporated in the feed line from the pump to the fuel rail ensures that the fuel supplied to the injectors is clean.

Refer to Section 6 for further information on the operation of the engine management system, and to Section 16 for information on the exhaust system.

 **Warning: Many of the procedures in this Chapter require the removal of fuel lines and connections,**

**2.2  Depress the sides of the quick-release fitting and detach the engine breather hose from the air cleaner lid**

**2.4  Turn the plastic retainer through 90° to release it**

*which may result in some fuel spillage. Before carrying out any operation on the fuel system, refer to the precautions given in 'Safety first!' at the beginning of this manual, and follow them implicitly. Petrol is a highly dangerous and volatile liquid, and the precautions necessary when handling it cannot be overstressed.*
**Note:** *Residual pressure will remain in the fuel lines long after the vehicle was last used. When disconnecting any fuel line, first depressurise the fuel system as described in Section 7.*

## 2  Air cleaner assembly and inlet ducts – removal and refitting

### Removal

1  Slacken the clip securing the air cleaner lid to the throttle housing **(see illustration)**.

2  Depress the sides of the quick-release fitting and detach the engine breather hose from the air cleaner lid **(see illustration)**.
3  Disconnect the plastic air inlet hose from the inlet duct or resonator at the front of the engine compartment, or from the base of the air cleaner assembly, according to model **(see illustration)**.
4  Release the plastic retainer securing the air cleaner to the support bracket by turning it through 90° **(see illustration)**.
5  Detach the air cleaner lid from the throttle housing, while at the same time lifting the air cleaner assembly upwards to release the lower mounting. Slide the unit sideways slightly and withdraw it from the engine compartment **(see illustrations)**. Recover the throttle housing sealing ring from the air cleaner lid.
6  To remove the air inlet duct or resonator, release the retaining clip and lift the duct or resonator upwards from the engine compartment.

### Refitting

7  Refitting is a reversal of the removal procedure, ensuring that all hoses and ducts are properly reconnected and correctly seated and, where necessary, securely held by their retaining clips.

## 3  Accelerator cable – removal, refitting and adjustment

**Note:** *An accelerator cable is only fitted to 1.1 litre models.*

### Removal

1  Working in the engine compartment, free the accelerator inner cable from the throttle housing cam, then pull the outer cable out from its mounting bracket rubber grommet. Recover the spring clip from the outer cable **(see illustration)**.
2  Working back along the length of the cable, free it from any retaining clips or ties, noting its correct routing.
3  Remove the lower facia panel on the driver's side. as described in Chapter 11.
4  Reach up behind the facia, squeeze together the sides of the retaining clip, then detach the inner cable from the top of the

**2.5a  Detach the air cleaner lid from the throttle housing . . .**

**2.5b  . . . then lift the air cleaner assembly upwards to release the lower mounting**

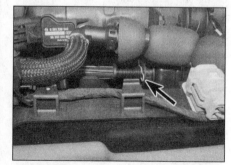

**3.1  Remove the spring clip (arrowed) from the accelerator outer cable**

accelerator pedal and pull out the clip securing the bulkhead grommet **(see illustration)**.

**5** Tie a length of string to the end of the cable.

**6** Return to the engine compartment, release the cable grommet from the bulkhead and withdraw the cable. When the end of the cable appears, untie the string and leave it in position – it can then be used to draw the cable back into position on refitting.

### Refitting

**7** Tie the string to the end of the cable, then use the string to draw the cable into position through the bulkhead. Once the cable end is visible, untie the string, then secure the inner cable into the pedal end.

**8** Refit the bulkhead grommet clip.

**9** From within the engine compartment, ensure the outer cable is correctly seated in the bulkhead grommet, then work along the cable, securing it in position with the retaining clips and ties, and ensuring that the cable is correctly routed.

**10** Pass the outer cable through its mounting bracket grommet, and reconnect the inner cable to the throttle cam. Adjust the cable as described below.

### Adjustment

**11** Remove the spring clip from the accelerator outer cable **(see illustration 3.1)**. Ensuring that the throttle cam is fully against its stop, gently pull the cable out of its grommet until all free play is removed from the inner cable.

**12** With the cable held in this position, refit the spring clip to the last exposed outer cable groove in front of the rubber grommet. When the clip is refitted and the outer cable is released, there should be only a small amount of free play in the inner cable.

**13** Have an assistant depress the accelerator pedal, and check that the throttle cam opens fully and returns smoothly to its stop.

## 4  Accelerator pedal –
removal and refitting

### Removal

#### Models with accelerator cable

**1** Detach the accelerator cable from the pedal as described in the previous Section.

**2** Remove the retaining clip and slide the accelerator pedal from the pedal pivot shaft. On left-hand drive models, recover the two pivot bushes from the pedal.

#### Models without accelerator cable

**3** Remove the lower facia panel on the driver's side, as described in Chapter 11.

**4** Disconnect the accelerator pedal position sensor wiring plug from the top of the pedal.

**5** Undo the three nuts and remove the pedal assembly **(see illustration)**.

### Refitting

**6** Refitting is a reversal of the removal

procedure. On models fitted with a cable, apply a little multi-purpose grease to the pedal pivot point, and adjust the accelerator cable as described in Section 3.

## 5  Unleaded petrol –
general information and usage

**Note:** *The information given in this Chapter is correct at the time of writing. If updated information is thought to be required, check with a Citroën dealer. If travelling abroad, consult one of the motoring organisations (or a similar authority) for advice on the fuel available.*

**1** The fuel recommended by Citroën is given in the Specifications Section of this Chapter, followed by the equivalent petrol currently on sale in the UK.

**2** All models are designed to run on fuel with a minimum octane rating of 95 (RON). All models have a catalytic converter, and so must be run on unleaded fuel only. Under no circumstances should leaded/lead replacement fuel (UK 4-star/LRP) be used, as this may damage the converter.

**3** Super unleaded petrol (98 octane) can also be used in all models if wished, though there is no advantage in doing so.

## 6  Engine management system
– general information

**Note:** *The fuel injection ECU is of the 'self-learning' type, meaning that as it operates, it also monitors and stores the settings which give optimum engine performance under all operating conditions. When the battery is disconnected, these settings are lost and the ECU reverts to the base settings programmed into its memory at the factory. On restarting, this may lead to the engine running/idling roughly for a short while, until the ECU has relearned the optimum settings. This process is best accomplished by taking the vehicle on a road test (for approximately 15 minutes), covering all engine speeds and loads, concentrating mainly in the 2500 to 3500 rpm region.*

On all engines, the fuel injection and ignition functions are combined into a single engine management system. The systems fitted are manufactured by Bosch, Magneti-Marelli and Sagem, and are very similar to each other in most respects, the only significant differences being in the software contained in the system ECU, and specific component location according to engine type. Each system incorporates a closed-loop catalytic converter and an evaporative emission control system, and complies with the latest emission control standards. Refer to Chapter 5B for information on the ignition side of each system; the fuel side of the system operates as follows.

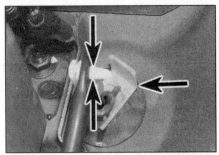

**3.4 Squeeze the tabs (arrowed), detach the inner cable from the accelerator pedal, then pull out the grommet clip (arrowed)**

The fuel pump supplies fuel from the tank to the fuel rail. The pump itself is mounted inside the tank, with the pump motor permanently immersed in fuel, to keep it cool. The fuel rail is mounted directly above the fuel injectors and acts as a fuel reservoir.

Fuel rail supply pressure is controlled by the pressure regulator, also located in the fuel tank. The regulator contains a spring-loaded valve, which lifts to allow excess fuel to recirculate within the tank when the optimum operating pressure of the fuel system is exceeded (eg, during low speed, light load cruising).

The fuel injectors are electromagnetic pintle valves, which spray atomised fuel into the combustion chambers under the control of the engine management system ECU. There are four injectors, one per cylinder, mounted in the inlet manifold close to the cylinder head. Each injector is mounted at an angle that allows it to spray fuel directly onto the back of the inlet valve(s). The ECU controls the volume of fuel injected by varying the length of time for which each injector is held open. The fuel injection systems are typically of the sequential type, whereby each injector operates individually in cylinder sequence.

The electrical control system consists of the ECU, along with the following sensors:

a) *Throttle potentiometer – informs the ECU of the throttle valve position, and the rate of throttle opening/closing.*

b) *Coolant temperature sensor – informs the ECU of engine temperature.*

c) *Inlet air temperature sensor – informs the ECU of the temperature of the air passing through the throttle housing.*

**4.5 Accelerator pedal mounting nuts (arrowed)**

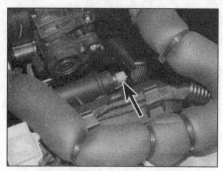

**7.2 Fuel pressure relief valve (arrowed)**

d) *Lambda (oxygen) sensors – inform the ECU of the oxygen content of the exhaust gases (explained in greater detail in Part C of this Chapter).*

e) *Manifold absolute pressure sensor – informs the ECU of the load on the engine (expressed in terms of inlet manifold vacuum).*

f) *Crankshaft position sensor – informs the ECU of engine speed and crankshaft angular position.*

g) *Vehicle speed sensor – informs the ECU of the vehicle speed (this function is performed by the wheel speed sensors on models with ABS).*

h) *Knock sensor – informs the ECU of pre-ignition (detonation) within the cylinders (not all models).*

i) *Accelerator pedal position sensor – informs the ECU of the pedal position and rate of change (Sagem and Bosch).*

j) *Throttle valve positioner motor – allows the ECU to control the throttle valve position (Sagem and Bosch).*

k) *Engine oil temperature sensor – informs the ECU of the engine oil temperature (not all models).*

l) *Clutch and brake pedal position sensor – informs the ECU of the pedal positions (not all models).*

Signals from each of the sensors are compared by the ECU and, based on this information, the ECU selects the response appropriate to those values, and controls the fuel injectors (varying the pulse width – the length of time the injectors are held open – to provide a richer or weaker air/fuel mixture, as appropriate). The air/fuel mixture is constantly varied by the ECU, to provide the best settings for cranking, starting (with either a hot or cold engine) and engine warm-up, idle, cruising and acceleration.

The ECU also has full control over the engine idle speed, via a stepper motor fitted to the throttle housing. The stepper motor either controls the amount of air passing through a bypass drilling at the side of the throttle or controls the position of the throttle valve itself, depending on model. On Sagem and Bosch systems, a sensor informs the ECU of the position, and rate of change, of the accelerator pedal. The ECU then controls the throttle valve by means of a throttle positioning motor integral with the throttle body – no accelerator cable is fitted. The ECU also carries out 'fine tuning' of the idle speed by varying the ignition timing to increase or reduce the torque of the engine as it is idling. This helps to stabilise the idle speed when electrical or mechanical loads (such as headlights, air conditioning, etc) are switched on and off.

The throttle housing is also fitted with an electric heating element. The heater is supplied with current by the ECU, warming the throttle housing on cold starts to help prevent icing of the throttle valve.

The exhaust and evaporative loss emission control systems are described in more detail in Chapter 4C.

If there is any abnormality in any of the readings obtained from the various, the ECU enters its 'back-up' mode. If this happens, the erroneous sensor signal is overridden, and the ECU assumes a preprogrammed 'back-up' value, which will allow the engine to continue running, albeit at reduced efficiency. If the ECU enters this mode, the warning lamp on the instrument panel will be illuminated, and the relevant fault code will be stored in the ECU memory.

If the warning light illuminates, the vehicle should be taken to a Citroën dealer or engine management diagnostic specialist at the earliest opportunity. Once there, a complete test of the engine management system can be carried out, using a special electronic diagnostic test unit, which is plugged into the system's diagnostic connector, located above the passenger's compartment fusebox.

## 7 Fuel system – depressurisation and pressurising

**Note:** *Refer to the warning note in Section 1 before proceeding.*

### Depressurisation

 *Warning: The following procedure will merely relieve the pressure in the fuel system – remember that fuel will still be present in the system components and take precautions accordingly before disconnecting any of them.*

**1** The fuel system referred to in this Section is defined as the tank-mounted fuel pump, the fuel injectors, the fuel rail and the pipes of the fuel lines between these components. All these contain fuel which will be under pressure while the engine is running, and/ or while the ignition is switched on. The pressure will remain for some time after the ignition has been switched off, and must be relieved in a controlled fashion when any of these components are disturbed for servicing work.

**2** Some models are equipped with a pressure relief valve on the fuel rail **(see illustration)**. Unscrew the cap from the valve and position a container beneath the valve. Hold a wad of rag over the valve and relieve the pressure in the system by depressing the valve core with a suitable screwdriver. Be prepared for the squirt of fuel as the valve core is depressed and catch it with the rag. Hold the valve core down until no more fuel is expelled from the valve. Once the pressure is relieved, securely refit the valve cap.

**3** Where no valve is fitted to the fuel rail, it will be necessary to release the pressure as the fuel pipe is disconnected. Place a container beneath the union and position a large rag around the union to catch any fuel spray which may be expelled. Slowly release and disconnect the fuel pipe and catch any spilt fuel in the container. Plug the pipe/union to minimise fuel loss and prevent the entry of dirt into the fuel system.

### Pressurising

**4** After any work is carried out on the fuel system, the system should be pressurised as follows.

**5** Depress the accelerator pedal fully then switch on the ignition. Hold the pedal depressed for approximately 1 second then release it. The ECU should then operate the fuel pump for between 20 and 30 seconds to refill the fuel system. Once the fuel pump stops the ignition can be switched off.

## 8 Fuel pump – removal and refitting

**Note:** *The fuel pump is only available as a complete assembly – no components are available separately.*

### Removal

**1** For access to the fuel pump, tilt or remove the rear seat cushion (see Chapter 11).

**2** Using a screwdriver, carefully release the three plastic access cover retaining clips at the points indicated by the small arrows, and remove the cover from the floor to expose the fuel pump/sender unit **(see illustration)**.

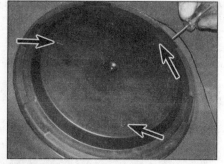

**8.2 Fuel pump access cover retaining clips release points (arrowed)**

**3** Disconnect the wiring connector from the fuel pump, and tape the connector to the vehicle body, to prevent it from disappearing behind the tank **(see illustration)**.

**4** Depressurise the fuel system as described in Section 7, then depress the retaining clip and detach the fuel pipe(s) from the top of the pump. Plug the pipe end(s) to minimise fuel loss and prevent the entry of dirt **(see illustration)**.

**5** Noting the alignment marks on the tank, pump cover and the locking ring, unscrew the ring and remove it from the tank. This is best accomplished by using a screwdriver on the raised ribs of the locking ring. Carefully tap the screwdriver to turn the ring anti-clockwise until it can be unscrewed by hand **(see illustration)**. Alternatively, a Citroën special tool is available which fits over the collar and allows it to be released using a ratchet and extension.

**6** Carefully lift the fuel pump assembly out of the fuel tank, taking great care not to damage the fuel gauge sender unit float arm, or to spill fuel onto the interior of the vehicle **(see illustration)**. Recover the rubber sealing ring and discard it – a new one must be used on refitting.

**7** If the fuel pump is going to be left out of the fuel tank for a while, screw the ring back to the top of the fuel tank to prevent it from going out of shape. Cover the access hole in the tank to prevent dirt ingress.

### Refitting

**8** Fit the new sealing ring to the top of the fuel tank **(see illustration)**.

**9** Carefully manoeuvre the pump assembly into the fuel tank, taking care not to damage the float arm.

**10** Align the arrow on the fuel pump cover with previously noted mark on the fuel tank and clip the pump assembly into position.

**11** Refit the locking ring and tighten it securely until its alignment mark aligns with the pump cover arrow **(see illustration)**.

**12** Securely reconnect the fuel pipe(s) to the pump cover then reconnect the pump wiring connector.

**13** Pressurise the fuel system (see Section 7). Start the engine and check the fuel pump hose unions for signs of leakage.

**14** If all is well, refit the plastic access cover ensuring its locating tab is at the front.

**15** Refit the rear seat cushion (see Chapter 11).

**9  Fuel gauge sender unit –**
  removal and refitting

The fuel gauge sender unit is an integral part of the fuel pump assembly and is not available separately. Refer to Section 8 for removal and refitting details.

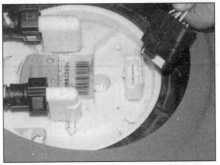

**8.3  Disconnect the pump wiring plug**

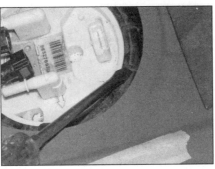

**8.5  Tap the screwdriver to rotate the locking ring anti-clockwise**

**10  Fuel tank –**
  removal and refitting

**Note:** *Refer to the warning note in Section 1 before proceeding.*

### Removal

**1** Before removing the fuel tank, all fuel must be drained from the tank. Since a fuel tank drain plug is not provided, it is therefore preferable to carry out the removal operation when the tank is nearly empty. Before proceeding, disconnect the battery (see Chapter 5A) and syphon or hand-pump the remaining fuel from the tank.

**2** Remove the rear seat cushion and, using a screwdriver, carefully release the three access

**8.8  Fit a new sealing ring to the top of the tank**

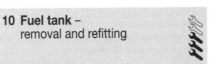

**8.4  Depress the release button and disconnect the fuel pipe**

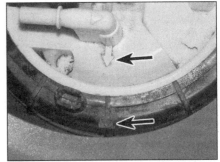

**8.6  Lift the fuel pump assembly, taking care not to damage the float arm**

cover retaining clips at the points indicated by the small arrows, and remove the cover from the floor to expose the fuel pump **(see illustration 8.2)**.

**3** Disconnect the wiring connector from the fuel pump, and tape the connector to the vehicle body, to prevent it from disappearing behind the tank **(see illustration 8.3)**.

**4** Depressurise the fuel system as described in Section 7, then depress the retaining clip and detach the fuel pipe(s) from the top of the pump **(see illustration 8.4)**. Plug the pipe end(s) to minimise fuel loss and prevent the entry of dirt.

**5** Chock the front wheels then jack up the rear of the vehicle and support it on axle stands (see *Jacking and vehicle support*). Remove the left-hand rear roadwheel.

**6** Prise out the stud fasteners and remove

**8.11  Rotate the locking ring until the mark aligns with the pump cover mark (arrowed)**

10.6a Prise out the stud fasteners . . .

10.6b . . . and remove the wheel arch liner

10.11 Unscrew the bolt (arrowed) securing the filler neck to the inner wheel arch

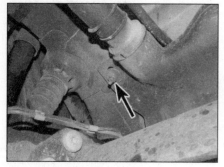

10.14a Fuel tank left-hand rear (arrowed) . . .

10.14b . . . and right-hand rear (arrowed) retaining nuts

## 11 Engine management system – testing and adjustment

### Testing

**1** If a fault appears in the engine management system, first ensure that all the system wiring connectors are securely connected and free of corrosion. Ensure that the fault is not due to poor maintenance; ie, check that the air cleaner filter element is clean, the spark plugs are in good condition and correctly gapped, the cylinder compression pressures are correct and that the engine breather hoses are clear and undamaged, referring to Chapters 1A, 2A and 5B for further information.

**2** If these checks fail to reveal the cause of the problem, the vehicle should be taken to a suitably-equipped Citroën dealer or engine management diagnostic specialist for testing. A diagnostic socket is located above the passenger's compartment fusebox, to which a fault code reader or other suitable test equipment can be connected **(see illustration)**. By using the code reader or test equipment, the engine management ECU (and the various other vehicle system ECUs) can be interrogated, and any stored fault codes can be retrieved. This will allow the fault to be quickly and simply traced, alleviating the need to test all the system components individually, which is a time-consuming operation that carries a risk of damaging the ECU.

### Adjustment

**3** Whilst it is possible to check the exhaust CO level and the idle speed, if these are found to be in need of adjustment, the car *must* be taken to a suitably-equipped Citroën dealer or specialist or further testing. Neither the mixture adjustment (exhaust gas CO level) nor the idle speed are adjustable, and should either be incorrect, a fault must be present in the engine management system.

the left-hand rear wheel arch liner **(see illustrations)**.

**7** Refer to Chapter 10 and remove the rear suspension coil springs.

**8** Remove the exhaust system as described in Section 16.

**9** Undo the nuts, release the plastic rivets and remove the plastic undershields from both sides of the fuel tank.

**10** Unscrew the retaining nuts, and remove the heat shield from the tank underside.

**11** Unscrew the bolt securing the filler neck to the inner wheel arch **(see illustration)**.

**12** Remove the rear suspension bump stop on the left-hand side.

**13** Place a trolley jack with an interposed block of wood beneath the tank, then raise the jack until it is supporting the weight of the tank.

**14** Slacken and remove the four nuts securing the fuel tank to the body **(see illustrations)**.

11.2 The diagnostic socket (arrowed) is located above the passenger's compartment fusebox

Release the filler neck seal from the body at the filler cap aperture.

**15** Slowly lower the fuel tank, ensuring the filler neck assembly is guided out of position without placing any stress on it.

**16** If the tank is contaminated with sediment or water, remove the fuel pump (Section 8), and swill the tank out with clean fuel. The tank is injection-moulded from a synthetic material – if seriously damaged, it should be renewed. However, in certain cases, it may be possible to have small leaks or minor damage repaired. Seek the advice of a specialist before attempting to repair the fuel tank.

**17** It is not possible to separate the filler neck from the tank. If damaged, the complete assembly must be renewed.

### Refitting

**18** Refitting is the reverse of the removal procedure, noting the following points:

a) Ensure the wiring connector and fuel pipes are securely reconnected and retained by all the relevant clips. When lifting the tank back into position, take care to ensure that the pipes/wiring do not become trapped between the tank and vehicle body.

b) Refit the rear suspension springs as described in Chapter 10.

c) Refit the exhaust as described in Section 16.

d) On completion, refill the tank with a small amount of fuel and pressurise the fuel system as described in Section 7. Check for signs of leakage prior to taking the vehicle out on the road.

**12.3 Disconnect the wiring connectors from the throttle housing components (1.1 litre engine)**

**12.4a Undo the three retaining screws (arrowed) . . .**

**12.4b . . . then remove the throttle housing from the manifold and recover the sealing ring (1.1 litre engine)**

## 12 Throttle housing – removal and refitting

### Removal

**1** Remove the air cleaner assembly as described in Section 2.

**2** Free the accelerator inner cable from the throttle cam (where fitted).

**3** Note their fitted positions, then depress the retaining clip and disconnect the wiring connectors from the throttle housing **(see illustration)**.

**4** Slacken and remove the retaining screws and remove the throttle housing from the inlet manifold **(see illustrations)**. Recover the sealing ring from manifold and discard it; a new one must be used on refitting.

### Refitting

**5** Refitting is a reversal of the removal procedure, noting the following points:

  a) *Fit a new sealing ring to the manifold, then refit the throttle housing and securely tighten its retaining screws.*

  b) *Ensure all wiring is correctly routed, and that the connectors are securely reconnected.*

  c) *On completion, adjust the accelerator cable (where fitted) as described in Section 3.*

## 13 Engine management system components – removal and refitting

### Fuel rail and injectors

**Note 1:** *Refer to the warning note in Section 1 before proceeding.*

**Note 2:** *If a faulty injector is suspected, before condemning the injector, it is worth trying the effect of one of the proprietary injector-cleaning treatments which are available from car accessory shops.*

**1** Before proceeding with removing any of the engine management system components, disconnect the battery (see Chapter 5A).

### SOHC engines

**2** Remove the ignition HT coil as described in Chapter 5B.

**3** Free the accelerator inner cable (where fitted) from the throttle housing cam, then pull the outer cable out from its mounting bracket rubber grommet, complete with its spring clip **(see illustration 3.1)**.

**4** Unscrew the bolts/nuts and remove the accelerator cable bracket, or manifold support bracket, from the manifold/cylinder head.

**5** Depressurise the fuel system as described in Section 7, then depress the retaining clip and disconnect the fuel pipe from the right-hand end of the fuel rail **(see illustration)**.

**6** Slacken and remove the two bolts securing the fuel rail to the cylinder head, and the nut securing the rail to the manifold. Loosen the bolt securing the fuel rail centre bracket to the inlet manifold, then lift off the bracket

(the bracket is slotted to ease removal) **(see illustrations)**.

**7** Disconnect the injector wiring harness connector, then unclip the connector from the rear of the inlet manifold. Also disconnect the wiring connectors from the throttle housing and position the wiring harness clear of the manifold so that it does not hinder fuel rail removal.

**8** Carefully ease the fuel rail and injector assembly out from the cylinder head and manoeuvre it out of position. Remove the seals from the end of each injector and discard them; they must be renewed whenever they are disturbed **(see illustration)**.

**9** Disconnect the wiring connector(s) then slide out the retaining clip(s) and remove the relevant injector(s) from the fuel rail. Remove the upper seal from each disturbed injector and discard; all disturbed seals must be renewed.

**13.5 Depress the retaining clip (arrowed) and disconnect the fuel hose from the fuel rail (SOHC engines)**

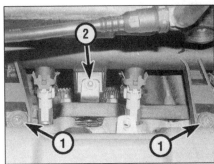

**13.6a Unscrew the fuel rail mounting bolts (1) and the nut (2) . . .**

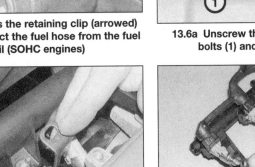

**13.6b . . . then slacken the bolt (arrowed) and lift off the centre bracket (SOHC engines)**

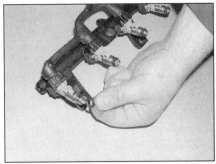

**13.8 Remove the seal from the end of each injector (SOHC engines)**

**13.12 Undo the two bolts (arrowed) and remove the injectors and fuel rail from the manifold (DOHC engines)**

**13.13 Slide off the retaining clip and remove the injector from the fuel rail (DOHC engines)**

**13.14 Renew all injector seals (arrowed) disturbed on removal (DOHC engines)**

**10** Refitting is a reversal of the removal procedure, noting the following points.
 a) *Fit new seals to all disturbed injector unions.*
 b) *Apply a smear of engine oil to the seals to aid installation, then ease the injectors and fuel rail into position ensuring that none of the seals are displaced.*
 c) *On completion, pressurise the fuel system as described in Section 7. Start the engine and check for fuel leaks.*

### DOHC engines

**11** Remove the inlet manifold as described in Section 14.
**12** Undo the two bolts and remove the fuel rail with injectors from the manifold **(see illustration)**.
**13** Disconnect the wiring connector(s) then slide out the retaining clip(s) and remove the relevant injector(s) from the fuel rail. Remove the seals from each disturbed injector and discard; all disturbed seals must be renewed **(see illustration)**.
**14** Refitting is a reversal of the removal procedure, noting the following points.
 a) *Fit new seals to all disturbed injector unions* **(see illustration)**.
 b) *Apply a smear of engine oil to the seals to aid installation, then ease the injectors and fuel rail into position ensuring that none of the seals are displaced.*
 c) *On completion, pressurise the fuel system as described in Section 7. Start the engine and check for fuel leaks.*

### Fuel pressure regulator

**15** The fuel pressure regulator is an integral part of the fuel pump assembly and is not available separately. Refer to Section 8 for removal and refitting details.

**13.16 Disconnect the throttle potentiometer wiring plug . . .**

**13.17 . . . then undo the retaining screws (arrowed) and remove it from the throttle housing (1.1 litre engine)**

### Throttle potentiometer

**Note:** *On 1.4 and 1.6 litre models, the throttle potentiometer is an integral part of the throttle housing and is not available separately.*
**16** Depress the retaining clip and disconnect the wiring connector from the throttle potentiometer **(see illustration)**.
**17** Slacken and remove the two retaining screws, then disengage the potentiometer from the throttle valve spindle and remove it from the vehicle **(see illustration)**.
**18** Refit in the reverse order of removal. Ensure that the potentiometer is correctly engaged with the throttle valve spindle.

### Electronic Control Unit (ECU)

**Note:** *If a new ECU is being fitted, the vehicle will not start until the immobiliser ECU has been matched to the engine management ECU. This can only be performed using dedicated test equipment. Consequently, entrust the procedure to a Citroën dealer or suitably-equipped specialist.*
**19** The ECU is located in the battery box on the left-hand side of the engine compartment.
**20** For improved access, remove the battery as described in Chapter 5A.
**21** Release the lever catches and disconnect the ECU wiring connectors **(see illustration)**.
**22** Disengage the mounting plate lower locating lugs and lift the ECU and mounting plate from the battery box **(see illustration)**.
**23** Undo the mounting bolts and separate the ECU from the mounting plate.
**24** Refitting is a reverse of the removal procedure ensuring the wiring connectors are securely reconnected.

### Idle speed stepper motor

**Note:** *On 1.4 and 1.6 litre models, the stepper motor is an integral part of the throttle housing and is not available separately.*
**25** The idle speed stepper motor is fitted to the rear of the throttle housing.
**26** Disconnect the wiring connector from the motor **(see illustration)**.
**27** Slacken and remove the retaining screws then remove the motor from the throttle housing **(see illustration)**. If necessary, remove the throttle potentiometer to improve access to the motor lower screw.

**13.21 Release the lever catches and disconnect the ECU wiring plugs**

**13.22 Lift the ECU up from the battery box**

13.26 Disconnect the idle speed stepper motor wiring plug (arrowed) (1.1 litre engine)

13.27 Undo the retaining screw(s) and remove the motor from the housing (1.1 litre engine)

13.30a Disconnect the wiring connector, undo the screw and remove the MAP sensor (arrowed) (SOHC engines) . . .

13.30b . . . and DOHC engines

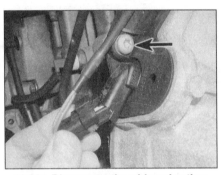

13.35a Disconnect the wiring plug then undo the retaining screw (arrowed) . . .

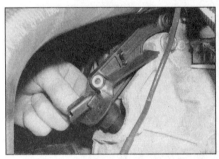

13.35b . . . then remove the crankshaft position sensor from the front of the transmission housing

**28** Refitting is a reversal of the removal procedure ensuring the seal is in good condition.

### Manifold absolute pressure sensor

**29** The MAP sensor is mounted on the front of the inlet manifold.
**30** Disconnect the wiring connector then undo the screw and remove the sensor from the manifold (see illustrations).
**31** Refitting is a reversal of the removal procedure ensuring the sensor seal is in good condition.

### Coolant temperature sensor

**32** The coolant temperature sensor is screwed into the coolant outlet housing on the left-hand end of the cylinder head. Refer to Chapter 3, Section 7, for removal and refitting information.

### Inlet air temperature sensor

**33** The inlet air temperature sensor is integral with the throttle housing and is not available separately.

### Crankshaft position sensor

**34** The crankshaft sensor is situated on the front face of the transmission clutch housing.
**35** Disconnect the sensor wiring connector and unclip the wiring. Undo the retaining bolt and remove the sensor and bracket assembly from the transmission unit (see illustrations).
**36** Refitting is reverse of the removal procedure.

### Vehicle speed sensor

**37** On models without ABS, the vehicle speed

sensor is an integral part of the speedometer drive. Refer to Chapter 7A for removal and refitting details. On other models, the ECU receives vehicle speed data from the wheel speed sensors, via the ABS ECU.

### Knock sensor

**38** Refer to Chapter 5B.

### Air conditioning pressure switch

**39** The air conditioning pressure switch is fitted to the refrigerant pipe located on the right-hand side of the engine compartment. Switch renewal requires the air conditioning system to be discharged and drained (see Chapter 3).

### Throttle valve positioner motor

**40** The throttle valve positioner motor (where

14.5a Disconnect the vacuum servo pipe (arrowed) . . .

fitted) is integral with the throttle housing, and is not available separately.

### Accelerator pedal position sensor

**41** The sensor is integral with the accelerator pedal assembly – see Section 4.

## 14 Inlet manifold – removal and refitting

### Removal

**Note:** *Refer to the warning note in Section 1 before proceeding.*

#### SOHC engines

**1** Remove the air cleaner assembly as described in Section 2.
**2** Remove the fuel rail and injectors as described in Section 13.
**3** If not already done, disconnect the wiring connectors from the throttle housing components then unclip the harness and position it clear of the manifold

#### DOHC engines

**4** Remove the throttle housing as described in Section 12.

#### All models

**5** Release the retaining clips and disconnect the vacuum servo unit pipe and purge valve pipe from the inlet manifold (see illustrations).
**6** Disconnect all wiring connectors from

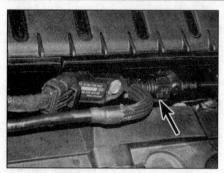

14.5b ... and purge valve pipe (arrowed) from the manifold (DOHC engines)

14.9a Inlet manifold nuts (arrowed) (SOHC engines)

14.9b Note the centre bracket (arrowed) fitted to the DOHC engines

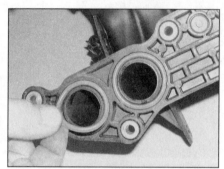

14.10 Ensure new manifold seals are fitted

the manifold, having first noted their fitted positions. Release the wiring from any retaining clips.

**7** Depress the release button and disconnect the fuel pipe and position it clear of the manifold.

**8** Where necessary, undo the retaining bolts and remove the support bracket from the underside of the manifold.

**9** Undo the manifold retaining nuts and withdraw the manifold from the engine compartment. Recover the four manifold seals and discard them; new ones must be used on refitting **(see illustrations)**.

### *Refitting*

**10** Refitting is a reverse of the relevant removal procedure, noting the following points:

a) Ensure that the manifold and cylinder head mating surfaces are clean and dry, then locate the new seals in their

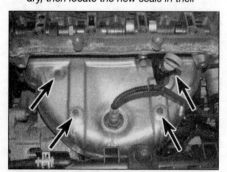

15.2a Undo the heat shield bolts (arrowed) ...

recesses in the manifold **(see illustration overleaf)**. Refit the manifold and tighten its retaining nuts to the specified torque.

b) Ensure that all relevant hoses are reconnected to their original positions and are securely held (where necessary) by the retaining clips.

c) Ensure the wiring is correctly routed and all connectors are securely reconnected.

d) Adjust the accelerator cable (where fitted) as described in Section 3.

### 15 Exhaust manifold – removal and refitting

### *Removal*

**1** Disconnect the battery, as described in Chapter 5A.

**2** Slacken and remove the retaining screws

15.2b ... and the dipstick guide tube bolt

and remove the shroud from the top of the exhaust manifold. It may be necessary to remove the engine lifting eye bracket from the left-hand end of the cylinder head, and undo the bolt and remove the oil dipstick tube **(see illustrations)**.

**3** Firmly apply the handbrake, then jack up the front of the vehicle and support it on axle stands (see *Jacking and vehicle support*). Release the screws and remove the engine undershield (where fitted).

**4** On some models, a second heat shield is fitted on the underside of the manifold, above the oil filter. Undo the bolts and remove the heat shield.

**5** Trace the lambda sensors wiring back to the connectors and disconnect them.

**6** Undo the nuts securing the exhaust front pipe/catalytic converter to the manifold, then remove the bolt securing the front pipe to its mounting bracket. Disconnect the front pipe from the manifold, and recover the gasket.

**7** Undo the retaining nuts securing the manifold to the head. Manoeuvre the manifold out of the engine compartment, and discard the manifold gasket(s).

### *Refitting*

**8** Refitting is the reverse of the removal procedure, noting the following points:

a) Examine all the exhaust manifold studs for signs of damage and corrosion; remove all traces of corrosion, and repair or renew any damaged studs.

b) Ensure that the manifold and cylinder head sealing faces are clean and flat, and fit the new manifold gasket(s). Tighten the manifold retaining nuts to the specified torque.

c) Reconnect the front pipe to the manifold using the information given in Section 16.

d) Where necessary, renew the oil dipstick tube O-ring.

### 16 Exhaust system – general information, removal and refitting

### *General information*

**1** On new vehicles, the exhaust system consists two sections; the front pipe with integral catalytic converter and the remaining system consisting of a silencer and tailpipe. The front pipe is secured to the manifold by nuts and bolts and the two sections are joined by a spring-loaded ball type joint to allow for movement in the system.

**2** For service replacements it is possible to obtain an intermediate section and a rear section (silencer and tailpipe) separately, however the original pipe must be cut with a hacksaw to accommodate either new section. The new sections are supplied with a clamping sleeve to allow connection to the original pipe.

**3** The system is suspended throughout its entire length by rubber mountings.

**4**  To remove the system or part of the system, first jack up the front or rear of the car and support it on axle stands (see *Jacking and vehicle support*). Alternatively, position the car over an inspection pit or on car ramps. If the complete system is to be removed, the rear beam axle must be lowered to allow room to withdraw the system from the rear of the car. Bear this in mind when considering how the car is to be positioned.

### Removal and refitting

#### Front pipe/catalytic converter

**Note:** *The catalytic converter is integral with the front pipe.*

**5**  Trace the wiring back from the post-catalyst lambda sensor to its wiring connector. Disconnect the connector and free the wiring from all its clips and ties so the sensor is free to be removed with the front pipe.

**6**  Slacken and remove the two nuts securing the front pipe flange joint to the intermediate/rear pipe. Recover the spring cups, springs, bolts and collars.

**7**  Undo the nuts securing the front pipe flange joint to the manifold, and the single bolt securing the front pipe to its mounting bracket. Separate the flange joint, collect the gasket, and withdraw the front pipe from underneath the vehicle.

**8**  Refitting is a reversal of the removal procedure. Ensure that the flange joint mating faces are clean and use a new gasket.

#### Whole system (minus front pipe)

**9**  If the complete system is to be removed, the rear beam axle must be lowered to allow room to withdraw the system from the rear of the car. To do this, remove the rear suspension coil springs as described in Chapter 10, and lower the beam axle as far as the mountings will permit.

**10**  Slacken and remove the two nuts securing the intermediate/rear pipe flange joint to the front pipe **(see illustration)**. Recover the spring cups, springs, bolts and collars.

**11**  Undo the nuts securing the exhaust system mounting brackets to the underbody. Lift the system over the beam axle and withdraw it from the rear of the car.

**12**  Refitting is a reversal of the removal procedure, bearing in mind the following points:

  a) *Inspect the rubber mountings for signs of damage or deterioration, and renew as necessary.*

  b) *Prior to tightening the exhaust system fasteners, ensure that all rubber mountings are correctly located, and that there is adequate clearance between the exhaust system and vehicle underbody.*

  c) *Refit the rear suspension coil springs as described in Chapter 10.*

#### Intermediate pipe (service replacement)

**13**  If a service replacement intermediate pipe is already installed, slacken and remove the two nuts securing the intermediate pipe flange joint to the front pipe. Recover the spring cups, springs, bolts and collars.

**14**  Undo the nuts securing the intermediate pipe mounting brackets to the underbody. Slacken the clamping sleeve nuts, withdraw the intermediate pipe from the clamping sleeve and remove the pipe from under the car.

**15**  Refitting is a reversal of removal, but inspect the rubber mountings for signs of damage or deterioration, and renew if necessary.

**16**  If a service replacement intermediate pipe is to be installed on an original system, locate the cutting point on the original pipe. The cutting point is located just forward of the rear beam axle and is identified by four circular indentations in the pipe.

**17**  Using a hacksaw, cut through the pipe at the cutting point.

**18**  Slacken and remove the two nuts securing the intermediate pipe flange joint to the front pipe. Recover the spring cups, springs, bolts and collars.

**19**  Undo the nuts securing the intermediate pipe mounting brackets to the underbody and remove the pipe from under the car.

**20**  Inspect the rubber mountings for signs of damage or deterioration, and renew if necessary. If satisfactory, transfer the mountings to the new intermediate pipe.

**21**  Using a pencil, make a mark on the tailpipe (remaining on the car) 40 mm from the cutting point. Slide the new clamping sleeve over the tailpipe and up to the mark. Fit the retaining bolts and nuts and tighten them just sufficiently to hold the sleeve in position.

**22**  Engage the new intermediate pipe with the clamping sleeve then refit the mounting bracket retaining nuts finger tight only at this stage.

**23**  Fit the flange joint collars, bolts springs and cups, then screw on the nuts and tighten the joint securely.

**24**  Check that the clamping sleeve is still positioned at the previously made mark and that the intermediate pipe is fully engaged. Securely tighten the clamping sleeve nuts, followed by the mounting bracket nuts.

#### Silencer/tailpipe (service replacement)

**25**  If a service replacement silencer/tailpipe is already installed, undo the nuts securing the silencer/tailpipe mounting bracket to the underbody. Slacken the clamping sleeve nuts, withdraw the silencer/tailpipe from the clamping sleeve and remove the pipe from under the car.

**26**  Refitting is a reversal of removal, but inspect the rubber mounting for signs of damage or deterioration, and renew if necessary.

**27**  If a service replacement silencer/tailpipe is to be installed on an original system, locate the cutting point on the original pipe. The cutting point is located just forward of the rear beam axle and is identified by four circular indentations in the pipe.

**16.10 Exhaust system flange joint retaining nuts (arrowed)**

**28**  Using a hacksaw, cut through the pipe at the cutting point.

**29**  Undo the nuts securing the silencer/tailpipe mounting bracket to the underbody and remove the pipe from under the car.

**30**  Inspect the rubber mountings for signs of damage or deterioration, and renew if necessary. If satisfactory, transfer the mounting to the new silencer/tailpipe.

**31**  Using a pencil, make a mark on the intermediate pipe (remaining on the car) 40 mm from the cutting point. Slide the new clamping sleeve over the intermediate pipe and up to the mark. Fit the retaining bolts and nuts and tighten them just sufficiently to hold the sleeve in position.

**32**  Engage the new silencer/tailpipe with the clamping sleeve then refit the mounting bracket retaining nuts.

**33**  Check that the clamping sleeve is still positioned at the previously made mark and that the silencer/tailpipe is fully engaged. Securely tighten the clamping sleeve nuts, followed by the mounting bracket nuts.

#### Heat shield(s)

**34**  The heat shields are secured to the underside of the body by various nuts and fasteners **(see illustration)**. If a shield is being removed to gain access to a component located behind it, remove the retaining nuts and/or fastener (unscrew the centre screw then pull out the complete fastener), and manoeuvre the shield out of position. On some models it may be necessary to free the exhaust system from its mountings to gain the clearance necessary to remove the larger heat shield.

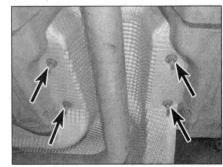

**16.34 Exhaust rear heat shield retaining nuts (arrowed)**

# Chapter 4 Part B:
# Fuel and exhaust systems – diesel models

## Contents

## Degrees of difficulty

| **Easy,** suitable for novice with little experience | **Fairly easy,** suitable for beginner with some experience | **Fairly difficult,** suitable for competent DIY mechanic | **Difficult,** suitable for experienced DIY mechanic | **Very difficult,** suitable for expert DIY or professional |
|---|---|---|---|---|

## Specifications

### Engine identification

| | Designation | Engine code |
|---|---|---|
| **1.4 litre:** | | |
| SOHC (8-valve). . . . . . . . . . . . . . . . . . . . . . . . . . . . . . . . . . . . . . . | DV4TD | 8HX and 8HZ |
| DOHC (16-valve). . . . . . . . . . . . . . . . . . . . . . . . . . . . . . . . . . . . . . | DV4TED4 | 8HY |
| **1.6 litre:** | | |
| DOHC (16-valve) with intercooler. . . . . . . . . . . . . . . . . . . . . . . . . | DV6ATED4 | 9HX |
| DOHC (16-valve) without intercooler . . . . . . . . . . . . . . . . . . . . . . | DV6TED4 | 9HY |
| DOHC (16-valve) without intercooler but with particulate filter . . . . . | DV6TED4 | 9HZ |

### General

System type . . . . . . . . . . . . . . . . . . . . . . . . . . . . . . . . . . . . . . . . . . . HDi (High-pressure Diesel injection) with full electronic control, direct injection and turbocharger

Designation:
  DV4TD 8-valve:
    8HX and 8HZ:
      Pre-2006. . . . . . . . . . . . . . . . . . . . . . . . . . . . . . . . . . . . . . . . Siemens SID 802/804/806
      2006-on. . . . . . . . . . . . . . . . . . . . . . . . . . . . . . . . . . . . . . . . Bosch EDC 16C34
  DV4TED4 16-valve 8HY . . . . . . . . . . . . . . . . . . . . . . . . . . . . . . . . Delphi C6
  DV6. . . . . . . . . . . . . . . . . . . . . . . . . . . . . . . . . . . . . . . . . . . . . . . Bosch EDC 16C34
Firing order. . . . . . . . . . . . . . . . . . . . . . . . . . . . . . . . . . . . . . . . . . . 1-3-4-2 (No 1 at flywheel end)
Fuel system operating pressure . . . . . . . . . . . . . . . . . . . . . . . . . . . 200 to 1800 bars (according to engine speed)
Idle speed. . . . . . . . . . . . . . . . . . . . . . . . . . . . . . . . . . . . . . . . . . . . 800 ± 20 rpm (controlled by ECU)
Engine cut-off speed . . . . . . . . . . . . . . . . . . . . . . . . . . . . . . . . . . . 5000 rpm (controlled by ECU)

### Injectors

Type . . . . . . . . . . . . . . . . . . . . . . . . . . . . . . . . . . . . . . . . . . . . . . . . Electromagnetic or Piezo

### Turbocharger

Type:
  DV4. . . . . . . . . . . . . . . . . . . . . . . . . . . . . . . . . . . . . . . . . . . . . . . KKK
  DV6TED4 . . . . . . . . . . . . . . . . . . . . . . . . . . . . . . . . . . . . . . . . . . Garrett GT1544V
  DV6ATED4 . . . . . . . . . . . . . . . . . . . . . . . . . . . . . . . . . . . . . . . . . MHI – TD025S2
Boost pressure (approximate) . . . . . . . . . . . . . . . . . . . . . . . . . . . . 0.9 bar @ 3500 rpm

## Torque wrench settings

| | Nm | lbf ft |
|---|---|---|
| Accumulator rail mounting bolts . . . . . . . . . . . . . . . . . . . . . . . . . . . . | 22 | 16 |
| Accumulator rail-to-fuel injector fuel pipe unions*: | | |
|     Stage 1 . . . . . . . . . . . . . . . . . . . . . . . . . . . . . . . . . . . . . . . . . . . . | 20 | 15 |
|     Stage 2 . . . . . . . . . . . . . . . . . . . . . . . . . . . . . . . . . . . . . . . . . . . . | 25 | 18 |
| Camshaft position sensor bolt . . . . . . . . . . . . . . . . . . . . . . . . . . . . . | 5 | 4 |
| Clamping ring nuts . . . . . . . . . . . . . . . . . . . . . . . . . . . . . . . . . . . . . . | 20 | 15 |
| Crankshaft speed/position sensor . . . . . . . . . . . . . . . . . . . . . . . . . . | 5 | 4 |
| Cylinder head cover bolts . . . . . . . . . . . . . . . . . . . . . . . . . . . . . . . . | 10 | 7 |
| Exhaust manifold nuts . . . . . . . . . . . . . . . . . . . . . . . . . . . . . . . . . . . | 25 | 18 |
| Exhaust system fasteners: | | |
|     Catalytic converter-to-manifold nuts . . . . . . . . . . . . . . . . . . . . . . | 40 | 30 |
|     Clamping ring nuts . . . . . . . . . . . . . . . . . . . . . . . . . . . . . . . . . . . | 20 | 15 |
| Fuel injector clamp bolt: | | |
|   8-valve engines: | | |
|     Stage 1 . . . . . . . . . . . . . . . . . . . . . . . . . . . . . . . . . . . . . . . . . . . . | 15 | 11 |
|     Stage 2 . . . . . . . . . . . . . . . . . . . . . . . . . . . . . . . . . . . . . . . . . . . . | Angle-tighten a further 70° | |
|   16-valve engines: | | |
|     Stage 1 . . . . . . . . . . . . . . . . . . . . . . . . . . . . . . . . . . . . . . . . . . . . | 4 | 3 |
|     Stage 2 . . . . . . . . . . . . . . . . . . . . . . . . . . . . . . . . . . . . . . . . . . . . | Angle-tighten a further 65° | |
| Fuel injector clamp stud . . . . . . . . . . . . . . . . . . . . . . . . . . . . . . . . . | 7 | 5 |
| Fuel pressure sensor to accumulator rail . . . . . . . . . . . . . . . . . . . . . | 45 | 33 |
| Fuel pump-to-accumulator rail fuel pipe unions*: | | |
|     Stage 1 . . . . . . . . . . . . . . . . . . . . . . . . . . . . . . . . . . . . . . . . . . . . | 20 | 15 |
|     Stage 2 . . . . . . . . . . . . . . . . . . . . . . . . . . . . . . . . . . . . . . . . . . . . | 25 | 18 |
| High-pressure fuel pump mounting bolts . . . . . . . . . . . . . . . . . . . . . | 20 | 15 |
| High-pressure fuel pump sprocket nut . . . . . . . . . . . . . . . . . . . . . . . | 50 | 37 |
| Inlet manifold retaining bolts (16-valve engines) . . . . . . . . . . . . . . . . | 10 | 7 |
| Knock sensor . . . . . . . . . . . . . . . . . . . . . . . . . . . . . . . . . . . . . . . . . | 20 | 15 |
| Turbocharger mounting nuts . . . . . . . . . . . . . . . . . . . . . . . . . . . . . . | 25 | 18 |
| Turbocharger oil feed pipe banjo bolts: | | |
|   8-valve engines . . . . . . . . . . . . . . . . . . . . . . . . . . . . . . . . . . . . . . | 20 | 15 |
|   16-valve engines . . . . . . . . . . . . . . . . . . . . . . . . . . . . . . . . . . . . . | 30 | 22 |

*These torque settings are using Citroën's crow's-foot adaptors – see Section 2*

---

## 1  General information and system operation

The fuel system consists of a rear-mounted fuel tank and fuel gauge sender unit, a fuel filter with integral water separator, a fuel cooler mounted under the car, and an electronically-controlled High-pressure Diesel injection (HDi) system, together with a turbocharger.

The exhaust system is conventional, but to meet the latest emission levels an unregulated catalytic converter and an exhaust gas recirculation system are fitted. On DV6TED4 (9HZ) 1.6 litre models, an exhaust emission particulate filter is fitted – refer to Chapter 4C for further details.

The HDi system (generally known as a 'common rail' system) derives its name from the fact that a common rail (referred to as an accumulator rail), or fuel reservoir, is used to supply fuel to all the fuel injectors. Instead of an in-line or distributor type injection pump, which distributes the fuel directly to each injector, a high-pressure pump is used, which generates a very high fuel pressure (1600 bars at high engine speed) in the accumulator rail. The accumulator rail stores fuel, and maintains a constant fuel pressure, with the aid of a pressure control valve. Each injector is supplied with high-pressure fuel from the accumulator rail, and the injectors are individually controlled via signals from the system electronic control unit (ECU). The injectors are electromagnetically-operated.

In addition to the various sensors used on models with a conventional fuel injection pump, common rail systems also have a fuel pressure sensor. The fuel pressure sensor allows the ECU to maintain the required fuel pressure, via the pressure control valve.

### System operation

For the purposes of describing the operation of a common rail injection system, the components can be divided into three sub-systems; the low-pressure fuel system, the high-pressure fuel system and the electronic control system.

### Low-pressure fuel system

The low-pressure fuel system consists of the following components:
a) Fuel tank.
b) Fuel cooler.
c) Fuel heater (not all models).
d) Fuel filter/water trap.
e) Low-pressure fuel lines.

The low-pressure system (fuel supply system) is responsible for supplying clean fuel to the high-pressure fuel system.

### High-pressure fuel system

The high-pressure fuel system consists of the following components:
a) High-pressure fuel pump with pressure control valve.
b) High-pressure fuel accumulator rail.
c) Fuel injectors.
d) High-pressure fuel lines.

After passing through the fuel filter, the fuel reaches the high-pressure pump, which forces it into the accumulator rail. As diesel fuel has a certain elasticity, the pressure in the accumulator rail remains constant, even though fuel leaves the rail each time one of the injectors operates. Additionally, a pressure control valve mounted on the high-pressure pump ensures that the fuel pressure is maintained within preset limits.

The pressure control valve is operated by the ECU. When the valve is opened, fuel is returned from the high-pressure pump to the tank, via the fuel return lines, and the pressure in the accumulator rail falls. To enable the ECU to trigger the pressure control valve correctly, the pressure in the accumulator rail is measured by a fuel pressure sensor.

The electromagnetically-controlled fuel injectors are operated individually, via signals from the ECU, and each injector injects fuel directly into the relevant combustion chamber.

The fact that high fuel pressure is always available allows very precise and highly flexible injection in comparison to a conventional injection pump: for example combustion during the main injection process can be improved considerably by the pre-injection of a very small quantity of fuel.

### Electronic control system

The electronic control system consists of the following components:

a) Electronic control unit (ECU).
b) Crankshaft speed/position sensor.
c) Camshaft position sensor.
d) Accelerator pedal position sensor.
e) Coolant temperature sensor.
f) Fuel temperature sensor.
g) Atmospheric pressure sensor (integral with the ECU on some models).
h) Manifold pressure sensor (early 16-valve engines).
i) Knock sensor (early 16-valve engines).
j) Air mass meter.
k) Fuel pressure sensor.
l) Fuel injectors.
m) Fuel pressure control valve.
n) Preheating control unit.
o) EGR solenoid valve.
p) Air temperature sensor.
q) Throttle housing in addition to the air mass meter (pre-2006 1.4 litre models with Siemens injection system, and all 1.6 litre models).

The information from the various sensors is passed to the ECU, which evaluates the signals. The ECU contains electronic 'maps' which enable it to calculate the optimum quantity of fuel to inject, the appropriate start of injection, and even pre- and post-injection fuel quantities, for each individual engine cylinder under any given condition of engine operation.

Additionally, the ECU carries out monitoring and self-diagnostic functions. Any faults in the system are stored in the ECU memory, which enables quick and accurate fault diagnosis using appropriate diagnostic equipment (such as a suitable fault code reader).

### System Components

#### Fuel lift pump

The fuel lift pump and integral fuel gauge sender unit is electrically-operated, and is mounted in the fuel tank.

#### High-pressure pump

The high-pressure pump is mounted on the engine in the position normally occupied by the conventional distributor fuel injection pump. The pump is driven at half engine speed by the timing belt, and is lubricated by the fuel which it pumps.

The high-pressure pump consists of three radially-mounted pistons and cylinders. The pistons are operated by an eccentric cam mounted on the pump drive spindle. As a piston moves down, fuel enters the cylinder through an inlet valve. When the piston reaches bottom dead centre (BDC), the inlet

valve closes, and as the piston moves back up the cylinder the fuel is compressed. When the pressure in the cylinder reaches the pressure in the accumulator rail, an outlet valve opens, and fuel is forced into the accumulator rail. When the piston reaches top dead centre (TDC), the outlet valve closes, due to the pressure drop, and the pumping cycle is repeated. The use of multiple cylinders provides a steady flow of fuel, minimising pulses and pressure fluctuations.

As the pump needs to be able to supply sufficient fuel under full-load conditions, it will supply excess fuel during idle and part-load conditions. This excess fuel is returned from the high-pressure circuit to the low-pressure circuit (to the tank) via the pressure control valve.

The pump incorporates a facility to effectively switch off one of its cylinders to improve efficiency and reduce fuel consumption when maximum pumping capacity is not required. When this facility is operated, a solenoid-operated needle holds the inlet valve in the relevant pump cylinder open during the delivery stroke, preventing the fuel from being compressed.

#### Accumulator rail

As its name suggests, the accumulator rail acts as an accumulator, storing fuel and preventing pressure fluctuations. Fuel enters the rail from the high-pressure pump, and each injector has its own connection to the rail. The fuel pressure sensor is mounted in the rail, and the rail also has a connection to the fuel pressure control valve on the pump.

#### Pressure control valve

The pressure control valve is operated by the ECU, and controls the system pressure. The valve is integral with the high-pressure pump and cannot be separated.

If the fuel pressure is excessive, the valve opens, and fuel flows back to the tank. If the pressure is too low, the valve closes, enabling the high-pressure pump to increase the pressure.

The valve is an electromagnetically-operated ball valve. The ball is forced against its seat, against the fuel pressure, by a powerful spring, and also by the force provided by the electromagnet. The force generated by the electromagnet is directly proportional to the current applied to it by the ECU. The desired pressure can therefore be set by varying the current applied to the electromagnet. Any pressure fluctuations are damped by the spring.

#### Fuel pressure sensor

The fuel pressure sensor is mounted in the accumulator rail, and provides very precise information on the fuel pressure to the ECU.

#### Fuel injector

The injectors are mounted on the engine in a similar manner to conventional diesel fuel injectors. The injectors are electromagnetically-operated via signals from the ECU, and fuel

is injected at the pressure existing in the accumulator rail. The injectors are high-precision instruments and are manufactured to very high tolerances.

Fuel flows into the injector from the accumulator rail, via an inlet valve and an inlet throttle, and an electromagnet causes the injector nozzle to lift from its seat, allowing injection. Excess fuel is returned from the injectors to the tank via a return line. The injector operates on a hydraulic servo principle: the forces resulting inside the injector due to the fuel pressure effectively amplify the effects of the electromagnet, which does not provide sufficient force to open the injector nozzle directly. The injector functions as follows. Five separate forces are essential to the operation of the injector.

a) A nozzle spring forces the nozzle needle against the nozzle seat at the bottom of the injector, preventing fuel from entering the combustion chamber.
b) In the valve at the top of the injector, the valve spring forces the valve ball against the opening to the valve control chamber. The fuel in the chamber is unable to escape through the fuel return.
c) When triggered, the electromagnet exerts a force which overcomes the valve spring force, and moves the valve ball away from its seat. This is the triggering force for the start of injection. When the valve ball moves off its seat, fuel enters the valve control chamber.
d) The pressure of the fuel in the valve control chamber exerts a force on the valve control plunger, which is added to the nozzle spring force.
e) A slight chamfer towards the lower end of the nozzle needle causes the fuel in the control chamber to exert a force on the nozzle needle.

When these forces are in equilibrium, the injector is in its rest (idle) state, but when a voltage is applied to the electromagnet, the forces work to lift the nozzle needle, injecting fuel into the combustion chamber. There are four phases of injector operation as follows:

a) Rest (idle) state – all forces are in equilibrium. The nozzle needle closes off the nozzle opening, and the valve spring forces the valve ball against its seat.
b) Opening – the electromagnet is triggered which opens the nozzle and triggers the injection process. The force from the electromagnet allows the valve ball to leave its seat. The fuel from the valve control chamber flows back to the tank via the fuel return line. When the valve opens, the pressure in the valve control chamber drops, and the force on the valve plunger is reduced. However, due to the effect of the input throttle, the pressure on the nozzle needle remains unchanged. The resulting force in the valve control chamber is sufficient to lift the nozzle from its seat, and the injection process begins.

**2.4 Typical plastic plug and cap set for sealing disconnected fuel pipes and components**

c) *Injection – within a few milliseconds, the triggering current in the electromagnet is reduced to a lower holding current. The nozzle is now fully open, and fuel is injected into the combustion chamber at the pressure present in the accumulator rail.*

d) *Closing – the electromagnet is switched off, at which point the valve spring forces the valve ball firmly against its seat, and in the valve control chamber, the pressure is the same as that at the nozzle needle. The force at the valve plunger increases, and the nozzle needle closes the nozzle opening. The forces are now in equilibrium once more, and the injector is once more in the idle state, awaiting the next injection sequence.*

### ECU and sensors

The ECU and sensors are described earlier in this Section – see *Electronic control system*.

### Air inlet sensor and turbocharger

An airflow sensor is fitted downstream of the air filter to monitor the quantity of air supplied to the turbocharger. On 1.6 litre models, air from the high-pressure side of the turbocharger is either channelled through the intercooler, or into the manifold without being intercooled, depending on the air temperature. The flow and routing of inlet air is controlled by the engine management ECU. On these models, an engine coolant-heated matrix is fitted to the base of the air cleaner housing to warm the incoming air, which decreases harmful exhaust emissions. The turbochargers are of the variable nozzle geometry type.

**3.1a Hand priming pump location (arrowed) on 8-valve engines . . .**

**2.7 Two crow's-foot adaptors will be necessary for tightening the fuel pipe unions**

## 2 High-pressure diesel injection system – special information

### Warnings and precautions

**1** It is essential to observe strict precautions when working on the fuel system components, particularly the high-pressure side of the system. Before carrying out any operations on the fuel system, refer to the precautions given in *Safety first!* at the beginning of this manual, and to the following additional information.

• *Do not carry out any repair work on the high-pressure fuel system unless you are competent to do so, have all the necessary tools and equipment required, and are aware of the safety implications involved.*

• *Before starting any repair work on the fuel system, wait at least 30 seconds after switching off the engine to allow the fuel circuit pressure to reduce.*

• *Never work on the high-pressure fuel system with the engine running.*

• *Keep well clear of any possible source of fuel leakage, particularly when starting the engine after carrying out repair work. A leak in the system could cause an extremely high-pressure jet of fuel to escape, which could result in severe personal injury.*

• *Never place your hands or any part of your body near to a leak in the high-pressure fuel system.*

• *Do not use steam cleaning equipment or compressed air to clean the engine or any of the fuel system components.*

**3.1b . . . 1.4 litre 16-valve engines . . .**

### Procedures and information

**2** Strict cleanliness must be observed at all times when working on any part of the fuel system. This applies to the working area in general, the person doing the work, and the components being worked on.

**3** Before working on the fuel system components, they must be thoroughly cleaned with a suitable degreasing fluid. Specific cleaning products may be obtained from Citroën dealers. Alternatively, a suitable brake cleaning fluid may be used. Cleanliness is particularly important when working on the fuel system connections at the following components:

a) *Fuel filter.*
b) *High-pressure fuel pump.*
c) *Accumulator rail.*
d) *Fuel injectors.*
e) *High-pressure fuel pipes.*

**4** After disconnecting any fuel pipes or components, the open union or orifice must be immediately sealed to prevent the entry of dirt or foreign material. Plastic plugs and caps in various sizes are available in packs from motor factors and accessory outlets, and are particularly suitable for this application **(see illustration)**. Fingers cut from disposable rubber gloves should be used to protect components such as fuel pipes, fuel injectors and wiring connectors, and can be secured in place using elastic bands. Suitable gloves of this type are available at no cost from most petrol station forecourts.

**5** Whenever any of the high-pressure fuel pipes are disconnected or removed, new pipes must be obtained for refitting.

**6** On the completion of any repair on the high-pressure fuel system, Citroën recommend the use of a leak-detecting compound. This is a powder which is applied to the fuel pipe unions and connections and turns white when dry. Any leak in the system will cause the product to darken indicating the source of the leak.

**7** The torque wrench settings given in the Specifications must be strictly observed when tightening component mountings and connections. This is particularly important when tightening the high-pressure fuel pipe unions. To enable a torque wrench to be used on the fuel pipe unions, two Citroën crow's-foot adaptors are required. Suitable alternatives are available from motor factors and accessory outlets **(see illustration)**.

## 3 Fuel system – priming and bleeding

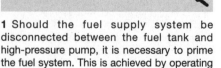

**1** Should the fuel supply system be disconnected between the fuel tank and high-pressure pump, it is necessary to prime the fuel system. This is achieved by operating the hand-priming pump (where fitted) until resistance is felt (1.6 litre models) or fuel appears in the transparent fuel supply pipe in the engine compartment (1.4 litre models).

Remove the plastic cover from the top of the engine to access the priming pump. Operate the hand-priming pump for approximately 2 minutes **(see illustrations)**.

**2** Where a hand-priming pump is not fitted, priming is achieved by connecting a suitable hose (if necessary, a special Citroën hose No 444-T may be available) from the fuel filter outlet pipe to the fuel return pipe and forcing fuel through the filter, into the return system. If the suitable hose is not available, it will suffice to connect a length of hose to the filter outlet, with the other end of the hose in a suitable container.

**3** With the system primed, reconnect the hoses, and then operate the starter until the engine starts.

### 4 Air cleaner assembly and inlet ducts – removal and refitting

## *Air cleaner and inlet ducts removal*

### 8-valve engines

**1** Disconnect the battery (see Chapter 5A).

**2** Release the diesel hand priming pump from its brackets at the right-hand end of the air cleaner housing.

**3** Slacken the retaining clip and disconnect the air inlet hose from the turbocharger **(see illustration)**.

**4** Disconnect the air mass meter wiring connector then undo the screw securing

**3.1c ... and 1.6 litre engines**

the air mass meter to the air inlet duct **(see illustration)**.

**5** Undo the two screws securing the air cleaner housing to the cylinder head cover **(see illustration)**.

**6** Disconnect the breather hose from the cylinder head cover, then lift the air cleaner assembly upwards to disengage the rear mounting lugs from the mounting rubbers.

**7** Reach behind the air cleaner assembly, release the clip and disconnect the air inlet hose from the base of the housing.

**8** Withdraw the air cleaner assembly from the engine, disconnecting any wiring plugs or hose clips as necessary as the unit is with-drawn.

**9** To remove the air inlet ducting, first remove the air cleaner assembly as described previously.

**10** Remove the air deflector by turning the plastic retainer through 90°. Withdraw the air

deflector from the front of the air inlet ducting **(see illustration)**.

**11** Pull out the centre of the plastic expansion rivet securing the air inlet ducting to the front panel, then pull out the entire rivet **(see illustration)**.

**12** Lift the front of the inlet ducting upward to release the mounting lug from the front of the battery box. Manipulate the rear of the inlet ducting out from under the fuel filter and remove the ducting from the car. For improved clearance, undo the fuel filter retaining screw and lift the filter from its mounting bracket slightly.

### 16-valve engines

**13** Disconnect the battery (see Chapter 5A), then remove the plastic cover from the top of the engine. The cover is retained by rubber grommets, and pulls upwards to release **(see illustration)**.

**14** Remove the air deflector at the left-hand front of the car, by turning the plastic retainer through 90°. Withdraw the air deflector from the front of the air inlet ducting **(see illustration 4.10)**.

**15** Pull out the centre of the plastic expansion rivet securing the air inlet ducting to the front panel, then pull out the entire rivet **(see illustration 4.11)**.

**16** Lift the front of the inlet ducting upward to release the mounting lug from the front of the battery box. At the same time, disengage the centre of the duct from the mounting stud located just in front of the fuel filter **(see illustration)**.

**17** Release the brake servo vacuum hose from

**4.3 Slacken the clip (arrowed) and disconnect the air inlet hose from the turbocharger (8-valve engines)**

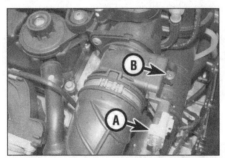

**4.4 Disconnect the air mass meter wiring connector (A) then undo the retaining screw (B) (8-valve engines)**

**4.5 Undo the two air cleaner housing screws (arrowed) (8-valve engines)**

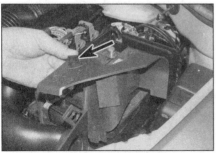

**4.10 Remove the air deflector by turning the plastic retainer (arrowed) through 90° (8-valve engines)**

**4.11 Pull out the centre of the plastic expansion rivet (arrowed) then pull out the entire rivet (8-valve engines)**

**4.13 Remove the plastic cover from the top of the engine (16-valve engines)**

**4.16 Disengage the centre of the air inlet duct from the mounting stud (arrowed) (16-valve engines)**

**4.17a Release the brake servo vacuum hose from the side of the air duct at the rear . . .**

**4.17b . . . then lift the duct off the elbow on the air cleaner housing (16-valve engines)**

**4.18 Slacken the clips and disconnect the air inlet duct from the turbocharger and air mass meter (16-valve engines)**

the side of the duct at the rear, then lift the duct off the elbow on the air cleaner housing and remove it from the car **(see illustrations)**.

**18** Slacken the retaining clips and disconnect the air inlet duct from the turbocharger and air mass meter **(see illustration)**.

**4.19 Disconnect the air mass meter wiring connector (16-valve engines)**

**19** Disconnect the air mass meter wiring connector **(see illustration)**.

**20** Using a small screwdriver, release the tabs securing the diesel hand priming pump support brackets to the front of the air cleaner lid **(see illustration)**. Move the priming pump

**4.20 Release the retaining tabs and move the hand priming pump clear of the air cleaner lid (16-valve engines)**

forwards slightly clear of the air cleaner assembly.

**21** Undo the three screws at the front securing the air cleaner lid to the base. Lift the air cleaner lid, complete with air mass meter upwards, disengage the locating lugs at the rear, and remove the lid **(see illustration)**. Lift out the filter element, noting which way up it was fitted.

**22** Remove the air cleaner support frame from within the air cleaner base **(see illustration)**.

**23** Lift the air cleaner base upwards to disengage the lower mounting lugs, then release the clips on each side. Separate the two parts of the air cleaner base and lift out the front part, followed by the rear part **(see illustrations)**.

### *Inlet air resonator removal*

#### 8-valve engines

**24** Slacken the retaining clip and disconnect the turbocharger air outlet hose from the inlet manifold **(see illustration)**.

**4.21 Undo the three screws and lift off the air cleaner lid (16-valve engines)**

**4.22 Remove the air cleaner support frame from the air cleaner base (16-valve engines)**

**4.23a Lift the air cleaner base upwards, then release the clips on each side (16-valve engines)**

**4.23b Separate the two part base and lift out the front part, followed by the rear part (16-valve engines)**

**4.24 Slacken the clip (arrowed) and disconnect the turbocharger outlet hose from the inlet manifold (8-valve engines)**

**4.26 Undo the retaining bolts (arrowed) . . .**

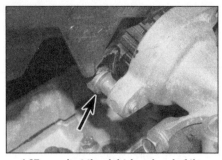

**4.27 . . . pivot the right-hand end of the resonator up and disengage it from the turbo outlet stud (arrowed) (8-valve engines)**

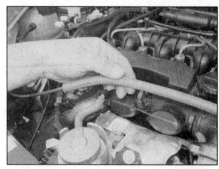

**4.29 Open the clips and free the coolant hose from the resonator (16-valve engines)**

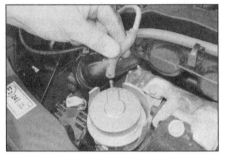

**4.30 Disconnect the vacuum hose from the turbocharger wastegate actuator (16-valve engines)**

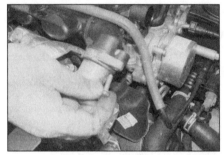

**4.31 Undo the bolt (arrowed) securing the resonator to the turbocharger outlet flange (16-valve engines)**

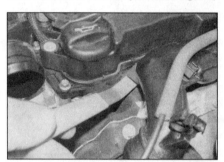

**4.32 Prise up the right-hand end of the resonator to free the mounting grommet from its stud (16-valve engines)**

**25** Release the small-bore coolant hose from the clips at the front of the resonator.

**26** Undo the bolt securing the resonator to the cylinder head cover and the bolt securing the resonator to the turbocharger outlet flange **(see illustration)**.

**27** Pivot the right-hand end of the resonator upwards, disengage it from the stud on the turbocharger flange and remove the resonator from the engine **(see illustration)**. Recover the O-ring seal.

### 16-valve engines

**28** Slacken the clip and disconnect the intercooler air inlet hose from the right-hand end of the resonator.

**29** Open the retaining clips and free the small-bore coolant hose from the resonator **(see illustration)**.

**30** Disconnect the vacuum hose from the turbocharger wastegate actuator **(see illustration)**.

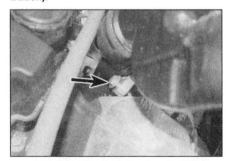

**4.33 Pivot the right-hand end of the resonator up and disengage it from the turbo outlet stud (arrowed) (16-valve engines)**

**31** Undo the bolt securing the resonator to the turbocharger outlet flange **(see illustration)**.

**32** Using a screwdriver or similar tool, lift up the right-hand end of the resonator to free the mounting grommet from its mounting stud **(see illustration)**.

**33** Pivot the right-hand end of the resonator upwards, disengage it from the stud on the turbocharger flange and remove the resonator from the engine **(see illustration)**. Recover the O-ring seal.

### Refitting

**34** Refitting is a reverse of the removal procedure. Examine the condition of the seals and retaining clips and renew if necessary.

### 5  Accelerator pedal – removal and refitting

Refer to Chapter 4A.

### 6  Fuel gauge sender unit – removal and refitting

The removal and refitting procedures for the fuel gauge sender unit are the same as described in Chapter 4A, Section 8, for the fuel pump, except that on diesel engines the assembly comprises the sender unit only.

### 7  Fuel tank and cooler – removal and refitting

## Fuel tank

Refer to Chapter 4A.

## Fuel cooler

### Removal

**1** The fuel cooler is located under the right-hand side of the vehicle. Jack up the rear of the vehicle, and support it on axle stands (see *Jacking and vehicle support*).

**2** Working underneath the vehicle, undo the two retaining nuts, and release the cooler from the locating holes **(see illustration)**.

**3** Depress the release buttons and disconnect the fuel feed and return hoses from the cooler. Be prepared for fuel spillage, and plug the

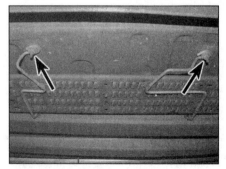

**7.2 Undo the two nuts (arrowed) securing the fuel cooler**

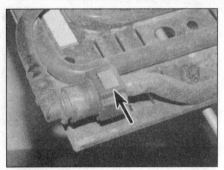

**7.3  Depress the release button (arrowed) and disconnect the hose**

hose and cooler openings to prevent dirt ingress **(see illustration)**.

### Refitting

**4**  Refitting is a reversal of removal,

### 8  High-pressure fuel pump – removal and refitting

> **Warning: Refer to the information contained in Section 2 before proceeding.**

**Note:** *A new fuel pump-to-accumulator rail high-pressure fuel pipe will be required for refitting.*

### Removal

#### 8-valve engines

**1**  Disconnect the battery (see Chapter 5A).

**8.3  Depress the release buttons (arrowed) and disconnect the fuel supply and return hoses from the pump (8-valve engines)**

**8.11a  Undo the two screws (arrowed) securing the EGR pipe to the inlet manifold ...**

**2**  Carry out the following operations using the information given in Chapter 2B:
  a) *Remove the cylinder head cover.*
  b) *Remove the timing belt. After removal of the timing belt, temporarily refit the right-hand engine mounting but do not fully tighten the bolts.*
  c) *Remove the fuel pump sprocket.*

**3**  Depress the quick-release fittings and disconnect the fuel supply and return hoses from the pump **(see illustration)**. Plug the end of the hoses and the pump outlets to prevent dirt ingress.

**4**  Thoroughly clean the high pressure fuel pipe unions on the fuel pump and accumulator rail. Using an open-ended spanner, unscrew the union nuts securing the high pressure fuel pipe to the fuel pump and accumulator rail. Counterhold the union on the pump with a second spanner, while unscrewing the union nut **(see illustration)**. Withdraw the high pressure fuel pipe and plug or cover the open unions to prevent dirt entry. Note that a new high pressure fuel pipe will be required for refitting.

**5**  Disconnect the wiring plugs from the pump, noting their fitted positions.

**6**  Undo the nuts/bolts and remove the pump support bracket from the rear of the pump.

**7**  Undo the three front mounting bolts, and remove the pump from its mounting bracket **(see illustration)**.

*Caution: The high-pressure fuel pump is manufactured to extremely close tolerances and must not be dismantled in any way. Do not unscrew the fuel pipe male union on the*

**8.4  Counterhold the union with a second spanner whilst slackening the accumulator-to-pump pipe union (8-valve engines)**

**8.11b  ... and the bolt (arrowed) securing the pipe to the rear of the cylinder head (16-valve engines)**

*rear of the pump, or attempt to remove the sensor, piston de-activator switch, or the seal on the pump shaft. No parts for the pump are available separately and if the unit is in any way suspect, it must be renewed.*

#### 16-valve engines

**8**  Disconnect the battery (see Chapter 5A).

**9**  Remove the air cleaner assembly and inlet ducts as described in Section 4.

**10**  Carry out the following operations using the information given in Chapter 2B or 2C:
  a) *Remove the timing belt. After removal of the timing belt, temporarily refit the right-hand engine mounting but do not fully tighten the bolts.*
  b) *Remove the fuel pump sprocket.*

**11**  Undo the two screws securing the EGR pipe to the inlet manifold, and the bolt securing the pipe to the rear of the cylinder head **(see illustrations)**.

**12**  Remove the clip securing the EGR pipe to the EGR valve. If the original crimped clip is still in place, cut it off; new clips are supplied by Citroën parts stockists with a screw clamp fixing. If a screw type is fitted, undo the screw and manipulate the clip off the pipe. Remove the EGR pipe from the rear of the engine **(see illustration)**. Recover the O-ring seal from the end of the pipe.

**13**  Undo the retaining nut and bolt and remove the air cleaner support bracket from the rear of the cylinder head **(see illustration)**.

**14**  Depress the quick-release fittings and disconnect the fuel supply and return hoses from the pump. Plug the end of the hoses and the pump outlets to prevent dirt ingress.

**8.7  High-pressure fuel pump front mounting bolts (arrowed)**

**8.12  Remove the EGR pipe-to-valve clip then withdraw the pipe from the engine (16-valve engines)**

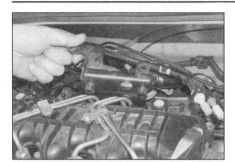

**8.13 Undo the retaining nut and bolt and remove the air cleaner support bracket (16-valve engines)**

**15** Thoroughly clean the high pressure fuel pipe unions on the fuel pump and accumulator rail. Using an open-ended spanner, unscrew the union nuts securing the high pressure fuel pipe to the fuel pump and accumulator rail. Counterhold the pump union with a second spanner, while unscrewing the union nut. Undo the pipe clamp retaining bolt, then withdraw the high pressure fuel pipe **(see illustration)**. Plug or cover the open unions to prevent dirt entry. Note that a new high pressure fuel pipe will be required for refitting.

**16** Disconnect the wiring connector from the pump solenoid valve.

**17** Undo the rear mounting bolt securing the pump to the support bracket **(see illustration)**.

**18** Undo the three front mounting bolts, and remove the pump from its mounting bracket **(see illustration 8.7)**.

*Caution: The high-pressure fuel pump is manufactured to extremely close tolerances and must not be dismantled in any way. Do not unscrew the fuel pipe male union on the rear of the pump, or attempt to remove the sensor, piston de-activator switch, or the seal on the pump shaft. No parts for the pump are available separately and if the unit is in any way suspect, it must be renewed.*

### Refitting

**19** Locate the pump in the mounting bracket, and refit the three mounting bolts. Tighten them to the specified torque.

**20** Refit the pump rear support bracket, tight-ening the bolts/nut to the specified torque.

**21** Remove the blanking plugs from the fuel pipe unions on the pump and accumulator rail. Locate a new high pressure fuel pipe over the unions and screw on the union nuts finger tight at this stage.

**22** Using a torque wrench and crow's-foot adaptor, tighten the fuel pipe union nuts to the specified torque. Counterhold the union on the pump with an open-ended spanner, while tightening the union nuts.

**23** Reconnect the pump wiring plugs, and the fuel hose unions.

**24** On 8-valve engines, refit the fuel pump sprocket, timing belt and cylinder head cover as described in Chapter 2B.

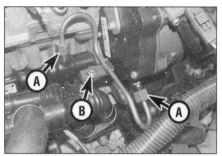

**8.15 Pump-to-accumulator rail high pressure fuel pipe unions (A) and pipe clamp bolt (B) (16-valve engines)**

**25** On 16-valve engines, refit the EGR pipe and air cleaner support bracket, then refit the fuel pump sprocket and timing belt as described in Chapter 2B or 2C. Refit the cleaner assembly and inlet ducts as described in Section 4.

**26** With everything reassembled and reconnected, and observing the precautions listed in Section 2, start the engine and allow it to idle. Check for leaks at the high-pressure fuel pipe unions with the engine idling. If satisfactory, increase the engine speed to 4000 rpm and check again for leaks.

**27** Take the car for a short road test and check for leaks once again on return. If any leaks are detected, obtain and fit another new high-pressure fuel pipe. **Do not** attempt to cure even the slightest leak by further tightening of the pipe unions. During the road test, initialise the engine management ECU as follows. Engage third gear and stabilise the engine at 1000 rpm, then accelerate fully up to 3500 rpm.

## 9 Accumulator rail – removal and refitting

> ⚠ *Warning: Refer to the information contained in Section 2 before proceeding.*

**Note:** *A complete new set of high-pressure fuel pipes will be required for refitting.*

### Removal

#### 8-valve engines

**1** Disconnect the battery (see Chapter 5A).

**9.4 Use a second spanner to counterhold the fuel injector unions whilst slackening the pipe unions (8-valve engines)**

**8.17 Undo the pump rear support bracket bolt (arrowed) (16-valve engines)**

**2** Remove the cylinder head cover as described in Chapter 2B.

**3** Thoroughly clean the area around the high pressure fuel pipes to and from the accumulator rail. Using an open-ended spanner, unscrew the union nuts securing the high pressure fuel pipe to the fuel pump and accumulator rail. Counterhold the union on the pump with a second spanner, while unscrewing the union nut **(see illustration 8.4)**. Withdraw the high pressure fuel pipe and plug or cover the open unions to prevent dirt entry. Note that a new high pressure fuel pipe will be required for refitting.

**4** Repeat the procedure on the accumulator rail-to-injector fuel pipes. Use a second spanner to counterhold the unions screwed into the injectors **(see illustration)**. These unions must not be allowed to move. Note their fitted locations and remove the pipes.

**5** Plug the openings in the accumulator rail and fuel injectors to prevent dirt ingress.

**6** Disconnect the pressure sensor wiring plug and fuel return pipe from the accumulator rail **(see illustration)**.

**7** Move the coolant hoses aside for access to the accumulator rail mounting bolts. Unscrew the two mounting bolts and manoeuvre the accumulator rail from its location **(see illustration)**. **Note:** *Citroën insist that the fuel pressure sensor on the accumulator rail must not be removed.*

#### 16-valve engines

**8** Disconnect the battery (see Chapter 5A).

**9** Remove the air cleaner assembly and inlet ducts as described in Section 4.

**9.6 Disconnect the accumulator rail pressure sensor wiring plug (8-valve engines)**

**9.7 Remove the accumulator rail mounting bolts (arrowed) (8-valve engines)**

10 Undo the two screws securing the EGR pipe to the inlet manifold, and the bolt securing the pipe to the rear of the cylinder head **(see illustrations 8.11a and 8.11b)**.

11 Remove the clip securing the EGR pipe to the EGR valve. If the original crimped clip is still in place, cut it off; new clips are supplied by Citroën parts stockists with a screw clamp fixing. If a screw type is fitted, undo the screw and manipulate the clip off the pipe. Remove the EGR pipe from the rear of the engine **(see illustration 8.12)**. Recover the O-ring seal from the end of the pipe.

12 Undo the retaining nut and bolt and remove the air cleaner support bracket from the rear of the cylinder head **(see illustration 8.13)**.

13 Undo the two bolts securing the high pressure fuel pipe clamps to the top of the inlet manifold **(see illustration)**.

**9.13 Undo the bolts (arrowed) securing the high pressure fuel pipe clamps to the inlet manifold (16-valve engines)**

**9.17 Disconnect the fuel pressure sensor wiring plug from the accumulator rail (16-valve engines)**

14 Thoroughly clean the high pressure fuel pipe unions on the fuel pump and accumulator rail. Using an open-ended spanner, unscrew the union nuts securing the high pressure fuel pipe to the fuel pump and accumulator rail. Counterhold the union on the pump with a second spanner, while unscrewing the union nut. Undo the pipe clamp retaining bolt, then withdraw the high pressure fuel pipe **(see illustration 8.15)**. Plug or cover the open unions to prevent dirt entry. Note that a new high pressure fuel pipe will be required for refitting.

15 Repeat the procedure on the accumulator rail-to-injector fuel pipes. Use a crow's-foot adaptor to unscrew the injector union nuts as clearance is limited **(see illustration)**. Note their fitted locations and remove the pipes.

16 Plug the openings in the accumulator rail and fuel injectors to prevent dirt ingress.

17 Disconnect the fuel pressure sensor wiring plug from the end of the accumulator rail **(see illustration)**.

18 Move the coolant hoses aside for access to the accumulator rail mountings. Unscrew the mounting nut and bolt and manoeuvre the accumulator rail from its location **(see illustration)**. **Note:** *Citroën insist that the fuel pressure sensor on the accumulator rail must not be removed.*

### Refitting

19 Locate the accumulator rail in position, refit and finger-tighten the mounting bolts/nuts.

**9.15 Use a crow's-foot adaptor to unscrew the injector fuel pipe union nuts (16-valve engines)**

**9.18 Unscrew the mounting nut and bolt and manoeuvre the accumulator rail from its location (16-valve engines)**

20 Reconnect the accumulator rail pressure sensor wiring plug.

21 Fit the new pump-to-rail high pressure pipe, and only finger-tighten the unions at first, then tighten the unions to the specified torque setting. Use a second spanner to counterhold the union screwed into the pump body.

22 Fit the new set of accumulator rail-to-injector high pressure pipes, and finger tighten the unions.

23 Tighten the accumulator rail mounting bolts/nuts to the specified torque.

24 Tighten the accumulator rail-to-injector pipe unions to the specified torque setting, using a second spanner to counterhold the injector unions on 8-valve engines.

25 The remainder of refitting is a reversal of removal, noting the following points:

a) On 8-valve engines, refit the cylinder head cover as described in Chapter 2B.

b) On 16-valve engines, refit the EGR pipe and air cleaner support bracket, then refit the air cleaner assembly and inlet ducts as described in Section 4.

c) Ensure all wiring connectors and harnesses are correctly refitting and secured.

d) Reconnect the battery as described in Chapter 5A.

e) Observing the precautions listed in Section 2, start the engine and allow it to idle. Check for leaks at the high-pressure fuel pipe unions with the engine idling. If satisfactory, increase the engine speed to 4000 rpm and check again for leaks. Take the car for a short road test and check for leaks once again on return. If any leaks are detected, obtain and fit additional new high-pressure fuel pipes as required. **Do not** attempt to cure even the slightest leak by further tightening of the pipe unions. During the road test, initialise the engine management ECU as follows. Engage third gear and stabilise the engine at 1000 rpm, then accelerate fully up to 3500 rpm.

## 10 Fuel injectors – removal and refitting

⚠️ *Warning: Refer to the information contained in Section 2 before proceeding.*

**Note:** *The following procedure describes the removal and refitting of the injectors as a complete set, however each injector may be removed individually if required. New copper washers, upper seals, injector clamp retaining nuts and a high-pressure fuel pipe will be required for each disturbed injector when refitting.*

### Removal

#### 8-valve engines

1 Remove the cylinder head cover as described in Chapter 2B.

2 Thoroughly clean the area around the high

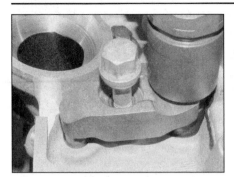

10.4a Undo the injector clamp bolt . . .

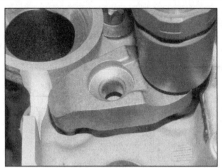

10.4b . . . and remove the clamp (8-valve engines)

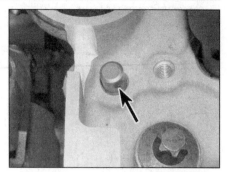

10.4c If it's loose, remove the locating dowel (arrowed) (8-valve engines)

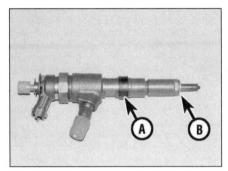

10.6 Fuel injector upper seal (A) and copper washer (B) (8-valve engines)

10.9a Unscrew the two retaining nuts . . .

10.9b . . . and remove the injector clamp (16-valve engines)

pressure fuel pipes between the injectors and the accumulator rail. Using an open-ended spanner, unscrew the union nuts securing the high pressure fuel pipes to the injectors and accumulator rail. Counterhold the union on the injectors with a second spanner, while unscrewing the union nuts **(see illustration 9.4)**. Note their fitted locations and remove the fuel pipes. Plug or cover the open unions to prevent dirt entry.

**3** Extract the retaining circlip and disconnect the leak-off pipe from each fuel injector.

**4** Unscrew the injector retaining bolt, and remove the clamp. If loose, recover the clamp locating dowel from the cylinder head **(see illustrations)**.

**5** Carefully pull or lever the injector from its location. Do not lever against or pull on the solenoid housing at the top of the injector.

**6** Remove the copper washer and the upper seal from each injector, or from the cylinder head if they remained in place during injector removal **(see illustration)**. New copper washers and upper seals will be required for refitting. Cover the injector hole in the cylinder head to prevent dirt ingress.

**7** Examine each injector visually for any signs of obvious damage or deterioration. If any defects are apparent, renew the injector(s). If the injectors are in a satisfactory condition, plug the fuel pipe union (if not already done) and suitably cover the electrical element and the injector nozzle.

*Caution: The injectors are manufactured to extremely close tolerances and must not be dismantled in any way. Do not unscrew the fuel pipe union on the side of the injector,*

*or separate any parts of the injector body. Do not attempt to clean carbon deposits from the injector nozzle or carry out any form of ultrasonic or pressure testing.*

### 16-valve engines

**8** Remove the inlet manifold as described in Section 12.

**9** Unscrew the two retaining nuts, and remove the injector clamp **(see illustrations)**. Note that new clamp nuts will be required for refitting.

**10** Using a spanner engaged with the flats on the injector body, twist the injector from side to side, while at the same time pulling it upwards. Once free, withdraw the injector from its location **(see illustrations)**. Cover the injector hole in the cylinder head to prevent dirt ingress.

**11** Remove the copper washer and the upper seal from each injector, or from the cylinder head if they remained in place during injector

removal. New copper washers and upper seals will be required for refitting.

*Caution: The injectors are manufactured to extremely close tolerances and must not be dismantled in any way. Do not unscrew the fuel pipe union on the side of the injector, or separate any parts of the injector body. Do not attempt to clean carbon deposits from the injector nozzle or carry out any form of ultrasonic or pressure testing.*

### Refitting

#### 8-valve engines

**12** Locate a new upper seal on the body of each injector, and place a new copper washer on the injector nozzle **(see illustrations)**.

**13** Refit the injector clamp locating dowels to the cylinder head.

**14** Place the injector clamp in the slot on each injector body and refit the injectors to the cylinder head. Guide the clamp over the

10.10a Twist the injector from side to side to free it . . .

10.10b . . . then withdraw the injector from the cylinder head (16-valve engines)

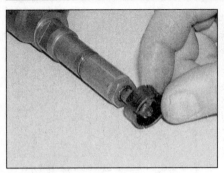

**10.12a Locate a new upper seal on the body of each injector . . .**

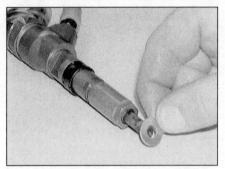

**10.12b . . . and place a new copper washer on the injector nozzle (8-valve engines)**

mounting stud and onto the locating dowel as each injector is inserted. Ensure the upper injector seals are correctly located in the cylinder head.

**15** Fit the washer and a new injector clamp retaining nut to each mounting stud. Tighten the nuts finger tight only at this stage.

**16** Working on one fuel injector at a time, remove the blanking plugs from the fuel pipe unions on the accumulator rail and the relevant injector. Locate a new high-pressure fuel pipe over the unions and screw on the union nuts. Take care not to cross-thread the nuts or strain the fuel pipes as they are fitted. Once the union nut threads have started, finger-tighten the nuts only at this stage.

**17** When all the fuel pipes are in place, tighten the injector clamp retaining nuts to the specified torque.

**18** Using an open-ended spanner, hold each fuel pipe union in turn and tighten the

union nut to the specified torque using a torque wrench and crow's-foot adaptor **(see illustration)**. Tighten all the disturbed union nuts in the same way.

**19** The remainder of refitting is a reversal of removal, noting the following points:
a) Refit the cylinder head cover as described in Chapter 2B.
b) Ensure all wiring connectors and harnesses are correctly refitting and secured.
c) Reconnect the battery as described in Chapter 5A.
d) Observing the precautions listed in Section 2, start the engine and allow it to idle. Check for leaks at the high-pressure fuel pipe unions with the engine idling. If satisfactory, increase the engine speed to 4000 rpm and check again for leaks. Take the car for a short road test and check for leaks once again on return. If any leaks

are detected, obtain and fit additional new high-pressure fuel pipes as required. **Do not** attempt to cure even the slightest leak by further tightening of the pipe unions. During the road test, initialise the engine management ECU as follows. Engage third gear and stabilise the engine at 1000 rpm, then accelerate fully up to 3500 rpm.

### 16-valve engines

**20** Locate a new upper seal on the body of each injector, and place a new copper washer on the injector nozzle **(see illustrations)**.
**21** Refit the injectors to the cylinder head, then refit the clamps and new retaining nuts. Tighten the nuts finger tight only at this stage.
**22** Reconnect the leak-off pipe to each injector **(see illustration)**. Temporarily lay the inlet manifold and cylinder head cover in place and ensure that there is sufficient clearance between these components and the leak-off pipes. If necessary turn the injector body to achieve the necessary clearance.
**23** With the injectors correctly positioned, tighten the retaining clamp nuts to the specified torque.
**24** The remainder of refitting is a reversal of removal, noting the following points:
a) Refit the inlet manifold as described in Section 12.
b) Ensure all wiring connectors and harnesses are correctly refitting and secured.
c) Reconnect the battery as described in Chapter 5A.
d) Observing the precautions listed in Section 2, start the engine and allow it to idle. Check for leaks at the high-pressure fuel pipe unions with the engine idling. If satisfactory, increase the engine speed to 4000 rpm and check again for leaks. Take the car for a short road test and check for leaks once again on return. If any leaks are detected, obtain and fit additional new high-pressure fuel pipes as required. **Do not** attempt to cure even the slightest leak by further tightening of the pipe unions. During the road test, initialise the engine management ECU as follows. Engage third gear and stabilise the engine at 1000 rpm, then accelerate fully up to 3500 rpm.

**10.18 Using a torque wrench and crow's-foot adaptor, tighten the fuel pipe union nuts (8-valve engines)**

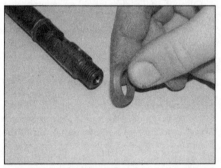

**10.20a Locate a new upper seal on the body of each injector . . .**

**11 Electronic control system components –** testing, removal and refitting

### Testing

**1** If a fault is suspected in the electronic control side of the system, first ensure that all the wiring connectors are securely connected and free of corrosion. Ensure that the suspected problem is not of a mechanical nature, or due to poor maintenance; ie, check that the air cleaner filter element is clean, the engine breather hoses are clear and undamaged, and that the cylinder compression pressures are correct, referring to Chapters 1B and 2B for further information.

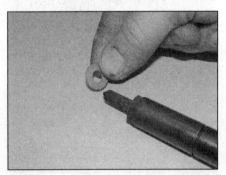

**10.20b . . . and place a new copper washer on the injector nozzle (16-valve engines)**

**10.22 Reconnect the leak-off pipe to each injector (16-valve engines)**

**11.3 The diagnostic socket (arrowed) is located above the passenger's compartment fusebox**

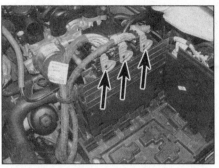

**11.6 Release the lever catches (arrowed) and disconnect the ECU wiring connectors**

**11.7 Disengage the lower locating lugs and lift the ECU and mounting plate from the battery box**

**2** If these checks fail to reveal the cause of the problem, the vehicle should be taken to a Citroën dealer or suitably-equipped engine management diagnostic specialist for testing.

**3** A diagnostic socket is located above the passenger's compartment fusebox, to which a fault code reader or other suitable test equipment can be connected **(see illustration)**. By using the code reader or test equipment, the engine management ECU (and the various other vehicle system ECUs) can be interrogated, and any stored fault codes can be retrieved. This will allow the fault to be quickly and simply traced, alleviating the need to test all the system components individually, which is a time-consuming operation that carries a risk of damaging the ECU.

### Electronic control unit (ECU)

**Note:** *If a new ECU is to be fitted, this work must be entrusted to a Citroën dealer or suitably-equipped specialist. It is necessary to initialise the new ECU after installation, which requires the use of dedicated Citroën diagnostic equipment.*

**Note:** *Before carrying out the following procedure, disconnect the battery (see Chapter 5A). Reconnect the battery on completion of refitting.*

**4** The ECU is located in the battery box on the left-hand side of the engine compartment.

**5** For improved access, remove the battery as described in Chapter 5A.

**6** Release the lever catches and disconnect the ECU wiring connectors **(see illustration)**. Open the clip and release the wiring harness from the side of the ECU.

**7** Disengage the mounting plate lower locating lugs and lift the ECU and mounting plate from the battery box **(see illustration)**.

**8** Undo the mounting bolts and separate the ECU from the mounting plate.

**9** Refitting is a reverse of the removal procedure ensuring the wiring connectors are securely reconnected.

### Crankshaft speed/ position sensor

**10** The crankshaft position sensor is located adjacent to the crankshaft pulley on the

**11.12 Disconnect the crankshaft position sensor wiring plug**

right-hand end of the engine. Slacken the right-hand front roadwheel bolts, then jack the front of the vehicle up and support it on axle stands (see *Jacking and vehicle support*). Remove the right-hand front roadwheel.

**11** Push in the centre pins a little, then prise out the rivets and remove the wheel arch liner.

**12** Disconnect the sensor wiring plug **(see illustration)**.

**13** Undo the bolt and remove the sensor.

**14** Refitting is a reversal of removal, tightening the sensor retaining bolt securely.

### Camshaft position sensor

**15** The camshaft position sensor is mounted on the camshaft bearing housing, directly behind the camshaft sprocket.

**16** Remove the upper timing belt cover, as described in Chapter 2B or 2C.

**17** Unplug the sensor wiring connector.

**18** Undo the retaining bolt and withdraw the sensor from its location **(see illustration)**.

**19** Upon refitting a used sensor, position the sensor so that the air gap between the sensor end and the webs of the signal wheel is 1.2 mm, measured with feeler gauges. If fitting a new sensor, the small tip of the sensor must be just touching one of the three webs of the signal wheel.

**20** Clearance for the feeler blades is limited with the timing belt and camshaft sprocket in place, but it is just possible if the feeler blades are bent through 90° so they can be inserted through the holes in the sprocket, to rest against the inner face of the signal wheel **(see illustration)**.

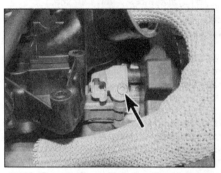

**11.18 Camshaft position sensor retaining bolt (arrowed)**

**21** With the feeler blades placed against the signal wheel, move the sensor toward the sprocket until it just contacts the feeler blades. Hold the sensor in this position and tighten the retaining bolt.

**22** With the gap correctly adjusted, reconnect the sensor wiring connector, then refit the timing belt upper cover as described in Chapter 2B or 2C.

### Accelerator pedal position sensor

**23** The pedal sensor is integral with the accelerator pedal assembly. Refer to the relevant Section of Chapter 4A for the pedal removal procedure.

### Coolant temperature sensor

**24** Refer to Chapter 3, Section 7.

**11.20 Insert feeler gauges bent 90° through the sprocket to measure the camshaft position sensor air gap**

**11.25 The air mass meter (arrowed) is located on the front of the air cleaner assembly (8-valve engines)**

### Air mass meter

#### 8-valve engines

**25** The air mass meter is located on the front of the air cleaner assembly **(see illustration)**.
**26** Remove the air cleaner assembly as described in Section 4.
**27** Slacken the clip and disconnect the turbocharger air inlet hose from the air mass meter.
**28** Undo the retaining screws and withdraw the meter from the air cleaner housing.
**29** Refitting is reverse of the removal procedure.

#### 1.4 and 1.6 litre 16-valve engines

**30** The air mass meter is located on the front of the air cleaner lid.
**31** Remove the plastic cover from the top of the engine. The cover is retained by rubber grommets, and pulls upwards to release.

**11.33 Disconnect the air inlet duct from the turbocharger and air mass meter (1.4 litre 16-valve engines)**

**11.35 Undo the three screws and remove the air cleaner lid (1.4 litre 16-valve engines)**

**11.32 Release the tabs securing the hand priming pump support brackets to the air cleaner lid (1.4 litre 16-valve engines)**

**32** Using a small screwdriver, release the tabs securing the diesel hand priming pump support brackets to the front of the air cleaner lid **(see illustration)**. Move the priming pump forwards slightly clear of the air cleaner assembly.
**33** Slacken the retaining clips and disconnect the air inlet duct from the turbocharger and air mass meter **(see illustration)**.
**34** Disconnect the air mass meter wiring connector **(see illustration)**.
**35** Undo the three screws at the front securing the air cleaner lid to the base. Lift the air cleaner lid upwards, disengage the locating lugs at the rear, and remove the lid **(see illustration)**.
**36** Undo the retaining screws and withdraw the meter from the air cleaner lid.
**37** Refitting is reverse of the removal procedure.

**11.34 Disconnect the air mass meter wiring connector (1.4 litre 16-valve engines)**

**11.39 Throttle potentiometer and air temperature sensor wiring plugs on the throttle housing (DV6 engines)**

### Throttle housing

#### 1.4 litre 16-valve engines with Seimens fuel system, and all 1.6 litre engines

**38** The throttle housing is located in the air ducting from the intercooler to the inlet manifold. **Note:** *1.6 litre DV6TED4 (9HZ) models fitted with a particulate filter up to RPO 11647 have a double-butterfly throttle housing which is attached to the intercooler inlet and outlet air pipes, however models from RPO 11648 reverted to a single-butterfly throttle housing in the intercooler-to-inlet manifold air hose.* First, remove the plastic cover from its mountings on top of the engine.
**39** Disconnect the wiring plug connector(s) from the throttle housing **(see illustration)**.
**40** Slacken the retaining clips and disconnect the air inlet ducting from either side of the throttle housing (two pipes each side on DV6TED4 9HZ engines). Plug or cover the turbocharger inlet duct(s), using clean rag to prevent any dirt or foreign material from entering. Where applicable, unbolt the throttle housing from the mounting bracket.
**41** Refitting is a reversal of removal.

### Fuel pressure sensor

**42** The fuel pressure sensor is integral with the accumulator rail, and is not available separately. Citroën insist that the sensor is not removed from the rail.

### Manifold pressure sensor

**43** The sensor is only fitted to early 1.4 litre 16-valve engines and is located on the right-hand end of the inlet manifold **(see illustration)**.
**44** Remove the plastic cover from the top of the engine. The cover is retained by rubber grommets, and pulls upwards to release.
**45** Disconnect the sensor wiring connector, unscrew the retaining bolt and remove the sensor from the manifold.
**46** Refitting is reverse of the removal procedure.

### Knock sensor

**47** The sensor is only fitted to early 1.4 litre 16-valve engines and is located on the rear of the cylinder block, directly below the accumulator rail. Access to the sensor is limited and is best reached from below.

**11.43 Manifold pressure sensor location (arrowed) (1.4 litre 16-valve engines)**

**48** Firmly apply the handbrake, then jack up the front of the car and support it securely on axle stands (see *Jacking and vehicle support*).
**49** Remove the engine undertray.
**50** Trace the wiring back from the sensor and disconnect the wiring connector.
**51** Undo the retaining bolt and remove the sensor from the cylinder block.
**52** Refitting is reverse of the removal procedure, but tighten the sensor retaining bolt to the specified torque.

### Fuel pressure control valve

**53** The fuel pressure control valve is integral with the high-pressure fuel pump and cannot be separated.

### Fuel temperature sensor

 **Warning: Refer to the information contained in Section 2 before proceeding.**
**54** The sensor is clipped in to the plastic fuel manifold at the right-hand rear end of the cylinder head. To remove the sensor, disconnect the wiring plug, and then unclip the sensor from the manifold. Be prepared for fuel spillage **(see illustration)**.
**55** Refitting is a reversal of removal.
**56** Observing the precautions listed in Section 2, start the engine and allow it to idle. Check for leaks at the fuel temperature sensor with the engine idling. If satisfactory, increase the engine speed to 4000 rpm and check again for leaks. Take the car for a short road test and check for leaks once again on return. If any leaks are detected, obtain and fit a new sensor.

### Preheating system control unit

**57** Refer to Chapter 5C.

### EGR solenoid valve

**58** Refer to Chapter 4C.

### Vehicle speed sensor

**59** On models without ABS, the vehicle speed sensor is an integral part of the speedometer drive. Refer to Chapter 7A for removal and refitting details. On other models, the ECU receives vehicle speed data from the wheel speed sensors, via the ABS ECU.

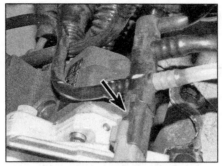

**11.54 Fuel temperature sensor (arrowed) – 1.4 litre engine**

### 12 Inlet manifold – removal and refitting

#### 1.4 litre 8-valve engines

**1** The inlet manifold is integral with the cylinder head cover. Refer to Chapter 2B.

#### 1.4 litre 16-valve engines

**Removal**

**2** Remove the air cleaner and inlet ducts, and the inlet air resonator as described in Section 4.
**3** Thoroughly clean the fuel feed and return pipe connections located above the timing belt upper cover. Depress the tabs on the side of the quick-release fittings and disconnect the two pipes **(see illustration)**. Plug the pipes and unions to prevent dirt ingress and fuel

**12.3 Depress the tabs on the quick-release fittings and disconnect the fuel pipes (1.4 litre 16-valve engines)**

loss. Release the fuel pipes from the retaining clips on the manifold.
**4** Disconnect the wiring connector at the pressure sensor on the inlet manifold **(see illustration)**.
**5** Slacken the retaining clip and disconnect the intercooler outlet duct from the manifold **(see illustration)**.
**6** Disconnect the main engine wiring harness connector located at the rear of the inlet manifold. The connector is retained by a horseshoe type locking collar which is released by pulling sideways **(see illustration)**. Undo the screws and release the wiring harness connector socket support bracket from the rear of the manifold.
**7** Trace the wiring harness from the socket to the EGR solenoid valve at the rear of the engine. Disconnect the solenoid valve wiring connector, then move the wiring harness and fuel/vacuum hoses clear of the manifold.
**8** Undo the two screws securing the EGR pipe to the inlet manifold, and the bolt securing the pipe to the rear of the cylinder head **(see illustrations 8.11a and 8.11b)**.
**9** Remove the clip securing the EGR pipe to the EGR valve. If the original crimped clip is still in place, cut it off; new clips are supplied by Citroën parts stockists with a screw clamp fixing. If a screw type is fitted, undo the screw and manipulate the clip off the pipe. Remove the EGR pipe from the rear of the engine **(see illustration 8.12)**. Recover the O-ring seal from the end of the pipe.
**10** Undo the bolt securing the right-hand end of the inlet manifold to the cylinder head **(see illustration)**.

**12.4 Disconnect the manifold pressure sensor wiring connector (1.4 litre 16-valve engines)**

**12.5 Disconnect the intercooler outlet duct from the manifold (1.4 litre 16-valve engines)**

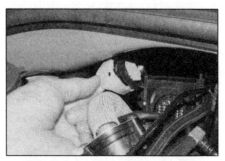

**12.6 Release the locking collar and disconnect the engine wiring harness connector (1.4 litre 16-valve engines)**

**12.10 Undo the bolt securing the right-hand end of the inlet manifold to the cylinder head (1.4 litre 16-valve engines)**

**12.13 Undo the seven bolts and withdraw the cylinder head cover from the camshaft bearing housing (1.4 litre 16-valve engines)**

**12.14 Pull off the leak-off pipe connector from each injector and remove the leak-off pipe assembly (1.4 litre 16-valve engines)**

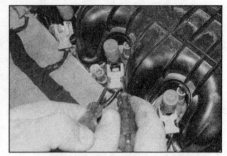

**12.15 Depress the sides of the locking clip and disconnect the fuel injector wiring connectors (1.4 litre 16-valve engines)**

**12.16a Remove the manifold from the cylinder head . . .**

**12.16b . . . and recover the O-ring seals from each of the manifold apertures (1.4 litre 16-valve engines)**

**11** Undo the two bolts securing the high pressure fuel pipe clamps to the top of the inlet manifold **(see illustration 9.13)**.

**12** Thoroughly clean the high pressure fuel pipe unions on the fuel injectors and accumulator rail. Using a crow's-foot adaptor, unscrew the union nuts securing the high pressure fuel pipes to the injectors and accumulator rail **(see illustration 9.15)**. Note that a complete set of new high pressure fuel pipes will be required for refitting. Note their fitted locations and remove the pipes. Plug the openings in the accumulator rail and fuel injectors to prevent dirt ingress.

**13** Undo the seven bolts and withdraw the cylinder head cover from the camshaft bearing housing **(see illustration)**. Cover the top of the camshaft bearing housing with a clean

cloth to prevent dirt entry while the cylinder head cover is removed.

**14** Pull the fuel injector leak-off pipe connector from each injector and remove the leak-off pipe assembly **(see illustration)**.

**15** Using two small screwdrivers, depress the sides of the locking clip and disconnect the wiring connectors from each fuel injector **(see illustration)**. Move the injector wiring harness clear of the manifold.

**16** Undo the two remaining rear retaining bolts, and remove the manifold from the cylinder head. Recover the O-ring seals from each of the manifold apertures **(see illustrations)**. Note that new O-rings will be required for refitting.

**17** Check the condition of the cylinder head cover rubber seal and renew it if there is any sign of deterioration.

### Refitting

**18** Thoroughly clean the inlet apertures in the cylinder head, and fit new O-ring seals to the inlet manifold. Lightly lubricate the O-ring seals with clean engine oil.

**19** Locate the inlet manifold in position on the cylinder head and fit the two rear retaining bolts, and the bolt at the right-hand front corner. Tighten the bolts finger tight only at this stage.

**20** Reconnect the wiring connectors to the fuel injectors, followed by the leak-off pipe connectors.

**21** Place the cylinder head cover in position and refit the retaining bolts. Tighten the retaining bolts in sequence to the specified torque **(see illustration)**. Tighten the two

manifold rear retaining bolts, and the bolt at the right-hand front corner to the specified torque.

**22** Fit the new set of accumulator rail-to-injector high pressure fuel pipes, and finger tighten the unions.

**23** Using a crow's-foot adaptor, tighten the union nuts at the injectors and accumulator rail to the specified torque.

**24** Refit the two bolts securing the high pressure fuel pipe clamps to the top of the inlet manifold.

**25** The remainder of refitting is a reversal of removal, noting the following points:

a) *Ensure all wiring connectors and harnesses are correctly refitting and secured.*

b) *Reconnect the battery as described in Chapter 5A.*

c) *Observing the precautions listed in Section 2, start the engine and allow it to idle. Check for leaks at the high-pressure fuel pipe unions with the engine idling. If satisfactory, increase the engine speed to 4000 rpm and check again for leaks. Take the car for a short road test and check for leaks once again on return. If any leaks are detected, obtain and fit additional new high-pressure fuel pipes as required. **Do not** attempt to cure even the slightest leak by further tightening of the pipe unions. During the road test, initialise the engine management ECU as follows. Engage third gear and stabilise the engine at 1000 rpm, then accelerate fully up to 3500 rpm.*

### 1.6 litre engines

**26** The inlet manifold is integral with the cylinder head cover. Refer to Chapter 2C.

## 13 Exhaust manifold – removal and refitting

### Removal

**1** Remove the turbocharger as described in Section 15.

**2** Undo the retaining nuts, recover the spacers, and remove the manifold. Recover the gasket **(see illustrations)**.

H45532

**12.21 Cylinder head cover tightening sequence (1.4 litre 16-valve engines)**

## Refitting

**3** Refitting is a reverse of the removal procedure, bearing in mind the following points:

a) *Ensure that the manifold and cylinder head mating faces are clean, with all traces of old gasket removed.*

b) *Use a new gasket and tighten the exhaust manifold retaining nuts to the specified torque.*

c) *Refit the turbocharger as described in Section 15.*

## 14 Turbocharger –
description and precautions

## Description

**1** A turbocharger is fitted to increase engine efficiency by raising the pressure in the inlet manifold above atmospheric pressure. Instead of the air simply being sucked into the cylinders, it is forced in.

**2** Energy for the operation of the turbocharger comes from the exhaust gas. The gas flows through a specially-shaped housing (the turbine housing) and, in so doing, spins the turbine wheel. The turbine wheel is attached to a shaft, at the end of which is another vaned wheel known as the compressor wheel. The compressor wheel spins in its own housing, and compresses the inlet air on the way to the inlet manifold.

**3** Boost pressure (the pressure in the inlet manifold) is limited by a wastegate, which diverts the exhaust gas away from the turbine wheel in response to a pressure-sensitive actuator. On later models, the turbocharger incorporates a variable inlet nozzle to improve boost pressure at low engine speeds.

**4** The turbo shaft is pressure-lubricated by an oil feed pipe from the main oil gallery. The shaft 'floats' on a cushion of oil. A drain pipe returns the oil to the sump.

## Precautions

**5** The turbocharger operates at extremely high speeds and temperatures. Certain precautions must be observed, to avoid premature failure of the turbo, or injury to the operator.

**6** Do not operate the turbo with any of its parts exposed, or with any of its hoses removed. Foreign objects falling onto the rotating vanes could cause excessive damage, and (if ejected) personal injury.

**7** Do not race the engine immediately after start-up, especially if it is cold. Give the oil a few seconds to circulate.

**8** Always allow the engine to return to idle speed before switching it off – do not blip the throttle and switch off, as this will leave the turbo spinning without lubrication.

**9** Allow the engine to idle for several minutes before switching off after a high-speed run.

**10** Observe the recommended intervals for oil and filter changing, and use a reputable oil of the specified quality. Neglect of oil

**13.2a  Undo the exhaust manifold nuts, recover the spacers, and remove the manifold**

**13.2b  Recover the manifold gasket**

changing, or use of inferior oil, can cause carbon formation on the turbo shaft, leading to subsequent failure.

## 15 Turbocharger –
removal, inspection and refitting

## Removal

**1** Disconnect the battery (see Chapter 5A).

**2** Apply the handbrake, then jack up the front of the vehicle and support it on axle stands (see *Jacking and vehicle support*). Undo the screws and remove the engine undershield.

### 1.4 litre engines

**3** Remove the inlet air resonator as described in Section 4.

**15.7a  Undo the four screws . . .**

**15.8  Undo the bolt each side and move the radiator/intercooler mounting frame forward**

**4** Remove the catalytic converter as described in Section 17.

**5** Slacken the retaining clip and disconnect the intercooler outlet duct from the inlet manifold.

**6** Remove the radiator grille.

**7** Undo the four screws and remove the upper front crossmember from the top of the radiator/intercooler mounting frame **(see illustrations)**.

**8** Undo the bolt each side securing the radiator/intercooler mounting frame to the front wings. Lift the mounting frame upwards to disengage the lower lugs and move it towards the front of the car as far as the hoses and attachments will allow **(see illustration)**.

**9** Undo the three retaining bolts and manipulate the exhaust manifold upper heat shield out from its location **(see illustration)**.

**15.7b  . . . and remove the crossmember from the radiator/intercooler mounting frame**

**15.9  Undo the three bolts and remove the exhaust manifold upper heat shield**

**15.10a Undo the turbocharger oil supply pipe banjo bolts from the cylinder block . . .**

**15.10b . . . and the turbocharger**

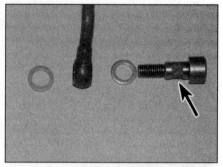

**15.10c Note the filter incorporated into the banjo bolt (arrowed)**

**15.11 Slacken the oil return hose clip (arrowed)**

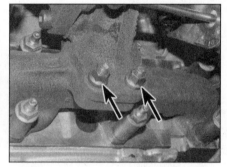

**15.12a Undo the lower nuts (arrowed) . . .**

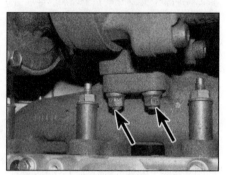

**15.12b . . . and upper nuts securing the turbocharger**

10 Undo the oil supply pipe banjo bolts and recover the sealing washers **(see illustrations)**.

11 Slacken the retaining clip and disconnect the oil return pipe from the turbocharger **(see illustration)**.

12 Unscrew the four nuts, and remove the turbocharger from the exhaust manifold **(see illustrations)**.

### 1.6 litre engines

13 Remove the engine top cover and place a piece of cardboard over the radiator to protect its fins.

14 Remove the catalytic converter/particulate filter (as applicable) as described in Section 17.

15 Loosen the clips and disconnect the inlet air duct and outlet noise attenuator from the turbocharger **(see illustration)**. Cover the turbocharger ports with cloth rags or tape.

16 Unscrew the bolts and remove the heat shield noting that the engine top cover stud is located towards the timing end of the engine.

17 Disconnect the vacuum hose from the turbocharger wastegate control assembly **(see illustration)**.

18 Undo the oil supply pipe banjo bolts, remove the pipe and recover the sealing washers **(see illustrations)**. **Note:** *The banjo bolt securing the oil supply pipe to the cylinder block must NOT have a strainer in its internal bore – if it has, remove it with a small screwdriver.*

**15.15 Inlet air duct on the turbocharger**

**15.17 Disconnect the vacuum pipe from the wastegate control assembly (arrowed)**

**15.18a Turbocharger oil supply and return pipes at the cylinder block end (arrowed)**

**15.18b Oil supply pipe on the turbocharger (arrowed)**

**15.20 Undo the 4 mounting nuts and the support nut and remove the turbocharger**

**19** Loosen the retaining clips and disconnect the oil return pipe from the turbocharger and cylinder block.
**20** Unscrew the four nuts, and the nut securing the support bracket, then remove the turbocharger from the exhaust manifold **(see illustration)**.

### Inspection

**21** With the turbocharger removed, inspect the housing for cracks or other visible damage.
**22** Spin the turbine or the compressor wheel, to verify that the shaft is intact and to feel for excessive shake or roughness. Some play is normal, since in use, the shaft is 'floating' on a film of oil. Check that the wheel vanes are undamaged.
**23** If oil contamination of the exhaust or induction passages is apparent, it is likely that turbo shaft oil seals have failed.
**24** No DIY repair of the turbo is possible and none of the internal or external parts are available separately. If the turbocharger is suspect in any way a complete new unit must be obtained.

### Refitting

**25** Refitting is a reverse of the removal procedure, bearing in mind the following points:
 a) *Renew the turbocharger retaining nuts and gaskets.*
 b) *If a new turbocharger is being fitted, change the engine oil and filter.*
 c) *Prime the turbocharger by injecting clean engine oil through the oil feed pipe union before reconnecting the union.*

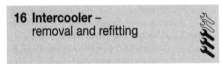

## 16 Intercooler –
### removal and refitting

**Note:** *An intercooler is only fitted to 16-valve engines.*

### Removal

**1** The intercooler is located at the front of the engine compartment, on the right-hand side of the radiator. First apply the handbrake, then jack up the front of the vehicle and support it on axle stands (see *Jacking and vehicle support*). Undo the screws and remove the engine undershield.

#### 1.4 litre engines

**2** Slacken the retaining clips and disconnect the inlet and outlet air ducts from the intercooler, inlet manifold and resonator.
**3** Remove the radiator grille.
**4** Undo the four screws and remove the upper front crossmember from the top of the radiator/intercooler mounting frame **(see illustrations 15.7a and 15.7b)**.
**5** Undo the bolt each side securing the radiator/intercooler mounting frame to the front wings. Lift the mounting frame upwards to disengage the lower lugs and move it towards the front of the car as far as the hoses and attachments will allow **(see illustration 15.8)**.

**16.6 Depress the tabs and release the intercooler upper plastic mounting bracket . . .**

**6** Using two screwdrivers, depress the tabs on each side of the intercooler upper plastic mounting bracket. Move the top of the intercooler towards the engine to free the bracket from its location, then lift it off the intercooler mounting stud **(see illustration)**.
**7** Lift the intercooler upwards to disengage the lower mounting lugs, then carefully remove it from the engine compartment **(see illustration)**. Recover the lower mounting rubbers.

#### 1.6 litre engines

**8** For improved access, remove the throttle housing as described in Section 11.
**9** Unbolt the resonator from the turbocharger outlet flange and disconnect the venting pipe.
**10** Loosen the clips and disconnect the inlet and outlet hoses from the top of the intercooler. If preferred, disconnect the hoses from the throttle housing and air resonator and remove the hoses from the intercooler later **(see illustrations)**.
**11** On models with air conditioning, remove the auxiliary drivebelt as described in Chapter 1B, then refer to Chapter 3 and unbolt the air conditioning compressor and support it to one side without disconnecting the refrigerant pipes. If necessary disconnect the wiring from the compressor.
**12** Using two screwdrivers, depress the tabs on each side of the intercooler upper plastic mounting bracket. Move the top of the intercooler towards the engine to free the bracket from its location, then lift it off the intercooler mounting stud.
**13** Lower the intercooler and withdraw from

**16.7 . . . then lift the intercooler from its location**

under the car. Recover the lower mounting rubbers.

### Refitting

**14** Refitting is a reversal of removal.

## 17 Exhaust system –
### general information
### and component renewal

### General information

**1** On new vehicles, the exhaust system consists two sections; the front pipe with integral catalytic converter and the remaining system consisting of a silencer and tailpipe. The catalytic converter is secured to the turbocharger and intermediate/rear section by clamping rings.
**2** For service replacements it is possible to obtain an intermediate section and a rear section (silencer and tailpipe) separately, however the original pipe must be cut with a hacksaw to accommodate either new section. The new sections are supplied with a clamping sleeve to allow connection to the original pipe.
**3** The system is suspended throughout its entire length by rubber mountings, and incorporates a flexible section at the forward end to cater for system movement.
**4** To remove the system or part of the system, first jack up the front or rear of the car and support it on axle stands (see *Jacking and vehicle support*). Alternatively, position the car over an inspection pit or on car ramps. If the complete system is to be removed, the rear

**16.10a Hose connections to the top of the intercooler . . .**

**16.10b . . . and to the throttle housing and air resonator**

**17.7a Slacken the clamp (arrowed) securing the catalytic converter to the turbocharger ...**

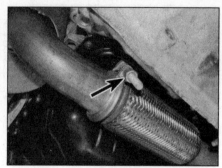

**17.7b ... and intermediate/rear pipe (arrowed)**

**17.8 Undo the two nuts (arrowed) and remove the catalytic converter**

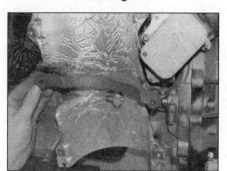

**17.9a Remove the spacer bracket ...**

**17.9b ... and inner heat shield from the cylinder block studs**

beam axle must be lowered to allow room to withdraw the system from the rear of the car. Bear this in mind when considering how the car is to be positioned.

### Removal and refitting

#### Catalytic converter – 1.4 litre engines

**5** Undo the screws and remove the engine undershield.

**6** Undo the six bolts and remove the lower heat shield from the front of the catalytic converter.

**7** Slacken the retaining clamps joining the catalytic converter to the turbocharger and intermediate/rear pipe **(see illustrations)**. Take care not to damage the intermediate/rear pipe flexible section.

**8** Undo the two nuts securing the catalytic converter to the cylinder block and manoeuvre it down and out of the engine compartment **(see illustration)**.

**9** Remove the spacer bracket and inner heat shield from the cylinder block studs **(see illustrations)**.

**10** Refitting is a reversal of the removal procedure, ensuring that the clamps are tightened to the specified torque.

#### Catalytic converter/particulate filter – 1.6 litre engines

**11** Undo the screws and remove the engine undershield.

**12** With the engine top cover removed, remove the air inlet duct from the right-hand corner of the engine compartment, then remove the air duct from between the air filter and turbocharger inlet.

**13** Disconnect the air hose from the resonator then unbolt it from the turbocharger.

**14** Loosen the clips and remove the air hoses from the intercooler and throttle housing.

**15** On models without a particulate filter,

place some cardboard or similar over the rear of the radiator to protect the fins.

**16** On models with a particulate filter, remove the radiator as described in Chapter 3.

**17** Undo the bolts and remove the outer heat shield from the catalytic converter/particulate filter.

**18** On models with a particulate filter, remove the pressure take-off pipes and the exhaust gas temperature sensor **(see illustrations)**.

**19** Unbolt and remove the upper heat shield and outer heat shield from the catalytic converter/particulate filter.

**20** Loosen the bolts and remove the clamp rings from the exhaust manifold and intermediate section.

**21** Unscrew the two nuts securing the catalytic converter/particulate filter to the cylinder block and manoeuvre it down and out of the engine compartment. Also remove the inner heat shield.

**22** On models with a particulate filter, note its fitted position, then loosen the clamp and detach the particulate filter from the base of the catalytic converter **(see illustration)**.

**23** Refitting is a reversal of removal.

#### Whole system (minus catalytic converter)

**24** If the complete system is to be removed, the rear beam axle must be lowered to allow room to withdraw the system from the rear of the car. To do this, remove the rear suspension coil springs as described in Chapter 10, and lower the beam axle as far as the mountings will permit.

**25** Slacken the retaining clamp joining the catalytic converter to the intermediate/rear pipe.

**26** Undo the nuts securing the exhaust system mounting brackets to the underbody. Lift the system over the beam axle and withdraw it from the rear of the car.

**27** Refitting is a reversal of the removal procedure, bearing in mind the following points:

a) *Inspect the rubber mountings for signs of damage or deterioration, and renew as necessary.*

b) *Prior to tightening the exhaust system clamps, ensure that all rubber mountings are correctly located,*

**17.18a Unscrew the pressure take-off union from the side of the catalytic converter ...**

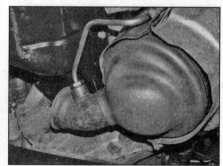

**17.18b ... and the one at the base of the particulate filter**

*and that there is adequate clearance between the exhaust system and vehicle underbody.*

*c) Refit the rear suspension coil springs as described in Chapter 10.*

### Intermediate pipe (service replacement)

**28** If a service replacement intermediate pipe is already installed, slacken the retaining clamp joining the intermediate pipe to the catalytic converter.

**29** Undo the nuts securing the intermediate pipe mounting brackets to the underbody. Slacken the clamping sleeve nuts, withdraw the intermediate pipe from the clamping sleeve and remove the pipe from under the car.

**30** Refitting is a reversal of removal, but inspect the rubber mountings for signs of damage or deterioration, and renew if necessary.

**31** If a service replacement intermediate pipe is to be installed on an original system, locate the cutting point on the original pipe. The cutting point is located just forward of the rear beam axle and is identified by four circular indentations in the pipe.

**32** Using a hacksaw, cut through the pipe at the cutting point.

**33** Slacken the retaining clamp joining the intermediate pipe to the catalytic converter.

**34** Undo the nuts securing the intermediate pipe mounting brackets to the underbody and remove the pipe from under the car.

**35** Inspect the rubber mountings for signs of damage or deterioration, and renew if necessary. If satisfactory, transfer the mountings to the new intermediate pipe.

**36** Using a pencil, make a mark on the tailpipe (remaining on the car) 40 mm from the cutting point. Slide the new clamping sleeve over the tailpipe and up to the mark. Fit the retaining bolts and nuts and tighten them just sufficiently to hold the sleeve in position.

**37** Engage the new intermediate pipe with the clamping sleeve then refit the mounting bracket retaining nuts finger tight only at this stage.

**17.22 Loosen the clamp (arrowed) and slide the particulate filter from the catalytic converter**

**38** Fit the retaining clamp joining the intermediate pipe to the catalytic converter and securely tighten the clamp bolt.

**39** Check that the clamping sleeve is still positioned at the previously made mark and that the intermediate pipe is fully engaged. Securely tighten the clamping sleeve nuts, followed by the mounting bracket nuts.

### Silencer/tailpipe (service replacement)

**40** If a service replacement silencer/tailpipe is already installed, undo the nuts securing the silencer/tailpipe mounting bracket to the underbody. Slacken the clamping sleeve nuts, withdraw the silencer/tailpipe from the clamping sleeve and remove the pipe from under the car.

**41** Refitting is a reversal of removal, but inspect the rubber mounting for signs of damage or deterioration, and renew if necessary.

**42** If a service replacement silencer/tailpipe is to be installed on an original system, locate the cutting point on the original pipe. The cutting point is located just forward of the rear beam axle and is identified by four circular indentations in the pipe.

**43** Using a hacksaw, cut through the pipe at the cutting point.

**44** Undo the nuts securing the silencer/tailpipe mounting bracket to the underbody and remove the pipe from under the car.

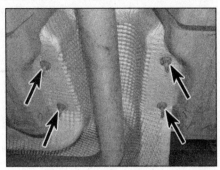

**17.49 Exhaust rear heat shield retaining nuts (arrowed)**

**45** Inspect the rubber mountings for signs of damage or deterioration, and renew if necessary. If satisfactory, transfer the mounting to the new silencer/tailpipe.

**46** Using a pencil, make a mark on the inter-mediate pipe (remaining on the car) 40 mm from the cutting point. Slide the new clamping sleeve over the intermediate pipe and up to the mark. Fit the retaining bolts and nuts and tighten them just sufficiently to hold the sleeve in position.

**47** Engage the new silencer/tailpipe with the clamping sleeve then refit the mounting bracket retaining nuts.

**48** Check that the clamping sleeve is still positioned at the previously made mark and that the silencer/tailpipe is fully engaged. Securely tighten the clamping sleeve nuts, followed by the mounting bracket nuts.

### Heat shield(s)

**49** The heat shields are secured to the under-side of the body by various nuts and fasteners **(see illustration)**. If a shield is being removed to gain access to a component located behind it, remove the retaining nuts and/or fastener (unscrew the centre screw then pull out the complete fastener), and manoeuvre the shield out of position. On some models it may be necessary to free the exhaust system from its mountings to gain the clearance necessary to remove the larger heat shield.

# Chapter 4 Part C:
# Emission control systems

## Contents

## Degrees of difficulty

| | | | | |
|---|---|---|---|---|
| **Easy,** suitable for novice with little experience | **Fairly easy,** suitable for beginner with some experience | **Fairly difficult,** suitable for competent DIY mechanic | **Difficult,** suitable for experienced DIY mechanic | **Very difficult,** suitable for expert DIY or professional |

---

### 1 General information

All petrol engines use unleaded petrol and also have various other features built into the fuel system to help minimise harmful emissions. In addition, all engines are equipped with the crankcase emission control system described below. All engines are also equipped with a catalytic converter and an evaporative emission control system.

All diesel engines are also designed to meet the strict emission requirements and are equipped with a crankcase emission control system and a catalytic converter. To further reduce exhaust emissions, all diesel engines are also fitted with an exhaust gas recirculation (EGR) system. Additionally, 1.6 litre DV6TED4 (9HZ) diesel engine models are equipped with a particulate emission filter which uses porous silicon carbide substrate to trap particulates of carbon as the exhaust gases pass through.

The emission control systems function as follows.

### Petrol engines

#### Crankcase emission control

To reduce the emission of unburned hydrocarbons from the crankcase into the atmosphere, the engine is sealed and the blow-by gases and oil vapour are drawn from inside the crankcase, through a wire mesh oil separator, into the inlet tract to be burned by the engine during normal combustion.

Under all conditions the gases are forced out of the crankcase by the (relatively) higher crankcase pressure; if the engine is worn, the raised crankcase pressure (due to increased blow-by) will cause some of the flow to return under all manifold conditions.

#### Exhaust emission control

To minimise the amount of pollutants which escape into the atmosphere, a catalytic converter is fitted in the exhaust system. The system is of the closed-loop type, in which lambda (oxygen) sensors in the exhaust system provide the engine management system ECU with constant feedback, enabling the ECU to adjust the mixture to provide the best possible conditions for the converter to operate.

The lambda sensors have a heating element built-in that is controlled by the ECU through the lambda sensor relay to quickly bring the sensor's tip to an efficient operating temperature. The sensor's tip is sensitive to oxygen and sends the ECU a varying voltage depending on the amount of oxygen in the exhaust gases; if the inlet air/fuel mixture is too rich, the exhaust gases are low in oxygen so the sensor sends a low-voltage signal, the voltage rising as the mixture weakens and the amount of oxygen rises in the exhaust gases. Peak conversion efficiency of all major pollutants occurs if the inlet air/fuel mixture is maintained at the chemically-correct ratio for the complete combustion of petrol of 14.7 parts (by weight) of air to 1 part of fuel (the 'stoichiometric' ratio). The sensor output voltage alters in a large step at this point, the ECU using the signal change as a reference point and correcting the inlet air/fuel mixture accordingly by altering the fuel injector pulse width.

#### Evaporative emission control

To minimise the escape into the atmosphere of unburned hydrocarbons, an evaporative emission control system is fitted. The fuel tank filler cap is sealed and a charcoal canister is mounted behind the wheel arch liner under the right-hand side rear wing to collect the petrol vapours generated in the tank when the car is parked. It stores them until they can be cleared from the canister (under the control of the engine management system ECU) via the purge valve into the inlet tract to be burned by the engine during normal combustion.

To ensure that the engine runs correctly when it is cold and/or idling and to protect the catalytic converter from the effects of an over-rich mixture, the purge control valve is not opened by the ECU until the engine has warmed-up, and the engine is under load; the valve solenoid is then modulated on and off to allow the stored vapour to pass into the inlet tract.

### Diesel engines

#### Crankcase emission control

Refer to the description for petrol engines.

#### Exhaust emission control

To minimise the level of exhaust pollutants released into the atmosphere, a catalytic converter is fitted in the exhaust system.

The catalytic converter consists of a canister containing a fine mesh impregnated with a catalyst material, over which the hot exhaust gases pass. The catalyst speeds up the oxidation of harmful carbon monoxide, unburnt hydrocarbons and soot, effectively reducing the quantity of harmful products released into the atmosphere via the exhaust gases.

#### Exhaust gas recirculation system

This system is designed to recirculate small quantities of exhaust gas into the inlet tract, and therefore into the combustion process. This process reduces the level of oxides of nitrogen present in the final exhaust gas which is released into the atmosphere.

The volume of exhaust gas recirculated is controlled by the engine management system ECU.

A vacuum-operated valve (early 1.4 litre models) or electrically-operated valve (later 1.4 and all 1.6 litre models) is fitted to the exhaust manifold, to regulate the quantity of exhaust gas recirculated. The valve is operated by the vacuum supplied by the solenoid valve.

#### Particulate filter system

The particulate filter is combined with the catalytic converter in the exhaust system, and its purpose it to trap particulates of carbon (soot) as the exhaust gases pass through, in order to comply with latest emission regulations.

The filter can be automatically regenerated (cleaned) by the system's ECU on-board the vehicle. The engine's high pressure injection

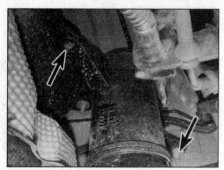

**2.4 Charcoal canister mounting nuts (arrowed)**

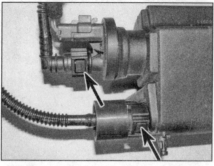

**2.5 Depress the quick-release buttons, and disconnect the hoses (arrowed)**

system is utilised to inject fuel into the exhaust gases during the post-injection period; this causes the filter temperature to increase sufficiently to oxidise the particulates, leaving an ash residue. The regeneration period is automatically controlled by the on-board ECU. Subsequently, at the correct service interval, the filter must be removed from the exhaust system and renewed. **Note:** *When driving in traffic jams or at prolonged reduced speed, a message warning that the particulate filter is clogged may be displayed. Should this occur, the filter may be regenerated by driving at a speed of at least 37 mph for a period of 5 minutes.*

To assist the combustion of the trapped carbon (soot) during the regeneration process, a fuel additive (cerium-based Eolys) is automatically mixed with the diesel fuel in the fuel tank. The additive is stored in a container attached to the right-hand side of the fuel

tank, and the ECU regulates the amount of additive to send to the fuel tank by means of an additive injector located on the top of the fuel tank.

## 2 Emission control systems – testing and component renewal

### Petrol engines

#### Crankcase emission control

**1** The components of this system require no attention other than to check that the hose(s) are clear and undamaged at regular intervals.

#### Evaporative emission control

**2** If the system is thought to be faulty, disconnect the hoses from the charcoal

canister and purge control valve and check that they are clear by blowing through them. If the purge control valve or charcoal canister are thought to be faulty, they must be renewed.

#### Charcoal canister renewal

**3** The charcoal canister is located under the rear wheel arch on the right-hand side. To gain access, slacken the right-hand rear roadwheel bolts, jack up the rear of the car and support it on axle stands (see *Jacking and vehicle support*). Remove the roadwheel, prise out the plastic expanding rivets, and remove the wheel arch liner.
**4** Undo the two mounting nuts and lower the canister from the top of the wheel arch **(see illustration)**.
**5** Identify the location of the hoses, then depress the quick-release button and disconnect the vapour hoses from the canister. Also disconnect the wiring plug connector from the purge valve **(see illustration)**.
**6** Refitting is a reverse of the removal procedure ensuring that the hoses are correctly reconnected.

#### Purge valve renewal

**7** The purge valve is mounted on the engine at the right-hand end of the cylinder head **(see illustrations)**.
**8** Disconnect the wiring connector and disconnect the vapour hoses from the valve. Where a crimped-type retaining clip is used, cut off the clip and use a worm-drive type when refitting.
**9** Withdraw the valve from its mounting bracket and remove it from the engine.
**10** Refitting is a reverse of the removal procedure ensuring that the hoses are correctly reconnected.

#### Exhaust emission control

**11** The performance of the catalytic converter can be checked only by measuring the exhaust gases using a good-quality, carefully-calibrated exhaust gas analyser.
**12** If the CO level at the tailpipe is too high, the vehicle should be taken to a Citroën dealer or specialist so that the complete fuel injection and ignition systems, including the lambda sensor, can be thoroughly checked using the special diagnostic equipment. Once these have been checked and are known to be free from faults, the fault must be in the catalytic converter, which must be renewed as described in Part A of this Chapter.

#### Catalytic converter renewal

**13** Refer to Part A of this Chapter.

#### Lambda (oxygen) sensor renewal

**Note:** *The lambda sensor is delicate and will not work if it is dropped or knocked, if its power supply is disrupted, or if any cleaning materials are used on it.*
**14** Trace the wiring back from the lambda sensors, which are located before and after the catalytic converters. One sensor is located in the exhaust manifold, and one after the catalytic converter **(see illustrations)**.

**2.7a Purge valve location (arrowed) on 1.1 and 1.4 litre engines . . .**

**2.7b . . . and on 1.6 litre engines (arrowed)**

**2.14a The lambda sensors are located in the exhaust manifold (arrowed) . . .**

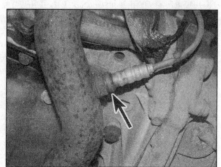

**2.14b . . . and in the front pipe (arrowed) after the catalytic converter**

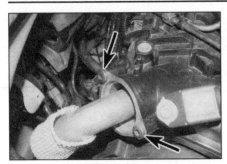

**2.23a Undo the two screws (arrowed) securing the EGR pipe to the inlet manifold . . .**

**2.23b . . . and the bolt (arrowed) securing the pipe to the rear of the cylinder head**

**2.24a Remove the EGR pipe-to-valve clip (arrowed) . . .**

**2.24b . . . then withdraw the pipe from the engine**

**2.28a EGR solenoid valve retaining nuts (arrowed) on 8-valve engines . . .**

**2.28b . . . and bolts (arrowed) on 16-valve engines**

Disconnect both wiring connectors and free the wiring from any relevant retaining clips or ties.

15 Unscrew the sensor from the exhaust system front pipe/manifold and remove it along with its sealing washer.

16 Refitting is a reverse of the removal procedure using a new sealing washer. Prior to installing the sensor apply a smear of high temperature grease to the sensor threads. Ensure that the sensor is securely tightened and that the wiring is correctly routed and in no danger of contacting either the exhaust system or engine.

### Diesel engines

#### Crankcase emission control

17 The components of this system require no attention other than to check that the hose(s) are clear and undamaged at regular intervals.

#### Exhaust emission control

18 The performance of the catalytic converter can be checked only by measuring the exhaust gases using a good-quality, carefully-calibrated exhaust gas analyser.

19 If the catalytic converter is thought to be faulty, before assuming the catalytic converter is faulty, it is worth checking the problem is not due to a faulty injector(s). Refer to your Citroën dealer for further information.

#### Catalytic converter renewal

20 Refer to Part B of this Chapter.

#### Exhaust gas recirculation system

21 Testing of the system should ideally be

entrusted to a Citroën dealer since a vacuum pump and vacuum gauge are required.

#### EGR valve renewal

22 Remove the air cleaner assembly and inlet ducts as described in Chapter 4B.

23 Undo the two screws securing the EGR pipe to the inlet manifold, and the bolt securing the pipe to the rear of the cylinder head (see illustrations).

24 Remove the clip securing the EGR pipe to the EGR valve. If the original crimped clip is still in place, cut it off; new clips are supplied by Citroën parts stockists with a screw clamp fixing. If a screw type is fitted, undo the screw and manipulate the clip off the pipe. Remove the EGR pipe from the rear of the engine (see illustrations). Recover the O-ring seal from the end of the pipe.

25 Disconnect the vacuum hose (early 1.4 litre engine) or wiring (later 1.4 and all 1.6 litre engines) from the EGR valve, then undo the two bolts and remove the valve from the rear of the engine. Recover the gasket.

26 Refitting is a reversal of removal, using a new gasket and O-ring.

#### EGR solenoid valve renewal (early 1.4 litre engine only)

27 The solenoid valve is located on the front facing side of the cylinder block on 8-valve engines and on the lower rear of the cylinder block on 16-valve engines.

28 To remove the valve, disconnect the two vacuum hoses and the wiring connector. Undo the mounting bracket bolts/nuts and remove the valve from the engine (see illustrations).

29 Refitting is a reversal of removal.

#### EGR heat exchanger (cooler) renewal

30 Disconnect the battery negative lead as described in Chapter 5A.

31 Remove the air cleaner housing as described in Chapter 4B.

32 Fit hose clamps to the hoses connected to the EGR heat exchanger on the rear of the engine.

33 Remove the heat shield over the EGR pipe (where applicable).

34 Undo the 2 bolts securing the EGR pipe, and release the clamp securing the pipe to the EGR cooler.

35 Release the clips and disconnect the coolant hoses from the cooler (see illustration), then undo the mounting bolts/nuts, remove the bracket, and manoeuvre it from place.

36 Refitting is a reversal of removal.

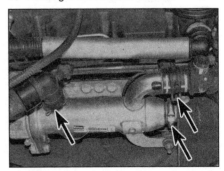

**2.35 EGR heat exchanger pipe clamp and coolant hoses (arrowed)**

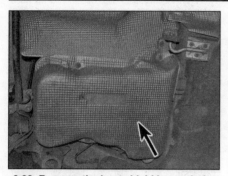

**2.39 Remove the heat shield beneath the additive reservoir (arrowed)**

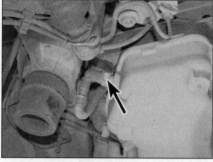

**2.40 Depress the release button (arrowed) and disconnect the breather hose**

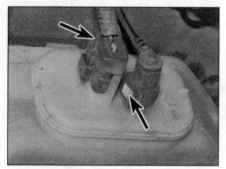

**2.41 Unclip the wiring plug and depress the hose release button (arrowed)**

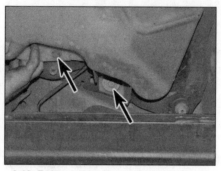

**2.42 Release the clip, undo the bolt and slide the reservoir to the left (arrowed)**

### Fuel additive system (vehicles with particulate filter)

37 It is possible to check the fuel additive system. However, this should be made by a Citroën dealer or suitably-equipped specialist due to the requirement for specialised diagnostic test equipment. A fuel cap presence sensor is fitted to the fuel filler neck, which informs the ECU when the filler cap is removed, to enable it to calculate the amount of fuel added, so that the correct amount of additive can be injected. A permanent magnet is fitted to the filler cap, which changes the resistance of the sensor when it's fitted. Bear this in mind should a filler cap be lost and a temporary replacement considered.

### Fuel additive reservoir renewal

**Note:** *Ideally, the additive reservoir should be empty before removing it, otherwise take precautions against spillage.*

 **Warning: Wear protective gloves and eye protection when handling the reservoir.**

38 To remove the fuel additive reservoir, chock the front wheels then jack up the rear of the vehicle and support on axle stands (see *Jacking and vehicle support*). The reservoir is attached to the left-hand side of the fuel tank.
39 Undo the fasteners and remove the heat shield from beneath the reservoir **(see illustration)**.

40 Disconnect the breather pipe at the connection to the left of the reservoir **(see illustration)**.
41 Disconnect the wiring plug and the pipe connection at the front of the reservoir **(see illustration)**. Tape over or plug the openings to prevent dirt ingress.
42 Undo the mounting bolt, release the retaining clip and slide the reservoir to the left-hand side and remove it **(see illustration)**.
43 Refitting is a reversal of removal.
44 Have the reservoir refilled by a Citroën dealer or suitably-equipped specialist.

### Particulate filter

45 Renewal of the particulate filter is described in Part B of this Chapter.

### Pressure differential sensor and pipes

46 This sensor measures the pressure at the particulate filter inlet and outlet, and is located beneath the double-throttle housing on the right-hand side of the engine.
47 Remove the right-hand front headlight as described in Chapter 12.
48 Disconnect the wiring plug from the sensor, then release the support clips from the pipes and unscrew the sensor mounting nuts.
49 Identify the hoses for position, then loosen the clips to remove the hoses and remove the sensor from the engine.

50 If it is required to remove the metal pipes, it will be necessary to raise the front of the car and support it on axle stands, then remove the engine undertray. Refer to Chapter 3 and unbolt the air conditioning compressor from the front of the engine without disconnecting the refrigerant lines. Unscrew the unions and detach the pipes from the particulate filter.
51 Refitting is a reversal of removal.

<table><tr><td>**3**</td><td>**Catalytic converter –** general information and precautions</td></tr></table>

1 The catalytic converter is a reliable and simple device which needs no maintenance in itself, but there are some facts of which an owner should be aware if the converter is to function properly for its full service life.

### Petrol engines

a) *DO NOT use leaded petrol or LRP (lead replacement petrol) – the lead will coat the precious metals, and will eventually destroy the converter.*
b) *Always keep the ignition and fuel systems well-maintained to the service schedule.*
c) *If the engine develops a misfire, do not drive the car at all (or at least as little as possible) until the fault is cured.*
d) *DO NOT push- or tow-start the car – this will soak the catalytic converter in unburned fuel, causing it to overheat when the engine does start.*
e) *DO NOT switch off the ignition at high engine speeds.*
f) *DO NOT use fuel or engine oil additives – these may contain substances harmful to the catalytic converter.*
g) *DO NOT continue to use the car if the engine burns oil to the extent of leaving a visible trail of blue smoke.*
h) *Remember that the catalytic converter operates at very high temperatures. DO NOT, therefore, park the car in dry undergrowth, over long grass or piles of dead leaves after a long run.*
i) *Remember that the catalytic converter is FRAGILE – do not strike it with tools.*
j) *In some cases a sulphurous smell (like that of rotten eggs) may be noticed from the exhaust. This is common to many catalytic converter-equipped cars and once the car has covered a few thousand miles the problem should disappear.*
k) *If the converter is no longer effective it must be renewed.*

### Diesel engines

2 Refer to parts f, g, h and i of the *petrol engines* information given above.

# Chapter 5 Part A:
## Starting and charging systems

## Contents

## Degrees of difficulty

| | | | | |
|---|---|---|---|---|
| **Easy,** suitable for novice with little experience  | **Fairly easy,** suitable for beginner with some experience | **Fairly difficult,** suitable for competent DIY mechanic | **Difficult,** suitable for experienced DIY mechanic | **Very difficult,** suitable for expert DIY or professional  |

## Specifications

**System type** .................................................. 12 volt, negative earth

**Battery**

Type .......................................................... Low maintenance or 'maintenance-free' sealed for life
Charge condition:
  Poor ....................................................... 12.5 volts
  Normal ..................................................... 12.6 volts
  Good ....................................................... 12.7 volts

**Alternator**

Type .......................................................... Denso, Valeo or Mitsubishi (depending on model)
Rating:
  Petrol engines ............................................. 60, 70, 80 or 90 amp
  Diesel engines ............................................. 80 or 150 amp

**Starter motor**

Type .......................................................... Mitsubishi, Valeo, Ducellier, Iskra, or Bosch (depending on model)

| **Torque wrench settings** | **Nm** | **lbf ft** |
|---|---|---|
| Alternator mounting bolts | 40 | 30 |
| Oil pressure switch | 30 | 22 |
| Starter motor | 35 | 26 |

---

### 1 General information and precautions

#### General information

The engine electrical system consists mainly of the charging and starting systems. Because of their engine-related functions, these components are covered separately from the body electrical devices such as the lights, instruments, etc (which are covered in Chapter 12). On petrol engine models refer to Part B for information on the ignition system, and on diesel models refer to Part C for information on the pre/post-heating system.

The electrical system is of the 12 volt negative earth type.

The battery is of the low maintenance or 'maintenance-free' (sealed for life) type and is charged by the alternator, which is belt-driven from the crankshaft pulley.

The starter motor is of the pre-engaged type incorporating an integral solenoid. On starting, the solenoid moves the drive pinion into engagement with the flywheel ring gear before the starter motor is energised. Once the engine has started, a one-way clutch prevents the motor armature being driven by the engine until the pinion disengages from the flywheel.

#### Precautions

Further details of the various systems are given in the relevant Sections of this Chapter. While some repair procedures are given, the usual course of action is to renew the component concerned. The owner whose interest extends beyond mere component renewal should obtain a copy of the *Automotive Electrical & Electronic Systems Manual*, available from the publishers of this manual.

It is necessary to take extra care when working on the electrical system to avoid damage to semi-conductor devices (diodes and transistors), and to avoid the risk of personal injury. In addition to the precautions given in *Safety first!* at the beginning of this manual, observe the following when working on the system:

• *Always remove rings, watches, etc, before working on the electrical system. Even with the battery disconnected, capacitive discharge could occur if a component's live terminal is earthed through a metal object. This could cause a shock or nasty burn.*

- *Do not reverse the battery connections. Components such as the alternator, electronic control units, or any other components having semi-conductor circuitry could be irreparably damaged.*
- *If the engine is being started using jump leads and a slave battery, connect the batteries positive-to-positive and negative-to-negative (see 'Jump starting'). This also applies when connecting a battery charger.*
- *Never disconnect the battery terminals, the alternator, any electrical wiring or any test instruments when the engine is running.*
- *Do not allow the engine to turn the alternator when the alternator is not connected.*
- *Never 'test' for alternator output by 'flashing' the output lead to earth.*
- *Never use an ohmmeter of the type incorporating a hand-cranked generator for circuit or continuity testing.*
- *Always ensure that the battery negative lead is disconnected when working on the electrical system.*
- *Before using electric-arc welding equipment on the car, disconnect the battery, alternator and components such as the various vehicle electronic control units to protect them from the risk of damage.*

## 2 Electrical fault finding
– general information

Refer to Chapter 12.

## 3 Battery –
testing and charging

### Testing

#### Standard and
#### low maintenance battery

**1** If the vehicle covers a small annual mileage, it is worthwhile checking the specific gravity of the electrolyte every three months to determine the state of charge of the battery. Use a hydrometer to make the check and compare the results with the following table. Note that the specific gravity readings assume an electrolyte temperature of 15°C (60°F); for every 10°C (18°F) below 15°C (60°F) subtract 0.007. For every 10°C (18°F) above 15°C (60°F) add 0.007.

| | Above 25°C | Below 25°C |
|---|---|---|
| **Fully-charged** | 1.210 to 1.230 | 1.270 to 1.290 |
| **70% charged** | 1.170 to 1.190 | 1.230 to 1.250 |
| **Discharged** | 1.050 to 1.070 | 1.110 to 1.130 |

**2** If the battery condition is suspect, first check the specific gravity of electrolyte in each cell. A variation of 0.040 or more between any cells indicates loss of electrolyte or deterioration of the internal plates.
**3** If the specific gravity variation is 0.040 or more, the battery should be renewed. If the

cell variation is satisfactory but the battery is discharged, it should be charged as described later in this Section.

#### Maintenance-free battery

**4** In cases where a 'sealed for life' maintenance-free battery is fitted, topping-up and testing of the electrolyte in each cell is not possible. The condition of the battery can therefore only be tested using a battery condition indicator or a voltmeter.
**5** Certain models may be fitted with a 'Delco' type maintenance-free battery, with a built-in charge condition indicator. The indicator is located in the top of the battery casing, and indicates the condition of the battery from its colour. If the indicator shows green, then the battery is in a good state of charge. If the indicator shows black, then the battery requires charging, as described later in this Section. If the indicator shows blue, then the electrolyte level in the battery is too low to allow further use, and the battery should be renewed.
*Caution: Do not attempt to charge, load or jump start a battery when the indicator shows clear/yellow.*
**6** If testing the battery using a voltmeter, connect the voltmeter across the battery and compare the result with those given in the Specifications under 'charge condition'. The test is only accurate if the battery has not been subjected to any kind of charge for the previous six hours. If this is not the case, switch on the headlights for 30 seconds, then wait four to five minutes before testing the battery after switching off the headlights. All other electrical circuits must be switched off, so check that the doors and tailgate are fully shut when making the test.
**7** If the voltage reading is less than 12.2 volts, then the battery is discharged, whilst a reading of 12.2 to 12.4 volts indicates a partially-discharged condition.
**8** If the battery is to be charged, remove it from the vehicle (Section 4) and charge it as described later in this Section.

### Charging

**Note:** *The following is intended as a guide only. Always refer to the manufacturer's recommendations (often printed on a label attached to a battery) before charging a battery.*

**4.3a Lift off the battery cover front section . . .**

#### Standard and
#### low maintenance battery

**9** Charge the battery at a rate of 3.5 to 4 amps and continue to charge the battery at this rate until no further rise in specific gravity is noted over a four hour period.
**10** Alternatively, a trickle charger charging at the rate of 1.5 amps can safely be used overnight.
**11** Specially rapid 'boost' charges which are claimed to restore the power of the battery in 1 to 2 hours are not recommended, as they can cause serious damage to the battery plates through overheating.
**12** While charging the battery, note that the temperature of the electrolyte should never exceed 37.8°C (100°F).

#### Maintenance-free battery

**13** This battery type takes considerably longer to fully recharge than the standard type, the time taken being dependent on the extent of discharge, but it can take anything up to three days.
**14** A constant voltage type charger is required to be set, when connected, to 13.9 to 14.9 volts with a charger current below 25 amps. Using this method, the battery should be usable within three hours, giving a voltage reading of 12.5 volts, but this is for a partially-discharged battery and, as mentioned, full charging can take considerably longer.
**15** If the battery is to be charged from a fully discharged state (condition reading less than 12.2 volts), have it recharged by your Citroën dealer or local automotive electrician, as the charge rate is higher and constant supervision during charging is necessary.

## 4 Battery –
disconnection, removal and refitting

**Note 1:** *The radio/cassette/CD player/auto-changer unit fitted as standard equipment by Citroën is equipped with an anti-theft system, to deter thieves. If the power source is disconnected, the audio unit will automatically recode itself as long as it is still fitted to the correct vehicle. If the unit is removed it will not operate in another vehicle.*
**Note 2:** *Prior to disconnecting the battery, wait at least two minutes after switching off the ignition.*

### Battery

#### Disconnection

**1** The battery is located on the left-hand side of the engine compartment.
**2** Prior to disconnecting the battery, close all windows and the sunroof, and ensure that the vehicle alarm system is deactivated (see Owner's Handbook or Chapter 12).
**3** Lift off the battery cover front section, followed by the rear section **(see illustrations)**.

4.3b . . . followed by the rear section

4.4 Slacken the clamp bolt nut and disconnect the negative lead from the battery terminal

4.14 Depress the locking catch on the battery box to disengage it from the base of the battery

**4** Slacken the clamp bolt nut and disconnect the negative lead from the battery terminal **(see illustration)**.

**5** Lift up the quick-release lever and disconnect the positive lead from the battery terminal.

### Reconnection

**6** Reconnect the battery leads, positive first and negative last. Smear petroleum jelly on the terminals after reconnecting the leads.

**7** With the battery reconnected, switch on the ignition and wait at least 1 minute before starting the engine. This will allow the vehicle electronic systems and control units to stabilise. Also refer to Chapter 12 on models with the anti-theft alarm system.

**8** Lock and unlock the tailgate to restore correct operation of the lock mechanism.

**9** Reprogram the audio unit station presets, and reset the parameters of the multifunction display.

**10** Re-initialise the 'anti-pinch' function on the electric front windows as follows:

a) Press the control switch to open the window fully.

b) Press the switch to close the window. It will start to close and then stop.

c) Press the switch again until the window closes completely.

**11** On models with a sunroof, re-initialise the sunroof mechanism as follows:

a) Turn the switch to the maximum opening position.

b) Keep the control switch pressed in for a further 1 second after the sunroof reaches the maximum opening position.

### Removal

**12** Disconnect the battery leads as described above.

**13** On diesel models, remove the air deflector, located in front of the battery box, by turning the plastic retainer through 90°. Withdraw the air deflector from the front of the air inlet ducting.

**14** Depress the plastic locking catch on the side of the battery box to disengage it from the base of the battery **(see illustration)**. Lift the battery upwards slightly, disengage the lower locating lugs and remove the battery from the battery box.

### Refitting

**15** Refitting is a reversal of removal, ensuring the battery correctly locates in the box. Reconnect the battery leads as described previously.

## *Battery box*

### Removal

**16** Remove the battery as described previously.

**17** According to model, remove the air cleaner and/or air inlet ducts as necessary for access to the battery tray.

**18** Disconnect the air intake tube from the front of the battery box, and release the wiring harness from the battery box clips **(see illustration)**.

**19** Remove the engine management electronic control unit from the battery box as described in Chapter 4A or 4B as applicable.

**20** Lift out the plastic partition panel located in front of the electric power steering ECU **(see illustration)**.

**21** Disconnect the three wiring connectors from the electric power steering ECU. To disconnect the large connector, pull out the retaining circlip, then slide out the locking catch **(see illustrations)**.

**22** Undo the two battery tray retaining bolts. Slide the tray towards the front of the car to release the rear locating lugs, then remove the tray complete with power steering ECU from the engine compartment.

### Refitting

**23** Refitting is a reversal of removal.

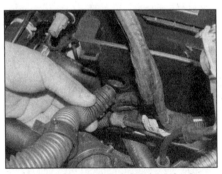

4.18 Disconnect the air intake tube from the front of the battery box

4.20 Lift out the plastic partition panel

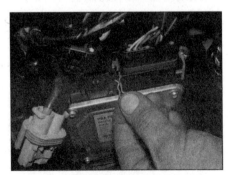

4.21a Pull out the wiring connector retaining circlip . . .

4.21b . . . then slide out the locking catch

**7.3 Undo the auxiliary drivebelt tensioner bolts (arrowed)**

### 5 Charging system – testing

**Note:** *Refer to the warnings given in 'Safety first!' and in Section 1 of this Chapter before starting work.*

1 If the ignition warning light fails to illuminate when the ignition is switched on, first check the alternator wiring connections for security. If satisfactory, check that the warning light bulb has not blown, and that the bulbholder is secure in its location in the instrument panel. If the light still fails to illuminate, check the continuity of the warning light feed wire from the alternator to the bulbholder. If all is satisfactory, the alternator is at fault and should be renewed or taken to an auto-electrician for testing and repair.

2 If the ignition warning light illuminates when the engine is running, stop the engine and check that the drivebelt is correctly fitted and tensioned (see Chapter 1A or 1B) and that the alternator connections are secure. If all is so far satisfactory, have the alternator checked by an auto-electrician for testing and repair.

3 If the alternator output is suspect even though the warning light functions correctly, the regulated voltage may be checked as follows.

4 Connect a voltmeter across the battery terminals and start the engine.

5 Increase the engine speed until the voltmeter reading remains steady; the reading should be approximately 12 to 13 volts, and no more than 14 volts.

**7.4 Prise out the rubber cover, then disconnect the alternator wiring and plug**

6 Switch on as many electrical accessories (eg, the headlights, heated rear window and heater blower) as possible, and check that the alternator maintains the regulated voltage of around 13 to 14 volts.

7 If the regulated voltage is not as stated, the fault may be due to worn brushes, weak brush springs, a faulty voltage regulator, a faulty diode, a severed phase winding or worn or damaged slip-rings. The alternator should be renewed or taken to an auto-electrician for testing and repair.

### 6 Alternator drivebelt – removal, refitting and tensioning

Refer to the procedure given for the auxiliary drivebelt in Chapter 1A or 1B.

### 7 Alternator – removal and refitting

#### Removal

1 Disconnect the battery (see Section 4).

2 Remove the auxiliary drivebelt as described in Chapter 1A or 1B. **Note:** *This work includes supporting the front of the car on axle stands and removing the roadwheel and wheel arch liner.* Additionally, on 1.4 litre ET3 petrol engines remove the exhaust manifold heat shield, and on diesel engines remove the throttle housing (where applicable) as described in Chapter 4B.

Also, on some diesel engines, it may be necessary to temporarily support the engine and remove the right-hand engine mounting for access to the auxiliary drivebelt tensioner (refer to Chapter 2B or 2C).

3 Where necessary and depending on engine and equipment fitted, either undo the three bolts and remove the auxiliary drivebelt tensioner assembly **(see illustration)**, or undo the bolts and remove the auxiliary drivebelt idler pulley bracket.

4 Remove the rubber cover from the alternator terminal, then unscrew the retaining nut and disconnect the wiring from the rear of the alternator **(see illustration)**. Release the wiring harness routed around the left-hand end of the alternator.

5 Unscrew the alternator mounting bolts and, where applicable, the bolt securing the adjuster bolt bracket to the alternator. Note that the left-hand bolt(s) act as centralisers and incorporate a spacer and cone **(see illustrations)**. To access the left-hand lower mounting bolt, unbolt the air conditioning compressor (where fitted) and move it to one side. **Do not** disconnect the refrigerant pipes.

6 Manoeuvre the alternator away from its mounting brackets and out from the engine compartment.

#### Refitting

7 Refitting is a reversal of removal, tightening the left-hand (centraliser) bolts first, followed by the right-hand bolts. Refit and tension the auxiliary drivebelt as described in Chapter 1A or 1B.

### 8 Alternator – testing and overhaul

If the alternator is thought to be suspect, it should be removed from the vehicle and taken to an auto-electrician for testing. Most auto-electricians will be able to supply and fit brushes at a reasonable cost. However, check on the cost of repairs before proceeding as it may prove more economical to obtain a new or exchange alternator.

**7.5a Alternator right-hand mounting bolts (arrowed) . . .**

**7.5b . . . and left-hand mounting bolts (arrowed)**

**7.5c The left-hand bolt(s) act as centralisers and incorporate a spacer and cone**

## 9 Starting system – testing

**Note:** *Refer to the precautions given in 'Safety first!' and in Section 1 of this Chapter before starting work.*

**1** If the starter motor fails to operate when the ignition key is turned to the appropriate position, the following possible causes may be to blame.

a) *The engine immobiliser is faulty.*
b) *The battery is faulty.*
c) *The electrical connections between the switch, solenoid, battery and starter motor are somewhere failing to pass the necessary current from the battery through the starter to earth.*
d) *The solenoid is faulty.*
e) *The starter motor is mechanically or electrically defective.*

**2** To check the battery, switch on the headlights. If they dim after a few seconds, this indicates that the battery is discharged – recharge (see Section 3) or renew the battery. If the headlights glow brightly, operate the ignition switch and observe the lights. If they dim, then this indicates that current is reaching the starter motor, therefore the fault must lie in the starter motor. If the lights continue to glow brightly (and no clicking sound can be heard from the starter motor solenoid), this indicates that there is a fault in the circuit or solenoid – see following paragraphs. If the starter motor turns slowly when operated, but the battery is in good condition, then this indicates that either the starter motor is faulty, or there is considerable resistance somewhere in the circuit.

**3** If a fault in the circuit is suspected, disconnect the battery leads (including the earth connection to the body), the starter/solenoid wiring and the engine/transmission earth strap – located on the to of the transmission housing **(see illustration)**. Thoroughly clean the connections and reconnect the leads and wiring, then use a voltmeter or test lamp to check that full battery voltage is available at the battery positive lead connection to the solenoid, and that the earth is sound. Smear petroleum jelly around the battery terminals to prevent corrosion –

corroded connections are amongst the most frequent causes of electrical system faults.

**4** If the battery and all connections are in good condition, check the circuit by disconnecting the wire from the solenoid blade terminal. Connect a voltmeter or test lamp between the wire end and a good earth (such as the battery negative terminal), and check that the wire is live when the ignition switch is turned to the 'start' position. If it is, then the circuit is sound – if not the circuit wiring can be checked as described in Chapter 12.

**5** The solenoid contacts can be checked by connecting a voltmeter or test lamp between the battery positive feed connection on the starter side of the solenoid, and earth. When the ignition switch is turned to the 'start' position, there should be a reading or lighted bulb, as applicable. If there is no reading or lighted bulb, the solenoid is faulty and should be renewed.

**6** If the circuit and solenoid are proved sound, the fault must lie in the starter motor. In this event, it may be possible to have the starter motor overhauled by a specialist, but check on the cost of spares before proceeding, as it may prove more economical to obtain a new or exchange motor.

## 10 Starter motor – removal and refitting

### Removal

**1** Disconnect the battery (see Section 4).

**2** So that access to the motor can be gained both from above and below, apply the handbrake then jack up the front of the vehicle and support it on axle stands (see *Jacking and vehicle support*). Release the screws and remove the engine undershield (where fitted).

### Petrol engines

**3** Remove the air cleaner assembly as described in Chapter 4A.

**4** Slacken and remove the two retaining nuts then disconnect the wiring from the starter motor solenoid. Recover the washers under the nuts.

**5** Undo the three mounting bolts (two at the rear of the motor, and one which comes through from the top of the transmission

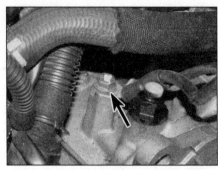

**9.3 Engine/transmission earth strap connection (arrowed)**

housing), supporting the motor as the bolts are withdrawn. Recover the washers from under the bolt heads and note the locations of any wiring or hose brackets secured by the bolts **(see illustration)**.

**6** Manoeuvre the starter motor out from underneath the engine and recover the locating dowel(s) from the motor/transmission (as applicable).

### Diesel engines

**Note:** *Access to the starter motor is extremely limited both from above and below. It will be necessary to disconnect or move aside various pipes, hoses and wiring harnesses to obtain the necessary clearance for removal.*

**7** Remove the air cleaner assembly and air inlet ducts as described in Chapter 4B, then remove the battery and battery box as described in Section 4 of this Chapter. On 1.6 litre models, also remove the engine management ECU (Chapter 4B) and power steering ECU (Chapter 10).

**8** Refer to Chapter 4B and disconnect the exhaust intermediate/rear pipe from the catalytic converter.

**9** On early 16-valve engines, note the location of the vacuum hose connections at the vacuum reservoir below the starter motor. Disconnect the hoses, then undo the two nuts and remove the reservoir.

**10** Slacken and remove the two retaining nuts and disconnect the wiring from the starter motor solenoid. Recover the washers under the nuts. Release the wiring loom from the retaining clips, then undo the bolt securing the wiring loom support plate above the starter motor **(see illustrations)**.

**10.5 Starter motor mounting bolts (arrowed)**

**10.10a Undo the two nuts (arrowed) and disconnect the starter motor wiring**

**10.10b Undo the bolt (arrowed) securing the wiring loom support plate**

**13.3 The oil pressure switch is located at the front of the cylinder block**

**11** Undo the three mounting bolts (two at the rear of the motor, and one which comes through from the top of the transmission housing), supporting the motor as the bolts are withdrawn. Recover the washers from under the bolt heads and note the locations of any wiring or hose brackets secured by the bolts **(see illustration 10.5)**.
**12** Move the exhaust to the left slightly and manoeuvre the starter motor out from underneath the engine. Recover the locating dowel(s) from the motor/transmission (as applicable).

### Refitting

**13** Refitting is a reversal of removal, ensuring that the locating dowel(s) are correctly positioned. Also make sure that any wiring or hose brackets are in place under the bolt heads as noted prior to removal.

## 11 Starter motor –
testing and overhaul

If the starter motor is thought to be suspect, it should be removed from the vehicle and taken to an auto-electrician for testing. Most auto-electricians will be able to supply and fit brushes at a reasonable cost. However, check on the cost of repairs before proceeding as it may prove more economical to obtain a new or exchange motor.

## 12 Ignition switch –
removal and refitting

The ignition switch is integral with the steering column lock, and can be removed as described in Chapter 10.

## 13 Oil pressure
warning light switch
– removal and refitting

### Removal

**1** The switch is fitted at the front of the cylinder block, in the following locations:
*Petrol engines: Screwed into the base of the oil filter housing.*
*Diesel engines: Adjacent to the oil dipstick guide tube.*
Note that on some models access to the switch may be improved if the vehicle is jacked up and supported on axle stands, and the engine undershield removed (where fitted), so that the switch can be reached from underneath (see *Jacking and vehicle support*).
**2** Remove the protective sleeve from the wiring plug (where applicable), then disconnect the wiring from the switch.
**3** Unscrew the switch from the cylinder block, and recover the sealing washer **(see illustration)**. Be prepared for oil spillage, and if the switch is to be left removed from the engine for any length of time, plug the hole in the cylinder block.

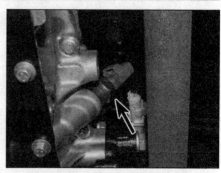

**14.2 Oil level sensor (arrowed)**

### Refitting

**4** Examine the sealing washer for signs of damage or deterioration and if necessary renew.
**5** Refit the switch, complete with washer, and tighten it securely. Reconnect the wiring connector.
**6** Lower the vehicle to the ground then check and, if necessary, top-up the engine oil as described in *Weekly Checks*.

## 14 Oil level sensor –
removal and refitting

**1** The sensor is fitted in the following locations:
*Petrol engines: Front side of the cylinder block adjacent to the oil filter housing.*
*Diesel engines: Rear side of the cylinder block, between cylinders 2 and 3.*
**2** The removal and refitting procedure is as described for the oil pressure switch in Section 13. Access is most easily obtained from underneath the vehicle **(see illustration)**.

# Chapter 5 Part B:
## Ignition system – petrol models

## Contents

## Degrees of difficulty

| Easy, suitable for novice with little experience  | Fairly easy, suitable for beginner with some experience  | Fairly difficult, suitable for competent DIY mechanic  | Difficult, suitable for experienced DIY mechanic  | Very difficult, suitable for expert DIY or professional  |
|---|---|---|---|---|

## Specifications

### General

System type . . . . . . . . . . . . . . . . . . . . . . . . . . . . . . . . . . . . . . . . .  Static (distributorless) ignition system controlled by engine management ECU
Firing order. . . . . . . . . . . . . . . . . . . . . . . . . . . . . . . . . . . . . . . . . .  1-3-4-2 (No 1 cylinder at transmission end)
Spark plugs . . . . . . . . . . . . . . . . . . . . . . . . . . . . . . . . . . . . . . . . .  See Chapter 1A Specifications
Ignition timing. . . . . . . . . . . . . . . . . . . . . . . . . . . . . . . . . . . . . . . .  Controlled by engine management ECU

| Torque wrench setting | Nm | lbf ft |
|---|---|---|
| Knock sensor securing bolt . . . . . . . . . . . . . . . . . . . . . . . . . . . . . . | 20 | 15 |

### 1 Ignition system – general information

The ignition system is integrated with the fuel injection system to form a combined engine management system under the control of one ECU (see Chapter 4A for further information). The ignition side of the system is of the static (distributorless) type, consisting of the ignition coils and spark plugs. The ignition coils are housed in a single unit mounted directly above the spark plugs. The coils are integral with the spark plug caps and are pushed directly onto the spark plugs, one for each plug. This removes the need for any HT leads connecting the coils to the plugs.

Under the control of the ECU, the ignition coils operate on the 'wasted spark' principle, ie, each plug sparks twice for every cycle of the engine, once during the compression stroke and once during the exhaust stroke. The spark voltage is greatest in the cylinder which is under compression; in the cylinder on its exhaust stroke the compression is low and this produces a very weak spark which has no effect on the exhaust gases.

The ECU uses its inputs from the various sensors to calculate the required ignition advance setting and coil charging time, depending on engine temperature, load and speed. At idle speeds, the ECU varies the ignition timing to alter the torque characteristic of the engine, enabling the idle speed to be controlled. This system operates in conjunction with the idle speed control motor – see Chapter 4A for additional details.

A knock sensor is also incorporated into the ignition system. Mounted onto the cylinder block, the sensor detects the high-frequency vibrations caused when the engine starts to pre-ignite, or 'pink'. Under these conditions, the knock sensor sends an electrical signal to the ECU which in turn retards the ignition advance setting in small steps until the 'pinking' ceases.

### 2 Ignition system – testing

**Warning: Due to the high voltages produced by the electronic ignition system, extreme care must be taken when working on the system with the ignition switched on. Persons with surgically-implanted cardiac pacemaker devices should keep well clear of the ignition circuits, components and test equipment.**

1 If a fault appears in the engine management system, first ensure that all the system wiring connectors are securely connected and free of corrosion. Ensure that the fault is not due to poor maintenance; ie, check that the air cleaner filter element is clean, the spark plugs are in good condition and correctly gapped, the cyl-inder compression pressures are correct and that the engine breather hoses are clear and undamaged, referring to Chapters 1A and 2A for further information. If the engine is running very roughly, check the compression pressures and the valve clearances as described in Chapter 2A.

2 If these checks fail to reveal the cause of the problem, the vehicle should be taken to a suitably-equipped Citroën dealer or engine management diagnostic specialist for testing. A diagnostic socket is located above the passenger's compartment fusebox, to which a fault code reader or other suitable test equipment can be connected **(see illustration)**.

**2.2 The diagnostic socket (arrowed) is located above the passenger's compartment fusebox**

**3.1a Disconnect the engine breather hose at the air cleaner air inlet duct . . .**

**3.1c . . . and inlet manifold (arrowed)**

**3.3a Undo the coil retaining nut (arrowed) and lift off the earth lead from the left-hand stud . . .**

By using the code reader or test equipment, the engine management ECU (and the various other vehicle system ECUs) can be interrogated, and any stored fault codes can be retrieved. This will allow the fault to be quickly and

**3.1b . . . cylinder head cover (arrowed) . . .**

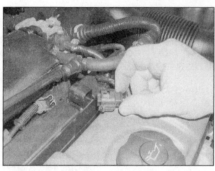

**3.2 Disconnect the wiring plug from the ignition HT coil**

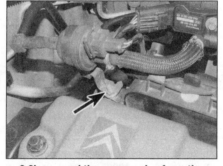

**3.3b . . . and the purge valve from the right-hand stud (arrowed)**

simply traced, alleviating the need to test all the system components individually, which is a time-consuming operation that carries a risk of damaging the ECU.

**3** The only ignition system checks which can

be carried out by the home mechanic are those described in Chapter 1A relating to the spark plugs.

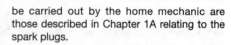

## 3  Ignition coil unit – removal, testing and refitting

### Removal

#### 1.1 and 1.4 litre SOHC engines

**1** Disconnect the engine breather hose at the quick-release connections on the air cleaner air inlet duct, cylinder head cover and inlet manifold **(see illustrations)**. Move the hose to one side.

**2** Unplug the wiring connector from the top of the ignition coil unit **(see illustration)**. Release the wiring harness from the clips on the coil unit.

**3** Undo the nut securing each end of the ignition coil unit to the mounting studs. Note that it is quite likely that the stud will be released with the nut. Lift off the earth lead from the left-hand stud, and the purge valve from the right-hand stud **(see illustrations)**.

**4** Lift the ignition coil unit upwards off the mounting studs and at the same time carefully ease the HT extension pillars away from the tops of the spark plugs. Lift the unit off the plugs and withdraw it from the engine **(see illustration)**.

#### 1.4 and 1.6 litre DOHC engines

**5** Undo the six screws and remove the plastic coil unit cover from the top of the engine between the two camshaft covers.

**6** Disconnect the wiring plug from the left-hand end of the ignition coil unit **(see illustration)**.

**7** Depress the clips and remove the two breather pipes from between the camshaft covers **(see illustration)**.

**8** Undo the four mounting screws securing the coil unit **(see illustration)**.

**9** Lift the ignition coil unit upwards and at the same time carefully ease the HT extension pillars away from the tops of the spark plugs. Lift the unit off the plugs and withdraw it from the engine.

**3.4 . . . then ease the ignition HT coil assembly off the spark plugs and remove it from the engine**

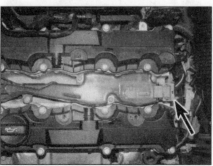

**3.6 Disconnect the wiring plug from the HT coils (arrowed)**

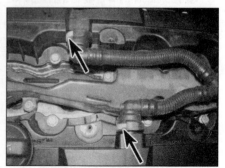

**3.7 Depress the clips (arrowed) and disconnect the breather pipes**

## Testing

**10** The circuitry arrangement of the ignition coil unit on these engines is such that testing of an individual coil in isolation from the remainder of the engine management system is unlikely to prove effective in diagnosing a particular fault. Should there be any reason to suspect a faulty individual coil, the engine management system should be tested by a Citroën dealer or specialist using diagnostic test equipment (see Section 2).

## Refitting

**11** Refitting is a reversal of the relevant removal procedure ensuring the wiring connectors are securely reconnected.

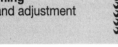

## 4 Ignition timing – checking and adjustment

**1** There are no timing marks on the flywheel or crankshaft pulley. The timing is constantly being monitored and adjusted by the engine management ECU, and nominal values cannot be given. Therefore, it is not possible for the home mechanic to check the ignition timing.
**2** The only way in which the ignition timing can be checked is using special electronic test equipment, connected to the engine management system diagnostic connector (see Section 2 or refer to Chapter 4A for further information).

## 5 Knock sensor – removal and refitting

## Removal

**1** The knock sensor is screwed into the rear face of the cylinder block.
**2** Firmly apply the handbrake, then jack up the front of the vehicle and support it securely on axle stands (see *Jacking and vehicle support*). Undo the screws and remove the engine undershield (where fitted).
**3** Depending on the type of knock sensor fitted, either trace the wiring back from the

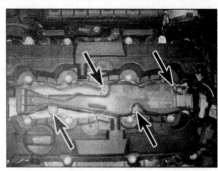

**3.8 Undo the four coil unit retaining screws (arrowed)**

sensor to its wiring connector, and disconnect it from the main loom, or disconnect the wiring connector directly from the sensor.
**4** Undo the sensor securing bolt and remove the sensor from the cylinder block.

## Refitting

**5** Refitting is a reversal of the removal procedure, ensuring that the sensor securing bolt is tightened to the specified torque.

# Chapter 5 Part C:
# Pre/post-heating system – diesel models

## Contents

## Degrees of difficulty

| **Easy,** suitable for novice with little experience | **Fairly easy,** suitable for beginner with some experience | **Fairly difficult,** suitable for competent DIY mechanic | **Difficult,** suitable for experienced DIY mechanic | **Very difficult,** suitable for expert DIY or professional |
|---|---|---|---|---|

## Specifications

### Glow plugs

| | |
|---|---|
| Resistance (typical) . . . . . . . . . . . . . . . . . . . . . . . . . . . . . . . . . . . . . . | 1 ohm approximately |
| Type . . . . . . . . . . . . . . . . . . . . . . . . . . . . . . . . . . . . . . . . . . . . . . . . . . | NGK YE04 |

### Torque wrench setting

| | Nm | lbf ft |
|---|---|---|
| Glow plugs: | | |
| SOHC engines . . . . . . . . . . . . . . . . . . . . . . . . . . . . . . . . . . . . . . . . | 8 | 6 |
| DOHC engines . . . . . . . . . . . . . . . . . . . . . . . . . . . . . . . . . . . . . . . . | 9 | 7 |

**1  Pre/post-heating system –**
   description and testing

### Description

**1** To assist cold starting, diesel engines are fitted with a preheating system, which consists of four of glow plugs (one per cylinder), a glow plug relay unit, a facia-mounted warning lamp, the engine management ECU, and the associated electrical wiring.
**2** The glow plugs are miniature electric heating elements, encapsulated in a metal case with a probe at one end and electrical connection at the other. Each combustion chamber has one glow plug threaded into it, with the tip of the glow plug probe positioned directly in line with incoming spray of fuel from the injectors. When the glow plug is energised, it heats up rapidly, causing the fuel passing over the glow plug probe to be heated to its optimum temperature, ready for combustion. In addition, some of the fuel passing over the glow plugs is ignited and this helps to trigger the combustion process.
**3** The preheating system begins to operate as soon as the ignition key is switched to the second position, but only if the engine coolant temperature is below 20°C and the engine is turned at more than 70 rpm for 0.2 seconds. A facia-mounted warning lamp informs the driver that preheating is

taking place. The lamp extinguishes when sufficient preheating has taken place to allow the engine to be started, but power will still be supplied to the glow plugs for a further period until the engine is started. If no attempt is made to start the engine, the power supply to the glow plugs is switched off after 10 seconds, to prevent battery drain and glow plug burn-out.
**4** With the electronically-controlled diesel injection systems fitted to all diesel models in this manual, the glow plug relay unit is controlled by the engine management system ECU, which determines the necessary preheating time based on inputs from the various system sensors. The system monitors the temperature of the intake air, then alters the preheating time (the length for which the glow plugs are supplied with current) to suit the conditions.
**5** Post-heating takes place after the ignition key has been released from the 'start' position, but only if the engine coolant temperature is below 20°C, the injected fuel flow is less than a certain rate, and the engine speed is less than 2000 rpm. The glow plugs continue to operate for a maximum of 60 seconds, helping to improve fuel combustion whilst the engine is warming-up, resulting in quieter, smoother running and reduced exhaust emissions.

### Testing

**6** If the system malfunctions, testing is ultimately by substitution of known good

units, but a preliminary check may be made as follows.
**7** To gain access to the glow plugs for testing, remove the following components, according to model:

#### 8-valve engines

a) Remove the cylinder head cover/manifold assembly as described in Chapter 2B.

#### 16-valve engines

a) Remove the air cleaner assembly and inlet ducts as described in Chapter 4B.
b) Remove the EGR pipe as described in Chapter 4C.
c) Undo the nut and retaining bolt and remove the air cleaner support bracket from the rear of the cylinder head.

**8** Disconnect the main supply cable and the interconnecting wire from the top of the glow plugs. Be careful not to drop the nuts and washers.
**9** Use a continuity tester, or a 12 volt test lamp connected to the battery positive terminal, to check for continuity between each glow plug terminal and earth. The resistance of a glow plug in good condition is very low (less than 1 ohm), so if the test lamp does not light or the continuity tester shows a high resistance, the glow plug is certainly defective.
**10** As a further check, the glow plugs can be removed and inspected as described in the following Section. On completion, refit the components removed for access, with reference to the Chapters indicated.

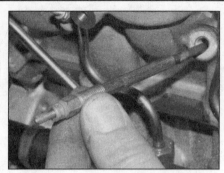

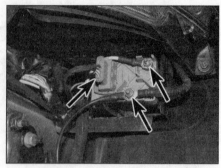

**2.2  Undo the nuts securing the glow plug connections (arrowed)**

**2.4  Unscrew the glow plugs from the cylinder head**

**3.4  Electrical connections (arrowed) at the pre/post-heating system relay unit**

### 2  Glow plugs – removal, inspection and refitting

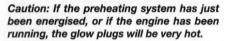

*Caution: If the preheating system has just been energised, or if the engine has been running, the glow plugs will be very hot.*

#### Removal

**1** To gain access to the glow plugs, remove the components described in Section 1, according to engine.

**2** Unscrew the nuts from the glow plug terminals, and recover the washers **(see illustration)**. Be careful not to drop the nuts and washers. Disconnect the main supply cable and the interconnecting wire from the top of the glow plugs.

**3** Where applicable, carefully move any obstructing pipes or wires to one side to enable access to the relevant glow plug(s).

**4** Unscrew the glow plug(s) and remove from the cylinder head **(see illustration)**.

#### Inspection

**5** Inspect each glow plug for physical damage. Burnt or eroded glow plug tips can be caused by a bad injector spray pattern. Have the injectors checked if this sort of damage is found.

**6** If the glow plugs are in good physical con-dition, check them electrically using a 12 volt test lamp or continuity tester as described in the previous Section.

**7** The glow plugs can be energised by applying 12 volts to them to verify that they heat up evenly and in the required time. Observe the following precautions.

*a) Support the glow plug by clamping it carefully in a vice or self-locking pliers. Remember it will become red-hot.*

*b) Make sure that the power supply or test lead incorporates a fuse or overload trip to protect against damage from a short-circuit.*

*c) After testing, allow the glow plug to cool for several minutes before attempting to handle it.*

**8** A glow plug in good condition will start to glow red at the tip after drawing current for 5 seconds or so. Any plug which takes much longer to start glowing, or which starts glowing in the middle instead of at the tip, is defective.

#### Refitting

**9** Refit by reversing the removal operations. Apply a smear of copper-based anti-seize compound to the plug threads and tighten the glow plugs to the specified torque. Do not overtighten, as this can damage the glow plug element.

**10** Refit the components removed for access, with reference to the Chapters indicated.

### 3  Pre/post-heating system relay unit – removal and refitting

#### Removal

**1** The unit is located under the bumper on the left-hand side of the car, behind the head-light.

**2** Disconnect the battery (see Chapter 5A).

**3** Remove the front bumper as described in Chapter 11, and the left-hand headlight unit as described in Chapter 12.

**4** Unscrew the two retaining nuts and free the main feed and supply wires from the unit, then disconnect the wiring connector **(see illustration)**.

**5** Unscrew the retaining nut securing the unit to the mounting bracket, then remove the unit from under the front wing.

#### Refitting

**6** Refitting is a reversal of removal, ensuring that the wiring connectors are correctly connected. Refit the headlight unit and front bumper as described in Chapters 12 and 11 respectively.

# Chapter 6
# Clutch

## Contents

## Degrees of difficulty

| | | | | |
|---|---|---|---|---|
| **Easy,** suitable for novice with little experience  | **Fairly easy,** suitable for beginner with some experience | **Fairly difficult,** suitable for competent DIY mechanic | **Difficult,** suitable for experienced DIY mechanic | **Very difficult,** suitable for expert DIY or professional  |

## Specifications

### Type
All models. . . . . . . . . . . . . . . . . . . . . . . . . . . . . . . . . . . . . . . . . . . . Single dry disc with diaphragm spring, hydraulic operation

### Clutch operation
All models. . . . . . . . . . . . . . . . . . . . . . . . . . . . . . . . . . . . . . . . . . . Hydraulic

### Friction disc diameter
Petrol engine models:
  SOHC engines . . . . . . . . . . . . . . . . . . . . . . . . . . . . . . . . . . . . . . 180 mm
  DOHC engines . . . . . . . . . . . . . . . . . . . . . . . . . . . . . . . . . . . . . . 200 mm
Diesel engine models:
  SOHC engines . . . . . . . . . . . . . . . . . . . . . . . . . . . . . . . . . . . . . . 200 mm
  DOHC engines:
    DV4TED4 . . . . . . . . . . . . . . . . . . . . . . . . . . . . . . . . . . . . . . . . 228 mm
    DV6TED4 (dual mass flywheel). . . . . . . . . . . . . . . . . . . . . . . . . 235 mm
    DV6ATED4 . . . . . . . . . . . . . . . . . . . . . . . . . . . . . . . . . . . . . . . 225 mm

### Torque wrench settings

| | Nm | lbf ft |
|---|---|---|
| Pressure plate retaining bolts: | | |
| SOHC petrol engine models. . . . . . . . . . . . . . . . . . . . . . . . . . . . . | 12 | 9 |
| DOHC petrol engine models. . . . . . . . . . . . . . . . . . . . . . . . . . . . . | 20 | 15 |
| Diesel engine models . . . . . . . . . . . . . . . . . . . . . . . . . . . . . . . . . . | 20 | 15 |

## 1 General information

The clutch consists of a friction disc, a pressure plate assembly, a release bearing and release fork; all of these components are contained in the large cast-aluminium alloy bellhousing, sandwiched between the engine and the transmission. The release mechanism is hydraulic on all models.

The friction disc is fitted between the engine flywheel and the clutch pressure plate, and is allowed to slide on the transmission input shaft splines.

The pressure plate assembly is bolted to the engine flywheel. When the engine is running, drive is transmitted from the crankshaft, via the flywheel, to the friction disc (these components being clamped securely together by the pressure plate assembly) and from the friction disc to the transmission input shaft.

To interrupt the drive, the spring pressure must be relaxed. This is done by means of the clutch release bearing, fitted concentrically around the transmission input shaft. The bearing is pushed onto the pressure plate assembly by means of the release fork actuated by the clutch slave cylinder pushrod.

The clutch pedal is connected to the clutch master cylinder by a short pushrod. The master cylinder is mounted on the engine side of the bulkhead in front of the driver and receives its hydraulic fluid supply from the brake master cylinder reservoir. Depressing the clutch pedal moves the piston in the master cylinder forwards, so forcing hydraulic fluid through the clutch hydraulic pipe to the slave cylinder. The piston in the slave cylinder moves forward on the entry of the fluid and actuates the clutch release fork by means of a short pushrod. The release fork pivots on its mounting stud, and the other end of the fork then presses the release bearing against the pressure plate spring fingers. This causes the springs to deform and releases the clamping force on the pressure plate.

On all models the clutch operating mechanism is self-adjusting, and no manual adjustment is required.

**2.3 Remove the dust cap from the bleed screw**

## 2  Clutch hydraulic system – bleeding

⚠️ *Warning: Hydraulic fluid is poisonous; wash off immediately and thoroughly in the case of skin contact, and seek immediate medical advice if any fluid is swallowed or gets into the eyes. Certain types of hydraulic fluid are inflammable, and may ignite when allowed into contact with hot components; when servicing any hydraulic system, it is safest to assume that the fluid IS inflammable, and to take precautions against the risk of fire as though it is petrol that is being handled. Hydraulic fluid is also an effective paint stripper, and will attack plastics; if any is spilt, it should be washed off immediately, using copious quantities of clean water. When topping-up or renewing the fluid, always use the recommended type, and ensure that it comes from a freshly-opened sealed container.*

1 Obtain a clean jar, a suitable length of rubber or clear plastic tubing, which is a tight fit over the bleed screw on the clutch slave cylinder, and a tin of the specified hydraulic fluid. The help of an assistant will also be required. (If a one-man do-it-yourself bleeding kit for bleeding the brake hydraulic system is available, this can be used quite satisfactorily for the clutch also. Full information on the use of these kits may be found in Chapter 9.)

2 Remove the filler cap from the brake master cylinder reservoir, and if necessary top-up the fluid. Keep the reservoir topped-up during subsequent operations.

3 Remove the dust cap from the slave cylinder bleed screw, located on the lower front facing side of the transmission **(see illustration)**.

4 Connect one end of the bleed tube to the bleed screw, and insert the other end of the tube in the jar containing sufficient clean hydraulic fluid to keep the end of the tube submerged.

5 Open the bleed screw half a turn and have your assistant depress the clutch pedal and then slowly release it. Continue this procedure until clean hydraulic fluid, free from air bubbles, emerges from the tube. Now tighten the bleed screw at the end of a downstroke. Make sure that the brake master cylinder reservoir is checked frequently to ensure that the level does not drop too far, allowing air into the system.

6 Check the operation of the clutch pedal. After a few strokes it should feel normal. Any sponginess would indicate air still present in the system.

7 On completion remove the bleed tube and refit the dust cover. Top-up the master cylinder reservoir if necessary and refit the cap. Fluid expelled from the hydraulic system should now be discarded as it will be contaminated with moisture, air and dirt, making it unsuitable for further use.

## 3  Clutch master cylinder – removal and refitting

**Note:** *Before starting work, refer to the note at the beginning of Section 2 concerning the dangers of hydraulic fluid.*

### Removal

1 Remove the lower facia panel on the driver's side, as described in Chapter 11.

2 On left-hand drive models, remove the battery and battery box as described in Chapter 5A.

3 Depress the clutch pedal until the end of the master cylinder pushrod is visible though the hole in the side of the pedal bracket. Using a screwdriver, prise the end of the pushrod from the pedal pin **(see illustration 5.2)**.

4 To minimise hydraulic fluid loss, remove the brake master cylinder reservoir filler cap then tighten it down onto a piece of polythene to obtain an airtight seal.

5 Place absorbent rags under the clutch master cylinder pipe connections in the engine compartment and be prepared for hydraulic fluid loss.

6 Release the master cylinder hydraulic pressure pipe from its retaining clips on the engine compartment bulkhead, then prise out the retaining wire clip and disconnect the pipe from the master cylinder **(see illustration)**. Suitably plug or cap the pipe end to prevent further fluid loss and dirt entry.

7 Disconnect the hydraulic fluid supply hose from the master cylinder and suitably plug or cap the hose end.

8 Rotate the master cylinder 90 degrees clockwise, and remove it from the bulkhead **(see illustration)**.

### Refitting

9 Refitting the master cylinder is the reverse sequence to removal, bearing in mind the following points.

   a) *Ensure all retaining clips are correctly refitted.*
   b) *Bleed the clutch hydraulic system as described in Section 2 on completion.*
   c) *Refit the components removed for access with reference to the Chapters indicated.*

## 4  Clutch slave cylinder – removal and refitting

**Note:** *Before starting work, refer to the note at the beginning of Section 2 concerning the dangers of hydraulic fluid.*

### Removal

1 To minimise hydraulic fluid loss, remove the brake master cylinder reservoir filler cap then tighten it down onto a piece of polythene to obtain an airtight seal.

2 Place absorbent rags under the clutch slave cylinder located on the lower front facing side of the transmission. Be prepared for hydraulic fluid loss.

3 Where necessary for access, release the wiring harness from the retaining clips and move the harness clear of the slave cylinder.

4 Lever out the retaining clip a little, then disconnect the hydraulic pipe from the side of the slave cylinder **(see illustration)**. Suitably

**3.6 Prise out the clip, and disconnect the pipe from the master cylinder**

**3.8 Turn the master cylinder 90° clockwise, and remove it from the bulkhead**

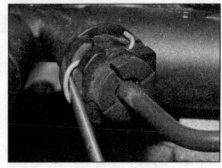

**4.4 Lever out the hydraulic pipe retaining clip**

**4.5 Undo the two bolts (arrowed) and remove the clutch slave cylinder**

**5.2 Prise the end of the pushrod from the pedal pin**

**5.4 The clutch pedal bolt (arrowed) is also the pivot for the brake pedal**

plug or cap the pipe end to prevent further fluid loss and dirt entry.

**5** Undo the two retaining bolts, and remove the cylinder from the transmission housing **(see illustration)**.

### Refitting

**6** Refitting the slave cylinder is the reverse sequence to removal, bearing in mind the following points.
a) Apply a little Molykote BR2 Plus grease to the end of the slave cylinder pushrod.
b) Bleed the clutch hydraulic system as described in Section 2 on completion.

## 5 Clutch pedal –
removal and refitting

### Removal

**1** Remove the lower facia panel on the driver's side, as described in Chapter 11.

**2** Depress the clutch pedal until the end of the master cylinder pushrod is visible though the hole in the side of the pedal bracket. Using a screwdriver, prise the end of the pushrod from the pedal pin **(see illustration)**.

**3** Using a screwdriver, compress the helper spring a little, and remove it from the pedal and pedal bracket.

**4** Undo the nut from the clutch pedal pivot bolt and withdraw the bolt **(see illustration)**. Note that the bolt also provides a pivot for the brake pedal.

**5** Remove the clutch pedal from the pedal bracket and recover the bush from the pedal pivot.

**6** Check the condition of the pedal, pivot bush and helper spring assembly and renew any components as necessary.

### Refitting

**7** Lubricate the pedal pivot bolt with multi-purpose grease, then locate the pedal in the bracket and insert the pivot bolt. Refit the pivot bolt nut and tighten it securely.

**8** Reconnect the helper spring to the pedal and pedal bracket.

**9** Depress the pedal two or three times and check the operation of the clutch release mechanism.

**10** Refit the lower facia panel as described in Chapter 11.

## 6 Clutch assembly –
removal, inspection and refitting

**⚠ Warning: Dust created by clutch wear and deposited on the clutch components may contain asbestos, which is a health hazard. DON'T blow it out with compressed air, nor inhale any of it. DO NOT use petrol or petroleum-based solvents to clean off the dust. Brake system cleaner or methylated spirit should be used to flush the dust into a suitable receptacle. After the clutch components are wiped clean with rags, dispose of the contaminated rags and cleaner in a sealed, marked container.**
Note: *Although most friction materials no longer contain asbestos, it is safest to assume that some still do, and to take precautions accordingly.*

### Removal

**1** Unless the complete engine/transmission unit is to be removed from the car and separated for major overhaul (see Chapter 2C), the clutch can be reached by removing the transmission as described in Chapter 7A.

**2** Before disturbing the clutch, use chalk or a marker pen to mark the relationship of the pressure plate assembly to the flywheel.

**3** Working in a diagonal sequence, slacken the pressure plate bolts by half a turn at a time,

**6.3 Undo the pressure plate bolts (arrowed)**

until spring pressure is released and the bolts can be unscrewed by hand **(see illustration)**.

**4** Prise the pressure plate assembly off its locating dowels, and collect the friction disc, noting which way round the disc is fitted.

### Inspection

Note: *Due to the amount of work necessary to remove and refit clutch components, it is considered good practice to renew the clutch friction disc, pressure plate assembly and release bearing as a matched set, even if only one of these is worn enough to require renewal. It is worth considering the renewal of the clutch components on a preventative basis if the engine and/or transmission have been removed for some other reason.*

**5** When cleaning clutch components, read first the warning at the beginning of this Section; remove dust using a clean, dry cloth, and working in a well-ventilated atmosphere.

**6** Check the friction disc facings for signs of wear, damage or oil contamination. If the friction material is cracked, burnt, scored or damaged, or if it is contaminated with oil or grease (shown by shiny black patches), the friction disc must be renewed.

**7** If the friction material is still serviceable, check that the centre boss splines are unworn, that the torsion springs are in good condition and securely fastened, and that all the rivets are tight. If any wear or damage is found, the friction disc must be renewed.

**8** If the friction material is fouled with oil, this must be due to an oil leak from the crankshaft left-hand oil seal, from the sump-to-cylinder block joint, or from the transmission input shaft. Renew the seal or repair the joint, as appropriate, as described in the relevant Part of Chapter 2 or 7, before installing the new friction disc.

**9** Check the pressure plate assembly for obvious signs of wear or damage; shake it to check for loose rivets or worn or damaged fulcrum rings, and check that the drive straps securing the pressure plate to the cover do not show signs (such as a deep yellow or blue discoloration) of overheating. If the diaphragm spring is worn or damaged, or if its pressure is in any way suspect, the pressure plate assembly should be renewed.

**10** Examine the machined bearing surfaces

**6.13 Fit the disc so the spring hub assembly faces away from the flywheel**

**6.16 Using a clutch aligning tool to centralise the friction disc**

used to eliminate the guesswork; these can be obtained from most accessory shops **(see illustration)**.

> **HAYNES HiNT** *A home-made aligning tool can be fabricated from a length of metal rod or wooden dowel which fits closely inside the crankshaft hole, and has insulating tape wound around it to match the diameter of the friction disc splined hole.*

of the pressure plate and of the flywheel; they should be clean, completely flat, and free from scratches or scoring. If either is discoloured from excessive heat, or shows signs of cracks, it should be renewed – although minor damage of this nature can sometimes be polished away using emery paper.

**11** Check that the release bearing contact surface rotates smoothly and easily, with no sign of noise or roughness. Also check that the surface itself is smooth and unworn, with no signs of cracks, pitting or scoring. If there is any doubt about its condition, the bearing must be renewed.

### Refitting

**12** On reassembly, ensure that the bearing surfaces of the flywheel and pressure plate are completely clean, smooth, and free from oil or grease. Use solvent to remove any protective grease from new components.

**13** Fit the friction disc so that its spring hub assembly faces away from the flywheel; there may be a marking showing which way round the disc is to be refitted **(see illustration)**.

**14** Refit the pressure plate assembly, aligning the marks made on dismantling (if the original pressure plate is re-used), and locating the pressure plate on its three locating dowels. Fit the pressure plate bolts, but tighten them only finger-tight, so that the friction disc can still be moved.

**15** The friction disc must now be centralised, so that when the transmission is refitted, its input shaft will pass through the splines at the centre of the friction disc.

**16** Centralisation can be achieved by passing a screwdriver or other long bar through the friction disc and into the hole in the crankshaft; the friction disc can then be moved around until it is centred on the crankshaft hole. Alternatively, a clutch-aligning tool can be

**17** When the friction disc is centralised, tighten the pressure plate bolts evenly and in a diagonal sequence to the specified torque setting.

**18** Apply a **thin** smear of molybdenum disulphide grease (Citroën recommend the use of Molykote BR2 Plus – available from your dealer) to the splines of the friction disc and the transmission input shaft, and also to the release bearing bore and release fork shaft.

**19** Refit the transmission as described in Chapter 7A.

### 7 Clutch release mechanism – removal, inspection and refitting

**Note:** *Refer to the warning concerning the dangers of asbestos dust at the beginning of Section 7.*

### Removal

**1** Unless the complete engine/transmission unit is to be removed from the car and separated for major overhaul (see Chapter 2C), the clutch release mechanism can be reached by removing the transmission only, as described in Chapter 7A.

**2** With the transmission removed, squeeze together the tabs of the retaining clip and pull the release fork off the pivot ball-stud. Recover the shim where fitted. The mounting stud unscrews from the transmission housing **(see illustrations)**.

**3** Slide the release bearing off the guide tube and disengage the arms of the release fork **(see illustration)**.

### Inspection

**4** Check that the release bearing contact surface rotates smoothly and easily, with no sign of noise or roughness, and that the surface itself is smooth and unworn, with no signs of cracks, pitting or scoring. If there is any doubt about its condition, the bearing must be renewed.

**5** Check the bearing surfaces and points of contact on the release fork and pivot ball-stud, renewing any component which is worn or damaged.

### Refitting

**6** Apply a smear of molybdenum disulphide grease to the pivot ball-stud.

**7.2a Squeeze the tabs of the retaining clip together and remove the release fork . . .**

**7.2b . . . recover the shim (arrowed) . . .**

**7.2c . . . then unscrew the pivot ball-stud**

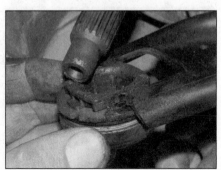

**7.3 Disengage the release bearing from the release fork**

**7** Insert the outer end of the release fork through the rubber boot in the side of the transmission bellhousing.

**8** Engage the arms of the release fork with the release bearing collar, then slide the release bearing onto the guide tube.

**9** Position the shim over the tabs of the pivot ball-stud clip, then push the fork over the stud, ensuring the tabs of the retaining clip engage correctly with the fork **(see illustration)**.

**10** Refit the transmission as described in Chapter 7A.

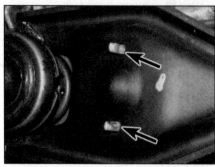

**7.9 Ensure the retaining tabs (arrowed) engage correctly with the release fork**

# Chapter 7 Part A:
# Manual transmission

## Contents

## Degrees of difficulty

| Easy, suitable for novice with little experience  | Fairly easy, suitable for beginner with some experience | Fairly difficult, suitable for competent DIY mechanic | Difficult, suitable for experienced DIY mechanic | Very difficult, suitable for expert DIY or professional  |

## Specifications

### General

| | |
|---|---|
| Type . . . . . . . . . . . . . . . . . . . . . . . . . . . . . . . . . . . . . . . . . . . . . . . . . | Manual, five forward speeds and reverse. Synchromesh on all forward speeds |

Designation:
  Petrol models . . . . . . . . . . . . . . . . . . . . . . . . . . . . . . . . . . . . . . . . .   MA5
  Diesel models:
    SOHC (8-valve) engines . . . . . . . . . . . . . . . . . . . . . . . . . . . . . . . .   MA5
    DOHC (16-valve) engines . . . . . . . . . . . . . . . . . . . . . . . . . . . . . . .   BE4/5
Transmission code:
  Petrol models:
    1.1 litre engines. . . . . . . . . . . . . . . . . . . . . . . . . . . . . . . . . . . . . .   20CF14
    1.4 litre engines. . . . . . . . . . . . . . . . . . . . . . . . . . . . . . . . . . . . . .   20CF15, 20CF16
    1.6 litre engines. . . . . . . . . . . . . . . . . . . . . . . . . . . . . . . . . . . . . .   20CN40
  Diesel models:
    SOHC (8-valve) engines . . . . . . . . . . . . . . . . . . . . . . . . . . . . . . . .   20CN33, 20CN36
    DOHC (16-valve) engines . . . . . . . . . . . . . . . . . . . . . . . . . . . . . . .   20DM25, 20DM26

**Note:** *Transmission code is stamped on either the front of the clutch housing, or on the front face of the transmission housing.*

### Lubrication

Capacity (after draining):
  MA5 . . . . . . . . . . . . . . . . . . . . . . . . . . . . . . . . . . . . . . . . . . . . . . . .   2.0 litres
  BE4/5 . . . . . . . . . . . . . . . . . . . . . . . . . . . . . . . . . . . . . . . . . . . . . .   1.8 litres
Recommended oil type . . . . . . . . . . . . . . . . . . . . . . . . . . . . . . . . . .   See *Lubricants and fluids*

### Torque wrench settings

| | Nm | lbf ft |
|---|---|---|
| **MA5 transmission** | | |
| Clutch release bearing guide sleeve bolts . . . . . . . . . . . . . . . . . . . . | 12 | 9 |
| Engine-to-transmission fixing bolts . . . . . . . . . . . . . . . . . . . . . . . . . . | 40 | 30 |
| Gearchange lever mounting nuts . . . . . . . . . . . . . . . . . . . . . . . . . . . | 8 | 6 |
| Left-hand engine/transmission mounting. . . . . . . . . . . . . . . . . . . . . . | Refer to Chapter 2A or 2B | |
| Oil drain plug . . . . . . . . . . . . . . . . . . . . . . . . . . . . . . . . . . . . . . . . . . | 33 | 24 |
| Oil filler/level plug (where fitted) . . . . . . . . . . . . . . . . . . . . . . . . . . . | 25 | 18 |
| Rear mounting link . . . . . . . . . . . . . . . . . . . . . . . . . . . . . . . . . . . . . . | Refer to Chapter 2A or 2B | |
| Reversing light switch . . . . . . . . . . . . . . . . . . . . . . . . . . . . . . . . . . . | 25 | 18 |
| Roadwheel bolts. . . . . . . . . . . . . . . . . . . . . . . . . . . . . . . . . . . . . . . . | 90 | 66 |
| Speedometer drive pinion bracket. . . . . . . . . . . . . . . . . . . . . . . . . . | 10 | 7 |

## Torque wrench settings (continued)

| | Nm | lbf ft |
|---|---|---|
| **BE4/5 transmission** | | |
| Clutch release bearing guide sleeve bolts . . . . . . . . . . . . . . . . . . . . . . | 12 | 9 |
| Engine-to-transmission fixing bolts . . . . . . . . . . . . . . . . . . . . . . . . . . . | 45 | 33 |
| Gearchange lever mounting nuts . . . . . . . . . . . . . . . . . . . . . . . . . . . . . | 8 | 6 |
| Left-hand engine/transmission mounting. . . . . . . . . . . . . . . . . . . . . . . | Refer to Chapter 2B or 2C | |
| Oil drain plug . . . . . . . . . . . . . . . . . . . . . . . . . . . . . . . . . . . . . . . . . . . . | 35 | 26 |
| Oil filler/level plug . . . . . . . . . . . . . . . . . . . . . . . . . . . . . . . . . . . . . . . . | 20 | 15 |
| Rear mounting link . . . . . . . . . . . . . . . . . . . . . . . . . . . . . . . . . . . . . . . . | Refer to Chapter 2B or 2C | |
| Reversing light switch . . . . . . . . . . . . . . . . . . . . . . . . . . . . . . . . . . . . | 25 | 18 |
| Roadwheel bolts. . . . . . . . . . . . . . . . . . . . . . . . . . . . . . . . . . . . . . . . . . | 90 | 66 |
| Speedometer drive housing bolts . . . . . . . . . . . . . . . . . . . . . . . . . . . . | 15 | 11 |

## 1  General information

**1** The transmission is contained in a cast-aluminium alloy casing bolted to the engine's left-hand end, and consists of the gearbox and final drive differential – often called a transaxle.
**2** Drive is transmitted from the crankshaft via the clutch to the input shaft, which has a splined extension to accept the clutch friction disc, and rotates in sealed ball-bearings. From the input shaft, drive is transmitted to the output shaft, which rotates in a roller bearing at its right-hand end, and a sealed ball-bearing at its left-hand end. From the output shaft, the drive is transmitted to the differential crownwheel, which rotates with the differential case and planetary gears, thus driving the sun gears and driveshafts. The rotation of the planetary gears on their shaft allows the inner

roadwheel to rotate at a slower speed than the outer roadwheel when the car is cornering.
**3** The input and output shafts are arranged side-by-side, parallel to the crankshaft and driveshafts, so that their gear pinion teeth are in constant mesh. In the neutral position, the output shaft gear pinions rotate freely, so that drive cannot be transmitted to the crownwheel.
**4** Gear selection is via a floor-mounted lever and cable mechanism **(see illustration)**. The selector/gearchange cables causes the appropriate selector fork to move its respective synchro-sleeve along the shaft, to lock the gear pinion to the synchro-hub. Since the synchro-hubs are splined to the output shaft, this locks the pinion to the shaft, so that drive can be transmitted. To ensure that gearchanging can be made quickly and quietly, a synchromesh system is fitted to all forward gears, consisting of baulk rings and spring-loaded fingers, as well as the gear pinions and synchro-hubs. The synchromesh

cones are formed on the mating faces of the baulk rings and gear pinions.
**5** Two different manual transmissions are used on the models covered in this manual; all petrol engine models and 8-valve diesel engine models have the MA5 transmission, whereas 16-valve diesel engine models are fitted with the BE4/5 unit.
**6** Both of the transmissions used are 'filled-for-life' with fluid – there's no recommended interval for changing the fluid, although it may be prudent to do so at some stage in the vehicle's life. During each service, it is advised to check around the transmission for signs of any leaks.

## 2  Manual transmission – draining and refilling

**Note:** *On later MA transmissions, the oil level cannot be checked, as there is no filler/level plug fitted. These transmissions do not require regular maintenance and are filled for life. If the transmission develops a leak or is removed for other work, the oil needs to be completely drained and the transmission refilled with the correct amount of oil. The transmission is then refilled through the vent/breather on the top of the transmission. For checking the level on earlier models, see Chapter 1A or 1B.*
**Note:** *A suitable square section wrench may be required to undo the transmission filler/level and drain plugs on some models. These wrenches can be obtained from most motor factors or your Citroën dealer.*
**1** This operation is much quicker and more efficient if the car is first taken on a journey of sufficient length to warm the engine/transmission up to normal operating temperature.
**2** Park the car on level ground, switch off the ignition and apply the handbrake firmly. For improved access, jack up the front of the car and support it securely on axle stands (see *Jacking and vehicle support*). Note that the car must be level to ensure accuracy when refilling and checking the oil level. Undo the screws and remove the engine undershield (where fitted).
**3** To improve access to the filler/level plug, remove the plastic rivets (push in the centre pin a little then remove the complete plastic rivet) and remove the left-hand wheel arch liner.
**Note:** *On later MA transmissions remove the air cleaner/air ducting as applicable for access to*

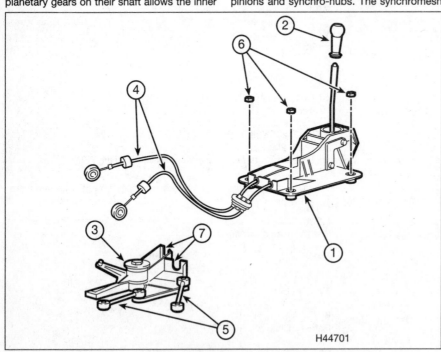

**1.4  Gearchange lever and cables**

| | | |
|---|---|---|
| 1 *Gearchange lever and housing* | 3 *Bracket* | 6 *Nuts* |
| | 4 *Cables* | 7 *Horseshoe clips* |
| 2 *Gearchange lever knob* | 5 *Gearchange links* | |

H44701

*the vent/breather on the top of the transmission
– pull the cap directly from the vent hole.*

**4** Wipe clean the area around the filler/
level plug, which is situated on the left-hand
end of the transmission, next to the end
cover. Unscrew the filler/level plug from the
transmission and recover the sealing washer
**(see illustrations)**.

**5** Position a suitable container under
the drain plug (situated at the rear of the
transmission) and unscrew the plug. On
MA5 gearboxes, the plug is on the left-hand
side of the differential housing; on BE4/5
gearboxes, it is on the base of the differential
housing **(see illustrations)**.

**6** Allow the oil to drain completely into the
container. If the oil is hot, take precautions
against scalding. Clean both the filler/level and
the drain plugs, being especially careful to wipe
any metallic particles off the magnetic inserts.
Discard the original sealing washers; they should
be renewed whenever they are disturbed.

**7** When the oil has finished draining, clean the
drain plug threads and those of the transmission
casing, fit a new sealing washer and refit the
drain plug, tightening it to the specified torque
wrench setting. Refit the undercover (where
fitted) then lower the vehicle to the ground.

**8** Refilling the transmission is an extremely
awkward operation. Above all, allow plenty of
time for the oil level to settle properly before
checking it. Note that the car must be parked on
flat level ground when checking the oil level.

**9** Refill the transmission with the exact amount
of the specified type of oil then check the
oil level as described in the relevant part of
Chapter 1; if the correct amount was poured
into the transmission and a large amount
flows out on checking the level, refit the filler/
level plug and take the car on a short journey
so that the new oil is distributed fully around
the transmission components, then check the
level again on your return. Once the oil level
is correct, securely refit the inner cover/wheel
arch liner/air cleaner/air ducting (as applicable).

---

### 3 Gearchange lever and cables – removal and refitting

#### Removal

**1** Firmly apply the handbrake, then jack up
the front of the vehicle and support it on axle
stands (see *Jacking and vehicle support*).

**2** Remove the centre console as described in
Chapter 11.

**3** Undo the four nuts securing the gearchange
lever housing to the floor **(see illustration)**.

**4** Remove the air cleaner assembly and inlet
ducts as described in Chapter 4A or 4B.

**5** Remove the battery and battery box, as
described in Chapter 5A.

**6** Working in the engine compartment, note
their fitted locations, then carefully prise the
two gearchange cable balljoints from the
selector levers on the transmission.

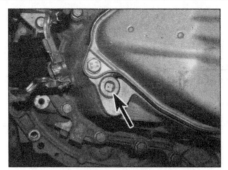
**2.4a  Oil filler/level plug (arrowed)
(MA5 transmission)**

**2.4b  Oil filler/level plug
(BE4/5 transmission)**

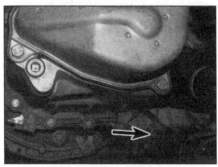
**2.5a  Oil drain plug (arrowed)
(MA5 transmission)**

**2.5b  Oil drain plug
(BE4/5 transmission)**

**7** Working underneath the vehicle, remove the
front exhaust pipe heat shield fasteners, and
allow the shield to rest on the exhaust pipe.

**8** Using a small screwdriver, press down the
two horseshoe-shaped retaining clips upper
tangs, then lever or pull the cables upwards

and release them from the support bracket
**(see illustrations)**.

**9** Release the cable sealing grommet from
the floor, and manoeuvre the lever, housing
and cables assembly from the vehicle **(see
illustration)**.

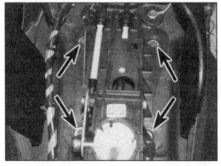
**3.3  Undo the four nuts (arrowed) securing
the gear lever housing to the floor**

**3.8a  Depress the clip tabs and lever the
cable outer upwards**

**3.8b  The cable retaining clip tabs
(arrowed) – shown with the cable removed**

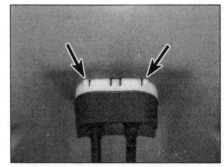
**3.9  Depress the clips (arrowed) and release
the cable sealing grommet from the floor**

**10** To release the cables from the lever housing, lever the cable balljoint from the lever, then depress the clips and pull the cable up from the housing (see illustrations)

**11** The gearchange lever is integral with the housing, and is not available separately.

### Refitting

**12** Refitting is a reversal of the removal procedure, noting the following points:

a) Tie the two cables together to make it easier to pass them through the floor to their correct locations.

b) Apply grease to the balljoints before refitting.

c) No adjustment of the gearchange cables is possible.

## 4 Oil seals – renewal

### Driveshaft oil seals

**1** Remove the appropriate driveshaft as described in Chapter 8.

**2** Carefully prise the oil seal out of the transmission, using a large flat-bladed screwdriver (see illustration).

**3** Remove all traces of dirt from the area around the oil seal aperture, then apply a smear of grease to the outer lip of the new oil seal. Fit the new seal into its aperture, and drive it squarely into position using a suitable tubular drift (such as a socket) which bears only on the hard outer edge of the seal, until it abuts its locating shoulder (see illustration).

**4.2 Use a large flat-bladed screwdriver to prise out the driveshaft oil seals**

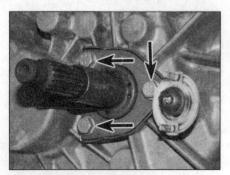

**4.7 Undo the three bolts (arrowed) securing the guide sleeve**

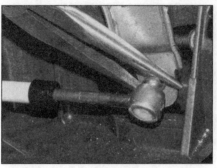

**3.10a Lever the cable balljoint from the lever . . .**

**4** Apply a thin film of grease to the oil seal lip.

**5** Refit the driveshaft as described in Chapter 8.

### Input shaft oil seal

**6** Remove the transmission as described in Section 7, and the clutch release mechanism as described in Chapter 6.

**7** Undo the three bolts securing the clutch release bearing guide sleeve in position, and slide the guide off the input shaft, along with its sealing ring or gasket (as applicable) (see illustration). Recover any shims or thrustwashers which have stuck to the rear of the guide sleeve, and refit them to the input shaft.

**8** Carefully lever the oil seal out of the guide using a suitable flat-bladed screwdriver (see illustration).

**9** Before fitting a new seal, check the input shaft's seal rubbing surface for signs of burrs,

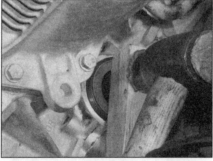

**4.3 Fit the new seal to the transmission, and tap it into position using a tubular drift**

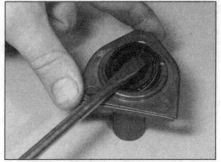

**4.8 Remove the input shaft seal from the guide sleeve**

**3.10b . . . then depress the clips and pull the cable up from the housing**

scratches or other damage, which may have caused the seal to fail in the first place. It may be possible to polish away minor faults of this sort using fine abrasive paper; however, more serious defects will require the renewal of the input shaft. Ensure that the input shaft is clean and greased, to protect the seal lips on refitting.

**10** Dip the new seal in clean oil, and fit it to the guide sleeve.

**11** Fit a new sealing ring or gasket (as applicable) to the rear of the guide sleeve, then carefully slide the sleeve into position over the input shaft. Refit the retaining bolts and tighten them securely (see illustration).

**12** Take the opportunity to inspect the clutch components if not already done (Chapter 6). Finally, refit the transmission as described in Section 7.

### Selector shaft oil seal

#### MA5 transmissions

**13** On these models, to renew the selector shaft seal, the transmission must be dismantled. This task should therefore be entrusted to a Citroën dealer or transmission specialist.

#### BE4/5 transmissions

**14** Park the car on level ground, apply the handbrake, slacken the left-hand front roadwheel bolts, then jack up the front of the vehicle and support it on axle stands (see Jacking and vehicle support). Remove the left-hand front roadwheel.

**15** Using a large flat-bladed screwdriver, lever the link rod balljoint off the transmission selector shaft, and disconnect the link rod.

**4.11 Fit a new O-ring/gasket (as applicable) to the guide sleeve**

**16** Using a large flat-bladed screwdriver, carefully prise the selector shaft seal out of the housing, and slide it off the end of the shaft.

**17** Before fitting a new seal, check the selector shaft's seal rubbing surface for signs of burrs, scratches or other damage, which may have caused the seal to fail in the first place. It may be possible to polish away minor faults of this sort using fine abrasive paper; however, more serious defects will require the renewal of the selector shaft.

**18** Apply a smear of grease to the new seal's outer edge and sealing lip, then carefully slide the seal along the selector rod. Press the seal fully into position in the transmission housing.

**19** Refit the link rod to the selector shaft, ensuring that its balljoint is pressed firmly onto the shaft. Lower the car to the ground.

## 5  Reversing light switch – testing, removal and refitting

### Testing

**1** The reversing light circuit is controlled by a plunger-type switch screwed into the top of the transmission casing. If a fault develops, first ensure that the circuit fuse has not blown.

**2** To gain access to the switch, remove the air cleaner assembly and inlet ducts as described in Chapter 4A or 4B.

**3** To test the switch, disconnect the wiring connector, and use a multimeter (set to the resistance function) or a battery-and-bulb test circuit to check that there is continuity between the switch terminals only when reverse gear is selected. If this is not the case, and there are no obvious breaks or other damage to the wires, the switch is faulty, and must be renewed.

### Removal

**4** To gain access to the switch, remove the air cleaner assembly and inlet ducts as described in Chapter 4A or 4B.

**5** Disconnect the wiring connector, then unscrew the switch from the transmission casing along with its sealing washer **(see illustration)**.

### Refitting

**6** Fit a new sealing washer to the switch, then screw it back into position in the top of the transmission housing and tighten it to the specified torque setting. Refit the wiring plug, and test the operation of the circuit. Refit the components removed for access.

## 6  Speedometer drive – removal and refitting

**Note:** *The speedometer drive assembly is only fitted to models without ABS. On models with ABS, the speedometer receives vehicle speed*

**5.5  Unscrew the reversing light switch from the transmission casing**

*data from the engine management ECU, supplied by the wheel speed sensors and the ABS ECU.*

### Removal

**1** Chock the rear wheels, firmly apply the handbrake, then jack up the front of the car and support it on axle stands (see *Jacking and vehicle support*). The speedometer drive is on the rear of the transmission housing, next to the inner end of the right-hand driveshaft. Undo the screws and remove the engine/transmission undershield (where fitted).

**2** Disconnect the wiring connector from the speedometer drive **(see illustration)**.

**3** Slacken and remove the retaining bolt and remove the heat shield (where fitted). Withdraw the speedometer drive and driven pinion assembly from the transmission housing, along with its sealing ring.

**4** If necessary, the pinion can be slid out of the housing, and the oil seal removed from the top of the housing. Examine the pinion for signs of damage, and renew if necessary. Renew the housing sealing ring as a matter of course.

**5** If the driven pinion is worn or damaged, also examine the drive pinion in the transmission housing for similar signs.

**6** To renew the drive pinion, the transmission must be dismantled and the differential gear removed. This task should therefore be entrusted to a Citroën dealer or a transmission specialist.

### Refitting

**7** Apply a smear of grease to the lips of the

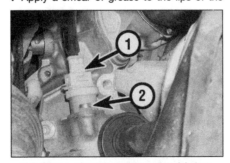

**6.2  Disconnect the wiring plug (1) then undo the retaining bolt (2) and withdraw the speedometer drive assembly**

seal and to the driven pinion shaft, and slide the pinion into position in the speedometer drive.

**8** Fit a new sealing ring to the speedometer drive and refit it to the transmission, ensuring that the drive and driven pinions are correctly engaged. Refit the drive retaining bolt, complete with heat shield (where fitted), and tighten securely.

**9** Reconnect the wiring connector to the speedometer drive then lower the vehicle to the ground.

## 7  Manual transmission – removal and refitting

### Removal

**1** Chock the rear wheels, then firmly apply the handbrake. Slacken both front roadwheel bolts. Jack up the front of the vehicle, and securely support it on axle stands (see *Jacking and vehicle support*). Remove both front roadwheels.

**2** Drain the transmission oil as described in Section 2, then refit the drain and filler plugs, and tighten to their specified torque settings.

**3** Remove the air cleaner assembly and inlet ducts as described in Chapter 4A or 4B.

**4** Remove the battery and battery box as described in Chapter 5A.

**5** Remove the catalytic converter (petrol models) or the main exhaust system (minus catalytic converter (diesel models) as described in Chapter 4A or 4B. On 1.6 litre diesel engine models with the 9HZ (particulate filter) engine, remove the exhaust gas pressure take-off and pressure sensor pipes, and disconnect the exhaust gas temperature sensor wiring.

**6** Remove both driveshafts as described in Chapter 8.

**7** Remove the starter motor (Chapter 5A).

**8** Detach the clutch slave cylinder from the transmission as described in Chapter 6. Note there is no need to disconnect the fluid pipe from the cylinder.

**9** Disconnect the gearchange cables from the transmission and support bracket as described in Section 3.

**10** Note their fitted positions, then disconnect all wiring plugs from the transmission. Note the harness routing and move the harness to one side.

**11** Undo the retaining bolt(s), and remove the flywheel lower cover plate (where fitted) from the transmission.

**12** Place a jack with a block of wood beneath the engine, to take the weight of the engine. Alternatively, attach a couple of lifting eyes to the engine, and fit a hoist or support bar to take the engine weight.

**13** Place a jack and block of wood beneath the transmission, and raise the jack to take the weight of the transmission.

**14** Slacken and remove the two bolts securing the left-hand engine/transmission mounting arm to the bracket on the transmission **(see**

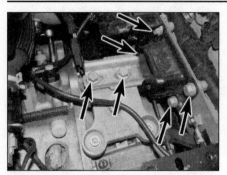

**7.14 Left-hand engine mounting retaining bolts (arrowed)**

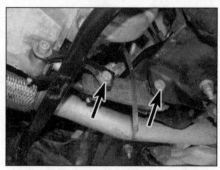

**7.15 Rear engine mounting connecting link through-bolts (arrowed)**

**7.16 On diesel engines, remove the mounting stud (arrowed) which obscures the transmission-to-engine bolt**

**illustration)**. Undo the four bolts securing the mounting to the body and remove the complete mounting assembly from the engine compartment.

**15** Unscrew and remove the two through-bolts securing the rear engine/transmission mounting connecting link to the subframe and transmission bracket **(see illustration)**.

**16** With the jack positioned beneath the transmission taking the weight, slacken and remove the remaining bolts securing the transmission housing to the engine. Note the correct fitted positions of each bolt and the necessary brackets, as they are removed, to use as a reference on refitting. On diesel engine models, unscrew the left-hand catalytic converter mounting stud to allow access to the front transmission-to-engine bolt **(see illustration)**.

**17** Make a final check that all components have been disconnected, and are positioned clear of the transmission so that they will not hinder the removal procedure.

**18** With the bolts removed, move the trolley jack and transmission to the left, to free it from its locating dowels. Lower the engine slightly to enable the transmission to be freed.

*Caution: Take great care not to damage the radiator if the engine is moved – place a sheet of thick cardboard over the rear face of the radiator. On models equipped with air conditioning, care must also be taken to ensure the auxiliary drivebelt pulleys do not damage the air conditioning pipes on the right-hand side of the engine compartment.*

**19** Once the transmission is free, lower the jack and manoeuvre the unit out from under the car. Remove the locating dowels from the transmission or engine if they are loose, and keep them in a safe place.

### Refitting

**20** The transmission is refitted by a reversal of the removal procedure, bearing in mind the following points:

a) *Prior to refitting, check the clutch assembly and release mechanism components (see Chapter 6). Lubricate the release bearing guide with a little high melting-point grease (Citroën recommend the use of Molykote BR2 Plus). Do not apply too much grease, otherwise there is a possibility of the grease contaminating the clutch friction disc, and ensure no grease is applied to the input shaft/friction disc splines.*

b) *Ensure that the locating dowels are correctly positioned prior to installation.*

c) *Tighten all nuts and bolts to the specified torque (where given).*

d) *Renew the driveshaft oil seals, then refit the driveshafts (see Chapter 8).*

e) *Refit the slave cylinder (see Chapter 6).*

f) *On completion, refill the transmission with the specified type and quantity of lubricant, as described in Section 2.*

## 8 Manual transmission overhaul – general information

**1** Overhauling a manual transmission is a difficult and involved job for the DIY home mechanic. In addition to dismantling and reassembling many small parts, clearances must be precisely measured and, if necessary, changed by selecting shims and spacers. Internal transmission components are also often difficult to obtain, and in many instances, extremely expensive. Because of this, if the transmission develops a fault or becomes noisy, the best course of action is to have the unit overhauled by a specialist repairer, or to obtain an exchange reconditioned unit.

**2** Nevertheless, it is not impossible for the more experienced mechanic to overhaul the transmission, provided the special tools are available, and the job is done in a deliberate step-by-step manner, so that nothing is overlooked.

**3** The tools necessary for an overhaul include internal and external circlip pliers, bearing pullers, a slide hammer, a set of pin punches, a dial test indicator, and possibly a hydraulic press. In addition, a large, sturdy workbench and a vice will be required.

**4** During dismantling of the transmission, make careful notes of how each component is fitted, to make reassembly easier and more accurate.

**5** Before dismantling the transmission, it will help if you have some idea what area is malfunctioning. Certain problems can be closely related to specific areas in the transmission, which can make component examination and renewal easier. Refer to the *Fault finding* Section for more information.

# Chapter 7 Part B:
# Automatic transmission

## Contents

## Degrees of difficulty

| **Easy,** suitable for novice with little experience | **Fairly easy,** suitable for beginner with some experience | **Fairly difficult,** suitable for competent DIY mechanic | **Difficult,** suitable for experienced DIY mechanic | **Very difficult,** suitable for expert DIY or professional |
|---|---|---|---|---|

## Specifications

### General

| | |
|---|---|
| Type | Auto-adaptive four-speed electronically-controlled automatic with three (normal, sport and snow) driving modes |
| Designation | AL4 |

### Lubrication

| | |
|---|---|
| Capacity: | |
| Refilling after draining | 3.0 litres |
| From dry | 6.0 litres |
| Recommended fluid | See *Lubricants and fluids* |

### Torque wrench settings

| | Nm | lbf ft |
|---|---|---|
| Fluid cooler centre bolt | 50 | 37 |
| Fluid drain plug | 33 | 24 |
| Fluid filler plug | 24 | 18 |
| Fluid level plug | 24 | 18 |
| Fluid pressure sensor bolts | 9 | 7 |
| Input shaft speed sensor bolt | 10 | 7 |
| Left-hand engine/transmission mounting | Refer to Chapter 2A | |
| Multi-function switch retaining bolts | 10 | 7 |
| Output shaft speed sensor bolt | 10 | 7 |
| Rear mounting link | Refer to Chapter 2A | |
| Roadwheel bolts | 90 | 66 |
| Torque converter-to-driveplate nuts: | | |
| Stage 1 | 10 | 7 |
| Stage 2 | 30 | 22 |
| Transmission-to-engine fixing bolts | 35 | 26 |

## 1 General information

**1** 1.4 litre petrol models are available with the option of a four-speed electronically-controlled automatic transmission, consisting of a torque converter, an epicyclic geartrain, and hydraulically-operated clutches and brakes. The unit is controlled by the electronic control unit (ECU) via the electrically-operated solenoid valves in the hydraulic block within the transmission unit. The transmission has three driving modes: Normal, Sport and Snow; the mode buttons are situated on the right-hand side of the selector lever and the mode indicator lights are incorporated in the instrument panel.

**2** The normal mode is the standard mode for driving in which the transmission shifts up at relatively low engine speeds to combine reasonable performance with economy. If the transmission unit is switched into sport mode, the transmission will shift up only at high engine speeds, giving improved acceleration and overtaking performance. In snow mode, the transmission will select 2nd gear when the vehicle pulls away from a standing start; this helps maintain traction on slippery surfaces.

**3** The torque converter provides a fluid coupling between the engine and transmission, which acts as an automatic clutch, and also provides a degree of torque multiplication when accelerating.

**4** The epicyclic geartrain provides either of the four forward or one reverse gear ratios, according to which of its component parts are held stationary or allowed to turn. The components of the geartrain are held or released by brakes and clutches which are controlled by the ECU via the electrically-operated solenoid valves in the hydraulic unit. A fluid pump within the transmission provides the necessary hydraulic pressure to operate the brakes and clutches.

**5** Driver control of the transmission is by a six-position selector lever. The transmission has a 'drive' position, and a 'hold' facility on the first three gear ratios. The 'drive' position D provides automatic changing throughout the range of all four gear ratios, and is the one to select for normal driving. An automatic kickdown facility shifts the transmission down a gear if the accelerator pedal is fully depressed. The 'hold' facility is very similar, but limits the number of gear ratios available – ie, when the selector lever is in the 3 position, only the first three ratios can be selected; in the 2 position, only the first two can be selected. When the lever is in the 2 position, the transmission can be locked in first gear using the button on the right-hand side of the selector lever. These lower ratio 'hold' settings are useful for providing engine braking when travelling down steep gradients, or for preventing unwanted selection of top gear on twisty roads. Note, however, that the transmission should never be shifted down at high engine speeds.

**6** On some models, the selector lever is equipped with a shift-lock function. This prevents the selector lever being moved from the P position unless the brake pedal is depressed.

**7** Due to the complexity of the automatic transmission, any repair or overhaul work must be left to a Citroën dealer with the necessary special equipment for fault diagnosis and repair. The contents of the following Sections are therefore confined to supplying general information, and any service information and instructions that can be used by the owner.

**Note:** *The automatic transmission unit is of the 'auto-adaptive' type. This means that it takes into account your driving style and modifies the transmission shift points to provide optimum performance and economy to suit. When the battery is disconnected, the transmission will lose its memory and will resort to one of its many base shift programs. The transmission will then relearn the optimum shift points when the vehicle is driven a few miles. During these first few miles of driving, there maybe a noticeable difference in performance whilst the transmission adapts to your individual style.*

## 2 Automatic transmission fluid – draining and refilling

**Note 1:** *A suitable square section wrench may be required to undo the transmission filler plug. These wrenches can be obtained from most motor factors or your Citroën dealer.*

**Note 2:** *The transmission unit is equipped with a fluid wear sensor to inform the driver when the fluid needs renewing (the ECU flashes the Sport and Snow mode indicator lights when fluid renewal is necessary). If the transmission unit is drained and refilled with new fluid, this sensor should be reset. This can only be done using Citroën diagnostic test equipment.*

### General

**1** Numerous modifications have been carried out to the AL4 automatic transmission since its introduction, the most significant of these being a change to the transmission fluid drain and level plugs, and to the draining and refilling procedure.

**2** On later transmissions a drain plug is no longer fitted, and the transmission is effectively 'sealed for life'. The information contained in this Section is therefore only applicable to early transmission units. It is advisable to seek the advice of a Citroën dealer as to the latest recommendations regarding fluid renewal on all transmissions, before continuing with this procedure.

### Draining

**Note:** *This is only possible on early models (see above).*

**3** This operation is much quicker and more efficient if the car is first taken on a journey of sufficient length to warm the engine/transmission up to normal operating temperature.

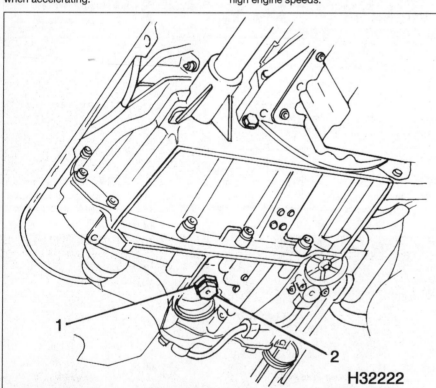

**2.5 Transmission fluid drain plug (1) and oil level plug (2), inside the drain plug (early type transmissions)**

**4** Park the car on level ground, switch off the ignition and apply the handbrake firmly. For improved access, jack up the front of the car and support it securely on axle stands (see *Jacking and vehicle support*). Undo the screws and remove the engine/transmission undershield (where fitted).

**5** Position a suitable container under the drain plug, situated on the base of the transmission. Unscrew the drain plug (the smaller plug in the centre of the drain plug is the level plug – see Chapter 1A) and recover the sealing washer **(see illustration opposite)**. Allow the fluid to drain completely into the container.

 **Warning: If the fluid is hot, take precautions against scalding.**

**6** Clean the drain plug, being especially careful to wipe off any metallic particles. Discard the sealing washer; it should be renewed whenever it is disturbed.

**7** When the fluid has finished draining, clean the drain plug threads and those of the transmission casing, fit a new sealing washer and refit the drain plug, tightening it to the specified torque wrench setting. If the car was raised for the draining operation, now lower it to the ground.

### Refilling

**8** To gain access to the filler plug, remove the air cleaner assembly as described in Chapter 4A.

**9** Wipe clean the area around the filler plug which is situated directly behind the transmission selector lever **(see illustration)**. Unscrew the filler plug from the transmission and recover the sealing washer.

***Caution: Do not unscrew the selector shaft bolt (located in front of the selector lever).***

**10** Carefully refill the transmission with the correct amount of the specified type of fluid. Fit the new sealing washer to the filler plug then refit the plug, tightening it to the specified torque. Refit the air cleaner assembly as described in Chapter 4A.

**11** Take the vehicle on a short journey to warm the transmission up to normal operating temperature.

**12** On your return, check the transmission fluid level as described in Chapter 1A.

### 3  Selector cable – adjustment

**1** To gain access to the transmission end of the selector cable, remove the air cleaner assembly as described in Chapter 4A.

**2** Position the selector lever firmly against its detent in the P (park) position.

**3** Pull up the yellow plastic locking clamp on the cable end fitting to unlock the adjustment system **(see illustration)**.

**4** Ensure that the selector lever on top of the transmission is fully forward, then press in the yellow locking clamp on the selector cable to lock it in position.

**2.9  Automatic transmission fluid filler plug (arrowed)**

**5** Check the operation of the selector lever before refitting the air cleaner assembly (Chapter 4A).

### 4  Selector lever and cable – removal and refitting

### Removal

**1** Remove the centre console as described in Chapter 11, then position the selector lever in the P position.

**2** Depress the tabs in the centre of the selector cable end fitting, then lift the end fitting from the balljoint on the selector lever **(see illustration)**.

**3** Using pointed-nose pliers, pull out the spring-loaded black pin and lift the outer cable

**4.2  Depress the tabs (arrowed) to release the selector cable end fitting**

**4.8a  Depress the tabs in the centre of the selector cable end fitting . . .**

**3.3  Pull up the yellow plastic locking clamp on the selector cable end fitting to unlock the adjustment system**

from the front of the selector lever housing **(see illustration)**.

**4** Note their fitted positions and disconnect all wiring plugs from the lever housing.

**5** Undo the four retaining nuts, lift the lever housing from its location and remove it from the car,

**6** Firmly apply the handbrake, then jack up the front of the vehicle and support it on axle stands (see *Jacking and vehicle support*).

**7** Remove the air cleaner assembly as described in Chapter 4A.

**8** Depress the tabs in the centre of the selector cable end fitting, then lift the end fitting from the balljoint on the transmission lever **(see illustrations)**.

**9** Pull out the spring-loaded black pin and lift the outer cable from the transmission bracket. Prise the cable sealing grommet from the floor and withdraw the cable assembly from inside the car.

**4.3  Pull out the spring-loaded black pin and lift the selector cable from the selector lever housing**

**4.8b  . . . then lift the end fitting from the balljoint on the transmission lever**

**7.4 Release the retaining clips and disconnect the coolant hoses (arrowed) from the fluid cooler (viewed from above)**

### Refitting

10 Refitting is the reverse of removal, but adjust the cable as described in Section 3 before refitting all components removed for access.

## 5 Speedometer drive –
### removal and refitting

Refer to Chapter 7A, Section 6.

## 6 Oil seals –
### renewal

### Driveshaft oil seals

1 Remove the appropriate driveshaft as described in Chapter 8.

#### Right-hand seal

2 Remove the O-ring from the differential sun gear shaft then carefully remove the oil seal from of the transmission, taking care not to damage the shaft or housing. To remove the seal, carefully punch or drill two small holes opposite each other into the seal. Screw a self-tapping screw into each hole and pull on the screws to extract the seal.

3 Remove all traces of dirt from the area around the oil seal aperture, then apply a smear of grease to the outer edge and sealing

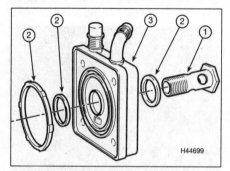

**7.5 Fluid cooler components**

| 1 Bolt | 3 Fluid cooler |
| 2 Seals | |

lip of the new oil seal. Ease the new seal onto the shaft, taking care not to damage its lip, and into its aperture. Drive the seal squarely into position using a suitable tubular drift (such as a socket) which bears only on the hard outer edge of the seal.

4 Once the seal is correctly installed, fit a new O-ring to the sun gear shaft and slide along until it abuts the seal.

5 Refit the driveshaft as described in Chapter 8.

#### Left-hand seal

6 Carefully prise the oil seal out of the transmission, using a large flat-bladed screwdriver.

7 Remove all traces of dirt from the area around the oil seal aperture, then apply a smear of grease to the outer lip of the new oil seal. Fit the new seal into its aperture, and drive it squarely into position using a suitable tubular drift (such as a socket) which bears only on the hard outer edge of the seal, until it abuts its locating shoulder. If the seal was supplied with a plastic protector sleeve, leave this in position until the driveshaft has been refitted.

8 Apply a thin film of grease to the oil seal lip.

9 Refit the driveshaft as described in Chapter 8.

### Selector shaft oil seal

10 To gain access to the transmission selector shaft, remove the air cleaner assembly as described in Chapter 4A.

11 Position the selector lever firmly against its detent mechanism in the P position.

12 Slacken and remove the nut and clamp bolt securing the selector lever to the transmission shaft. Make alignment marks between the shaft and lever then free the lever from the shaft.

13 Pull out the spring-loaded black pin and lift the selector cable from the transmission bracket. Position the cable clear of the selector shaft.

14 Make alignment marks between the multi-function switch and transmission unit then unscrew the retaining bolts and remove the switch.

15 Carefully remove the oil seal from the top of the transmission, taking care not to damage the shaft or housing. To remove the seal, carefully punch or drill two small holes opposite each other into the seal. Screw a self-tapping screw into each hole and pull on the screws to extract the seal.

16 Remove all traces of dirt from the area around the oil seal aperture, then apply a smear of grease to the outer edge and sealing lip of the new oil seal. Ease the new seal onto the shaft, taking care not to damage its lip, and press it squarely into its aperture.

17 Locate the multi-function switch back on the selector shaft. Align the marks made prior to removal then refit the switch bolts, tightening them to the specified torque.

18 Seat the selector cable in the transmission bracket and engage the selector lever with the

transmission shaft. Ensure the marks made on removal are correctly aligned then refit the lever clamp bolt and nut and tighten securely.

19 Adjust the cable as described in Section 3, then refit all components removed for access.

### Torque converter seal

20 Remove the transmission unit as described in Section 9.

21 Carefully slide the torque converter off the transmission shaft whilst being prepared for fluid spillage.

22 Note the correct fitted position of the seal in the housing then carefully lever it out of position, taking care not to mark the housing or shaft.

23 Remove all traces of dirt from the area around the oil seal aperture. Ease the new seal into its aperture, ensuring its sealing lip is facing inwards, then press it squarely into position.

24 Engage the torque converter with the transmission shaft splines and slide it into position, taking care not to damage the oil seal.

25 Refit the transmission unit as described in Section 9.

## 7 Fluid cooler –
### removal and refitting

*Caution: Be careful not to allow dirt into the transmission unit during this procedure.*

### Removal

1 The fluid cooler is mounted on the rear of the transmission housing. To gain access to the cooler, remove the battery and battery box as described in Chapter 5A.

2 Remove all traces of dirt from around the fluid cooler before proceeding.

3 Using a hose clamp or similar, clamp both the fluid cooler coolant hoses to minimise coolant loss during subsequent operations.

4 Release the retaining clips, and disconnect both coolant hoses from the fluid cooler – be prepared for some coolant spillage (see illustration). Wash off any spilt coolant immediately with cold water, and dry the surrounding area before proceeding further.

5 Slacken and remove the fluid cooler centre bolt, and remove the cooler from the transmission. Remove the seal from the centre bolt, and the two seals fitted to the rear of the cooler, and discard them; new ones must be used on refitting (see illustration).

### Refitting

6 Lubricate the new seals with clean automatic transmission fluid, then fit the two new seals to the rear of the fluid cooler, and a new seal to the centre bolt.

7 Locate the fluid cooler on the rear of transmission housing then refit the centre bolt. Ensure the cooler is correctly positioned then tighten the centre bolt to the specified torque setting.

**8** Reconnect the coolant hoses to the fluid cooler, and secure them in position with their retaining clips. Remove the hose clamps.

**9** Refit the battery and battery box (see Chapter 5A).

**10** Top-up the cooling system as described in *Weekly checks* and check the transmission unit fluid level as described in Chapter 1A.

---

### 8 Transmission control system components – removal and refitting

## *Electronic control unit (ECU)*

**Note:** *The automatic transmission electronic control system relies on accurate communication between the engine management ECU and the automatic transmission ECU. If either ECU is renewed, then both ECUs must be 'initialised'. The initialisation procedure requires access to specialised electronic test equipment and it is recommended that this operation is entrusted to a suitably-equipped Citroën dealer or specialist.*

### Removal

**1** The ECU is mounted on the front face of the transmission, below the radiator top hose.

**2** Disconnect the battery (see Chapter 5A).

**3** Firmly apply the handbrake, then jack up the front of the car and support it securely on axle stands (see *Jacking and vehicle support*).

**4** From under the car, disengage the lower locating tabs of the plastic ECU cover, and remove the cover from the ECU mounting plate **(see illustration)**.

**5** Slide out the locking catch and disconnect the wiring connector from the ECU **(see illustration)**.

**6** Release the wiring harness from the ECU mounting plate then undo the three bolts securing the mounting plate to the transmission. There is one bolt on the front of the transmission, and two on the side **(see illustration)**.

**7** Withdraw the ECU and mounting plate from the front of the transmission, then undo the mounting stud nuts and separate the ECU from the mounting plate.

### Refitting

**8** Refitting is the reverse of removal, ensuring the wiring connector is securely reconnected.

## *Output shaft speed sensor*

*Caution: Be careful not to allow dirt into the transmission unit during this procedure.*

### Removal

**9** The output shaft sensor is fitted to the rear of the transmission unit.

**10** To gain access to the sensor, jack up the front of the vehicle and support it securely on axle stands (see *Jacking and vehicle support*). Undo the screws and remove the engine/transmission undershield (where fitted).

**11** Trace the sensor wiring back to its

---

**8.4 Disengage the lower locating tabs, and remove the cover from the ECU mounting plate**

connector, located next to the transmission main wiring harness connector. Unclip the connector from its bracket then disconnect it.

**12** Wipe clean the area around the sensor then slacken and remove the sensor retaining bolt. Remove the sensor along with its sealing ring; discard the sealing ring, a new one must be used on refitting.

### Refitting

**13** Refitting is the reverse of removal, noting the following points.
   a) *Fit a new sealing ring to the sensor and tighten the sensor bolt to the specified torque.*
   b) *On completion, check the transmission fluid level as described in Chapter 1A.*

## *Input shaft speed sensor*

*Caution: Be careful not to allow dirt into the transmission unit during this procedure.*

### Removal

**14** The input shaft speed sensor is located on the left-hand end of the transmission unit.

**15** To gain access to the sensor, chock the rear wheels, firmly apply the handbrake, then jack up the front of the vehicle and securely support it on axle stands (see *Jacking and vehicle support*).

**16** To gain access to the main wiring connector, remove the battery and battery box (see Chapter 5A).

**17** Lift the retaining clip and disconnect the main wiring connector from the top of the transmission unit.

**18** Unscrew the two bolts and free the main wiring connector from the transmission unit. Cut the cable tie securing the wiring to the connector cover then release the clips and slide the cover off the connector.

**19** Trace the wiring back from the sensor being removed, freeing it from all the relevant retaining clips and ties, to the main wiring connector. Carefully release the retaining clips then slide the sensor connector out from the rear of the main connector, noting which way around it is fitted.

**20** Wipe clean the area around the sensor. Slacken and remove the retaining bolt then remove the sensor, along with its sealing ring. Discard the sealing ring, a new one must be used on refitting.

---

**8.5 Slide out the locking catch (arrowed) and disconnect the ECU wiring connector**

### Refitting

**21** Refitting is the reverse of removal, noting the following points.
   a) *Fit a new sealing ring to the sensor and tighten the sensor bolt to the specified torque.*
   b) *Ensure the sensor wiring is correctly routed and retained by all the necessary clips and ties.*
   c) *Clip the sensor wiring back into the main wiring connector, ensuring it is fitted the right way around. Slide the cover back onto the main connector, ensuring it is clipped securely in position, and secure the wiring to the cover with a new cable tie. Secure the connector to the transmission unit with the retaining bolts.*
   d) *On completion, check the transmission fluid level as described in Chapter 1A.*

## *Fluid pressure sensor*

*Caution: Be careful not to allow dirt into the transmission unit during this procedure.*

### Removal

**22** The fluid pressure sensor is located on the base of the transmission unit.

**23** To gain access to the sensor, chock the rear wheels, firmly apply the handbrake then jack up the front of the vehicle and securely support it on axle stands (see *Jacking and vehicle support*).

**24** Remove the battery and battery box as described in Chapter 5A.

**25** Unscrew the two bolts and free the main wiring connector from the transmission unit.

**8.6 ECU mounting plate front retaining bolt (arrowed)**

**8.27 The fluid pressure sensor is secured to the base of the transmission by two bolts (arrowed)**

Cut the cable tie securing the wiring to the connector cover then release the clips and slide the cover off the connector.

**26** Trace the wiring back from the sensor being removed, freeing it from all the relevant retaining clips and ties, to the main wiring connector. Carefully release the retaining clips then slide the green 3-way sensor connector out from the rear of the main connector, noting which way around it is fitted.

**27** Wipe clean the area around the sensor. Slacken and remove the retaining bolts then remove the sensor, along with its sealing ring **(see illustration)**. Discard the sealing ring, a new one must be used on refitting. Be prepared for fluid spillage, and plug the opening to minimise fluid loss.

### Refitting

**28** Refitting is the reverse of removal, noting the following points.

  a) *Fit a new sealing ring to the sensor and tighten the sensor bolts to the specified torque.*
  b) *Ensure the sensor wiring is correctly routed and retained by all the necessary clips and ties.*
  c) *Clip the sensor wiring back into the main wiring connector, ensuring it is fitted the right way around. Slide the cover back onto the main connector, ensuring it is clipped*

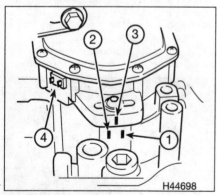

**8.46 Multi-function switch adjustment**

  1 *1st alignment mark*
  2 *2nd alignment mark*
  3 *Switch body alignment mark*
  4 *Switch external contacts*

*securely in position, and secure the wiring to the cover with a new cable tie.*
  d) *On completion, check the transmission fluid level as described in Chapter 1A.*

### Multi-function switch

**Note:** *The multi-function switch is slotted to allow for adjustment. Accurate adjustment requires the use an accurate multimeter – see the text later in this Section.*

### Removal

**29** Remove the battery and battery box/tray (see Chapter 5A).

**30** Position the selector lever firmly against its detent mechanism in the P position.

**31** Slacken and remove the nut and clamp bolt securing the selector lever to the transmission shaft. Make alignment marks between the shaft and lever then free the lever from the shaft.

**32** Pull out the spring-loaded black pin and lift the selector cable from the transmission bracket. Position the cable clear of the selector shaft.

**33** Unscrew the two bolts and free the main wiring connector from the transmission unit. Cut the cable tie securing the wiring to the connector cover then release the clips and slide the cover off the connector.

**34** Trace the wiring back from the switch to the main wiring connector, freeing it from all the relevant retaining clips and ties. Carefully release the retaining clips then slide the green 12-way connector out from the rear of the main connector, noting which way around it is fitted.

**35** Make accurate alignment marks between the multi-function switch and transmission unit then unscrew the retaining bolts and remove the switch.

### Refitting

**36** Locate the multi-function switch back on the selector shaft. Align the marks made prior to removal then refit the switch bolts, tightening them to the specified torque.

**37** Clip the wiring back into the main wiring connector, ensuring it is fitted the right way around. Slide the cover back onto the main connector, ensuring it is clipped securely in position, and secure the wiring to the cover with a new cable tie. Locate the connector on the transmission unit and securely tighten its retaining bolts.

**38** Reconnect the main wiring connector to the transmission unit.

**39** Seat the selector cable in the transmission bracket and engage the selector lever with the transmission shaft. Ensure the marks made on removal are correctly aligned then refit the lever clamp bolt and nut, and tighten securely.

**40** Adjust the cable as described in Section 3, and the multi-function switch as described next.

### Adjustment

**41** Slacken the switch mounting bolts and rotate the switch fully anti-clockwise as far as it will go.

**42** Set the multimeter to measure ohms, and connect the meter terminals to the external switch contacts.

**43** Slowly rotate the switch clockwise until the switch contacts close (the meter should register zero ohms – no resistance).

**44** In this position, make an alignment mark between the switch and the transmission casing.

**45** Continue to rotate the switch clockwise until the contacts open (the meter should register infinite ohms or similar)

**46** Make another alignment mark between the transmission casing and the mark made previously on the switch **(see illustration)**.

**47** Rotate the switch until the alignment mark on the switch body is exactly half-way between the two marks made on the transmission casing. Tighten the switch mounting bolts to the specified torque.

**48** Refit the battery and battery box as described in Chapter 5A.

**49** Check that the selector lever position corresponds to the display on the instrument panel.

---

**9  Automatic transmission**
– removal and refitting

---

### Removal

**1** Chock the rear wheels, then firmly apply the handbrake. Slacken both front roadwheel bolts. Jack up the front of the vehicle, and securely support it on axle stands (see *Jacking and vehicle support*). Remove both front roadwheels.

**2** Remove the air cleaner housing and inlet duct as described in Chapter 4A.

**3** Remove the battery and battery box as described in Chapter 5A.

**4** Remove the automatic transmission ECU as described in Section 8.

**5** Remove the catalytic converter as described in Chapter 4A.

**6** Remove both driveshafts as described in Chapter 8.

**7** Remove the starter motor (Chapter 5A).

**8** Slacken and remove the nut and clamp bolt securing the selector lever to the transmission shaft. Make alignment marks between the shaft and lever then free the lever from the shaft.

**9** Pull out the spring-loaded black pin and lift the selector cable from the transmission bracket. Position the cable clear of the selector shaft.

**10** Using a hose clamp or similar, clamp both the fluid cooler coolant hoses to minimise coolant loss. Release the retaining clips and disconnect both coolant hoses from the fluid cooler – be prepared for some coolant spillage. Wash off any spilt coolant immediately with cold water, and dry the surrounding area before proceeding further.

**11** Lift the retaining clip and disconnect the main wiring connector from the transmission wiring block, located at the rear of the unit. Also disconnect the output shaft speed sensor wiring connector (located next to the main connector) then position the wiring harness clear of the transmission unit.

**12** Undo the retaining nut/bolt(s), and disconnect the earth straps from the top of the transmission housing. Free the wiring from any relevant retaining clips, and position it clear of the transmission.

**13** Undo the retaining bolts and remove the lower driveplate cover plate (where fitted) from the transmission.

**14** Access to the torque converter retaining nuts is gained via an access hole above the right-hand driveshaft on the back of the cylinder block. Use a socket and extension bar to rotate the crankshaft pulley to align the first nut with the aperture **(see illustration)**. Unscrew the nut then rotate the crankshaft 120°. Remove the second nut then rotate the crankshaft another 120° Unscrew the third and final nut and discard all three nuts; new ones must be used on refitting.

**15** To ensure that the torque converter does not fall out as the transmission is removed, secure it in position using a length of metal strip bolted to one of the starter motor bolt holes.

**16** Place a jack with a block of wood beneath the engine, to take the weight of the engine. Alternatively, attach a couple of lifting eyes to the engine, and fit a hoist or support bar to take the engine weight.

**17** Place a jack and block of wood beneath the transmission, and raise the jack to take the weight of the transmission.

**18** Slacken and remove the two bolts securing the left-hand engine/transmission mounting arm to the bracket on the transmission. Undo the four bolts securing the mounting to the body and remove the complete mounting assembly from the engine compartment.

**19** Unscrew and remove the two through-bolts securing the rear engine/transmission mounting connecting link to the subframe and transmission bracket.

**20** With the jack positioned beneath the transmission taking the weight, slacken and remove the remaining bolts securing the transmission housing to the engine. Note the correct fitted positions of each bolt and the necessary brackets as they are removed, to use as a reference on refitting. Make a final check that all components have been disconnected, and are positioned clear of the transmission so that they will not hinder the removal procedure.

**21** With the bolts removed, move the trolley jack and transmission to the left, to free it from its locating dowels. If necessary, lower the engine slightly to enable the transmission to be freed.

**22** Once the transmission is free, lower the jack and manoeuvre the unit out from under the car. Remove the locating dowels from the transmission or engine if they are loose, and keep them in a safe place.

## Refitting

**23** Ensure that the bush fitted to the centre of the crankshaft is in good condition, and apply a little Molykote BR2 grease to the torque converter centring pin.

**Caution: Do not apply too much, otherwise there is a possibility of the grease contaminating the torque converter.**

**24** Ensure that the engine/transmission locating dowels are correctly positioned then raise the transmission unit into position. Align the torque converter studs with the driveplate holes then engage the transmission unit with the engine.

**Caution: Do not allow the weight of the transmission unit to hang on the torque converter as the unit is installed.**

**25** With the transmission and engine correctly joined, refit the transmission-to-engine unit bolts and tighten them to the specified torque.

**26** Screw the new nuts onto the torque converter studs, tightening them lightly only, rotating the crankshaft as necessary. Tighten all three nuts to the specified Stage 1 torque

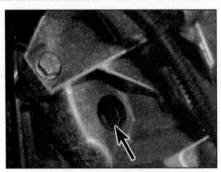

**9.14 Access to the torque converter nuts is gained via the access hole (arrowed) above the driveshaft**

setting. Once all have been tightened to the Stage 1 torque, go around and tighten them to the specified Stage 2 torque setting.

**27** The remainder of refitting is the reverse of removal, noting the following.
a) *Tighten all nuts and bolts to the specified torque (where given).*
b) *Renew the driveshaft oil seals, then refit the driveshafts (see Chapter 8).*
c) *Reconnect the selector cable and adjust as described in Section 3.*
d) *On completion, check the transmission fluid level as described in Chapter 1A.*

## 10 Automatic transmission overhaul – general information

**1** In the event of a fault occurring with the transmission, it is first necessary to determine whether it is of an electrical, mechanical or hydraulic nature and, to do this, special test equipment is required. It is therefore essential to have the work carried out by a Citroën dealer or specialist if a transmission fault is suspected.

**2** Do not remove the transmission from the car for possible repair before professional fault diagnosis has been carried out, since most tests require the transmission to be in the vehicle.

# Chapter 8
# Driveshafts

## Contents

## Degrees of difficulty

| Easy, suitable for novice with little experience  | Fairly easy, suitable for beginner with some experience | Fairly difficult, suitable for competent DIY mechanic | Difficult, suitable for experienced DIY mechanic | Very difficult, suitable for expert DIY or professional  |
|---|---|---|---|---|

## Specifications

### Lubrication (overhaul only – see text)

| | |
|---|---|
| Lubricant type/specification. . . . . . . . . . . . . . . . . . . . . . . . . . . . . . . . . | Use only special grease supplied in sachets with gaiter kits – joints are otherwise pre-packed with grease and sealed |

Lubricant quantity:
| | |
|---|---|
| Outer CV joint. . . . . . . . . . . . . . . . . . . . . . . . . . . . . . . . . . . . . . . . . . | 160 g |
| Inner CV joint . . . . . . . . . . . . . . . . . . . . . . . . . . . . . . . . . . . . . . . . . . | 130 g |

### Torque wrench settings

| | Nm | lbf ft |
|---|---|---|
| Driveshaft retaining nut*. . . . . . . . . . . . . . . . . . . . . . . . . . . . . . . . . . . | 245 | 181 |
| Lower suspension arm balljoint clamp bolt nut* . . . . . . . . . . . . . . . . . | 40 | 30 |
| Right-hand driveshaft intermediate bearing retaining bolt nuts. . . . . . . | 20 | 15 |
| Roadwheel bolts. . . . . . . . . . . . . . . . . . . . . . . . . . . . . . . . . . . . . . . . . | 90 | 66 |
| Track rod balljoint retaining nut*. . . . . . . . . . . . . . . . . . . . . . . . . . . . . | 35 | 26 |

* New nuts must be used.

## 1 General information

Drive is transmitted from the differential to the front wheels by means of two unequal-length driveshafts.

Both driveshafts are splined at their outer ends, to accept the wheel hubs, and are threaded so that each hub can be fastened by a large nut. The inner end of each driveshaft is splined, to accept the differential sun gear.

Constant velocity (CV) joints are fitted to each end of the driveshafts, to ensure the smooth and efficient transmission of power at all suspension and steering angles. The outer constant velocity joints are of the ball-and-cage type, with the inner constant velocity joints being of the tripod type.

On 16-valve diesel engine models, the right-hand inner constant velocity joint is situated approximately halfway along the shaft's length, and an intermediate support bearing is mounted in a bracket attached to the rear of the engine. The inner end of the driveshaft passes through the bearing (which prevents any lateral movement of the driveshaft inner end) and the inner constant velocity joint outer member.

## 2 Driveshafts – removal and refitting

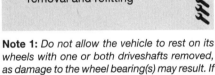

Note 1: Do not allow the vehicle to rest on its wheels with one or both driveshafts removed, as damage to the wheel bearing(s) may result. If moving the vehicle is unavoidable, temporarily insert the outer end of the driveshaft(s) in the hub(s) and tighten the hub nut(s): in this case, the inner end(s) of the driveshaft(s) must be supported, for example by suspending with string from the vehicle underbody. Do not allow the driveshaft to hang down under its own weight.

Note 2: A new driveshaft retaining nut, lower arm balljoint clamp bolt nut and track rod balljoint retaining nut must be used on refitting.

### Removal

1 Firmly apply the handbrake, then jack up the front of the car and support it securely on axle stands (see Jacking and vehicle support). Remove the appropriate front roadwheel.

2 On manual transmission models, drain the transmission oil as described in Chapter 7A. On automatic transmission models, there is no need to drain the transmission fluid.

3 Release the hydraulic brake hose and, where fitted, the ABS wheel speed sensor wiring harness from the support brackets on the suspension strut.

4 On models where the driveshaft nut is staked, using a hammer and a chisel or similar tool, tap up the staking securing the driveshaft nut in position (see illustration). On models where the driveshaft nut is secured by an

2.4 Tap up the staking securing the driveshaft retaining nut in position

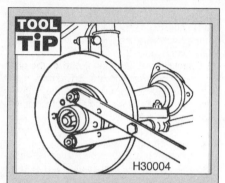

**TOOL TiP**

H30004

*A tool to hold the front hub stationary whilst the driveshaft retaining nut is slackened can be fabricated from two lengths of steel strip (one long, one short) and a nut and bolt; the nut and bolt forming the pivot of a forked tool.*

R-clip, withdraw the R-clip and remove the locking cap from the driveshaft nut. Note that a new retaining nut must be used on refitting.

5 Refit at least two roadwheel bolts to the front hub, and tighten them securely. Have an assistant firmly depress the brake pedal to prevent the front hub from rotating, then using a socket and a long extension bar, slacken and remove the driveshaft retaining nut. Alternatively, a tool can be fabricated from two lengths of steel strip (one long, one short) and a nut and bolt; the nut and bolt forming the pivot of a forked tool. Bolt the tool to the hub using two wheel bolts, and

hold the tool to prevent the hub from rotating as the driveshaft retaining nut is undone **(see Tool Tip)**. This nut is very tight; make sure that there is no risk of pulling the car off the axle stands.

6 Slacken and remove the nut securing the steering gear track rod balljoint to the hub carrier, and release the balljoint tapered shank using a balljoint separator. Note that a new retaining nut must be used on refitting.

7 Slacken and remove the nut, then withdraw the lower suspension arm balljoint clamp bolt from the hub carrier **(see illustration)**. Note that a new retaining nut must be used on refitting.

8 Tap a small chisel into the split on the hub carrier, to spread the hub slightly and allow the balljoint shank to be withdrawn. Pull the lower suspension arm downwards to release the balljoint shank from the hub carrier. To do this it will be necessary to use a long bar and block of wood which will engage under the front subframe. Attach the bar to the suspension arm, preferably with a chain, or alternatively with a stout strap or rope. Lever down on the bar to release the balljoint from the hub carrier **(see illustration)**.

9 Once the balljoint is free, remove the protector plate which is fitted to the balljoint shank.

### Left-hand driveshaft

10 Carefully pull the hub carrier assembly outwards, and withdraw the driveshaft outer constant velocity joint from the hub assembly.

If necessary, the shaft can be tapped out of the hub using a soft-faced mallet.

11 Support the driveshaft, then withdraw the inner constant velocity joint from the transmission, taking care not to damage the driveshaft oil seal. Remove the driveshaft from the vehicle.

### Right-hand driveshaft

12 Loosen the two intermediate bearing retaining bolt nuts, then rotate the bolts through 90°, so that their offset heads are clear of the bearing outer race **(see illustration)**.

13 Carefully pull the hub carrier assembly outwards, and withdraw the driveshaft outer constant velocity joint from the hub assembly. If necessary, the shaft can be tapped out of the hub using a soft-faced mallet.

14 Support the outer end of the driveshaft, then pull on the inner end of the shaft to free the shaft from the transmission, and the intermediate bearing from its mounting bracket. Remove the driveshaft from the vehicle.

### *Refitting*

15 Before installing the driveshaft, examine the driveshaft oil seal in the transmission for signs of damage or deterioration and, if necessary, renew it as described in Chapter 7A or 7B. (Having got this far it is worth renewing the seal as a matter of course.)

16 Thoroughly clean the driveshaft splines, and the apertures in the transmission and hub assembly. Apply a thin film of grease to the oil seal lips, and to the driveshaft splines and shoulders. Check that all gaiter clips are securely fastened.

### Left-hand driveshaft

17 Offer up the driveshaft, and locate the joint splines with those of the differential sun gear, taking great care not to damage the oil seal. Push the joint fully into position.

18 Locate the outer constant velocity joint splines with those of the hub carrier, and slide the joint back into position in the hub.

19 Refit the protector plate to the lower arm balljoint then, using the method employed on removal, locate the balljoint shank in the hub carrier, ensuring that the lug on the protector plate is correctly located in the clamp split. Insert the balljoint clamp bolt (from the front of the hub carrier), then fit the new retaining nut and tighten it to the specified torque.

20 Engage the track rod balljoint in the hub carrier, then fit a new retaining nut and tighten it to the specified torque.

21 Lubricate the inner face and threads of the driveshaft retaining nut with clean engine oil, and refit it to the end of the driveshaft. Use the method employed on removal to prevent the hub from rotating, and tighten the driveshaft retaining nut to the specified torque. Check that the hub rotates freely.

22 On models where the driveshaft nut is staked, stake the new nut into the driveshaft groove using a hammer and punch **(see illustration)**. On models where the driveshaft

**2.7 Undo the nut and withdraw the lower suspension arm balljoint clamp bolt from the hub carrier**

**2.8 Pull the lower suspension arm downwards using a bar and chain or similar arrangement, pivoting on the subframe**

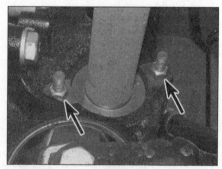

**2.12a On the right-hand driveshaft, slacken the intermediate bearing retaining nuts (arrowed) . . .**

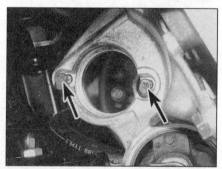

**2.12b . . . then turn the bolts through 90° so the offset heads (arrowed) are clear of the outer race (driveshaft removed for clarity)**

nut is secured by an R-clip, engage the locking cap with the driveshaft nut so that one of its cut-outs is aligned with the driveshaft hole. Secure the cap in position with the R-clip.
**23** Refit the hydraulic brake hose and, where fitted, the ABS wheel sensor wiring harness to the support brackets on the suspension strut.
**24** Refill the manual transmission with the specified type and quantity of oil as described in Chapter 7A.
**25** On completion, refit the roadwheel, then lower the vehicle to the ground and tighten the roadwheel bolts to the specified torque.

### Right-hand driveshaft

**26** Check that the intermediate bearing rotates smoothly, without any sign of roughness or undue free play between its inner and outer races. If necessary, renew the bearing as described in Section 5.
**27** Apply a smear of grease to the outer race of the intermediate bearing, then pass the inner end of the driveshaft through the bearing mounting bracket.
**28** Carefully locate the inner driveshaft splines with those of the differential sun gear, taking care not to damage the oil seal. Align the intermediate bearing with its mounting bracket, and push the driveshaft fully into position. If necessary, use a soft-faced mallet to tap the outer race of the bearing into position in the mounting bracket.
**29** Locate the outer constant velocity joint splines with those of the hub carrier, and slide the joint back into position in the hub.
**30** Ensure that the intermediate bearing is correctly seated, then rotate its retaining bolts

**2.22 Stake the nut firmly into the driveshaft grooves using a hammer and punch**

back through 90°, so that their offset heads are resting against the bearing outer race. Tighten the retaining nuts to the specified torque.
**31** Carry out the operations described above in paragraphs 19 to 25.

### 3 Driveshaft rubber gaiters – renewal

**Note:** *From around the end of 2004 the driveshaft joints are not removable from the shafts. Any problem with the joint requires a reconditioned or new shaft. A split boot requires a special tool to stretch the boot over the joint.*

### Outer joint

**1** Remove the driveshaft from the car as described in Section 2.

**3.5a Sharply strike the edge of the outer joint to compress the internal circlip . . .**

**2** Release the rubber gaiter inner and outer retaining clips by cutting through them using a junior hacksaw **(see illustration)**. Spread the clips and remove them from the gaiter.
**3** Check to see if the inner end of the gaiter locates in a groove in the driveshaft. If not, mark the position of the end of the gaiter on the driveshaft using quick-drying paint or typist's correction fluid.
**4** Slide the rubber gaiter down the shaft, to expose the outer constant velocity joint then scoop out the excess grease. It is advisable to wear disposable rubber gloves during this operation.
**5** Have an assistant securely hold the driveshaft, or clamp it in a vice equipped with soft jaws. Using a mallet, sharply strike the edge of the outer joint to drive it off the end of the shaft **(see illustrations)**. The joint is retained on the driveshaft by an internal circlip, and striking the joint in this manner forces the circlip into its groove, so allowing the joint to slide off.
**6** Once the joint assembly has been removed, remove the circlip from the groove in the driveshaft splines, and discard it **(see illustration)**. A new circlip must be fitted on reassembly.
**7** Withdraw the rubber gaiter from the driveshaft.
**8** With the constant velocity joint removed from the driveshaft, wipe away as much of the old grease as possible (do not use any solvent) to allow the joint components to be inspected.
**9** Move the inner splined driving member from side-to-side, to expose each ball in turn at the top of its track. Examine the balls for cracks, flat spots, or signs of surface pitting.
**10** Inspect the ball tracks on the inner and outer members. If the tracks have widened, the balls will no longer be a tight fit. At the same time, check the ball cage windows for wear or cracking between the windows.
**11** If any of the constant velocity joint components are found to be worn or damaged, it will be necessary to renew the complete joint assembly. If the joint is in satisfactory condition, obtain a repair kit consisting of a new gaiter, circlip, retaining clips, and the correct type and quantity of grease **(see illustration)**.

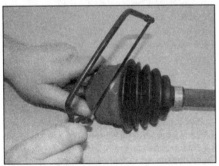

**3.2 Release the rubber gaiter retaining clips by cutting through them with a hacksaw**

**3.5b . . . then withdraw the joint off the end of the shaft**

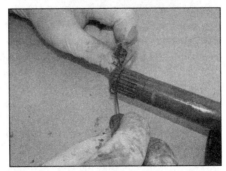

**3.6 Remove the circlip from the groove in the driveshaft splines**

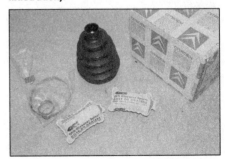

**3.11 Obtain a repair kit consisting of a new gaiter, circlip, retaining clips, and the correct type and quantity of grease**

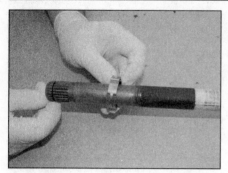

3.12a Slide the new gaiter inner retaining clip on the driveshaft . . .

3.12b . . . followed by the new gaiter

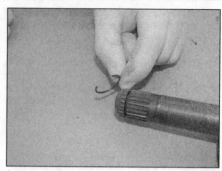

3.12c Locate a new circlip in the driveshaft groove . . .

3.12d . . . then compress the circlip using a cable tie. Use side-cutters to pull the cable tie tight, then cut off the end

3.12e Slide the CV joint onto the splines, and position the inner member up against the cable tie

3.12f Strike the end of the joint sharply to displace the cable tie and force the inner member over the circlip. With the joint in place, cut off the cable tie

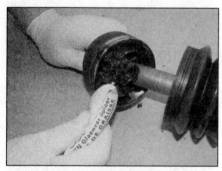

3.12g Pack the joint with half the recommended quantity of grease, working it well into the ball tracks

3.12h Fill the gaiter with the remaining grease, then slide the gaiter over the joint outer member, engaging it with the locating groove

3.12i Locate the gaiter inner end in the shaft groove or against the mark made on removal, slide the clip in place and compress the raised portion using pincers or side-cutters

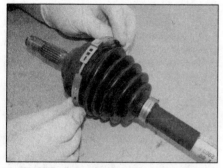

3.12j Slide the outer retaining clip over the gaiter . . .

3.12k . . . then compress the raised portion using pincers or side-cutters

3.15 Measure and record the distance between the inner edges of the driveshaft inner and outer gaiters

**3.17 Withdraw the joint outer member from the tripod**

**12** To install the new gaiter, perform the operations shown **(see illustrations)**. Be sure to stay in order, and follow the captions carefully. Note that different types of gaiter retaining clips may be encountered, but the fitting procedures will be similar to those shown.

**13** Check that the constant velocity joint moves freely in all directions, then refit the driveshaft to the car as described in Section 2.

*Inner joint*

**14** Remove the driveshaft from the vehicle as described in Section 2.

**15** Measure the distance between the inner edges of the driveshaft inner and outer rubber gaiters and record this dimension for use when refitting.

**16** Release the rubber gaiter inner and outer retaining clips by cutting through them using a junior hacksaw. Spread the clips and remove them from the gaiter.

**17** Withdraw the joint outer member from the tripod, and recover the spring and thrust cap from inside the outer member **(see illustration)**. As the outer member is withdrawn, check whether the tripod bearing rollers are staked to the tripod, or secured by circlips. If the rollers are not secured to the tripod, wrap adhesive tape around the rollers to hold them in position.

**18** Wipe away as much of the excess grease as possible from the tripod and bearing rollers. It is advisable to wear disposable rubber gloves during this operation.

**19** The tripod joint will either be staked to the end of the driveshaft or retained by means of a circlip. If a circlip is used, extract the circlip using circlip pliers.

**20** The tripod joint can now be removed using a two- or three-legged hydraulic bearing puller or a press. If a puller is being used, ensure that the legs of the puller are located behind the tripod, and not in contact with the joint rollers. If a press is being used, support the underside of the tripod, and press the driveshaft out of the joint. With the tripod removed, slide the gaiter off the end of the driveshaft.

**21** Wipe away as much of the old grease as possible (do not use any solvent) to allow the joint components to be inspected. Examine

the tripod, bearing rollers and outer member for any signs of scoring or wear, and for smoothness of movement of the rollers on the tripod stems. If any of the components are found to be worn or damaged, it will be necessary to renew the complete joint assembly. If the joint is in satisfactory condition, obtain a repair kit consisting of a new gaiter, retaining clips, and the correct type and quantity of grease.

**22** Slide the new inner retaining clip and the gaiter onto the driveshaft.

**23** Mount the driveshaft in a vice, engage the tripod over the splines and tap it fully into position.

**24** If the tripod was retained by a circlip, refit the circlip ensuring that it fully engages with the groove in the driveshaft. If a circlip was not used, stake the tripod to the driveshaft in three places using a small punch.

**25** Pack the tripod and the gaiter with half the recommended quantity of the grease, working it well into the bearing rollers.

**26** Refit the spring and thrust cap to the outer member, then pack the outer member with the remaining grease.

**27** Locate the outer member over the tripod, and engage the gaiter with the outer member groove.

**28** Push the outer member fully into position over the tripod, while lifting the gaiter inner end to expel the trapped air.

**29** Position the outer retaining clip over the gaiter and compress the raised portion using pincers or side-cutters.

**30** Position the gaiter inner end at the dimension recorded during removal, slip on the clip and compress the raised portion in the same way.

**31** Check that the constant velocity joint moves freely in all directions, then refit the driveshaft to the car as described in Section 2.

## 4 Driveshaft overhaul – general information

**Note:** *From around the end of 2004 the driveshaft joints are not removable from the shafts. Any problem with the joint requires a reconditioned or new shaft.*

**1** If any of the checks described in Chapter 1A or 1B reveal possible wear in any driveshaft joint, carry out the following procedures to identify the source of the problem.

**2** On models with a staked driveshaft nut, if the staking is still effective, the driveshaft nut should be correctly tightened; if in doubt, relieve the staking, then tighten the nut to the specified torque and restake it into the driveshaft grooves. Refit the roadwheel trim or centre cap (as applicable), and repeat the check on the remaining driveshaft nut.

**3** On models where the driveshaft nut is secured by an R-clip, if the R-clip is fitted, the driveshaft nut should be correctly tightened. If

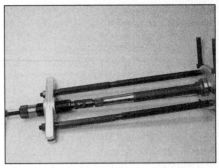

**5.3 Using a long-reach bearing puller to remove the intermediate bearing from the right-hand driveshaft**

in doubt, remove the R-clip and locking cap, and use a torque wrench to check that the nut is securely fastened. Once tightened, refit the locking cap and R-clip, and then refit the centre cap or trim. Repeat this check on the remaining driveshaft nut.

**4** Road test the vehicle, and listen for a metallic clicking from the front as the vehicle is driven slowly in a circle on full-lock. If a clicking noise is heard, this indicates wear in the outer constant velocity joint. This means that the joint must be renewed; reconditioning is not possible.

**5** If vibration, consistent with roadspeed, is felt through the car when accelerating, there is a possibility of wear in the inner constant velocity joints.

**6** To check the joints for wear, remove the driveshafts, then dismantle them as described in Section 3; if any wear or free play is found, the affected joint must be renewed.

## 5 Right-hand driveshaft intermediate bearing – renewal

**Note:** *A suitable bearing puller will be required, to draw the bearing and collar off the driveshaft end.*

**1** Remove the right-hand driveshaft as described in Section 2 of this Chapter.

**2** Check that the bearing outer race rotates smoothly and easily, without any signs of roughness or undue free play between the inner and outer races. If necessary, renew the bearing as follows.

**3** Using a long-reach universal bearing puller, carefully draw the collar and intermediate bearing off the driveshaft inner end **(see illustration)**. Apply a smear of grease to the inner race of the new bearing, then fit the bearing over the end of the driveshaft. Using a hammer and suitable piece of tubing which bears only on the bearing inner race, tap the new bearing into position on the driveshaft, until it abuts the constant velocity joint outer member. Once the bearing is correctly positioned, tap the bearing collar onto the shaft until it contacts the bearing inner race.

**4** Check that the bearing rotates freely, then refit the driveshaft as described in Section 2.

# Chapter 9
# Braking system

## Contents

## Degrees of difficulty

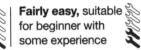

| **Easy,** suitable for novice with little experience | **Fairly easy,** suitable for beginner with some experience | **Fairly difficult,** suitable for competent DIY mechanic | **Difficult,** suitable for experienced DIY mechanic | **Very difficult,** suitable for expert DIY or professional |
|---|---|---|---|---|

## Specifications

### Front brakes

Type:
| | |
|---|---|
| 1.1 and 1.4 litre petrol engine, and 8-valve diesel engine models | Solid disc, with single-piston sliding caliper |
| 1.6 litre petrol engine and 16-valve diesel engine models | Ventilated disc, with single-piston sliding caliper |
| Disc diameter | 266.0 mm |

Disc thickness:
| | **New** | **Minimum** |
|---|---|---|
| Solid disc | 13.0 mm | 11.0 mm |
| Ventilated disc | 22.0 mm | 20.0 mm |

| | |
|---|---|
| Maximum disc run-out | 0.05 mm |

Brake pad friction material thickness:
| | |
|---|---|
| New | 13.0 mm |
| Minimum | 2.0 mm |

### Rear brakes

Type:
| | |
|---|---|
| 1.1 and 1.4 litre petrol engine, and 8-valve diesel engine models | Single leading shoe drum |
| 1.6 litre petrol engine and 16-valve diesel engine models | Solid disc, with single-piston sliding caliper |

Drum diameter:
| | |
|---|---|
| New | 203.0 mm |
| Maximum | 205.0 mm |
| Brake shoe friction material minimum thickness | 2.0 mm |
| Disc diameter | 247.0 mm |

Disc thickness:
| | |
|---|---|
| New | 9.0 mm |
| Minimum thickness | 7.0 mm |
| Maximum disc run-out | 0.05 mm |

Brake pad friction material thickness:
| | |
|---|---|
| New | 11.0 mm |
| Minimum | 2.0 mm |

### Anti-lock braking system

| | |
|---|---|
| Type | Teves Mk. 60 |

## Torque wrench settings

| | Nm | lbf ft |
|---|---|---|
| ABS system components: | | |
|    Modulator unit bolts | 10 | 7 |
|    Wheel speed sensor retaining bolts | 10 | 7 |
| Crossover linkage housing nuts and bolts (right-hand drive models) | 25 | 18 |
| Disc retaining screws | 10 | 7 |
| Front brake caliper: | | |
|    Guide pin bolts* | 30 | 22 |
|    Mounting bracket bolts* | 105 | 77 |
| Handbrake lever nuts | 15 | 12 |
| Hydraulic hose/pipe union nuts | 15 | 12 |
| Master cylinder retaining nuts | 20 | 15 |
| Rear brake caliper: | | |
|    Guide pin bolts* | 38 | 28 |
|    Mounting bracket bolts* | 50 | 37 |
| Rear hub nut* | 200 | 148 |
| Roadwheel bolts | 90 | 66 |
| Vacuum pump mounting bolts | 18 | 13 |
| Vacuum servo unit mounting nuts | 20 | 15 |

*\* New nuts/bolts must be used.*

## 1 General information

The braking system is of the servo-assisted, dual-circuit hydraulic type. The arrangement of the hydraulic system is such that each circuit operates one front and one rear brake from a tandem master cylinder. Under normal circumstances, both circuits operate in unison. However, in the event of hydraulic failure in one circuit, full braking force will still be available at two wheels.

All models are equipped with disc brakes on the front wheels and either disc or drum brakes on the rear wheels, according to model. ABS is fitted as standard on most models, and is optionally available on all others (refer to Section 22 for further information on ABS operation). Some later models are available with ESP (Electronic Stability Program). This system is designed to maintain the stability of the vehicle during extreme braking manoeuvres by operating the wheel brakes independently of each other. The system utilises the same wheel speed sensor/brake operating components as the ABS system, with the addition of a lateral acceleration sensor (Yaw rate) and a steering angle sensor.

The disc brakes are actuated by single-piston sliding type calipers, which ensure that equal pressure is applied to each disc pad.

On models with rear drum brakes, the rear brakes incorporate leading and trailing shoes, which are actuated by twin-piston wheel cylinders. The wheel cylinders incorporate integral pressure-regulating valves, which control the hydraulic pressure applied to the rear brakes. The regulating valves help to prevent rear wheel lock-up during emergency braking. A self-adjust mechanism is incorporated, to automatically compensate for brake shoe wear. As the brake shoe linings wear, the footbrake operation automatically operates the adjuster mechanism, which effectively lengthens the shoe strut and repositions the brake shoes, to reduce the lining-to-drum clearance.

On models with rear disc brakes, the brakes are actuated by single-piston sliding calipers which incorporate mechanical handbrake mechanisms. The hydraulic pressure applied to the rear brakes is regulated by the ABS hydraulic modulator under all braking conditions.

On all models, the handbrake provides an independent mechanical means of rear brake application.

On diesel engines, there is insufficient vacuum in the inlet manifold to operate the braking system servo effectively at all times. To overcome this problem, a vacuum pump is fitted to the engine, to provide sufficient vacuum to operate the servo unit. The vacuum pump is mounted on the end of the cylinder head, and is driven directly off the end of the camshaft.

**Note:** *When servicing any of the system, work carefully and methodically; also observe scrupulous cleanliness when overhauling any of the hydraulic system. Always renew components (in axle sets, where applicable) if in doubt about their condition, and use only genuine Citroën parts, or at least those of known good quality. Note the warnings given in 'Safety first!' and at relevant points in this Chapter concerning the dangers of asbestos dust and hydraulic fluid.*

## 2 Hydraulic system – bleeding

**Warning: Hydraulic fluid is poisonous; wash off immediately and thoroughly in the case of skin contact, and seek immediate medical advice if any fluid is swallowed or gets into the eyes. Certain types of hydraulic fluid are inflammable, and may ignite when allowed into contact with hot components; when servicing any hydraulic system, it is safest to assume that the fluid is inflammable, and to take precautions against the risk of fire as though it is petrol that is being handled. Hydraulic fluid is also an effective paint stripper, and will attack plastics; if any is spilt, it should be washed off immediately, using copious quantities of fresh water. Finally, it is hygroscopic (it absorbs moisture from the air) – old fluid may be contaminated and unfit for further use. When topping-up or renewing the fluid, always use the recommended type, and ensure that it comes from a freshly-opened sealed container.**

*Caution: Ensure the ignition is switched off before starting the bleeding procedure, to avoid any possibility of voltage being applied to the ABS hydraulic modulator before the bleeding procedure is complete. Ideally, the battery should be disconnected. If voltage is applied to the modulator before the bleeding procedure is complete, this will effectively drain the hydraulic fluid in the modulator, rendering the unit unserviceable. Do not, therefore, attempt to 'run' the modulator in order to bleed the brakes.*

**Note 1:** *If difficulty is experienced in bleeding the braking circuit, this maybe due to air being trapped in the ABS modulator unit. If this is the case then the vehicle should be taken to a Citroën dealer or suitably-equipped specialist so that the system can be bled using special electronic test equipment.*

**Note 2:** *A hydraulic clutch shares its fluid reservoir with the braking system, and may also need to be bled (see Chapter 6).*

### General

1 The correct operation of any hydraulic system is only possible after removing all air from the components and circuit; this is achieved by bleeding the system.

2 During the bleeding procedure, add only clean, unused hydraulic fluid of the recommended type; never re-use fluid that has already been bled from the system. Ensure that sufficient fluid is available before starting work.

3 If there is any possibility of incorrect fluid being already in the system, the brake

components and circuit must be flushed completely with uncontaminated, correct fluid, and new seals should be fitted to the various components.

**4** If hydraulic fluid has been lost from the system, or air has entered because of a leak, ensure that the fault is cured before proceeding further.

**5** Park the vehicle on level ground, switch off the engine and select first or reverse gear, then chock the wheels and release the handbrake.

**6** Check that all pipes and hoses are secure, unions tight and bleed screws closed. Clean any dirt from around the bleed screws.

**7** Unscrew the master cylinder reservoir cap, and top the master cylinder reservoir up to the MAX level line; refit the cap loosely, and remember to maintain the fluid level at least above the MIN level line throughout the procedure, or there is a risk of further air entering the system.

**8** There is a number of one-man, do-it-yourself brake bleeding kits currently available from motor accessory shops. It is recommended that one of these kits is used whenever possible, as they greatly simplify the bleeding operation, and also reduce the risk of expelled air and fluid being drawn back into the system. If such a kit is not available, the basic (two-man) method must be used, which is described in detail below.

**9** If a kit is to be used, prepare the vehicle as described previously, and follow the kit manufacturer's instructions, as the procedure may vary slightly according to the type being used; generally, they are as outlined below in the relevant sub-section.

**10** Whichever method is used, the same sequence must be followed (paragraphs 11 and 12) to ensure that the removal of all air from the system.

### *Bleeding*

#### Sequence

**11** If the system has been only partially disconnected, and suitable precautions were taken to minimise fluid loss, it should be necessary only to bleed that of the system (ie, the primary or secondary circuit).

**12** If the complete system is to be bled, then it should be done working in the following sequence:

   *a) Left-hand front brake.*
   *b) Right-hand front brake.*
   *c) Left-hand rear brake.*
   *d) Right-hand rear brake.*

#### Basic (two-man) method

**13** Collect a clean glass jar, a suitable length of plastic or rubber tubing which is a tight fit over the bleed screw, and a ring spanner to fit the screw. The help of an assistant will also be required.

**14** Remove the dust cap from the first screw in the sequence. Fit the spanner and tube to the screw, place the other end of the tube in the jar, and pour in sufficient fluid to cover the end of the tube.

**15** Ensure that the master cylinder reservoir fluid level is maintained at least above the MIN level line throughout the procedure.

**16** Have the assistant fully depress the brake pedal several times to build-up pressure, then maintain it on the final downstroke.

**17** While pedal pressure is maintained, unscrew the bleed screw (approximately one turn) and allow the compressed fluid and air to flow into the jar. The assistant should maintain pedal pressure, following it down to the floor if necessary, and should not release it until instructed to do so. When the flow stops, tighten the bleed screw again, have the assistant release the pedal slowly, and recheck the reservoir fluid level.

**18** Repeat the steps given in paragraphs 16 and 17 until the fluid emerging from the bleed screw is free from air bubbles. If the master cylinder has been drained and refilled, and air is being bled from the first screw in the sequence, allow approximately five seconds between cycles for the master cylinder passages to refill.

**19** When no more air bubbles appear, tighten the bleed screw securely, remove the tube and spanner, and refit the dust cap. Do not overtighten the bleed screw.

**20** Repeat the procedure on the remaining screws in the sequence, until all air is removed from the system and the brake pedal feels firm again.

#### Using a one-way valve kit

**21** As their name implies, these kits consist of a length of tubing with a one-way valve fitted, to prevent expelled air and fluid being drawn back into the system; some kits include a translucent container which can be positioned so that the air bubbles can be more easily seen flowing from the end of the tube.

**22** The kit is connected to the bleed screw, which is then opened **(see illustration)**. The user returns to the driver's seat, depresses the brake pedal with a smooth, steady stroke, and slowly releases it; this is repeated until the expelled fluid is clear of air bubbles.

**23** Note that these kits simplify work so much that it is easy to forget the master cylinder reservoir fluid level; ensure that this is maintained at least above the MIN level line at all times.

**2.22 Connect the kit to the bleed screw**

#### Using a pressure-bleeding kit

**24** These kits are usually operated by the reservoir of pressurised air contained in the spare tyre. However, note that it will probably be necessary to reduce the pressure to a lower level than normal; refer to the instructions supplied with the kit.

**25** By connecting a pressurised, fluid-filled container to the master cylinder reservoir, bleeding can be carried out simply by opening each screw in turn (in the specified sequence), and allowing the fluid to flow out until no more air bubbles can be seen in the expelled fluid.

**26** This method has the advantage that the large reservoir of fluid provides an additional safeguard against air being drawn into the system during bleeding.

**27** Pressure-bleeding is particularly effective when bleeding 'difficult' systems, or when bleeding the complete system at the time of routine fluid renewal.

#### All methods

**28** When bleeding is complete, and firm pedal feel is restored, wash off any spilt fluid, tighten the bleed screws securely, and refit their dust caps.

**29** Check the hydraulic fluid level in the master cylinder reservoir, and top-up if necessary (see *Weekly checks*).

**30** Discard any hydraulic fluid that has been bled from the system; it will not be fit for re-use.

**31** Check the feel of the brake pedal. If it feels at all spongy, air must still be present in the system, and further bleeding is required. Failure to bleed satisfactorily after a reasonable repetition of the bleeding procedure may be due to worn master cylinder seals.

---

**3  Hydraulic pipes and hoses**
   **– renewal**

---

*Caution: Ensure the ignition is switched off before disconnecting any braking system hydraulic union and do not switch it on until after the hydraulic system has been bled. Failure to do this could lead to air entering the ABS hydraulic modulator requiring the unit to be bled using special Citroën test equipment (see Section 2).*

**Note:** *Before starting work, refer to the note at the beginning of Section 2 concerning the dangers of hydraulic fluid.*

**1** If any pipe or hose is to be renewed, minimise fluid loss by first removing the master cylinder reservoir cap, then tightening it down onto a piece of polythene to obtain an airtight seal. Alternatively, flexible hoses can be sealed, if required, using a proprietary brake hose clamp; metal brake pipe unions can be plugged (if care is taken not to allow dirt into the system) or capped immediately they are disconnected. Place a wad of rag under any union that is to be disconnected, to catch any spilt fluid.

**4.2 Push the piston into its bore by carefully levering the caliper outwards**

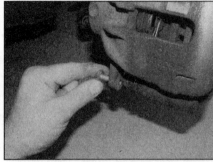

**4.3 Slacken and remove the caliper lower guide pin bolt**

**4.4 Pivot the caliper upwards off the brake pads and mounting bracket**

**4.5 Withdraw the inner and outer brake pads from the caliper mounting bracket**

**2** If a flexible hose is to be disconnected, unscrew the brake pipe union nut before removing the spring clip which secures the hose to its mounting bracket.

**3** To unscrew the union nuts, it is preferable to obtain a brake pipe spanner of the correct size; these are available from most large motor accessory shops. Failing this, a close-fitting open-ended spanner will be required, though if the nuts are tight or corroded, their flats may be rounded-off if the spanner slips. In such a case, a self-locking wrench is often the only way to unscrew a stubborn union, but it follows that the pipe and the damaged nuts must be renewed on reassembly. Always clean a union and surrounding area before disconnecting it. If disconnecting a component with more than one union, make a careful note of the connections before disturbing any of them.

**4** If a brake pipe is to be renewed, it can be

obtained, cut to length and with the union nuts and end flares in place, from Citroën dealers. All that is then necessary is to bend it to shape, following the line of the original, before fitting it to the car. Alternatively, most motor accessory shops can make up brake pipes from kits, but this requires very careful measurement of the original, to ensure that the new one is of the correct length. The safest answer is usually to take the original to the shop as a pattern.

**5** On refitting, do not overtighten the union nuts. It is not necessary to exercise brute force to obtain a sound joint.

**6** Ensure that the pipes and hoses are correctly routed, with no kinks, and that they are secured in the clips or brackets provided. After fitting, remove the polythene from the reservoir, and bleed the hydraulic system as described in Section 2. Wash off any spilt fluid, and check carefully for fluid leaks.

**4.9a Use a suitable tool to retract the caliper piston . . .**

**4.9b . . . and with the bleed nipple open, collect the expelled fluid in a container**

## 4 Front brake pads – renewal

⚠️ **Warning: Renew both sets of front brake pads at the same time – never renew the pads on only one wheel, as uneven braking may result. Note that the dust created by wear of the pads may contain asbestos, which is a health hazard. Never blow it out with compressed air, and don't inhale any of it. An approved filtering mask should be worn when working on the brakes. DO NOT use petrol or petroleum-based solvents to clean brake parts; use brake cleaner or methylated spirit only.**

**Note:** *New guide pin bolts must be used on refitting.*

**1** Apply the handbrake, slacken the front roadwheel bolts, then jack up the front of the vehicle and support it on axle stands. Remove the front roadwheels.

**2** Push the piston into its bore by carefully levering the caliper outwards **(see illustration)**.

**3** Hold the caliper lower guide pin with a spanner, then slacken and remove the guide pin bolt with a second spanner **(see illustration)**. Discard the guide pin bolt – a new one must be used on refitting.

**4** With the lower guide pin bolt removed, pivot the caliper away from the brake pads and mounting bracket, and tie it to the suspension strut using a suitable piece of wire **(see illustration)**.

**5** Withdraw the two brake pads from the caliper mounting bracket; the shims (where fitted) should be bonded to the pad, but may have come unstuck in use **(see illustration)**.

**6** First measure the thickness of each brake pad's friction material. If either pad is worn at any point to the specified minimum thickness or less, all four pads must be renewed. Also, the pads should be renewed if any are fouled with oil or grease; there is no satisfactory way of degreasing friction material, once contaminated. If any of the brake pads are worn unevenly, or are fouled with oil or grease, trace and rectify the cause before reassembly.

**7** If the brake pads are still serviceable, carefully clean them using a clean, fine wire brush or similar, paying particular attention to the sides and back of the metal backing. Clean out the grooves in the friction material, and pick out any large embedded particles of dirt or debris. Carefully clean the pad locations in the caliper mounting bracket.

**8** Prior to fitting the pads, check that the guide pins are free to slide easily in the caliper mounting bracket, and check that the rubber guide pin gaiters are undamaged. Brush the dust and dirt from the caliper and piston, but **do not** inhale it, as it is a health hazard. Inspect the dust seal around the piston for damage, and the piston for evidence of fluid leaks, corrosion or damage. If attention to any of these components is necessary, refer to Section 8.

9 If new brake pads are to be fitted, the caliper piston must be pushed back into the cylinder to make room for them. Either use a G-clamp or similar tool, or use suitable pieces of wood as levers. Clamp off the flexible brake hose leading to the caliper then connect a brake bleeding kit to the caliper bleed nipple. Open the bleed nipple as the piston is retracted, the surplus brake fluid will then be collected in the bleed kit vessel **(see illustrations)**. Close the bleed nipple just before the caliper piston is pushed fully into the caliper. This should ensure no air enters the hydraulic system. **Note:** *The ABS modulator contains hydraulic components that are very sensitive to impurities in the brake fluid. Even the smallest particles can cause the system to fail through blockage. The pad retraction method described here prevents any debris in the brake fluid expelled from the caliper from being passed back to the ABS modulator, as well as preventing any chance of damage to the master cylinder seals.*

10 Check to make sure the shims at the top and bottom of the caliper bracket are correctly fitted **(see illustration)**.

11 Ensuring that the friction material of each pad is against the brake disc, fit the pads to the caliper mounting bracket. If the shims (where fitted) have become detached, ensure that they are correctly positioned on each pads backing plate.

12 Pivot the caliper down into position over the pads. If the threads of the new guide pin bolt are not already precoated with locking compound, apply a suitable thread-locking compound to them (Citroën recommend Loctite Frenetanch – available from your dealer). Press the caliper into position, then install the guide pin bolt, tightening it to the specified torque setting.

13 Depress the brake pedal repeatedly, until the pads are pressed into firm contact with the brake disc, and normal (non-assisted) pedal pressure is restored.

14 Repeat the above procedure on the remaining front brake caliper.

15 Refit the roadwheels, then lower the vehicle to the ground and tighten the roadwheel bolts to the specified torque.

16 Check the hydraulic fluid level as described in *Weekly checks*.

*Caution: New pads will not give full braking*

**4.10  Ensure that the shims at the top and bottom of the caliper bracket are correctly fitted**

*efficiency until they have bedded-in. Be prepared for this, and avoid hard braking as far as possible for the first hundred miles or so after pad renewal.*

## 5  Rear brake pads – renewal

⚠ *Warning: Renew both sets of rear brake pads at the same time – never renew the pads on only one wheel, as uneven braking may result. Note that the dust created by wear of the pads may contain asbestos, which is a health hazard. Never blow it out with compressed air, and don't inhale any of it. An approved filtering mask should be worn when working on the brakes. DO NOT use petrol or petroleum-based solvents to clean brake parts; use brake cleaner or methylated spirit only.*

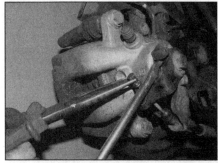

**5.2a  Release the handbrake cable from the caliper lever . . .**

**Note:** *New guide pin bolts must be fitted on reassembly.*

1 Chock the front wheels, slacken the rear roadwheel bolts, then jack up the rear of the vehicle and support it on axle stands (see *Jacking and vehicle support*). Remove the rear roadwheels.

2 Using a pair of pliers, release the handbrake cable from the caliper lever. Compress the clip and pull the cable from the support bracket **(see illustrations)**.

3 Slacken and remove the caliper upper and lower guide pin bolts, using a second spanner to retain the guide pin **(see illustration)**. Slide the caliper off the mounting bracket and brake pads, and tie it to the road spring using a suitable piece of wire.

4 Withdraw the inner and outer pads from the caliper bracket, and note the location of any shims fitted between the pads and caliper **(see illustrations)**.

5 First measure the thickness of the friction material of each brake pad. If either pad is worn at any point to the specified minimum thickness or less, all four pads must be renewed. Also, the pads should be renewed if any are fouled with oil or grease; there is no satisfactory way of degreasing friction material, once contaminated. If any of the brake pads are worn unevenly, or fouled with oil or grease, trace and rectify the cause before reassembly. Examine the retaining pins for signs of wear and renew if necessary. New brake pads and retaining pin kits are available from Citroën dealers.

6 If the brake pads are still serviceable,

**5.2b  . . . then compress the clip and pull the cable from the support bracket**

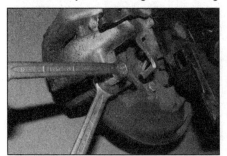

**5.3  Slacken and remove the caliper upper and lower guide pin bolts, using a second spanner to retain the guide pin**

**5.4a  Withdraw the inner and outer pads from the caliper bracket . . .**

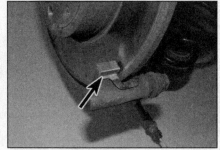

**5.4b  . . . noting the fitted location of any shims (arrowed) fitted between the pads and caliper**

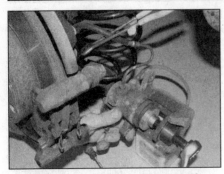

**5.8 Use a retraction tool to rotate the piston whilst pushing at the same time**

carefully clean them using a clean, fine wire brush or similar, paying particular attention to the sides and back of the metal backing. Clean out the grooves in the friction material, and pick out any large embedded particles of dirt or debris. Carefully clean the pad locations in the caliper body/mounting bracket.

7 Prior to fitting the pads, check that the guide pins are free to slide easily in the caliper body, and check that the rubber guide pin gaiters are undamaged. Brush the dust and dirt from the caliper and piston, but **do not** inhale it, as it is a health hazard. Inspect the dust seal around the piston for damage, and the piston for evidence of fluid leaks, corrosion or damage. If attention to any of these components is necessary, refer to Section 9.

8 If new brake pads are to be fitted, the caliper piston must be pushed back into the cylinder to make room for them. In order to retract the piston, the piston must be turned clockwise as it is pushed into the caliper. Citroën tool No 0805.JZ is available to retract the pistons, as are several available from good accessory/parts retailers **(see illustration)**. Clamp off the flexible brake hose leading to the caliper then connect a brake bleeding kit to the caliper bleed nipple. Open the bleed nipple as the piston is retracted, the surplus brake fluid will then be collected in the bleed kit vessel. Close the bleed nipple just before the caliper piston is pushed fully into the caliper. This should ensure no air enters the hydraulic system. **Note:** *The ABS modulator contains hydraulic components that are very sensitive to impurities in the brake fluid. Even the smallest particles can cause the system*

*to fail through blockage. The pad retraction method described here prevents any debris in the brake fluid expelled from the caliper from being passed back to the ABS modulator, as well as preventing any chance of damage to the master cylinder seals.*

9 Slide the brake pads into position in the caliper bracket, ensuring each pad's friction material is facing the brake disc. If the shims (where fitted) have become detached, ensure that they are correctly positioned on each pad's backing plate.

10 Slide the caliper back into position over the pads. Insert the new caliper guide pin bolts, and tighten them to the specified torque.

11 Slide the handbrake cable into the support bracket and reconnect the cable end fitting.

12 Depress the brake pedal repeatedly until the pads are pressed into firm contact with the brake disc, and normal (non-assisted) pedal pressure is restored.

13 Repeat the above procedure on the remaining rear brake caliper.

14 Check the operation of the handbrake, and if necessary, carry out the adjustment procedure as described in Section 17.

15 Refit the roadwheels, then lower the vehicle to the ground and tighten the roadwheel bolts to the specified torque setting.

16 Check the hydraulic fluid level as described in *Weekly checks*.

*Caution: New pads will not give full braking efficiency until they have bedded-in. Be prepared for this, and avoid hard braking as far as possible for the first hundred miles or so after pad renewal.*

## 6 Front brake disc – inspection, removal and refitting

**Note:** *Before starting work, refer to the note at the beginning of Section 4 concerning the dangers of asbestos dust.*

### Inspection

**Note:** *If either disc requires renewal, BOTH should be renewed at the same time, to ensure even and consistent braking. New brake pads should also be fitted.*

1 Apply the handbrake, slacken the front

roadwheel bolts, then jack up the front of the car and support it on axle stands (see *Jacking and vehicle support*). Remove the appropriate front roadwheel.

2 Slowly rotate the brake disc so that the full area of both sides can be checked; remove the brake pads if better access is required to the inboard surface. Light scoring is normal in the area swept by the brake pads, but if heavy scoring or cracks are found, the disc must be renewed.

3 It is normal to find a lip of rust and brake dust around the disc's perimeter; this can be scraped off if required. If, however, a lip has formed due to excessive wear of the brake pad swept area, then the disc's thickness must be measured using a micrometer. Take measurements at several places around the disc, at the inside and outside of the pad swept area; if the disc has worn at any point to the specified minimum thickness or less, the disc must be renewed **(see illustration)**.

4 If the disc is thought to be warped, it can be checked for run-out. Either use a dial gauge mounted on any convenient fixed point, while the disc is slowly rotated, or use feeler blades to measure (at several points all around the disc) the clearance between the disc and a fixed point, such as the caliper mounting bracket **(see illustration)**. If the measurements obtained are at the specified maximum or beyond, the disc is excessively warped, and must be renewed; however, it is worth checking first that the hub bearing is in good condition (Chapter 1A or 1B). Also try the effect of removing the disc and turning it through 180°, to reposition it on the hub; if the run-out is still excessive, the disc must be renewed.

5 Check the disc for cracks, especially around the wheel bolt holes, and any other wear or damage, and renew if necessary.

### Removal

**Note:** *New caliper mounting bracket bolts will be required on reassembly.*

6 Slacken and remove the two bolts securing the brake caliper mounting bracket to the hub carrier **(see illustration)**. Slide the assembly off the disc and tie it to the coil spring, using a piece of wire or string, to avoid placing any strain on the hydraulic brake hose.

**6.3 Use a micrometer to measure the disc thickness**

**6.4 Check the disc run-out using a dial gauge**

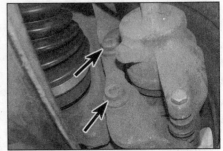

**6.6 Slacken and remove the two bolts (arrowed) securing the brake caliper mounting bracket to the hub carrier**

**7** Use chalk or paint to mark the relationship of the disc to the hub, then remove the screws securing the brake disc to the hub, and remove the disc. If it is tight, lightly tap its rear face with a hide or plastic mallet.

### Refitting

**8** Refitting is the reverse of the removal procedure, noting the following points:
  a) *Ensure that the mating surfaces of the disc and hub are clean and flat.*
  b) *Align (if applicable) the marks made on removal, and tighten the disc retaining screws to the specified torque setting.*
  c) *If a new disc has been fitted, use a suitable solvent to wipe any preservative coating from the disc, before refitting the caliper.*
  d) *Refit the roadwheel then lower the vehicle to the ground and tighten the wheel bolts to the specified torque. Apply the footbrake several times to force the pads back into contact with the disc before driving the vehicle.*

---

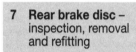 **7  Rear brake disc –** inspection, removal and refitting

**Note:** *Before starting work, refer to the note at the beginning of Section 5 concerning the dangers of asbestos dust.*

### Inspection

**Note:** *If either disc requires renewal, BOTH should be renewed at the same time, to ensure even and consistent braking. New brake pads should also be fitted.*
**1** Firmly chock the front wheels, slacken the appropriate rear roadwheel bolts, then jack up the rear of the car and support it on axle stands (see *Jacking and vehicle support*). Remove the relevant rear roadwheel.
**2** Inspect the disc as described in Section 6.

### Removal

**Note:** *New caliper mounting bracket bolts will be required on reassembly.*
**3** Remove the brake pads as described in Section 5.
**4** Undo the two Torx bolts securing the caliper mounting bracket to the stub axle, and lift off the bracket **(see illustration).**
**5** Use chalk or paint to mark the relationship of the disc to the hub, then undo the screw(s) securing the disc to the hub. If necessary, gently tap the disc from behind and release it from the hub **(see illustration).**

### Refitting

**6** Refitting is the reverse of the removal procedure, noting the following points:
  a) *Ensure that the mating surfaces of the disc and hub are clean and flat.*
  b) *Align (if applicable) the marks made on removal, and tighten the disc retaining screws to the specified torque.*
  c) *If a new disc has been fitted, use a*

**7.4  Slacken the two caliper mounting bracket Torx bolts (arrowed)**

*suitable solvent to wipe any preservative coating from the disc, before refitting the caliper.*
  d) *Refit the roadwheel, then lower the vehicle to the ground and tighten the roadwheel bolts to the specified torque. Depress the brake pedal several times to force the pads back into contact with the disc.*

---

 **8  Front brake caliper –** removal, overhaul and refitting

**Caution: Ensure the ignition is switched off before disconnecting any braking system hydraulic union and do not switch it on until after the hydraulic system has been bled. Failure to do this could lead to air entering the ABS hydraulic modulator requiring the unit to be bled using special Citroën test equipment (see Section 2).**
**Note 1:** *Before starting work, refer to the note at the beginning of Section 2 concerning the dangers of hydraulic fluid, and to the warning at the beginning of Section 4 concerning the dangers of asbestos dust.*
**Note 2:** *New caliper guide pin bolts and caliper mounting bracket bolts will be required on reassembly.*

### Removal

**1** Apply the handbrake, slacken the relevant front roadwheel bolts, then jack up the front of the vehicle and support it on axle stands (see *Jacking and vehicle support*). Remove the appropriate roadwheel.
**2** Minimise fluid loss by first removing the master cylinder reservoir cap, and then tightening it down onto a piece of polythene, to obtain an airtight seal. Alternatively, use a brake hose clamp, a G-clamp or a similar tool to clamp the flexible hose **(see illustration).**
**3** Clean the area around the caliper hose union, then loosen the union.
**4** Slacken and remove the upper and lower caliper guide pin bolts **(see illustration 4.3).** Discard the bolts, new ones must be used on refitting. Lift the caliper away from the brake disc, then unscrew the caliper from the end of the brake hose. Note that the brake pads need not be disturbed, and can be left in position in the caliper mounting bracket.

**7.5  Undo the Torx screws and remove the disc**

**5** If required, the caliper mounting bracket can be unbolted from the hub carrier. Discard the bolts as new ones must be fitted.

### Overhaul

**Note:** *Check the availability of repair kits for the caliper before dismantling.*
**6** With the caliper on the bench, wipe away all traces of dust and dirt, but *avoid inhaling the dust, as it is a health hazard.*
**7** Withdraw the partially ejected piston from the caliper body, and remove the dust seal.

> **HAYNES HiNT** *If the piston cannot be withdrawn by hand, it can be pushed out by applying compressed air to the brake hose union hole. Only low pressure should be required, such as is generated by a foot pump. As the piston is expelled, take great care not to trap your fingers between the piston and caliper.*

**8** Using a small screwdriver, extract the piston hydraulic seal, taking great care not to damage the caliper bore.
**9** Thoroughly clean all components, using only methylated spirit, isopropyl alcohol or clean hydraulic fluid as a cleaning medium. Never use mineral-based solvents such as petrol or paraffin, as they will attack the hydraulic system's rubber components. Dry the components immediately, using compressed air or a clean, lint-free cloth. Use compressed air to blow clear the fluid passages.

**8.2  To minimise fluid loss, fit a brake hose clamp to the flexible hose**

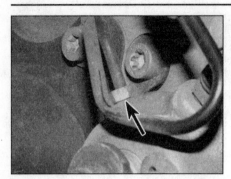

**9.4 Unscrew the union nut (arrowed)**

**10** Check all components, and renew any that are worn or damaged. Check particularly the cylinder bore and piston; these should be renewed (note that this means the renewal of the complete body assembly) if they are scratched, worn or corroded in any way. Similarly check the condition of the guide pins and their gaiters; both pins should be undamaged and (when cleaned) a reasonably tight sliding fit in the caliper bracket. If there is any doubt about the condition of any component, renew it.

**11** If the assembly is fit for further use, obtain the appropriate repair kit; the components should be available from Citroën dealers in various combinations. All rubber seals should be renewed as a matter of course; these should never be re-used.

**12** On reassembly, ensure that all components are clean and dry.

**13** Soak the piston and the new piston (fluid) seal in clean brake fluid. Smear clean fluid on the cylinder bore surface.

**14** Fit the new piston (fluid) seal, using only your fingers (no tools) to manipulate it into the cylinder bore groove.

**15** Fit the new dust seal to the rear of the piston and seat the outer lip of the seal in the caliper body groove. Carefully ease the piston squarely into the cylinder bore using a twisting motion. Press the piston fully into position, and seat the inner lip of the dust seal in the piston groove.

**16** If the guide pins are being renewed, lubricate the pin shafts with the special grease supplied in the repair kit, and fit the gaiters to the pin grooves. Insert the pins into the caliper

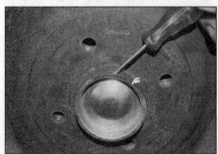

**10.2 Using a suitable screwdriver, carefully prise the dust cap out of the centre of the brake drum**

bracket and seat the gaiters correctly in the bracket grooves.

### Refitting

**17** If previously removed, refit the caliper mounting bracket to the hub carrier, and tighten the new bolts to the specified torque.

**18** Screw the caliper body fully onto the flexible hose union.

**19** Ensure that the brake pads are correctly fitted in the caliper mounting bracket and refit the caliper (see Section 4).

**20** If the threads of the new guide pin bolts are not already precoated with locking compound, apply a suitable locking compound to them (Citroën recommend Loctite Frenetanch – available from your dealer). Fit the new lower guide pin bolt, then press the caliper into position and fit the new upper guide pin bolt. Tighten both guide pin bolts to the specified torque.

**21** Tighten the brake hose union nut to the specified torque, then remove the brake hose clamp or polythene (where fitted).

**22** Bleed the hydraulic system as described in Section 2. Note that, providing the precautions described were taken to minimise brake fluid loss, it should only be necessary to bleed the relevant front brake.

**23** Refit the roadwheel, then lower the vehicle to the ground and tighten the roadwheel bolts to the specified torque.

## 9 Rear brake caliper – removal, overhaul and refitting

*Caution: Ensure the ignition is switched off before disconnecting any braking system hydraulic union and do not switch it on until after the hydraulic system has been bled. Failure to do this could lead to air entering the ABS hydraulic modulator requiring the unit to be bled using special Citroën test equipment (see Section 2).*

**Note 1:** *Before starting work, refer to the note at the beginning of Section 2 concerning the dangers of hydraulic fluid, and to the warning at the beginning of Section 5 concerning the dangers of asbestos dust.*

**Note 2:** *New caliper mounting bracket bolts and guide pin bolts when be required on reassembly.*

### Removal

**1** Chock the front wheels, slacken the relevant rear roadwheel bolts, then jack up the rear of the vehicle and support on axle stands (see *Jacking and vehicle support*). Remove the relevant rear wheel.

**2** Remove the brake pads (see Section 5).

**3** Minimise fluid loss by first removing the master cylinder reservoir cap, and then tightening it down onto a piece of polythene, to obtain an airtight seal. Alternatively, use a brake hose clamp, a G-clamp or a similar tool to clamp the flexible hose at the nearest convenient point to the brake caliper.

**4** Wipe away all traces of dirt around the brake pipe union on the caliper. Unscrew the union nut and disconnect the brake pipe from the caliper **(see illustration)**. Plug the pipe and caliper unions to minimise fluid loss and prevent dirt entry.

**5** Withdraw the caliper from the vehicle. If required, the caliper mounting bracket can be unbolted from the hub carrier. Discard the bolts as new ones must be fitted.

### Overhaul

**6** Check that spare parts are available before deciding to overhaul the caliper. Although Citroën dealers do not supply internal parts for the caliper (apart from guide pin bolts, guide pins and guide pin gaiters), it may be possible to obtain a repair kit from specialist motor factors. Ensure that the correct repair kit is obtained for the caliper being worked on. Note the locations of all components to ensure correct refitting, and lubricate the new seals using clean brake fluid. Follow the assembly instructions supplied with the repair kit.

### Refitting

**7** If previously removed, refit the caliper mounting bracket to the hub carrier, and tighten the new bolts to the specified torque.

**8** Refit the brake pads as described in Section 5.

**9** Refit the caliper and insert the new guide pin bolts, tightening them to the specified torque settings.

**10** Reconnect the brake pipe to the caliper, and tighten the brake hose union nut to the specified torque. Remove the brake hose clamp or polythene (where fitted).

**11** Bleed the hydraulic system as described in Section 2. Note that, providing the precautions described were taken to minimise brake fluid loss, it should only be necessary to bleed the relevant rear brake.

**12** Refit the roadwheel, then lower the vehicle to the ground and tighten the roadwheel bolts to the specified torque.

## 10 Rear brake drum – removal, inspection and refitting

**Note 1:** *Before starting work, refer to the warning at the beginning of Section 5 concerning the dangers of asbestos dust.*

**Note 2:** *A new rear hub nut and dust cap must be used on refitting.*

### Removal

**1** Chock the front wheels, then jack up the rear of the vehicle and support it on axle stands (see *Jacking and vehicle support*). Remove the appropriate rear wheel and release the handbrake.

**2** Using a suitable screwdriver, carefully prise the dust cap out of the centre of the brake drum **(see illustration)**. Discard the cap – a new one must be used on refitting.

**3** Using a hammer and a suitable cold chisel or punch, relieve the staking on the rear hub nut.

 **Warning: Wear suitable eye protection.**

**4** Using a socket and long bar, slacken and remove the rear hub nut, and withdraw the thrustwasher **(see illustrations)**. Discard the hub nut – a new nut must used on refitting.

**5** It should now be possible to withdraw the brake drum assembly from the stub axle by hand **(see illustration)**. It may be difficult to remove the drum, due to the tightness of the hub bearing on the stub axle, or due to the brake shoes binding on the inner circumference of the drum. If the bearing is tight, tap the periphery of the drum using a hide or plastic mallet, or use a universal puller, secured to the drum with the wheel bolts, to pull it off. If the brake shoes are binding, first check that the handbrake is fully released. Referring to Section 17 for further information, fully slacken the handbrake adjuster nut to obtain maximum free play in the cable. It should now be possible to remove the drum.

### Inspection

**Note:** *If either drum requires renewal, BOTH should be renewed at the same time, to ensure even and consistent braking. New brake shoes should also be fitted.*

**6** Working carefully, remove all traces of brake dust from the drum, but *avoid inhaling the dust, as it is a health hazard.*

**7** Clean the outside of the drum, and check it for obvious signs of wear or damage, such as cracks around the roadwheel bolt holes; renew the drum if necessary.

**8** Carefully examine the inside of the drum. Light scoring of the friction surface is normal, but if heavy scoring is found, the drum must be renewed. It is usual to find a lip on the drum's inboard edge which consists of a mixture of rust and brake dust; this should be scraped away, to leave a smooth surface which can be polished with fine (120- to 150-grade) emery paper. If, however, the lip is due to the friction surface being recessed by excessive wear, then the drum must be renewed.

**9** If the drum is thought to be excessively worn, or oval, its internal diameter must be measured at several points using an internal micrometer. Take measurements in pairs, the second at right-angles to the first, and compare the two, to check for signs of ovality. Provided that it does not enlarge the drum to beyond the specified maximum diameter, it may be possible to have the drum refinished by skimming or grinding; if this is not possible, the drums on both sides must be renewed. Note that if the drum is to be skimmed, BOTH drums must be refinished, to maintain a consistent internal diameter on both sides.

### Refitting

**10** If a new brake drum is to be installed, use a suitable solvent to remove any preservative

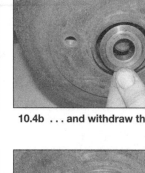

**10.4a Slacken and remove the rear hub nut . . .**

**10.4b . . . and withdraw the thrustwasher**

**10.5 Withdraw the brake drum assembly from the stub axle**

**10.12 Stake the hub nut into the stub axle groove to secure it in position**

coating that may have been applied to its internal friction surfaces. Note that it may also be necessary to shorten the adjuster strut length, by rotating the strut wheel, to allow the drum to pass over the brake shoes.

**11** Ensure that the handbrake lever stop-peg is correctly repositioned against the edge of the brake shoe web, then apply a smear of clean engine oil to the stub axle, and slide on the drum assembly.

**12** Fit the thrustwasher and new hub nut, and tighten the hub nut to the specified torque. Stake the nut firmly into the groove on the stub axle, to secure it in position **(see illustration)**.

**13** Tap the new dust cover into place in the centre of the brake drum.

**14** Depress the footbrake several times to operate the self-adjusting mechanism.

**15** Repeat the above procedure on the remaining rear brake assembly (where necessary), then check and, if necessary, adjust the handbrake cable as described in Section 17.

**16** On completion, refit the roadwheel(s), then lower the vehicle to the ground and tighten the roadwheel bolts to the specified torque.

## 11 Rear brake shoes – renewal

 **Warning: Renew BOTH sets of rear brake shoes at the same time – NEVER renew the shoes on only one wheel, as uneven braking may result. Note that the dust created by wear**

*of the shoes may contain asbestos, which is a health hazard. Never blow it out with compressed air, and don't inhale any of it. An approved filtering mask should be worn when working on the brakes. DO NOT use petrol or petroleum-based solvents to clean brake parts; use brake cleaner or methylated spirit only.*

**Note:** *The components encountered may vary in detail, but the principles described in the following paragraphs are equally applicable to all models. Make a careful note of the fitted positions of all components before dismantling.*

**HAYNES HINT** *Complete all work on one rear drum at a time – in other words, renew the shoes on one side, before starting work on the other side. In this way, you will always have an assembled set of shoes to use as a reference.*

**1** Remove the rear brake drums, as described in Section 10.

**2** Working on one side of the vehicle, brush the dirt and dust from the brake backplate and drum. **Do not** inhale the dust, as it may be a health hazard.

**3** Note the position of each shoe, and the location of the return and steady springs.

**4** Using pliers, release the handbrake lever helper spring from the handbrake lever, then disengage the helper spring from the brake shoe and lower return spring (see illustrations).

11.4a Release the helper spring from the handbrake lever . . .

11.4b . . . then disengage the helper spring from the brake shoe and lower return spring

11.5 Depress the hold-down spring clips while pushing on the pin from behind the backplate

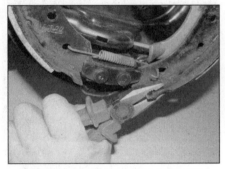

11.6a Disengage the lower ends of the shoes from the bottom anchor . . .

11.6b . . . and pull the upper ends of the shoes from the wheel cylinder pistons

11.6c Withdraw the shoe assembly, and unhook the handbrake cable from the lever on the trailing shoe

5 Remove the brake shoe hold-down spring clips. Use pliers to depress the spring clips while pushing on the pin from behind the backplate with your finger **(see illustration)**. Slide the spring clips off the pins, then remove the pins from the rear of the backplate.

6 Disengage the lower ends of the shoes from the bottom anchor, and pull the upper ends of the shoes from the wheel cylinder pistons. Withdraw the shoe assembly, and unhook the handbrake cable from the lever on the trailing brake shoe **(see illustrations)**.

7 Position a rubber band or a cable-tie over the wheel cylinder, to prevent the pistons from being ejected.

8 With the brake shoe assembly on the bench, Unhook the lower return spring from the leading shoe, then remove it from the trailing shoe.

9 Spread the shoes apart at the bottom and disengage the adjuster strut from the handbrake lever and leading brake shoe.

10 Remove the upper return spring, then remove the adjuster lever return spring and adjuster lever from the leading shoe.

11 Withdraw the forked end from the strut, and carefully examine the assembly for signs of wear or damage. Pay particular attention to the threads and the knurled adjuster wheel, and renew if necessary. All return springs should be renewed, regardless of their apparent condition; spring kits are available from Citroën dealers.

12 Peel back the rubber protective caps, and check the wheel cylinder for fluid leaks or other damage; check that both cylinder pistons are free to move easily. Refer to Section 12, if necessary, for information on wheel cylinder renewal.

13 Prior to installation, clean the backplate, and apply a thin smear of high-temperature brake grease or anti-seize compound to all those surfaces of the backplate which bear on the shoes, particularly the wheel cylinder pistons and lower pivot point. Do not allow the lubricant to foul the friction material.

14 Place the shoes on the bench in their correct positions, and place the adjuster lever over its locating peg on the leading brake shoe. Engage the long end of the adjuster lever return spring into its hole, through the back of the brake shoe, then hook the other end over the adjuster lever **(see illustrations)**.

15 Screw in the adjuster wheel until the minimum adjuster strut length is obtained, then engage the strut end with the leading shoe and adjuster lever **(see illustration)**.

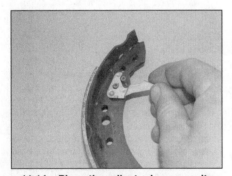

11.14a Place the adjuster lever over its locating peg on the leading brake shoe . . .

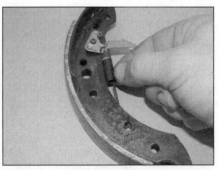

11.14b . . . then fit the return spring to the shoe and adjuster lever

11.15 Engage the adjuster strut end with the leading shoe and adjuster lever

**11.16a Engage the longer straight end of the upper return spring with the hole in the leading shoe . . .**

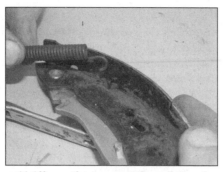

**11.16b . . . then engage the coiled end with the trailing shoe**

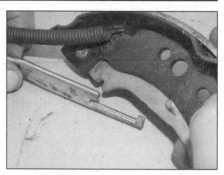

**11.17 Locate the other end of the adjuster strut into the handbrake lever**

**16** Engage the longer straight end of the upper return spring with the hole in the leading shoe, then engage the coiled end with the trailing shoe **(see illustrations)**.

**17** Spread the shoes apart at the bottom and locate the adjuster strut into the handbrake lever **(see illustration)**.

**18** Hook the larger looped end of the lower return spring into its hole, through the back of the trailing shoe **(see illustration)**.

**19** Check that the adjuster strut is still correctly located, pull the shoes together at the bottom and connect the lower return spring to the leading shoe **(see illustration)**.

**20** Check that all the springs are seated correctly and the adjuster strut is engaged with the leading shoe and handbrake lever **(see illustration)**.

**21** Transfer the assembly to the car and connect the handbrake cable to the handbrake lever. Locate the shoes on the backplate with their upper ends engaged with the wheel cylinder pistons.

**22** Locate the leading shoe in the bottom anchor, then pull the lower end of the trailing shoe into position on the bottom anchor.

**23** Refit the hold-down spring pins to the backplate. Use pliers to depress the spring clips while pushing on the pin from behind the backplate with your finger. Slide the spring clips into position on the pins.

**24** Engage the handbrake lever helper spring with the hole on the training shoe and with the lower return spring end. Pull the other end of the helper spring into engagement with the handbrake lever.

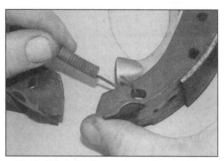

**11.18 Hook the larger looped end of the lower return spring into its hole, through the back of the trailing shoe**

**25** Move the upper ends of the brake shoes outward slightly and cut off the rubber band retaining the wheel cylinder pistons **(see illustration)**.

**26** Using a screwdriver, turn the strut adjuster wheel to expand the shoes to obtain a diameter of 202.5 mm, then check that the brake drum just slides over the shoes **(see illustration)**.

**27** Refit the brake drum as described in Section 10.

**28** Repeat the above procedure on the remaining rear brake.

**29** Once both sets of rear shoes have been renewed, adjust the lining-to-drum clearance by repeatedly depressing the brake pedal. Whilst depressing the pedal, have an assistant listen to the rear drums, to check that the adjuster strut is functioning correctly; if so, a clicking sound will be emitted by the strut as the pedal is depressed.

**11.19 Pull the shoes together at the bottom and connect the lower return spring to the leading shoe**

**30** Check and, if necessary, adjust the handbrake as described in Section 17

**31** On completion, check the hydraulic fluid level as described in *Weekly checks*.

*Caution: New brake shoes will not give full braking efficiency until they have bedded-in. Be prepared for this, and avoid hard braking as far as possible for the first hundred miles or so after shoe renewal.*

**12 Rear wheel cylinder –**
removal, overhaul and refitting

### Removal

**1** Remove the brake shoes as described in Section 11.

**2** Minimise fluid loss by first removing the master cylinder reservoir cap, then tightening it down onto a piece of polythene, to obtain

**11.20 Check that all components are correctly engaged and seated**

**11.25 With the shoes in place, cut off the rubber band retaining the wheel cylinder pistons**

**11.26 Turn the strut adjuster wheel to expand the shoes to the specified diameter**

an airtight seal. Alternatively, use a brake hose clamp, a G-clamp or a similar tool to clamp the flexible hose (connected between the metal pipe sections on the rear axle and trailing arm) at the nearest convenient point to the wheel cylinder.

3 Wipe away all traces of dirt around the brake pipe union at the rear of the wheel cylinder, and unscrew the union nut. Carefully ease the pipe out of the wheel cylinder, and plug or tape over its end to prevent dirt entry. Wipe off any spilt fluid immediately.

4 Unscrew the two wheel cylinder retaining bolts from the rear of the backplate, and remove the cylinder.

### Overhaul

#### Non-ABS models

5 On non-ABS models, the rear brake pressure-regulating valves are integral with the rear wheel cylinders, and the cylinders **must not** be dismantled. No spare parts are available, and if a cylinder is faulty or damaged, the complete assembly must be renewed.

#### ABS models

6 Clean the exterior of the cylinder to remove all traces of dirt and brake dust.

7 Pull the dust seals from the ends of the cylinder.

8 Extract the pistons, seals spring seats and, where fitted, the return spring, noting the locations of all components to ensure correct refitting.

9 Examine the surfaces of the cylinder bore and pistons for signs of scoring and corrosion, and if evident, renew the complete wheel cylinder. If the components are in good condition, discard the seals and obtain a repair kit, which will contain all the necessary renewable components.

10 Clean the pistons and the cylinder with methylated spirit or clean brake fluid, and reassemble in the reverse order to dismantling, making sure that the components are fitted in the correct sequence and orientated correctly, as noted before removal. Ensure that the lips of the seals face into the cylinder.

11 On completion, wipe the outer surfaces of the dust seals to remove any excess brake fluid.

### Refitting

12 Clean the backplate, then place the wheel cylinder in position, and refit the bolts, tightening them securely.

13 Reconnect the brake pipe to the rear of the wheel cylinder, taking care not to allow dirt into the system.

14 Refit the rear brake shoes as described in Section 11.

15 On completion, remove the brake hose clamp, or remove the polythene from the fluid reservoir, as applicable, and bleed the hydraulic system as described in Section 2. Note that, providing the precautions described were taken to minimise brake fluid loss, it should only be necessary to bleed the relevant rear brake circuit.

## 13 Master cylinder – removal, overhaul and refitting

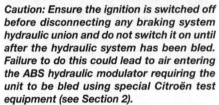

**Caution: Ensure the ignition is switched off before disconnecting any braking system hydraulic union and do not switch it on until after the hydraulic system has been bled. Failure to do this could lead to air entering the ABS hydraulic modulator requiring the unit to be bled using special Citroën test equipment (see Section 2).**

**Note:** *Before starting work, refer to the warning at the beginning of Section 2 concerning the dangers of hydraulic fluid.*

### Removal

1 Remove the battery and battery box as described in Chapter 5A.

2 Remove the master cylinder reservoir cap and filter, and syphon the hydraulic fluid from the reservoir. **Note:** *Do not syphon the fluid by mouth, as it is poisonous; use a syringe or an old antifreeze tester.* Alternatively, open any convenient bleed screw in the system, and gently pump the brake pedal to expel the fluid through a plastic tube connected to the screw until the reservoir is emptied (see Section 2).

3 Disconnect the clutch master cylinder fluid supply pipe from the reservoir and drain the remaining fluid into a container. Plug the pipe opening to prevent dirt ingress.

4 Wipe clean the area around the brake pipe unions on the side of the master cylinder, and place absorbent rags beneath the pipe unions to catch any surplus fluid. Make a note of the correct fitted positions of the unions, then unscrew the union nuts and carefully withdraw the pipes. Plug or tape over the pipe ends and master cylinder orifices to minimise the loss of brake fluid, and to prevent the entry of dirt into the system. Wash off any spilt fluid immediately with cold water.

5 Slacken and remove the two nuts securing the master cylinder to the vacuum servo unit, then withdraw the unit from the engine compartment. If the sealing ring fitted to the rear of the master cylinder shows signs of damage or deterioration, it must be renewed. If required, undo the retaining screw and pull the reservoir from the master cylinder.

**14.2 Slide off the clevis pin retaining clip (arrowed)**

### Overhaul

6 Check that spare parts are available before deciding to overhaul the master cylinder. Although Citroën dealers do not supply internal parts for the master cylinder, it may be possible to obtain a repair kit from specialist motor factors. Ensure that the correct repair kit is obtained for the master cylinder being worked on. Note the locations of all components to ensure correct refitting, and lubricate the new seals using clean brake fluid. Follow the assembly instructions supplied with the repair kit.

### Refitting

7 Remove all traces of dirt from the master cylinder and servo unit mating surfaces and ensure that the sealing ring is correctly fitted to the rear of the master cylinder.

8 Fit the master cylinder to the servo unit. Refit the master cylinder mounting nuts, and tighten them to the specified torque.

9 Wipe clean the brake pipe unions and refit them to the master cylinder ports, tightening them to the specified torque.

10 If removed, carefully ease the fluid reservoir back into position, ensuring that it is fully seated on the rubber seals. Refit the retaining screw and tighten it securely.

11 Reconnect the clutch master cylinder supply pipe, and level sensor wiring plug.

12 Refit the components removed for access, then refill the master cylinder reservoir with new fluid. Bleed the complete hydraulic system as described in Section 2. **Note:** *A hydraulic clutch shares its fluid reservoir with the braking system, and may also need to be bled (see Chapter 6).*

## 14 Brake pedal – removal and refitting

### Removal

1 Remove the driver's side lower facia panel above the pedals, as described in Chapter 11.

2 Slide off the retaining clip and withdraw the clevis pin securing the pedal crossover linkage pushrod (right-hand drive models), or vacuum servo unit pushrod (left-hand drive models) to the pedal **(see illustration)**. Discard the clevis pin, a new one must be fitted.

3 Slacken and remove the pivot bolt and nut **(see illustration)**, and remove the brake pedal from the vehicle. Slide the spacer and washer (where fitted) out from the pedal pivot. Examine all components for signs of wear or damage, renewing them as necessary.

### Refitting

4 Apply a smear of multi-purpose grease to the spacer and washer, and insert it into the pedal pivot bore.

5 Manoeuvre the pedal into position, making sure it is correctly engaged with the pushrod, and insert the pivot bolt. Refit the nut to the pivot bolt and tighten it securely.

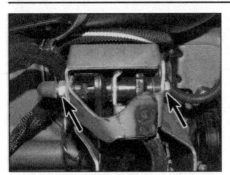

**14.3 Slacken and remove the pivot bolt and nut (arrowed)**

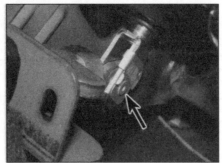

**15.8 Rotate the clip (arrowed) then pull it from place**

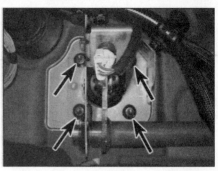

**15.9 Undo the four servo mounting nuts (arrowed)**

**6** Align the pedal with the pushrod and insert the new clevis pin, securing it in position with the retaining clip(s).

**7** Refit the lower panel to the facia.

## 15 Vacuum servo unit – testing, removal and refitting

### Testing

**1** To test the operation of the servo unit, depress the footbrake several times to exhaust the vacuum, then start the engine whilst keeping the pedal firmly depressed. As the engine starts, there should be a noticeable 'give' in the brake pedal as the vacuum builds-up. Allow the engine to run for at least two minutes, then switch it off. If the brake pedal is now depressed it should feel normal, but further applications should result in the pedal feeling firmer, with the pedal stroke decreasing with each application.

**2** If the servo does not operate as described, first inspect the servo unit check valve as described in Section 16. On diesel engine models, also check the operation of the vacuum pump as described in Section 25.

**3** If the servo unit still fails to operate satisfactorily, the fault lies within the unit itself. Repairs to the unit are not possible – if faulty, the servo unit must be renewed.

### Removal

**4** Remove the master cylinder as described in Section 13.

**5** Release the wiring harness adjacent to the servo from its retaining clips, and move it to one side.

**6** Depress the tabs on the side of the quick-release fitting, and disconnect the vacuum pipe from the servo unit check valve.

**7** Remove the carpet trim panel from under the left-hand side of the facia.

**8** Rotate the crossover shaft-to-servo pushrod clevis pin (right-hand drive models), or vacuum servo unit pushrod clevis pin (left-hand drive models) and remove it from the linkage **(see illustration)**. Discard the clevis pin, a new one must be fitted.

**9** Slacken and remove the four nuts securing the housing to the bulkhead **(see illustration)**.

**10** Manoeuvre the servo unit out of position, along with its gasket which is fitted between the servo and housing. Renew the gasket if it shows signs of damage.

### Refitting

**11** Refitting is the reverse of removal, noting the following points.

*a) Lubricate all crossover linkage pivot points with multi-purpose grease.*

*b) Tighten the servo unit and mounting bracket nuts and bolts to their specified torque settings.*

*c) Refit the master cylinder as described in Section 13 and bleed the complete hydraulic system as described in Section 2.*

*d) Always renew the crossover shaft clevis pins.*

## 16 Vacuum servo unit check valve – removal, testing and refitting

### Removal

**1** Depress the tabs on the side of the quick-release fitting, and disconnect the vacuum pipe from the servo unit check valve.

**2** Withdraw the valve from its rubber sealing grommet, using a pulling and twisting motion **(see illustration)**. Remove the grommet from the servo.

### Testing

**3** Examine the check valve for signs of damage, and renew if necessary. The valve

**16.2 Servo unit check valve**

may be tested by blowing through it in both directions. Air should flow through the valve in one direction only – when blown through from the servo unit end of the valve. Renew the valve if this is not the case.

**4** Examine the rubber sealing grommet and flexible vacuum hose for signs of damage or deterioration, and renew as necessary.

### Refitting

**5** Fit the sealing grommet into position in the servo unit.

**6** Carefully ease the check valve into position, taking great care not to displace or damage the grommet. Reconnect the vacuum hose to the valve.

**7** On completion, start the engine and check for air leaks from the check valve-to-servo unit connection.

## 17 Handbrake – adjustment

**1** To check the handbrake adjustment, applying normal moderate pressure, pull the handbrake lever to the fully-applied position, counting the number of clicks emitted from the handbrake ratchet mechanism. If adjustment is correct, there should be 2 clicks before the brakes begins to apply, and no more than 8 before the handbrake is fully applied. If this is not the case, adjust as follows.

**2** Using a small screwdriver, carefully prise the handbrake lever cover panel from the centre console **(see illustration)**.

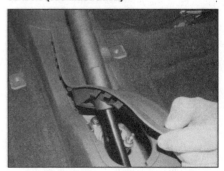

**17.2 Carefully prise the handbrake lever cover panel from the centre console**

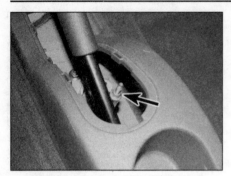

**17.7 Handbrake cable adjuster nut (arrowed)**

**3** Chock the front wheels, then jack up the rear of the vehicle and support it on axle stands (see *Jacking and vehicle support*).

**4** Start the engine then, with the handbrake released, press and release the brake pedal slowly 3 or 4 times.

**5** Fully apply the handbrake firmly 4 or 5 times then release it.

**6** On models with rear brake drums remove both rear drums as described in Section 10.

**7** On models with rear brake discs, using feeler blades measure the clearance between the handbrake lever on each rear brake caliper and the stop. On models with rear drum brakes, measure the clearance between the handbrake lever on the inner side of each trailing shoe and the stop. The clearance should be between 1.0 mm (max) and 0.5 mm (min). If not, turn the cable adjuster nut on the side of the handbrake lever until it is correct **(see illustration)**.

**8** On models with rear brake drums, temporarily locate the drums over the rear brake shoes.

**9** Fully apply the handbrake firmly 8 times then release it.

**10** Repeat paragraphs 6 and 7 and check that the clearance is still between 1.0 mm (max) and 0.5 mm (min). Adjust the cable if necessary.

**11** Refit the brake drums if applicable (see Section 10), then refit the handbrake lever cover and lower the car to the ground.

**19.7 Withdraw the handbrake outer cable out from the drum brake backplate**

## 18 Handbrake lever – removal and refitting

### Removal

**1** Chock the front wheels then jack up the rear of the vehicle and support it on axle stands (see *Jacking and vehicle support*).

**2** Remove the centre console as described in Chapter 11.

**3** Release the handbrake lever, then unscrew and remove the cable adjuster nut on the side of the handbrake lever. Pull the cable out from the equaliser plate and remove it from the lever.

**4** Disconnect the wiring connector from the handbrake warning light switch, and release the cable from its retaining clip.

**5** Undo and remove the three retaining nuts and remove the lever assembly from the car.

### Refitting

**6** Refitting is a reversal of removal. Tighten the lever retaining nuts to the specified torque, and adjust the handbrake (see Section 17).

## 19 Handbrake cables – removal and refitting

### Removal

**1** The handbrake cable consists of a left-hand section and a right-hand section connecting the rear brakes to the adjuster mechanism on the handbrake lever. The cables can be removed separately.

**2** Firmly chock the front wheels, slacken the relevant rear roadwheel bolts, then jack up the rear of the vehicle and support it on axle stands (see *Jacking and vehicle support*). Remove the relevant rear roadwheel.

**3** Remove the centre console as described in Chapter 11.

**4** Slacken the handbrake adjuster nut sufficiently to be able to disengage the relevant cable end fitting from the equaliser plate with reference to Section 17.

**5** Undo the nuts, release the plastic rivets and remove the relevant plastic undershield from the side of the fuel tank.

**6** Separate the outer cable at the point where it joins the metal guide tube.

**7** On models with rear drum brakes, remove the rear brake shoes from the relevant side as described in Section 11, then withdraw the outer cable out from the brake backplate **(see illustration)**.

**8** On models with rear disc brakes, using a pair of pliers, release the handbrake cable from the caliper lever. Compress the clip and pull the cable from the support bracket **(see illustrations 5.2a and 5.2b)**.

**9** Working back along the length of the cable, free it from the retaining clips and the support

on the trailing arm. Pull the front end of the inner cable out of the metal guide tube and remove the cable from underneath the vehicle.

### Refitting

**10** Refitting is a reversal of the removal procedure, adjusting the handbrake as described in Section 17.

## 20 Stop-light switch – removal, refitting and adjustment

**1** The stop-light switch is located on the pedal crossover shaft bracket behind the passenger side of the facia. Where two switches are fitted to the bracket, the stop-light switch is the right-hand of the two.

### Removal

**2** Working in the passenger's footwell, prise up the centre pins, lever out the complete plastic rivets, and remove the trim beneath the passenger's glovebox.

**3** Disconnect the wiring, then rotate the switch 90 degrees anti-clockwise and remove it from the bracket.

### Refitting and adjustment

**4** Pull the switch plunger out to its full extent, then depress the brake pedal by hand.

**5** Refit the switch back into position in the mounting bracket, then release the brake pedal, and pull it up as far as it will go. The switch should now be correctly positioned.

**6** Reconnect the wiring connector, and check the operation of the stop-lights. Refit the glovebox.

## 21 Handbrake 'on' warning light switch – removal and refitting

### Removal

**1** Remove the centre console as described in Chapter 11.

**2** Disconnect the wiring connector from the warning light switch, and release the cable from its retaining clip **(see illustration)**.

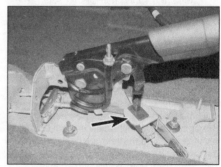

**21.2 Handbrake warning light switch location (arrowed)**

**3** Unclip the switch from the lever and remove it from the car.

### Refitting

**4** Refitting is a reversal of the removal procedure.

---

### 22 Anti-lock braking system (ABS) – general information

ABS is fitted as standard on most models and is optionally available on all others. The system comprises a hydraulic modulator unit and the four wheel speed sensors. The modulator unit contains the electronic control unit (ECU), the hydraulic solenoid valves and the electrically-driven return pump. The purpose of the system is to prevent the wheel(s) locking during heavy braking. This is achieved by automatic release of the brake on the relevant wheel, followed by re-application of the brake.

The solenoid valves are controlled by the ECU, which itself receives signals from the four wheel speed sensors which monitor the speed of rotation of each wheel. By comparing these signals, the ECU can determine the speed at which the vehicle is travelling. It can then use this speed to determine when a wheel is decelerating at an abnormal rate, compared to the speed of the vehicle, and therefore predicts when a wheel is about to lock. During normal operation, the system functions in the same way as a non-ABS braking system.

If the ECU senses that a wheel is about to lock, it closes the relevant outlet solenoid valves in the hydraulic unit, which then isolates the relevant brake(s) on the wheel(s) which is/are about to lock from the master cylinder, effectively sealing-in the hydraulic pressure.

If the speed of rotation of the wheel continues to decrease at an abnormal rate, the ECU opens the inlet solenoid valves on the relevant brake(s), and operates the electrically-driven return pump which pumps the hydraulic fluid back into the master cylinder, releasing the brake. Once the speed of rotation of the wheel returns to an acceptable rate, the pump stops; the solenoid valves switch again, allowing the hydraulic master cylinder pressure to return to the caliper or wheel cylinder, which then re-applies the brake. This cycle can be carried out many times a second.

The action of the solenoid valves and return pump creates pulses in the hydraulic circuit. When the ABS system is functioning, these pulses can be felt through the brake pedal.

The operation of the ABS system is entirely dependent on electrical signals. To prevent the system responding to any inaccurate signals, a built-in safety circuit monitors all signals received by the ECU. If an inaccurate signal or low battery voltage is detected, the ABS system is automatically shut-down, and the warning light on the instrument panel is illuminated, to inform the driver that the ABS

system is not operational. Normal braking should still be available, however.

The Citroën C3 is also equipped with additional safety features built around the ABS system. These systems are EBFD (Electronic Brake Force Distribution), which automatically apportions braking effort between the front and rear wheels, EBA (Emergency Brake Assist) which guarantees full braking effort in the event of an emergency stop by monitoring the rate at which the brake pedal is depressed and (on some models) ESP (Electronic Stability Program) which monitors the vehicles cornering forces and steering wheel angle, then applies the braking force to the appropriate roadwheel to enhance the stability of the vehicle.

If a fault does develop in the any of these systems, the vehicle must be taken to a Citroën dealer or suitably-equipped specialist for fault diagnosis and repair.

---

### 23 Anti-lock braking system (ABS) components – removal and refitting

#### Hydraulic modulator

*Caution: Disconnect the battery (see Chapter 5A) before disconnecting the modulator hydraulic unions, and do not reconnect the battery until after the hydraulic system has been bled. Also ensure that the unit is stored upright (in the same position as it is fitted to the vehicle) and is not tipped onto its side or upside down. Failure to do this could lead to air entering the modulator requiring the unit to be bled using special Citroën test equipment on refitting (see Section 2).*
**Note:** *Before starting work, refer to the warning at the beginning of Section 2 concerning the dangers of hydraulic fluid.*

#### Removal

**1** Disconnect the battery (see Chapter 5A).
**2** The modulator assembly is located in the front left-hand corner of the engine compartment. Slacken the left-hand front roadwheel bolts, jack up the front of the vehicle and support it securely on axle stands (see *Jacking and vehicle support*). Remove the roadwheel.
**3** Prise out the plastic rivets, undo the screws and remove the left-hand front wheel arch liner.
**4** Cut the cable tie securing the protective boot over the modulator main wiring connector. Peel back the boot, lift the locking lever and disconnect the wiring connector **(see illustration)**.
**5** Mark the locations of the hydraulic fluid pipes to ensure correct refitting, then unscrew the union nuts, and disconnect the pipes from the modulator assembly. Be prepared for fluid spillage, and plug the open ends of the pipes and the modulator to prevent dirt ingress and further fluid loss.
**6** Slacken and remove the three modulator

**23.4 Peel back the boot, lift the locking lever and disconnect the modulator wiring connector**

mounting bolts and remove the assembly from the engine compartment **(see illustration)**. Renew the mountings if they show signs of wear or damage.

#### Refitting

**7** Manoeuvre the modulator into position, refit the mounting bolts and tighten them to the specified torque setting.
**8** Reconnect the hydraulic pipes to the correct unions on the modulator and tighten the union nuts to the specified torque.
**9** Pull out the old cable tie from the wiring connector protective boot, and feed in a new cable tie.
**10** Reconnect the wiring connector to the modulator, then locate the boot in position and secure with the cable tie.
**11** Bleed the complete hydraulic system as described in Section 2. Once the system is correctly bled, refit the wheel arch liner and roadwheel, then reconnect the battery.

#### Electronic control unit (ECU)

#### Removal

**12** Remove the hydraulic modulator as described previously.
**13** Undo the two screws located on either side of the return pump and withdraw the ECU from the modulator.

#### Refitting

**14** Locate the ECU in position on the modulator and secure with the two screws, tightened securely.
**15** Refit the modulator as described previously.

**23.6 Slacken and remove the three modulator mounting bolts**

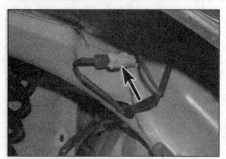

**23.19a Disconnect the front wheel speed sensor wiring connector at the top of the wheel arch (arrowed) . . .**

**23.19b . . . and release the wiring from the support brackets on the inner wing and suspension strut**

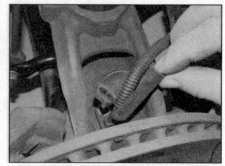

**23.20 Undo the sensor retaining bolt and lift off the sensor guard**

### Front wheel speed sensor

#### Removal

**16** Ensure the ignition is turned off.

**17** Apply the handbrake, slacken the appropriate front roadwheel bolts, then jack up the front of the vehicle and support securely on axle stands (see *Jacking and vehicle support*). Remove the roadwheel.

**18** Prise out the plastic rivets, undo the screws and remove the relevant front wheel arch liner.

**19** Disconnect the wiring connector located at the top of the wheel arch. Feed the wiring harness through the apertures in the inner wing and release it from the support brackets on the inner wing and suspension strut **(see illustrations)**.

**20** Undo the sensor retaining bolt and lift off the sensor guard **(see illustration)**.

**21** Carefully attempt to pull the sensor out of the hub carrier using pliers – it will be tight **(see illustration)**. If this fails, attempt to prise it free using two small screwdrivers under the mounting flange. The sensor body is made of plastic and any attempt to twist it free or use excessive force, is likely to result in breakage. As a last resort, remove the hub carrier as described in Chapter 10, and push the sensor out from the underside of the hub carrier.

#### Refitting

**22** Ensure that the mating faces of the sensor and the hub carrier are clean, and apply a little anti-seize grease to the hub carrier bore before refitting.

**23** Make sure the sensor tip is clean and ease it into position in the hub carrier.

**24** Clean the threads of the sensor retaining bolt and apply a few drops of thread-locking

compound (Citroën recommend Loctite Frenetanch – available from your dealer). Refit the sensor guard and retaining bolt and tighten the bolt to the specified torque.

**25** Work along the sensor wiring, making sure it is correctly routed and located in the support brackets. Reconnect the wiring connector.

**26** Refit the wheel arch liner and roadwheel, then lower the vehicle and tighten the wheel bolts to the specified torque.

### Rear wheel speed sensor

#### Removal

**27** Ensure the ignition is turned off.

**28** Chock the front wheels, slacken the appropriate rear roadwheel bolts, then jack up the rear of the vehicle and support it on axle stands (see *Jacking and vehicle support*). Remove the appropriate roadwheel.

**29** Disconnect the wiring connector, located adjacent to the rear beam axle mounting bracket **(see illustration)**. For improved access, undo the nuts, release the plastic rivets and remove the relevant plastic undershield from the side of the fuel tank.

**30** Release the wiring harness from all the relevant clips and ties whilst noting its correct routing.

**31** Undo the sensor retaining bolt, then carefully prise it out using two small screwdrivers under the mounting flange **(see illustrations)**.

#### Refitting

**32** Ensure that the mating faces of the sensor and the hub are clean, and apply a little anti-seize grease to the hub bore before refitting.

**33** Make sure the sensor tip is clean and ease it into position.

**34** Clean the threads of the sensor bolt and apply a few drops of thread-locking compound (Citroën recommend Loctite Frenetanch – available from your dealer). Refit the retaining bolt and tighten it to the specified torque.

**35** Work along the sensor wiring, making sure it is correctly routed, securing it in position with all the relevant clips and ties. Reconnect the wiring connector, then lower the vehicle and (where necessary) tighten the wheel bolts to the specified torque.

**23.21 Carefully attempt to pull the sensor out of the hub carrier**

**23.29 Left-hand rear wheel speed sensor wiring connector (arrowed)**

**23.31a Undo the sensor retaining bolt (arrowed) . . .**

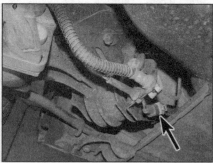

**23.31b . . . then carefully prise it out using two small screwdrivers**

### Yaw rate sensor

#### Removal

**36** Remove the centre console as described in Chapter 11.
**37** Release the clip then disconnect the wiring plug **(see illustration)**.

#### Refitting

**38** Undo the two nuts and remove the sensor.
**39** Refitting is a reversal of removal, ensuring the arrow on the top of the sensor points to the front of the vehicle.

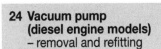

## 24 Vacuum pump (diesel engine models) – removal and refitting

### Removal

**1** The pump is located at the left-hand end of the cylinder head. To gain access to the vacuum pump, remove the air cleaner air inlet ducts as described in Chapter 4B.
**2** Depress the tabs on the side of the quick-release fitting, and disconnect the vacuum pipe from the pump.
**3** Slacken and remove the retaining bolts/nut (as applicable) securing the pump to the left-hand end of the cylinder head, then remove the pump **(see illustration)**. Discard the sealing rings – new ones must be used on refitting.

### Refitting

**4** Fit new sealing ring(s) to the pump recess(es), then align the drive dog with the slot in the end of the camshaft, and refit the pump to the cylinder head, ensuring that the sealing ring(s) remain correctly seated **(see illustrations)**.
**5** Refit the pump mounting bolts/nut (as applicable) and tighten them to the specified torque.
**6** Reconnect the vacuum hose to the pump, ensuring its retaining clip engages correctly, and refit the air inlet ducts.

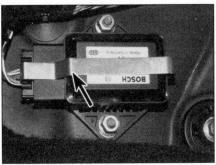

**23.37 Release the clip (arrowed) and disconnect the Yaw rate sensor wiring plug**

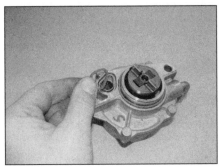

**24.4a Fit new seals to the vacuum pump**

## 25 Vacuum pump (diesel engine models) – testing

**1** The operation of the braking system vacuum pump can be checked using a vacuum gauge.
**2** Disconnect the vacuum pipe from the pump, and connect the gauge to the pump union using a suitable length of hose.
**3** Start the engine and allow it to idle, then measure the vacuum created by the pump.

**24.3 Vacuum pump mounting bolts (arrowed)**

**24.4b Ensure the pump drive dog engages with the slot in the end of the camshaft (arrowed)**

As a guide, after one minute, a minimum of approximately 500 mm Hg should be recorded. If the vacuum registered is significantly less than this, it is likely that the pump is faulty. However, seek the advice of a Citroën dealer before condemning the pump.
**4** Overhaul of the vacuum pump is not possible, since no components are available separately for it. If faulty, the complete pump assembly must be renewed.

# Chapter 10
# Suspension and steering

## Contents

## Degrees of difficulty

| **Easy,** suitable for novice with little experience | **Fairly easy,** suitable for beginner with some experience | **Fairly difficult,** suitable for competent DIY mechanic | **Difficult,** suitable for experienced DIY mechanic | **Very difficult,** suitable for expert DIY or professional |
|---|---|---|---|---|

## Specifications

### Wheel alignment and steering angles

Front wheel:
Toe setting . . . . . . . . . . . . . . . . . . . . . . . . . . . . . . . . . . . . . . . . . . . . . 0 ± 1.0 mm
Camber. . . . . . . . . . . . . . . . . . . . . . . . . . . . . . . . . . . . . . . . . . . . . . . . –0° ± 30'
Castor (dependant on body style and tyre size). . . . . . . . . . . . . . . . 3° 95' ± 30' (nominal)
King pin inclination . . . . . . . . . . . . . . . . . . . . . . . . . . . . . . . . . . . . . . 11° 40' ± 30'
Rear wheel:
Toe setting . . . . . . . . . . . . . . . . . . . . . . . . . . . . . . . . . . . . . . . . . . . . . 5.5 ± 1.0 (toe-in)
Camber. . . . . . . . . . . . . . . . . . . . . . . . . . . . . . . . . . . . . . . . . . . . . . . . –1° 30' ± 30'

### Roadwheels

Type . . . . . . . . . . . . . . . . . . . . . . . . . . . . . . . . . . . . . . . . . . . . . . . . . . . Pressed-steel or aluminium alloy (depending on model)
Tyre pressures . . . . . . . . . . . . . . . . . . . . . . . . . . . . . . . . . . . . . . . . . . See end of Weekly checks on page 0•16

### Torque wrench settings

| | Nm | lbf ft |
|---|---|---|
| **Front suspension** | | |
| Anti-roll bar: | | |
| Connecting link nuts*. . . . . . . . . . . . . . . . . . . . . . . . . . . . . . . . . . | 45 | 33 |
| Mounting clamp bolts. . . . . . . . . . . . . . . . . . . . . . . . . . . . . . . . . | 180 | 133 |
| Brake caliper mounting bracket bolts*. . . . . . . . . . . . . . . . . . . . . . . | 105 | 77 |
| Driveshaft retaining nut*. . . . . . . . . . . . . . . . . . . . . . . . . . . . . . . . . | 245 | 181 |
| Hub carrier to strut. . . . . . . . . . . . . . . . . . . . . . . . . . . . . . . . . . . . . | 54 | 40 |
| Lower arm-to-subframe mounting bolt nuts . . . . . . . . . . . . . . . . . | 40 | 30 |
| Lower balljoint: | | |
| Balljoint to lower arm*. . . . . . . . . . . . . . . . . . . . . . . . . . . . . . . . . | 40 | 30 |
| Clamp bolt nut*. . . . . . . . . . . . . . . . . . . . . . . . . . . . . . . . . . . . . . | 40 | 30 |
| Subframe mounting bolts. . . . . . . . . . . . . . . . . . . . . . . . . . . . . . . . | 90 | 66 |
| Subframe bracing strut. . . . . . . . . . . . . . . . . . . . . . . . . . . . . . . . . . | 65 | 48 |
| Suspension strut: | | |
| Upper mounting plate nut. . . . . . . . . . . . . . . . . . . . . . . . . . . . . . | 65 | 48 |
| Upper spring seat nut. . . . . . . . . . . . . . . . . . . . . . . . . . . . . . . . . | 65 | 48 |

## Torque wrench settings (continued)

| | Nm | lbf ft |
|---|---|---|
| **Rear suspension** | | |
| Caliper mounting bracket bolts* | 50 | 37 |
| Hub nut* | 200 | 148 |
| Rear axle mounting bracket-to-body nuts | 100 | 74 |
| Rear axle-to-mounting bracket | 76 | 56 |
| Shock absorber: | | |
| Lower mounting nut* | 106 | 78 |
| Upper mounting bolt | 42 | 31 |
| **Steering** | | |
| Column-to-steering rack pinch-bolt | 22 | 16 |
| Steering column mounting bolts | 22 | 16 |
| Steering rack mounting nuts* | 80 | 59 |
| Steering rack mounting studs | 80 | 59 |
| Steering wheel bolt | 33 | 24 |
| Track rod: | | |
| Balljoint-to-hub carrier nut* | 35 | 26 |
| Balljoint locknut | 40 | 30 |
| Inner balljoint to steering rack | 80 | 59 |
| **Roadwheels** | | |
| Wheel bolts | 90 | 66 |

*New nuts/bolts must be used.*

## 1 General information

The independent front suspension is of the MacPherson strut type, incorporating coil springs and integral telescopic shock absorbers. The MacPherson struts are located by transverse lower suspension arms, which utilise rubber inner mounting bushes. The front hub carriers, which carry the wheel bearings, brake calipers and the hub/disc assemblies, are bolted to the MacPherson struts, and connected to the lower arms via the balljoints. A front anti-roll bar is fitted to all models. The anti-roll bar is rubber-mounted onto the subframe, and is connected to the front suspension struts by link rods.

The rear suspension has separate telescopic shock absorbers and coil springs fitted between the beam axle and the vehicle body. The rear beam axle has an integral anti-roll bar, and pivots around rubber bushes which are bolted to the front mounting brackets.

The steering column has a universal joint

fitted to its lower end, which is connected to the steering rack pinion by means of a clamp bolt.

The steering rack is mounted onto the front subframe, and is connected by two track rods, with balljoints at their outer ends, to the steering arms projecting rearwards from the hub carriers. The track rod ends are threaded, to facilitate adjustment. The power steering system is electrically operated by means of an electric motor incorporated in the steering rack. The motor is controlled by an electronic control unit located in the battery box.

## 2 Front hub carrier assembly – removal and refitting

**Note:** *Always renew any self-locking nuts when working on the suspension/steering components.*

### Removal

**1** Remove the front suspension strut as described in Section 4.

**2** Undo the nut and withdraw the hub carrier-

to-suspension strut clamp bolt, noting that the bolt fits from the rear of the vehicle **(see illustration)**.

**3** Tap a small chisel into the split on the hub carrier to spread the hub slightly, then withdraw the hub carrier from the base of the strut. It may be necessary to gently tap the hub carrier off the strut using a soft-faced mallet if it is tight.

### Refitting

**4** Refit the suspension strut to the hub carrier and engage the lug on the strut with the hub carrier split **(see illustration)**. Ensure that the strut is pushed fully into the hub carrier, up to the shoulder.

**5** Refit the clamp bolt, screw on a new nut and tighten the nut to the specified torque.

**6** Refit the suspension strut to the car as described in Section 4.

## 3 Front hub bearings – renewal

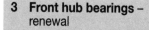

**Note 1:** *The bearing is a sealed, pre-adjusted and pre-lubricated, double-row roller type, and is intended to last the car's entire service life without maintenance or attention. Once removed from the hub carrier, a new bearing must always be fitted. A new bearing retaining circlip must also be used.*

**Note 2:** *A press will be required to dismantle and rebuild the assembly; if such a tool is not available, a large bench vice and spacers (such as large sockets) will serve as an adequate substitute. The bearing's inner races are an interference fit on the hub; if the inner race remains on the hub when it is pressed out of the hub carrier, a knife-edged bearing puller will be required to remove it.*

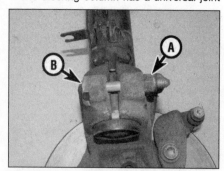

**2.2 Undo the nut (A) and withdraw the hub carrier-to-suspension strut clamp bolt (B)**

**2.4 Engage the lug (arrowed) on the strut with the hub carrier split**

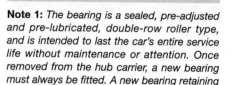

**3.2 Press the hub flange from the bearing**

**3.3 Extract the circlip from the inner side of the hub carrier**

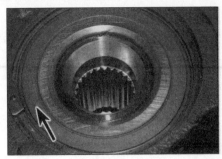

**3.7 Take great care not to damage the seal in the bearing (arrowed) – it contains the encoder for the wheel speed sensor**

**1** Remove the hub carrier assembly as described in Section 2.

**2** Support the hub carrier securely on blocks or in a vice. Using a tubular spacer which bears only on the inner end of the hub flange, press the hub flange out of the bearing **(see illustration)**. If the bearing's outboard inner race remains on the hub, remove it using a bearing puller (see note above).

**3** Extract the bearing retaining circlip from the inner end of the hub carrier assembly **(see illustration)**.

**4** Where necessary, refit the inner race back in position over the ball cage, and securely support the inner face of the hub carrier. Using a tubular spacer which bears only on the inner race, press the complete bearing assembly out of the hub carrier.

**5** Thoroughly clean the hub and hub carrier, removing all traces of dirt and grease, and polish away any burrs or raised edges which might hinder reassembly. Check both for cracks or any other signs of wear or damage, and renew them if necessary. Renew the circlip, regardless of its apparent condition.

**6** On reassembly, apply a light film of oil (Citroën recommend Molykote 321R – available from your dealer) to the bearing outer race and hub flange shaft, to aid installation of the bearing.

**7** Securely support the hub carrier, and locate the bearing in the hub. Press the bearing fully into position, ensuring that it enters the hub squarely, using a tubular spacer which bears only on the bearing outer race. Note that on models with ABS, the bearing is equipped with a magnetic encoder on its inboard face. When fitting the bearing ensure this face is inboard adjacent to the ABS wheel speed sensor **(see illustration)**. Take care not to damage this encoder, or place it adjacent to a magnetic source. Ensure the encoder face is clean.

**8** Once the bearing is correctly seated, secure the bearing in position with the new circlip, ensuring that it is correctly located in the groove in the hub carrier. **Note:** *Align the gap between the ends of the circlip with the gap for the ABS wheel speed sensor.*

**9** Securely support the outer face of the hub flange, and locate the hub carrier bearing inner race over the end of the hub flange. Press the bearing onto the hub, using a tubular spacer

which bears only on the inner race of the hub bearing, until it seats against the hub shoulder. Check that the hub flange rotates freely, and wipe off any excess oil or grease.

**10** Refit the hub carrier assembly as described in Section 2.

## 4 Front suspension strut – removal and refitting

**Note:** *Always renew any self-locking nuts when working on the suspension/steering components.*

### Removal

**1** Chock the rear wheels, then firmly apply the handbrake. Jack up the front of the vehicle, and support it on axle stands (see *Jacking and vehicle support*). Remove the appropriate front roadwheel.

**2** Using a hammer and a chisel-nosed tool, tap up the staking securing the driveshaft retaining nut in position. Note that a new nut must be used on refitting.

**3** Refit at least two roadwheel bolts to the front hub, and tighten them securely. Have an assistant firmly depress the brake pedal, to prevent the front hub from rotating, then using a socket and extension bar, slacken and remove the driveshaft retaining nut. Alternatively, a tool can be fabricated from two lengths of steel strip (one long, one short) and a nut and bolt; the nut and bolt forming the pivot of a forked tool. Bolt the tool to the hub using two wheel bolts, and hold the tool to

**4.4 Release the hydraulic brake hose from the support bracket on the suspension strut**

prevent the hub from rotating as the driveshaft nut is undone (see Chapter 8, Section 2).

**4** Release the hydraulic brake hose from the support bracket on the suspension strut **(see illustration)**.

**5** On models with ABS, remove the wheel speed sensor from the hub carrier as described in Chapter 9.

**6** Unscrew the nut securing the anti-roll bar connecting link to the strut, and position the link clear of the strut; if necessary, retain the balljoint shank with a Torx bit to prevent rotation whilst the nut is slackened. Discard the nut, a new one should be used on refitting.

**7** Refer to the procedures contained in Chapter 9 and remove the brake caliper from its mounting bracket, noting that it is not necessary to disconnect the hydraulic brake hose. If the hub bearings are to be disturbed, remove the caliper and the mounting bracket, then remove the brake disc. Using a piece of wire or string, tie the caliper to a convenient place under the wheel arch, to avoid placing any strain on the brake hose.

**8** Slacken and remove the nut securing the steering gear track rod balljoint to the hub carrier, and release the balljoint tapered shank using a balljoint separator **(see illustration)**.

**9** Slacken and remove the nut, then withdraw the lower suspension arm balljoint clamp bolt from the hub carrier **(see illustration)**. Discard the nut – a new one must be used on refitting.

**10** Tap a small chisel into the split on the hub carrier to spread the hub slightly, and allow the balljoint shank to be withdrawn. Pull the

**4.8 Slacken and remove the nut securing the steering gear track rod balljoint to the hub carrier**

**4.9  Slacken and remove the nut, then withdraw the lower suspension arm balljoint clamp bolt from the hub carrier**

**4.10  Pull the lower suspension arm downwards using a bar and chain or similar arrangement, pivoting on the subframe**

**4.12  Pull the strut assembly outwards to release it from the driveshaft outer constant velocity joint splines**

**4.13  Slacken and remove the strut upper mounting nut**

lower suspension arm downwards to release the balljoint shank from the hub carrier. To do this it will be necessary to use a long bar and block of wood which will engage under the front subframe. Attach the bar to the suspension arm, preferably with a chain, or alternatively with a stout strap or rope. Lever down on the bar to release the balljoint from the hub carrier **(see illustration)**.

**11**  Once the balljoint is free, remove the protector plate which is fitted to the balljoint shank.

**12**  Pull the strut assembly outwards to release it from the driveshaft outer constant velocity joint splines **(see illustration)**.

**13**  Working in the scuttle aperture, remove the protective cap, then slacken and remove the strut upper mounting nut, counterholding the strut rod with an Allen key located in the

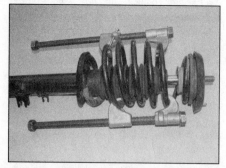

**5.1  Fit spring compressor and compress the coil spring until all tension is relieved from the spring seats**

end of the rod **(see illustration)**. Lift off the upper mounting plate and withdraw the strut from under the wheel arch.
*Caution: As soon as the upper mounting nut is removed, the strut will be unsupported.*
**14**  To separate the suspension strut from the hub carrier, undo the nut and withdraw the hub carrier-to-suspension strut clamp bolt, noting that the bolt fits from the rear of the vehicle **(see illustration 2.2)**.
**15**  Tap a small chisel into the split on the hub carrier to spread the hub slightly, then withdraw the hub carrier from the base of the strut. It may be necessary to gently tap the hub carrier off the strut using a soft-faced mallet if it is tight.

### Refitting

**16**  Refit the suspension strut to the hub carrier and engage the lug on the strut with the hub carrier split **(see illustration 2.4)**. Ensure that the strut is pushed fully into the hub carrier, up to the shoulder.
**17**  Refit the clamp bolt, screw on a new nut and tighten the nut to the specified torque.
**18**  Manoeuvre the strut assembly into position, ensuring that the peg on the strut upper mounting is correctly located in the corresponding outer hole in the inner wing. Fit the upper mounting plate and a new retaining nut and tighten it to the specified torque. Refit the protective cap.
**19**  Ensure that the driveshaft outer constant velocity joint and hub splines are clean, then slide the hub fully onto the driveshaft splines.
**20**  Refit the protector plate to the lower arm

balljoint then, using the method employed on removal, locate the balljoint shank in the hub carrier, ensuring that the lug on the protector plate is correctly located in the clamp split. Insert the balljoint clamp bolt (from the front of the hub carrier), then fit the new retaining nut and tighten it to the specified torque.
**21**  Engage the track rod balljoint in the hub carrier, then fit a new retaining nut and tighten it to the specified torque.
**22**  Referring to Chapter 9, refit the brake disc to the hub (if removed), then refit the brake caliper mounting bracket and/or brake caliper, as applicable.
**23**  Where applicable, refit the ABS wheel sensor as described in Chapter 9.
**24**  Refit the hydraulic brake hose to the support bracket on the suspension strut.
**25**  Reconnect the anti-roll bar connecting link to the strut using a new retaining nut. Tighten the nut to the specified torque.
**26**  Lubricate the inner face and threads of the new driveshaft retaining nut with clean engine oil, and refit it to the end of the driveshaft. Use the method employed on removal to prevent the hub from rotating, and tighten the driveshaft retaining nut to the specified torque. Check that the hub rotates freely.
**27**  Stake the nut firmly into the driveshaft grooves using a hammer and punch.
**28**  Refit the roadwheel, then lower the vehicle to the ground and tighten the roadwheel bolts to the specified torque.

## 5  Front suspension strut – overhaul

**⚠ Warning: Before attempting to dismantle the suspension strut, a suitable tool to hold the coil spring in compression must be obtained. Adjustable coil spring compressors which can be positively secured to the spring coils are readily available, and are recommended for this operation. Any attempt to dismantle the strut without such a tool is likely to result in damage or personal injury.**

**Note:** *Always renew any self-locking nuts when working on the suspension/steering components.*
**1**  With the strut removed from the car (as described in Section 4), clean away all external dirt, then mount it upright in a vice. Fit the spring compressor and compress the coil spring until all tension is relieved from the spring seats **(see illustration)**.
**2**  Slacken and remove the upper spring seat nut whilst retaining the shock absorber piston with a suitable Allen key **(see illustration)**.
**3**  Remove the nut then lift off the thrust bearing followed by the spring seat **(see illustrations)**. Note that a new nut will be required for reassembly.
**4**  Lift off the coil spring and remove the cap, dust gaiter and rubber bump stop from the shock absorber piston **(see illustrations)**.

5 Examine the shock absorber for signs of fluid leakage. Check the piston for signs of pitting along its entire length, and check the shock body for signs of damage. While holding it in an upright position, test the operation of the shock absorber by moving the piston through a full stroke, and then through short strokes of 50 to 100 mm. In both cases, the resistance felt should be smooth and continuous. If the resistance is jerky, or uneven, or if there is any visible sign of wear or damage to the shock absorber, renewal is necessary.

6 Inspect all other components for signs of damage or deterioration, and renew any that are suspect.

7 Slide the rubber bump stop onto the piston. Fit the dust gaiter and cap, making sure the lower end of gaiter is correctly positioned over the shock absorber end.

8 Refit the coil spring, making sure its lower end is correctly seated against the spring seat stop **(see illustration)**. Fit the upper spring seat, aligning its stop with the spring end, then the thrust bearing. Position the thrust bearing so that the locating peg will be towards the outside of the car when the strut is refitted.

9 Fit the new nut. Retain the shock absorber piston and tighten the upper spring seat nut to the specified torque.

## 6 Front suspension lower arm –
removal, overhaul and refitting

**Note:** *Always renew any self-locking nuts when working on the suspension/steering components.*

### Removal

1 Chock the rear wheels then jack up the front of the vehicle and support it on axle stands (see *Jacking and vehicle support*). Remove the appropriate front roadwheel.

2 Slacken and remove the nut, then withdraw the lower suspension arm balljoint clamp bolt from the hub carrier **(see illustration 4.9)**. Discard the nut – a new one must be used on refitting.

3 Tap a small chisel into the split on the hub carrier to spread the hub slightly, and allow the balljoint shank to be withdrawn. Pull the lower suspension arm downwards to release the balljoint shank from the hub carrier. To do this it will be necessary to use a long bar and block of wood which will engage under the front subframe. Attach the bar to the suspension arm, preferably with a chain, or alternatively with a stout strap or rope. Lever down on the bar to release the balljoint from the hub carrier **(see illustration 4.10)**.

4 Once the balljoint is free, remove the protector plate which is fitted to the balljoint shank.

5 Unscrew the lower arm front and rear mounting bolt nuts. Retain the mounting bolt with a Torx bit to prevent rotation whilst the nut is unscrewed. Withdraw the mounting bolts from the subframe.

**5.2 Slacken the upper spring seat nut whilst retaining the rod with an Allen key**

**5.3b ... the thrust bearing ...**

6 Manoeuvre the lower arm assembly out from underneath the vehicle.

### Overhaul

**Note:** *If the lower arm balljoint is renewed, new retaining nuts must be used on refitting.*

**5.4a ... followed by the cap ...**

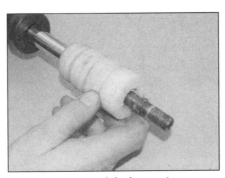
**5.4c ... and the bump stop**

**5.3a Remove the nut ...**

**5.3c ... the spring seat ...**

7 Thoroughly clean the lower arm and the area around the arm mountings, removing all traces of dirt and underseal if necessary, then check carefully for cracks, distortion or any other signs of wear or damage, paying particular attention to the

**5.4b ... the dust gaiter ...**

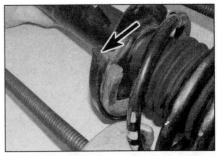
**5.8 Ensure the lower end of the spring locates correctly against the spring seat stop (arrowed)**

**7.5 Slacken and remove the three lower balljoint retaining nuts**

mounting bushes, and renew components as necessary.

**8** Renewal of the mounting bushes will require the use of a hydraulic press and several Citroën special tools and should therefore be entrusted to a dealer or specialist with access to the necessary equipment.

**9** Check that the lower arm balljoint moves freely, without any sign of roughness; check also that the balljoint dust cover shows no sign of deterioration, and is free from cracks and splits. If renewal is necessary, slacken and remove its retaining bolts, and remove the balljoint from the arm. Fit the new balljoint, and insert its retaining bolts. Fit new nuts to the bolts, and tighten them to the specified torque.

### Refitting

**10** Manoeuvre the lower arm assembly into position in the subframe and insert the mounting bolts. Refit the retaining nuts and tighten them to the specified torque.

**11** Refit the protector plate to the lower arm balljoint, then locate the balljoint shank in the hub carrier. Ensure that the lug on the protector plate is correctly located in the clamp split.

**12** Insert the balljoint clamp bolt (from the front of the hub carrier), then fit the new retaining nut and tighten it to the specified torque.

**13** Refit the roadwheel, then lower the vehicle and tighten the roadwheel bolts to the specified torque.

**8.2 Slacken and remove the nuts securing the connecting links to the anti-roll bar**

## 7 Front suspension lower balljoint – removal and refitting

**Note:** *Always renew any self-locking nuts when working on the suspension/steering components.*

### Removal

**1** Chock the rear wheels then jack up the front of the vehicle and support it on axle stands (see *Jacking and vehicle support*). Remove the appropriate front roadwheel.

**2** Slacken and remove the nut, then withdraw the lower suspension arm balljoint clamp bolt from the hub carrier **(see illustration 4.9)**. Discard the nut – a new one must be used on refitting.

**3** Tap a small chisel into the split on the hub carrier to spread the hub slightly, and allow the balljoint shank to be withdrawn. Pull the lower suspension arm downwards to release the balljoint shank from the hub carrier. To do this it will be necessary to use a long bar and block of wood which will engage under the front subframe. Attach the bar to the suspension arm, preferably with a chain, or alternatively with a stout strap or rope. Lever down on the bar to release the balljoint from the hub carrier **(see illustration 4.10)**.

**4** Once the balljoint is free, remove the protector plate which is fitted to the balljoint shank.

**5** Slacken and remove the three nuts, then withdraw the balljoint retaining bolts and remove the balljoint from the lower arm **(see illustration)**. Discard the nuts – new ones must be used on refitting.

**6** Check that the lower arm balljoint moves freely, without any sign of roughness. Check also that the balljoint dust cover shows no sign of deterioration, and is free from cracks and splits. Renew worn or damaged components as necessary.

### Refitting

**7** Locate the balljoint in the end of the suspension arm, and insert the three retaining bolts. Fit new nuts to the bolts, and tighten them to the specified torque.

**8** Refit the protector plate to the lower arm

**8.4 Slacken the anti-roll bar mounting clamp retaining bolts (arrowed) – shown with the subframe removed**

balljoint then, using the method employed on removal, locate the balljoint shank in the hub carrier, ensuring that the lug on the protector plate is correctly located in the clamp split. Insert the balljoint clamp bolt (from the front of the hub carrier), then fit the new retaining nut and tighten it to the specified torque.

**9** Refit the roadwheel, then lower the vehicle and tighten the roadwheel bolts to the specified torque.

## 8 Front suspension anti-roll bar – removal and refitting

**Note:** *Always renew any self-locking nuts when working on the suspension/steering components.*

### Removal

**1** Chock the rear wheels, firmly apply the handbrake, slacken the front roadwheel bolts, then jack up the front of the vehicle and support on axle stands (see *Jacking and vehicle support*). Remove both front roadwheels.

**2** Slacken and remove the nuts securing the left- and right-hand connecting links to the anti-roll bar, and position the links clear of the bar; if necessary, retain the balljoint shank with a Torx bit to prevent rotation whilst the nut is slackened **(see illustration)**. Discard the nuts, new ones should be used on refitting.

**3** Refer to Section 10 and partially lower the front subframe to gain access to the anti-roll bar mounting clamps.

**4** Slacken the two anti-roll bar mounting clamp retaining bolts, and remove both clamps from the top of the subframe **(see illustration)**.

**5** Manoeuvre the anti-roll bar out from underneath the vehicle, and remove the mounting bushes from the bar.

**6** Carefully examine the anti-roll bar components for signs of wear, damage or deterioration, paying particular attention to the mounting bushes. Renew worn components as necessary.

### Refitting

**7** Fit the rubber mounting bushes to the anti-roll bar. Position each bush so that its internal flats are correctly engaged with the flats on the anti-roll bar and the raised portion of the bush is uppermost.

**8** Offer up the anti-roll bar, and manoeuvre it into position on the subframe. Refit the mounting clamps and secure with the retaining bolts, tightened to the specified torque.

**9** Refit the front subframe as described in Section 10.

**10** Engage the connecting links with the ends of the anti-roll bar, fit the new retaining nuts and tighten them to the specified torque setting.

**11** Refit the roadwheels, then lower the vehicle to the ground and tighten the wheel bolts to the specified torque.

## 9  Front suspension anti-roll bar connecting link – removal and refitting

**Note:** *Always renew any self-locking nuts when working on the suspension/steering components.*

### Removal

**1** Chock the rear wheels, firmly apply the handbrake, slacken the relevant roadwheel bolts, then jack up the front of the vehicle and support on axle stands (see *Jacking and vehicle support*). Remove the relevant roadwheel.
**2** Slacken and remove the nuts securing the connecting link to the anti-roll bar and suspension strut and remove the link from the vehicle; if necessary, retain the balljoint shanks with a Torx bit to prevent rotation whilst each nut is slackened **(see illustration 8.2)**. Discard the nuts, new ones should be used on refitting.
**3** Inspect the link for signs of wear or damage and renew if necessary.

### Refitting

**4** Refitting is the reverse of removal, using new nuts and tightening them to the specified torque setting.

## 10  Front suspension subframe – removal and refitting

**Note:** *Always renew any self-locking nuts when working on the suspension/steering components.*

### Removal

**1** Chock the rear wheels, firmly apply the handbrake, slacken the front roadwheel bolts, and then jack up the front of the vehicle and support it on axle stands (see *Jacking and vehicle support*). Remove both front roadwheels.
**2** Remove the battery as described in Chapter 5A.
**3** From within the battery box, lift out the plastic partition panel located in front of the electric power steering ECU **(see illustration)**.

**10.3  Lift out the plastic partition panel**

**4** Disconnect the two smaller wiring connectors from the power steering ECU **(see illustration)**. Release the wiring harness from its retaining clips so that it is free to be removed with the subframe and steering gear.
**5** Working in the driver's footwell, make alignment marks between the steering column universal joint and the steering rack pinion. Release the retaining clip, then undo and remove the pinch-bolt/nut from the joint at the base of the column **(see illustration)**. Pull the steering column shaft upwards to disengage the universal joint from the pinion.
**6** Slacken and remove the nuts securing the left- and right-hand connecting links to the anti-roll bar, and position the links clear of the bar; if necessary, retain the balljoint shank with a Torx bit to prevent rotation whilst the nut is slackened **(see illustration 8.2)**. Discard the nuts, new ones should be used on refitting.
**7** Slacken and remove the nut, then withdraw the left-hand lower suspension arm balljoint clamp bolt from the hub carrier **(see illustration 4.9)**. Discard the nut – a new one must be used on refitting.
**8** Tap a small chisel into the split on the hub carrier to spread the hub slightly, and allow the balljoint shank to be withdrawn. Pull the lower suspension arm downwards to release the balljoint shank from the hub carrier. To do this it will be necessary to use a long bar and block of wood which will engage under the front subframe. Attach the bar to the suspension arm, preferably with a chain, or alternatively with a stout strap or rope. Lever down on the bar to release the balljoint from the hub carrier **(see illustration 4.10)**.

**10.4  Disconnect the two smaller wiring connectors (arrowed) from the power steering ECU**

**9** Once the balljoint is free, remove the protector plate which is fitted to the balljoint shank.
**10** Repeat paragraphs 7 to 9 on the right-hand side.
**11** Refer to Chapter 4A or 4B as applicable, and separate the exhaust system from the front pipe/catalytic converter. Undo the nuts securing the exhaust system mountings to the underbody and lower the system, clear of the subframe.
**12** Remove the rear engine/transmission mounting as described in Chapter 2A or 2B, as applicable.
**13** Place a jack beneath the subframe, and raise the jack until it is just taking the weight of the subframe.
**14** Undo the bolt each side securing the rear of the subframe to the underbody **(see illustration)**.
**15** Working through the aperture in the suspension lower arm, undo the bolt each side securing the front of the subframe to the underbody **(see illustration)**.
**16** With the aid of an assistant, slowly lower the jack and guide the subframe out from under the car. Take care not to trap the power steering wiring harness as the subframe is removed.

### Refitting

**17** Refitting is a reversal of the removal procedure, noting the following points:
  a) *Use new self-locking nuts on all disturbed fittings.*
  b) *Refer to the component refitting procedures in this Chapter and all other Chapters indicated.*
  c) *Tighten all nuts and bolts to the specified torque settings (where given).*

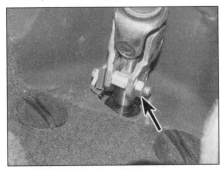

**10.5  Release the retaining clip then remove the pinch-bolt nut (arrowed)**

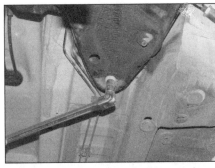

**10.14  Undo the bolt each side securing the rear of the subframe to the underbody**

**10.15  Undo the bolt each side securing the front of the subframe to the underbody**

11.2 Prise the cap from the hub

11.3 Unstake the retaining nut

11.5 Use a puller to remove the hub

11.8a Stake the new nut . . .

11.8b . . . then fit a new hub cap using a large socket

## 11 Rear hub assembly – removal and refitting

### Models with rear disc brakes

**Note:** *Do not remove the hub assembly unless it is absolutely necessary. A puller will be required to draw the hub assembly off the stub axle, and the hub bearing will be damaged by the removal procedure, necessitating renewal of the hub assembly. A new hub nut and centre cap must be used on refitting.*

#### Removal

1 Remove the rear brake disc as described in Chapter 9.

2 Prise out the cap from the centre of the hub and discard; a new cap should be used on refitting **(see illustration)**.

3 Using a hammer and punch, tap up the staking securing the hub retaining nut to the groove in the stub axle **(see illustration)**.

4 Using a socket and long bar, unscrew the rear hub nut and discard it; a new hub nut should be used on refitting. Remove the washer from behind the hub nut.

5 Using a puller, draw the hub assembly off the stub axle, along with the outer bearing race **(see illustration)**. With the hub removed, use the puller to draw the inner bearing race off the stub axle, then remove the spacer.

#### Refitting

6 Lubricate the stub axle shaft with molybdenum disulphide grease, then refit the spacer.

7 Fit the new hub/bearing assembly, tapping it fully onto the stub axle using a hammer and a tubular drift which bears only on the flat inside edge of the bearing inner race.

8 Fit the washer and new hub nut and tighten it to the specified torque. Stake the nut firmly into the groove on the stub axle to secure it in position, then tap the new hub cap into place in the centre of the hub **(see illustrations)**.

9 Refit the rear brake disc as described in Chapter 9.

### Models with rear drum brakes

10 The rear hub is an integral part of the brake drum. Refer to Chapter 9 for brake drum removal and refitting details.

## 12 Rear hub bearings – renewal

### Models with rear disc brakes

1 The hub bearing is an integral part of the hub assembly and is not available separately. If the bearing is worn, renew the complete hub assembly as described in Section 11.

### Models with rear drum brakes

**Note:** *Citroën tool 0540, or a suitable equivalent will be required for this operation.*

2 Remove the rear brake drum as described in Chapter 9.

3 Using the Citroën special tool, or a suitable equivalent, extract the bearing retaining circlip from the brake drum.

4 Prise the oil seal from the hub. Note that on models equipped with ABS, the oil seal incorporates a magnetic encoder on its edge, which provides the magnetic signals for the wheel speed sensor **(see illustration)**.

5 Securely support the drum hub, then press or drive the bearing out of position, using a tubular drift which bears on the bearing inner race. Alternatively, the bearing can be removed using an improvised tool made up from a suitable socket or tube, washers, nut and a suitable long bolt or threaded rod.

6 Thoroughly clean the hub, removing all traces of dirt and grease, and polish away any burrs or raised edges which might hinder reassembly. Check the hub for cracks or any other signs of wear or damage, and renew them if necessary. The bearing and its circlip must be renewed whenever they are disturbed. Note that a bearing kit, which consists of the bearing, circlip and spacer, is available from Citroën dealers.

7 Carefully prise the oil seal from the stub axle, and fit the new seal supplied in the bearing kit. Note the spacer fitted behind the oil seal.

8 Examine the stub axle shaft for signs of wear or damage. If stub axle shaft is worn, it will be necessary to renew the complete trailing arm, as the shaft is not available separately. Trailing arm renewal entails the use of numerous special tools and must be entrusted to a Citroën dealer.

9 On reassembly, apply a light film of clean engine oil to the bearing outer race, to aid installation of the bearing.

12.4 On models with ABS, the oil seal (arrowed) incorporates the magnetic encoder for the wheel speed sensor

**10** Securely support the drum, and locate the bearing in the hub. Press the bearing fully into position, ensuring it enters the hub squarely, using a tubular spacer which bears only on the bearing outer race. Alternatively, the bearing can be drawn into position with the improvised tool used previously, but note that a different socket or tube will be required to bear on the bearing outer race.

**11** Ensure that the bearing is correctly seated against the hub shoulder, and secure it in position with the new circlip. Ensure that the circlip is correctly seated in its hub groove.

**12** Press the new oil seal seating ring into position in the hub, taking care not to damage the oil seal seating surface. Note that two different-sized oil seal seating rings may be supplied in the bearing kit – ensure the correct ring is used. On ABS models, take care not to damage the encoder, incorporated in the oil seal, or place it adjacent to a magnetic source. Ensure the encoder face is clean.

**13** Refit the brake drum as described in Chapter 9.

## 13 Rear suspension shock absorber – removal, testing and refitting

**Note:** *Always renew any self-locking nuts when working on the suspension/steering components.*

### Removal

**1** Chock the front wheels, slacken the relevant rear roadwheel bolts, then jack up the rear of the vehicle and support it on axle stands (see *Jacking and vehicle support*). Remove the relevant rear roadwheel.

**2** Prise out the stud fasteners and remove the rear wheel arch liner **(see illustrations)**.

**3** Using a trolley jack positioned under the spring cup, raise the trailing arm until the rear suspension coil spring is slightly compressed.

**4** Working in the wheel arch, undo the shock absorber upper mounting bolt **(see illustration)**.

**5** Undo the nut, remove the lower mounting bolt then manoeuvre the shock absorber out of position **(see illustration)**. Discard the nut; a new should be used on refitting.

### Testing

**6** Examine the shock absorber for signs of fluid leakage or damage. Test the operation of the shock absorber, while holding it in an upright position, by moving the piston through a full stroke and then through short strokes of 50 to 100 mm. In both cases, the resistance felt should be smooth and continuous. If the resistance is jerky, or uneven, or if there is any visible sign of wear or damage, renewal is necessary. Also check the rubber mountings for damage and deterioration. Renew worn components as necessary. Inspect the shank of the mounting bolt for signs of wear or damage, and renew as necessary. The self-locking nuts should be renewed as a matter of course.

**13.2a Prise out the stud fasteners...**

### Refitting

**7** Prior to refitting the shock absorber, mount it upright in the vice, and operate it fully through several strokes in order to prime it. Apply a smear of multi-purpose grease to the lower mounting bolt and contact face of the new nut (Citroën recommend Molykote G Rapide Plus – available from your dealer).

**8** Fully extend the piston and manoeuvre the assembly into position. Refit the upper mounting bolt, and tighten it to the specified torque.

**9** Align the shock absorber lower mounting with the trailing arm hole and refit the mounting bolt. Screw on the new nut, tightening it lightly only at this stage.

**10** Refit the wheel arch liner and rear roadwheel then lower the vehicle to the ground and tighten the wheel bolts to the specified torque. Rock the vehicle to settle the shock absorber in position then tighten the shock absorber lower mounting to the specified torque.

## 14 Rear suspension coil spring – removal and refitting

**Note:** *Always renew any self-locking nuts when working on the suspension/steering components.*

### Removal

**1** Chock the front wheels, slacken the rear roadwheel bolts, then jack up the rear of the vehicle and support it on axle stands (see

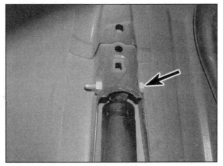

**13.4 Undo the shock absorber upper mounting bolt (arrowed)**

**13.2b ... and remove the rear wheel arch liner**

*Jacking and vehicle support*). Remove the rear roadwheels.

**2** Position a trolley jack underneath the spring cup of one of the trailing arms and raise the arm until the rear suspension coil spring on that side is slightly compressed.

**3** Unscrew the shock absorber lower mounting bolt/nut and withdraw the bolt. Discard the nut; a new should be used on refitting.

**4** Slowly lower the jack as far as the trailing arm will go, then position the jack under the trailing arm spring cup on the other side, and raise the arm until the coil spring on that side is slightly compressed.

**5** Slacken and remove the shock absorber lower mounting bolt/nut. Again, discard the nut a new one must be fitted.

**6** Lower the jack until all tension in the springs is released, then remove the springs.

**7** Inspect the coil spring and its seats for signs of wear or damage and renew if necessary.

### Refitting

**8** Fit the lower spring seat in position on the trailing arm, and seat the upper seat on top of the coil spring. Lubricate the shanks of the shock absorber and trailing arm bolts and the contact faces of the new nuts with multi-purpose grease (Citroën recommend Molykote G Rapide Plus – available from your dealer).

**9** Manoeuvre the springs into position and carefully raise one trailing arm with the jack, ensuring that the coil spring ends are correctly aligned with both seats.

**10** Align the shock absorber with the trailing arm and refit its mounting bolt. Fit the new

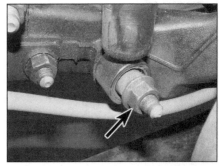

**13.5 Undo the nut (arrowed) and remove the shock absorber lower mounting bolt**

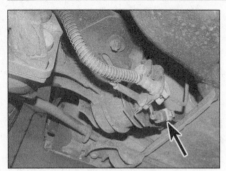

**15.3 Left-hand ABS wheel speed sensor wiring connector (arrowed)**

nut to the bolt, tightening it lightly only at this stage.

**11** Remove the jack from underneath the trailing arm, and position it under the trailing arm spring cup on the remaining side.

**12** Raise the jack and align the lower mounting of the shock absorber with the arm. Insert the bolt, and fit a new nut, tightening it lightly only at this stage.

**13** Refit the rear roadwheel then lower the vehicle to the ground and tighten the wheel bolts to the specified torque. Rock the vehicle to settle the trailing arms in position then tighten the shock absorber lower mounting bolts/nuts to their specified torque settings.

## 15 Rear beam axle – removal, overhaul and refitting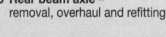

**Note:** *Always renew any self-locking nuts when working on the suspension/steering components.*

### Removal

**1** Remove the coil springs as described in Section 14.

**2** Undo the nuts, release the plastic rivets and remove the plastic undershields from each side of the fuel tank.

**3** Where fitted, disconnect the ABS wheel speed sensor wiring connectors, located adjacent to the beam axle mounting brackets **(see illustration)**.

**4** Clamp the flexible brake hose, and undo the hose union where the flexible hose connects to the rigid hose **(see illustration)**. Plug the

**16.3 Slacken and remove the steering wheel retaining bolt (arrowed)**

end of the hose/pipe to prevent dirt ingress. Repeat this procedure on the remaining side.

**5** On models with rear drum brakes, remove the rear brake shoes as described in Chapter 9, then withdraw the handbrake cables from the brake backplates.

**6** On models with rear disc brakes, working as described in Chapter 9, using a pair of pliers, release the handbrake cables from the caliper levers. Compress the clip and pull each outer cable from its caliper support bracket.

**7** Working back along the length of the cable on each side, free it from the retaining clips and the support on the trailing arm.

**8** Make alignment marks between the axle mounting brackets and the vehicle body to aid refitment. Undo the 3 bolts each side securing the mounting brackets to the vehicle body, and lower the axle to the floor. If the axle is to be renewed, transfer the braking system components to the new axle with reference to Chapter 9.

### Overhaul

**9** Thoroughly clean the axle and the area around the axle mountings, removing all traces of dirt and underseal if necessary, then check carefully for cracks, distortion or any other signs of wear or damage, paying particular attention to the pivot bushes.

**10** Renewal of the pivot bushes will require the use of a hydraulic press and several spacers, and should therefore be entrusted to a Citroën dealer or specialist with access to the necessary equipment.

### Refitting

**11** Lubricate the shanks of the axle mounting bracket bolts with multi-purpose grease (Citroën recommend Molykote G Rapide Plus – available from your dealer).

**12** Offer up the axle and mounting brackets, aligning the previously made marks, and insert the retaining bolts. Tighten them to the specified torque.

**13** Refit the handbrake cables to their retaining clips on the axle, and reconnect the cable ends to the brake shoes or caliper levers (see Chapter 9).

**14** Reconnect the ABS wiring connectors and the rear brake flexible hoses, tightening the hose/pipe unions securely. Remove the hose clamps.

**15.4 Undo the nut where the metal brake pipe joins the flexible pipe**

**15** Refit the plastic undershields on each side of the fuel tank.

**16** Refit the coil springs with reference to Section 14. On completion bleed the brakes as described in Chapter 9.

## 16 Steering wheel – removal and refitting

⚠ **Warning: Refer to the precautions given in Chapter 12 before proceeding.**

### Removal

**1** Remove the airbag unit as described in Chapter 12.

**2** Position the front wheels in the straight-ahead position and engage the steering lock.

**3** Slacken and remove the steering wheel retaining bolt then mark the steering wheel and steering column shaft in relation to each other **(see illustration)**.

**4** Lift the steering wheel off the column splines, feeding the airbag wires through the aperture in the steering wheel as it is withdrawn.

> **HAYNES HiNT** *If the wheel is tight, tap it up near the centre, using the palm of your hand, or twist it from side-to-side, whilst carefully pulling it upwards to release it from the shaft splines.*

### Refitting

**5** Prior to refitting the steering wheel, ensure that the front wheels are still in the straight-ahead position.

**6** Refitting is a reversal of removal, noting the following points:

a) Prior to refitting, ensure that the indicator switch stem is in its central position. Failure to do this could lead to the steering wheel lug breaking the switch tab as the steering wheel is refitted.

b) On refitting, align the marks made on removal, taking great care not to damage the airbag unit wiring, then tighten the retaining bolt to the specified torque.

c) On completion, refit the airbag unit as described in Chapter 12.

## 17 Steering column – removal, inspection and refitting

**Note 1:** *As all models are equipped with a driver's airbag, refer to the precautions given in Chapter 12 before proceeding.*

**Note 2:** *A new pinch-bolt nut will be needed on refitting.*

### Removal

**1** Remove the steering wheel as described in Section 16.

**2** Move the driver's seat as far back as possible.

**3** Working in the driver's footwell, make alignment marks between the universal joint and the steering rack pinion, release the retaining clip, then undo and remove the pinch-bolt/nut from the joint at the base of the column **(see illustration 10.5)**.

**4** Remove the combination switches from the top of the steering column as described in Chapter 12.

**5** Remove the driver's side lower facia panel as described in Chapter 11.

**6** Trace the wiring back from the ignition switch and disconnect it at the wiring connectors.

**7** Where applicable, undo the retaining bolt and free the wiring retaining bracket from the column. Note its fitted position, then release the wiring from its retaining clips and position it clear so that it does not hinder column removal.

**8** Slacken and remove the four mounting bolts from the top of the column **(see illustration)**. Slide the column assembly upwards, free it from the steering rack pinion, and remove it from the vehicle.

### Inspection

**9** Before refitting the steering column, examine the column and mountings for signs of damage and deformation, and renew as necessary. Check the steering shaft for signs of free play in the column bushes, and check the universal joints for signs of damage or roughness in the joint bearings. If any damage or wear is found on the steering column universal joint or shaft bushes, the column must be renewed as an assembly.

### Refitting

**10** Align the marks made prior to removal and engage the column universal joint with the steering rack pinion.

**11** Slide the column assembly into position making sure its mounting bracket is correctly engaged with the facia bracket. Refit the column mounting bolts and tighten them to the specified torque setting.

**12** Refit the universal joint pinch-bolt and nut, tighten them to the specified torque setting, then refit the retaining clip.

**13** The remainder of refitting is a reversal of the removal procedure, noting the following.

a) *Ensure that all wiring is correctly routed and retained by all the necessary clips and ties.*

b) *Refit the steering wheel as described in Section 16.*

## 18 Ignition switch/lock cylinder/steering lock – removal and refitting

### *Ignition switch/steering lock*

#### Removal

**1** Disconnect the battery (see Chapter 5A).

**2** Remove the driver's side lower facia panel as described in Chapter 11.

**3** Undo the retaining screws securing the steering column lower shroud in position **(see illustration)**. Disengage the lower shroud from the pegs on the upper shroud then slide it towards the rear to disengage the lower locating lug from the steering column. Lift the rear edge of the upper shroud, and release it from the two retaining clips at its front edge.

**4** Release the ignition switch wiring harness from the retaining clip on the underside of the column.

**5** Use a centre punch to mark the centre of the lock housing retaining screw then, using a drill and an extractor, remove the screw. Obviously a new screw will be required.

**6** Lift the two retaining clips and carefully pull the transponder immobiliser unit to release it from the ignition switch housing **(see illustration)**. The transponder can then be put to one side, with its wiring still connected. Take care not to damage the transponder assembly.

**7** Note its routing, then trace the wiring back from the ignition switch, and disconnect its wiring connectors from the main wiring harness.

**8** Insert the key into the steering lock and turn it to the first position.

**9** Use a small screwdriver to depress the locating peg and slide the assembly from the steering column housing **(see illustration)**.

**10** Manoeuvre the ignition switch complete with the wiring block connectors out from the column.

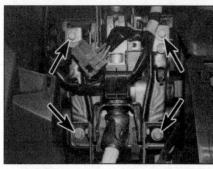

**17.8 Steering column mounting bolts (arrowed)**

#### Refitting

**11** Refitting is a reversal of removal, noting the following points:

a) *Ensure all wiring is correctly routed, and securely clipped back into its original positions.*

b) *Refit the steering lock housing with a new screw, tightening it until it shears.*

### *Lock cylinder*

**12** At the time of writing, the lock cylinder was not available separately from the ignition switch assembly.

## 19 Steering rack assembly – removal, overhaul and refitting

**Note:** *Always renew any self-locking nuts when working on the suspension/steering components.*

### *Removal*

**1** Position the front wheels in the straight-ahead position and engage the steering lock.

**2** Firmly apply the handbrake, slacken the front roadwheel bolts, then jack up the front of the vehicle and support it on axle stands (see *Jacking and vehicle support*). Remove both front roadwheels.

**3** Remove the battery as described in Chapter 5A.

**4** From within the battery box, lift out the plastic partition panel located in front of the electric power steering ECU **(see illustration 10.3)**.

**18.3 Undo the lower shroud retaining screws (arrowed)**

**18.6 Lift the transponder ring clips (upper arrowed) and slide it from the ignition switch**

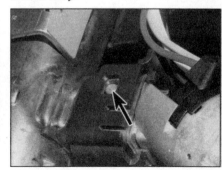

**18.9 Depress the peg (arrowed) and slide the switch from the steering column**

**20.2 Drill out the rivets (arrowed) securing the power steering ECU to the battery box**

**5** Disconnect the two smaller wiring connectors from the power steering ECU **(see illustration 10.4)**. Release the wiring harness from its retaining clips so that it is free to be removed with the steering gear.

**6** Working in the driver's footwell, make alignment marks between the steering column universal joint and the steering rack pinion. Release the retaining clip, then undo and remove the pinch-bolt/nut from the joint at the base of the column **(see illustration 10.5)**. Pull the steering column shaft upwards to disengage the universal joint from the pinion.

**7** Slacken and remove the nuts securing the steering rack track rod balljoints to the hub carriers. Release the balljoint tapered shanks using a universal balljoint separator. Discard the nuts, new ones will be needed on refitting.

**8** Refer to Chapter 4A or 4B as applicable, and separate the exhaust system from the front pipe/catalytic converter. Undo the nuts securing the exhaust system mountings to the underbody and lower the system, clear of the subframe.

**9** Remove the rear engine/transmission mounting as described in Chapter 2A or 2B, as applicable.

**10** Undo the nut each side securing the steering rack to the subframe, noting that new nuts will be required for refitting. Using a suitable Torx bit, unscrew the mounting studs from the rack and recover the washers fitted between the rack and subframe.

**11** Place a jack beneath the subframe, and raise the jack until it is just taking the weight of the subframe.

**22.3 Release the balljoint tapered shank using a universal balljoint separator**

**12** Undo the bolt each side securing the rear of the subframe to the underbody **(see illustration 10.14)**.

**13** Working through the aperture in the suspension lower arm, undo the bolt each side securing the front of the subframe to the underbody **(see illustration 10.15)**.

**14** Lower the subframe until there is sufficient clearance to withdraw the steering rack from the driver's side wheel arch. As the rack is being removed, feed the wiring harness down from the engine compartment.

### Overhaul

**15** The only components which can be renewed separately are the steering rack gaiters and the track rod balljoints which are covered elsewhere in this Chapter.

### Refitting

**16** Manoeuvre the steering rack onto the subframe and slide the washers into position between the subframe and the rack.

**17** Insert the mounting studs and tighten them to the specified torque. Fit the new mounting nuts to the studs and tighten these to the specified torque.

**18** The remainder of refitting is a reversal of removal, noting the following points:
  a) *Use new self-locking nuts on all disturbed fittings.*
  b) *Refer to the component refitting procedures in this Chapter and all other Chapters indicated.*
  c) *Tighten all nuts and bolts to the specified torque settings (where given).*
  d) *On completion have the front wheel alignment checked as described in Section 23.*

### 20 Power steering electronic control unit – removal and refitting

**Note:** *If a new ECU is being fitted, it must be initialised so it can communicate with the other vehicle system ECUs. This initialisation can only be performed using dedicated test equipment. Consequently, entrust the procedure to a Citroën dealer or suitably-equipped specialist.*

### Removal

**1** Remove the battery and battery box as described in Chapter 5A.

**2** Drill out the rivets securing the power steering ECU to the battery box and remove the ECU from the box **(see illustration)**.

### Refitting

**3** Locate the unit in the battery box and secure with new pop rivets.

**4** Refit the battery and battery box as described in Chapter 5A.

### 21 Steering rack rubber gaiters – renewal

**1** Remove the track rod balljoint as described in Section 22.

**2** Mark the correct fitted position of the gaiter on the track rod, then release the retaining clips and slide the gaiter off the steering rack housing and track rod.

**3** Thoroughly clean the track rod and the steering rack housing, using fine abrasive paper to polish off any corrosion, burrs or sharp edges, which might damage the new gaiter's sealing lips on installation. Scrape off all the grease from the old gaiter, and apply it to the track rod inner balljoint. (This assumes that grease has not been lost or contaminated as a result of damage to the old gaiter. Use fresh grease if in doubt.)

**4** Carefully slide the new gaiter onto the track rod end, and locate it on the steering rack housing. Align the outer edge of the gaiter with the mark made on the track rod prior to removal, then secure it in position with new retaining clips (where fitted).

**5** Refit the track rod balljoint as described in Section 22.

### 22 Track rod balljoint – removal and refitting

**Note:** *Always renew any self-locking nuts when working on the suspension/steering components.*

### Removal

**1** Apply the handbrake, slacken the appropriate front roadwheel bolts, then jack up the front of the vehicle and support it on axle stands (see *Jacking and vehicle support*). Remove the appropriate front roadwheel.

**2** Hold the balljoint, and unscrew the track rod locknut by a quarter of a turn. Do not move the locknut from this position, as it will serve as a handy reference mark on refitting.

**3** Slacken and remove the nut securing the track rod balljoint to the hub carrier; discard the nut, a new one will be needed on refitting. Release the balljoint tapered shank using a universal balljoint separator **(see illustration)**.

**4** Counting the **exact** number of turns necessary to do so, unscrew the balljoint from the track rod.

**5** Carefully clean the balljoint and the threads. Renew the balljoint if its movement is sloppy or too stiff, is excessively worn, or is damaged in any way; carefully check the stud taper and threads. If the balljoint gaiter is damaged, the complete balljoint assembly must be renewed; it is not possible to obtain the gaiter separately.

### Refitting

**6** Screw the balljoint into the track rod by

the number of turns noted on removal. This should bring the balljoint to within a quarter of a turn of the locknut.

**7** Locate the balljoint shank in the hub carrier. Fit a new retaining nut and tighten it to the specified torque.

**8** Tighten the track rod locknut to retain the balljoint.

**9** Refit the roadwheel, then lower the vehicle to the ground and tighten the roadwheel bolts to the specified torque.

**10** Have the front wheel alignment checked as described in Section 23.

---

**23 Wheel alignment and steering angles** – definitions, checking and adjustment

### Definitions

**1** A car's steering and suspension geometry is defined in four basic settings – all angles are expressed in degrees (toe settings are also expressed as a measurement); the steering axis is defined as an imaginary line drawn through the axis of the suspension strut, extended where necessary to contact the ground.

**2 Camber** is the angle between each roadwheel and a vertical line drawn through its centre and tyre contact patch, when viewed from the front or rear of the car. Positive camber is when the roadwheels are tilted outwards from the vertical at the top; negative camber is when they are tilted inwards. The camber angle is not adjustable.

**3 Castor** is the angle between the steering axis and a vertical line drawn through each roadwheel's centre and tyre contact patch, when viewed from the side of the car. Positive castor is when the steering axis is tilted so that it contacts the ground ahead of the vertical; negative castor is when it contacts the ground behind the vertical. The castor angle is not adjustable.

**4 Toe** is the difference, viewed from above, between lines drawn through the roadwheel centres and the car's centre-line. 'Toe-in' is when the roadwheels point inwards, towards each other at the front, while 'toe-out' is when they splay outwards from each other at the front.

**5** The front wheel toe setting is adjusted by screwing the track rod in or out of its balljoints, to alter the effective length of the track rod assembly.

**6** Rear wheel toe setting is not adjustable.

### Checking and adjustment

**7** Due to the special measuring equipment necessary to check the wheel alignment and steering angles, and the skill required to use it properly, the checking and adjustment of these settings is best left to a Citroën dealer or similar expert. Note that most tyre-fitting shops now possess sophisticated checking equipment.

# Chapter 11
# Bodywork and fittings

## Contents

## Degrees of difficulty

| Easy, suitable for novice with little experience | Fairly easy, suitable for beginner with some experience | Fairly difficult, suitable for competent DIY mechanic | Difficult, suitable for experienced DIY mechanic | Very difficult, suitable for expert DIY or professional |
|---|---|---|---|---|

## Specifications

| Torque wrench setting | Nm | lbf ft |
|---|---|---|
| Seat belt mountings | 25 | 18 |

---

### 1 General information

The bodyshell is made of pressed-steel sections, and is available as a five-door Hatchback. Most components are welded together, but some use is made of structural adhesives. The front wings are bolted on.

The bonnet, doors and some other vulnerable panels are made of zinc-coated metal, and are further protected by being coated with an anti-chip primer prior to being sprayed.

Extensive use is made of plastic materials, mainly in the interior, but also in exterior components. The front and rear bumpers and the front grille are injection-moulded from a synthetic material which is very strong, yet light. Plastic components such as wheel arch liners are fitted to the underside of the vehicle, to improve the body's resistance to corrosion.

### 2 Maintenance – bodywork and underframe

The general condition of a vehicle's bodywork is the one thing that significantly affects its value. Maintenance is easy, but needs to be regular. Neglect, particularly after minor damage, can lead quickly to further deterioration and costly repair bills. It is important also to keep watch on those parts of the vehicle not immediately visible, for instance the underside, inside all the wheel arches, and the lower part of the engine compartment.

The basic maintenance routine for the bodywork is washing – preferably with a lot of water, from a hose. This will remove all the loose solids which may have stuck to the vehicle. It is important to flush these off in such a way as to prevent grit from scratching the finish. The wheel arches and underframe

need washing in the same way, to remove any accumulated mud which will retain moisture and tend to encourage rust. Paradoxically enough, the best time to clean the underframe and wheel arches is in wet weather, when the mud is thoroughly wet and soft. In very wet weather, the underframe is usually cleaned of large accumulations automatically, and this is a good time for inspection.

Periodically, except on vehicles with a wax-based underbody protective coating, it is a good idea to have the whole of the underframe of the vehicle steam-cleaned, engine compartment included, so that a thorough inspection can be carried out to see what minor repairs and renovations are necessary. Steam-cleaning is available at many garages, and is necessary for the removal of the accumulation of oily grime, which sometimes is allowed to become thick in certain areas. If steam-cleaning facilities are not available, there are one or two excellent grease solvents available, which can be brush-applied; the dirt can then be simply hosed off. Note that these methods should not be used on vehicles with wax-based underbody protective coating, or the coating will be removed. Such vehicles should be inspected annually, preferably just prior to winter, when the underbody should be washed down, and any damage to the wax coating repaired using underseal. Ideally, a completely fresh coat should be applied. It would also be worth considering the use of wax-based protection for injection into door panels, sills, box sections, etc, as an additional safeguard against rust damage, where such protection is not provided by the vehicle manufacturer.

After washing paintwork, wipe off with a chamois leather to give an unspotted clear finish. A coat of clear protective wax polish will give added protection against chemical pollutants in the air. If the paintwork sheen has dulled or oxidised, use a cleaner/ polisher combination to restore the brilliance of the shine. This requires a little effort, but such dulling is usually caused because regular washing has been neglected. Care needs to be taken with metallic paintwork, as a special non-abrasive cleaner/polisher is required to avoid damage to the finish. Always check that the door and ventilator opening drain holes and pipes are completely clear, so that water can be drained out. Brightwork should be treated in the same way as paintwork. Windscreens and windows can be kept clear of the smeary film which often appears, by the use of proprietary glass cleaner. Never use any form of wax or other body or chromium polish on glass.

## 3 Maintenance – upholstery and carpets

Mats and carpets should be brushed or vacuum-cleaned regularly, to keep them free of grit. If they are badly stained, remove them from the vehicle for scrubbing or sponging, and make quite sure they are dry before refitting. Seats and interior trim panels can be kept clean by wiping with a damp cloth and a proprietary upholstery cleaner. If they do become stained (which can be more apparent on light-coloured upholstery), use a little liquid detergent and a soft nail brush to scour the grime out of the grain of the material. Do not forget to keep the headlining clean in the same way as the upholstery. When using liquid cleaners inside the vehicle, do not over-wet the surfaces being cleaned. Excessive damp could get into the seams and padded interior, causing stains, offensive odours or even rot. If the inside of the vehicle gets wet accidentally, it is worthwhile taking some trouble to dry it out properly, particularly where carpets are involved. *Caution: Do not leave oil or electric heaters inside the vehicle for this purpose.*

## 4 Minor body damage – repair

### Scratches

If the scratch is very superficial, and does not penetrate to the metal of the bodywork, repair is very simple. Lightly rub the area of the scratch with a paintwork renovator, or a very fine cutting paste, to remove loose paint from the scratch, and to clear the surrounding bodywork of wax polish. Rinse the area with clean water.

Apply touch-up paint to the scratch using a fine paint brush; continue to apply fine layers of paint until the surface of the paint in the scratch is level with the surrounding paintwork. Allow the new paint at least two weeks to harden, then blend it into the surrounding paintwork by rubbing the scratch area with a paintwork renovator or a very fine cutting paste. Finally apply wax polish.

Where the scratch has penetrated right through to the metal of the bodywork, causing the metal to rust, a different repair technique is required. Remove any loose rust from the bottom of the scratch with a penknife, then apply rust-inhibiting paint, to prevent the formation of rust in the future. Using a rubber or nylon applicator, fill the scratch with bodystopper paste. If required, this paste can be mixed with cellulose thinners, to provide a very thin paste which is ideal for filling narrow scratches. Before the stopper-paste in the scratch hardens, wrap a piece of smooth cotton rag around the top of a finger. Dip the finger in cellulose thinners, and quickly sweep it across the surface of the stopper-paste in the scratch; this will ensure that the surface of the stopper-paste is slightly hollowed. The scratch can now be painted over as described earlier in this Section.

### Dents

When deep denting of the vehicle's bodywork has taken place, the first task is to pull the dent out, until the affected bodywork almost attains its original shape. There is little point in trying to restore the original shape completely, as the metal in the damaged area will have stretched on impact, and cannot be reshaped fully to its original contour. It is better to bring the level of the dent up to a point which is about 3 mm below the level of the surrounding bodywork. In cases where the dent is very shallow anyway, it is not worth trying to pull it out at all. If the underside of the dent is accessible, it can be hammered out gently from behind, using a mallet with a wooden or plastic head. Whilst doing this, hold a suitable block of wood firmly against the outside of the panel, to absorb the impact from the hammer blows and thus prevent a large area of the bodywork from being 'belled-out'.

Should the dent be in a section of the bodywork which has a double skin, or some other factor making it inaccessible from behind, a different technique is called for. Drill several small holes through the metal inside the area – particularly in the deeper section. Then screw long self-tapping screws into the holes, just sufficiently for them to gain a good purchase in the metal. Now the dent can be pulled out by pulling on the protruding heads of the screws with a pair of pliers.

The next stage of the repair is the removal of the paint from the damaged area, and from an inch or so of the surrounding 'sound' bodywork. This is accomplished most easily by using a wire brush or abrasive pad on a power drill, although it can be done just as effectively by hand, using sheets of abrasive paper. To complete the preparation for filling, score the surface of the bare metal with a screwdriver or the tang of a file, or alternatively, drill small holes in the affected area. This will provide a really good 'key' for the filler paste.

To complete the repair, see the Section on filling and respraying.

### Rust holes or gashes

Remove all paint from the affected area, and from an inch or so of the surrounding 'sound' bodywork, using an abrasive pad or a wire brush on a power drill. If these are not available, a few sheets of abrasive paper will do the job most effectively. With the paint removed, you will be able to judge the severity of the corrosion, and therefore decide whether to renew the whole panel (if this is possible) or to repair the affected area. New body panels are not as expensive as most people think, and it is often quicker and more satisfactory to fit a new panel than to attempt to repair large areas of corrosion.

Remove all fittings from the affected area, except those which will act as a guide to the original shape of the damaged bodywork (eg headlight shells etc). Then, using tin snips or a hacksaw blade, remove all loose metal and any other metal badly affected by corrosion. Hammer the edges of the hole inwards, in order to create a slight depression for the filler paste.

Wire-brush the affected area to remove the powdery rust from the surface of the remaining metal. Paint the affected area with rust-inhibiting paint; if the back of the rusted area is accessible, treat this also.

Before filling can take place, it will be necessary to block the hole in some way. This can be achieved by the use of aluminium or plastic mesh, or aluminium tape.

Aluminium or plastic mesh, or glass-fibre matting, is probably the best material to use for a large hole. Cut a piece to the approximate size and shape of the hole to be filled, then position it in the hole so that its edges are below the level of the surrounding bodywork. It can be retained in position by several blobs of filler paste around its periphery.

Aluminium tape should be used for small or very narrow holes. Pull a piece off the roll, trim it to the approximate size and shape required, then pull off the backing paper (if used) and stick the tape over the hole; it can be overlapped if the thickness of one piece is insufficient. Burnish down the edges of the tape with the handle of a screwdriver or similar, to ensure that the tape is securely attached to the metal underneath.

### Filling and respraying

Before using this Section, see the Sections on dent, minor scratch, rust holes and gash repairs.

Many types of bodyfiller are available, but generally speaking, those proprietary kits which contain a tin of filler paste and a tube of resin hardener are best for this type of repair; some can be used directly from the tube. A wide, flexible plastic or nylon applicator will be found invaluable for imparting a smooth and well-contoured finish to the surface of the filler.

Mix up a little filler on a clean piece of card or board – measure the hardener carefully (follow the maker's instructions on the pack), otherwise the filler will set too rapidly or too slowly. Using the applicator, apply the filler paste to the prepared area; draw the applicator across the surface of the filler to achieve the correct contour and to level the surface. As soon as a contour that approximates to the correct one is achieved, stop working the paste – if you carry on too long, the paste will become sticky and begin to 'pick-up' on the applicator. Continue to add thin layers of filler paste at 20-minute intervals, until the level of the filler is just proud of the surrounding bodywork.

Once the filler has hardened, the excess can be removed using a metal plane or file. From then on, progressively-finer grades of abrasive paper should be used, starting with a 40-grade production paper, and finishing with a 400-grade wet-and-dry paper. Always wrap the abrasive paper around a flat rubber, cork, or wooden block – otherwise the surface of the filler will not be completely flat. During the smoothing of the filler surface, the wet-and-dry paper should be periodically rinsed in water. This will ensure that a very smooth finish is imparted to the filler at the final stage.

At this stage, the 'dent' should be surrounded by a ring of bare metal, which in turn should be encircled by the finely 'feathered' edge of the good paintwork. Rinse the repair area with clean water, until all of the dust produced by the rubbing-down operation has gone.

Spray the whole area with a light coat of primer – this will show up any imperfections in the surface of the filler. Repair these imperfections with fresh filler paste or bodystopper, and once more smooth the surface with abrasive paper. If bodystopper is used, it can be mixed with cellulose thinners, to form a really thin paste which is ideal for filling small holes. Repeat this spray-and-repair procedure until you are satisfied that the surface of the filler, and the feathered edge of the paintwork, are perfect. Clean the repair area with clean water, and allow to dry fully.

The repair area is now ready for final spraying. Paint spraying must be carried out in a warm, dry, windless and dust-free atmosphere. This condition can be created artificially if you have access to a large indoor working area, but if you are forced to work in the open, you will have to pick your day very carefully. If you are working indoors, dousing the floor in the work area with water will help to settle the dust which would otherwise be in the atmosphere. If the repair area is confined to one body panel, mask off the surrounding panels; this will help to minimise the effects of a slight mismatch in paint colours. Bodywork fittings (eg chrome strips, door handles etc) will also need to be masked off. Use genuine masking tape, and several thicknesses of newspaper, for the masking operations.

Before commencing to spray, agitate the aerosol can thoroughly, then spray a test area (an old tin, or similar) until the technique is mastered. Cover the repair area with a thick coat of primer; the thickness should be built up using several thin layers of paint, rather than one thick one. Using 400 grade wet-and-dry paper, rub down the surface of the primer until it is really smooth. While doing this, the work area should be thoroughly doused with water, and the wet-and-dry paper periodically rinsed in water. Allow to dry before spraying on more paint.

Spray on the top coat, again building up the thickness by using several thin layers of paint. Start spraying at the top of the repair area, and then, using a side-to-side motion, work downwards until the whole repair area and about 2 inches of the surrounding original paintwork is covered. Remove all masking material 10 to 15 minutes after spraying on the final coat of paint.

Allow the new paint at least two weeks to harden, then, using a paintwork renovator or a very fine cutting paste, blend the edges of the paint into the existing paintwork. Finally, apply wax polish.

### Plastic components

With the use of more and more plastic body components by the vehicle manufacturers (eg bumpers. spoilers, and in some cases major body panels), rectification of more serious damage to such items has become a matter of either entrusting repair work to a specialist in this field, or renewing complete components. Repair of such damage by the DIY owner is not really feasible, owing to the cost of the equipment and materials required for effecting such repairs. The basic technique involves making a groove along the line of the crack in the plastic, using a rotary burr in a power drill. The damaged part is then welded back together, using a hot air gun to heat up and fuse a plastic filler rod into the groove. Any excess plastic is then removed, and the area rubbed down to a smooth finish. It is important that a filler rod of the correct plastic is used, as body components can be made of a variety of different types (eg polycarbonate, ABS, polypropylene).

Damage of a less serious nature (abrasions, minor cracks etc) can be repaired by the DIY owner using a two-part epoxy filler repair material. Once mixed in equal proportions, this is used in similar fashion to the bodywork filler used on metal panels. The filler is usually cured in twenty to thirty minutes, ready for sanding and painting.

If the owner is renewing a complete component himself, or if he has repaired it with epoxy filler, he will be left with the problem of finding a suitable paint for finishing which is compatible with the type of plastic used. At one time, the use of a universal paint was not possible, owing to the complex range of plastics encountered in body component applications. Standard paints, generally speaking, will not bond to plastic or rubber satisfactorily. However, it is now possible to obtain a plastic body parts finishing kit which consists of a pre-primer treatment, a primer and coloured top coat. Full instructions are normally supplied with a kit, but basically, the method of use is to first apply the pre-primer to the component concerned, and allow it to dry for up to 30 minutes. Then the primer is applied, and left to dry for about an hour before finally applying the special-coloured top coat. The result is a correctly-coloured component, where the paint will flex with the plastic or rubber, a property that standard paint does not normally posses.

### 5 Major body damage – repair

Where serious damage has occurred, or large areas need renewal due to neglect, it means that complete new panels will need welding-in, and this is best left to professionals. If the damage is due to impact, it will also be necessary to check completely the alignment of the bodyshell, and this can only be carried out accurately by a Citroën dealer, or accident repair specialist, using special jigs. If the body is left misaligned, it is primarily dangerous, as the car will not handle properly, and secondly, uneven stresses will be imposed on the steering, suspension and possibly transmission, causing abnormal wear, or complete failure, particularly to such items as the tyres.

### 6 Front bumper – removal and refitting

**Note:** *The help of an assistant is useful to support the bumper during the removal and refitting procedure.*

### Removal

**1** Firmly apply the handbrake, then jack up the front of the vehicle and support it securely on axle stands (see *Jacking and vehicle support*). To improve access to the bumper fasteners, remove both front roadwheels.
**2** Remove the radiator grille as described in Section 22.

**6.4 Undo the screw each side, securing the base of the wheel arch liner to the bumper**

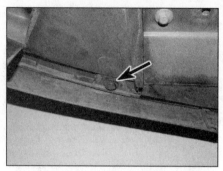

**6.5 Pull out the plastic rivet (arrowed) at the front of the bumper on each side**

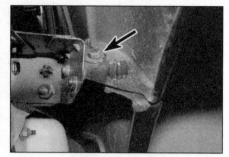

**6.6 Undo the bolt each side (arrowed) securing the rear edge of the bumper to the front wing**

**6.7 Undo the screws (arrowed) securing the upper front edge of the bumper to the bracket**

**6.9 Carefully pull the bumper forward and off the car**

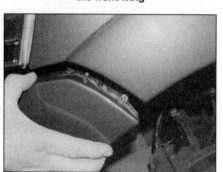

**6.11 Ensure that the two pegs each side correctly engage with the front wings**

**3** Turn the fasteners a quarter turn and remove the engine undershield (where fitted).
**4** Undo the screw each side, securing the base of the wheel arch liner to the bumper **(see illustration)**.
**5** Using a forked tool, pull out the plastic rivet at the front of the bumper on each side **(see illustration)**.
**6** Reach up behind the wheel arch liner and undo the bolt securing the rear edge of the bumper to the front wing **(see illustration)**.
**7** Undo the three screws securing the upper front edge of the bumper to the bumper bracket **(see illustration)**.
**8** On models equipped with foglights, disconnect the foglight wiring connectors, and release the wiring from the bumper clips.
**9** Release the tangs below each headlight then, with the help of an assistant, carefully pull the bumper forward and off the car **(see illustration)**.

**10** To remove the bumper bracket, undo the three bolts each side and lift the bracket from its location.

### Refitting

**11** Refitting is a reversal of removal, ensuring that the two pegs each side correctly engage with the front wings as it is located in position **(see illustration)**.

## 7 Rear bumper – removal and refitting

**Note:** *The help of an assistant is useful to support the bumper during the removal and refitting procedure.*

### Removal

**1** Chock the front wheels, then jack up the rear of the vehicle and support securely on axle stands (see *Jacking and vehicle support*).
**2** Remove the rear light cluster on both sides as described in Chapter 12, Section 5.
**3** Using a forked tool pull out the plastic rivet at the rear of the bumper on each side **(see illustration)**.
**4** Undo the two lower centre screws securing the bumper to the bumper bracket **(see illustration)**.
**5** Working through the slot in the wheel arch liner, undo the bolt each side securing the bumper to the rear wing **(see illustration)**.
**6** Undo the bolt each side at the upper edge of the bumper **(see illustration)**.
**7** Release the three tangs along the upper edge of the bumper then, with the help of an assistant, carefully pull the bumper rearward and off the car. On models equipped with the parking aid system, disconnect the ultrasound sensor wiring.

**7.3 Pull out the plastic rivet at the rear of the bumper on each side**

**7.4 Undo the lower centre screws securing the bumper to the bracket**

**7.5 Undo the bolt (arrowed) each side securing the bumper to the rear wing**

**8** To remove the bumper bracket, undo the bolts and lift the bracket from its location.

### Refitting

**9** Refitting is a reversal of removal, ensuring that the pegs each side correctly engage with the rear wings as it is located in position **(see illustration)**.

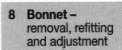

## 8 Bonnet –
### removal, refitting and adjustment

### Removal

**1** Open the bonnet and have an assistant support it then, using a pencil or felt tip pen, mark the outline of each bonnet hinge relative to the bonnet, to use as a guide on refitting.

**2** Disconnect the washer jet supply tubing from the right-hand jet and release the supply tubing from the retaining clips **(see illustration)**.

**3** Unscrew the bonnet-to-hinge retaining bolts each side **(see illustration)**. With the help of the assistant, carefully lift the bonnet from the vehicle. Store the bonnet out of the way in a safe place.

**4** Inspect the bonnet hinges for signs of wear and free play at the pivots, and if necessary renew. Each hinge is secured to the body by two bolts. On refitting, apply a smear of multi-purpose grease to the hinges.

### Refitting and adjustment

**5** With the aid of an assistant, offer up the bonnet, and engage the retaining bolts. Align the hinges with the marks made on removal, then tighten the retaining bolts securely. Reconnect the washer jet tubing.

**6** Close the bonnet, and check for alignment with the adjacent panels. If necessary, slacken the hinge bolts and re-align the bonnet to suit. When correctly aligned, tighten the hinge bolts securely.

**7** Once the bonnet is correctly aligned, check that the bonnet fastens and releases in a satisfactory manner. If adjustment is necessary, slacken the bonnet lock retaining bolts, and adjust the position of the lock to suit. Once the lock is operating correctly, securely tighten its retaining bolts.

## 9 Bonnet lock
### and release cable –
removal and refitting

### Removal

**1** Undo the two bolts securing the bonnet lock to the radiator support frame. Withdraw the lock and disconnect the release cable **(see illustrations)**.

**2** Work along the length of the cable in the engine compartment, note their fitted locations, and release the cable retaining clips.

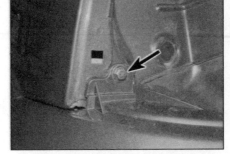

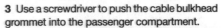

**7.6 Undo the bolt (arrowed) each side at the upper edge of the bumper**

**3** Use a screwdriver to push the cable bulkhead grommet into the passenger compartment.

**4** Working under the facia on the left-hand side, unscrew the two release lever retaining nuts, and withdraw the lever assembly from its location.

**5** Tie a length of string to the end of the cable in the engine compartment, note its routing, then carefully pull the cable through into the passenger compartment. Untie the string from the end of the cable, and leave it in position to aid refitting.

### Refitting

**6** Locate the cable in position in the passenger compartment.

**7** Tie the end of the new cable to the string, and pull it through into the engine compartment.

**8** Check that the bulkhead grommet is securely seated, then remove the string and connect the cable to the bonnet lock lever.

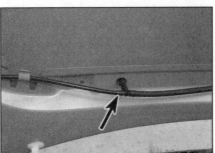

**8.2 Disconnect the washer jet supply tubing (arrowed) from the right-hand jet**

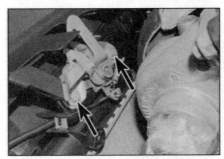

**9.1a Undo the two bolts (arrowed) securing the bonnet lock to the radiator support frame**

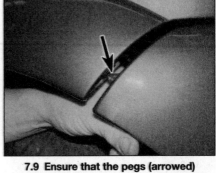

**7.9 Ensure that the pegs (arrowed) correctly engage with the rear wings**

**9** Secure the release lever in place, tightening its retaining nuts securely.

**10** Reconnect the cable to the bonnet lock then refit the lock, tightening its retaining bolts securely.

**11** Secure the cable in place with its retaining clips. Check the operation of the lock and, if necessary, adjust the position of the lock within the elongated bolt holes to achieve satisfactory operation prior to closing the bonnet.

## 10 Door –
### removal, refitting and adjustment

### Front door

#### Removal

**1** Release the protective rubber boot from the door wiring harness guide.

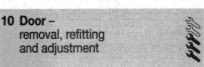

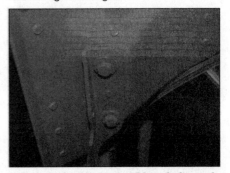

**8.3 Undo the two bonnet hinge bolts each side**

**9.1b Withdraw the lock and disconnect the release cable**

**10.2 Squeeze the tabs of the harness guide and pull the assembly from the body**

2 Squeeze the internal tabs of the guide and pull the assembly from the body **(see illustration)**.

3 Prise up the locking catch and disconnect the door wiring connector.

4 Unscrew the securing bolt, and disconnect the door check strap from the door pillar **(see illustration)**.

5 Ensure that the door is adequately supported, slide out the hinge pin clips, then remove the upper and lower hinge pins. Carefully lift the door from the vehicle.

### Refitting

6 Refitting is a reversal of removal.

## Rear door

7 The procedure is as described for the front doors, but the hinge-to-body bolts are accessed for adjustment with the front door open.

**11.1a Carefully prise off the door pull handle trim . . .**

**11.3 Work around the edge of the trim panel, and release the securing clips**

**10.4 Undo the door check strap bolt**

### 11 Door inner trim panel – removal and refitting

## Front door

### Removal

1 On pre-2006 models, use a small screwdriver to prise off the door pull handle trim, then undo the two retaining screws **(see illustrations)**. On 2006-on models, undo the single screw located beneath the door pull.

2 Undo the two screws securing the rear edge of the panel to the door **(see illustration)**. Note: *Some early models do not have these screws fitted.*

3 Using a suitable forked tool, work around the edge of the trim panel, and release the securing clips **(see illustration)**.

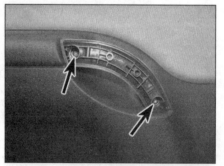

**11.1b . . . then undo the two retaining screws (arrowed)**

**11.4 Pull the panel outwards, lift it up and remove it from the door**

4 Pull the panel outwards, lift it up and remove it from the door **(see illustration)**.

### Refitting

5 Before refitting, check whether any of the trim panel retaining studs were broken on removal. Renew the panel retaining studs as necessary, then refit the panel using a reversal of removal. Ensure that the tabs on the inner face of the panel locate in the slots of the interior handle as the panel is fitted **(see illustration)**.

## Rear door

### Removal

6 The procedure is the same as for the front door trim panel, with the following exceptions:
a) *Pull the window regulator handle off the regulator shaft.*
b) *There are no screws at the rear edge of the panel.*

### Refitting

7 Refitting is a reversal of removal, after first renewing any broken panel retaining studs as necessary.

### 12 Door handle and lock components – removal and refitting

## Interior door handle

### Removal

Note: *A new door sealing sheet will be required for refitting.*

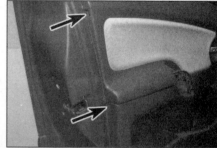

**11.2 Undo the two screws (arrowed) securing the rear edge of the panel to the door**

**11.5 Ensure that the tabs on the panel (arrowed) locate in the slots of the interior handle when refitting**

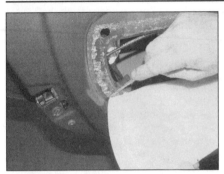

**12.3  Carefully release the self-adhesive plastic sealing sheet from the door**

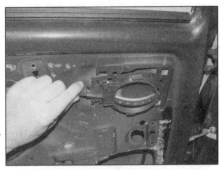

**12.4  Release the interior handle by sliding it towards the rear**

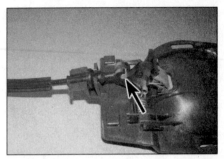

**12.5  Release the operating cable from the handle, then slip the cable end (arrowed) out of the lever**

**12.8  Slide the white lever forwards so the handle no longer engages with it**

**12.9  Pull the rear of the handle outwards, and disengage the front end from the pivot pin**

**12.10a Unclip the plastic lock cylinder cover . . .**

**1** Remove the door inner trim panel, as described in Section 11.

**2** Remove the door loudspeaker as described in Chapter 12.

**3** Using a sharp knife, carefully release the self-adhesive plastic sealing sheet and remove the sheet from the door **(see illustration)**. The sheet will be irreparably damaged during removal and a new sheet will be required for refitting.

**4** Release the handle from its location by sliding it towards the rear **(see illustration)**.

**5** Release the operating cable from the handle, then slip the cable end out of the handle lever **(see illustration)**.

### Refitting

**6** Refitting is a reversal of removal but ensure that the operating cable is correctly reconnected. Remove all traces of old adhesive from the door and fit a new sealing sheet. Refit the door loudspeaker as described

in Chapter 12, then refit the inner trim panel as described in Section 11.

### Front door lock and exterior handle

**Note:** *The exterior handle mounting bracket is riveted to the door. Ensure that new rivets of the correct size are available for refitting.*

### Removal

**7** Remove the interior door handle as described previously.

**8** Slide the white plastic operating lever forward so that the locking clip engages in the groove, and the rear of the exterior handle no longer engages with it **(see illustration)**.

**9** Pull the rear of the exterior handle outwards, and disengage the front of the handle from the front pivot pin **(see illustration)**. Remove the handle from the door.

**10** Unclip the plastic lock cylinder exterior

cover then, using a 5.0 mm diameter drill bit, drill off the rivet heads securing the handle mounting bracket to the door **(see illustrations)**.

**11** Undo the three screws securing the lock assembly to the edge of the door **(see illustration)**.

**12** Disconnect the central locking motor wiring plug and remove the lock and exterior handle mounting bracket as an assembly through the door aperture **(see illustration)**.

**13** To separate the door lock from the exterior handle mounting bracket, lift up the arm of the retaining collar, and release the collar from the door lock. Slide the retaining collar off the lock cylinder operating arm, and disengage the operating arm from the door lock **(see illustrations)**.

**14** Release the door lock operating cable from handle mounting bracket, then slip the cable end out of the handle lever.

**12.10b  . . . then drill off the rivet heads securing the handle mounting bracket to the door**

**12.11  Undo the three screws securing the lock assembly to the door**

**12.12  Disconnect the wiring plug and remove the lock and exterior handle mounting bracket as an assembly**

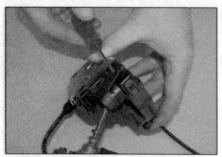

**12.13a Lift up the arm of the retaining collar, and release the collar from the door lock**

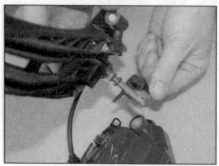

**12.13b Slide the collar off the lock cylinder arm, and disengage the arm from the lock**

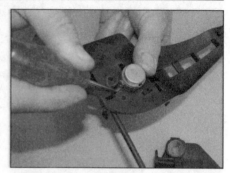

**12.17a Depress the tab on the side of the lock cylinder . . .**

**12.17b . . . and withdraw the cylinder from the handle mounting bracket**

**12.23 Undo the three screws securing the lock assembly to the door**

**12.24 Release the wiring harness clip from the door panel**

### Refitting

**15** Refitting is a reversal of removal, using new pop rivets to secure the handle mounting bracket.

## Front door lock cylinder

### Removal

**16** Remove the front door lock and exterior handle as described previously.
**17** Depress the tab on the side of the lock cylinder, and withdraw the cylinder from the exterior handle mounting bracket **(see illustrations)**.

### Refitting

**18** Refitting is a reversal of removal

## Rear door lock and exterior handle

**Note:** *The exterior handle mounting bracket is*

**12.25 Withdraw the lock and exterior handle mounting bracket through the door aperture**

*riveted to the door. Ensure that new rivets of the correct size are available for refitting.*

### Removal

**19** Remove the interior door handle as described previously.
**20** Slide the white plastic operating lever forward so that the locking clip engages in the groove, and the rear of the exterior handle no longer engages with it **(see illustration 12.8)**.
**21** Pull the rear of the exterior handle outwards, and disengage the front of the handle from the front pivot pin **(see illustration 12.9)**. Remove the handle from the door.
**22** Unclip the plastic exterior cover at the end of the exterior handle mounting bracket. Then, using a 5.0 mm diameter drill bit, drill off the rivet heads securing the handle mounting bracket to the door **(see illustration 12.10)**.
**23** Undo the three screws securing the

**12.26 Hook the cable end out of the handle lever**

lock assembly to the edge of the door **(see illustration)**.
**24** Release the wiring harness clip from the door panel **(see illustration)**.
**25** Withdraw the lock and exterior handle mounting bracket as an assembly through the door aperture, and disconnect the central locking motor wiring plug **(see illustration)**.
**26** To separate the door lock from the exterior handle mounting bracket, release the door lock operating cable from handle mounting bracket, then hook the cable end out of the handle lever **(see illustration)**.

### Refitting

**27** Refitting is a reversal of removal, using new pop rivets to secure the handle mounting bracket.

## 13 Door window glass, regulator and quarter light – removal and refitting

## Front door window glass

**Note:** *A new door sealing sheet will be required on refitting.*

### Removal

**1** Remove the door inner trim panel as described in Section 11.
**2** Remove the door loudspeaker as described in Chapter 12.
**3** Using a sharp knife, carefully release the self-adhesive plastic sealing sheet and remove the sheet from the door **(see illustration 12.3)**.

**13.5 Depress the tab (arrowed) on the regulator lifting channel, and free the glass from the support**

**13.6 Lower the glass at the front and remove it from the outside of the door frame**

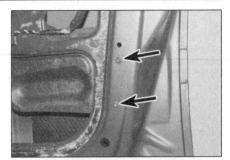

**13.10a Undo the screws (arrowed) securing the window glass rear guide channel to the door**

**13.10b Withdraw the inner damper pad and guide channel, out through the door aperture**

**13.11 Remove the outer damper pad through the door aperture**

**13.12 Disconnect the wiring connector from the regulator motor**

The sheet will be irreparably damaged during removal and a new sheet will be required for refitting.

**4** Position the window approximately three-quarters of the way down.

**5** Depress the tab on the window regulator lifting channel, lift the glass slightly and free the glass from the support **(see illustration)**.

**6** Lower the glass at the front and remove it from the outside of the door frame **(see illustration)**.

### Refitting

**7** Refitting is a reversal of removal. Remove all traces of old adhesive from the door and fit a new sealing sheet. Refit the door loudspeaker as described in Chapter 12, then refit the inner trim panel as described in Section 11.

### *Front door window regulator*

**Note 1:** *A new door sealing sheet will be required on refitting.*

**Note 2:** *The regulator assembly is riveted to the door. Ensure that new rivets of the correct size are available for refitting.*

### Removal

**8** Release the window glass from the regulator lifting channel as described in paragraphs 1 to 5 above.

**9** Slide the window glass up to the fully-closed position and secure it in this position with masking tape over the top of the door frame.

**10** Undo the two screws securing the window glass rear guide channel to the door. Withdraw

the inner damper pad, complete with guide channel, out through the door aperture **(see illustrations)**.

**11** Remove the outer damper pad through the door aperture **(see illustration)**.

**12** Disconnect the wiring connector from the regulator motor **(see illustration)**.

**13** Using a 5.0 mm diameter drill bit, drill off the four rivet heads securing the regulator assembly to the door **(see illustration)**.

**14** Manipulate the regulator assembly out through the door aperture **(see illustration)**.

### Refitting

**15** Refitting is a reversal of removal. Remove all traces of old adhesive from the door and fit a new sealing sheet. Refit the door loudspeaker as described in Chapter 12, then refit the inner trim panel as described in Section 11.

**13.13 Drill off the rivet heads (arrowed) securing the regulator assembly to the door**

### *Rear door window glass*

**Note:** *A new door sealing sheet will be required on refitting.*

### Removal

**16** Remove the door inner trim panel as described in Section 11.

**17** Remove the door loudspeaker as described in Chapter 12.

**18** Using a sharp knife, carefully release the self-adhesive plastic sealing sheet and remove the sheet from the door **(see illustration 12.3)**. The sheet will be irreparably damaged during removal and a new sheet will be required for refitting.

**19** Undo the two screws at the rear of the door frame securing the window guide channel, and withdraw the guide channel **(see illustrations)**.

**20** Carefully prise up the forward end of the plastic trim from the rear lower corner of

**13.14 Manipulate the regulator assembly out through the door aperture**

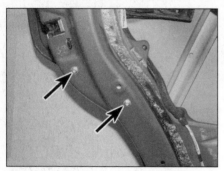

**13.19a Undo the screws (arrowed) securing the window guide channel . . .**

**13.19b . . . and withdraw the guide channel**

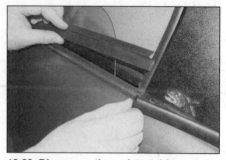

**13.20 Disengage the waist seal from under the plastic trim, then remove the waist seal from the window aperture**

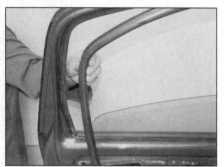

**13.21 Remove the window aperture channel seal from the door frame**

**13.22 Position the window so the attachment to the lifting channel (arrowed) is accessible through the door aperture**

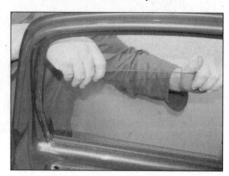

**13.26 Lift the rear of the window glass upwards and remove it from the door**

the window outer aperture. Disengage the exterior waist seal from under the plastic trim, then remove the waist seal from the window aperture **(see illustration)**.

**21** Beginning in the rear lower corner, carefully remove the window aperture channel seal from the door frame **(see illustration)**.

**22** Temporarily refit the regulator handle, and position the window so the attachment to the lifting channel is accessible through the door aperture **(see illustration)**.

**23** Depress the tab on the window regulator lifting channel, lift the glass slightly and free the glass from the support **(see illustration 13.5)**.

**24** Slide the window up to the fully-closed position and secure it in this position with masking tape over the top of the door frame.

**25** Using the regulator handle, fully lower the regulator mechanism.

**26** Fully lower the window, then lift the rear

of the window glass upwards and remove it from the door **(see illustration)**. Take care not to damage the paintwork on the door.

**Refitting**

**27** Refitting is a reversal of removal. Remove all traces of old adhesive from the door and fit a new sealing sheet. Refit the door loudspeaker as described in Chapter 12, then refit the inner trim panel as described in Section 11.

### Rear door window regulator

**Note 1:** *A new door sealing sheet will be required on refitting.*

**Note 2:** *The regulator assembly is riveted to the door. Ensure that new rivets of the correct size are available for refitting.*

**Removal**

**28** Remove the door inner trim panel as described in Section 11.

**29** Remove the door loudspeaker as described in Chapter 12.

**30** Using a sharp knife, carefully release the self-adhesive plastic sealing sheet and remove the sheet from the door **(see illustration 12.3)**. The sheet will be irreparably damaged during removal and a new sheet will be required for refitting.

**31** Temporarily refit the regulator handle, and position the window so the attachment to the lifting channel is accessible through the door aperture **(see illustration 13.22)**.

**32** Depress the tab on the window regulator lifting channel, lift the glass slightly and free the glass from the support **(see illustration 13.5)**.

**33** Slide the window glass upwards by hand, and tape it to the top of the door frame to secure it in the raised position.

**34** Fully lower the window regulator mechanism using the handle.

**35** Using a 5.0 mm diameter drill bit, drill off the four rivet heads securing the regulator assembly to the door **(see illustration)**.

**36** Manipulate the regulator assembly out through the door aperture **(see illustration)**.

**Refitting**

**37** Refitting is a reversal of removal. Remove all traces of old adhesive from the door and fit a new sealing sheet. Refit the door loudspeaker as described in Chapter 12, then refit the inner trim panel as described in Section 11.

### Front door quarter light

**Note:** *The quarter light is riveted to the door. Ensure that new rivets of the correct size are available for refitting.*

**13.35 Drill off the four rivet heads (arrowed) securing the regulator assembly to the door**

**13.36 Manipulate the regulator assembly out through the door aperture**

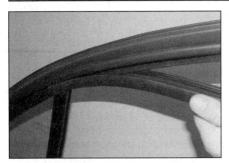

**13.40  Remove the window aperture channel seal from the door frame, up to the quarter light**

**13.41  Ease the channel seal away from the door frame and drill off the head of the upper rivet**

**13.42  Drill off the head of the lower rivet, working through the door aperture**

## Removal

**38**  Remove the front door window glass as described earlier in this Section.

**39**  Remove the exterior mirror from the door as described in Section 17.

**40**  Prise up and remove the interior and exterior waist seals from the window aperture, then carefully remove the window aperture channel seal from the top of the door frame, up to the quarter light (**see illustration**).

**41**  Using a small screwdriver, ease the window aperture channel seal away from the door frame directly above the quarter light window frame. Using a 5.0 mm diameter drill bit, drill off the head of the upper retaining rivet now exposed (**see illustration**).

**42**  Similarly drill off the head of the lower retaining rivet, working through the aperture in the door (**see illustration**).

**43**  Undo the centre retaining screw located below the exterior mirror mounting (**see illustration**).

**44**  Pull the quarter light rearward to free the channel seal from the front of the door frame, then manipulate the quarter light from the door (**see illustration**).

## Refitting

**45**  Refitting is a reversal of removal.

**13.43  Undo the screw located below the exterior mirror mounting**

harness cover from the left-hand edge of the tailgate (**see illustration**). Release the grommet from the tailgate and withdraw the wiring harness.

**5**  Remove the high-level brake light as described in Chapter 12, Section 5.

**6**  Unscrew the two bolts each side securing the hinges to the tailgate, and carefully lift the tailgate from the vehicle.

## Refitting

**7**  If a new tailgate is to be fitted, transfer all serviceable components (lock mechanism, wiper motor, etc) to it, with reference to the relevant procedures in this Chapter, and in Chapter 12.

**8**  Refitting is a reversal of removal, bearing in mind the following points:

a) *If necessary, adjust the rubber buffers to obtain a good fit when the tailgate is shut.*
b) *If necessary, adjust the position of*

**13.44  Pull the quarter light rearward, then manipulate the quarter light from the door**

*the tailgate lock and/or hinge bolts within their elongated holes to achieve satisfactory lock operation.*

### Support struts

## Removal

**9**  Support the tailgate in the open position, with the help of an assistant, or using a stout piece of wood.

**10**  Using a small screwdriver, release the spring clip, and pull the support strut from its balljoint on the tailgate (**see illustration**).

**11**  Similarly, release the strut from the balljoint on the body, and withdraw the strut from the vehicle.

## Refitting

**12**  Refitting is a reversal of removal, but ensure the spring clips are correctly engaged.

## 14  Tailgate and support struts
– removal and refitting

### Tailgate

## Removal

**1**  Remove the tailgate trim panels as described in Section 25.

**2**  Disconnect the wiring harness connectors at the tailgate internal components, referring to the relevant procedures contained in Chapter 12.

**3**  With the aid of an assistant, suitably support the tailgate, then prise out the support strut spring clips, and pull the struts from the balljoints on the tailgate.

**4**  Undo the screws and remove the wiring

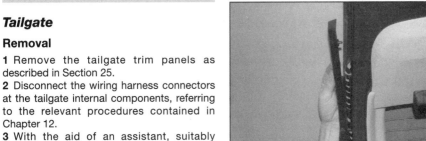

**14.4  Remove the wiring harness cover from the left-hand edge of the tailgate**

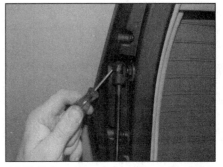

**14.10  Release the spring clip, and pull the support strut from its tailgate balljoint**

**15.2 Undo the two screws securing the lock to the tailgate**

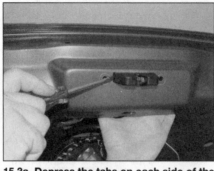

**15.3a Depress the tabs on each side of the lock and pull the lock into the tailgate**

## 16 Central locking components – removal and refitting

### Control unit

**1** The central locking system is controlled by the Built-in Systems Interface (BSI) which is the vehicle central computer controlling the main body electrical system functions. The unit is located under the facia on the left-hand side. Refer to Chapter 12 for further information.

**2** Should any problems be experienced with the operation of the central locking system or any of the other functions controlled by the BSI, the vehicle should be taken to a Citroën dealer for diagnostic investigation.

### Door lock motor

**3** The motor is integral with the door lock assembly. Removal and refitting of the lock assembly is described in Section 12.

### Tailgate lock motor

**4** Removal of the tailgate lock motor is described as part of the tailgate lock removal and refitting procedure described in Section 15.

### Remote control transmitter

#### Battery renewal

**5** Using a small screwdriver, undo the screw, carefully prise the two halves of the transmitter apart, and remove the battery.

**6** Fit the new battery and reassemble the transmitter.

#### Initialisation

**7** To initialise the unit after renewing the battery, switch off the ignition, then switch on the ignition and immediately press the locking button. Switch off the ignition and remove the key from the ignition lock.

**15.3b Withdraw the lock and disconnect the wiring connector**

**15.6 Unscrew the two bolts (arrowed) and remove the tailgate striker**

the tailgate lock striker as necessary to obtain satisfactory closure.

### Tailgate lock striker

#### Removal

**5** Undo the screws and remove the tailgate aperture lower panel (see Section 25) for access to the striker plate retaining bolts.

**6** Mark the position of the striker on the body, for use when refitting. Unscrew the two securing bolts, and remove the striker from the body **(see illustration)**.

#### Refitting

**7** Refitting is a reversal of removal. Before tightening the securing bolts, the position of the striker should be altered (the securing bolt holes are elongated) until satisfactory lock operation is obtained. Use the marks made prior to removal, if appropriate.

## 17 Exterior mirrors and mirror glass – removal and refitting

### Exterior mirror assembly

**1** Ensure the ignition is turned off.

**2** Remove the door inner trim panel as described in Section 11, then carefully prise off the mirror trim panel **(see illustration)**.

**3** Disconnect the mirror wiring connectors.

**4** Undo the three retaining screws and remove the mirror from the door frame **(see illustration)**.

**5** Refitting is a reversal of removal.

### Exterior mirror glass

**6** Working through the gap at the outer edge of the mirror glass, using a screwdriver, release the plastic lugs which secure the glass to the mirror body **(see illustrations)**.

**7** Withdraw the glass, and disconnect the wiring connector (where fitted).

**8** Push the mirror glass into the mirror until it locks into position.

## 15 Tailgate lock components – removal and refitting

### Tailgate lock

#### Removal

**1** Remove the tailgate trim panels as described in Section 25.

**2** Undo the two screws securing the lock to the tailgate **(see illustration)**.

**3** Depress the tabs on each side of the lock and pull the lock into the tailgate. Withdraw the lock through the tailgate aperture and disconnect the wiring connector **(see illustrations)**.

#### Refitting

**4** Refitting is a reversal of removal, but adjust

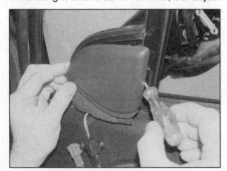

**17.2 Carefully prise off the mirror trim panel**

**17.4 Undo the retaining screws (arrowed) and remove the mirror from the door**

## 18 Windscreen, tailgate and fixed side window glass – general information

These areas of glass are secured by the tight fit of the weatherstrip in the body aperture, and are bonded in position with a special adhesive. Renewal of such fixed glass is a difficult, messy and time-consuming task, which is considered beyond the scope of the home mechanic. It is difficult, unless one has plenty of practice, to obtain a secure, waterproof fit. Furthermore, the task carries a high risk of breakage; this applies especially to the laminated glass windscreen. In view of this, owners are strongly advised to have this sort of work carried out by one of the many specialist windscreen fitters.

## 19 Sunroof – general information

The factory-fitted sunroof is of the electric tilt/slide type.

Due to the complexity of the sunroof mechanism, considerable expertise is required to repair, renew or adjust the sunroof components successfully. Removal of the roof first requires the headlining to be removed, which is a tedious operation, and not a task to be undertaken lightly. Any problems with the sunroof should be referred to a Citroën dealer.

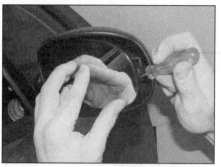

17.6a  Working through the gap at the outer edge of the mirror glass . . .

## 20 Body exterior fittings – removal and refitting

### Wheel arch liners/mud shields

1 The wheel arch liners are secured by expanding plastic rivets. To remove the liners, push in the centre pins, or pull out the raised centre portion (according to type), then prise the complete rivet from its location. With all the rivets removed, manoeuvre the liner from the wheel arch (see illustrations).

### Body trim strips and badges

2 The various body trim strips and badges are held in position with a special adhesive membrane. Removal requires the trim/badge to be heated, to soften the adhesive, and then cut away from the surface. Due to the high risk

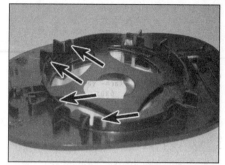

17.6b  . . . release the plastic lugs (arrowed) securing the glass to the mirror body

of damage to the vehicle paintwork during this operation, it is recommended that this task should be entrusted to a Citroën dealer.

## 21 Scuttle grille panel – removal and refitting

### Removal

1 Open the bonnet and support it in the highest position.
2 Remove the windscreen wiper arms as described in Chapter 12.
3 Pull off the bonnet rubber sealing strip from the front edge of the scuttle aperture (see illustration).
4 Undo the five screws securing the outer panel to the inner panels (see illustration).
5 Depress the retaining tab and lift off the outer panel (see illustration).

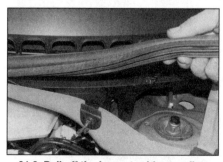

20.1a  Pull out the plastic rivet raised centre portion then prise out the complete rivet

20.1b  With all the rivets removed, manoeuvre the front liner . . .

20.1c  . . . or rear liner from the wheel arch

21.3  Pull off the bonnet rubber sealing strip from the front edge of the scuttle aperture

21.4  Undo the five screws securing the outer scuttle panel to the inner panels

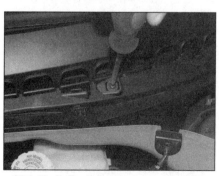

21.5  Depress the retaining tab and lift off the outer panel

**21.6 Release the left-hand inner panel from the windscreen rubber strip and lift off the panel**

6 Release the left-hand inner panel from the rubber strip at the base of the windscreen and lift off the panel **(see illustration)**.
7 Remove the rubber grommet from the windscreen wiper spindle, then remove the right-hand inner panel **(see illustration)**.

### Refitting

8 Refitting is a reversal of removal.

## 22 Radiator grille –
removal and refitting

### Removal

1 Open and support the bonnet.
2 Undo the screws/bolts along the top edge securing the grille in position **(see illustrations)**.
3 On early models, release the plastic retainer

**21.7 Remove the rubber grommet from the windscreen wiper spindle, then remove the right-hand inner panel**

each side, located adjacent to the lower edge of the headlight.
4 Lift the grille upward to disengage the lower locating pegs/supports and remove the grille from the car **(see illustration)**.

### Refitting

5 Refitting is a reversal of removal.

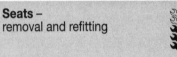

## 23 Seats –
removal and refitting

## Front seats

⚠ **Warning: The front seats are equipped with side airbags built into the outer sides of the seats. Refer to Chapter 12 for the precautions which should be observed when dealing with an airbag system. Do not tamper**

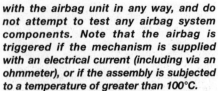

with the airbag unit in any way, and do not attempt to test any airbag system components. Note that the airbag is triggered if the mechanism is supplied with an electrical current (including via an ohmmeter), or if the assembly is subjected to a temperature of greater than 100°C.

1 De-activate the airbag system (see Chapter 12) before attempting to remove the seat.
2 Move the seat fully forwards.
3 Remove the bolts (one on each side) securing the rear of the seat rails to the vehicle floor **(see illustration)**.
4 Move the seat fully rearwards.
5 Remove the bolts (one bolt on each side) securing the front of the seat frame to the floor **(see illustration)**.
6 Tip the seat backwards and disconnect the seat wiring plugs **(see illustration)**. Release the wiring harness from the retaining clips on the seat then remove the seat from the passenger compartment.
7 Refitting is a reversal of removal, but observe the following precautions before reconnecting the battery.
   a) Ensure that there are no occupants in the vehicle, and that there are no loose objects around the vicinity of the seats.
   b) Ensure that the ignition is switched off then reconnect the airbag ECU and the battery.
   c) Open the driver's door and switch on the ignition. Check that the airbag warning light illuminates briefly then extinguishes.
   d) Switch off the ignition.
   e) If the airbag warning light does not

**22.2a Undo the radiator grille retaining screws . . .**

**22.2b . . . and the bolt on each side (early models)**

**22.4 Lift the grille upward to disengage the lower locating pegs**

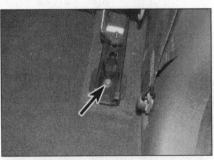

**23.3 Remove the bolt (arrowed) on each side securing the rear of the seat rails to the floor**

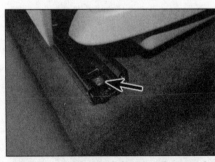

**23.5 Remove the bolt (arrowed) on each side securing the front of the seat frame to the floor**

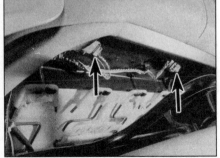

**23.6 Tip the seat backwards and disconnect the wiring plugs (arrowed)**

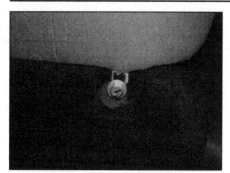

**23.8 Lift off the trim caps then undo the three seat cushion front mounting bolts**

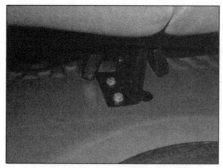

**23.10 Undo the two bolts securing the seat back centre mounting to the floor**

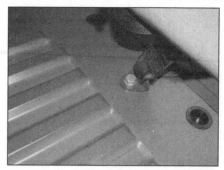

**23.11 Unscrew the bolt securing the seat belt anchorage to the floor**

*operate as described in paragraph c), consult a Citroën dealer before driving the vehicle.*

### Rear seats removal

#### Seat cushion

**8** Lift off the trim caps then undo the three seat cushion front mounting bolts **(see illustration)**. Pull and tilt the seat towards the front then remove it from the car.

#### Seat backs

**9** Where fitted, remove the Moduboard from the luggage compartment.
**10** Undo the two bolts securing the centre mounting to the floor **(see illustration)**.
**11** Tip the seat backs forward and unscrew the bolt securing the seat belt anchorage to the floor **(see illustration)**.
**12** Using a forked tool, extract the seat back side mounting retaining pegs **(see illustration)**.
**13** Manipulate the side mounting pivot bracket from its location then remove the left- and right-hand seat backs from the car **(see illustration)**.
**14** To separate the two seat backs, undo the two mounting bolts and the seat belt buckle retaining nut and pull the seats apart.

### Rear seats refitting

**15** Refitting is a reversal of removal, tightening the seat belt mounting bolts to the specified torque.

---

## 24 Seat belt components –
removal and refitting

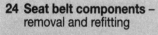

**Note:** *Record the positions of the washers and spacers on the seat belt anchors, and ensure they are refitted in their original positions.*

### Front seat belt

⚠ *Warning: The front seat belt buckles and inertia reels are equipped with a pyrotechnic pretensioner mechanism. Refer to the airbag system precautions contained in Chapter 12 which apply equally to the seat belt pretensioners. Do not tamper with the pretensioner unit*

**23.12 Extract the seat back side mounting retaining pegs**

*in any way, and do not attempt to test the unit. Note that the unit is triggered if the mechanism is supplied with an electrical current (including via an ohmmeter), or if the assembly is subjected to a temperature of greater than 100°C. Once removed from the car the pyrotechnic components should be stored in a suitable area in accordance with applicable safety regulations.*

**1** De-activate the airbag system (which will also de-activate the pyrotechnic pretensioner mechanism) as described in Chapter 12 before attempting to remove the seat belt.
**2** Remove the relevant front seat as described in Section 23.
**3** Remove the B-pillar trim panels as described in Section 25.
**4** Disconnect the wiring connector from the inertia reel pretensioner unit.
**5** Undo the inertia reel anchor bolt, and recover the washers **(see illustration)**.

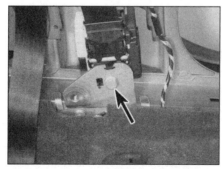

**24.5 Front seat belt inertia reel anchor bolt (arrowed)**

**23.13 Manipulate the side mounting pivot bracket from its location**

**6** Withdraw the inertia reel from the door pillar, and remove the seat belt assembly from the vehicle.
**7** To remove the pretensioner seat belt buckle, prise off the trim panel on the side of the seat. Undo the retaining bolt and remove the pretensioner from the seat frame.
**8** Refitting is a reversal of removal, but observe the following precautions before reconnecting the battery.
 a) *Ensure that there are no occupants in the vehicle, and that there are no loose objects around the vicinity of the seats.*
 b) *Ensure that the ignition is switched off then reconnect the battery.*
 c) *Open the driver's door and switch on the ignition. Check that the airbag warning light illuminates briefly then extinguishes.*
 d) *Switch off the ignition.*
 e) *If the airbag warning light does not operate as described in paragraph c), consult a Citroën dealer before driving the vehicle.*
 f) *Tighten the seat belt mountings to the specified torque.*

### Rear seat belts

**9** Remove the luggage compartment side trim panels as described in Section 25.
**10** Undo the anchor bolt securing the seat belt inertia reel to the vehicle body and remove the reel and seat belt from the car **(see illustration)**.
**11** To remove the seat belt buckles, fold forward the rear seat cushions, and undo the nut securing the buckles to the rear seat mounting, and the bolt securing the seat belt anchorage to the floor.

24.10 Rear seat belt inertia reel anchor bolt (arrowed)

**12** To remove the centre seat belt inertia reel, the seat must be partially dismantled. This work should be entrusted to a Citroën dealer.
**13** Refitting is a reversal of removal. Tighten the seat belt mounting bolts to the specified torque.

## 25 Interior trim – removal and refitting

### Door inner trim

**1** Refer to Section 11.

### *A-pillar trim*

#### Removal

**2** Prise the weatherstrip from the front door aperture in the vicinity of the A-pillar.

25.3b . . . to release the internal retaining lugs

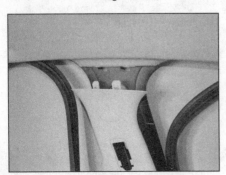

25.9 Lower the trim to disengage the upper locating lugs

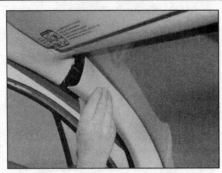

25.3a Starting at the top, carefully pull the trim away from the A-pillar . . .

**3** Starting at the top, carefully pull the trim away from the A-pillar, to release the internal retaining lugs **(see illustrations)**.
**4** Lift the trim up to disengage it from the side of the facia and remove it from the vehicle.

#### Refitting

**5** Refitting is a reversal of removal, but ensure that all retaining clips are fully engaged and that the weatherstrip is fully seated.

### *Upper B-pillar trim*

#### Removal

**6** Prise the weatherstrip from the front and rear door apertures in the vicinity of the B-pillar.
**7** Remove the trim cap, then unscrew the front seat belt upper mounting bolt **(see illustration)**.
**8** Carefully prise the base of the upper trim

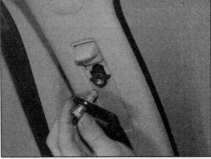

25.7 Remove the trim cap, then unscrew the front seat belt upper mounting bolt

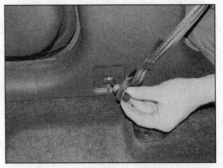

25.12 Remove the trim cap, then unscrew the front seat belt lower anchor bolt

panel away from the pillar, to release the internal clips **(see illustration)**.
**9** Lower the trim to disengage the upper locating lugs, and remove the trim panel from the car **(see illustration)**.

#### Refitting

**10** Refitting is a reversal of removal, but ensure that all retaining clips are fully engaged and that the weatherstrip is fully seated.

### *Lower B-pillar trim*

#### Removal

**11** Remove the upper B-pillar trim as described previously.
**12** Remove the trim cap, then unscrew the front seat belt lower anchor bolt **(see illustration)**.
**13** Carefully lift the rear edge of the front sill trim upwards. Release the front edge of the rear sill trim in the same way **(see illustration)**.
**14** Carefully prise the lower trim panel away from the pillar, to release the internal clips, then disengage the seat belt and remove the trim panel.

#### Refitting

**15** Refitting is a reversal of removal, but ensure that all retaining clips are fully engaged.

### *Front door sill trim*

#### Removal

**16** Prise the weatherstrip from the lower edge of the front door aperture.

25.8 Carefully prise the base of the upper trim panel away from the pillar, to release the internal clips

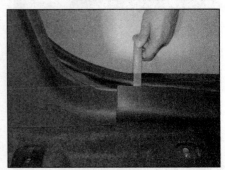

25.13 Carefully lift the rear edge of the front sill trim upwards

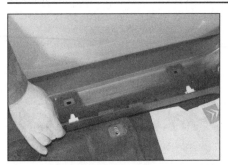

**25.17 Carefully prise the front door sill trim away from the sill to release its retaining clips**

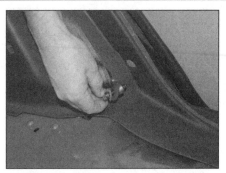

**25.22 Remove the trim cap, then unscrew the rear seat belt lower anchor bolt**

**25.23 Carefully prise the rear door sill trim away from its location, to release the internal clips**

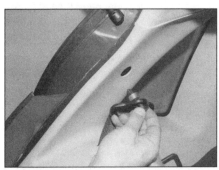

**25.26 Remove the trim cap, then unscrew the rear seat belt upper mounting bolt**

**25.27 Lift up the trim cap over the seat belt entry into the panel, and disengage it from the seat belt**

**25.29 Carefully prise the upper side panel away from the body, to release the internal clips**

**17** Carefully prise the front door sill trim away from the sill to release its retaining clips and remove it from the car **(see illustration)**.

### Refitting

**18** Refitting is a reversal of removal, but ensure that all retaining clips are fully engaged and that the weatherstrip is fully seated.

## Rear door sill trim

### Removal

**19** Remove the rear seat backs as described in Section 23.
**20** Remove the luggage compartment upper side panel as described below.
**21** Prise the weatherstrip from the rear side and lower edge of the rear door aperture.
**22** Remove the trim cap, then unscrew the rear seat belt lower anchor bolt **(see illustration)**.
**23** Carefully prise the sill trim panel away from its location, to release the internal clips, and remove the panel **(see illustration)**.

### Refitting

**24** Refitting is a reversal of removal, but ensure that all retaining clips are fully engaged and that the weatherstrip is fully seated.

## Luggage area upper side panel

### Removal

**25** Prise the weatherstrip from the tailgate a̶ ̶ture in the vicinity of the upper side panel.
**26** Remove the trim cap, then unscrew the rear seat belt upper mounting bolt **(see illustration)**.

**27** Lift up the trim cap over the seat belt entry into the panel, and disengage it from the seat belt **(see illustration)**.
**28** Release the interior light from the side panel and disconnect the wiring connector.
**29** Carefully prise the upper side panel away from the body, to release the internal clips, then disengage the seat belt and remove the trim panel **(see illustration)**.

### Refitting

**30** Refitting is a reversal of removal, but ensure that all retaining clips are fully engaged and that the weatherstrip is fully seated.

## Luggage area lower side panel

### Removal

**31** Remove the rear door sill trim as described previously.
**32** Remove the tailgate aperture lower panel as described below.

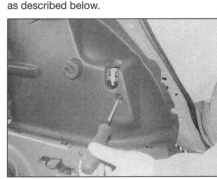

**25.33 Undo the front retaining screw securing the lower side panel to the body**

**33** Undo the front retaining screw securing the side panel to the body **(see illustration)**.
**34** Carefully prise the lower side panel away from the body, to release the internal clips, and remove the panel from the car **(see illustration)**.

### Refitting

**35** Refitting is a reversal of removal, but ensure that all retaining clips are fully engaged.

## Tailgate trim panels

### Removal

**36** Disengage the parcel shelf cords from the lifting pins.
**37** Working on one side at a time, push in the centre of the lifting pin, then pull the pin body from the tailgate **(see illustrations)**. It is quite likely that the lifting pin centre will drop into the tailgate as the pin is removed. If this

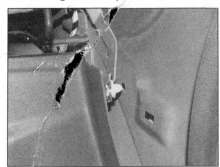

**25.34 Release the internal clips, and remove the lower side panel**

**25.37a Push in the centre of the parcel shelf lifting pin . . .**

**25.37b . . . then pull the pin body from the tailgate**

**25.38 Carefully prise the side trim panel from the tailgate to release the internal plastic clips**

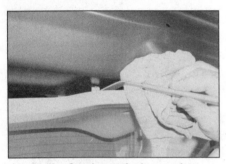

**25.40a Starting at the lower edge, carefully lever the centre trim panel away from the tailgate . . .**

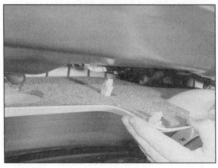

**25.40b . . . to release the internal plastic clips**

**25.43 Prise the weatherstrip from the tailgate aperture in the vicinity of the lower panel**

happens, it should be possible to retrieve it through one of the tailgate apertures, once the trim panels are removed.

**38** Carefully prise the side trim panel from the tailgate to release the internal plastic clips **(see illustration)**.

**39** Repeat paragraphs 37 and 38 to remove the panel on the other side.

**40** Starting at the lower edge, carefully lever the centre trim panel away from the tailgate to release the internal plastic clips **(see illustrations)**.

**41** Once the clips are released, move the panel upward, to disengage the upper locating pegs from the brackets on the tailgate.

### Refitting

**42** Refitting is a reversal of removal, but ensure that all retaining clips are fully engaged.

### Tailgate aperture lower panel

#### Removal

**43** Prise the weatherstrip from the tailgate aperture in the vicinity of the lower panel **(see illustration)**.

**44** Undo the screws securing the panel to the luggage compartment floor **(see illustration)**.

**45** Carefully prise the panel upwards to release its retaining clips and remove it from the car **(see illustration)**.

#### Refitting

**46** Refitting is a reversal of removal, but ensure that all retaining clips are fully engaged and that the weatherstrip is fully seated.

### Headlining

**Note:** *Headlining removal requires considerable skill and experience if it is to be*

carried out without damage, and is therefore best entrusted to a Citroën dealer or bodywork specialist. A general overview of the procedure is given below for those with the expertise to attempt the operation on a DIY basis.

**47** The headlining is clipped and glued to the roof, and can be withdrawn only once all fittings such as the grab handles, courtesy lights, sun visors, sunroof (if fitted), pillar trim panels, and associated additional panels have been removed. The door, tailgate and sunroof aperture weatherstrips will also have to be prised clear and any additional screws and clips removed. Once the headlining attachments are released, the adhesive bonding in the centre panels must be broken using a hot air gun and spatula, starting at the front and working rearwards.

**48** When refitting, a coat of neoprene adhesive (available from Citroën dealers) must be applied to the centre panels in the locations noted during removal. Position the headlining carefully and refit all components disturbed during removal. Clean the headlining with soap and water or white spirit on completion.

### 26 Centre console – removal and refitting

#### Removal

**1** On manual transmission models, twist and remove the gear lever knob off the gear lever **(see illustration)**.

**25.44 Undo the screws securing the panel to the luggage compartment floor**

**25.45 Carefully prise the panel upwards to release its retaining clips**

26.1  On manual transmission models, twist and remove the gear lever knob off the gear lever

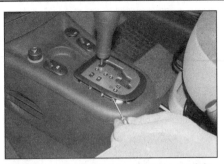

26.2a  On automatic transmission models, prise the selector lever trim from the retaining clips . . .

26.2b  . . . and remove the trim from the lever base

26.3  Carefully prise the handbrake lever cover panel from the centre console

26.4a  Prise off the lower front cover panel at the base of the facia . . .

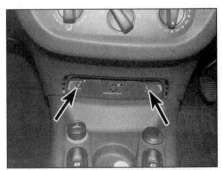

26.4b  . . . and undo the two screws (arrowed) now exposed

**2** On automatic transmission models, release the selector lever trim from the retaining clips and remove the trim from the lever base **(see illustrations)**.

**3** Using a small screwdriver, carefully prise the handbrake lever cover panel from the centre console **(see illustration)**.

**4** Carefully prise off the lower front cover panel at the base of the facia, and undo the two screws now exposed **(see illustrations)**.

**5** Extract the trim moulding at the rear of the console and undo the rear retaining nut now exposed **(see illustration)**.

**6** Lift the console up and disconnect the wiring at the console switches **(see illustration)**.

**7** Lift the console up and over the handbrake lever and remove it from the car.

### Refitting

**8** Refitting is a reversal of removal.

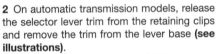

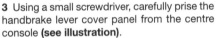
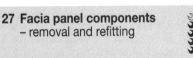

**27 Facia panel components**
– removal and refitting

## Multi-function display surround

### Removal

**1** Protect the area in front of the display with masking tape to protect the facia.

**2** Slide a thin plastic spatula or similar tool under the lower edge of the surround to compress the internal plastic retaining tabs **(see illustrations)**.

**3** Pull the lower edge of the surround forward,

then lift it up to disengage the rear locating lugs **(see illustration)**.

### Refitting

**4** Refitting is a reversal of removal.

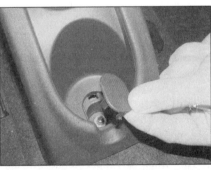

26.5  Extract the trim moulding and undo the console rear retaining nut

27.2a  Slide a thin plastic spatula under the multi-function display surround . . .

## Passenger side glovebox

### Removal

**5** Open the glovebox and remove the fusebox cover **(see illustration)**.

26.6  Lift the console up and disconnect the wiring at the console switches

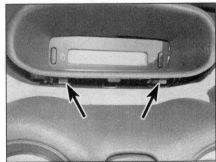

27.2b  . . . to compress the internal plastic retaining tabs (arrowed)

**27.3 Pull the lower edge of the surround forward, then lift it up to disengage the rear locating lugs**

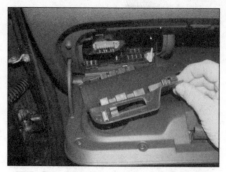

**27.5 Open the glovebox and remove the fusebox cover**

**27.6 Slide the hinge pins toward the centre of the glovebox to release them from the facia**

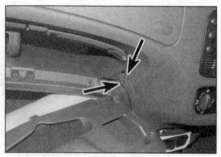

**27.7 Compress the ends of the glovebox stays (arrowed) and release them from the slots in the facia**

**27.8 Undo the five screws and withdraw the glovebox from the facia**

**27.10 Undo the two screws (arrowed) securing the steering column lower shroud**

6 Using a small screwdriver, slide the hinge pins toward the centre of the glovebox to release them from the facia **(see illustration)**.
7 Compress the ends of the glovebox stays and release them from the slots in the facia

(see illustration). Remove the lid.
8 Undo the five screws and withdraw the glovebox from the facia. As the glovebox is withdrawn, reach up and detach the air duct **(see illustration)**.

### Refitting

9 Refitting is a reversal of removal.

### Steering column shrouds

#### Removal

10 Undo the two screws securing the lower shroud in position **(see illustration)**.
11 Disengage the lower shroud from the pegs on the upper shroud, then slide it towards the rear to disengage the lower locating lug from the steering column **(see illustration)**.
12 Lift the upper shroud, and release the inner portion from the two retaining clips on the steering column **(see illustration)**.

#### Refitting

13 Refitting is a reversal of removal.

### Driver's side lower facia panel

#### Removal

14 Carefully prise the upper edge of the panel away from the facia to release the two upper tabs **(see illustration)**.
15 Reach under the facia and compress the legs of the locating peg, then withdraw the panel from the facia **(see illustration)**.

#### Refitting

16 Refitting is a reversal of removal.

### Instrument panel

17 Refer to Chapter 12.

### Complete facia assembly

**Note:** *This is an involved operation entailing the removal of numerous components and*

**27.11 Disengage the lower locating lug (arrowed) from the steering column**

**27.12 Release the upper shroud from the retaining clips (arrowed) on the steering column**

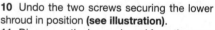

**27.14 Prise the lower facia panel away from the facia to release the two upper tabs**

**27.15 Reach under the facia and compress the legs of the locating peg**

27.24a Push out the storage compartment . . .

27.24b . . . to release the retaining lugs (arrowed) each side

27.25a Push the heater/ventilation control panel in at the top to release the upper lugs . . .

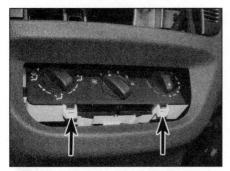

27.25b . . . then move the unit upwards to free the lower lugs (arrowed)

27.26 Undo the two earth lead securing bolts (arrowed)

27.27 Undo the lower bolt and upper nut (arrowed) and remove the strengthening bracket

*assemblies, and the disconnection of a multitude of wiring connectors. Make notes of the location of all disconnected wiring, or attach labels to the connectors, to avoid confusion when refitting.*

## Removal

**18** Disconnect the battery (see Chapter 5A).
**19** Move the front seats as far back as possible. Set the steering wheel in the straight-ahead position, and engage the steering lock.
**20** Remove the following facia panels as described previously in this Section:
 a) *Passenger side glovebox.*
 b) *Steering column shrouds.*
 c) *Driver's side lower facia panel.*
**21** Remove the centre console as described in Section 26.
**22** Remove the steering column as described in Chapter 10.

**23** Remove the following components as described in Chapter 12:
 a) *Instrument panel.*
 b) *Audio unit.*
 c) *Passenger's air bag.*
**24** Reach in through the audio unit aperture and push out the storage compartment to release the retaining lugs each side **(see illustrations)**.
**25** Push the heater/ventilation control panel in at the top to release the upper locating lugs, then move the unit upwards to free the lower lugs **(see illustrations)**. Move the control panel forwards and engage it with the supports on the front of the heater unit.
**26** Undo the two bolts securing the earth leads at the front of the gear selector housing **(see illustration)**.
**27** Undo the lower bolt and upper nut and

remove the strengthening bracket from the base of the facia **(see illustration)**.
**28** Undo the facia attachments in the following locations **(see illustrations)**:
 a) *Two screws and one bolt in the instrument panel aperture.*
 b) *Two screws in the audio unit aperture.*
 c) *Two screws below the heater/ventilation controls.*
**29** Prise off the cover panels at each end of the facia and undo the two mounting bolts, each side **(see illustrations)**.
**30** With the help of an assistant, lift the facia from its location and move it rearward. As soon as sufficient clearance exists, disconnect all the facia wiring connectors, noting their fitted positions. Note the wiring harness routing and release it from the various retaining clips.

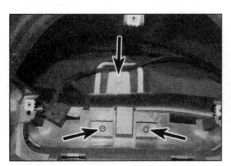

27.28a Undo the two screws and one bolt (arrowed) in the instrument panel aperture . . .

27.28b . . . the two screws (arrowed) in the audio unit aperture . . .

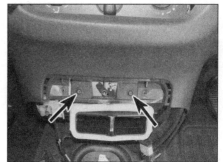

27.28c . . . and the two screws (arrowed) below the heater/ventilation controls

**27.29a Prise off the cover panels at each end of the facia . . .**

**27.29b . . . and undo the two mounting bolts (arrowed) each side**

**31** Check that everything is disconnected and moved clear, then remove the facia from the vehicle.

### Refitting

**32** Refitting is a reversal of removal ensuring that all wiring is correctly reconnected and all mountings securely tightened.

# Chapter 12
## Body electrical systems

## Contents

## Degrees of difficulty

| Easy, suitable for novice with little experience | Fairly easy, suitable for beginner with some experience | Fairly difficult, suitable for competent DIY mechanic | Difficult, suitable for experienced DIY mechanic | Very difficult, suitable for expert DIY or professional |
|---|---|---|---|---|

## Specifications

### General
System type . . . . . . . . . . . . . . . . . . . . . . . . . . . . . . . . . . . . 12 volt negative earth

### Bulbs

| | Type | Wattage |
|---|---|---|
| Direction indicator light | Bayonet | 21 |
| Direction indicator side repeater | Push-fit | 5 |
| Front foglight | H1 | 55 |
| Front sidelights | Push-fit | 5 |
| Headlights: | | |
| Main beam bulbs | H1 | 55 |
| Dip beam bulbs | H7 | 55 |
| High-level stop-light | Push-fit | 16 |
| Interior/courtesy lights | Push-fit | 5 |
| Luggage compartment light | Push-fit | 5 |
| Number plate light | Push-fit | 5 |
| Rear foglight | Bayonet | 21 |
| Reversing light | Bayonet | 21 |
| Stop/tail light | Bayonet | 21/5 |
| Tail light | Bayonet | 5 |

### Torque wrench setting

| | Nm | lbf ft |
|---|---|---|
| Airbag control unit retaining nuts | 8 | 6 |

## 1 General information

⚠️ **Warning: Before carrying out any work on the electrical system, read through the precautions given in 'Safety first!' at the beginning of this manual, and in Chapter 5A.**

The electrical system is of 12 volt negative earth type. Power for the lights and all electrical accessories is supplied by a lead-acid type battery, which is charged by the alternator.

Many of the body electrical systems are controlled by individual electronic control units (ECUs) and these are in turn controlled by a main ECU known as a Built-in Systems Interface (BSI). The various ECUs and the BSI exchange data with each other via a multiplex network. The multiplex network is a two-wire system linking the BSI with the system ECUs and is termed by Citroën as CAN (controlled area network) and VAN (vehicle area network). Essentially this means that the BSI and the ECUs controlling the 'comfort' systems, safety systems, security systems, and entertainment systems in the vehicle, are all interconnected via Vehicle Area Networks.

An ECU connected to the multiplex network only receives some of the data needed for it to operate directly, with the remaining data being supplied by the other ECUs on the network. Because the ECUs share information via the network, several ECUs can control the operation of the same system. Also, one ECU can control several systems in an autonomous manner. The BSI is the manager of this information interchange as well as also being responsible for the control of certain vehicle systems itself. The BSI has a full diagnostic capability whereby any fault in any of the ECUs on the multiplex network can be traced using diagnostic equipment connected to the vehicle diagnostic connector. Should any fault develop with a system on the network, have the self-diagnosis facility interrogated by a Citroën dealer or suitably-equipped specialist.

This Chapter covers repair and service procedures for the various electrical components not associated with the engine. Information on the battery, alternator and starter motor can be found in Chapter 5A.

It should be noted that, prior to working on any component in the electrical system, the battery should first be disconnected, to prevent the possibility of electrical short-circuits (see Chapter 5A).

## 2 Electrical fault finding
### – general information

**Note:** *Refer to the precautions given in 'Safety first!' and in Chapter 5A before starting work. The following tests relate to testing of the main*

electrical circuits, and should not be used to test delicate electronic circuits (such as anti-lock braking systems), particularly where an electronic control unit (ECU) or multiplexing is used (see Section 1).*

### General

1 A typical electrical circuit consists of an electrical component, any switches, relays, motors, fuses, fusible links or circuit breakers related to that component, and the wiring and connectors which link the component to both the battery and the chassis. To help to pinpoint a problem in an electrical circuit, wiring diagrams are included at the end of this Chapter.

2 Before attempting to diagnose an electrical fault, first study the appropriate wiring diagram, to obtain a more complete understanding of the components included in the particular circuit concerned. The possible sources of a fault can be narrowed down by noting whether other components related to the circuit are operating properly. If several components or circuits fail at one time, the problem is likely to be related to a shared fuse or earth connection.

3 Electrical problems usually stem from simple causes, such as loose or corroded connections, a faulty earth connection, a blown fuse, a melted fusible link, or a faulty relay (refer to Section 3 for details of testing relays). Visually inspect the condition of all fuses, wires and connections in a problem circuit before testing the components. Use the wiring diagrams to determine which terminal connections will need to be checked, in order to pinpoint the trouble-spot.

4 The basic tools required for electrical fault finding include a circuit tester or voltmeter; an ohmmeter (to measure resistance); a battery and set of test leads; and a jumper wire, preferably with a circuit breaker or fuse incorporated, which can be used to bypass suspect wires or electrical components. Before attempting to locate a problem with test instruments, use the wiring diagram to determine where to make the connections.

5 To find the source of an intermittent wiring fault (usually due to a poor or dirty connection, or damaged wiring insulation), a 'wiggle' test can be performed on the wiring. This involves wiggling the wiring by hand, to see if the fault occurs as the wiring is moved. It should be possible to narrow down the source of the fault to a particular section of wiring. This method of testing can be used in conjunction with any of the tests described in the following sub-Sections.

6 Apart from problems due to poor connections, two basic types of fault can occur in an electrical circuit – open-circuit, or short-circuit.

7 Open-circuit faults are caused by a break somewhere in the circuit, which prevents current from flowing. An open-circuit fault will prevent a component from working, but will not cause the relevant circuit fuse to blow.

8 Short-circuit faults are caused by a 'short' somewhere in the circuit, which allows the current flowing in the circuit to 'escape' along an alternative route, usually to earth. Short-circuit faults are normally caused by a breakdown in wiring insulation, which allows a feed wire to touch either another wire, or an earthed component such as the bodyshell. A short-circuit fault will normally cause the relevant circuit fuse to blow. **Note:** *As an aid to economy and to prevent battery discharge, certain functions of the electrical system can only be used for 30 minutes after the engine has been stopped. Bear this in mind when tracing power supply faults on these systems.*

### Functions affected

*Windscreen wipers.*
*Electric windows.*
*Sunroof.*
*Courtesy lights.*
*Audio equipment.*
*After this period the BSI (Built-in Systems Interface) cuts the power to these circuits. To restore power, start the engine.*
*It is also possible for the BSI to turn off certain functions (heater blower and heated rear window) depending on the state of charge of the battery. When tracing a fault, ensure the battery is in a good state of charge.*

### Finding an open-circuit

9 To check for an open-circuit, connect one lead of a voltmeter to either the negative battery terminal or a known good earth.

10 Connect the other lead to a connector in the circuit being tested, preferably nearest to the battery or fuse.

11 Switch on the circuit, bearing in mind that some circuits are live only when the ignition switch is moved to a particular position.

12 If voltage is present (indicated either by the tester bulb lighting or a voltmeter reading, as applicable), this means that the section of the circuit between the relevant connector and the battery is problem-free.

13 Continue to check the remainder of the circuit in the same fashion.

14 When a point is reached at which no voltage is present, the problem must lie between that point and the previous test point with voltage. Most problems can be traced to a broken, corroded or loose connection.

### Finding a short-circuit

15 To check for a short-circuit, first disconnect the load(s) from the circuit (loads are the components which draw current from a circuit, such as bulbs, motors, heating elements, etc).

16 Remove the relevant fuse from the circuit, and connect a circuit tester or voltmeter to the fuse connections.

17 Switch on the circuit, bearing in mind that some circuits are live only when the ignition switch is moved to a particular position.

18 If voltage is present (indicated either by

**3.3a Lift off the cover to gain access to the facia fuses**

**3.3b Additional fuses and relays are located in the engine compartment fuse/relay box**

**3.4 Use the plastic tool provided to remove a fuse**

the tester bulb lighting or a voltmeter reading, as applicable), this means that there is a short-circuit.

**19** If no voltage is present, but the fuse still blows with the load(s) connected, this indicates an internal fault in the load(s).

### *Finding an earth fault*

**20** The battery negative terminal is connected to 'earth' – the metal of the engine/transmission and the car body – and most systems are wired so that they only receive a positive feed, the current returning via the metal of the car body. This means that the component mounting and the body form part of that circuit. Loose or corroded mountings can therefore cause a range of electrical faults, ranging from total failure of a circuit, to a puzzling partial fault. In particular, lights may shine dimly (especially when another circuit sharing the same earth point is in operation), motors (eg, wiper motors or the radiator cooling fan motor) may run slowly, and the operation of one circuit may have an apparently-unrelated effect on another. Note that on many vehicles, earth straps are used between certain components, such as the engine/transmission and the body, usually where there is no metal-to-metal contact between components, due to flexible rubber mountings, etc.

**21** To check whether a component is properly earthed, disconnect the battery, and connect one lead of an ohmmeter to a known good earth point. Connect the other lead to the wire or earth connection being tested. The resistance reading should be zero; if not, check the connection as follows.

**22** If an earth connection is thought to be faulty, dismantle the connection, and clean back to bare metal both the bodyshell and the wire terminal or the component earth connection mating surface. Be careful to remove all traces of dirt and corrosion, then use a knife to trim away any paint, so that a clean metal-to-metal joint is made. On reassembly, tighten the joint fasteners securely; if a wire terminal is being refitted, use serrated washers between the terminal and the bodyshell, to ensure a clean and secure connection. When the connection is remade, prevent the onset of corrosion in the future by applying a coat of petroleum jelly or

silicone-based grease, or by spraying on (at regular intervals) a proprietary ignition sealer or water-dispersant lubricant.

### 3  Fuses and relays – general information

#### *Fuses*

**1** Fuses are designed to break a circuit when a predetermined current is reached, in order to protect the components and wiring which could be damaged by excessive current flow. Any excessive current flow will be due to a fault in the circuit, usually a short-circuit (see Section 2).

**2** The majority of fuses are located on the left-hand side of the facia, inside the glovebox (right-hand drive models), or behind a detachable panel (left-hand drive models). Additional fuses (including the larger, higher-rated maxi-fuses) are located in the fuse/relay box on the left-hand side of the engine compartment.

**3** To gain access to the facia fuses, open the glovebox (or remove the lower facia panel) and

lift off the fusebox cover. To gain access to the fuses in the engine compartment, simply unclip the cover from the fuse/relay box **(see illustrations)**. The main fuses and relays are in the upper part of the box, with the maxi-fuses located below.

**4** To remove a fuse, first switch off the circuit concerned (or the ignition), then pull the fuse out of its terminals **(see illustration)**. The wire within the fuse should be visible; if the fuse has blown it will be broken or melted.

**5** Always renew a fuse with one of the correct rating, never use a fuse with a different rating from that specified. The fuse rating is stamped on the top of the fuse, the fuses are also colour-coded as follows. Refer to the accompanying illustrations and the wiring diagrams for details of the fuse locations, fuse ratings and the circuits protected **(see illustrations)**.

| Colour | Rating |
|---|---|
| Orange | 5A |
| Red | 10A |
| Blue | 15A |
| Yellow | 20A |
| Clear or white | 25A |
| Green | 30A |

**6** Never renew a fuse more than once without tracing the source of the trouble. If the new

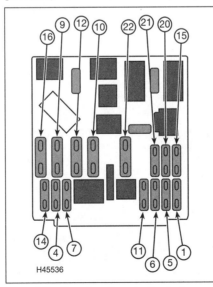

**3.5a Fuse locations in the facia fusebox . . .**

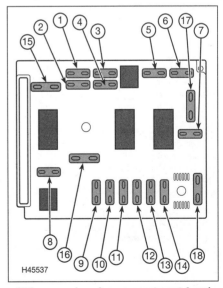

**3.5b . . . and engine compartment fuse/relay box**

**4.5 Steering column switch assembly clamp bolt (arrowed)**

**4.8 The rotary contact circular aperture (A) must be aligned with the triangle (B)**

fuse blows immediately, find the cause before renewing it again; a short to earth as a result of faulty insulation is most likely. Where a fuse protects more than one circuit, try to isolate the fault by switching on each circuit in turn (where possible) until the fuse blows again. Always carry a supply of spare fuses of each relevant rating on the vehicle; a spare of each rating should be clipped into the fusebox.

## Relays

**7** The majority of relay functions are incorporated into the built-in system interface (BSI) unit (see Section 23). Other relays are located in the fuse/relay box in the engine compartment or in an additional relay box, located behind the front bumper on the left-hand side. On certain models, the cooling fan relay(s) is/are located in front panel above the radiator.

**8** If a circuit or system controlled by a relay develops a fault and the relay is suspect, operate the system. If the relay is functioning, it should be possible to hear it 'click' as it is energised. If this is the case, the fault lies with the components or wiring of the system. If the relay is not being energised, then either the relay is not receiving a main supply or a switching voltage, or the relay itself is faulty. Testing is by the substitution of a known good unit, but be careful – while some relays are identical in appearance and in operation, others look similar but perform different functions.

**9** To remove a relay, first ensure that the relevant circuit is switched off. The relay can then simply be pulled out from the socket, and pushed back into position.

## 4 Switches – removal and refitting

**Note:** *Disconnect the battery before removing any switch, and reconnect the lead after refitting the switch (see Chapter 5A).*

### Ignition switch

**1** Refer to Chapter 10.

### Steering column switches

**2** Remove the driver's airbag as described in Section 22.
**3** Remove the steering wheel as described in Chapter 10.
**4** Remove the steering column lower and upper shrouds as described in Section 27 of Chapter 11.
**5** Slacken the switch assembly retaining clamp then, using a small screwdriver, carefully prise the retaining catches away from the column and lift off the switch assembly **(see illustration)**. Disconnect the three wiring plugs as the assembly is withdrawn.
*Caution: Take great care not damage the switch assembly retaining catches.*
**6** Although refitting is a reversal of removal, the airbag contact unit built into the switch assembly must be set in the correct position as follows:
**7** Ensure the wheels are in the straight-ahead position.
**8** Check that the letter O can be seen in the circular viewing aperture on the front of the rotary contact **(see illustration)**. If the letter D

appears, turn the rotary contact anti-clockwise until O can be seen. If the letter G appears, turn the rotary contact clockwise until O can be seen. With the letter O visible, position the aperture adjacent to the triangle on the switch body.
**Note:** *If a new switch assembly is fitted to a vehicle with ESP (Electronic Stability Programme) the unit must be initialised using dedicated test equipment. Entrust this task to a Citroën dealer or suitably-equipped specialist.*

### Facia switches

#### Centre-mounted

**9** The facia centre-mounted switches are located between the centre air vents, and on either side of the audio unit. The switches are removed by pushing them out from behind the facia as follows.
**10** Remove the audio unit as described in Section 17.
**11** Reach in through the audio unit aperture and push out the storage compartment (where fitted), to release the retaining lugs each side.
**12** Push the relevant switch from its location and disconnect the wiring plug as the switch is withdrawn **(see illustrations)**.
**13** Refitting is the reverse of removal.

#### Side-mounted

**14** The facia side-mounted switches are located alongside the steering column on the driver's side. The switches are removed by pushing them out from behind the facia as follows.
**15** Remove the driver's side lower facia panel as described in Chapter 11, Section 27.
**16** Reach in through the facia aperture, push the relevant switch from its location and disconnect the wiring plug as the switch is withdrawn **(see illustration)**.
**17** Refitting is the reverse of removal.

### Heating/ventilation control

**18** The switches are an integral part of the heater/ventilation control panel, and cannot be renewed separately. If any switch is faulty, the complete control panel must be renewed – refer to Chapter 3 for details.

### Stop-light switch

**19** Refer to Chapter 9.

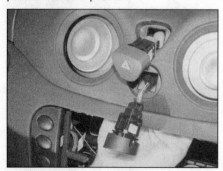

**4.12a Push out the switches located between the centre air vents . . .**

**4.12b . . . and on either side of the audio unit from behind the facia**

**4.16 Push out the side-mounted switches, working through the facia aperture**

**4.24a Depress the tab at the rear of the centre console switches . . .**

**4.24b . . . and remove the relevant switch from the console**

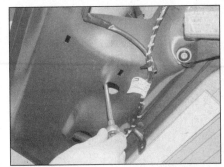

**4.27 Undo the outer nuts each side securing the exterior handle to the tailgate**

**4.28 Disconnect the lock switch wiring connector, then undo the two inner nuts (arrowed)**

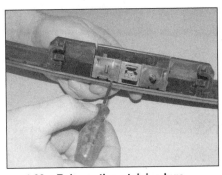

**4.29a Release the retaining lugs . . .**

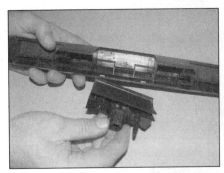

**4.29b . . . and remove the lock switch from the exterior handle**

### Handbrake warning switch

**20** Refer to Chapter 9.

### Courtesy light switch

**21** The courtesy light switches are an integral part of the door lock assemblies. Refer to Chapter 11 for door lock removal and refitting details.

### Luggage area light switch

**22** The luggage compartment light switch function is integral with the tailgate lock assembly. For tailgate lock removal, refer to Chapter 11.

### Centre console switches

**23** Remove the centre console as described in Chapter 11.
**24** Using a small screwdriver, depress the tab at the rear of the relevant switch and push the switch from its location **(see illustrations)**.
**25** Refitting is the reverse of removal.

### Tailgate lock switch

**26** Remove the tailgate trim panel as described in Chapter 11, Section 25.
**27** Working through the apertures in the tailgate undo the nut each side securing the outer edges of the exterior handle to the tailgate **(see illustration)**.
**28** Disconnect the lock switch wiring connector, then undo the two inner nuts securing exterior handle to the tailgate **(see illustration)**. Withdraw the handle from the tailgate.
**29** Using a small screwdriver, release the

retaining lugs and remove the lock switch from the exterior handle **(see illustrations)**.
**30** Refitting is the reverse of removal.

### 5  Bulbs (exterior lights) – renewal

#### General

**1** Whenever a bulb is renewed, note the following points:
a) Remember that, if the light has just been in use, the bulb may be extremely hot.
b) Always check the bulb contacts and holder, ensuring that there is clean metal-to-metal contact between the bulb and its live(s) and earth. Clean off any corrosion or dirt before fitting a new bulb.

**5.3a Lift up the wire locking clip . . .**

c) Wherever bayonet-type bulbs are fitted (see Specifications), ensure that the live contact(s) bear firmly against the bulb contact.
d) Always ensure that the new bulb is of the correct rating, and that it is completely clean before fitting it; this applies particularly to headlight/foglight bulbs (see below).

#### Headlight

**2** To improve access to the left-hand headlight unit, remove the battery cover, then remove the air cleaner air inlet duct components behind the headlight as described in Chapter 4A or 4B as applicable.
**3** Reach behind the headlight unit, lift up the wire locking clip and lift off the access cover **(see illustrations)**.
**4** Disconnect the wiring plug from the relevant

**5.3b . . . and lift off the headlight bulb access cover**

**5.4 Disconnect the wiring plug from the headlight bulb**

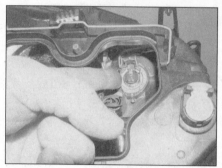

**5.5a Release the bulb retaining clip . . .**

**5.5b . . . and withdraw the headlight bulb**

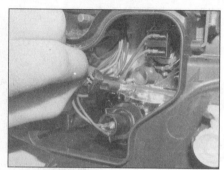

**5.11 Pull the sidelight bulbholder from the headlight unit**

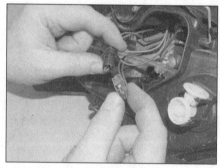

**5.12 Remove the push-fit bulb from the bulbholder**

bulb **(see illustration)**. The main beam is the outer bulb and the dipped beam is the inner bulb.

**5** Release the bulb retaining clip, and withdraw the bulb **(see illustrations)**.

**6** When handling the new bulb, use a tissue or clean cloth to avoid touching the glass with the fingers; moisture and grease from the skin can cause blackening and rapid failure of this type of bulb. If the glass is accidentally touched, wipe it clean using methylated spirit.

**7** Install the new bulb, ensuring that its locating tabs are correctly seated in the light cut-outs, and secure it in position with the retaining clip.

**8** Refit the access cover and secure with the retaining clip.

**9** Refit the components disturbed for access.

### Front sidelight

**10** Proceed as described in paragraphs 2 and 3.

**11** Pull the bulbholder from the rear of the headlight unit **(see illustration)**.

**12** The bulb is of the capless (push-fit) type, and can be removed by simply pulling it out of the holder **(see illustration)**.

**13** Refit the bulbholder and turn it clockwise to secure.

**14** Refit the access cover and secure with the retaining clip.

**15** Refit the components disturbed for access.

### Front foglight

**16** Open the access cover at the base of the front wheel arch liner, directly beneath the foglight unit.

**17** Disconnect the wiring connector on the light unit cover, then turn the cover anticlockwise to release it **(see illustrations)**.

**18** Disconnect the wiring connector from the foglight bulb.

**19** Unhook the end of the bulb retaining clip and release it from the rear of the foglight unit **(see illustration)**. Withdraw the bulb.

**20** When handling the new bulb, use a tissue or clean cloth to avoid touching the glass with the fingers; moisture and grease from the skin can cause blackening and rapid failure of this type of bulb. If the glass is accidentally touched, wipe it clean using methylated spirit.

**21** Install the new bulb, ensuring that its locating tabs are correctly seated in the light cut-outs. Secure the bulb in position with the retaining clip then reconnect the wiring connector.

**22** Ensure the seal is in good condition then securely refit the cover to the rear of the light unit.

**23** Refit the wiring connector, then close the access cover.

### Front indicator

**24** Proceed as described in paragraphs 2 and 3.

**25** Rotate the bulbholder anti-clockwise, and free it from the rear of the headlight unit. The bulb is a bayonet-fit in the holder, and can be removed by pressing it in and rotating it anti-clockwise **(see illustrations)**.

**26** Refit the bulbholder and turn it clockwise to secure.

**27** Refit the access cover and secure with the retaining clip.

**28** Refit the components disturbed for access.

### Indicator side repeater

**29** Push the light unit forward to free its rear

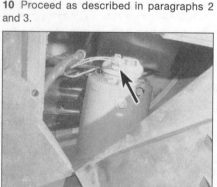

**5.17a Disconnect the foglight wiring connector (arrowed) . . .**

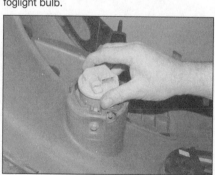

**5.17b . . . then turn the cover anti-clockwise to release it**

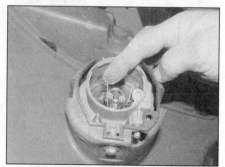

**5.19 Unhook the bulb retaining clip and release it from the light unit**

**5.25a  Rotate the direction indicator bulbholder anti-clockwise and release it from the headlight unit**

**5.25b  . . . then remove the bayonet-fit bulb**

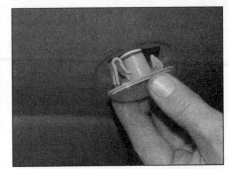

**5.29  Push the side repeater light unit forward, then ease it out from the wing**

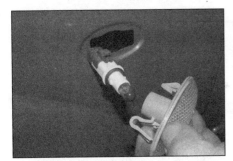

**5.30a  Rotate the bulbholder anti-clockwise to release it from the light unit . . .**

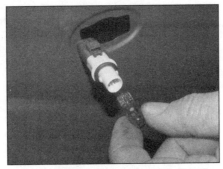

**5.30b  . . . then remove the push-fit bulb from the bulbholder**

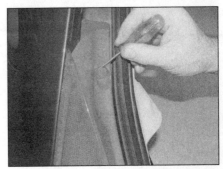

**5.32a  Prise out the trim cap at the top of the light unit . . .**

retaining clip, then ease it out from the front wing **(see illustration)**.

30  Rotate the bulbholder anti-clockwise and free it from the rear of the light unit. The bulb is of the capless (push-fit) type, and can be removed by simply pulling it out of the holder **(see illustrations)**.

31  Refitting is a reversal of the removal procedure.

### Rear light cluster

32  Open the tailgate and carefully prise out the trim cap at the top of the light unit. Undo the retaining nut now exposed **(see illustrations)**.

33  Working through the aperture in the luggage compartment side trim, undo the light unit lower retaining nut **(see illustration)**.

34  Withdraw the light unit from the body and disconnect the wiring connector **(see illustration)**.

35  Carefully release the retaining catches and remove the bulbholder from the light unit **(see illustrations)**.

36  All the bulbs have bayonet fittings. The relevant bulb can be removed by pressing

it in and rotating it anti-clockwise **(see illustration)**.

37  Refitting is the reverse of removal, ensuring the light unit and bulbholder seals are in good condition.

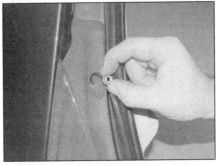

**5.32b  . . . and undo the retaining nut now exposed**

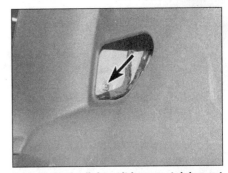

**5.33  Undo the light unit lower retaining nut (arrowed) through the trim panel aperture**

**5.34  Withdraw the light unit and disconnect the wiring connector**

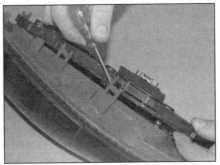

**5.35a  Carefully release the retaining catches . . .**

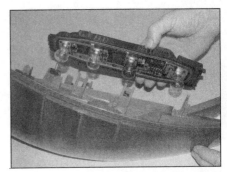

**5.35b  . . . and remove the bulbholder from the light unit**

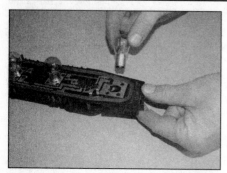

**5.36 Remove the relevant bayonet-fit bulb from the bulbholder**

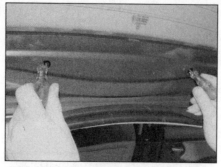

**5.38 Use two screwdrivers to release the high-level stop-light retaining spring clips**

**5.39 Withdraw the light unit and disconnect the bulbholder wiring plug**

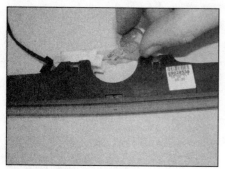

**5.40 Remove the push-fit bulb from the bulbholder**

**5.42a Carefully prise out the number plate light lens . . .**

**5.42b . . . and remove the push-fit bulb from the light unit**

### High-level stop-light

**38** Open the tailgate and, using two screwdrivers, release the light unit retaining spring clips, working through the access holes in the tailgate **(see illustration)**.

**39** Withdraw the light unit from the outside and disconnect the wiring plug from the bulbholder **(see illustration)**.
**40** The bulb is of the capless (push-fit) type, and can be removed by simply pulling it out of the bulbholder **(see illustration)**.

**41** Refitting is the reverse of removal.

### Number plate light

**42** Using a small flat-bladed screwdriver, carefully prise the side of the lens out, and remove it. The bulb is of the capless (push-fit) type, and can be removed by simply pulling it out of the light unit **(see illustrations)**.
**43** Refitting is the reverse of the removal procedure, ensuring that the lens is securely clipped in position.

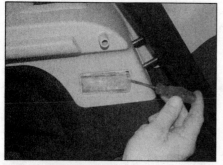

**6.2 Carefully prise the interior light lens from the light unit**

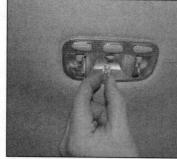

**6.3 Remove the relevant push-fit bulb from the light unit**

## 6 Bulbs (interior lights) – renewal

### General

**1** Refer to Section 5, paragraph 1.

### Passenger compartment lights

**2** Using a small screwdriver, carefully prise the lens from the light unit **(see illustration)**.
**3** The bulbs are of the capless (push-fit) type, and can be removed by simply pulling them out of the bulbholders **(see illustration)**.
**4** Refitting is the reverse of the removal procedure.

### Luggage compartment light

**5** Using a small screwdriver, carefully prise the light unit from the side trim panel and disconnect the wiring connector **(see illustrations)**.
**6** The bulb is of the capless (push-fit) type, and can be removed by simply pulling it out of the bulbholder **(see illustration)**.

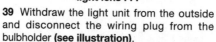

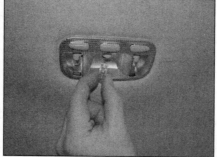

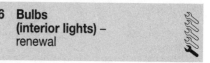

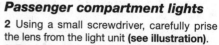

**6.5a Carefully prise the light unit from the side trim panel . . .**

**6.5b . . . and disconnect the wiring connector**

**6.6  Remove the push-fit bulb from the light unit**

**6.10a  Reach in through the audio unit aperture and push out the storage compartment . . .**

**6.10b  . . . to release the retaining lugs (arrowed) each side**

**6.11a  Release the control unit upper locating lugs . . .**

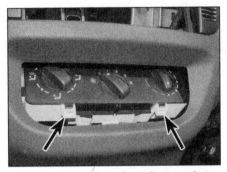

**6.11b  . . . then move the unit upwards to free the lower lugs (arrowed)**

**6.12a  Rotate the bulbholders anti-clockwise to remove them from the control unit . . .**

**7** Refitting is the reverse of the removal procedure.

### Instrument panel lights

**8** The instrument panel and warning lights are illuminated by integral LEDs. It is not possible to renew them independently of the panel. Instrument panel renewal is described in Section 9.

### Heating/ventilation control illumination

**9** Remove the audio unit as described in Section 17.
**10** Reach in through the audio unit aperture and push out the storage compartment, to release the retaining lugs each side (**see illustrations**).
**11** Push the heater/ventilation control panel in at the top to release the upper locating lugs,

then move the unit upwards to free the lower lugs (**see illustrations**).
**12** Turn the control panel over and, using pointed-nose pliers, rotate the bulbholders anti-clockwise to remove them. The capless bulbs simply pull from the bulbholders (**see illustrations**).
**13** Refitting is the reverse of the removal procedure.

### Multi-function display illumination

**14** Remove the multi-function display as described in Section 10.
**15** Rotate the bulbholders anti-clockwise and remove them. The capless bulbs simply pull from the bulbholder (**see illustration**).

### Switch illumination

**16** All of the switches that are illuminated, are

done so by LEDs. These LEDs are an integral part of the switch and cannot be renewed separately. Renewal will therefore require renewal of the complete switch assembly (see Section 4).

### Vanity mirror illumination

**17** Carefully prise the lens and mirror from the sunvisor.
**18** Prise the festoon bulb(s) from place.

---

**7  Exterior light units –** removal and refitting

---

### Headlight

**1** Remove the front bumper (see Chapter 11).
**2** Undo the two lower mounting bolts securing the headlight unit to the body (**see illustration**).

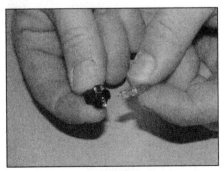

**6.12b  . . . then remove the push-fit bulbs from the bulbholders**

**6.15  Remove the multi-function display bulbholders then remove the push-fit bulbs**

**7.2  Undo the two headlight unit lower mounting bolts (arrowed)**

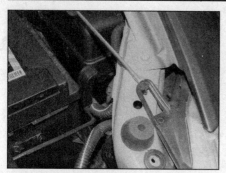

**7.3 Lift the upper locating tab to release it from the front wing**

**7.4 Withdraw the headlight from the front wing and disconnect the wiring connector**

**7.6 Ensure that the peg (arrowed) on the headlight engages with the slot in the wing**

**7.13 Undo the retaining bolt (arrowed) then push the foglight unit out of the bumper**

**7.17 Prise the number plate light unit from the tailgate and disconnect the wiring connector**

3 Using a small screwdriver, lift the upper locating tab to release it from the front wing **(see illustration)**. **Note:** *On later models a bolt is used instead of the tab.*
4 Withdraw the headlight from the front wing and disconnect the wiring connector **(see illustration)**.
5 Offer up the headlight unit and securely reconnect its wiring connector.
6 Position the headlight in its aperture, ensuring that the peg on the rear of the unit engages with the slot in the wing **(see illustration)**.
7 Refit and tighten the headlight mounting bolts.
8 Check the operation of the headlight, then refit the front bumper.
9 Check the headlight beam alignment using the information given in Section 8.

### Indicator side repeater

10 The procedure is described as part of the bulb renewal procedure in Section 5.

### Front foglight

11 Open the access cover at the base of the front wheel arch liner, directly beneath the foglight unit.
12 Disconnect the wiring connector on the light unit cover.
13 Undo the lower retaining bolt, then unclip and push the light unit forward out of the bumper **(see illustration)**.
14 Refitting is the reverse of the removal procedure.

### Rear light unit

15 The procedure is described as part of the bulb renewal procedure in Section 5.

### High-level stop-light

16 The procedure is described as part of the bulb renewal procedure in Section 5.

### Number plate light

17 Using a small screwdriver, carefully prise the light unit from the tailgate and disconnect the wiring connector **(see illustration)**.
18 Refit the wiring connector and push the unit back into its location.

## 8 Headlight beam alignment – general information

1 Accurate adjustment of the headlight beam is only possible using optical beam-setting equipment, and this work should therefore be carried out by a Citroën dealer or suitably-equipped workshop.
2 On models equipped with headlight levelling, ensure the adjuster switch is set to position 0 before the headlights are adjusted.

## 9 Instrument panel – removal and refitting

### Removal

1 Disconnect the battery as described in Chapter 5A.
2 Carefully detach the instrument panel surround from the facia **(see illustration)**.
3 Undo the three retaining screws and withdraw the panel from the facia **(see illustration)**.
4 Disconnect the wiring connectors and remove the instrument panel.

### Refitting

5 Refitting is a reversal of removal.

## 10 Clock/multi-function unit – removal and refitting

### Removal

1 Ensure the ignition is switched off.

**9.2 Carefully detach the instrument panel surround from the facia**

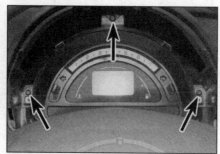

**9.3 Undo the three retaining screws (arrowed) and withdraw the panel from the facia**

**2** Remove the multi-function display surround as described in Chapter 11, Section 27.

**3** Undo the two retaining screws, withdraw the unit from the facia and disconnect the wiring plug **(see illustration)**.

### Refitting

**4** Refitting is a reversal of removal.

## 11 Cigarette lighter/ accessory socket – removal and refitting

### Removal

**1** Remove the centre console as described in Chapter 11.

**2** Carefully release the retaining clips and slide the illumination light assembly off the base of the lighter, taking great care not to break its electrical contacts.

**3** Pull out the lighter element then release the tangs and push out the metal insert/accessory socket. The plastic outer section can then be removed from the console.

### Refitting

**4** Align the plastic outer section tab with the cut-out then insert it into the console.

**5** Align the bulbholder contact on the metal insert with the holder tangs on the plastic outer then clip the insert into position.

**6** Slide the illumination light assembly onto the metal insert and clip it securely onto the plastic outer.

**7** Ensure the cigarette lighter is correctly assembled then refit the centre console.

## 12 Horn – removal and refitting

### Removal

**1** The horn is located behind the front bumper, on the left-hand side.

**2** Remove the front bumper as described in Chapter 11.

**3** Disconnect the wiring connector(s) then slacken the mounting nut and remove the horn from the vehicle **(see illustration)**.

### Refitting

**4** Refitting is a reversal of removal.

## 13 Wiper arm – removal and refitting

**Note:** *The wiper arms are a very tight fit on their spindles and it is likely that a puller will be needed to remove them safely and without damage.*

### Removal

**1** Operate the wiper motor, then switch it off

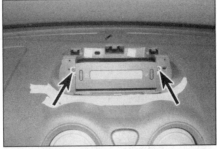

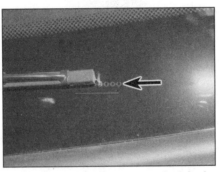

**10.3 Undo the multi-function unit retaining screws (arrowed) and withdraw the unit from the facia**

**13.1 Wiper arm alignment mark etched into the windscreen (arrowed)**

so that the wiper arm returns to the at-rest position. Stick tape to the screen alongside the wiper blade to ensure correct refitment. There is also an alignment mark provided on the windscreen **(see illustration)**.

**2** Lift up the wiper arm spindle nut cover then slacken and remove the spindle nut **(see illustration)**.

**3** Lift the blade off the glass, and pull the wiper arm off its spindle. If the arm is very tight, free it from the spindle using a suitable puller.

**4** When removing the tailgate wiper arm, recover the spacer from the motor spindle, once the arm is removed **(see illustration)**.

### Refitting

**5** Ensure that the wiper arm and spindle splines are clean and dry, then refit the arm to the spindle, aligning the wiper blade with the

**13.4 Recover the spacer from the tailgate motor spindle, once the arm is removed**

**12.3 Horn mounting nut (arrowed)**

**13.2 Lift up the wiper arm spindle nut cover then slacken and remove the spindle nut**

tape fitted on removal, or the alignment marks provided.

**6** Refit the spindle nut, tightening it securely, and clip the nut cover (where fitted) back into position.

## 14 Windscreen wiper motor and linkage – removal and refitting

### Removal

**1** Remove the scuttle grille panel as described in Chapter 11.

**2** Lift off the foam insulation pad and undo the nut securing the linkage frame to the body **(see illustrations)**.

**3** At the other end of the assembly, undo the two bolts securing the mechanism to the body **(see illustration)**.

**14.2a Lift off the foam insulation pad . . .**

14.2b  . . . then undo the nut (arrowed) securing one end of the linkage frame to the body

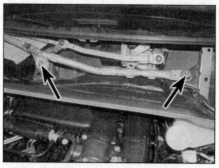

14.3  Undo the remaining linkage retaining bolts (arrowed)

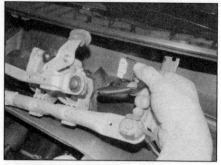

14.4  Withdraw the motor and linkage and disconnect the wiring plug

14.5  Prise the linkage off the balljoint crank arm

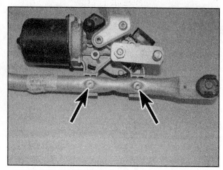

14.6  Undo the two bolts (arrowed) and remove the motor from the linkage frame

**4** Withdraw the motor and linkage assembly from the scuttle and disconnect the wiring plug **(see illustration)**.
**5** To separate the motor from the linkage, prise the linkage off the balljoint crank arm **(see illustration)**.
**6** Undo the two bolts and remove the motor from the linkage frame **(see illustration)**.

### Refitting

**7** Refitting is a reversal of removal.

### 15 Tailgate window wiper motor – removal and refitting

**Note:** *A pop rivet gun and suitable rivets will be required on refitting.*

### Removal

**1** Ensure the ignition is turned off.

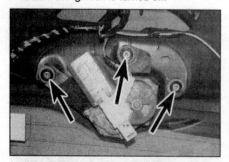

15.4  Drill the heads off the pop rivets (arrowed) securing the wiper motor bracket to the tailgate

**2** Remove the wiper arm (see Section 13).
**3** Remove the tailgate trim panel as described in Chapter 11, Section 25.
**4** Using a 8 mm drill bit, carefully drill the heads off the pop rivets securing the wiper motor bracket to the tailgate **(see illustration)**.
*Caution: Take care not to damage the motor and tailgate when drilling out the rivets.*
**5** With the three rivets removed, disconnect the wiring connector and remove the wiper motor from the tailgate. Take care not to lose the collars from the motor mounting rubbers.
**6** Remove the wiper motor sealing grommet from the tailgate glass.
**7** Recover the remnants of each rivet from the motor bracket/tailgate. Ensure all traces of rivet are removed.
**8** The wiper motor is not available separately. If faulty renew the assembly as a whole.

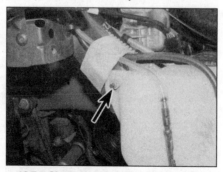

16.7a  Slacken and remove the washer reservoir upper retaining nut (arrowed) . . .

### Refitting

**9** Prior to refitting check the sealing grommet and rubber mountings for signs of damage or deterioration and renew as necessary.
**10** Ensure the rubber grommet is correctly fitted to the tailgate glass, and the rubber mountings and collars are correctly fitted to the motor mounting bracket.
**11** Manoeuvre the wiper motor into position and secure it in position with new pop rivets.
**12** Reconnect the wiring connector to the motor then refit the trim panel to the tailgate. Turn on the ignition, then operate the wiper and allow it to stop in the park position.
**13** Refit the wiper arm as described in Section 13.

### 16 Washer system components – removal and refitting

**1** The washer reservoir is located behind the right-hand front wing and supplies both the windscreen and tailgate washers via the same pump.

### Washer fluid reservoir

**2** Slacken the right-hand front roadwheel bolts. Jack up the front of the vehicle, and support it securely on axle stands (see *Jacking and vehicle support*). Remove the right-hand roadwheel.
**3** Remove the front right-hand wheel arch liner. The liner is secured by several expanding plastic rivets. Push the centre pins a little, or lift the raised portion, then prise the complete rivet from place, and manoeuvre the liner out from underneath the wing.
**4** Pull the reservoir filler neck upwards from the reservoir.
**5** Note the correct fitted location of the washer hoses (if necessary, mark them for identification purposes) then disconnect the hoses from the washer pump(s).
**6** Disconnect the wiring connector(s) from the washer pump(s).
**7** Slacken and remove the upper retaining nut, and lower retaining bolt, then manoeuvre the reservoir out from underneath the wing **(see illustrations)**.
**8** Refitting is the reverse of removal, ensuring

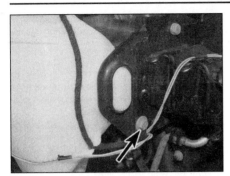

**16.7b . . . and lower retaining bolt (arrowed)**

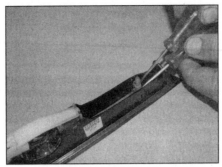

**16.17 Free the washer jet from the stop-light light unit by releasing the two retaining clips**

**17.3 Insert the removal tools into the holes on the audio unit and withdraw the unit from the facia**

that the hoses are securely reconnected. Refill the reservoir and check for leaks.

### Washer pump

**9** Proceed as described in paragraphs 2 to 6 and disconnect the hose(s) and wiring connector from the pump.
**10** Position a container beneath the reservoir to catch the washer fluid as the pump is removed.
**11** Carefully ease the pump out from the reservoir, and recover its sealing grommet. Wash off any spilt fluid with cold water.
**12** Refitting is the reverse of removal, using a new sealing grommet if the original shows signs of damage or deterioration. Refill the reservoir and check the pump grommet for leaks on completion.

### Windscreen washer jet

**13** Open and support the bonnet.
**14** Disconnect the washer hose(s) from the relevant jet, then depress the retaining clips and ease the jet out of position.
**15** On refitting, clip the jet into the bonnet and reconnect the hose. The aim of the washer jets is not adjustable.

### Tailgate washer jet

**16** Remove the high-level stop-light unit as described in Section 7.
**17** Disconnect the washer hose from the jet, then free the jet from the light unit by releasing the two retaining clips **(see illustration)**. Recover the jet O-ring.
**18** Refitting is the reverse of removal.

### 17 Audio unit – removal and refitting

**Note:** *The following procedure is for the range of equipment fitted by Citroën.*

### Removal

**1** Ensure the audio unit and ignition is switched off.
**2** The audio units fitted by Citroën have DIN standard fixings. Two special tools, obtainable from most car accessory retailers, are required for removal. Alternatively, suitable tools can

be fabricated from 3 mm diameter wire, such as welding rod.
**3** Insert the tools into the holes on each side of the audio unit and push them in until they snap into place. The audio unit can be slid out of the facia **(see illustration)**.
**4** Once the unit has been withdrawn from the facia, disconnect the wiring connections and aerial lead from the rear, and remove the unit from the vehicle.

### Refitting

**5** Securely reconnect the aerial lead and wiring connectors then slide the unit back into position, taking care not to trap the wiring.

### 18 Loudspeakers – removal and refitting

### Removal

#### Door speakers

**1** Remove the front or rear door inner trim panel as described in Chapter 11.
**2** Using a 5 mm drill bit. Drill out the rivets securing the speaker to the door **(see illustration)**.
**3** Withdraw the speaker and disconnect the wiring plug **(see illustration)**.

#### Front tweeter

**4** Carefully prise the tweeter cover from the facia and remove it along with the tweeter. Disconnect the wiring plug as it is withdrawn.

**5** Rotate the tweeter speaker clockwise to free it from the cover.

### Refitting

**6** Refitting is a reversal of removal. Ensure the trim panels are clipped securely in position and are correctly located behind the edges of the sealing strips.

### 19 Radio aerial – removal and refitting

### Removal

**1** The aerial is a screw-fit in its base and is easily removed.
**2** To remove the complete aerial, open the tailgate then free the tailgate sealing strip from the top of its aperture. Carefully release the rear of the headlining to gain access to the aerial nut.
**3** Disconnect the wiring plug, undo the nut and remove the aerial.

### Refitting

**4** Refitting is the reverse of removal.

### 20 Parking aid components – general, removal and refitting

### General information

**1** The parking aid system is available on all later models. Four ultrasound sensors located

**18.2 Drill out the rivets securing the speaker to the door**

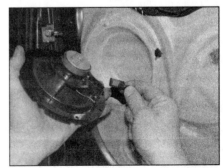

**18.3 Withdraw the speaker and disconnect the wiring plug**

in the rear bumper measure the distance to the closest object behind the car, and inform the driver using acoustic signals from the rear loudspeakers. The nearer the object, the more frequent the acoustic signals.

2 The system includes a control unit and self-diagnosis program, and therefore, in the event of a fault, the vehicle should be taken to a Citroën dealer or suitably-equipped specialist who will be able to interrogate the system.

### Electronic control unit

#### Removal

3 The control unit is located beneath the right-hand front seat. Remove the seat as described in Chapter 11.

4 Undo the 2 retaining screws, and remove the ECU from its mounting bracket.

5 Disconnect the wiring plugs and remove the control unit from inside the car.

#### Refitting

6 Refitting is a reversal of removal.

### Range/distance sensor

#### Removal

7 Chock the front roadwheels, then jack up the rear of the car and support it on axle stands (see Jacking and vehicle support).

8 Reach up behind the rear bumper and disconnect the sensor wiring plug, then push the retaining clips apart, and pull the sensor from position.

#### Refitting

9 Refitting is a reversal of removal. Press the sensor firmly into position until the retaining clips engage.

### 21 Engine immobiliser and anti-theft alarm system – general information

Note: This information is applicable only to the systems fitted by Citroën as standard equipment.

### Engine immobiliser

1 An engine immobiliser system is fitted as standard to all models and the system is operated automatically every time the ignition key is inserted/removed.

2 The immobiliser system ensures the vehicle can only be started using the original Citroën ignition key. The key contains an electronic chip (transponder) which is programmed with a code. When the key is inserted into the ignition switch it uses the current present in the sensor ring (which is fitted to the ignition switch housing) to send a signal to the immobiliser electronic control unit (ECU). The ECU is incorporated into the built-in systems interface (BSI) unit (see Section 24). The ECU checks this code every time the ignition is switched on. If the key code does not match the ECU code, the ECU will disable the starter, fuel and ignition (as applicable) to prevent the engine being started.

3 When the vehicle is new, a confidential security card is supplied along with the other vehicle documentation. This card contains the security code which your Citroën dealer requires when carrying out any work on the immobiliser system. Keep this card in a safe place at home; never store it in the vehicle. If the ignition key is lost, a new one can be obtained from a Citroën dealer. Take the confidential security card and all the existing keys along to your Citroën dealer who will supply a new key and reprogram all the keys with a new security code; this will render the lost key useless.

Caution: Without the confidential security card, it will not be possible to have the keys and immobiliser system reprogrammed.

> **HAYNES HINT** If you have purchased the vehicle second-hand, as a precaution have all the keys and the immobiliser system reprogrammed with a new security code. This will ensure the keys in your possession are the only ones able to start the vehicle and render all other keys useless.

4 Any problems with the engine immobiliser system should be referred to a Citroën dealer.

### Anti-theft alarm system

5 Most models covered in this manual were equipped with an anti-theft alarm system as standard equipment. The system was available as a option on all other models. The alarm is automatically armed when the deadlocking is set using the remote central locking transmitter and is disarmed when the doors are unlocked using the remote transmitter. The alarm system has switches on the bonnet, tailgate and each of the doors and also has ultrasonic sensing, which detects movement inside the vehicle, via sensors mounted on either side of the vehicle interior.

6 Details of the alarm system operation are given in the Owner's Handbook. For obvious security reasons, they are not given here.

7 Should the alarm system become faulty, the vehicle should be taken to a Citroën dealer for examination.

**23.2 Depress the internal spring retainers and pull the airbag unit away from the steering wheel**

### 22 Airbag system – general information and precautions

1 All models in the range are fitted with a driver's airbag, passenger's airbag, side-front airbags, and side curtain airbags.

2 The airbag system is triggered in the event of a heavy frontal impact above a pre-determined force, depending on the point of impact. The airbag is then inflated within milliseconds, and forms a safety cushion between the cabin occupants and the vehicle interior. This prevents contact between the upper body and vehicle interior, and therefore greatly reduces the risk of injury. The airbag then deflates almost immediately. The control unit also operates the front seat belt tensioner mechanisms at the same time (see Chapter 11).

3 The side airbags are fitted to the seat back of each front seat. Each airbag unit has its own lateral acceleration sensor which is mounted onto the vehicle body. The side airbags are not linked in any way and operate individually.

4 The curtain airbags are fitted behind the windscreen pillars and headlining on each side of the passenger cabin.

5 Every time the ignition is switched on, the airbag control unit performs a self-test. The self-test takes approximately six seconds and during this time the warning light in the instrument panel will be illuminated. After the self-test is complete, the warning light will go out (unless the passenger airbag unit has been deactivated – see paragraph 6). If the warning light fails to come on, remains illuminated after the self-test period, or comes on at any time when the vehicle is being driven, there is a fault in the airbag system. The vehicle should be taken to a Citroën dealer for examination at the earliest possible opportunity.

6 Most vehicles with a passenger airbag are equipped with a disabling switch fitted to the edge of the facia. The switch is operated using the ignition key and switches off the passenger airbag (it is not possible to disable the driver's or side/curtain airbags) to enable a rear-facing child seat to be installed in the passenger seat. Whilst the passenger airbag is disabled, the airbag warning light on the instrument panel will remain illuminated all the time.

⚠ **Warning: Before carrying out any operations on the airbag system, disconnect the battery (see Chapter 5A) and wait at least two minutes. Remove the centre console (see Chapter 11) then release the retaining clip and disconnect the wiring connector(s) from the airbag control unit. When the operations are complete, securely reconnect the control unit then refit the centre console (see Chapter 11). Make sure no one is inside the vehicle when the battery is reconnected then, with the driver's door open, switch the ignition on from outside vehicle and check the operation of the airbag warning light.**

**Warning:** *Do not subject the area of the body around the control unit to any form of shock which could trigger the system.*

**Warning:** *Note that the airbags must not be subjected to temperatures in excess of 100ºC. When the airbag is removed, ensure that it is stored pad upwards to prevent possible inflation.*

**Warning:** *Do not allow any solvents or cleaning agents to contact the airbag assemblies. They must be cleaned using only a damp cloth.*

**Warning:** *The airbags and control unit are both sensitive to impact. If either is dropped or damaged they should be renewed.*

**Warning:** *Disconnect the airbag control unit wiring connector prior to using arc welding equipment on the vehicle.*

**Warning:** *Never fit a rear-facing child seat to the front passenger seat unless the passenger airbag has been disabled (paragraph 6).*

**Warning:** *Citroën recommend that the airbag units be renewed every ten years.*

## 23 Airbag system components – removal and refitting

**Warning:** *Refer to the precautions given in Section 21 before carrying out the following operations.*

### Driver's airbag

#### Removal

**1** Disconnect the battery (see Chapter 5A). Remove the centre console (see Chapter 11) then release the retaining clip and disconnect the wiring connector(s) from the airbag control unit **(see illustration 23.13)**.

**2** Insert a screwdriver into the holes on both sides of the steering wheel, to depress the internal spring retainers, and at the same time pull the airbag unit away from the steering wheel to release it **(see illustration)**.

**3** Release the locking clip, then disconnect the airbag wiring connector and the horn push earth connector **(see illustration)**. Remove the airbag unit.

**Warning:** *Do not knock or drop the airbag unit and store it with its padded surface uppermost.*

#### Refitting

**4** Securely reconnect the wiring connectors then seat the airbag unit in the steering wheel, ensuring the wiring does not become trapped.

**5** Fit the airbag unit, press it into place until the retaining clips engage.

**6** Securely reconnect the airbag control unit wiring connector(s). Refit the centre console (see Chapter 11). Make sure no one is inside the vehicle then reconnect the battery. With

**23.3 Release the locking clip, then disconnect the airbag wiring connector**

the driver's door open, switch the ignition on from outside vehicle and check the operation of the warning light.

### Passenger airbag

#### Removal

**7** Disconnect the battery and wait at least two minutes. Remove the centre console (see Chapter 11) then release the retaining clip and disconnect the wiring connector(s) from the airbag control unit **(see illustration 23.13)**.

**8** Remove the glovebox as described in Chapter 11, Section 27.

**9** Working in the glovebox aperture, undo the three airbag retaining bolts **(see illustration)**.

**10** Disconnect the wiring connector and remove the airbag unit from the facia **(see illustration)**.

#### Refitting

**11** Fit the airbag unit to the facia, ensuring the wiring is correctly routed, and the bolts are securely tightened.

**12** The remainder of refitting is the reverse of removal. On completion, securely reconnect the airbag control unit wiring connector(s). Refit the centre console (see Chapter 11). Make sure no one is inside the vehicle then reconnect the battery. With the driver's door open, switch the ignition on from outside vehicle and check the operation of the warning light.

### Airbag control unit

#### Removal

**13** Disconnect the battery (see Chapter 5A)

**23.10 Disconnect the wiring connector and remove the airbag unit from the facia**

**23.9 Undo the three passenger airbag retaining bolts (arrowed)**

and wait at least two minutes. Remove the centre console (see Chapter 11) then release the retaining clip and disconnect the wiring connector(s) from the airbag control unit **(see illustration)**.

**14** Unscrew the retaining nuts then remove the control unit from the vehicle.

#### Refitting

**15** Refit the control unit, making sure the arrow on the top of the unit is pointing towards the front of the vehicle. Refit the control unit retaining nuts and tighten them to the specified torque.

**16** Securely reconnect the airbag control unit wiring connector(s).

**17** Refit the centre console (see Chapter 11). Make sure no one is inside the vehicle then reconnect the battery. With the driver's door open, switch the ignition on from outside vehicle and check the operation of the warning light.

### Side airbag

**18** Removal and refitting of the side airbag units should be entrusted to a Citroën dealer. The seat must be dismantled to enable the airbag unit to removed/refitted.

### Curtain airbag

**19** Removal and refitting of the curtain airbag units should be entrusted to a Citroën dealer. The headlining must be partially removed to enable the airbag unit to removed/refitted.

**23.13 Disconnect the wiring connector from the airbag control unit**

## 24 Built-in systems interface (BSI) unit/fusebox – general, removal and refitting

### General information

1 The built-in systems interface (BSI) unit is an electronic control unit which controls a variety of functions, normally controlled by individual control units and relays. The BSI unit is located in the left-hand side of the facia where it is situated directly beneath the fusebox. The BSI unit controls the following functions (not all functions are fitted to all models).

   a) *Direction indicator/hazard warning lights.*
   b) *Windscreen/tailgate wiper motors.*
   c) *Rear screen heating element.*
   d) *Immobiliser system.*
   e) *Anti-theft alarm system.*
   f) *Lights-on/ignition key warning buzzer.*
   g) *Central locking/deadlocking, including the remote central locking receiver.*
   h) *Door open indicator.*
   i) *Courtesy light delay timer.*
   j) *Automatic transmission audible warning system.*

2 Should any of the above functions become faulty, first check the condition of the fuses. If this fails to locate the problem, take the vehicle to a Citroën dealer for testing.

### Removal

3 Disconnect the battery (see Chapter 5A).
4 Refer to Chapter 11, Section 27, and remove the passenger side glovebox (right-hand drive models) or the driver's side lower facia panel (left-hand drive models).
5 Rotate the two white plastic fasteners 90 degrees anti-clockwise, and prise the fusebox outwards slightly.
6 Lower the rear edge of the unit, then lift up the front edge and slide it from place.
7 Note their fitted positions, then release the retaining clips then disconnect all the wiring connectors and remove the BSI unit from the vehicle. Note that there are several different designs of locking catches for the various connectors. Take your time to study the wiring connectors, and release them without using excessive force as they are easily damaged.

### Refitting

8 Refitting is the reverse of removal, ensuring the wiring connectors are all securely reconnected. Note that the connector colours are listed adjacent to their respective sockets on the BSI.

## CITROEN C3

Diagram 1

## Fuse table

### Engine fuse box

| Maxi Fuses | Rating | Circuit protected |
|---|---|---|
| MF1 | 20-80A | Engine cooling |
| MF2 | 20-80A | ABS |
| MF3 | 20-80A | ABS |
| MF4 | 20-80A | Built-in system interface |
| MF5 | 20-80A | Built-in system interface |
| MF6 | 20-80A | Heated seats |
| MF7 | 20-80A | Ignition switch |
| MF8 | 20-80A | Power steering |

| Fuses | Rating | Circuit protected |
|---|---|---|
| F1 | 10A | Diesel pre heating, reversing lights, air conditioning |
| F2 | 15A | Fuel pump |
| F3 | 10A | ABS |

| Fuses | Rating | Circuit protected |
|---|---|---|
| F4 | 10A | Power steering, engine cooling engine management, cruise control |
| F6 | 15A | Front foglights |
| F7 | 20A | Headlight washer |
| F8 | 20A | Engine management, power steering |
| F9 | 15A | LH dipped beam |
| F10 | 15A | RH dipped beam |
| F11 | 10A | LH main beam |
| F12 | 10A | RH main beam |
| F13 | 15A | Horn |
| F14 | 10A | Wash/wipe |
| F15 | 30A | Engine management |
| F16 | 30A | Air pump |
| F17 | 30A | Wash/wipe |
| F18 | 40A | Heater blower |

### Built-in system interface fuses

| Fuses | Rating | Circuit protected |
|---|---|---|
| F1 | 15A | Navigation, diagnostic socket |
| F4 | 20A | Steering wheel switches, clock, display, radio, automatic transmission |
| F5 | 15A | Alarm |
| F6 | 10A | Steering wheel sensor |
| F7 | 15A | Rain sensor, alarm |
| F10 | 40A | Heated rear window, heated mirrors |
| F11 | 15A | Rear wiper |
| F12 | 30A | Electric windows and mirrors, sunroof |
| F14 | 10A | Steering wheel switches, airbag, radio |
| F15 | 15A | Instrument panel, radio, air conditioning |
| F16 | 30A | Central locking |
| F20 | 10A | RH brake light |
| F21 | 15A | LH brake light, high level brake light |
| F22 | 30A | 12V socket, cigarette lighter, interior lights, radio, number plate lights |

## Key to circuits

| | |
|---|---|
| Diagram 1 | Information for wiring diagrams |
| Diagram 2 | Starting and charging, built-in system interface supply and airbag |
| Diagram 3 | ABS, central locking, cigarette lighter and accessory socket |
| Diagram 4 | Electric windows, horn, radio with CD player, electric and heated mirrors |
| Diagram 5 | Wash/wipe, sunroof and heated rear window |
| Diagram 6 | Engine cooling, power steering and cruise control |
| Diagram 7 | Brake lights, fog lights, headlights, sidelights and licence plate lights |
| Diagram 8 | Direction indicators, reversing lights, interior lights and headlight leveling |
| Diagram 9 | Air conditioning |
| Diagram 10 | Heater blower, instrument panel |

## Earth points

| | | | |
|---|---|---|---|
| E1 | Battery earth | E10 | Above RH rear wheel arch |
| E2 | Behind LH headlight | E11 | LH of handbrake lever |
| E3 | Behind LH headlight | E12 | LH of tailgate |
| E4 | Bottom of LH A pillar | E13 | LH engine bulkhead |
| E5 | Bottom of LH A pillar | E14 | RH engine compartment |
| E6 | Halfway up LH A pillar | E15 | RH of handbrake lever |
| E7 | Between front seats | E16 | LH wing behind battery |
| E8 | Bottom of RH A pillar | E17 | Above LH rear wheel arch |
| E9 | Behind LH headlight | E18 | Right of battery |

## Key to symbols

|  | |  | |  | |
|---|---|---|---|---|---|
| Bulb | —⊗— | Item no. | 2 | Connecting wires | |
| Switch | | Pump/motor | (M) | Wire joint | |
| Fuse/fusible link and current rating | F5 10A | Earth point and location | (E12) | Wire colour (brown with black tracer) | Mr/Nr |
| Multiple contact switch (ganged) | | Solenoid actuator | | Screened cable | |
| Resistor | | Diode | | Dashed outline denotes part of a larger item, containing in this case an electronic or solid state device. Pin types: | |
| Variable resistor | | Light emitting diode (LED) | | 2 - Unspecified colour connector, pin 2. | |
| Speaker | | Heater | | 2Mr 1 - Brown two pin connector, pin 1. | |

## Please Note

*The power supply to the Built-in system interface is shown on Diagram 2.*
*Reference should therefore be made to Diagram 2 for power supply details on diagrams including the Built-in system interface.*
*This power supply circuit has not been replicated in every circuit due to space considerations.*

*The prime method of wire identification is by using the terminal pin numbers (moulded into each component or connector and shown in the diagrams) together with the number code printed on each wire. To relate each diagram to the vehicle wiring, locate the relevant component or connector illustrated and find the wire(s) connected to the terminal pin(s) as shown in the diagram.*

*Caution: Whilst a number (indicating the function of that wire) may be printed on each wire, this is not always the case, and in such instances, this is reflected by the absence of such wire numbering on our diagrams. Similarly, numbering of the connector/component terminal pins is not always available from the manufacturers' source information and may also be missing from our diagrams. In these cases, it may be necessary to refer to your local dealer for further information.*

*Note that the conventional method of using colour coding does not apply – whilst the wires on the vehicle will be coloured, the wire colour has no relevance.*

H33139/a

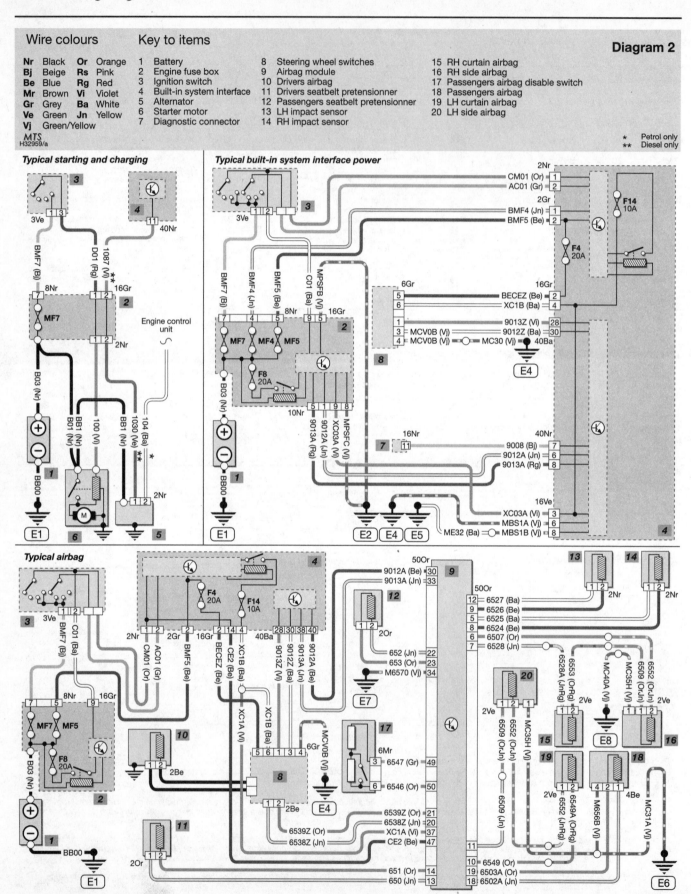

## Wire colours

| | | | |
|---|---|---|---|
| **Nr** | Black | **Or** | Orange |
| **Bj** | Beige | **Rs** | Pink |
| **Be** | Blue | **Rg** | Red |
| **Mr** | Brown | **Vi** | Violet |
| **Gr** | Grey | **Ba** | White |
| **Ve** | Green | **Jn** | Yellow |
| **Vj** | Green/Yellow | | |

MTS
H32959/a

## Key to items

1 Battery
2 Engine fuse box
3 Ignition switch
4 Built-in system interface
5 Alternator
6 Starter motor
7 Diagnostic connector
8 Steering wheel switches
9 Airbag module
10 Drivers airbag
11 Drivers seatbelt pretensionner
12 Passengers seatbelt pretensionner
13 LH impact sensor
14 RH impact sensor
15 RH curtain airbag
16 RH side airbag
17 Passengers airbag disable switch
18 Passengers airbag
19 LH curtain airbag
20 LH side airbag

## Diagram 2

★ Petrol only
★★ Diesel only

**Typical starting and charging**

**Typical built-in system interface power**

**Typical airbag**

## Wire colours

| | | | |
|---|---|---|---|
| **Nr** | Black | **Or** | Orange |
| **Bj** | Beige | **Rs** | Pink |
| **Be** | Blue | **Rg** | Red |
| **Mr** | Brown | **Vi** | Violet |
| **Gr** | Grey | **Ba** | White |
| **Ve** | Green | **Jn** | Yellow |
| **Vj** | Green/Yellow | | |

## Key to items

1 Battery
2 Engine fuse box
3 Ignition switch
4 Built-in system interface
7 Diagnostic connector
21 ABS module
22 Front LH wheel sensor
23 Front RH wheel sensor
24 Rear LH wheel sensor
25 Rear RH wheel sensor
26 Brake fluid level switch
27 Cigarette lighter
28 Front accessory socket
29 Rear accessory socket
30 Rear LH door lock
31 Front LH door lock
32 Rear RH door lock
33 Front RH door lock
34 Tailgate lock
35 Tailgate lock switch
36 Child safety relay
37 Switches RH of driver
38 Door lock switch

**Diagram 3**

MTS
H33141/a

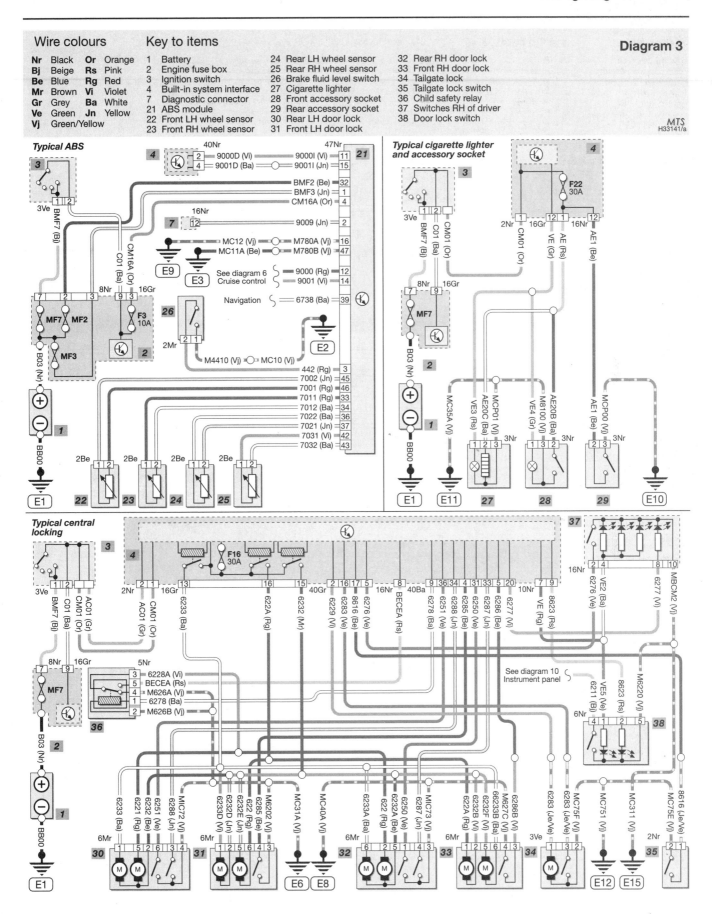

Typical ABS

Typical cigarette lighter and accessory socket

Typical central locking

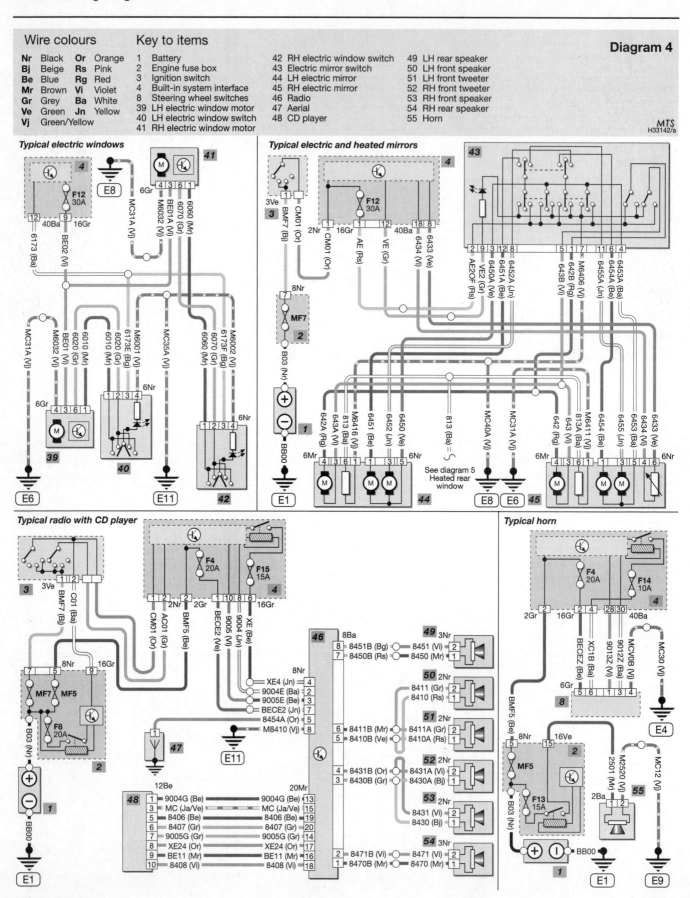

**Diagram 4**

## Wire colours

| | | | |
|---|---|---|---|
| **Nr** | Black | **Or** | Orange |
| **Bj** | Beige | **Rs** | Pink |
| **Be** | Blue | **Rg** | Red |
| **Mr** | Brown | **Vi** | Violet |
| **Gr** | Grey | **Ba** | White |
| **Ve** | Green | **Jn** | Yellow |
| **Vj** | Green/Yellow | | |

## Key to items

1 Battery
2 Engine fuse box
3 Ignition switch
4 Built-in system interface
8 Steering wheel switches
39 LH electric window motor
40 LH electric window switch
41 RH electric window motor
42 RH electric window switch
43 Electric mirror switch
44 LH electric mirror
45 RH electric mirror
46 Radio
47 Aerial
48 CD player
49 LH rear speaker
50 LH front speaker
51 LH front tweeter
52 RH front tweeter
53 RH front speaker
54 RH rear speaker
55 Horn

MTS
H33142/a

*Typical electric windows*

*Typical electric and heated mirrors*

*Typical radio with CD player*

*Typical horn*

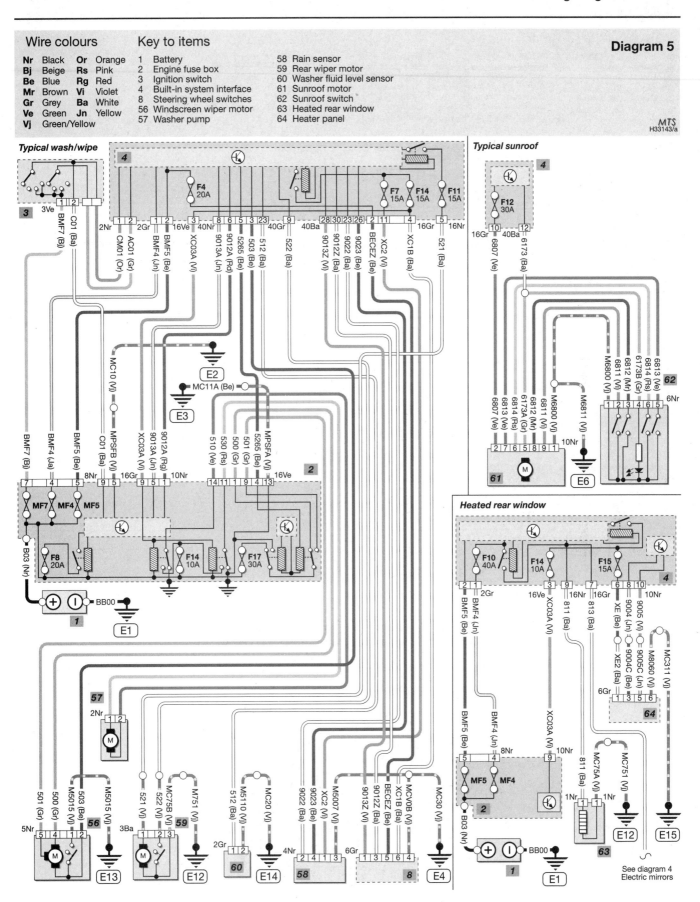

## Wire colours

| | | | |
|---|---|---|---|
| **Nr** | Black | **Or** | Orange |
| **Bj** | Beige | **Rs** | Pink |
| **Be** | Blue | **Rg** | Red |
| **Mr** | Brown | **Vi** | Violet |
| **Gr** | Grey | **Ba** | White |
| **Ve** | Green | **Jn** | Yellow |
| **Vj** | Green/Yellow | | |

## Key to items

1 Battery
2 Engine fuse box
3 Ignition switch
4 Built-in system interface
8 Steering wheel switches
56 Windscreen wiper motor
57 Washer pump
58 Rain sensor
59 Rear wiper motor
60 Washer fluid level sensor
61 Sunroof motor
62 Sunroof switch
63 Heated rear window
64 Heater panel

**Diagram 5**

MTS
H33143/a

*Typical wash/wipe*

*Typical sunroof*

*Heated rear window*

See diagram 4
Electric mirrors

## Wire colours

| | | | |
|---|---|---|---|
| Nr | Black | Or | Orange |
| Bj | Beige | Rs | Pink |
| Be | Blue | Rg | Red |
| Mr | Brown | Vi | Violet |
| Gr | Grey | Ba | White |
| Ve | Green | Jn | Yellow |
| Vj | Green/Yellow | | |

## Key to items

1  Battery
2  Engine fuse box
3  Ignition switch
4  Built-in system interface
7  Diagnostic connector
8  Steering wheel switches
65  Engine cooling fan relay
66  Engine cooling fan
67  Engine coolant level switch
68  Power steering unit
69  Power steering motor
70  Power steering torque sensor
71  Cruise control clutch switch
72  Cruise control brake switch
73  Accelerator pedal position sensor
74  Brake light switch
75  Engine speed sensor
76  Throttle valve position motor
77  Cruise control switches
78  Engine control unit

*   KFV only
**  8HY only

**Diagram 6**

H33144/a

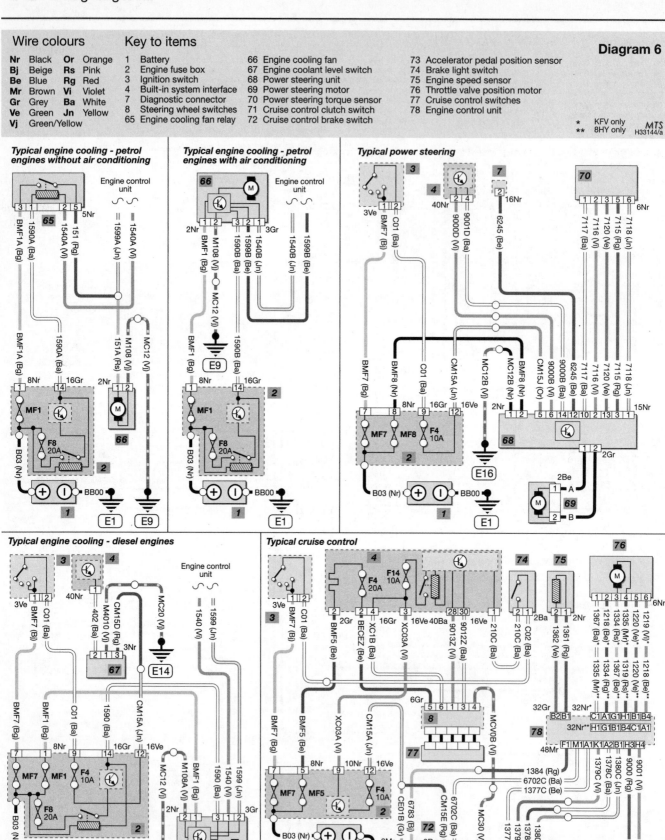

Typical engine cooling - petrol engines without air conditioning

Typical engine cooling - petrol engines with air conditioning

Typical power steering

Typical engine cooling - diesel engines

Typical cruise control

## Wire colours

| Nr | Black | Or | Orange |
|----|-------|----|--------|
| Bj | Beige | Rs | Pink |
| Be | Blue | Rg | Red |
| Mr | Brown | Vi | Violet |
| Gr | Grey | Ba | White |
| Ve | Green | Jn | Yellow |
| Vj | Green/Yellow | | |

## Key to items

1  Battery
2  Engine fuse box
3  Ignition switch
4  Built-in system interface
8  Steering wheel switches
74 Brake light switch
79 LH rear light cluster
  a) tail light

b) brake light
c) fog light
80 RH rear light cluster
  (as 79)
81 LH front headlight cluster
  a) side light
  b) dipped beam
  c) main beam

82 RH front headlight cluster
  (as 81)
83 LH number plate light
84 RH number plate light
85 High level brake light
86 LH front fog light
87 RH front fog light

**Diagram 7**

MTS
H33145/a

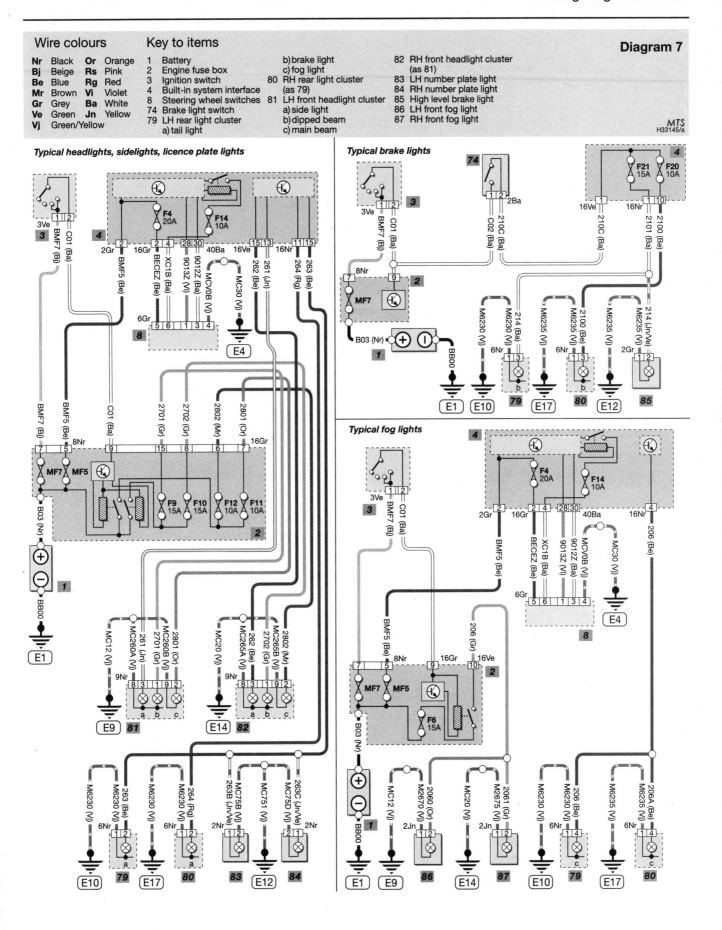

*Typical headlights, sidelights, licence plate lights*

*Typical brake lights*

*Typical fog lights*

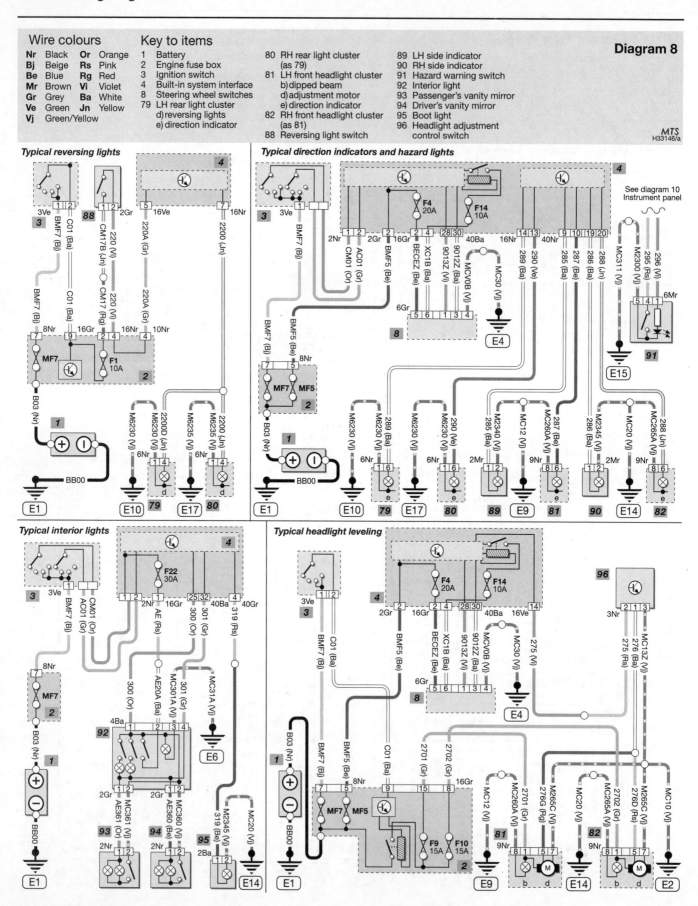

## Wire colours

| | | | |
|---|---|---|---|
| **Nr** | Black | **Or** | Orange |
| **Bj** | Beige | **Rs** | Pink |
| **Be** | Blue | **Rg** | Red |
| **Mr** | Brown | **Vi** | Violet |
| **Gr** | Grey | **Ba** | White |
| **Ve** | Green | **Jn** | Yellow |
| **Vj** | Green/Yellow | | |

## Key to items

1 Battery
2 Engine fuse box
3 Ignition switch
4 Built-in system interface
8 Steering wheel switches
79 LH rear light cluster
  d) reversing lights
  e) direction indicator

80 RH rear light cluster
  (as 79)
81 LH front headlight cluster
  b) dipped beam
  d) adjustment motor
  e) direction indicator
82 RH front headlight cluster
  (as 81)
88 Reversing light switch

89 LH side indicator
90 RH side indicator
91 Hazard warning switch
92 Interior light
93 Passenger's vanity mirror
94 Driver's vanity mirror
95 Boot light
96 Headlight adjustment
  control switch

**Diagram 8**

MTS
H33146/a

*Typical reversing lights*

*Typical direction indicators and hazard lights*

*Typical interior lights*

*Typical headlight leveling*

## Wire colours

| | | | |
|---|---|---|---|
| Nr | Black | Or | Orange |
| Bj | Beige | Rs | Pink |
| Be | Blue | Rg | Red |
| Mr | Brown | Vi | Violet |
| Gr | Grey | Ba | White |
| Ve | Green | Jn | Yellow |
| Vj | Green/Yellow | | |

## Key to items

| | |
|---|---|
| 1 | Battery |
| 2 | Engine fuse box |
| 3 | Ignition switch |
| 4 | Built-in system interface |
| 21 | ABS module |
| 75 | Engine speed sensor |
| 78 | Engine control unit |
| 97 | Evaporator temperature sensor |
| 98 | Air conditioning fluid pressure sensor |
| 99 | Engine coolant temperature sensor |
| 100 | Engine temperature switch |
| 101 | Air conditioning control panel |
| 102 | Heater blower resistor |
| 103 | Heater blower motor |
| 104 | Vehicle speed sensor |
| 105 | Air conditioning clutch |
| 106 | Air flap reduction motor |

**Diagram 9**

\* Not ABS

MTS
H33147/a

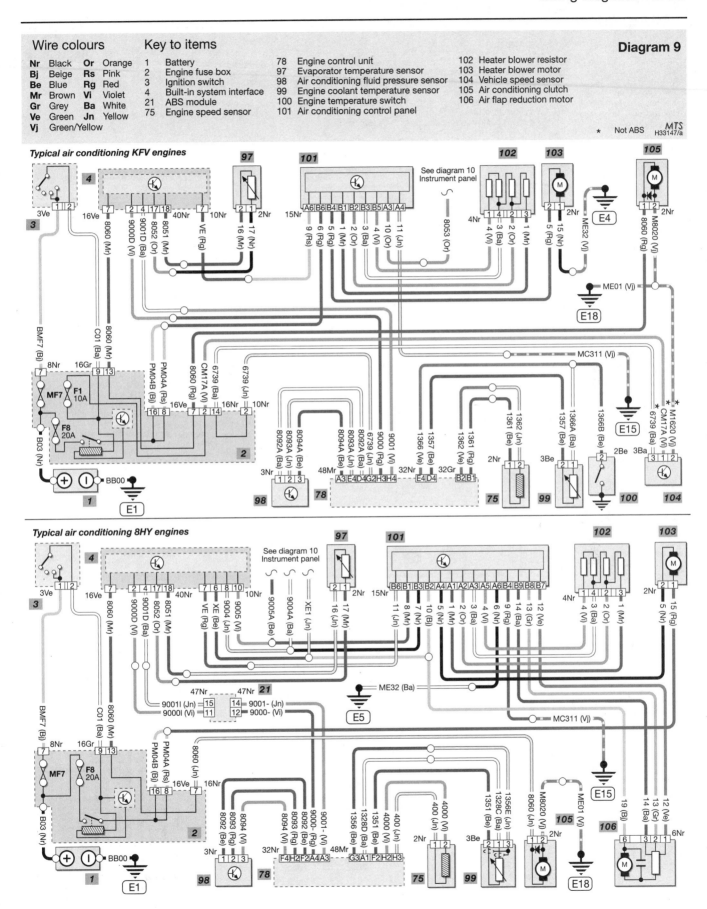

*Typical air conditioning KFV engines*

*Typical air conditioning 8HY engines*

## Wire colours

| | | | |
|---|---|---|---|
| Nr | Black | Or | Orange |
| Bj | Beige | Rs | Pink |
| Be | Blue | Rg | Red |
| Mr | Brown | Vi | Violet |
| Gr | Grey | Ba | White |
| Ve | Green | Jn | Yellow |
| Vj | Green/Yellow | | |

## Key to items

1 Battery
2 Engine fuse box
3 Ignition switch
4 Built-in system interface
8 Steering wheel switches
78 Engine control unit
101 Air conditioning control panel

102 Heater blower resistor
103 Heater blower motor
106 Air flap reduction motor
107 Instrument panel
108 Ignition key in lock sensor
109 Fuel pump with level sensor
110 Oil level sensor

111 Oil pressure switch
112 Seat belt switch
113 Handbrake switch
114 Low brake fluid level switch
115 Low coolant level switch
116 Coolant temperature sensor

**Diagram 10**

MTS
H33148/a

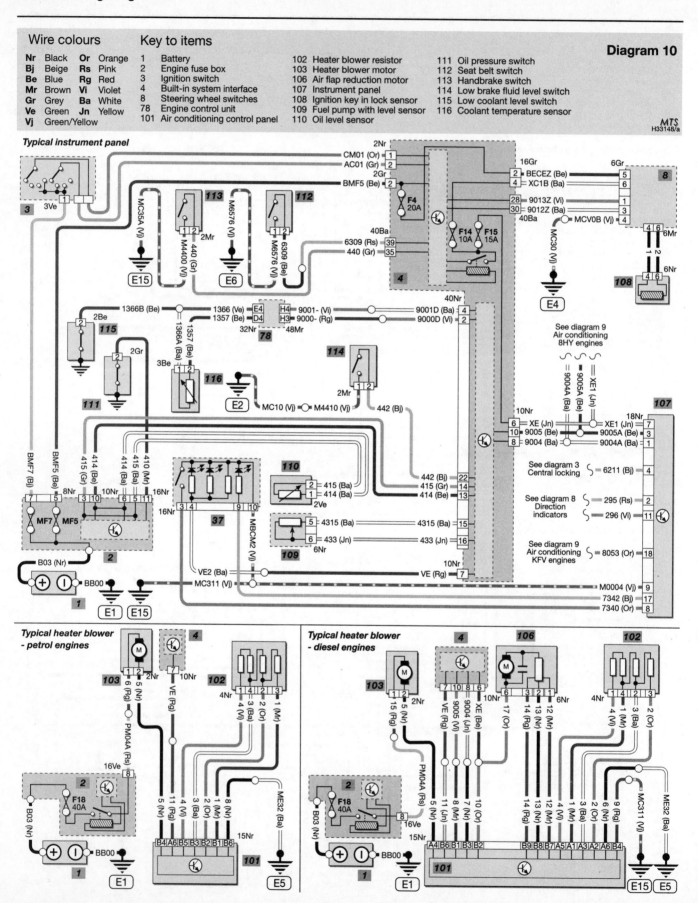

Typical instrument panel

Typical heater blower - petrol engines

Typical heater blower - diesel engines

# Dimensions and weights

## Dimensions

| | |
|---|---|
| Overall length . . . . . . . . . . . . . . . . . . . . . . . . . . . . . . . | 3850 mm |
| Overall width (excluding mirrors) . . . . . . . . . . . . . . . . . . . | 1667 mm |
| Overall height (unladen) . . . . . . . . . . . . . . . . . . . . . . . . | 1519 mm |
| Wheelbase . . . . . . . . . . . . . . . . . . . . . . . . . . . . . . . . . . | 2460 mm |
| Front track . . . . . . . . . . . . . . . . . . . . . . . . . . . . . . . . . . | 1438 mm |
| Rear track. . . . . . . . . . . . . . . . . . . . . . . . . . . . . . . . . . . | 1435 mm |

## Weights

Kerb weight (without optional equipment):
Petrol engine models:

| | |
|---|---|
| 1.1 litre engine . . . . . . . . . . . . . . . . . . . . . . . . . . . . | 1053 kg |

1.4 litre engine:

| | |
|---|---|
| With manual transmission. . . . . . . . . . . . . . . . . . . . . | 1080 kg |
| With automatic transmission . . . . . . . . . . . . . . . . . . | 1114 kg |
| 1.6 litre engine . . . . . . . . . . . . . . . . . . . . . . . . . . . . | 1133 kg |

Diesel engine models:

| | |
|---|---|
| 8-valve engine. . . . . . . . . . . . . . . . . . . . . . . . . . . . . | 1097 kg |
| 16-valve engine. . . . . . . . . . . . . . . . . . . . . . . . . . . . | 1147 kg |

Maximum gross vehicle weight*:
Petrol engine models:

| | |
|---|---|
| 1.1 litre engine . . . . . . . . . . . . . . . . . . . . . . . . . . . . | 1463 kg |

1.4 litre engine:

| | |
|---|---|
| With manual transmission. . . . . . . . . . . . . . . . . . . . . | 1470 kg |
| With automatic transmission . . . . . . . . . . . . . . . . . . | 1507 kg |
| 1.6 litre engine . . . . . . . . . . . . . . . . . . . . . . . . . . . . | 1525 kg |

Diesel engine models:

| | |
|---|---|
| 8-valve engine. . . . . . . . . . . . . . . . . . . . . . . . . . . . . | 1501 kg |
| 16-valve engine. . . . . . . . . . . . . . . . . . . . . . . . . . . . | 1539 kg |

Maximum gross train (vehicle and trailer) weight*:
Petrol engine models:

| | |
|---|---|
| 1.1 litre engine . . . . . . . . . . . . . . . . . . . . . . . . . . . . | 2113 kg |

1.4 litre engine:

| | |
|---|---|
| With manual transmission. . . . . . . . . . . . . . . . . . . . . | 2370 kg |
| With automatic transmission . . . . . . . . . . . . . . . . . . | 2407 kg |
| 1.6 litre engine . . . . . . . . . . . . . . . . . . . . . . . . . . . . | 2425 kg |

Diesel engine models:

| | |
|---|---|
| 8-valve engine. . . . . . . . . . . . . . . . . . . . . . . . . . . . . | 2401 kg |
| 16-valve engine. . . . . . . . . . . . . . . . . . . . . . . . . . . . | 2439 kg |

Maximum towing weight**:
Unbraked trailer:

| | |
|---|---|
| 1.1 litre petrol engine model. . . . . . . . . . . . . . . . . . . | 526 kg |

1.4 litre petrol engine model:

| | |
|---|---|
| With manual transmission. . . . . . . . . . . . . . . . . . . . . | 540 kg |
| With automatic transmission . . . . . . . . . . . . . . . . . . | 557 kg |
| 1.6 litre petrol engine model. . . . . . . . . . . . . . . . . . . | 566 kg |
| 8-valve diesel engine model. . . . . . . . . . . . . . . . . . . | 548 kg |
| 16-valve diesel engine model. . . . . . . . . . . . . . . . . . | 573 kg |

Braked trailer:

| | |
|---|---|
| 1.1 litre petrol engine model. . . . . . . . . . . . . . . . . . . | 926 kg |
| All other models . . . . . . . . . . . . . . . . . . . . . . . . . . . | 1175 kg |

*Refer to the Vehicle Identification Plate for the exact figures for your vehicle – see 'Vehicle identification numbers'.*

**Ensure the combined weight of the trailer and vehicle never exceeds the gross train weight when towing.*

# Fuel economy

Although depreciation is still the biggest part of the cost of motoring for most car owners, the cost of fuel is more immediately noticeable. These pages give some tips on how to get the best fuel economy.

## Working it out

### Manufacturer's figures

Car manufacturers are required by law to provide fuel consumption information on all new vehicles sold. These 'official' figures are obtained by simulating various driving conditions on a rolling road or a test track. Real life conditions are different, so the fuel consumption actually achieved may not bear much resemblance to the quoted figures.

### How to calculate it

Many cars now have trip computers which will

display fuel consumption, both instantaneous and average. Refer to the owner's handbook for details of how to use these.

To calculate consumption yourself (and maybe to check that the trip computer is accurate), proceed as follows.

1. Fill up with fuel and note the mileage, or zero the trip recorder.
2. Drive as usual until you need to fill up again.
3. Note the amount of fuel required to refill the tank, and the mileage covered since the previous fill-up.
4. Divide the mileage by the amount of fuel used to obtain the consumption figure.

*For example:*

    Mileage at first fill-up (a) = 27,903
    Mileage at second fill-up (b) = 28,346
    Mileage covered (b - a) = 443
    Fuel required at second fill-up = 48.6 litres

The half-completed changeover to metric units in the UK means that we buy our fuel

in litres, measure distances in miles and talk about fuel consumption in miles per gallon. There are two ways round this: the first is to convert the litres to gallons before doing the calculation (by dividing by 4.546, or see Table 1). So in the example:

    48.6 litres ÷ 4.546 = 10.69 gallons
    443 miles ÷ 10.69 gallons = 41.4 mpg

The second way is to calculate the consumption in miles per litre, then multiply that figure by 4.546 (or see Table 2).

*So in the example, fuel consumption is:*

    443 miles ÷ 48.6 litres = 9.1 mpl
    9.1 mpl x 4.546 = 41.4 mpg

The rest of Europe expresses fuel consumption in litres of fuel required to travel 100 km (l/100 km). For interest, the conversions are given in Table 3. In practice it doesn't matter what units you use, provided you know what your normal consumption is and can spot if it's getting better or worse.

**Table 1: conversion of litres to Imperial gallons**

| litres | 1 | 2 | 3 | 4 | 5 | 10 | 20 | 30 | 40 | 50 | 60 | 70 |
|---|---|---|---|---|---|---|---|---|---|---|---|---|
| gallons | 0.22 | 0.44 | 0.66 | 0.88 | 1.10 | 2.24 | 4.49 | 6.73 | 8.98 | 11.22 | 13.47 | 15.71 |

**Table 2: conversion of miles per litre to miles per gallon**

| miles per litre | 5 | 6 | 7 | 8 | 9 | 10 | 11 | 12 | 13 | 14 |
|---|---|---|---|---|---|---|---|---|---|---|
| miles per gallon | 23 | 27 | 32 | 36 | 41 | 46 | 50 | 55 | 59 | 64 |

**Table 3: conversion of litres per 100 km to miles per gallon**

| litres per 100 km | 4 | 4.5 | 5 | 5.5 | 6 | 6.5 | 7 | 8 | 9 | 10 |
|---|---|---|---|---|---|---|---|---|---|---|
| miles per gallon | 71 | 63 | 56 | 51 | 47 | 43 | 40 | 35 | 31 | 28 |

# Maintenance

A well-maintained car uses less fuel and creates less pollution. In particular:

### Filters

Change air and fuel filters at the specified intervals.

### Oil

Use a good quality oil of the lowest viscosity specified by the vehicle manufacturer (see *Lubricants and fluids*). Check the level often and be careful not to overfill.

### Spark plugs

When applicable, renew at the specified intervals.

### Tyres

Check tyre pressures regularly. Under-inflated tyres have an increased rolling resistance. It is generally safe to use the higher pressures specified for full load conditions even when not fully laden, but keep an eye on the centre band of tread for signs of wear due to over-inflation.

When buying new tyres, consider the 'fuel saving' models which most manufacturers include in their ranges.

# Driving style

### Acceleration

Acceleration uses more fuel than driving at a steady speed. The best technique with modern cars is to accelerate reasonably briskly to the desired speed, changing up through the gears as soon as possible without making the engine labour.

### Air conditioning

Air conditioning absorbs quite a bit of energy from the engine – typically 3 kW (4 hp) or so. The effect on fuel consumption is at its worst in slow traffic. Switch it off when not required.

### Anticipation

Drive smoothly and try to read the traffic flow so as to avoid unnecessary acceleration and braking.

### Automatic transmission

When accelerating in an automatic, avoid depressing the throttle so far as to make the transmission hold onto lower gears at higher speeds. Don't use the 'Sport' setting, if applicable.

When stationary with the engine running, select 'N' or 'P'. When moving, keep your left foot away from the brake.

### Braking

Braking converts the car's energy of motion into heat – essentially, it is wasted. Obviously some braking is always going to be necessary, but with good anticipation it is surprising how much can be avoided, especially on routes that you know well.

### Carshare

Consider sharing lifts to work or to the shops. Even once a week will make a difference.

### Electrical loads

Electricity is 'fuel' too; the alternator which charges the battery does so by converting some of the engine's energy of motion into electrical energy. The more electrical accessories are in use, the greater the load on the alternator. Switch off big consumers like the heated rear window when not required.

### Freewheeling

Freewheeling (coasting) in neutral with the engine switched off is dangerous. The effort required to operate power-assisted brakes and steering increases when the engine is not running, with a potential lack of control in emergency situations.

In any case, modern fuel injection systems automatically cut off the engine's fuel supply on the overrun (moving and in gear, but with the accelerator pedal released).

### Gadgets

Bolt-on devices claiming to save fuel have been around for nearly as long as the motor car itself. Those which worked were rapidly adopted as standard equipment by the vehicle manufacturers. Others worked only in certain situations, or saved fuel only at the expense of unacceptable effects on performance, driveability or the life of engine components.

The most effective fuel saving gadget is the driver's right foot.

### Journey planning

Combine (eg) a trip to the supermarket with a visit to the recycling centre and the DIY store, rather than making separate journeys.

When possible choose a travelling time outside rush hours.

### Load

The more heavily a car is laden, the greater the energy required to accelerate it to a given speed. Remove heavy items which you don't need to carry.

One load which is often overlooked is the contents of the fuel tank. A tankful of fuel (55 litres / 12 gallons) weighs 45 kg (100 lb) or so. Just half filling it may be worthwhile.

### Lost?

At the risk of stating the obvious, if you're going somewhere new, have details of the route to hand. There's not much point in achieving record mpg if you also go miles out of your way.

### Parking

If possible, carry out any reversing or turning manoeuvres when you arrive at a parking space so that you can drive straight out when you leave. Manoeuvering when the engine is cold uses a lot more fuel.

Driving around looking for free on-street parking may cost more in fuel than buying a car park ticket.

### Premium fuel

Most major oil companies (and some supermarkets) have premium grades of fuel which are several pence a litre dearer than the standard grades. Reports vary, but the consensus seems to be that if these fuels improve economy at all, they do not do so by enough to justify their extra cost.

### Roof rack

When loading a roof rack, try to produce a wedge shape with the narrow end at the front. Any cover should be securely fastened – if it flaps it's creating turbulence and absorbing energy.

Remove roof racks and boxes when not in use – they increase air resistance and can create a surprising amount of noise.

### Short journeys

The engine is at its least efficient, and wear is highest, during the first few miles after a cold start. Consider walking, cycling or using public transport.

### Speed

The engine is at its most efficient when running at a steady speed and load at the rpm where it develops maximum torque. (You can find this figure in the car's handbook.) For most cars this corresponds to between 55 and 65 mph in top gear.

Above the optimum cruising speed, fuel consumption starts to rise quite sharply. A car travelling at 80 mph will typically be using 30% more fuel than at 60 mph.

### Supermarket fuel

It may be cheap but is it any good? In the UK all supermarket fuel must meet the relevant British Standard. The major oil companies will say that their branded fuels have better additive packages which may stop carbon and other deposits building up. A reasonable compromise might be to use one tank of branded fuel to three or four from the supermarket.

### Switch off when stationary

Switch off the engine if you look like being stationary for more than 30 seconds or so. This is good for the environment as well as for your pocket. Be aware though that frequent restarts are hard on the battery and the starter motor.

### Windows

Driving with the windows open increases air turbulence around the vehicle. Closing the windows promotes smooth airflow and

reduced resistance. The faster you go, the more significant this is.

### And finally . . .

Driving techniques associated with good fuel economy tend to involve moderate acceleration and low top speeds. Be considerate to the needs of other road users who may need to make brisker progress; even if you do not agree with them this is not an excuse to be obstructive.

Safety must always take precedence over economy, whether it is a question of accelerating hard to complete an overtaking manoeuvre, killing your speed when confronted with a potential hazard or switching the lights on when it starts to get dark.

# Conversion factors

## Length (distance)

| | | | | | |
|---|---|---|---|---|---|
| Inches (in) | x 25.4 | = Millimetres (mm) | x 0.0394 | = | Inches (in) |
| Feet (ft) | x 0.305 | = Metres (m) | x 3.281 | = | Feet (ft) |
| Miles | x 1.609 | = Kilometres (km) | x 0.621 | = | Miles |

## Volume (capacity)

| | | | | | |
|---|---|---|---|---|---|
| Cubic inches (cu in; in³) | x 16.387 | = Cubic centimetres (cc; cm³) | x 0.061 | = | Cubic inches (cu in; in³) |
| Imperial pints (Imp pt) | x 0.568 | = Litres (l) | x 1.76 | = | Imperial pints (Imp pt) |
| Imperial quarts (Imp qt) | x 1.137 | = Litres (l) | x 0.88 | = | Imperial quarts (Imp qt) |
| Imperial quarts (Imp qt) | x 1.201 | = US quarts (US qt) | x 0.833 | = | Imperial quarts (Imp qt) |
| US quarts (US qt) | x 0.946 | = Litres (l) | x 1.057 | = | US quarts (US qt) |
| Imperial gallons (Imp gal) | x 4.546 | = Litres (l) | x 0.22 | = | Imperial gallons (Imp gal) |
| Imperial gallons (Imp gal) | x 1.201 | = US gallons (US gal) | x 0.833 | = | Imperial gallons (Imp gal) |
| US gallons (US gal) | x 3.785 | = Litres (l) | x 0.264 | = | US gallons (US gal) |

## Mass (weight)

| | | | | | |
|---|---|---|---|---|---|
| Ounces (oz) | x 28.35 | = Grams (g) | x 0.035 | = | Ounces (oz) |
| Pounds (lb) | x 0.454 | = Kilograms (kg) | x 2.205 | = | Pounds (lb) |

## Force

| | | | | | |
|---|---|---|---|---|---|
| Ounces-force (ozf; oz) | x 0.278 | = Newtons (N) | x 3.6 | = | Ounces-force (ozf; oz) |
| Pounds-force (lbf; lb) | x 4.448 | = Newtons (N) | x 0.225 | = | Pounds-force (lbf; lb) |
| Newtons (N) | x 0.1 | = Kilograms-force (kgf; kg) | x 9.81 | = | Newtons (N) |

## Pressure

| | | | | | |
|---|---|---|---|---|---|
| Pounds-force per square inch (psi; lbf/in²; lb/in²) | x 0.070 | = Kilograms-force per square centimetre (kgf/cm²; kg/cm²) | x 14.223 | = | Pounds-force per square inch (psi; lbf/in²; lb/in²) |
| Pounds-force per square inch (psi; lbf/in²; lb/in²) | x 0.068 | = Atmospheres (atm) | x 14.696 | = | Pounds-force per square inch (psi; lbf/in²; lb/in²) |
| Pounds-force per square inch (psi; lbf/in²; lb/in²) | x 0.069 | = Bars | x 14.5 | = | Pounds-force per square inch (psi; lbf/in²; lb/in²) |
| Pounds-force per square inch (psi; lbf/in²; lb/in²) | x 6.895 | = Kilopascals (kPa) | x 0.145 | = | Pounds-force per square inch (psi; lbf/in²; lb/in²) |
| Kilopascals (kPa) | x 0.01 | = Kilograms-force per square centimetre (kgf/cm²; kg/cm²) | x 98.1 | = | Kilopascals (kPa) |
| Millibar (mbar) | x 100 | = Pascals (Pa) | x 0.01 | = | Millibar (mbar) |
| Millibar (mbar) | x 0.0145 | = Pounds-force per square inch (psi; lbf/in²; lb/in²) | x 68.947 | = | Millibar (mbar) |
| Millibar (mbar) | x 0.75 | = Millimetres of mercury (mmHg) | x 1.333 | = | Millibar (mbar) |
| Millibar (mbar) | x 0.401 | = Inches of water (inH₂O) | x 2.491 | = | Millibar (mbar) |
| Millimetres of mercury (mmHg) | x 0.535 | = Inches of water (inH₂O) | x 1.868 | = | Millimetres of mercury (mmHg) |
| Inches of water (inH₂O) | x 0.036 | = Pounds-force per square inch (psi; lbf/in²; lb/in²) | x 27.68 | = | Inches of water (inH₂O) |

## Torque (moment of force)

| | | | | | |
|---|---|---|---|---|---|
| Pounds-force inches (lbf in; lb in) | x 1.152 | = Kilograms-force centimetre (kgf cm; kg cm) | x 0.868 | = | Pounds-force inches (lbf in; lb in) |
| Pounds-force inches (lbf in; lb in) | x 0.113 | = Newton metres (Nm) | x 8.85 | = | Pounds-force inches (lbf in; lb in) |
| Pounds-force inches (lbf in; lb in) | x 0.083 | = Pounds-force feet (lbf ft; lb ft) | x 12 | = | Pounds-force inches (lbf in; lb in) |
| Pounds-force feet (lbf ft; lb ft) | x 0.138 | = Kilograms-force metres (kgf m; kg m) | x 7.233 | = | Pounds-force feet (lbf ft; lb ft) |
| Pounds-force feet (lbf ft; lb ft) | x 1.356 | = Newton metres (Nm) | x 0.738 | = | Pounds-force feet (lbf ft; lb ft) |
| Newton metres (Nm) | x 0.102 | = Kilograms-force metres (kgf m; kg m) | x 9.804 | = | Newton metres (Nm) |

## Power

| | | | | | |
|---|---|---|---|---|---|
| Horsepower (hp) | x 745.7 | = Watts (W) | x 0.0013 | = | Horsepower (hp) |

## Velocity (speed)

| | | | | | |
|---|---|---|---|---|---|
| Miles per hour (miles/hr; mph) | x 1.609 | = Kilometres per hour (km/hr; kph) | x 0.621 | = | Miles per hour (miles/hr; mph) |

## Fuel consumption*

| | | | | | |
|---|---|---|---|---|---|
| Miles per gallon, Imperial (mpg) | x 0.354 | = Kilometres per litre (km/l) | x 2.825 | = | Miles per gallon, Imperial (mpg) |
| Miles per gallon, US (mpg) | x 0.425 | = Kilometres per litre (km/l) | x 2.352 | = | Miles per gallon, US (mpg) |

## Temperature

Degrees Fahrenheit = (°C x 1.8) + 32          Degrees Celsius (Degrees Centigrade; °C) = (°F - 32) x 0.56

*It is common practice to convert from miles per gallon (mpg) to litres/100 kilometres (l/100km), where mpg x l/100 km = 282*

Spare parts are available from many sources, including maker's appointed garages, accessory shops, and motor factors. To be sure of obtaining the correct parts, it will sometimes be necessary to quote the vehicle identification number. If possible, it can also be useful to take the old parts along for positive identification. Items such as starter motors and alternators may be available under a service exchange scheme – any parts returned should be clean.

Our advice regarding spare parts is as follows.

## Officially appointed garages

This is the best source of parts which are peculiar to your car, and which are not otherwise generally available (eg, badges, interior trim, certain body panels, etc). It is also the only place at which you should buy parts if the car is still under warranty.

## Accessory shops

These are very good places to buy materials and components needed for the maintenance of your car (oil, air and fuel filters, light bulbs, drivebelts, greases, brake pads, touch-up paint, etc). Components of this nature

sold by a reputable shop are usually of the same standard as those used by the car manufacturer.

Besides components, these shops also sell tools and general accessories, usually have convenient opening hours, charge lower prices, and can often be found close to home. Some accessory shops have parts counters where components needed for almost any repair job can be purchased or ordered.

## Motor factors

Good factors will stock all the more important components which wear out comparatively quickly, and can sometimes supply individual components needed for the overhaul of a larger assembly (eg, brake seals and hydraulic parts, bearing shells, pistons, valves). They may also handle work such as cylinder block reboring, crankshaft regrinding, etc.

## Engine reconditioners

These specialise in engine overhaul and can also supply components. It is recommended that the establishment is a member of the Federation of Engine Re-Manufacturers, or a similar society.

## Tyre and exhaust specialists

These outlets may be independent, or members of a local or national chain. They frequently offer competitive prices when compared with a main dealer or local garage, but it will pay to obtain several quotes before making a decision. When researching prices, also ask what extras may be added – for instance fitting a new valve, balancing the wheel and tyre disposal all both commonly charged on top of the price of a new tyre.

## Other sources

Beware of parts or materials obtained from market stalls, car boot sales, on-line auctions or similar outlets. Such items are not invariably sub-standard, but there is little chance of compensation if they do prove unsatisfactory. In the case of safety-critical components such as brake pads, there is the risk not only of financial loss, but also of an accident causing injury or death.

Second-hand components or assemblies obtained from a car breaker can be a good buy in some circumstances, but this sort of purchase is best made by the experienced DIY mechanic.

# Vehicle identification numbers

Modifications are a continuing and unpublicised process in vehicle manufacture, quite apart from major model changes. Spare parts manuals and lists are compiled upon a numerical basis, the individual vehicle identification numbers being essential for correct identification of the part concerned.

When ordering spare parts, always give as much information as possible. Quote the car model, year of manufacture, VIN and engine numbers, as appropriate.

The *vehicle identification number (VIN)* is located on a plate riveted onto the door pillar on the left-hand side. The plate carries the vehicle identification number (VIN) and vehicle weight information **(see illustration)**.

The *vehicle identification number (VIN)* is also stamped onto a plate visible through the base of the windscreen.

The engine number is situated on the front face of the cylinder block, and can be found in the following locations:

a) *On petrol engines the engine number is located on the left-hand side of the cylinder block. The number is either stamped directly onto the block or is stamped onto a plate which is riveted to the block.*

b) *On diesel engines the engine number is stamped on the base of the cylinder block on the flat surface located on the right-hand side of the oil filter/cooler.*

**Note:** *The first part of the engine number gives the engine code, eg KFV.*

H45538

**Vehicle identification details**

| | | | |
|---|---|---|---|
| 1 | Chassis number | 3/4 | Colour code, tyre pressures and tyre information |
| 2 | Manufacturer's chassis plate (also contains the VIN number) and other information | 5 | VIN number (on the windscreen) |
| | | 6 | Gearbox number |
| | | 7 | Engine number |

Whenever servicing, repair or overhaul work is carried out on the car or its components, observe the following procedures and instructions. This will assist in carrying out the operation efficiently and to a professional standard of workmanship.

## Joint mating faces and gaskets

When separating components at their mating faces, never insert screwdrivers or similar implements into the joint between the faces in order to prise them apart. This can cause severe damage which results in oil leaks, coolant leaks, etc upon reassembly. Separation is usually achieved by tapping along the joint with a soft-faced hammer in order to break the seal. However, note that this method may not be suitable where dowels are used for component location.

Where a gasket is used between the mating faces of two components, a new one must be fitted on reassembly; fit it dry unless otherwise stated in the repair procedure. Make sure that the mating faces are clean and dry, with all traces of old gasket removed. When cleaning a joint face, use a tool which is unlikely to score or damage the face, and remove any burrs or nicks with an oilstone or fine file.

Make sure that tapped holes are cleaned with a pipe cleaner, and keep them free of jointing compound, if this is being used, unless specifically instructed otherwise.

Ensure that all orifices, channels or pipes are clear, and blow through them, preferably using compressed air.

## Oil seals

Oil seals can be removed by levering them out with a wide flat-bladed screwdriver or similar implement. Alternatively, a number of self-tapping screws may be screwed into the seal, and these used as a purchase for pliers or some similar device in order to pull the seal free.

Whenever an oil seal is removed from its working location, either individually or as part of an assembly, it should be renewed.

The very fine sealing lip of the seal is easily damaged, and will not seal if the surface it contacts is not completely clean and free from scratches, nicks or grooves. If the original sealing surface of the component cannot be restored, and the manufacturer has not made provision for slight relocation of the seal relative to the sealing surface, the component should be renewed.

Protect the lips of the seal from any surface which may damage them in the course of fitting. Use tape or a conical sleeve where possible. Where indicated, lubricate the seal lips with oil before fitting and, on dual-lipped seals, fill the space between the lips with grease.

Unless otherwise stated, oil seals must be fitted with their sealing lips toward the lubricant to be sealed.

Use a tubular drift or block of wood of the appropriate size to install the seal and, if the seal housing is shouldered, drive the seal down to the shoulder. If the seal housing is unshouldered, the seal should be fitted with its face flush with the housing top face (unless otherwise instructed).

## Screw threads and fastenings

Seized nuts, bolts and screws are quite a common occurrence where corrosion has set in, and the use of penetrating oil or releasing fluid will often overcome this problem if the offending item is soaked for a while before attempting to release it. The use of an impact driver may also provide a means of releasing such stubborn fastening devices, when used in conjunction with the appropriate screwdriver bit or socket. If none of these methods works, it may be necessary to resort to the careful application of heat, or the use of a hacksaw or nut splitter device. Before resorting to extreme methods, check that you are not dealing with a left-hand thread!

Studs are usually removed by locking two nuts together on the threaded part, and then using a spanner on the lower nut to unscrew the stud. Studs or bolts which have broken off below the surface of the component in which they are mounted can sometimes be removed using a stud extractor.

Always ensure that a blind tapped hole is completely free from oil, grease, water or other fluid before installing the bolt or stud. Failure to do this could cause the housing to crack due to the hydraulic action of the bolt or stud as it is screwed in.

For some screw fastenings, notably cylinder head bolts or nuts, torque wrench settings are no longer specified for the latter stages of tightening, "angle-tightening" being called up instead. Typically, a fairly low torque wrench setting will be applied to the bolts/nuts in the correct sequence, followed by one or more stages of tightening through specified angles.

When checking or retightening a nut or bolt to a specified torque setting, slacken the nut or bolt by a quarter of a turn, and then retighten to the specified setting. However, this should not be attempted where angular tightening has been used.

## Locknuts, locktabs and washers

Any fastening which will rotate against a component or housing during tightening should always have a washer between it and the relevant component or housing.

Spring or split washers should always be renewed when they are used to lock a critical component such as a big-end bearing retaining bolt or nut. Locktabs which are folded over to retain a nut or bolt should always be renewed.

Self-locking nuts can be re-used in non-critical areas, providing resistance can be felt when the locking portion passes over the bolt or stud thread. However, it should be noted that self-locking stiffnuts tend to lose their effectiveness after long periods of use, and should then be renewed as a matter of course.

Split pins must always be replaced with new ones of the correct size for the hole.

When thread-locking compound is found on the threads of a fastener which is to be re-used, it should be cleaned off with a wire brush and solvent, and fresh compound applied on reassembly.

## Special tools

Some repair procedures in this manual entail the use of special tools such as a press, two or three-legged pullers, spring compressors, etc. Wherever possible, suitable readily-available alternatives to the manufacturer's special tools are described, and are shown in use. In some instances, where no alternative is possible, it has been necessary to resort to the use of a manufacturer's tool, and this has been done for reasons of safety as well as the efficient completion of the repair operation. Unless you are highly-skilled and have a thorough understanding of the procedures described, never attempt to bypass the use of any special tool when the procedure described specifies its use. Not only is there a very great risk of personal injury, but expensive damage could be caused to the components involved.

## Environmental considerations

When disposing of used engine oil, brake fluid, antifreeze, etc, give due consideration to any detrimental environmental effects. Do not, for instance, pour any of the above liquids down drains into the general sewage system, or onto the ground to soak away. Many local council refuse tips provide a facility for waste oil disposal, as do some garages. You can find your nearest disposal point by calling the Environment Agency on 08708 506 506 or by visiting www.oilbankline.org.uk.

**Note: It is illegal and anti-social to dump oil down the drain. To find the location of your local oil recycling bank, call 08708 506 506 or visit www.oilbankline.org.uk.**

The jack supplied with the vehicle should only be used for changing the roadwheels – see *Wheel changing* at the front of this manual. When carrying out any other kind of work, raise the vehicle using a hydraulic (or 'trolley') jack, and always supplement the jack with axle stands at the vehicle jacking points.

When using a hydraulic jack or axle stands, always position the jack head or axle stand head under one of the relevant jacking points; the jacking point is the area in below the cut-out on the sill **(see illustration)**. Use a block of wood between the jack or axle stand and the sill – the block of wood should have a groove cut into it, into which the welded flange of the sill will locate.

Do not attempt to jack the vehicle under the front crossmember, the sump, or any of the suspension components.

The jack supplied with the vehicle locates in the jacking points on the underside of the sills – see *Wheel changing*. Ensure that the jack head is correctly engaged before attempting to raise the vehicle.

**Never** work under, around, or near a raised vehicle, unless it is adequately supported in at least two places.

**The jacking and supporting point is indicated by a triangle on the sill**

### Introduction

A selection of good tools is a fundamental requirement for anyone contemplating the maintenance and repair of a motor vehicle. For the owner who does not possess any, their purchase will prove a considerable expense, offsetting some of the savings made by doing-it-yourself. However, provided that the tools purchased meet the relevant national safety standards and are of good quality, they will last for many years and prove an extremely worthwhile investment.

To help the average owner to decide which tools are needed to carry out the various tasks detailed in this manual, we have compiled three lists of tools under the following headings: *Maintenance and minor repair*, *Repair and overhaul*, and *Special*. Newcomers to practical mechanics should start off with the *Maintenance and minor repair* tool kit, and confine themselves to the simpler jobs around the vehicle. Then, as confidence and experience grow, more difficult tasks can be undertaken, with extra tools being purchased as, and when, they are needed. In this way, a *Maintenance and minor repair* tool kit can be built up into a *Repair and overhaul* tool kit over a considerable period of time, without any major cash outlays. The experienced do-it-yourselfer will have a tool kit good enough for most repair and overhaul procedures, and will add tools from the *Special* category when it is felt that the expense is justified by the amount of use to which these tools will be put.

### Maintenance and minor repair tool kit

The tools given in this list should be considered as a minimum requirement if routine maintenance, servicing and minor repair operations are to be undertaken. We recommend the purchase of combination spanners (ring one end, open-ended the other); although more expensive than open-ended ones, they do give the advantages of both types of spanner.

☐ *Combination spanners:*
  *Metric - 8 to 19 mm inclusive*
☐ *Adjustable spanner - 35 mm jaw (approx.)*
☐ *Spark plug spanner (with rubber insert) - petrol models*
☐ *Spark plug gap adjustment tool - petrol models*
☐ *Set of feeler gauges*
☐ *Brake bleed nipple spanner*
☐ *Screwdrivers:*
  *Flat blade - 100 mm long x 6 mm dia*
  *Cross blade - 100 mm long x 6 mm dia*
  *Torx - various sizes (not all vehicles)*
☐ *Combination pliers*
☐ *Hacksaw (junior)*
☐ *Tyre pump*
☐ *Tyre pressure gauge*
☐ *Oil can*
☐ *Oil filter removal tool (if applicable)*
☐ *Fine emery cloth*
☐ *Wire brush (small)*
☐ *Funnel (medium size)*
☐ *Sump drain plug key (not all vehicles)*

### Repair and overhaul tool kit

These tools are virtually essential for anyone undertaking any major repairs to a motor vehicle, and are additional to those given in the *Maintenance and minor repair* list. Included in this list is a comprehensive set of sockets. Although these are expensive, they will be found invaluable as they are so versatile - particularly if various drives are included in the set. We recommend the half-inch square-drive type, as this can be used with most proprietary torque wrenches.

The tools in this list will sometimes need to be supplemented by tools from the *Special* list:

☐ *Sockets to cover range in previous list (including Torx sockets)*
☐ *Reversible ratchet drive (for use with sockets)*
☐ *Extension piece, 250 mm (for use with sockets)*
☐ *Universal joint (for use with sockets)*
☐ *Flexible handle or sliding T "breaker bar" (for use with sockets)*
☐ *Torque wrench (for use with sockets)*
☐ *Self-locking grips*
☐ *Ball pein hammer*
☐ *Soft-faced mallet (plastic or rubber)*
☐ *Screwdrivers:*
  *Flat blade - long & sturdy, short (chubby), and narrow (electrician's) types*
  *Cross blade – long & sturdy, and short (chubby) types*
☐ *Pliers:*
  *Long-nosed*
  *Side cutters (electrician's)*
  *Circlip (internal and external)*
☐ *Cold chisel - 25 mm*
☐ *Scriber*
☐ *Scraper*
☐ *Centre-punch*
☐ *Pin punch*
☐ *Hacksaw*
☐ *Brake hose clamp*
☐ *Brake/clutch bleeding kit*
☐ *Selection of twist drills*
☐ *Steel rule/straight-edge*
☐ *Allen keys (inc. splined/Torx type)*
☐ *Selection of files*
☐ *Wire brush*
☐ *Axle stands*
☐ *Jack (strong trolley or hydraulic type)*
☐ *Light with extension lead*
☐ *Universal electrical multi-meter*

**Sockets and reversible ratchet drive**

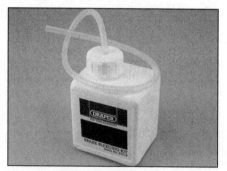

**Brake bleeding kit**

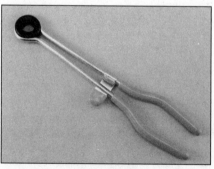

**Hose clamp**

**Angular-tightening gauge**

**Torx key, socket and bit**

## Special tools

The tools in this list are those which are not used regularly, are expensive to buy, or which need to be used in accordance with their manufacturers' instructions. Unless relatively difficult mechanical jobs are undertaken frequently, it will not be economic to buy many of these tools. Where this is the case, you could consider clubbing together with friends (or joining a motorists' club) to make a joint purchase, or borrowing the tools against a deposit from a local garage or tool hire specialist.

The following list contains only those tools and instruments freely available to the public, and not those special tools produced by the vehicle manufacturer specifically for its dealer network. You will find occasional references to these manufacturers' special tools in the text of this manual. Generally, an alternative method of doing the job without the vehicle manufacturers' special tool is given. However, sometimes there is no alternative to using them. Where this is the case and the relevant tool cannot be bought or borrowed, you will have to entrust the work to a dealer.

- ☐ Angular-tightening gauge
- ☐ Valve spring compressor
- ☐ Valve grinding tool
- ☐ Piston ring compressor
- ☐ Piston ring removal/installation tool
- ☐ Cylinder bore hone
- ☐ Balljoint separator
- ☐ Coil spring compressors (where applicable)
- ☐ Two/three-legged hub and bearing puller
- ☐ Impact screwdriver
- ☐ Micrometer and/or vernier calipers
- ☐ Dial gauge
- ☐ Tachometer
- ☐ Fault code reader
- ☐ Cylinder compression gauge
- ☐ Hand-operated vacuum pump and gauge
- ☐ Clutch plate alignment set
- ☐ Brake shoe steady spring cup removal tool
- ☐ Bush and bearing removal/installation set
- ☐ Stud extractors
- ☐ Tap and die set
- ☐ Lifting tackle

## Buying tools

Reputable motor accessory shops and superstores often offer excellent quality tools at discount prices, so it pays to shop around.

Remember, you don't have to buy the most expensive items on the shelf, but it is always advisable to steer clear of the very cheap tools. Beware of 'bargains' offered on market stalls, on-line or at car boot sales. There are plenty of good tools around at reasonable prices, but always aim to purchase items which meet the relevant national safety standards. If in doubt, ask the proprietor or manager of the shop for advice before making a purchase.

## Care and maintenance of tools

Having purchased a reasonable tool kit, it is necessary to keep the tools in a clean and serviceable condition. After use, always wipe off any dirt, grease and metal particles using a clean, dry cloth, before putting the tools away. Never leave them lying around after they have been used. A simple tool rack on the garage or workshop wall for items such as screwdrivers and pliers is a good idea. Store all normal spanners and sockets in a metal box. Any measuring instruments, gauges, meters, etc, must be carefully stored where they cannot be damaged or become rusty.

Take a little care when tools are used. Hammer heads inevitably become marked, and screwdrivers lose the keen edge on their blades from time to time. A little timely attention with emery cloth or a file will soon restore items like this to a good finish.

## Working facilities

Not to be forgotten when discussing tools is the workshop itself. If anything more than routine maintenance is to be carried out, a suitable working area becomes essential.

It is appreciated that many an owner-mechanic is forced by circumstances to remove an engine or similar item without the benefit of a garage or workshop. Having done this, any repairs should always be done under the cover of a roof.

Wherever possible, any dismantling should be done on a clean, flat workbench or table at a suitable working height.

Any workbench needs a vice; one with a jaw opening of 100 mm is suitable for most jobs. As mentioned previously, some clean dry storage space is also required for tools, as well as for any lubricants, cleaning fluids, touch-up paints etc, which become necessary.

Another item which may be required, and which has a much more general usage, is an electric drill with a chuck capacity of at least 8 mm. This, together with a good range of twist drills, is virtually essential for fitting accessories.

Last, but not least, always keep a supply of old newspapers and clean, lint-free rags available, and try to keep any working area as clean as possible.

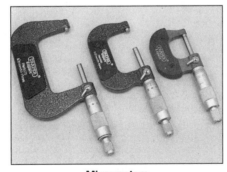

**Micrometers**

**Dial test indicator ("dial gauge")**

**Oil filter removal tool (strap wrench type)**

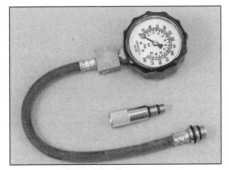

**Compression tester**

**Bearing puller**

This is a guide to getting your vehicle through the MOT test. Obviously it will not be possible to examine the vehicle to the same standard as the professional MOT tester. However, working through the following checks will enable you to identify any problem areas before submitting the vehicle for the test.

It has only been possible to summarise the test requirements here, based on the regulations in force at the time of printing. Test standards are becoming increasingly stringent, although there are some exemptions for older vehicles.

An assistant will be needed to help carry out some of these checks.

*The checks have been sub-divided into four categories, as follows:*

**1** Checks carried out **FROM THE DRIVER'S SEAT**

**2** Checks carried out **WITH THE VEHICLE ON THE GROUND**

**3** Checks carried out **WITH THE VEHICLE RAISED AND THE WHEELS FREE TO TURN**

**4** Checks carried out on **YOUR VEHICLE'S EXHAUST EMISSION SYSTEM**

---

**1** Checks carried out **FROM THE DRIVER'S SEAT**

### Handbrake (parking brake)

☐ Test the operation of the handbrake. Excessive travel (too many clicks) indicates incorrect brake or cable adjustment.
☐ Check that the handbrake cannot be released by tapping the lever sideways. Check the security of the lever mountings.

☐ If the parking brake is foot-operated, check that the pedal is secure and without excessive travel, and that the release mechanism operates correctly.
☐ Where applicable, test the operation of the electronic handbrake. The brake should engage and disengage without excessive delay. If the warning light does not extinguish when the brake is disengaged, this could indicate a fault which will need further investigation.

### Footbrake

☐ Depress the brake pedal and check that it does not creep down to the floor, indicating a master cylinder fault. Release the pedal,

wait a few seconds, then depress it again. If the pedal travels nearly to the floor before firm resistance is felt, brake adjustment or repair is necessary. If the pedal feels spongy, there is air in the hydraulic system which must be removed by bleeding.

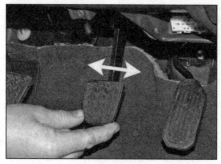

☐ Check that the brake pedal is secure and in good condition. Check also for signs of fluid leaks on the pedal, floor or carpets, which would indicate failed seals in the brake master cylinder.
☐ Check the servo unit (when applicable) by operating the brake pedal several times, then keeping the pedal depressed and starting the engine. As the engine starts, the pedal will move down slightly. If not, the vacuum hose or the servo itself may be faulty.

### Steering wheel and column

☐ Examine the steering wheel for fractures or looseness of the hub, spokes or rim.
☐ Move the steering wheel from side to side and then up and down. Check that the steering wheel is not loose on the column, indicating wear or a loose retaining nut. Continue moving the steering wheel as before, but also turn it slightly from left to right.

☐ Check that the steering wheel is not loose on the column, and that there is no abnormal movement of the steering wheel, indicating wear in the column support bearings or couplings.
☐ Check that the ignition lock (where fitted) engages and disengages correctly.
☐ Steering column adjustment mechanisms (where fitted) must be able to lock the column securely in place with no play evident.

### Windscreen, mirrors and sunvisor

☐ The windscreen must be free of cracks or other significant damage within the driver's field of view. (Small stone chips are acceptable.) Rear view mirrors must be secure, intact, and capable of being adjusted.

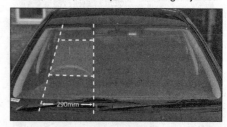

☐ The driver's sunvisor must be capable of being stored in the "up" position.

### Seat belts and seats

**Note:** *The following checks are applicable to all seat belts, front and rear.*

☐ Examine the webbing of all the belts (including rear belts if fitted) for cuts, serious fraying or deterioration. Fasten and unfasten each belt to check the buckles. If applicable, check the retracting mechanism. Check the security of all seat belt mountings accessible from inside the vehicle, ensuring any height adjustable mountings lock securely in place.

☐ Seat belts with pre-tensioners, once activated, have a "flag" or similar showing on the seat belt stalk. This, in itself, is not a reason for test failure.

☐ The front seats themselves must be securely attached and the backrests must lock in the upright position.

### Doors

☐ Both front doors must be able to be opened and closed from outside and inside, and must latch securely when closed.

### Bonnet and boot/tailgate

☐ The bonnet and boot/tailgate must latch securely when closed.

## 2 Checks carried out WITH THE VEHICLE ON THE GROUND

### Vehicle identification

☐ Number plates must be in good condition, secure and legible, with letters and numbers correctly spaced – spacing at (A) should be 33 mm and at (B) 11 mm. At the front, digits must be black on a white background and at the rear black on a yellow background. Other background designs (such as honeycomb) are not permitted.

☐ The VIN plate and/or homologation plate must be permanently displayed and legible.

### Electrical equipment

☐ Switch on the ignition and check the operation of the horn.

☐ Check the windscreen washers and wipers, examining the wiper blades; renew damaged or perished blades. Also check the operation of the stop-lights.

☐ Check the operation of the sidelights and number plate lights. The lenses and reflectors must be secure, clean and undamaged.

☐ Check the operation and alignment of the headlights. The headlight reflectors must not be tarnished and the lenses must be undamaged.

☐ Switch on the ignition and check the operation of the direction indicators (including the instrument panel tell-tale) and the hazard warning lights. Operation of the sidelights and stop-lights must not affect the indicators - if it does, the cause is usually a bad earth at the rear light cluster. Indicators should flash at a rate of between 60 and 120 times per minute – faster or slower than this could indicate a fault with the flasher unit or a bad earth at one of the light units.

☐ Check the operation of the rear foglight(s), including the warning light on the instrument panel or in the switch.

☐ The ABS warning light must illuminate in accordance with the manufacturers' design. For most vehicles, the ABS warning light should illuminate when the ignition is switched on, and (if the system is operating properly) extinguish after a few seconds. Refer to the owner's handbook.

### Footbrake

☐ Examine the master cylinder, brake pipes and servo unit for leaks, loose mountings, corrosion or other damage. If ABS is fitted, this unit should also be examined for signs of leaks or corrosion.

☐ The fluid reservoir must be secure and the fluid level must be between the upper (A) and lower (B) markings.

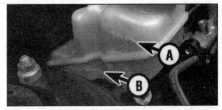

☐ Inspect both front brake flexible hoses for cracks or deterioration of the rubber. Turn the steering from lock to lock, and ensure that the hoses do not contact the wheel, tyre, or any part of the steering or suspension mechanism. With the brake pedal firmly depressed, check the hoses for bulges or leaks under pressure.

### Steering and suspension

☐ Have your assistant turn the steering wheel from side to side slightly, up to the point where the steering gear just begins to transmit this movement to the roadwheels. Check for excessive free play between the steering wheel and the steering gear, indicating wear or insecurity of the steering column joints, the column-to-steering gear coupling, or the steering gear itself.

☐ Have your assistant turn the steering wheel more vigorously in each direction, so that the roadwheels just begin to turn. As this is done, examine all the steering joints, linkages, fittings and attachments. Renew any component that shows signs of wear or damage. On vehicles with power steering, check the security and condition of the steering pump, drivebelt and hoses.

☐ Check that the vehicle is standing level, and at approximately the correct ride height.

### Shock absorbers

☐ Depress each corner of the vehicle in turn, then release it. The vehicle should rise and then settle in its normal position. If the vehicle continues to rise and fall, the shock absorber is defective. A shock absorber which has seized will also cause the vehicle to fail.

## Exhaust system

☐ Start the engine. With your assistant holding a rag over the tailpipe, check the entire system for leaks. Repair or renew leaking sections.

**3** Checks carried out **WITH THE VEHICLE RAISED AND THE WHEELS FREE TO TURN**

*Jack up the front and rear of the vehicle, and securely support it on axle stands. Position the stands clear of the suspension assemblies. Ensure that the wheels are clear of the ground and that the steering can be turned from lock to lock.*

## Steering mechanism

☐ Have your assistant turn the steering from lock to lock. Check that the steering turns smoothly, and that no part of the steering mechanism, including a wheel or tyre, fouls any brake hose or pipe or any part of the body structure.
☐ Examine the steering rack rubber gaiters for damage or insecurity of the retaining clips. If power steering is fitted, check for signs of damage or leakage of the fluid hoses, pipes or connections. Also check for excessive stiffness or binding of the steering, a missing split pin or locking device, or severe corrosion of the body structure within 30 cm of any steering component attachment point.

## Front and rear suspension and wheel bearings

☐ Starting at the front right-hand side, grasp the roadwheel at the 3 o'clock and 9 o'clock positions and rock gently but firmly. Check for free play or insecurity at the wheel bearings, suspension balljoints, or suspension mount-ings, pivots and attachments.
☐ Now grasp the wheel at the 12 o'clock and 6 o'clock positions and repeat the previous inspection. Spin the wheel, and check for roughness or tightness of the front wheel bearing.

☐ If excess free play is suspected at a component pivot point, this can be confirmed by using a large screwdriver or similar tool and levering between the mounting and the component attachment. This will confirm whether the wear is in the pivot bush, its retaining bolt, or in the mounting itself (the bolt holes can often become elongated).

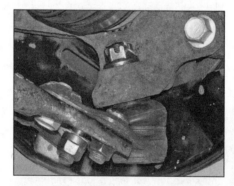

☐ Carry out all the above checks at the other front wheel, and then at both rear wheels.

## Springs and shock absorbers

☐ Examine the suspension struts (when applicable) for serious fluid leakage, corrosion, or damage to the casing. Also check the security of the mounting points.
☐ If coil springs are fitted, check that the spring ends locate in their seats, and that the spring is not corroded, cracked or broken.
☐ If leaf springs are fitted, check that all leaves are intact, that the axle is securely attached to each spring, and that there is no deterioration of the spring eye mountings, bushes, and shackles.

☐ The same general checks apply to vehicles fitted with other suspension types, such as torsion bars, hydraulic displacer units, etc. Ensure that all mountings and attachments are secure, that there are no signs of excessive wear, corrosion or damage, and (on hydraulic types) that there are no fluid leaks or damaged pipes.
☐ Inspect the shock absorbers for signs of serious fluid leakage. Check for wear of the mounting bushes or attachments, or damage to the body of the unit.

## Driveshafts (fwd vehicles only)

☐ Rotate each front wheel in turn and inspect the constant velocity joint gaiters for splits or damage. Also check that each driveshaft is straight and undamaged.

## Braking system

☐ If possible without dismantling, check brake pad wear and disc condition. Ensure that the friction lining material has not worn excessively, (A) and that the discs are not fractured, pitted, scored or badly worn (B).

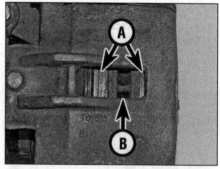

☐ Examine all the rigid brake pipes underneath the vehicle, and the flexible hose(s) at the rear. Look for corrosion, chafing or insecurity of the pipes, and for signs of bulging under pressure, chafing, splits or deterioration of the flexible hoses.
☐ Look for signs of fluid leaks at the brake calipers or on the brake backplates. Repair or renew leaking components.
☐ Slowly spin each wheel, while your assistant depresses and releases the footbrake. Ensure that each brake is operating and does not bind when the pedal is released.

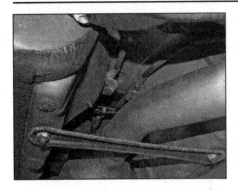

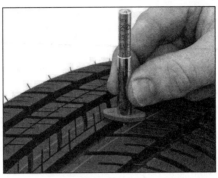

□Examine the handbrake mechanism, checking for frayed or broken cables, excessive corrosion, or wear or insecurity of the linkage. Check that the mechanism works on each relevant wheel, and releases fully, without binding.

□It is not possible to test brake efficiency without special equipment, but a road test can be carried out later to check that the vehicle pulls up in a straight line.

## Fuel and exhaust systems

□Inspect the fuel tank (including the filler cap), fuel pipes, hoses and unions. All components must be secure and free from leaks. Locking fuel caps must lock securely and the key must be provided for the MOT test.

□Examine the exhaust system over its entire length, checking for any damaged, broken or missing mountings, security of the retaining clamps and rust or corrosion.

## Wheels and tyres

□Examine the sidewalls and tread area of each tyre in turn. Check for cuts, tears, lumps, bulges, separation of the tread, and exposure of the ply or cord due to wear or damage. Check that the tyre bead is correctly seated on the wheel rim, that the valve is sound and properly seated, and that the wheel is not distorted or damaged.

□Check that the tyres are of the correct size for the vehicle, that they are of the same size and type on each axle, and that the pressures are correct.

□Check the tyre tread depth. The legal minimum at the time of writing is 1.6 mm over the central three-quarters of the tread width. Abnormal tread wear may indicate incorrect front wheel alignment or wear in steering or suspension components.

□If the spare wheel is fitted externally or in a separate carrier beneath the vehicle, check that mountings are secure and free of excessive corrosion.

## Body corrosion

□Check the condition of the entire vehicle structure for signs of corrosion in load-bearing areas. (These include chassis box sections, side sills, cross-members, pillars, and all suspension, steering, braking system and seat belt mountings and anchorages.) Any corrosion which has seriously reduced the thickness of a load-bearing area (or is within 30 cm of safety-related components such as steering or suspension) is likely to cause the vehicle to fail. In this case professional repairs are likely to be needed.

□Damage or corrosion which causes sharp or otherwise dangerous edges to be exposed will also cause the vehicle to fail.

## Towbars

□Check the condition of mounting points (both beneath the vehicle and within boot/hatchback areas) for signs of corrosion, ensuring that all fixings are secure and not worn or damaged. There must be no excessive play in detachable tow ball arms or quick-release mechanisms.

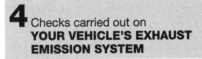

**4** Checks carried out on **YOUR VEHICLE'S EXHAUST EMISSION SYSTEM**

## Petrol models

□The engine should be warmed up, and running well (ignition system in good order, air filter element clean, etc).

□Before testing, run the engine at around 2500 rpm for 20 seconds. Let the engine drop to idle, and watch for smoke from the exhaust. If the idle speed is too high, or if dense blue or black smoke emerges for more than 5 seconds, the vehicle will fail. Typically, blue smoke signifies oil burning (engine wear); black smoke means unburnt fuel (dirty air cleaner element, or other fuel system fault).

□An exhaust gas analyser for measuring carbon monoxide (CO) and hydrocarbons (HC) is now needed. If one cannot be hired or borrowed, have a local garage perform the check.

## CO emissions (mixture)

□The MOT tester has access to the CO limits for all vehicles. The CO level is measured at idle speed, and at 'fast idle' (2500 to 3000 rpm). The following limits are given as a general guide:

*At idle speed* – Less than 0.5% CO
*At 'fast idle'* – Less than 0.3% CO
*Lambda reading* – 0.97 to 1.03

□If the CO level is too high, this may point to poor maintenance, a fuel injection system problem, faulty lambda (oxygen) sensor or catalytic converter. Try an injector cleaning treatment, and check the vehicle's ECU for fault codes.

## HC emissions

□The MOT tester has access to HC limits for all vehicles. The HC level is measured at 'fast idle' (2500 to 3000 rpm). The following limits are given as a general guide:

*At 'fast idle'* – Less then 200 ppm

□Excessive HC emissions are typically caused by oil being burnt (worn engine), or by a blocked crankcase ventilation system ('breather'). If the engine oil is old and thin, an oil change may help. If the engine is running badly, check the vehicle's ECU for fault codes.

## Diesel models

□The only emission test for diesel engines is measuring exhaust smoke density, using a calibrated smoke meter. The test involves accelerating the engine at least 3 times to its maximum unloaded speed.

**Note:** *On engines with a timing belt, it is VITAL that the belt is in good condition before the test is carried out.*

□With the engine warmed up, it is first purged by running at around 2500 rpm for 20 seconds. A governor check is then carried out, by slowly accelerating the engine to its maximum speed. After this, the smoke meter is connected, and the engine is accelerated quickly to maximum speed three times. If the smoke density is less than the limits given below, the vehicle will pass:

*Non-turbo vehicles*: 2.5m-1
*Turbocharged vehicles*: 3.0m-1

□If excess smoke is produced, try fitting a new air cleaner element, or using an injector cleaning treatment. If the engine is running badly, where applicable, check the vehicle's ECU for fault codes. Also check the vehicle's EGR system, where applicable. At high mileages, the injectors may require professional attention.

## Engine

- ☐ Engine fails to rotate when attempting to start
- ☐ Engine rotates, but will not start
- ☐ Engine difficult to start when cold
- ☐ Eng ine difficult to start when hot
- ☐ Starter motor noisy or excessively-rough in engagement
- ☐ Engine starts, but stops immediately
- ☐ Engine idles erratically
- ☐ Engine misfires at idle speed
- ☐ Engine misfires throughout the driving speed range
- ☐ Engine hesitates on acceleration
- ☐ Engine stalls
- ☐ Engine lacks power
- ☐ Engine backfires
- ☐ Oil pressure warning light on with engine running
- ☐ Engine runs-on after switching off
- ☐ Engine noises

## Cooling system

- ☐ Overheating
- ☐ Overcooling
- ☐ External coolant leakage
- ☐ Internal coolant leakage
- ☐ Corrosion

## Fuel and exhaust systems

- ☐ Excessive fuel consumption
- ☐ Fuel leakage and/or fuel odour
- ☐ Excessive noise or fumes from exhaust system

## Clutch

- ☐ Pedal travels to floor – no pressure or very little resistance
- ☐ Clutch fails to disengage (unable to select gears)
- ☐ Clutch slips (engine speed rises, with no increase in vehicle speed)
- ☐ Judder as clutch is engaged
- ☐ Noise when depressing or releasing clutch pedal

## Manual transmission

- ☐ Noisy in neutral with engine running
- ☐ Noisy in one particular gear
- ☐ Difficulty engaging gears
- ☐ Jumps out of gear
- ☐ Vibration
- ☐ Lubricant leaks

## Automatic transmission

- ☐ Fluid leakage
- ☐ Transmission fluid brown, or has burned smell
- ☐ General gear selection problems
- ☐ Transmission will not downshift (kickdown) on full throttle
- ☐ Engine won't start in any gear, or starts in gears other than P or N
- ☐ Transmission slips, shifts roughly, is noisy, or has no drive in forward or reverse gears

## Driveshafts

- ☐ Clicking or knocking noise on turns (at slow speed on full-lock)
- ☐ Vibration when accelerating or decelerating

## Braking system

- ☐ Vehicle pulls to one side under braking
- ☐ Noise (grinding or high-pitched squeal) when brakes applied
- ☐ Excessive brake pedal travel
- ☐ Brake pedal feels spongy when depressed
- ☐ Excessive brake pedal effort required to stop vehicle
- ☐ Judder felt through brake pedal or steering wheel when braking
- ☐ Brakes binding
- ☐ Rear wheels locking under normal braking

## Suspension and steering systems

- ☐ Vehicle pulls to one side
- ☐ Wheel wobble and vibration
- ☐ Excessive pitching and/or rolling around corners, or during braking
- ☐ Wandering or general instability
- ☐ Excessively-stiff steering
- ☐ Excessive play in steering
- ☐ Lack of power assistance
- ☐ Tyre wear excessive

## Electrical system

- ☐ Battery will not hold a charge for more than a few days
- ☐ Ignition/no-charge warning light stays on with engine running
- ☐ Ignition/no-charge warning light fails to come on
- ☐ Lights inoperative
- ☐ Instrument readings inaccurate or erratic
- ☐ Horn inoperative, or unsatisfactory in operation
- ☐ Windscreen/tailgate wipers failed, or unsatisfactory in operation
- ☐ Windscreen/tailgate washers failed, or unsatisfactory in operation
- ☐ Electric windows inoperative, or unsatisfactory in operation
- ☐ Central locking system inoperative, or unsatisfactory in operation

# Introduction

The vehicle owner who does his or her own maintenance according to the recommended service schedules should not have to use this section of the manual very often. Modern component reliability is such that, provided those items subject to wear or deterioration are inspected or renewed at the specified intervals, sudden failure is comparatively rare. Faults do not usually just happen as a result of sudden failure, but develop over a period of time. Major mechanical failures in particular are usually preceded by characteristic symptoms over hundreds or even thousands of miles. Those components which do occasionally fail without warning are often small and easily carried in the vehicle.

With any fault-finding, the first step is to decide where to begin investigations. Sometimes this is obvious, but on other occasions, a little detective work will be necessary. The owner who makes half a dozen haphazard adjustments or replacements may be successful in curing a fault (or its symptoms), but will be none the wiser if the fault recurs, and ultimately may have spent more time and money than was necessary. A calm and logical approach will be found to be more satisfactory in the long run. Always take into account any warning signs or abnormalities that may have been noticed in the period preceding the fault – power loss, high or low gauge readings, unusual smells, etc – and remember that failure of components such as fuses or spark plugs may only be pointers to some underlying fault.

The pages which follow provide an easy-reference guide to the more common problems which may occur during the operation of the vehicle. These problems and their possible causes are grouped under headings denoting various components or systems, such as Engine, Cooling system, etc. The general Chapter which deals with the problem is also shown in brackets; refer to the relevant part of that Chapter for system-specific information. Whatever the fault, certain basic principles apply. These are as follows:

*Verify the fault.* This is simply a matter of being sure that you know what the symptoms are before starting work. This is particularly important if you are investigating a fault for someone else, who may not have described it very accurately.

*Don't overlook the obvious.* For example, if the vehicle won't start, is there fuel in the tank? (Don't take anyone else's word on this particular point, and don't trust the fuel gauge either!) If an electrical fault is indicated, look for loose or broken wires before digging out the test gear.

*Cure the disease, not the symptom.* Substituting a flat battery with a fully-charged one will get you off the hard shoulder, but if the underlying cause is not attended to, the new battery will go the same way. Similarly, changing oil-fouled spark plugs (petrol models) for a new set will get you moving again, but remember that the reason for the fouling (if it wasn't simply an incorrect grade of plug) will have to be found and corrected.

*Don't take anything for granted.* Particularly, don't forget that a 'new' component may itself be defective (especially if it's been rattling around in the boot for months), and don't leave components out of a fault diagnosis sequence just because they are new or recently-fitted. When you do finally diagnose a difficult fault, you'll probably realise that all the evidence was there from the start.

## *Diesel fault diagnosis*

The majority of starting problems on small diesel engines are electrical in origin. The mechanic who is familiar with petrol engines but less so with diesel may be inclined to view the diesel's injectors and pump in the same light as the spark plugs and distributor, but this is generally a mistake.

When investigating complaints of difficult starting for someone else, make sure that the correct starting procedure is understood and is being followed. Some drivers are unaware of the significance of the preheating warning light – many modern engines are sufficiently forgiving for this not to matter in mild weather, but with the onset of winter, problems begin. Glow plugs in particular are often neglected – just one faulty plug will make cold-weather starting very difficult.

As a rule of thumb, if the engine is difficult to start but runs well when it has finally got going, the problem is electrical (battery, starter motor or preheating system). If poor performance is combined with difficult starting, the problem is likely to be in the fuel system. The low-pressure (supply) side of the fuel system should be checked before suspecting the injectors and high-pressure pump. The most common fuel supply problem is air getting into the system, and any pipe from the fuel tank forwards must be scrutinised if air leakage is suspected.

# Engine

### Engine fails to rotate when attempting to start

- ☐ Battery terminal connections loose or corroded (*Weekly checks*).
- ☐ Battery discharged or faulty (Chapter 5A).
- ☐ Broken, loose or disconnected wiring in the starting circuit (Chapter 5A).
- ☐ Defective starter motor (Chapter 5A).
- ☐ Starter pinion or flywheel/driveplate ring gear teeth loose or broken (Chapter 2A, 2B, 2C and 5A).
- ☐ Engine earth strap broken or disconnected (Chapter 5A and 12).

### Engine rotates, but will not start

- ☐ Fuel tank empty.
- ☐ Battery discharged (engine rotates slowly) (Chapter 5A).
- ☐ Battery terminal connections loose or corroded (*Weekly checks*).
- ☐ Worn, faulty or incorrectly-gapped spark plugs – petrol models (Chapter 1A).
- ☐ Pre/post-heating system faulty – diesel models (Chapter 5C).
- ☐ Engine management system fault (Chapter 4A or 4B).
- ☐ Air in fuel system – diesel models (Chapter 4B).
- ☐ High pressure fuel system fault – diesel models (Chapter 4B).
- ☐ Low cylinder compressions (Chapter 2A, 2B or 2C).
- ☐ Major mechanical failure (eg camshaft drive) (Chapter 2A, 2B or 2C).

### Engine difficult to start when cold

- ☐ Battery discharged (Chapter 5A).
- ☐ Battery terminal connections loose or corroded (*Weekly checks*).
- ☐ Worn, faulty or incorrectly-gapped spark plugs – petrol models (Chapter 1A).
- ☐ Pre/post-heating system faulty – diesel models (Chapter 5C).
- ☐ Engine management system fault (Chapter 4A or 4B).
- ☐ High pressure fuel system fault – diesel models (Chapter 4B).
- ☐ Low cylinder compressions (Chapter 2A, 2B or 2C).

### Engine difficult to start when hot

- ☐ Engine management system fault (Chapter 4A or 4B).
- ☐ High pressure fuel system fault – diesel models (Chapter 4B).
- ☐ Low cylinder compressions (Chapter 2A, 2B or 2C).

### Starter motor noisy or excessively-rough in engagement

- ☐ Starter pinion or flywheel/driveplate ring gear teeth loose or broken (Chapter 2A, 2B, 2C and 5A).
- ☐ Starter motor mounting bolts loose or missing (Chapter 5A).
- ☐ Defective starter motor (Chapter 5A).

### Engine starts, but stops immediately

- ☐ Vacuum leak at the throttle housing/inlet manifold – petrol models (Chapter 4A).
- ☐ Engine management system fault (Chapter 4A or 4B).
- ☐ Air in fuel system – diesel models (Chapter 4B).
- ☐ High pressure fuel system fault – diesel models (Chapter 4B).

### Engine idles erratically

- ☐ Vacuum leak at the throttle housing/inlet manifold – petrol models (Chapter 4A).
- ☐ Worn, faulty or incorrectly-gapped spark plugs – petrol models (Chapter 1A).
- ☐ Engine management system fault (Chapter 4A or 4B).
- ☐ Air in fuel system – diesel models (Chapter 4B).
- ☐ High pressure fuel system fault – diesel models (Chapter 4B).
- ☐ Uneven or low cylinder compressions (Chapter 2A, 2B or 2C).
- ☐ Camshaft lobes worn (Chapter 2A, 2B or 2C).
- ☐ Timing belt/chain incorrectly fitted (Chapter 2A, 2B or 2C).

### Engine misfires at idle speed

- ☐ Worn, faulty or incorrectly-gapped spark plugs – petrol models (Chapter 1A).
- ☐ Vacuum leak at the throttle housing/inlet manifold – petrol models (Chapter 4A).
- ☐ Engine management system fault (Chapter 4A or 4B).
- ☐ High pressure fuel system fault – diesel models (Chapter 4B).
- ☐ Uneven or low cylinder compressions (Chapter 2A, 2B or 2C).
- ☐ Disconnected, leaking, or perished crankcase ventilation hoses (Chapter 4C).

### Engine misfires throughout the driving speed range

- ☐ Fuel filter blocked (Chapter 1A or 1B).
- ☐ Fuel pump faulty – petrol models (Chapter 4A).
- ☐ Fuel tank vent blocked, or fuel pipes restricted (Chapter 4A or 4B).
- ☐ Worn, faulty or incorrectly-gapped spark plugs – petrol models (Chapter 1A).
- ☐ Vacuum leak at the throttle housing/inlet manifold – petrol models (Chapter 4A).
- ☐ Engine management system fault (Chapter 4A or 4B).
- ☐ High pressure fuel system fault – diesel models (Chapter 4B).
- ☐ Faulty ignition HT coil – petrol models (Chapter 5B).
- ☐ Uneven or low cylinder compressions (Chapter 2A, 2B or 2C).

# Engine (continued)

### Engine hesitates on acceleration

☐ Worn, faulty or incorrectly-gapped spark plugs – petrol models (Chapter 1A).
☐ Vacuum leak at the throttle housing/inlet manifold – petrol models (Chapter 4A).
☐ Engine management system fault (Chapter 4A or 4B).
☐ High pressure fuel system fault – diesel models (Chapter 4B).

### Engine stalls

☐ Fuel filter blocked (Chapter 1A or 1B).
☐ Fuel pump faulty – petrol models (Chapter 4A).
☐ Fuel tank vent blocked, or fuel pipes restricted (Chapter 4A or 4B).
☐ Worn, faulty or incorrectly-gapped spark plugs – petrol models (Chapter 1A).
☐ Vacuum leak at the throttle housing/inlet manifold – petrol models (Chapter 4A).
☐ Engine management system fault (Chapter 4A or 4B).
☐ High pressure fuel system fault – diesel models (Chapter 4B).

### Engine lacks power

☐ Timing belt/chain incorrectly fitted (Chapter 2A, 2B or 2C).
☐ Fuel filter blocked (Chapter 1A or 1B).
☐ Fuel pump faulty – petrol models (Chapter 4A).
☐ Uneven or low cylinder compressions (Chapter 2A, 2B or 2C).
☐ Worn, faulty or incorrectly-gapped spark plugs – petrol models (Chapter 1A).
☐ Vacuum leak at the throttle housing/inlet manifold – petrol models (Chapter 4A).
☐ Engine management system fault (Chapter 4A or 4B).
☐ High pressure fuel system fault – diesel models (Chapter 4B).
☐ Brakes binding (Chapter 1A, 1B and 9).
☐ Clutch slipping (Chapter 6).

### Engine backfires

☐ Timing belt/chain incorrectly fitted (Chapter 2A, 2B or 2C).
☐ Vacuum leak at the throttle housing/inlet manifold – petrol models (Chapter 4A).
☐ Engine management system fault (Chapter 4A or 4B).

### Oil pressure warning light on with engine running

☐ Low oil level, or incorrect oil grade (Weekly checks).

☐ Faulty oil pressure warning light switch (Chapter 5A).
☐ Worn engine bearings and/or oil pump (Chapter 2D).
☐ High engine operating temperature (Chapter 3).
☐ Oil pressure relief valve defective (Chapter 2A, 2B or 2C).
☐ Oil pick-up strainer clogged (Chapter 2A, 2B or 2C).

### Engine runs-on after switching off

☐ Excessive carbon build-up in engine (Chapter 2A, 2B, 2C or 2D).
☐ High engine operating temperature (Chapter 3).
☐ Engine management system fault (Chapter 4A or 4B).
☐ High pressure fuel system fault – diesel models (Chapter 4B).

### Engine noises

#### Pre-ignition (pinking) or knocking during acceleration or under load

☐ Engine management system fault (Chapter 4A or 4B).
☐ Incorrect grade of spark plug – petrol models (Chapter 1A).
☐ Incorrect grade of fuel – petrol models (Chapter 4A).
☐ Vacuum leak at the throttle housing/inlet manifold – petrol models (Chapter 4A).
☐ Excessive carbon build-up in engine (Chapter 2A, 2B, 2C or 2D).

#### Whistling or wheezing noises

☐ Leaking inlet manifold or throttle housing gasket – petrol models (Chapter 4A).
☐ Leaking vacuum hose (Chapters 4A, 4B, 4C and 9).
☐ Blowing cylinder head gasket (Chapter 2A, 2B or 2C).

#### Tapping or rattling noises

☐ Worn valve gear or camshaft (Chapter 2A, 2B or 2C).
☐ Ancillary component fault (coolant pump, alternator, etc) (Chapters 3, 5A, etc).

#### Knocking or thumping noises

☐ Worn big-end bearings (regular heavy knocking, perhaps less under load) (Chapter 2D).
☐ Worn main bearings (rumbling and knocking, perhaps worsening under load) (Chapter 2D).
☐ Piston slap (most noticeable when cold) (Chapter 2D).
☐ Ancillary component fault (coolant pump, alternator, etc) (Chapters 3, 5A, etc).

# Cooling system

### Overheating

- [ ] Insufficient coolant in system (*Weekly checks*).
- [ ] Thermostat faulty (stuck closed) (Chapter 3).
- [ ] Radiator core blocked, or grille restricted (Chapter 3).
- [ ] Electric cooling fan or sensor faulty (Chapter 3).
- [ ] Pressure cap faulty (Chapter 3).
- [ ] Inaccurate temperature gauge/sensor (Chapter 3).
- [ ] Airlock in cooling system (Chapter 1A or 1B).
- [ ] Engine management system fault (Chapter 4A or 4B).

### Overcooling

- [ ] Thermostat faulty (stuck open) (Chapter 3).
- [ ] Inaccurate temperature gauge/sensor (Chapter 3).

### External coolant leakage

- [ ] Deteriorated or damaged hoses or hose clips (Chapter 1A or 1B).
- [ ] Radiator core or heater matrix leaking (Chapter 3).
- [ ] Pressure cap faulty (Chapter 3).
- [ ] Coolant pump leaking (Chapter 3).
- [ ] Boiling due to overheating (Chapter 3).
- [ ] Core plug leaking (Chapter 2D).

### Internal coolant leakage

- [ ] Leaking cylinder head gasket (Chapter 2A or 2B).
- [ ] Cracked cylinder head or cylinder bore (Chapter 2A, 2B or 2C).

### Corrosion

- [ ] Infrequent draining and flushing (Chapter 1A or 1B).
- [ ] Incorrect coolant mixture or inappropriate coolant type (Chapter 1A or 1B).

# Fuel and exhaust systems

### Excessive fuel consumption

- [ ] Air filter element dirty or clogged (Chapter 1A or 1B).
- [ ] Engine management system fault (Chapter 4A or 4B).
- [ ] High pressure fuel system fault – diesel models (Chapter 4B).
- [ ] Tyres under-inflated (*Weekly checks*).
- [ ] Brakes binding (Chapters 1A, 1B and 9).

### Fuel leakage and/or fuel odour

- [ ] Damaged or corroded fuel tank, pipes or connections (Chapter 4A or 4B).

### Excessive noise or fumes from exhaust system

- [ ] Leaking exhaust system or manifold joints (Chapters 1A or 1B and 4A or 4B).
- [ ] Leaking, corroded or damaged silencers or pipe (Chapters 1A or 1B and 4A or 4B).
- [ ] Broken mountings causing body or suspension contact (Chapters 1A or 1B and 4A or 4B).

# Clutch

### Pedal travels to floor – no pressure or very little resistance

- ☐ Air in hydraulic system/faulty master or slave cylinder (Chapter 6).
- ☐ Broken clutch release bearing or fork (Chapter 6).
- ☐ Broken diaphragm spring in clutch pressure plate (Chapter 6).

### Clutch fails to disengage (unable to select gears)

- ☐ Air in hydraulic system/faulty master or slave cylinder (Chapter 6).
- ☐ Clutch disc sticking on gearbox input shaft splines (Chapter 6).
- ☐ Clutch disc sticking to flywheel or pressure plate (Chapter 6).
- ☐ Faulty pressure plate assembly (Chapter 6).
- ☐ Clutch release mechanism worn or incorrectly assembled (Chapter 6).

### Clutch slips (engine speed rises, with no increase in vehicle speed)

- ☐ Faulty hydraulic release system (Chapter 6).
- ☐ Clutch disc linings excessively worn (Chapter 6).
- ☐ Clutch disc linings contaminated with oil or grease (Chapter 6).
- ☐ Faulty pressure plate or weak diaphragm spring (Chapter 6).

### Judder as clutch is engaged

- ☐ Clutch disc linings contaminated with oil or grease (Chapter 6).
- ☐ Clutch disc linings excessively worn (Chapter 6).
- ☐ Faulty or distorted pressure plate or diaphragm spring (Chapter 6).
- ☐ Worn or loose engine or gearbox mountings (Chapter 2A, 2B or 2C).
- ☐ Clutch disc hub or gearbox input shaft splines worn (Chapter 6).

### Noise when depressing or releasing clutch pedal

- ☐ Worn clutch release bearing (Chapter 6).
- ☐ Worn or dry clutch pedal bushes (Chapter 6).
- ☐ Faulty pressure plate assembly (Chapter 6).
- ☐ Pressure plate diaphragm spring broken (Chapter 6).
- ☐ Broken clutch disc cushioning springs (Chapter 6).

# Manual transmission

### Noisy in neutral with engine running

- ☐ Input shaft bearings worn (noise apparent with clutch pedal released, but not when depressed) (Chapter 7A).*
- ☐ Clutch release bearing worn (noise apparent with clutch pedal depressed, possibly less when released) (Chapter 6).

### Noisy in one particular gear

- ☐ Worn, damaged or chipped gear teeth (Chapter 7A).*

### Difficulty engaging gears

- ☐ Clutch fault (Chapter 6).
- ☐ Worn or damaged gear selection cables (Chapter 7A).
- ☐ Worn synchroniser units (Chapter 7A).*

### Jumps out of gear

- ☐ Worn or damaged gear selection cables (Chapter 7A).
- ☐ Worn synchroniser units (Chapter 7A).*
- ☐ Worn selector forks (Chapter 7A).*

### Vibration

- ☐ Lack of oil (Chapters 1A, 1B and 7A).
- ☐ Worn bearings (Chapter 7A).*

### Lubricant leaks

- ☐ Leaking differential output oil seal (Chapter 7A).
- ☐ Leaking housing joint (Chapter 7A).*
- ☐ Leaking input shaft oil seal (Chapter 7A).

*Although the corrective action necessary to remedy the symptoms described is beyond the scope of the home mechanic, the above information should be helpful in isolating the cause of the condition, so that the owner can communicate clearly with a professional mechanic.*

# Automatic transmission

**Note:** *Due to the complexity of the automatic transmission, it is difficult for the home mechanic to properly diagnose and service this unit. For problems other than the following, the vehicle should be taken to a Citroën dealer service department or suitably equipped specialist.*

### Fluid leakage

☐ Automatic transmission fluid is usually dark in colour. Fluid leaks should not be confused with engine oil, which can easily be blown onto the transmission by airflow.

☐ To determine the source of a leak, first remove all built-up dirt and grime from the transmission housing and surrounding areas using a degreasing agent, or by steam-cleaning. Drive the vehicle at low speed, so airflow will not blow the leak far from its source. Raise and support the vehicle, and determine where the leak is coming from.

### Transmission fluid brown, or has burned smell

☐ Transmission fluid level low, or fluid in need of renewal (Chapter 1A and 7B).

### General gear selection problems

☐ Chapter 7B deals with checking and adjusting the selector cable on automatic transmissions. The following are common problems which may be caused by a poorly-adjusted cable:

a) Engine starting in gears other than Park or Neutral.
b) Indicator panel showing a gear other than that being used.
c) Vehicle moves when in Park or Neutral.
d) Poor gear shift quality or erratic gear changes.
☐ Refer to Chapter 7B for the selector cable adjustment procedure.

### Transmission will not downshift (kickdown) at full throttle

☐ Low transmission fluid level (Chapter 1A).
☐ Incorrect selector cable adjustment (Chapter 7B).

### Engine won't start in any gear, or starts in gears other than Park or Neutral

☐ Incorrect multi-function switch adjustment (Chapter 7B).
☐ Incorrect selector cable adjustment (Chapter 7B).

### Transmission slips, shifts roughly, is noisy, or has no drive in forward or reverse gears

☐ There are many probable causes for the above problems, but the home mechanic should be concerned with only one possibility – fluid level. Before taking the vehicle to a dealer or transmission specialist, check the fluid level as described in Chapter 1A. Correct the fluid level as necessary, or change the fluid. If the problem persists, professional help will be necessary.

# Driveshafts

### Clicking or knocking noise on turns (at slow speed on full-lock)

☐ Lack of constant velocity joint lubricant, possibly due to damaged gaiter (Chapter 8).
☐ Worn outer constant velocity joint (Chapter 8).

### Vibration when accelerating or decelerating

☐ Worn inner constant velocity joint (Chapter 8).
☐ Bent or distorted driveshaft (Chapter 8).
☐ Worn intermediate bearing (where fitted) (Chapter 8).

# Braking system

**Note:** *Before assuming that a brake problem exists, make sure that the tyres are in good condition and correctly inflated, that the front wheel alignment is correct, and that the vehicle is not loaded with weight in an unequal manner. Apart from checking the condition of all pipe and hose connections, any faults occurring on the anti-lock braking system should be referred to a Citroën dealer for diagnosis.*

## Vehicle pulls to one side under braking

☐ Worn, defective, damaged or contaminated brake pads/shoes on one side (Chapter 9).
☐ Seized or partially-seized front brake caliper (Chapter 9).
☐ A mixture of brake pad/shoe materials fitted between sides (Chapter 9).
☐ Brake caliper mounting bolts loose (Chapter 9).
☐ Worn or damaged steering or suspension components (Chapters 1A, 1B and 10).

## Noise (grinding or high-pitched squeal) when brakes applied

☐ Brake pad/shoe material worn down to metal backing (Chapters 1A, 1B and 9).
☐ Excessive corrosion of brake disc/drum. May be apparent after the vehicle has been standing for some time (Chapter 9).
☐ Foreign object (stone chipping, etc) trapped between brake disc and shield (Chapter 9).

## Excessive brake pedal travel

☐ Faulty master cylinder (Chapter 9).
☐ Air in hydraulic system (Chapter 9).
☐ Faulty vacuum servo unit (Chapter 9).

## Brake pedal feels spongy when depressed

☐ Air in hydraulic system (Chapter 9).
☐ Deteriorated flexible rubber brake hoses (Chapters 1A, 1B and 9).
☐ Master cylinder mounting nuts loose (Chapter 9).
☐ Faulty master cylinder (Chapter 9).

## Excessive brake pedal effort required to stop vehicle

☐ Faulty vacuum servo unit (Chapter 9).
☐ Disconnected, damaged or insecure brake servo vacuum hose (Chapter 9).
☐ Primary or secondary hydraulic circuit failure (Chapter 9).
☐ Seized brake caliper or wheel cylinder (Chapter 9).
☐ Brake pads/shoes incorrectly fitted (Chapter 9).
☐ Incorrect grade of brake pads/shoes fitted (Chapter 9).
☐ Brake pads/shoes contaminated (Chapter 9).

## Judder felt through brake pedal or steering wheel when braking

☐ Excessive run-out or distortion of discs or drums (Chapters 9).
☐ Brake pads/shoes worn (Chapters 1A or 1B and 9).
☐ Brake caliper mounting bolts loose (Chapter 9).
☐ Wear in suspension or steering components or mountings (Chapters 1A, 1B and 10).

## Brakes binding

☐ Seized brake caliper or wheel cylinder (Chapter 9).
☐ Incorrectly-adjusted handbrake mechanism (Chapter 9).
☐ Faulty master cylinder (Chapter 9).

## Rear wheels locking under normal braking

☐ Rear brake pads contaminated (Chapters 1A, 1B and 9).
☐ Faulty rear wheel cylinder - models without ABS (Chapter 9).
☐ ABS system fault (Chapter 9).

# Suspension and steering

**Note:** *Before diagnosing suspension or steering faults, be sure that the trouble is not due to incorrect tyre pressures, mixtures of tyre types, or binding brakes.*

## Vehicle pulls to one side

☐ Defective tyre (*Weekly checks*).
☐ Excessive wear in suspension or steering components (Chapters 1A, 1B and 10).
☐ Incorrect front wheel alignment (Chapter 10).
☐ Damage to steering or suspension components (Chapter 1A or 1B).

## Wheel wobble and vibration

☐ Front roadwheels out of balance (vibration felt mainly through the steering wheel) (*Weekly checks*).
☐ Rear roadwheels out of balance (vibration felt throughout the vehicle) (*Weekly checks*).
☐ Roadwheels damaged or distorted (*Weekly checks*).
☐ Faulty or damaged tyre (*Weekly checks*).
☐ Worn steering or suspension joints, bushes or components (Chapters 1A, 1B and 10).
☐ Wheel bolts loose (Chapters 1A, 1B and 10).

## Excessive pitching and/or rolling around corners, or during braking

☐ Defective shock absorbers (Chapters 1A, 1B and 10).
☐ Broken or weak spring and/or suspension part (Chapters 1A, 1B and 10).
☐ Worn or damaged anti-roll bar or mountings (Chapter 10).

## Wandering or general instability

☐ Incorrect front wheel alignment (Chapter 10).
☐ Worn steering or suspension joints, bushes or components (Chapters 1A, 1B and 10).
☐ Roadwheels out of balance (*Weekly checks*).
☐ Faulty or damaged tyre (*Weekly checks*).
☐ Wheel bolts loose (Chapters 1A, 1B and 10).
☐ Defective shock absorbers (Chapters 1A, 1B and 10).

## Excessively-stiff steering

☐ Electric power steering system fault (Chapter 10).
☐ Seized track rod end balljoint or suspension balljoint (Chapters 1A, 1B and 10).
☐ Incorrect front wheel alignment (Chapter 10).
☐ Steering rack or column bent or damaged (Chapter 10).

## Excessive play in steering

☐ Worn steering column universal joint (Chapter 10).
☐ Worn steering track rod end balljoints (Chapters 1A, 1B and 10).
☐ Worn steering rack (Chapter 10).
☐ Worn steering or suspension joints, bushes or components (Chapters 1A, 1B and 10).

## Lack of power assistance

☐ Electric power steering system fault (Chapter 10).
☐ Faulty steering rack (Chapter 10).

## Tyre wear excessive

### Tyre treads exhibit feathered edges

☐ Incorrect toe setting (Chapter 10).

### Tyres worn in centre of tread

☐ Tyres over-inflated (*Weekly checks*).

### Tyres worn on inside and outside edges

☐ Tyres under-inflated (*Weekly checks*).

### Tyres worn on inside or outside edges

☐ Incorrect camber/castor angles (wear on one edge only) (Chapter 10).
☐ Worn steering or suspension joints, bushes or components (Chapters 1A, 1B and 10).
☐ Excessively-hard cornering.
☐ Accident damage.

### Tyres worn unevenly

☐ Tyres/wheels out of balance (*Weekly checks*).
☐ Excessive wheel or tyre run-out (Chapter 1A or 1B).
☐ Worn shock absorbers (Chapters 1A, 1B and 10).
☐ Faulty tyre (*Weekly checks*).

# Electrical system

**Note:** *For problems associated with the starting system, refer to the faults listed under 'Engine' earlier in this Section.*

## Battery won't hold a charge for more than a few days

- [ ] Battery defective internally (Chapter 5A).
- [ ] Battery terminal connections loose or corroded (*Weekly checks*).
- [ ] Auxiliary drivebelt broken, worn or incorrectly adjusted (Chapter 1A or 1B).
- [ ] Alternator not charging at correct output (Chapter 5A).
- [ ] Alternator or voltage regulator faulty (Chapter 5A).
- [ ] Short-circuit causing continual battery drain (Chapters 5A and 12).

## Ignition/no-charge warning light stays on with engine running

- [ ] Auxiliary drivebelt broken, worn, or incorrectly adjusted (Chapter 1A or 1B).
- [ ] Internal fault in alternator or voltage regulator (Chapter 5A).
- [ ] Broken, disconnected, or loose wiring in charging circuit (Chapter 5A).

## Ignition/no-charge warning light fails to come on

- [ ] Warning light bulb blown (Chapter 12).
- [ ] Broken, disconnected, or loose wiring in warning light circuit (Chapter 12).
- [ ] Alternator faulty (Chapter 5A).

## Lights inoperative

- [ ] Bulb blown (Chapter 12).
- [ ] Corrosion of bulb or bulbholder contacts (Chapter 12).
- [ ] Blown fuse (Chapter 12).
- [ ] Faulty relay (Chapter 12).
- [ ] Broken, loose, or disconnected wiring (Chapter 12).
- [ ] Faulty switch (Chapter 12).

## Instrument readings inaccurate or erratic

### Fuel or temperature gauges give no reading

- [ ] Faulty gauge sensor/sender unit (Chapter 3 or 4).
- [ ] Wiring open-circuit (Chapter 12).
- [ ] Faulty gauge (Chapter 12).
- [ ] Built-in Systems Interface (BSI) faulty (Chapter 12).

### Fuel or temperature gauges give continuous maximum reading

- [ ] Faulty gauge sensor/sender unit (Chapter 3 or 4).
- [ ] Wiring short-circuit (Chapter 12).
- [ ] Faulty gauge (Chapter 12).
- [ ] Built-in Systems Interface (BSI) faulty (Chapter 12).

## Horn inoperative, or unsatisfactory in operation

### Horn operates all the time

- [ ] Horn push either earthed or stuck down (Chapter 12).
- [ ] Horn cable-to-horn push earthed (Chapter 12).

### Horn fails to operate

- [ ] Blown fuse (Chapter 12).
- [ ] Cable or cable connections loose, broken or disconnected (Chapter 12).
- [ ] Faulty horn (Chapter 12).

### Horn emits intermittent or unsatisfactory sound

- [ ] Cable connections loose (Chapter 12).
- [ ] Horn mountings loose (Chapter 12).
- [ ] Faulty horn (Chapter 12).

## Windscreen/tailgate wipers failed, or unsatisfactory in operation

### Wipers fail to operate, or operate very slowly

- [ ] Wiper blades stuck to screen, or linkage seized or binding (Chapters 1A, 1B and 12).
- [ ] Blown fuse (Chapter 12).
- [ ] Cable or cable connections loose, broken or disconnected (Chapter 12).
- [ ] Built-in Systems Interface (BSI) faulty (Chapter 12).
- [ ] Faulty wiper motor (Chapter 12).

### Wiper blades sweep over too large or too small an area of the glass

- [ ] Wiper arms incorrectly positioned on spindles (Chapter 12).
- [ ] Excessive wear of wiper linkage (Chapter 12).
- [ ] Wiper motor or linkage mountings loose or insecure (Chapter 12).

### Wiper blades fail to clean the glass effectively

- [ ] Wiper blade rubbers worn or perished (*Weekly checks*).
- [ ] Wiper arm tension springs broken, or arm pivots seized (Chapter 12).
- [ ] Insufficient windscreen washer additive to adequately remove road film (*Weekly checks*).

## Windscreen/tailgate washers failed, or unsatisfactory in operation

### One or more washer jets inoperative

- [ ] Blocked washer jet (*Weekly checks*).
- [ ] Disconnected, kinked or restricted fluid hose (Chapter 12).
- [ ] Insufficient fluid in washer reservoir (*Weekly checks*).

# Electrical system (continued)

### Washer pump fails to operate

- [ ] Broken or disconnected wiring or connections (Chapter 12).
- [ ] Blown fuse (Chapter 12).
- [ ] Faulty washer switch (Chapter 12).
- [ ] Faulty washer pump (Chapter 12).

## Electric windows inoperative, or unsatisfactory in operation

### Window glass will only move in one direction

- [ ] Faulty switch (Chapter 12).

### Window glass slow to move

- [ ] Regulator seized or damaged, or in need of lubricant (Chapter 11).
- [ ] Door internal components or trim fouling regulator (Chapter 11).
- [ ] Faulty motor (Chapter 11).

### Window glass fails to move

- [ ] Blown fuse (Chapter 12).
- [ ] Broken or disconnected wiring or connections (Chapter 12).
- [ ] Faulty motor (Chapter 11).
- [ ] Built-in Systems Interface (BSI) faulty (Chapter 12).

## Central locking system inoperative, or unsatisfactory in operation

### Complete system failure

- [ ] Blown fuse (Chapter 12).
- [ ] Broken or disconnected wiring or connections (Chapter 12).
- [ ] Built-in Systems Interface (BSI) faulty (Chapter 12).

### Door/tailgate locks but will not unlock, or unlocks but will not lock

- [ ] Broken or disconnected link rod(s) (Chapter 11).
- [ ] Faulty lock motor (Chapter 11).

### One lock fails to operate

- [ ] Broken or disconnected wiring or connections (Chapter 12).
- [ ] Faulty lock motor (Chapter 11).
- [ ] Broken, binding or disconnected link rod(s) (Chapter 11).

## A

**ABS (Anti-lock brake system)** A system, usually electronically controlled, that senses incipient wheel lockup during braking and relieves hydraulic pressure at wheels that are about to skid.

**Air bag** An inflatable bag hidden in the steering wheel (driver's side) or the dash or glovebox (passenger side). In a head-on collision, the bags inflate, preventing the driver and front passenger from being thrown forward into the steering wheel or windscreen.

**Air cleaner** A metal or plastic housing, containing a filter element, which removes dust and dirt from the air being drawn into the engine.

**Air filter element** The actual filter in an air cleaner system, usually manufactured from pleated paper and requiring renewal at regular intervals.

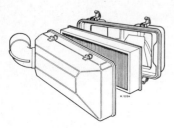

*Air filter*

**Allen key** A hexagonal wrench which fits into a recessed hexagonal hole.

**Alligator clip** A long-nosed spring-loaded metal clip with meshing teeth. Used to make temporary electrical connections.

**Alternator** A component in the electrical system which converts mechanical energy from a drivebelt into electrical energy to charge the battery and to operate the starting system, ignition system and electrical accessories.

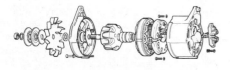

*Alternator (exploded view)*

**Ampere (amp)** A unit of measurement for the flow of electric current. One amp is the amount of current produced by one volt acting through a resistance of one ohm.

**Anaerobic sealer** A substance used to prevent bolts and screws from loosening. Anaerobic means that it does not require oxygen for activation. The Loctite brand is widely used.

**Antifreeze** A substance (usually ethylene glycol) mixed with water, and added to a vehicle's cooling system, to prevent freezing of the coolant in winter. Antifreeze also contains chemicals to inhibit corrosion and the formation of rust and other deposits that would tend to clog the radiator and coolant passages and reduce cooling efficiency.

**Anti-seize compound** A coating that reduces the risk of seizing on fasteners that are subjected to high temperatures, such as exhaust manifold bolts and nuts.

*Anti-seize compound*

**Asbestos** A natural fibrous mineral with great heat resistance, commonly used in the composition of brake friction materials. Asbestos is a health hazard and the dust created by brake systems should never be inhaled or ingested.

**Axle** A shaft on which a wheel revolves, or which revolves with a wheel. Also, a solid beam that connects the two wheels at one end of the vehicle. An axle which also transmits power to the wheels is known as a live axle.

*Axle assembly*

**Axleshaft** A single rotating shaft, on either side of the differential, which delivers power from the final drive assembly to the drive wheels. Also called a driveshaft or a halfshaft.

## B

**Ball bearing** An anti-friction bearing consisting of a hardened inner and outer race with hardened steel balls between two races.

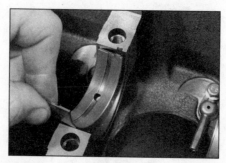

*Bearing*

**Bearing** The curved surface on a shaft or in a bore, or the part assembled into either, that permits relative motion between them with minimum wear and friction.

**Big-end bearing** The bearing in the end of the connecting rod that's attached to the crankshaft.

**Bleed nipple** A valve on a brake wheel cylinder, caliper or other hydraulic component that is opened to purge the hydraulic system of air. Also called a bleed screw.

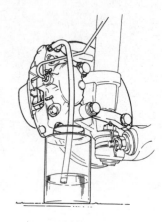

*Brake bleeding*

**Brake bleeding** Procedure for removing air from lines of a hydraulic brake system.

**Brake disc** The component of a disc brake that rotates with the wheels.

**Brake drum** The component of a drum brake that rotates with the wheels.

**Brake linings** The friction material which contacts the brake disc or drum to retard the vehicle's speed. The linings are bonded or riveted to the brake pads or shoes.

**Brake pads** The replaceable friction pads that pinch the brake disc when the brakes are applied. Brake pads consist of a friction material bonded or riveted to a rigid backing plate.

**Brake shoe** The crescent-shaped carrier to which the brake linings are mounted and which forces the lining against the rotating drum during braking.

**Braking systems** For more information on braking systems, consult the *Haynes Automotive Brake Manual*.

**Breaker bar** A long socket wrench handle providing greater leverage.

**Bulkhead** The insulated partition between the engine and the passenger compartment.

## C

**Caliper** The non-rotating part of a disc-brake assembly that straddles the disc and carries the brake pads. The caliper also contains the hydraulic components that cause the pads to pinch the disc when the brakes are applied. A caliper is also a measuring tool that can be set to measure inside or outside dimensions of an object.

**Camshaft** A rotating shaft on which a series of cam lobes operate the valve mechanisms. The camshaft may be driven by gears, by sprockets and chain or by sprockets and a belt.

**Canister** A container in an evaporative emission control system; contains activated charcoal granules to trap vapours from the fuel system.

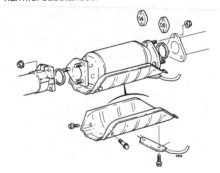

*Canister*

**Carburettor** A device which mixes fuel with air in the proper proportions to provide a desired power output from a spark ignition internal combustion engine.

*Carburettor*

**Castellated** Resembling the parapets along the top of a castle wall. For example, a castellated balljoint stud nut.

*Castellated nut*

**Castor** In wheel alignment, the backward or forward tilt of the steering axis. Castor is positive when the steering axis is inclined rearward at the top.

**Catalytic converter** A silencer-like device in the exhaust system which converts certain pollutants in the exhaust gases into less harmful substances.

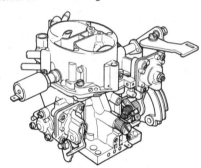

*Catalytic converter*

**Circlip** A ring-shaped clip used to prevent endwise movement of cylindrical parts and shafts. An internal circlip is installed in a groove in a housing; an external circlip fits into a groove on the outside of a cylindrical piece such as a shaft.

**Clearance** The amount of space between two parts. For example, between a piston and a cylinder, between a bearing and a journal, etc.

**Coil spring** A spiral of elastic steel found in various sizes throughout a vehicle, for example as a springing medium in the suspension and in the valve train.

**Compression** Reduction in volume, and increase in pressure and temperature, of a gas, caused by squeezing it into a smaller space.

**Compression ratio** The relationship between cylinder volume when the piston is at top dead centre and cylinder volume when the piston is at bottom dead centre.

**Constant velocity (CV) joint** A type of universal joint that cancels out vibrations caused by driving power being transmitted through an angle.

**Core plug** A disc or cup-shaped metal device inserted in a hole in a casting through which core was removed when the casting was formed. Also known as a freeze plug or expansion plug.

**Crankcase** The lower part of the engine block in which the crankshaft rotates.

**Crankshaft** The main rotating member, or shaft, running the length of the crankcase, with offset "throws" to which the connecting rods are attached.

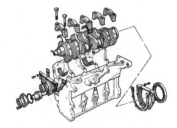

*Crankshaft assembly*

**Crocodile clip** See Alligator clip

# D

**Diagnostic code** Code numbers obtained by accessing the diagnostic mode of an engine management computer. This code can be used to determine the area in the system where a malfunction may be located.

**Disc brake** A brake design incorporating a rotating disc onto which brake pads are squeezed. The resulting friction converts the energy of a moving vehicle into heat.

**Double-overhead cam (DOHC)** An engine that uses two overhead camshafts, usually one for the intake valves and one for the exhaust valves.

**Drivebelt(s)** The belt(s) used to drive accessories such as the alternator, water pump, power steering pump, air conditioning compressor, etc. off the crankshaft pulley.

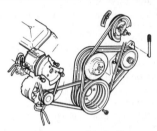

*Accessory drivebelts*

**Driveshaft** Any shaft used to transmit motion. Commonly used when referring to the axleshafts on a front wheel drive vehicle.

*Driveshaft*

**Drum brake** A type of brake using a drum-shaped metal cylinder attached to the inner surface of the wheel. When the brake pedal is pressed, curved brake shoes with friction linings press against the inside of the drum to slow or stop the vehicle.

*Drum brake assembly*

# E

**EGR valve** A valve used to introduce exhaust gases into the intake air stream.

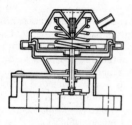

*EGR valve*

**Electronic control unit (ECU)** A computer which controls (for instance) ignition and fuel injection systems, or an anti-lock braking system. For more information refer to the *Haynes Automotive Electrical and Electronic Systems Manual*.

**Electronic Fuel Injection (EFI)** A computer controlled fuel system that distributes fuel through an injector located in each intake port of the engine.

**Emergency brake** A braking system, independent of the main hydraulic system, that can be used to slow or stop the vehicle if the primary brakes fail, or to hold the vehicle stationary even though the brake pedal isn't depressed. It usually consists of a hand lever that actuates either front or rear brakes mechanically through a series of cables and linkages. Also known as a handbrake or parking brake.

**Endfloat** The amount of lengthwise movement between two parts. As applied to a crankshaft, the distance that the crankshaft can move forward and back in the cylinder block.

**Engine management system (EMS)** A computer controlled system which manages the fuel injection and the ignition systems in an integrated fashion.

**Exhaust manifold** A part with several passages through which exhaust gases leave the engine combustion chambers and enter the exhaust pipe.

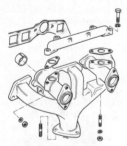

*Exhaust manifold*

# F

**Fan clutch** A viscous (fluid) drive coupling device which permits variable engine fan speeds in relation to engine speeds.

**Feeler blade** A thin strip or blade of hardened steel, ground to an exact thickness, used to check or measure clearances between parts.

*Feeler blade*

**Firing order** The order in which the engine cylinders fire, or deliver their power strokes, beginning with the number one cylinder.

**Flywheel** A heavy spinning wheel in which energy is absorbed and stored by means of momentum. On cars, the flywheel is attached to the crankshaft to smooth out firing impulses.

**Free play** The amount of travel before any action takes place. The "looseness" in a linkage, or an assembly of parts, between the initial application of force and actual movement. For example, the distance the brake pedal moves before the pistons in the master cylinder are actuated.

**Fuse** An electrical device which protects a circuit against accidental overload. The typical fuse contains a soft piece of metal which is calibrated to melt at a predetermined current flow (expressed as amps) and break the circuit.

**Fusible link** A circuit protection device consisting of a conductor surrounded by heat-resistant insulation. The conductor is smaller than the wire it protects, so it acts as the weakest link in the circuit. Unlike a blown fuse, a failed fusible link must frequently be cut from the wire for replacement.

# G

**Gap** The distance the spark must travel in jumping from the centre electrode to the side

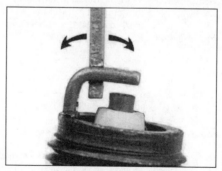

*Adjusting spark plug gap*

electrode in a spark plug. Also refers to the spacing between the points in a contact breaker assembly in a conventional points-type ignition, or to the distance between the reluctor or rotor and the pickup coil in an electronic ignition.

**Gasket** Any thin, soft material - usually cork, cardboard, asbestos or soft metal - installed between two metal surfaces to ensure a good seal. For instance, the cylinder head gasket seals the joint between the block and the cylinder head.

*Gasket*

**Gauge** An instrument panel display used to monitor engine conditions. A gauge with a movable pointer on a dial or a fixed scale is an analogue gauge. A gauge with a numerical readout is called a digital gauge.

# H

**Halfshaft** A rotating shaft that transmits power from the final drive unit to a drive wheel, usually when referring to a live rear axle.

**Harmonic balancer** A device designed to reduce torsion or twisting vibration in the crankshaft. May be incorporated in the crankshaft pulley. Also known as a vibration damper.

**Hone** An abrasive tool for correcting small irregularities or differences in diameter in an engine cylinder, brake cylinder, etc.

**Hydraulic tappet** A tappet that utilises hydraulic pressure from the engine's lubrication system to maintain zero clearance (constant contact with both camshaft and valve stem). Automatically adjusts to variation in valve stem length. Hydraulic tappets also reduce valve noise.

# I

**Ignition timing** The moment at which the spark plug fires, usually expressed in the number of crankshaft degrees before the piston reaches the top of its stroke.

**Inlet manifold** A tube or housing with passages through which flows the air-fuel mixture (carburettor vehicles and vehicles with throttle body injection) or air only (port fuel-injected vehicles) to the port openings in the cylinder head.

## J

**Jump start** Starting the engine of a vehicle with a discharged or weak battery by attaching jump leads from the weak battery to a charged or helper battery.

## L

**Load Sensing Proportioning Valve (LSPV)** A brake hydraulic system control valve that works like a proportioning valve, but also takes into consideration the amount of weight carried by the rear axle.

**Locknut** A nut used to lock an adjustment nut, or other threaded component, in place. For example, a locknut is employed to keep the adjusting nut on the rocker arm in position.

**Lockwasher** A form of washer designed to prevent an attaching nut from working loose.

## M

**MacPherson strut** A type of front suspension system devised by Earle MacPherson at Ford of England. In its original form, a simple lateral link with the anti-roll bar creates the lower control arm. A long strut - an integral coil spring and shock absorber - is mounted between the body and the steering knuckle. Many modern so-called MacPherson strut systems use a conventional lower A-arm and don't rely on the anti-roll bar for location.

**Multimeter** An electrical test instrument with the capability to measure voltage, current and resistance.

## N

**NOx** Oxides of Nitrogen. A common toxic pollutant emitted by petrol and diesel engines at higher temperatures.

## O

**Ohm** The unit of electrical resistance. One volt applied to a resistance of one ohm will produce a current of one amp.

**Ohmmeter** An instrument for measuring electrical resistance.

**O-ring** A type of sealing ring made of a special rubber-like material; in use, the O-ring is compressed into a groove to provide the sealing action.

*O-ring*

**Overhead cam (ohc) engine** An engine with the camshaft(s) located on top of the cylinder head(s).

**Overhead valve (ohv) engine** An engine with the valves located in the cylinder head, but with the camshaft located in the engine block.

**Oxygen sensor** A device installed in the engine exhaust manifold, which senses the oxygen content in the exhaust and converts this information into an electric current. Also called a Lambda sensor.

## P

**Phillips screw** A type of screw head having a cross instead of a slot for a corresponding type of screwdriver.

**Plastigage** A thin strip of plastic thread, available in different sizes, used for measuring clearances. For example, a strip of Plastigage is laid across a bearing journal. The parts are assembled and dismantled; the width of the crushed strip indicates the clearance between journal and bearing.

*Plastigage*

**Propeller shaft** The long hollow tube with universal joints at both ends that carries power from the transmission to the differential on front-engined rear wheel drive vehicles.

**Proportioning valve** A hydraulic control valve which limits the amount of pressure to the rear brakes during panic stops to prevent wheel lock-up.

## R

**Rack-and-pinion steering** A steering system with a pinion gear on the end of the steering shaft that mates with a rack (think of a geared wheel opened up and laid flat). When the steering wheel is turned, the pinion turns, moving the rack to the left or right. This movement is transmitted through the track rods to the steering arms at the wheels.

**Radiator** A liquid-to-air heat transfer device designed to reduce the temperature of the coolant in an internal combustion engine cooling system.

**Refrigerant** Any substance used as a heat transfer agent in an air-conditioning system. R-12 has been the principle refrigerant for many years; recently, however, manufacturers have begun using R-134a, a non-CFC substance that is considered less harmful to the ozone in the upper atmosphere.

**Rocker arm** A lever arm that rocks on a shaft or pivots on a stud. In an overhead valve engine, the rocker arm converts the upward movement of the pushrod into a downward movement to open a valve.

**Rotor** In a distributor, the rotating device inside the cap that connects the centre electrode and the outer terminals as it turns, distributing the high voltage from the coil secondary winding to the proper spark plug. Also, that part of an alternator which rotates inside the stator. Also, the rotating assembly of a turbocharger, including the compressor wheel, shaft and turbine wheel.

**Runout** The amount of wobble (in-and-out movement) of a gear or wheel as it's rotated. The amount a shaft rotates "out-of-true." The out-of-round condition of a rotating part.

## S

**Sealant** A liquid or paste used to prevent leakage at a joint. Sometimes used in conjunction with a gasket.

**Sealed beam lamp** An older headlight design which integrates the reflector, lens and filaments into a hermetically-sealed one-piece unit. When a filament burns out or the lens cracks, the entire unit is simply replaced.

**Serpentine drivebelt** A single, long, wide accessory drivebelt that's used on some newer vehicles to drive all the accessories, instead of a series of smaller, shorter belts. Serpentine drivebelts are usually tensioned by an automatic tensioner.

*Serpentine drivebelt*

**Shim** Thin spacer, commonly used to adjust the clearance or relative positions between two parts. For example, shims inserted into or under bucket tappets control valve clearances. Clearance is adjusted by changing the thickness of the shim.

**Slide hammer** A special puller that screws into or hooks onto a component such as a shaft or bearing; a heavy sliding handle on the shaft bottoms against the end of the shaft to knock the component free.

**Sprocket** A tooth or projection on the periphery of a wheel, shaped to engage with a chain or drivebelt. Commonly used to refer to the sprocket wheel itself.

**Starter inhibitor switch** On vehicles with an automatic transmission, a switch that prevents starting if the vehicle is not in Neutral or Park.

**Strut** See MacPherson strut.

# T

**Tappet** A cylindrical component which transmits motion from the cam to the valve stem, either directly or via a pushrod and rocker arm. Also called a cam follower.

**Thermostat** A heat-controlled valve that regulates the flow of coolant between the cylinder block and the radiator, so maintaining optimum engine operating temperature. A thermostat is also used in some air cleaners in which the temperature is regulated.

**Thrust bearing** The bearing in the clutch assembly that is moved in to the release levers by clutch pedal action to disengage the clutch. Also referred to as a release bearing.

**Timing belt** A toothed belt which drives the camshaft. Serious engine damage may result if it breaks in service.

**Timing chain** A chain which drives the camshaft.

**Toe-in** The amount the front wheels are closer together at the front than at the rear. On rear wheel drive vehicles, a slight amount of toe-in is usually specified to keep the front wheels running parallel on the road by offsetting other forces that tend to spread the wheels apart.

**Toe-out** The amount the front wheels are closer together at the rear than at the front. On front wheel drive vehicles, a slight amount of toe-out is usually specified.

**Tools** For full information on choosing and using tools, refer to the *Haynes Automotive Tools Manual*.

**Tracer** A stripe of a second colour applied to a wire insulator to distinguish that wire from another one with the same colour insulator.

**Tune-up** A process of accurate and careful adjustments and parts replacement to obtain the best possible engine performance.

**Turbocharger** A centrifugal device, driven by exhaust gases, that pressurises the intake air. Normally used to increase the power output from a given engine displacement, but can also be used primarily to reduce exhaust emissions (as on VW's "Umwelt" Diesel engine).

# U

**Universal joint or U-joint** A double-pivoted connection for transmitting power from a driving to a driven shaft through an angle. A U-joint consists of two Y-shaped yokes and a cross-shaped member called the spider.

# V

**Valve** A device through which the flow of liquid, gas, vacuum, or loose material in bulk may be started, stopped, or regulated by a movable part that opens, shuts, or partially obstructs one or more ports or passageways. A valve is also the movable part of such a device.

**Valve clearance** The clearance between the valve tip (the end of the valve stem) and the rocker arm or tappet. The valve clearance is measured when the valve is closed.

**Vernier caliper** A precision measuring instrument that measures inside and outside dimensions. Not quite as accurate as a micrometer, but more convenient.

**Viscosity** The thickness of a liquid or its resistance to flow.

**Volt** A unit for expressing electrical "pressure" in a circuit. One volt that will produce a current of one ampere through a resistance of one ohm.

# W

**Welding** Various processes used to join metal items by heating the areas to be joined to a molten state and fusing them together. For more information refer to the *Haynes Automotive Welding Manual*.

**Wiring diagram** A drawing portraying the components and wires in a vehicle's electrical system, using standardised symbols. For more information refer to the *Haynes Automotive Electrical and Electronic Systems Manual*.

**Note:** *References throughout this index are in the form* **"Chapter number"** • **"Page number".** *So, for example, 2C•15 refers to page 15 of Chapter 2C.*

Note: *References throughout this index are in the form* **"Chapter number"** • **"Page number"**. *So, for example, 2C•15 refers to page 15 of Chapter 2C.*

**Note:** *References throughout this index are in the form* **"Chapter number"** • **"Page number"**. *So, for example, 2C•15 refers to page 15 of Chapter 2C.*

**Note:** *References throughout this index are in the form* **"Chapter number"** • **"Page number"**. *So, for example, 2C•15 refers to page 15 of Chapter 2C.*

# Haynes Manuals – The Complete UK Car List

| Title | Book No. |
|---|---|
| **ALFA ROMEO** Alfasud/Sprint (74 - 88) up to F * | 0292 |
| Alfa Romeo Alfetta (73 - 87) up to E * | 0531 |
| **AUDI** 80, 90 & Coupe Petrol (79 - Nov 88) up to F | 0605 |
| Audi 80, 90 & Coupe Petrol (Oct 86 - 90) D to H | 1491 |
| Audi 100 & 200 Petrol (Oct 82 - 90) up to H | 0907 |
| Audi 100 & A6 Petrol & Diesel (May 91 - May 97) H to P | 3504 |
| Audi A3 Petrol & Diesel (96 - May 03) P to 03 | 4253 |
| Audi A4 Petrol & Diesel (95 - 00) M to X | 3575 |
| Audi A4 Petrol & Diesel (01 - 04) X to 54 | 4609 |
| **AUSTIN** A35 & A40 (56 - 67) up to F * | 0118 |
| Austin/MG/Rover Maestro 1.3 & 1.6 Petrol (83 - 95) up to M | 0922 |
| Austin/MG Metro (80 - May 90) up to G | 0718 |
| Austin/Rover Montego 1.3 & 1.6 Petrol (84 - 94) A to L | 1066 |
| Austin/MG/Rover Montego 2.0 Petrol (84 - 95) A to M | 1067 |
| Mini (59 - 69) up to H * | 0527 |
| Mini (69 - 01) up to X | 0646 |
| Austin/Rover 2.0 litre Diesel Engine (86 - 93) C to L | 1857 |
| Austin Healey 100/6 & 3000 (56 - 68) up to G * | 0049 |
| **BEDFORD** CF Petrol (69 - 87) up to E | 0163 |
| Bedford/Vauxhall Rascal & Suzuki Supercarry (86 - Oct 94) C to M | 3015 |
| **BMW** 316, 320 & 320i (4-cyl) (75 - Feb 83) up to Y * | 0276 |
| BMW 320, 320i, 323i & 325i (6-cyl) (Oct 77 - Sept 87) up to E | 0815 |
| BMW 3- & 5-Series Petrol (81 - 91) up to J | 1948 |
| BMW 3-Series Petrol (Apr 91 - 99) H to V | 3210 |
| BMW 3-Series Petrol (Sept 98 - 03) S to 53 | 4067 |
| BMW 520i & 525e (Oct 81 - June 88) up to E | 1560 |
| BMW 525, 528 & 528i (73 - Sept 81) up to X * | 0632 |
| BMW 5-Series 6-cyl Petrol (April 96 - Aug 03) N to 03 | 4151 |
| BMW 1500, 1502, 1600, 1602, 2000 & 2002 (59 - 77) up to S * | 0240 |
| **CHRYSLER** PT Cruiser Petrol (00 - 03) W to 53 | 4058 |
| **CITROËN** 2CV, Ami & Dyane (67 - 90) up to H | 0196 |
| Citroën AX Petrol & Diesel (87 - 97) D to P | 3014 |
| Citroën Berlingo & Peugeot Partner Petrol & Diesel (96 - 05) P to 55 | 4281 |
| Citroën BX Petrol (83 - 94) A to L | 0908 |
| Citroën C15 Van Petrol & Diesel (89 - Oct 98) F to S | 3509 |
| Citroën C3 Petrol & Diesel (02 - 05) 51 to 05 | 4197 |
| Citroen C5 Petrol & Diesel (01-08) Y to 08 | 4745 |
| Citroën CX Petrol (75 - 88) up to F | 0528 |
| Citroën Saxo Petrol & Diesel (96 - 04) N to 54 | 3506 |
| Citroën Visa Petrol (79 - 88) up to F | 0620 |
| Citroën Xantia Petrol & Diesel (93 - 01) K to Y | 3082 |
| Citroën XM Petrol & Diesel (89 - 00) G to X | 3451 |
| Citroën Xsara Petrol & Diesel (97 - Sept 00) R to W | 3751 |
| Citroën Xsara Picasso Petrol & Diesel (00 - 02) W to 52 | 3944 |
| Citroen Xsara Picasso (03-08) | 4784 |
| Citroën ZX Diesel (91 - 98) J to S | 1922 |
| Citroën ZX Petrol (91 - 98) H to S | 1881 |
| Citroën 1.7 & 1.9 litre Diesel Engine (84 - 96) A to N | 1379 |
| **FIAT** 126 (73 - 87) up to E * | 0305 |
| Fiat 500 (57 - 73) up to M * | 0090 |
| Fiat Bravo & Brava Petrol (95 - 00) N to W | 3572 |
| Fiat Cinquecento (93 - 98) K to R | 3501 |
| Fiat Panda (81 - 95) up to M | 0793 |
| Fiat Punto Petrol & Diesel (94 - Oct 99) L to V | 3251 |
| Fiat Punto Petrol (Oct 99 - July 03) V to 03 | 4066 |
| Fiat Punto Petrol (03-07) 03 to 07 | 4746 |
| Fiat Regata Petrol (84 - 88) A to F | 1167 |
| Fiat Tipo Petrol (88 - 91) E to J | 1625 |
| Fiat Uno Petrol (83 - 95) up to M | 0923 |
| Fiat X1/9 (74 - 89) up to G * | 0273 |
| **FORD** Anglia (59 - 68) up to G * | 0001 |

| Title | Book No. |
|---|---|
| Ford Capri II (& III) 1.6 & 2.0 (74 - 87) up to E * | 0283 |
| Ford Capri II (& III) 2.8 & 3.0 V6 (74 - 87) up to E | 1309 |
| Ford Cortina Mk I & Corsair 1500 ('62 - '66) up to D* | 0214 |
| Ford Cortina Mk III 1300 & 1600 (70 - 76) up to P * | 0070 |
| Ford Escort Mk I 1100 & 1300 (68 - 74) up to N * | 0171 |
| Ford Escort Mk I Mexico, RS 1600 & RS 2000 (70 - 74) up to N * | 0139 |
| Ford Escort Mk II Mexico, RS 1800 & RS 2000 (75 - 80) up to W * | 0735 |
| Ford Escort (75 - Aug 80) up to V * | 0280 |
| Ford Escort Petrol (Sept 80 - Sept 90) up to H | 0686 |
| Ford Escort & Orion Petrol (Sept 90 - 00) H to X | 1737 |
| Ford Escort & Orion Diesel (Sept 90 - 00) H to X | 4081 |
| Ford Fiesta (76 - Aug 83) up to Y | 0334 |
| Ford Fiesta Petrol (Aug 83 - Feb 89) A to F | 1030 |
| Ford Fiesta Petrol (Feb 89 - Oct 95) F to N | 1595 |
| Ford Fiesta Petrol & Diesel (Oct 95 - Mar 02) N to 02 | 3397 |
| Ford Fiesta Petrol & Diesel (Apr 02 - 07) 02 to 57 | 4170 |
| Ford Focus Petrol & Diesel (98 - 01) S to Y | 3759 |
| Ford Focus Petrol & Diesel (Oct 01 - 05) 51 to 05 | 4167 |
| Ford Galaxy Petrol & Diesel (95 - Aug 00) M to W | 3984 |
| Ford Granada Petrol (Sept 77 - Feb 85) up to B * | 0481 |
| Ford Granada & Scorpio Petrol (Mar 85 - 94) B to M | 1245 |
| Ford Ka (96 - 02) P to 52 | 3570 |
| Ford Mondeo Petrol (93 - Sept 00) K to X | 1923 |
| Ford Mondeo Petrol & Diesel (Oct 00 - Jul 03) X to 03 | 3990 |
| Ford Mondeo Petrol & Diesel (July 03 - 07) 03 to 56 | 4619 |
| Ford Mondeo Diesel (93 - 96) L to N | 3465 |
| Ford Orion Petrol (83 - Sept 90) up to H | 1009 |
| Ford Sierra 4-cyl Petrol (82 - 93) up to K | 0903 |
| Ford Sierra V6 Petrol (82 - 91) up to J | 0904 |
| Ford Transit Petrol (Mk 2) (78 - Jan 86) up to C | 0719 |
| Ford Transit Petrol (Mk 3) (Feb 86 - 89) C to G | 1468 |
| Ford Transit Diesel (Feb 86 - 99) C to T | 3019 |
| Ford Transit Diesel (00-06) | 4775 |
| Ford 1.6 & 1.8 litre Diesel Engine (84 - 96) A to N | 1172 |
| Ford 2.1, 2.3 & 2.5 litre Diesel Engine (77 - 90) up to H | 1606 |
| **FREIGHT ROVER** Sherpa Petrol (74 - 87) up to E | 0463 |
| **HILLMAN** Avenger (70 - 82) up to Y | 0037 |
| Hillman Imp (63 - 76) up to R * | 0022 |
| **HONDA** Civic (Feb 84 - Oct 87) A to E | 1226 |
| Honda Civic (Nov 91 - 96) J to N | 3199 |
| Honda Civic Petrol (Mar 95 - 00) M to X | 4050 |
| Honda Civic Petrol & Diesel (01 - 05) X to 55 | 4611 |
| Honda CR-V Petrol & Diesel (01-06) | 4747 |
| Honda Jazz (01 - Feb 08) 51 - 57 | 4735 |
| **HYUNDAI** Pony (85 - 94) C to M | 3398 |
| **JAGUAR** E Type (61 - 72) up to L * | 0140 |
| Jaguar MkI & II, 240 & 340 (55 - 69) up to H * | 0098 |
| Jaguar XJ6, XJ & Sovereign; Daimler Sovereign (68 - Oct 86) up to D | 0242 |
| Jaguar XJ6 & Sovereign (Oct 86 - Sept 94) D to M | 3261 |
| Jaguar XJ12, XJS & Sovereign; Daimler Double Six (72 - 88) up to F | 0478 |
| **JEEP** Cherokee Petrol (93 - 96) K to N | 1943 |
| **LADA** 1200, 1300, 1500 & 1600 (74 - 91) up to J | 0413 |
| Lada Samara (87 - 91) D to J | 1610 |
| **LAND ROVER** 90, 110 & Defender Diesel (83 - 07) up to 56 | 3017 |
| Land Rover Discovery Petrol & Diesel (89 - 98) G to S | 3016 |
| Land Rover Discovery Diesel (Nov 98 - Jul 04) S to 04 | 4606 |
| Land Rover Freelander Petrol & Diesel (97 - Sept 03) R to 53 | 3929 |
| Land Rover Freelander Petrol & Diesel (Oct 03 - Oct 06) 53 to 56 | 4623 |

| Title | Book No. |
|---|---|
| Land Rover Series IIA & III Diesel (58 - 85) up to C | 0529 |
| Land Rover Series II, IIA & III 4-cyl Petrol (58 - 85) up to C | 0314 |
| **MAZDA** 323 (Mar 81 - Oct 89) up to G | 1608 |
| Mazda 323 (Oct 89 - 98) G to R | 3455 |
| Mazda 626 (May 83 - Sept 87) up to E | 0929 |
| Mazda B1600, B1800 & B2000 Pick-up Petrol (72 - 88) up to F | 0267 |
| Mazda RX-7 (79 - 85) up to C * | 0460 |
| **MERCEDES-BENZ** 190, 190E & 190D Petrol & Diesel (83 - 93) A to L | 3450 |
| Mercedes-Benz 200D, 240D, 240TD, 300D & 300TD 123 Series Diesel (Oct 76 - 85) | 1114 |
| Mercedes-Benz 250 & 280 (68 - 72) up to L * | 0346 |
| Mercedes-Benz 250 & 280 123 Series Petrol (Oct 76 - 84) up to B * | 0677 |
| Mercedes-Benz 124 Series Petrol & Diesel (85 - Aug 93) C to K | 3253 |
| Mercedes-Benz A-Class Petrol & Diesel (98-04) S to 54 | 4748 |
| Mercedes-Benz C-Class Petrol & Diesel (93 - Aug 00) L to W | 3511 |
| Mercedes-Benz C-Class (00-06) | 4780 |
| **MGA** (55 - 62) * | 0475 |
| MGB (62 - 80) up to W | 0111 |
| MG Midget & Austin-Healey Sprite (58 - 80) up to W * | 0265 |
| **MINI** Petrol (July 01 - 05) Y to 05 | 4273 |
| **MITSUBISHI** Shogun & L200 Pick-Ups Petrol (83 - 94) up to M | 1944 |
| **MORRIS** Ital 1.3 (80 - 84) up to B | 0705 |
| Morris Minor 1000 (56 - 71) up to K | 0024 |
| **NISSAN** Almera Petrol (95 - Feb 00) N to V | 4053 |
| Nissan Almera & Tino Petrol (Feb 00 - 07) V to 56 | 4612 |
| Nissan Bluebird (May 84 - Mar 86) A to C | 1223 |
| Nissan Bluebird Petrol (Mar 86 - 90) C to H | 1473 |
| Nissan Cherry (Sept 82 - 86) up to D | 1031 |
| Nissan Micra (83 - Jan 93) up to K | 0931 |
| Nissan Micra (93 - 02) K to 52 | 3254 |
| Nissan Micra Petrol (03-07) 52 to 57 | 4734 |
| Nissan Primera Petrol (90 - Aug 99) H to T | 1851 |
| Nissan Stanza (82 - 86) up to D | 0824 |
| Nissan Sunny Petrol (May 82 - Oct 86) up to D | 0895 |
| Nissan Sunny Petrol (Oct 86 - Mar 91) D to H | 1378 |
| Nissan Sunny Petrol (Apr 91 - 95) H to N | 3219 |
| **OPEL** Ascona & Manta (B Series) (Sept 75 - 88) up to F * | 0316 |
| Opel Ascona Petrol (81 - 88) | 3215 |
| Opel Astra Petrol (Oct 91 - Feb 98) | 3156 |
| Opel Corsa Petrol (83 - Mar 93) | 3160 |
| Opel Corsa Petrol (Mar 93 - 97) | 3159 |
| Opel Kadett Petrol (Nov 79 - Oct 84) up to B | 0634 |
| Opel Kadett Petrol (Oct 84 - Oct 91) | 3196 |
| Opel Omega & Senator Petrol (Nov 86 - 94) | 3157 |
| Opel Rekord Petrol (Feb 78 - Oct 86) up to D | 0543 |
| Opel Vectra Petrol (Oct 88 - Oct 95) | 3158 |
| **PEUGEOT** 106 Petrol & Diesel (91 - 04) J to 53 | 1882 |
| Peugeot 205 Petrol (83 - 97) A to P | 0932 |
| Peugeot 206 Petrol & Diesel (98 - 01) S to X | 3757 |
| Peugeot 206 Petrol & Diesel (02 - 06) 51 to 06 | 4613 |
| Peugeot 306 Petrol & Diesel (93 - 02) K to 02 | 3073 |
| Peugeot 307 Petrol & Diesel (01 - 04) Y to 54 | 4147 |
| Peugeot 309 Petrol (86 - 93) C to K | 1266 |
| Peugeot 405 Petrol (88 - 97) E to P | 1559 |
| Peugeot 405 Diesel (88 - 97) E to P | 3198 |
| Peugeot 406 Petrol & Diesel (96 - Mar 99) N to T | 3394 |
| Peugeot 406 Petrol & Diesel (Mar 99 - 02) T to 52 | 3982 |

* Classic reprint

| Title | Book No. |
|---|---|
| Peugeot 505 Petrol (79 - 89) up to G | 0762 |
| Peugeot 1.7/1.8 & 1.9 litre Diesel Engine (82 - 96) up to N | 0950 |
| Peugeot 2.0, 2.1, 2.3 & 2.5 litre Diesel Engines (74 - 90) up to H | 1607 |
| PORSCHE 911 (65 - 85) up to C | 0264 |
| Porsche 924 & 924 Turbo (76 - 85) up to C | 0397 |
| PROTON (89 - 97) F to P | 3255 |
| RANGE ROVER V8 Petrol (70 - Oct 92) up to K | 0606 |
| RELIANT Robin & Kitten (73 - 83) up to A * | 0436 |
| RENAULT 4 (61 - 86) up to D * | 0072 |
| Renault 5 Petrol (Feb 85 - 96) B to N | 1219 |
| Renault 9 & 11 Petrol (82 - 89) up to F | 0822 |
| Renault 18 Petrol (79 - 86) up to D | 0598 |
| Renault 19 Petrol (89 - 96) F to N | 1646 |
| Renault 19 Diesel (89 - 96) F to N | 1946 |
| Renault 21 Petrol (86 - 94) C to M | 1397 |
| Renault 25 Petrol & Diesel (84 - 92) B to K | 1228 |
| Renault Clio Petrol (91 - May 98) H to R | 1853 |
| Renault Clio Diesel (91 - June 96) H to N | 3031 |
| Renault Clio Petrol & Diesel (May 98 - May 01) R to Y | 3906 |
| Renault Clio Petrol & Diesel (June '01 - '05) Y to 55 | 4168 |
| Renault Espace Petrol & Diesel (85 - 96) C to N | 3197 |
| Renault Laguna Petrol & Diesel (94 - 00) L to W | 3252 |
| Renault Laguna Petrol & Diesel (Feb 01 - Feb 05) X to 54 | 4283 |
| Renault Mégane & Scénic Petrol & Diesel (96 - 99) N to T | 3395 |
| Renault Mégane & Scénic Petrol & Diesel (Apr 99 - 02) T to 52 | 3916 |
| Renault Megane Petrol & Diesel (Oct 02 - 05) 52 to 55 | 4284 |
| Renault Scenic Petrol & Diesel (Sept 03 - 06) 53 to 06 | 4297 |
| ROVER 213 & 216 (84 - 89) A to G | 1116 |
| Rover 214 & 414 Petrol (89 - 96) G to N | 1689 |
| Rover 216 & 416 Petrol (89 - 96) G to N | 1830 |
| Rover 211, 214, 216, 218 & 220 Petrol & Diesel (Dec 95 - 99) N to V | 3399 |
| Rover 25 & MG ZR Petrol & Diesel (Oct 99 - 04) V to 54 | 4145 |
| Rover 414, 416 & 420 Petrol & Diesel (May 95 - 98) M to R | 3453 |
| Rover 45 / MG ZS Petrol & Diesel (99 - 05) V to 55 | 4384 |
| Rover 618, 620 & 623 Petrol (93 - 97) K to P | 3257 |
| Rover 75 / MG ZT Petrol & Diesel (99 - 06) S to 06 | 4292 |
| Rover 820, 825 & 827 Petrol (86 - 95) D to N | 1380 |
| Rover 3500 (76 - 87) up to E * | 0365 |
| Rover Metro, 111 & 114 Petrol (May 90 - 98) G to S | 1711 |
| SAAB 95 & 96 (66 - 76) up to R * | 0198 |
| Saab 90, 99 & 900 (79 - Oct 93) up to L | 0765 |
| Saab 900 (Oct 93 - 98) L to R | 3512 |
| Saab 9000 (4-cyl) (85 - 98) C to S | 1686 |
| Saab 9-3 Petrol & Diesel (98 - Aug 02) R to 02 | 4614 |
| Saab 9-3 Petrol & Diesel (02-07) 52 to 57 | 4749 |
| Saab 9-5 4-cyl Petrol (97 - 04) R to 54 | 4156 |
| SEAT Ibiza & Cordoba Petrol & Diesel (Oct 93 - Oct 99) L to V | 3571 |
| Seat Ibiza & Malaga Petrol (85 - 92) B to K | 1609 |
| SKODA Estelle (77 - 89) up to G | 0604 |
| Skoda Fabia Petrol & Diesel (00 - 06) W to 06 | 4376 |
| Skoda Favorit (89 - 96) F to N | 1801 |
| Skoda Felicia Petrol & Diesel (95 - 01) M to X | 3505 |
| Skoda Octavia Petrol & Diesel (98 - Apr 04) R to 04 | 4285 |
| SUBARU 1600 & 1800 (Nov 79 - 90) up to H * | 0995 |

| Title | Book No. |
|---|---|
| SUNBEAM Alpine, Rapier & H120 (67 - 74) up to N * | 0051 |
| SUZUKI SJ Series, Samurai & Vitara (4-cyl) Petrol (82 - 97) up to P | 1942 |
| Suzuki Supercarry & Bedford/Vauxhall Rascal (86 - Oct 94) C to M | 3015 |
| TALBOT Alpine, Solara, Minx & Rapier (75 - 86) up to D | 0337 |
| Talbot Horizon Petrol (78 - 86) up to D | 0473 |
| Talbot Samba (82 - 86) up to D | 0823 |
| TOYOTA Avensis Petrol (98 - Jan 03) R to 52 | 4264 |
| Toyota Carina E Petrol (May 92 - 97) J to P | 3256 |
| Toyota Corolla (80 - 85) up to C | 0683 |
| Toyota Corolla (Sept 83 - Sept 87) A to E | 1024 |
| Toyota Corolla (Sept 87 - Aug 92) E to K | 1683 |
| Toyota Corolla Petrol (Aug 92 - 97) K to P | 3259 |
| Toyota Corolla Petrol (July 97 - Feb 02) P to 51 | 4286 |
| Toyota Hi-Ace & Hi-Lux Petrol (69 - Oct 83) up to A | 0304 |
| Toyota RAV4 Petrol & Diesel (94-06) L to 55 | 4750 |
| Toyota Yaris Petrol (99 - 05) T to 05 | 4265 |
| TRIUMPH GT6 & Vitesse (62 - 74 ) up to N * | 0112 |
| Triumph Herald (59 - 71) up to K * | 0010 |
| Triumph Spitfire (62 - 81) up to X | 0113 |
| Triumph Stag (70 - 78) up to T * | 0441 |
| Triumph TR2, TR3, TR3A, TR4 & TR4A (52 - 67) up to F * | 0028 |
| Triumph TR5 & 6 (67 - 75) up to P * | 0031 |
| Triumph TR7 (75 - 82) up to Y * | 0322 |
| VAUXHALL Astra Petrol (80 - Oct 84) up to B | 0635 |
| Vauxhall Astra & Belmont Petrol (Oct 84 - Oct 91) B to J | 1136 |
| Vauxhall Astra Petrol (Oct 91 - Feb 98) J to R | 1832 |
| Vauxhall/Opel Astra & Zafira Petrol (Feb 98 - Apr 04) R to 04 | 3758 |
| Vauxhall/Opel Astra & Zafira Diesel (Feb 98 - Apr 04) R to 04 | 3797 |
| Vauxhall/Opel Astra Petrol (04 - 08) | 4732 |
| Vauxhall/Opel Astra Diesel (04 - 08) | 4733 |
| Vauxhall/Opel Calibra (90 - 98) G to S | 3502 |
| Vauxhall Carlton Petrol (Oct 78 - Oct 86) up to D | 0480 |
| Vauxhall Carlton & Senator Petrol (Nov 86 - 94) D to L | 1469 |
| Vauxhall Cavalier Petrol (81 - Oct 88) up to F | 0812 |
| Vauxhall Cavalier Petrol (Oct 88 - 95) F to N | 1570 |
| Vauxhall Chevette (75 - 84) up to B | 0285 |
| Vauxhall/Opel Corsa Diesel (Mar 93 - Oct 00) K to X | 4087 |
| Vauxhall Corsa Petrol (Mar 93 - 97) K to R | 1985 |
| Vauxhall/Opel Corsa Petrol (Apr 97 - Oct 00) P to X | 3921 |
| Vauxhall/Opel Corsa Petrol & Diesel (Oct 00 - Sept 03) X to 53 | 4079 |
| Vauxhall/Opel Corsa Petrol & Diesel (Oct 03 - Aug 06) 53 to 06 | 4617 |
| Vauxhall/Opel Frontera Petrol & Diesel (91 - Sept 98) J to S | 3454 |
| Vauxhall Nova Petrol (83 - 93) up to K | 0909 |
| Vauxhall/Opel Omega Petrol (94 - 99) L to T | 3510 |
| Vauxhall/Opel Vectra Petrol & Diesel (95 - Feb 99) N to S | 3396 |
| Vauxhall/Opel Vectra Petrol & Diesel (Mar 99 - May 02) T to 02 | 3930 |
| Vauxhall/Opel Vectra Petrol & Diesel (June 02 - Sept 05) 02 to 55 | 4618 |
| Vauxhall/Opel 1.5, 1.6 & 1.7 litre Diesel Engine (82 - 96) up to N | 1222 |
| VW 411 & 412 (68 - 75) up to P * | 0091 |
| VW Beetle 1200 (54 - 77) up to S | 0036 |
| VW Beetle 1300 & 1500 (65 - 75) up to P | 0039 |

| Title | Book No. |
|---|---|
| VW 1302 & 1302S (70 - 72) up to L * | 0110 |
| VW Beetle 1303, 1303S & GT (72 - 75) up to P | 0159 |
| VW Beetle Petrol & Diesel (Apr 99 - 07) T to 57 | 3798 |
| VW Golf & Jetta Mk 1 Petrol 1.1 & 1.3 (74 - 84) up to A | 0716 |
| VW Golf, Jetta & Scirocco Mk 1 Petrol 1.5, 1.6 & 1.8 (74 - 84) up to A | 0726 |
| VW Golf & Jetta Mk 1 Diesel (78 - 84) up to A | 0451 |
| VW Golf & Jetta Mk 2 Petrol (Mar 84 - Feb 92) A to J | 1081 |
| VW Golf & Vento Petrol & Diesel (Feb 92 - Mar 98) J to R | 3097 |
| VW Golf & Bora Petrol & Diesel (April 98 - 00) R to X | 3727 |
| VW Golf & Bora 4-cyl Petrol & Diesel (01 - 03) X to 53 | 4169 |
| VW Golf & Jetta Petrol & Diesel (04 - 07) 53 to 07 | 4610 |
| VW LT Petrol Vans & Light Trucks (76 - 87) up to E | 0637 |
| VW Passat & Santana Petrol (Sept 81 - May 88) up to E | 0814 |
| VW Passat 4-cyl Petrol & Diesel (May 88 - 96) E to P | 3498 |
| VW Passat 4-cyl Petrol & Diesel (Dec 96 - Nov 00) P to X | 3917 |
| VW Passat Petrol & Diesel (Dec 00 - May 05) X to 05 | 4279 |
| VW Polo & Derby (76 - Jan 82) up to X | 0335 |
| VW Polo (82 - Oct 90) up to H | 0813 |
| VW Polo Petrol (Nov 90 - Aug 94) H to L | 3245 |
| VW Polo Hatchback Petrol & Diesel (94 - 99) M to S | 3500 |
| VW Polo Hatchback Petrol (00 - Jan 02) V to 51 | 4150 |
| VW Polo Petrol & Diesel (02 - May 05) 51 to 05 | 4608 |
| VW Scirocco (82 - 90) up to H * | 1224 |
| VW Transporter 1600 (68 - 79) up to V | 0082 |
| VW Transporter 1700, 1800 & 2000 (72 - 79) up to V * | 0226 |
| VW Transporter (air-cooled) Petrol (79 - 82) up to Y * | 0638 |
| VW Transporter (water-cooled) Petrol (82 - 90) up to H | 3452 |
| VW Type 3 (63 - 73) up to M * | 0084 |
| VOLVO 120 & 130 Series (& P1800) (61 - 73) up to M * | 0203 |
| Volvo 142, 144 & 145 (66 - 74) up to N * | 0129 |
| Volvo 240 Series Petrol (74 - 93) up to K | 0270 |
| Volvo 262, 264 & 260/265 (75 - 85) up to C * | 0400 |
| Volvo 340, 343, 345 & 360 (76 - 91) up to J | 0715 |
| Volvo 440, 460 & 480 Petrol (87 - 97) D to P | 1691 |
| Volvo 740 & 760 Petrol (82 - 91) up to J | 1258 |
| Volvo 850 Petrol (92 - 96) J to P | 3260 |
| Volvo 940 petrol (90 - 98) H to R | 3249 |
| Volvo S40 & V40 Petrol (96 - Mar 04) N to 04 | 3569 |
| Volvo S40 & V50 Petrol & Diesel (Mar 04 - Jun 07) 04 to 07 | 4731 |
| Volvo S60 Petrol & Diesel (01-08) | 4793 |
| Volvo S70, V70 & C70 Petrol (96 - 99) P to V | 3573 |
| Volvo V70 / S80 Petrol & Diesel (98 - 05) S to 55 | 4263 |

### DIY MANUAL SERIES

| | |
|---|---|
| The Haynes Air Conditioning Manual | 4192 |
| The Haynes Car Electrical Systems Manual | 4251 |
| The Haynes Manual on Bodywork | 4198 |
| The Haynes Manual on Brakes | 4178 |
| The Haynes Manual on Carburettors | 4177 |
| The Haynes Manual on Diesel Engines | 4174 |
| The Haynes Manual on Engine Management | 4199 |
| The Haynes Manual on Fault Codes | 4175 |
| The Haynes Manual on Practical Electrical Systems | 4267 |
| The Haynes Manual on Small Engines | 4250 |
| The Haynes Manual on Welding | 4176 |

* Classic reprint

All the products featured on this page are available through most motor accessory shops, cycle shops and book stores. Our policy of continuous updating and development means that titles are being constantly added to the range. For up-to-date information on our complete list of titles, please telephone: (UK) +44 1963 442030 • (USA) +1 805 498 6703 • (Sweden) +46 18 124016 • (Australia) +61 3 9763 8100

CL24.08/09

# Preserving Our Motoring Heritage

> The Model J Duesenberg Derham Tourster. Only eight of these magnificent cars were ever built – this is the only example to be found outside the United States of America

Almost every car you've ever loved, loathed or desired is gathered under one roof at the Haynes Motor Museum. Over 300 immaculately presented cars and motorbikes represent every aspect of our motoring heritage, from elegant reminders of bygone days, such as the superb Model J Duesenberg to curiosities like the bug-eyed BMW Isetta. There are also many old friends and flames. Perhaps you remember the 1959 Ford Popular that you did your courting in? The magnificent 'Red Collection' is a spectacle of classic sports cars including AC, Alfa Romeo, Austin Healey, Ferrari, Lamborghini, Maserati, MG, Riley, Porsche and Triumph.

## A Perfect Day Out

Each and every vehicle at the Haynes Motor Museum has played its part in the history and culture of Motoring. Today, they make a wonderful spectacle and a great day out for all the family. Bring the kids, bring Mum and Dad, but above all bring your camera to capture those golden memories for ever. You will also find an impressive array of motoring memorabilia, a comfortable 70 seat video cinema and one of the most extensive transport book shops in Britain. The Pit Stop Cafe serves everything from a cup of tea to wholesome, home-made meals or, if you prefer, you can enjoy the large picnic area nestled in the beautiful rural surroundings of Somerset.

> John Haynes O.B.E., Founder and Chairman of the museum at the wheel of a Haynes Light 12.

> Graham Hill's Lola Cosworth Formula 1 car next to a 1934 Riley Sports.

The Museum is situated on the A359 Yeovil to Frome road at Sparkford, just off the A303 in Somerset. It is about 40 miles south of Bristol, and 25 minutes drive from the M5 intersection at Taunton.
Open 9.30am - 5.30pm (10.00am - 4.00pm Winter) 7 days a week, *except Christmas Day, Boxing Day and New Years Day*
Special rates available for schools, coach parties and outings  Charitable Trust No. 292048